"...an outstanding model of centering lived experi   ... theory and in practice."

— *Eli R. Green, CSES, The Transgender Training Institute, USA*

"An extensive chronicle of the systems of oppression baked into our current structures and the everyday discrimination experienced by transgender and nonbinary communities."

— *Kimberly Bender, University of Denver, USA*

"For providers who honestly wish to engage in healing work in the transgender community I know of no better resource."

— *Greta Gustava Martela, Trans Lifeline founder, USA*

"Grounded in the most recent research and thinking about trans and nonbinary people...this is a book which every practitioner should not only have on their bookshelves, but one that they should actually read and incorporate into their practice."

— *Gerald Mallon, Hunter College, USA*

Social Work and Health Care Practice with Transgender and Nonbinary Individuals and Communities

This book examines issues across the lifespan of transgender and nonbinary individuals whilst synthesizing conceptual work, empirical evidence, pedagogical content, educational experiences, and the voices of transgender and nonbinary individuals. It highlights the resilience and resistance of transgender and nonbinary individuals and communities to challenge narratives relying on one-dimensional perspectives of risk and tragic lives.

While there is currently unprecedented visibility and increasing support, members of these communities still face shockingly high rates of violence, victimization, unemployment, discrimination, and family rejection. Significant need for services and support coupled with social, clinical, and medical service systems ill-equipped to provide culturally responsive care illustrates the critical need for quality education and training of educators, practitioners, and service providers in best practices of working with members of the transgender and nonbinary community.

Organized into six sections:

- Health
- Areas of Practice
- Coming Out and Family
- Relationships and Sexuality
- Communities
- Multiply Marginalized Identities and Populations,

this book offers a current, comprehensive, and intersectional guide for students, practitioners, and researchers across a variety of professions, including social work, psychology, public policy, and health care.

Shanna K. Kattari (she/her/hers) is Assistant Professor at the University of Michigan School of Social Work and Department of Women's and Gender Studies (by courtesy), USA.

M. Killian Kinney (they/them) is a doctoral candidate and associate faculty in the School of Social Work at Indiana University, USA.

Leonardo Kattari (he/him/his) is a doctoral student in the School of Social Work at Michigan State University, USA.

N. Eugene Walls (he/him) is Professor in the Graduate School of Social Work at the University of Denver, USA.

Social Work and Health Care Practice with Transgender and Nonbinary Individuals and Communities

Voices for Equity, Inclusion, and Resilience

Edited by Shanna K. Kattari,
M. Killian Kinney, Leonardo Kattari,
and N. Eugene Walls

Routledge
Taylor & Francis Group

LONDON AND NEW YORK

First published 2021
by Routledge
2 Park Square, Milton Park, Abingdon, Oxon OX14 4RN

and by Routledge
52 Vanderbilt Avenue, New York, NY 10017

Routledge is an imprint of the Taylor & Francis Group, an informa business

British Library Cataloguing-in-Publication Data
A catalogue record for this book is available from the British Library

Library of Congress Cataloging-in-Publication Data
Names: Kattari, Shanna K., editor.
Title: Social work and health care practice with transgender and nonbinary
    individuals and communities : voices for equity, inclusion, and resilience /
    edited by Shanna K. Kattari, M. Killian Kinney, Leonardo Kattari and
    N. Eugene Walls.
Description: Abingdon, Oxon ; New York, NY : Routledge, 2020. |
    Includes bibliographical references and index.
Identifiers: LCCN 2020012412 (print) | LCCN 2020012413 (ebook) | ISBN
    9781138336216 (hardback) | ISBN 9781138336223 (paperback) | ISBN
    9780429443176 (ebook)
Subjects: LCSH: Transgender people—Civil rights. | Transgender people-
Social aspects. | Gender-nonconforming people. | Social work
    with transgender people.
Classification: LCC HQ77.9 .S635 2020 (print) | LCC HQ77.9 (ebook) |
    DDC 306.76/8—dc23
LC record available at https://lccn.loc.gov/2020012412
LC ebook record available at https://lccn.loc.gov/2020012413

ISBN: 978-1-138-33621-6 (hbk)
ISBN: 978-1-138-33622-3 (pbk)
ISBN: 978-0-429-44317-6 (ebk)

Typeset in Sabon and Helvetica Neue
by Swales & Willis, Exeter, Devon, UK

To all the trans, transgender, nonbinary, agender, two-spirit, genderqueer, transfeminine, transmasculine, gender fluid, gender diverse, gender awesome, gender expansive, and other people whose gender exists outside of the cisnormative binary. Your resistance and resilience in the face of a world that does not always recognize your beauty and strength is awe-inspiring. Thank you for sharing your stories and experiences with us; we hope that this book creates more ripples in the pond as we move towards a more just world.

Contents

Tables

Contributors

Mere Abrams (they/them/theirs) is a researcher, writer, educator, consultant, and Licensed Clinical Social Worker. Mere reaches a worldwide audience through direct service, public speaking, publications, clinical research, and social media, supporting individuals and communities seeking to understand and explore gender beyond the binary. Mere uses their diverse professional background to guide institutions, organizations, and businesses in identifying opportunities to demonstrate gender literacy and inclusion in policies, branding, products, services, programs, projects, and content.

Isaac M. Akapnitis (he/they) is a Social Worker, advocate, and educator. They earned their MSSW from the University of Texas at Austin, USA, and have worked with LGBTQ populations for over ten years. Their primary interests are in suicide prevention, provider education, community development, and policy change. They are currently a Field Instructor and Faculty Associate in the School of Social Work at Arizona State University, USA. In all settings, they strive to create safe and affirming environments for LGBTQ communities.

Lynne M. Alexander (they/them/theirs) is a graduate student at the University of Connecticut, USA, pursuing a dual Master of Public Administration and Master of Social Work with a concentration in Practice with Individuals, Groups and Families. They work with the University of Connecticut Women's, Gender and Sexuality Studies Program as a Graduate Instructor. They currently serve as the Vice President of the Board of Directors for the Connecticut TransAdvocacy Coalition (CTAC), a grassroots-oriented organization charged with making Connecticut a safe and tolerant place for the TNB individuals through education and social advocacy. Their research interests include queer pedagogy, classroom inclusion, and culturally-centric and trauma-focused health care for LGBTQIA+ individuals and survivors of gender-based violence.

Heather Arnold-Renicker (she/her/hers) is an Assistant Clinical Faculty at the Graduate School of Social Work where she serves as the Coordinator for the Organizational Leadership and Policy Practice concentration. Heather has been involved in organizing, campaign work, and social justice work for over 15 years. Her primary area of focus is anti-oppression and organizational culture and change.

Brittanie Atteberry-Ash (she/her/hers) is Assistant Professor in the School of Social Work at the University of Texas, Arlington, USA. Brittanie's work relies heavily on an intersectional lens to deepen the discipline's understanding of risk and resilience among people who live at the crossroads of marginalized identities. Brittanie also focuses on promoting justice and inclusion within classroom and field education experiences, identifying strategies for educators to more fully integrate a critical social justice lens into their pedagogy and field supervision of students. Believing in the power of social work education to transform students into practitioners dedicated to a just world, she is passionate about her work as a critical social work scholar advancing the discipline's commitment to social justice.

Matthew Bakko (he/him/his and they/them/their) is a doctoral student in the Joint PhD Program in Social Work and Sociology at the University of Michigan, USA. Matthew's research interests include social welfare and health policy, human service organizations, philanthropy and funding dynamics, and gender and sexuality.

Richard A. Brandon-Friedman (he/him/his) is Assistant Professor in the Indiana University School of Social Work and the Social Work Services Supervisor for the Gender Health Program at Riley Children's Health at IU Health, USA. As a Clinician, he has worked with youth in schools and in child welfare for over ten years and has worked with youth who identify as sexual minorities for over 15 years. His research focuses on sexual orientation and sexual and gender identity development among youth and their impact on youth's sexual well-being.

Heather Brydie Harris (they/them/theirs) is a PhD candidate in Pan-African Studies at the University of Louisville, USA. They hold degrees in Social Justice and Ethics (MA) from Iliff School of Theology and Women and Gender Studies (BA) from Metropolitan State University of Denver. Brydie is a Black, multiracial, nonbinary femme, poet and scholar-activist. Their interests and research are based in the Black queer experience through the framework of womanist and quare theology via transcontinental social justice imaginaries and Afrofuturistic thought.

Leonardo Candelario-Pérez (they/them/theirs) is a Latinx, nonbinary femme Licensed Psychologist, Sexual Health Consultant and Therapist within Urology, and Adolescent Care Co-Chair and Therapist for Gender Services at Health Partners MN. Additionally, they are Co-Educational Consultant at the National Center for Gender Spectrum Health. Their clinical, administrative, and research interests include sexual and gender health and wellness, mental health as it relates to issues of sexuality and gender identity, language and LGBTQI identity formation, and the intersections of race/ethnicity, gender, and sexual orientation.

K. Tajhi Claybren (she/her/hers) is the Coordinator of Therapy Services at the Broadway Youth Center. Her role includes providing brief counseling and crisis counseling with LGBTQ youth aged 12–24 who are experiencing homelessness and/or housing instability along with coordinating the strategic integration and implementation of mental health services. She is committed to supporting the healing, self-actualization, and mental wellness of Black, Indigenous and People of Color (BIPOC) LGBTQ communities, especially Black trans women and femmes.

Christine Cocker (she/her/hers) is a Senior Lecturer/Associate Professor in Social Work at the University of East Anglia, UK. Christine researches and writes about social work and sexuality, and social work with looked-after children, and has published numerous books and journal articles on these topics.

Jessie Rose Cohen (they/them/she/her/J/J's) is a TransNonBinary identified Clinician who has worked with children, families, and youth for over two decades. J serves as Director of Community-based Clinical Services and Training for the UCSF Child and Adolescent Gender Center and Clinical Supervisor and Consultant for the SF LGBT Center. J's passion and commitment to the field is to work from a Family Systems, trauma healing, anti-bias, gender affirming model and train other clinicians in this area.

Kate M. Curley (they/them/theirs) is a scholar-practitioner who recently completed their doctorate in Educational Leadership at Eastern Michigan University and is currently a Learning and Development Consultant at HealthPartners, a large health care nonprofit in the Minnesota-Wisconsin area. Their research interests look at the intersection of religion, secularity, and spirituality and LGBTQ+ identities in applied contexts with a focus on the trans-ing and queering of quantitative approaches.

Jonah P. DeChants (he/him/his) is a postdoctoral fellow for Inclusive Excellence and Health and Well-being Disparities at Colorado State University's School of Social Work. DeChants uses community-based research methods to study the experiences of youth and young adults experiencing homelessness, particularly those who identify as lesbian, gay, bisexual, transgender, or queer (LGBTQ). He is interested in youth participatory action research (YPAR) methods and including young people in collaborative investigations of issues which impact them. Jonah worked for the Philadelphia Department of Human Services, supervising a federal planning grant which examined risk and protective factors of homelessness among youth aging out of foster care. He earned his Master of Social Policy from the University of Pennsylvania's School of Social Policy and Practice and his Bachelor of Arts from Kalamazoo College. He is also an alum of the AmeriCorps VISTA program.

Gio Dolcecore (they/them) is a registered Social Worker residing on the traditional territory of Treaty 7, named by the Blackfoot people as Mohkinstsis, today recognized as the City of Calgary. Gio is a Therapist for a non-for-profit and through private practice, working primarily with gender and sexual diverse identities, specializing in complex trauma, addiction, and mental health. As an Instructor for the University of Calgary, Gio supports the Faculty of Social Work students to not only learn about diversity, but challenges them to be active allies professionally and personally.

Kelly L. Donahue (she/her/hers) is an Assistant Professor of Clinical Pediatrics at the Indiana University School of Medicine. She is a Licensed Clinical Psychologist and serves as Co-Director of the multidisciplinary Gender Health Program at Riley Hospital for Children. She is a member of several professional organizations, including the World Professional Association for Transgender Health. She is also the founding Co-Chair of the Gender Health Special Interest Group for the Society of Pediatric Psychology.

Simon Adriane Ellis (they/them/theirs) is a queer, trans, and nonbinary identified Certified Nurse Midwife in full scope practice at Kaiser Permanente in Seattle. Simon's clinical focus is on providing sexual and reproductive health services across the lifespan for people of all gender identities. They have clinical specialties in abortion care, LGBTQ family building, and gender affirming care.

Twiggy Pucci Garcon (she/her/hers) is the Senior Program Director at True Colors United, where she leads their Youth Collaboration programs, aimed at not only elevating youth voices but also creating space for partnerships with young adults to lead the movement to end youth homelessness. In addition to her activism and advocacy work, Twiggy has worked as a model and runway trainer, performance artist, and Special Events and Talent Management Coordinator. Twiggy was a featured subject in Timothy Greenfield-Sanders' and HBO's documentary feature film *The OUT List*, is the co-writer and one of seven subjects in the Sundance-selected, award-winning documentary *KIKI*, and is the runway choreographer for the award-winning series *Pose*.

Rachel Lynn Golden (she/her/hers) is an Assistant Professor of Clinical Medical Psychology (in Psychiatry) at Columbia University Irving Medical Center, USA. Her research and clinical work explores sexual development and gender across the lifespan and is centered in intersectional practice. She aims to promote safe and healthy sexuality, affirm and support individuals of all genders, and reduce barriers to psychological and medical care. Rachel received her doctoral degree in Clinical Psychology from the University of Denver. She also holds bachelor's degrees in Psychology (University of Colorado, Denver) and Romance Languages (Carleton College).

Jaime M. Grant (she/her/hers) is principal researcher and co-author of *Injustice at Every Turn: A Report of the National Transgender Discrimination Survey (NTDS)*, and served as the Policy Institute Director of the National LGBTQ Task Force during a pivotal moment in trans resistance and organizing. A lesbian feminist social justice researcher and educator, Grant has been active in LGBTQ, women's, and racial justice movements since the early 90s, working as part of the founding team of the ground-breaking Equal Justice Works fellowship program (1992) and later the Ford Foundation's grassroots signature awards program (2004–2007), Leadership for A Changing World. Grant's sexual liberation workshop, *Desire Mapping*, has been produced on college campuses and at LGBTQ and feminist leadership conferences around the world. Her podcast based on the workshop, *Just Sex: Mapping Your Desire*, captures everyday sex stories told by Desire Mappers from Beijing to Capetown, from Dallas to Denver to DC.

Trish Hafford-Letchfield (she/her/hers) is Professor of Social Work at the University of Strathclyde, Scotland. Her main research interests lie in the experience of aging in marginalized communities. Trish is a founder member of the International Social Work and Sexuality Network. Her research is applied and draws on co-production methods often using the arts and other collaborative techniques. Trish has written several key educational textbooks on management, leadership, and organizational development in social work and social care. She has also published widely on practice issues in social work and social care which impact on gender and sexual minority communities' experiences of services.

Seventy F. Hall (he/him/his or they/them/theirs) is a combined MSW/PhD student at the University at Buffalo School of Social Work, USA. His research focuses on the intersecting influences of adultism, heterosexism, and cissexism on homelessness and child welfare involvement among lesbian, gay, bisexual, transgender, and queer (LGBTQ+) youth. Seventy's philosophic orientation borrows from the critical youth studies discipline and incorporates an emphasis on adultism as a factor that both contributes to disproportionality among homeless and child welfare-involved LGBTQ+ youth and shapes their experiences and trajectories.

Vern Harner (they/them/theirs) is a trans and chronically ill PhD candidate in Social Welfare at the University of Washington, USA. Drawing on their broad experience advocating for trans and queer issues, Vern's current work focuses on trans intracommunity support (i.e., knowledge and support sharing within trans communities).

Kyle Inselman (he/him/his) is a Career Advisor and Instructor at the University of Denver working with liberal arts undergraduates. Kyle has written and spoken on LGBTQ issues for over ten years, with a primary focus on trans inclusion in higher education.

Ejay Jack (he/him/his) is the Transgender Care Coordinator and Community Liaison at the Comprehensive Gender Care program at the University of Minnesota. Ejay, who has worked in LGBTQ health care and HIV care and prevention for the last 15 years, is a trans-identified Licensed Graduate Social Worker with a master's degree in Public Administration.

G. Trey Jenkins (he/him) is a Senior Research and Evaluation Specialist at the Center for Applied Behavioral Health Policy at Arizona State University. He is the Co-Chair for the Queer Resource Collective and Board Member for Recovery Empowerment Network in Phoenix, AZ. Trey is an alumnus of Arizona Leading for Change Fellowship, class of 2019. His research and policy interests include culturally responsive data collection, health disparities, and health equity. In particular, Trey is interested in the well-being, safety, and health of transgender and nonbinary individuals.

Ian M. Johnson (he/him/his) is a queer Licensed Clinical Social Worker, critical aging and disability scholar, and social work educator. Through his work, Ian hopes to create more inclusive, emancipatory, and sustainable health and mental interventions for older disabled people.

T. J. Jourian (he/him/his) is an independent scholar and Consultant with Trans*Formational Change. His research, advocacy, and pedagogy center queer and trans people of color, while engaging with equity, intersectionality, and student leadership and activism. Additionally, he is the Events and Resources Coordinator at Philadelphia Yearly Meeting and a member of the Trans*forming Higher Education (T.H.E.) Collaborative.

Ryan Karnoski (he/him/his) is a social welfare researcher from Seattle, WA, with a background in direct clinical practice with gender and sexual minority youth and their families. He holds a Bachelor of Arts in Social Welfare and Gender, Women and Sexuality Studies, and a Master of Social Work degree from the University of Washington, where he specialized in Children, Youth and Family Social Work. He is currently a doctoral student at the University of California, Berkeley, where he researches the experiences of gender and sexual minority youth in public child welfare systems.

Leonardo Kattari (he/him/his) is a doctoral student in the School of Social Work at Michigan State University. He conducts research on health equity and policy across the lifespan, specifically focusing on health access and outcomes among transgender and gender diverse individuals and communities.

Shanna K. Kattari (she/her/hers) is an Assistant Professor at the University of Michigan School of Social Work and Department of Women's and Gender Studies (by courtesy), and is the Director of the [Sexuality|Relationships|Gender] Research Collective (www.SRGcollective.com). A queer, White, Jewish, cisgender, disabled, neurodiverse, chronically ill Femme, her practice and community background is as a Board Certified Sexologist, Certified Sexuality Educator, and social justice advocate. Her research focuses on understanding how power, privilege, and oppression systematically marginalize, exclude, and discriminate against people regarding their identities/expressions through negative attitudes, policies reinforcing oppression, oppressive actions, and isolation. Her work currently focuses on experiences of queer and trans affirming health care practice, disability and ableism, and non-mainstream sexuality. Please see www.ShannaKattari.com.

Aaron Kemmerer (he/him/his) is a student, organizer, and social work researcher in Richmond, Virginia. He has worked with community groups including Advocates for Richmond Youth (ARY), Southerners on New Ground (SONG), YWCA Richmond, and Girls Rock! RVA. Aaron has a passion for addressing the needs of youth experiencing unstable housing and has used his voice to increase visibility for issues facing transgender people in the US South and beyond.

alex kime (they/them/theirs) is a transdisciplinary writer, researcher, performer, and facilitator from Ann Arbor, Michigan. They received their Master of Social Work degree from the University of Michigan with a concentration in Social Policy and Evaluation, and they are currently a Lecturer for the Program on Intergroup Relations.

M. Killian Kinney (they/them) is a doctoral candidate and associate faculty in the School of Social Work at Indiana University. Mx. Kinney is a queer, White, currently able-bodied, neurodiverse, nonbinary person. Their community-driven research centers on transgender and nonbinary populations regarding health outcomes, policy implications, and promotive and corrosive factors of well-being. As a practitioner, Mx. Kinney's experience spans multidisciplinary gender health programming with adolescents, therapeutic groups with nonbinary adults, and LGBTQIA consultation and training. Please see www.KillianKinney.com

Cary Leonard Klemmer (he/they) holds a PhD in Social Work. He recently defended his dissertation, which uses mixed-methods to examine the schooling experiences of transgender young people and identifies challenges that they navigate and the resilience they exhibit. Cary hopes to promote a society supportive of lesbian, gay, bisexual, transgender, and queer people through social work practice, teaching, and research.

K. Abel Knochel (they/them/theirs) is Assistant Professor in the University of Minnesota Duluth Social Work Department. They conduct community-based research with transgender and nonbinary older adults and serve on the American Society on Aging's LGBT Aging Issues Network (LAIN) Council. Abel dreams of organizing a fierce, multigenerational trans/nonbinary/queer community that cares for its own like the best kind of family, and always welcomes one more.

Ashley Lacombe-Duncan (she/her/hers) is Assistant Professor at the University of Michigan School of Social Work. Her research centers on health care access and health equity, with a particular focus on health care access for people who experience multiple forms of intersecting oppressions. Through qualitative, quantitative, and mixed-methods community-based participatory research she explores: (1) barriers to access to care, including HIV care, for LGBTQ people; (2) interventions to increase HIV care engagement among LGBTQ people living with HIV; and, (3) LGBTQ affirming social work practice from an intersectional approach.

Lisa Langenderfer-Magruder (she/her/hers) is a jointly appointed postdoctoral scholar at the Florida State University College of Social Work and the Florida Institute for Child Welfare. Her research focuses on systemic approaches to addressing victimization and workforce-related issues, particularly in the contexts of intimate partner violence and child maltreatment.

Yoseñio V. Lewis (he/him/his) is a Latino of African Descent (Panamanian) female to male transsexual who has been a social justice activist since he was 13 years old.

A health educator, speaker, writer, performer, trainer, facilitator, and spiritual hugger, Yoseñio is also an out poly and kinky person. Yoseñio believes there can be no Art without Activism and no Activism without Art.

Will R. Logan (they/them) is 34, white, currently able-bodied, queer, nonbinary/trans, and a first-generation college student from a rural, working-class family. They have a master's degree in Social Work and a postgraduate certificate in Marriage and Family Therapy. Will is a Licensed Clinical Social Worker in private practice in Denver, Colorado, where they work with individuals, partners, and families. They specialize in trauma and attachment work with a focus on sex, gender, and sexuality.

Rebecca Manning (she/her/hers) is a registered Mental Health Nurse and manages mental health services in an NHS Trust. She is also a Specialist Advisor for the Care Quality Commission. She is currently completing an MBA and has won awards for her social enterprise designed to support TNB communities. Rebecca has an interest in research in relation to mental health, TNB students in higher education, and older people.

Keira McCormack (she/her/hers) is an independent Domestic Violence Advisor for a large national charity and an experienced Counsellor and Counselling Coordinator. She has a long history as an LGBT activist and advocate specializing in domestic violence, rape, and sexual abuse in England and Northern Ireland and is the Project Manager for Gender Essence, a specialist counseling and support organization that promotes awareness and offers therapeutic support and training to those from the TNB, Gender Variant, and Intersex community.

Nyx McLean (they/them/theirs) is a researcher of LGBTQIA+ and marginalized identities, digital culture, and online communities. Their core focus is on the significance of the internet and digital technologies for enabling change and creating safe spaces with a specific focus on gender, sexual, and LGBTQIA+ identities. Their work is informed by an anti-racist queer feminist lens.

Eric T. Meininger (he/him) is an Associate Professor of Clinical Pediatrics at the Indiana University School of Medicine, Division of Adolescent Medicine. His research interests include program evaluation and implementation of best practices for marginalized youth, improving the quality of care for gender and sexual minority youth, as well as young adults with childhood-onset disabilities. Dr. Meininger is also a Co-Director of the Gender Health program at Riley Children's Hospital at IU Health and has been working with transgender and gender diverse patients since 1999.

Rory P. O'Brien, MSW, MPH, (they/them/their) is a doctoral student in the Suzanne Dworak-Peck School of Social Work at the University of Southern California. Rory conducts research on LGBTQ, and especially trans and nonbinary, youth health, school climate, violence prevention, and policy implementation.

Megan S. Paceley (she/her) is an Assistant Professor and Coordinator for Diversity, Equity, and Inclusion at the University of Kansas School of Social Welfare. She is accountable to queer and trans young people through her research on the relationship between youth's social environments and their health and well-being. Utilizing community-based, qualitative, and mixed-methods research, she aims to transform stigmatizing environments, such as families, schools, and communities, that diminish well-being into affirming and supportive environments that promote healthy development and well-being for all queer and trans youth.

Jessie Read (he/him) is 30, queer, AFAB, transmasculine, white, currently able-bodied, and from an upper-middle-class background. Jessie is a Licensed Professional Counselor Candidate and has a therapy practice in Denver, Colorado. His work focuses on anti-oppressive practice with trans, nonbinary, and questioning community members of all ages and identities. Jessie practices from a lens of narrative therapy and queer theory.

G. Nic Rider (they/them/theirs) is an Asian American nonbinary/transmasculine Assistant Professor at the Program in Human Sexuality at the University of Minnesota Medical School and Co-Associate Director of Research at the National Center for Gender Spectrum Health. Their clinical and research interests include sexual and gender identity development, sexual and mental health, minority/intersectional stressors and resilience, and health and health care disparities. They serve on the editorial board of multiple journals, including the *International Journal of Transgender Health*, and are Co-Chair of the Asian American Psychological Association's Division on Lesbian, Gay, Bisexual, Transgender, Queer and Questioning.

Jennifer Rivera (she/her/hers) is a communications and nonprofit professional and current MSW candidate at the University of Denver. Jenn spent several years in program and grant management with community-based organizations across Indian Country. She has also consulted nonprofit organizations in their pursuit of culturally responsive and inclusive organizational practices.

Lee Roosevelt (she/her/hers) is a queer identified Certified Nurse Midwife in full scope practice with a clinical focus on sexual and reproductive health. She is a Clinical Assistant Professor at the University of Michigan School of Nursing. Her current midwifery practice is with Planned Parenthood of Michigan as well as St. Joseph Mercy Hospital in Ypsilanti, Michigan. She completed her doctoral studies in 2015 in nursing and also holds a master's in Public Health and a graduate certificate in Women's Studies. Her current research focuses on fear of childbirth, pregnancy loss, and LGBTQIA+ utilization of sexual and reproductive health services.

Jennifer J. Schwartz (she/they) is a Licensed Clinical Social Worker, and has worked as a Therapist specializing in serving the LGBTQ community, and specifically PLWHA, for the past eight years. Additionally, Jennifer is a speaker, group facilitator, educator, and advocate for the consensually non-monogamous, LGBTQ, and fat-liberation communities. Jennifer currently leads the Behavioral Health Services department at Corktown Health Center/Health Emergency Lifeline Program in Detroit, Michigan, as well as maintaining a private practice in Royal Oak, MI.

Andrew Seeber (he/him/his) is a part-time faculty member at the University of the Virgin Islands and an independent Instructional Design and Course Development Consultant for UVI Online. His research focuses on the experiences of trans people throughout the life course, using an intersectional approach to analysis in areas such as family relationships, employment, housing, and health care.

Kristie L. Seelman (she/her/hers) is an Associate Professor in the School of Social Work at Georgia State University. Her research focuses on understanding and addressing LGBTQ+ health disparities across the life course, improving health services and education settings for LGBTQ+ people, and developing LGBTQ+ affirming policies. Her goal is for her research and teaching to center social work values, promote LGBTQ+ equity and inclusion, and challenge cisgender normativity to create a more just future.

Jama Shelton (they/them/theirs) is an Assistant Professor at the Silberman School of Social Work at Hunter College and the Associate Director for the Silberman Center for Sexuality and Gender. Dr. Shelton's research focuses on LGBTQ youth homelessness. In particular, Shelton is interested in identifying and addressing systemic barriers rooted in cis/heterosexism that frequently constrain the successful transition out of homelessness for transgender and nonbinary youth and young adults.

Jennifer A. Vencill (she/her/hers) is a White, bisexual, cisgender femme Assistant Professor, Licensed Psychologist, and AASECT-certified Sex Therapist at the Mayo Clinic in Rochester, Minnesota. Her clinical and research interests include sexual health and functioning, sexuality and aging, health disparities and minority stress in marginalized sexual and gender communities, couples/relationship dynamics, and LGBTQ mental and sexual health. She serves on the editorial board of the *Journal of Positive Sexuality* and is past-president of the Society for the Psychology of Women's Section on Lesbian, Bisexual, and Transgender Concerns.

Stephen von Merz (he/him/his) is a Clinical Associate Professor at the University of Denver Graduate School of Social Work, and serves as Coordinator of GSSW's Family Systems Practice concentration, in addition to his role as GSSW Faculty Co-Chair. With over 20 years of bilingual (English/Spanish) clinical social work practice in a number of clinical and community settings, he is highly practiced in implementing intensive in-home therapy and outpatient therapy that includes using empirically based models of treatment such as trauma-focused structural family therapy, solution-focused brief therapy, and multisystemic family therapy. He provides bilingual clinical supervision and consultation with an emphasis on culturally responsive family therapy in social work practice and holds certificates in multisystemic therapy (MST), hand-drumming therapy with psychotherapy, and secondary trauma resiliency training.

M. Alex Wagaman (she/her/hers) is an Associate Professor in the School of Social Work at Virginia Commonwealth University. Most of her practice and research experience has included youth and young adults, many of whom are LGBTQ+. Over the last five years she has worked with a participatory action research team, Advocates for Richmond Youth, to blend research and action to mobilize the local community to work to end youth homelessness. Dr. Wagaman has dedicated much of her career to enhancing the ways that service providers and researchers engage young people as leaders in their own care and communities.

Rebecca Waletich (she/her/hers) has been serving the gender diverse community since 1999, providing individual, couples, family, and group therapy. She is a Certified Therapist with the World Professional Association for Transgender Health (WPATH). Outside of her practice, she is active in advocacy, professional training, and networking efforts.

N. Eugene Walls (he/him) is a Professor in the Graduate School of Social Work at the University of Denver whose practice experience includes direct and administrative work with LGBTQ youth and adults, individuals experiencing homelessness, disabled children and adults including those living with HIV, and children and youth in foster care. A gay, White, first-generation college student, cisgender, polyamorous, atheist, currently able-bodied male, his teaching and research focuses primarily on issues of social justice and the LGBQ and transgender/nonbinary community. His work is driven by a deep sense of commitment to and passion for a world where justice and equity are lived out in the day-to-day experiences of marginalized people and communities.

Rand Warden (they/them/theirs) is a Lecturer for Indiana University School of Social Work. Their work centers on and lifts up anti-oppressive social work education and praxis. Myranda has been working in, with, and for the TNB community locally and nationally for over a decade, serving as Therapist, Consultant, Peer Mentor, and more.

Sage Marie Tyler Warren (he/him/his) is a Social Worker for Sacramento County where he resides with his wife, Amy, and their children, Ashley and Ari. Sage completed his higher education at UC Davis and Sacramento State University, during which he worked with local LGBTQ nonprofits, passed three bills in the California State Assembly, and served as a Director on the Board of the Capitol LGBTQ Association.

Darren L. Whitfield (he/him/his) is an Assistant Professor of Social Work and Psychiatry at the University of Pittsburgh School of Social Work and Department of Psychiatry. His research focuses on the areas of psychosocial, sociocultural, and structural factors associated with health outcomes for gay and bisexual men of color and health disparities among LGBTQ communities.

Cameron T. Whitley (he/him/his or they/them/their) is an Assistant Professor in the Department of Sociology at Western Washington University. They study issues concerning the environment, science and technology, human-animal relationships, and gender and sexuality. They conduct research on a variety of questions within transgender studies and is currently working on several papers exploring how individuals form opinions about transgender rights and how an understanding of science informs these perspectives. Their work has been published in over 40 peer-reviewed articles and book chapters.

Sara E. Wiener (she/her) leads the mental health component of Child and Adolescent Gender Services at C.S. Mott Children's Hospital in Ann Arbor, Michigan. Ms. Wiener has been working with young people with diverse gender identities for a decade, and she is passionate about building parents' and caregivers' support of their child's gender identity.

Cassie Withey-Rila (they/them) is a postgraduate researcher completing a Master's of Public Health in the Department of Preventive and Social Medicine at the University of Otago. Their project is exploring the positive experiences of transgender, nonbinary, and gender diverse adults with their GPs in Aotearoa. After an undergraduate degree in English at Texas Woman's University, Cassie was doing volunteer work as a queer-inclusive sex educator in Texas, when they found their calling in public health. In addition to academia, Cassie spends their time working with queer communities both on and off campus.

Acknowledgements

Thank you to all of those that supported the creation of this book along the way.

To the friends, family, colleagues, and other helping professionals, we put our trust in you to create a world that helps gender diverse individuals and communities to thrive. Together we can create spaces for individuals to know that they are seen and appreciated, to access health care that is not harmful, and to navigate public spaces safely. Be the person who upholds accountability, who insists on inclusive and affirming policies, and who will advocate with us.

Glossary

CONSIDERATIONS FOR THE LANGUAGE USED IN THIS BOOK

> We support every person's right to self-identify, with or without labels. People might prefer one of many different labels. Or to use more than one label. These labels may not mean the same thing to everyone. In our research, we try to provide opportunities for individuals to describe themselves, and we often use those self-descriptions …
>
> (Riggle & Rostosky, 2011, p. 8)

As an editorial team, we discussed best-practices in terminology and, to the best of our current knowledge, decided on the language used in this book. We realize that language evolves over time, that there are regional and cultural variations in the meaning of terms, and that language is frequently imperfect in capturing lived experiences. Even still, we need language in order to express ourselves, find commonalities, and challenge oppressive structures.

Definitions in this glossary are drawn from numerous sources, including Adams (2017), Beemyn (n.d.), Demisexual Resource Center (2015), Human Rights Campaign (2020), The National LGBT Health Education Center (2010), Transgender Hub (2017), and Trans Student Educational Resources (2020). Definitions represent the most generally agreed-upon definition; however, some individuals have different meanings for the terms.

DEFINITIONS

Affectional orientation: See romantic/emotional orientation.

Agender: An umbrella term for some gender identities that do not align with man, woman, or any other gender. Many agender people identify as transgender. It is best if you ask how someone defines agender for themselves.

Ally: Someone who advocates and supports a community other than their own. Allies are not part of the communities they help. A person should not self-identify as an ally but demonstrate that they are one through their action. People may want to consider being an *accomplice* in changing our society to be more inclusive and affirming, or a *co-conspirator* in actions lead by members of marginalized communities.

Androgyne: Someone whose gender identity is both man and woman, or neither man nor woman. A person might present as androgynous and/or sometimes masculinely and sometimes femininely. Pronouns may vary or match the societal expectations connected with their gender presentation at that time.

Androgynous: Identifying and/or presenting as neither distinguishably masculine nor feminine.

Aromantic: The lack of romantic attraction, or one identifying with this orientation. May be used as an umbrella term for other romantic/emotional orientations such as *demiromantic*.

Asexual: The lack of sexual attraction or desire, or one identifying with this orientation. May be used as an umbrella term for other sexual orientations such as *demisexual* or *greysexual*.

Assigned female at birth/AFAB: Also sometimes *designated female at birth*. No one, whether *cis* or *trans*, gets to choose what sex they are assigned at birth. This term is preferred to *biological female*, *female-bodied*, *natal female*, and *born female*, which are defamatory and inaccurate.

Assigned male at birth/AMAB: Also sometimes *designated male at birth*. No one, whether *cis* or *trans*, gets to choose what sex they are assigned at birth. This term is preferred to *biological male*, *male-bodied*, *natal male*, and *born male*, which are defamatory and inaccurate.

Bigender: Refers to those who identify as two genders. Can also identify as *multigender*.

Binary: The gender binary is a system of viewing gender as consisting solely of two gender identities (man and woman) and two sexes (male and female). Since the binary genders are the only ones recognized by general society as being legitimate, they are given an unearned privileged status.

Binding: Compressing one's chest (with a binder, sports bras, ace bandages, or other mechanisms) to appear more flat or masculine. Can cause some health issues if done incorrectly.

Biphobia: Prejudice, fear, or hatred directed toward bisexual people.

Bisexual/bisexuality: A person emotionally, romantically, or sexually attracted to more than one gender, although not necessarily simultaneously, in the same way, or to the same degree. There is often debate about whether this is transphobic; it is not, and there are many TNB bisexual people. Many *nonbinary* people explain it as being attracted to both people of the same gender (also nonbinary) and other genders (those who are not nonbinary).

Boi: A term used with some queer communities of color to refer to sexual orientation, gender, and/or aesthetic among people assigned female at birth. Boi often designates queer women who present with masculinity (although, this depends on location and usage), and has become more common among *transmasculine* and *nonbinary* individuals.

Bottom surgery: Medical interventions that some *transgender/nonbinary* folx get to align their body with their gender identity, and may include genital surgeries such as hysterectomy, vaginoplasty, phalloplasty, or metoidioplasty. See *surgery*.

Butch: An identity or presentation that leans toward masculinity. Although commonly associated with masculine, queer/lesbian women, it's used by many to describe a distinct gender identity and/or expression, and does not necessarily imply that one also identifies as a woman or not.

Cis/cisgender/cisgender/cissexual individuals: People whose gender identity matches social and cultural assumptions connected to their sex assigned at birth. Coined by Julia Serano, coming from the scientific term "cis" as in to move in the same direction, compared to trans, which means to cross directions or to move over.

Cisgender privilege: The set of unearned advantages and/or immunities that people who are or who are perceived as gender conforming benefit from on a daily basis.

Cissexism, cisgenderism, cisnormativity: Systemic prejudice in favor of cisgender people.

Cissimilation: The expectation for TNB people assimilating to cisgender (and often heteronormative) standards of appearance and performance.

Closeted: Describes an *LGBTQIA2S+* person who has not disclosed their sexual orientation or gender identity.

Coming out: The process in which a person first acknowledges, accepts, and appreciates their sexual orientation or gender identity and begins to share that with others. *Coming out* may have a different meaning for LGBQ individuals and TNB individuals.

Cross-dresser: Individuals who, regardless of motivation, wear clothing, makeup, etc. that is considered by their culture to not be appropriate for the gender/sex they were assigned at birth. *Transvestite* is often considered a pejorative term with the same meaning. Drag performers are cross-dressing performers who take on exaggerated gender presentations (although not all drag performers identify as cross-dressers). Cross-dressing and drag are forms of gender expression and are not necessarily tied to erotic activity, nor are they indicative of one's sexual orientation or gender identity.

Dead name or birth name: How some transgender people refer to their given name at birth. To "*dead name*" someone is to refer to them by their birth name instead of their correct name.

Demiromantic: Describes the condition of romantic attraction felt only in the presence of a pre-existing emotional bond. Generally, someone who is demiromantic will not get crushes on strangers or anyone with whom the individual does not already feel close to.

Demisexual: Sexual orientation in which a person feels sexual and romantic attraction only to people with whom they have an emotional bond. Many demisexuals feel sexual attraction rarely compared to the general population and some have little to no interest in sexual activity.

Disorders of sex development (DSD): See *intersex.*

Drag/drag king/drag queen: Exaggerated, theatrical, and/or performative gender presentation. Although most commonly used to refer to cross-dressing performers (drag queens and drag kings), anyone of any gender can do any form of drag. Performing drag does not necessarily have anything to do with one's sex assigned at birth, gender identity, or sexual orientation.

Dyadic or Endox: Someone whose assigned sex characteristics fall under the "male" or "female" category, not *intersex.*

Enby: See *nonbinary.*

Equality: A state in which everyone is equal. This ignores the difference in identity/community and history.

Equity/liberation/justice: A state in which marginalized people and communities are free. This differs greatly from equality.

Facial feminization surgery: See *surgery.*

Femme: An identity or presentation that leans towards femininity. Although commonly associated with feminine, lesbian/queer women, it is used by many to describe a distinct gender identity and/or expression, and does not necessarily imply that one also identifies as a woman or not.

Folx: A queer reuse of the word folks that has been used among queer and trans individuals, especially people of color, to denote shared radicalized, politicized identities – as in *"folx* like us" (Kapitan, 2016). Similar to the use of *Latinx* rather than Latina/Latino to be queer and trans-inclusive.

FTM: Female-to-male transgender people. Some trans men reject being seen as FTM, arguing that they have always been male and are only making this identity visible to other people (instead, they may call themselves *MTM*). This language is falling out of use, as the sex of someone is often less salient and relevant than their gender.

Gay: A person who is physically, romantically, and/or sexually attracted to other people of the same gender. Can be used to refer to people of all genders, though it is used most commonly to refer to cisgender males.

Gender: The beliefs, feelings, and behaviors that a specific culture attributes to individuals based on their gender assigned at birth. It can involve gender roles (the expectations imposed on someone based on their gender identity and gender expression), gender attribution (how others perceive someone's gender), and gender identity (how someone defines their own gender).

Gender affirmation surgery/gender affirming surgery: Surgical procedures that change one's body to conform to one's gender identity. Only the minority of transgender people choose to and can afford to have surgeries. The following terms are inaccurate, offensive, or outdated: *sex change operation, gender reassignment/realignment surgery* (gender is not changed due to surgery), and *sex reassignment/realignment surgery* (as it insinuates a single surgery is required to transition along with sex being an ambiguous term).

Gender binary: A system of viewing gender as consisting solely of two opposite categories, termed *man* and *woman*, in which no other possibilities for gender or anatomy are believed to exist. This system is oppressive to anyone who does not fit neatly into one of the two standard categories.

Gender blind: Without regard for gender.

Gender diverse/Gender nonconforming: Broad terms referring to people whose gender does not align with or conform to the gender associated with the sex they were assigned at birth, or whose gender expression does not fit neatly into a category.

Gender dysphoria: Anxiety and/or discomfort regarding one's sex assigned at birth. Clinically defined as significant and durational distress. Per the American Psychiatric Association's Diagnostic and Statistical Manual of Mental Disorders (DSM), it is defined as a "marked incongruence between one's experienced/expressed gender and assigned gender." Many transgender people object to being listed in the DSM, arguing that the inclusion serves to dehumanize and pathologize them. Replaced "gender identity disorder" in the DSM-5.

Gender expansive: Conveys a wider, more flexible range of gender identity and/or expression than typically associated with the binary gender system.

Gender expression/presentation: External appearance of one's gender identity, usually expressed through behavior, clothing, accessories, makeup, haircut, body language, and/or voice, and which may or may not conform to socially defined behaviors and characteristics typically associated with being either masculine or feminine. Gender expression is not an indicator of sexual orientation or gender identity.

Gender euphoria: A sense of elation, fulfilment, or joy that comes from living as the gender one understands oneself to be.

Gender fluid: A person who does not identify with a single fixed gender, and expresses a fluid or unfixed gender identity. One's expression may shift and change depending on context.

Gender identity: A person's innermost concept of self as man, woman, a blend of both, or additional genders outside of the gender binary. How individuals perceive themselves and what they call themselves. One's gender identity can be aligned with or different from the gender associated with their sex assigned at birth, and is not necessarily visible to others.

Gender identity disorder/GID: A controversial DSM-3 and DSM-4 diagnosis given to transgender and other gender nonconforming people. Because it labels people as disordered, gender identity disorder is often considered offensive. The diagnosis is frequently given to children who do not conform to expected gender norms in terms of dress, play, or behavior. Such children are often subjected to intense psychotherapy, behavior modification, and/or institutionalization. The terms were replaced by the term *gender dysphoria* in the DSM-5.

Gender minority: Used to describe people whose gender expression and/or gender identity does not match traditional societal norms. *Sexual minority* should not be used as a synonym for, or as inclusive of *gender minority.*

Gender variant: A general term for individuals who do not fit into traditional binary categories of gender. Considered offensive by some for labeling one's gender as outside of norms or other. Alternative language include gender expansive (often used with youth), gender nonconforming, and gender diverse.

Gender questioning: A person who may be processing, questioning, or exploring how they want to express their gender identity.

Gender reassignment surgery (GRS), gender realignment surgery (GRS), gender confirmation surgery (GCS): Outdated terms that are considered offensive and have been replaced. See instead *gender affirmation surgery.*

Gender transition: The process by which some people strive to more closely align their outward appearance with their internal gender identity. Some people socially transition, whereby they might begin presenting in different ways, using new names and pronouns, and/or be socially recognized as another gender. Others undergo physical transitions in which they modify their bodies through medical interventions.

Gender X: A designation available in some countries (e.g., Australia, Bangladesh, Canada, Germany, Nepal, New Zealand, Pakistan), and some states in the US (e.g., California, Oregon, Vermont, Washington), for official government documentation that encompasses a gender that is not exclusively male or female, and may include *intersex, agender, gender fluid,* and *transgender* among other *nonbinary* identities.

Genderism: The societal, institutional, and individual beliefs and practices that privilege cisgender people, and subordinate and disparage transgender and gender nonconforming people.

Genderqueer/genderqueer individuals: A term for people who reject notions of static categories of gender and embrace a fluidity of gender identity and often, though not always, sexual orientation. People who identify as genderqueer may see themselves as being both man and woman, neither man nor woman, or as falling completely outside these categories. Not everyone who identifies as genderqueer identifies as trans or nonbinary. This term is generally used in two ways: (1) as an umbrella term that includes all people whose gender varies from the traditional norm, akin to the use of the word "queer" to refer to people whose sexual orientation is not heterosexual only; or (2) to describe a subset of individuals who are assigned female or male at birth, but feel their gender identity is neither female nor male.

Genital reconstruction surgery (GRS): Term that is increasingly falling into disuse that represents a cluster of *genital surgeries* that some transgender/nonbinary folx get to align their body with their gender identity. See instead *surgery.*

Getting clocked/being read: When people are not perceived as the gender they are presenting (e.g., based on their dress and mannerisms match according to social norms).

Gray-romantic/grey-romantic/gray-aromantic/grey-aromantic/gray/grey: A romantic orientation on the *aromantic* spectrum. A person who is gray-romantic may identify with some elements of aromanticism or as being on the aromantic spectrum without identifying solely as aromantic. Gray-romantic people may be indifferent, repulsed, or favorable toward romance and may identify with any sexual orientation.

Greysexual/greysexual/grey asexual/gray asexual/grey-A/gray-A/gray-ace/grace: A sexual orientation where someone identifies strongly with *asexuality,* but doesn't feel like asexual is the most correct word for them. Someone who identifies somewhere between *asexual* and *sexual.* A greysexual person may feel sexual attraction, but only infrequently and/or of low intensity and/or only in specific circumstances.

Hermaphrodite: Previously used to describe *intersex.* Now considered pejorative and outdated.

Heteronormative/heteronormativity: These terms refer to the assumption that heterosexuality is the norm, which plays out in interpersonal interactions and society and furthers the marginalization of queer people.

Homophobia: The fear and hatred of or discomfort with people who are attracted to members of the same gender.

Informed consent model: An alternative to the *Standards of Care for the Health of Transsexual, Transgender, and Gender Nonconforming People* which allows *transgender/nonbinary* individuals to access hormone treatments and surgical interventions without being under a mental health evaluation or receiving a referral from a mental health specialist (Schulz, 2018).

Intersex: An umbrella term used to describe a wide range of natural bodily variations. In some cases, these traits are visible at birth, and in others, they are not apparent until puberty. Some chromosomal variations of this type may not be physically apparent at all. Parents and medical professionals usually coercively assign intersex infants a sex and have, in the past, been medically permitted to perform surgical operations to conform the infant's genitalia to that assignment. This practice has become increasingly controversial as intersex adults speak out against the practice. The term *intersex* is not interchangeable with or a synonym for *transgender* (although some intersex people do identify as transgender). Sometimes referred to in medical texts as *DSD* (disorders of sexual development), though many intersex people reject this language.

Lesbian: A woman who is emotionally, physically, and/or romantically attracted to some other women.

LGBTQ: An acronym for lesbian, gay, bisexual, transgender, and queer.

LGBTQQIAPP+: An expanded acronym for a collection of identities for lesbian, gay, bisexual, trans, queer, questioning, intersex, asexual, aromantic, pansexual, polysexual.

LGBTQIA2S+: An expanded acronym for a collection of identities for lesbian, gay, bisexual, trans, queer, questioning, intersex, asexual/aromantic, two-spirit, and other.

Living openly: A state in which LGBTQIA2S+ people are comfortably out about their sexual orientation or gender identity – where and when it feels appropriate to them. It is important to remember that not all LGBTQIA2S+ people have the safety and/or resources that permit one to live openly.

Lower surgery: See *bottom surgery.*

Microaggression: The concept of microaggressions emerged in the 1970s in the context of racial microaggressions (Pierce, Carew, Pierce-Gonzalez, & Willis, 1978), which were defined as "brief and commonplace daily verbal, behavioral, or environmental indignities, whether intentional or unintentional, that communicate hostile, derogatory, or negative racial slights and insults to the target person or group", and have since been applied to other marginalized populations (Sue & Constantine, 2007, p. 273). The concept of microaggressions emerged in the 1970s in the context of racial microaggressions as defined as "subtle, stunning, often automatic, and non-verbal exchanges which are 'put downs'" (Pierce, Carew, Pierce-Gonzalez, & Willis, 1978, p. 65).

Misgender: Referring to or addressing someone using pronouns that do not correctly reflect the gender with which the person identifies.

Monosexual: Umbrella term for sexual orientations that are directed towards one gender (includes gay, lesbian, heterosexual).

MTF: Male-to-female transgender people. Some transwomen reject being seen as MTF, arguing that they have always been female and are only making this identity visible to other people. Instead, they may call themselves *FTF*. This language is falling out of use, as the sex of someone is often less salient and relevant than their gender.

Multigender: Describes someone who experiences more than one gender identity. The term can be used as a gender identity in its own right or can be an umbrella term for identities that fit this description. Identities include *bigender, trigender, polygender, pangender, two-spirit (Indigenous people only),* and *genderfluid,* among others.

Multisexual or non-monosexual: Umbrella term for sexual orientations attracted to multiple genders (includes bisexual, pansexual, queer, etc.)

Neo-vagina: While this is a technical term for when a vagina is surgically created and is suitable for use when having a discussion with another medical professional, it is not a term that should be used with a client during routine office visits, or in social contexts. A clinician need not remind a female client that she has a *neo-vagina,* but rather should simply say *vagina.*

Nonbinary (also non-binary)/nonbinary individual/enby: Umbrella term for all genders that fall outside of the binary system of woman/man. Nonbinary people may identify as being both a man and a woman, somewhere in between, or as falling completely outside these categories. Should be used as an adjective (e.g., Suze is a nonbinary person). Not all nonbinary people identify as trans, and not all trans people identify as nonbinary.

Omnisexual: Describes someone who has the potential for sexual attraction to people of any gender, taking into account their gender, though not necessarily simultaneously, in the same way, or to the same degree. Sometimes the term *pansexual* is used as a synonym; however, there are nuanced differences. While *pansexual* individuals are considered *gender blind, omnisexual* individuals are not.

Outing: The unauthorized disclosure by one person of another person's gender, gender identity, or sexual orientation without their permission. Outing someone can have serious repercussions on employment, economic stability, personal safety, religious affiliations, or family situations. In the political world, *outing* has been used by some activists to expose the hypocrisy of opposing pro-LGBTQIA2S+ policies and laws while secretly being LGBTQIA2S+ or engaging in same-sex sexual/affectional behaviors. *Outing* in the political world is controversial and there is significant disagreement on its use by activists.

Packing: Wearing a penile prosthesis.

Pangender: See *nonbinary* and *genderqueer.*

Pansexual: Describes someone who has the potential for sexual attraction to people of any gender regardless of their gender, though not necessarily simultaneously, in the same way, or to the same degree. Sometimes the term *omnisexual* is used in the same manner; however, there are nuanced differences. While *pansexual* individuals are considered *gender blind*, *omnisexual* individuals are not.

Passing: Being perceived by others as a particular identity that one identifies as (e.g., passing as heterosexual, passing as a cisgender woman). This term has become controversial as it can be understood to imply that one is not genuinely what they are passing as.

Polygender: Describes someone who experiences multiple gender identities, either simultaneously or varying between them. These may be male, female, and/or any nonbinary identities. Polygender people may also identify as *multigender, nonbinary*, and/or *transgender*. If a polygender person experiences their gender identity as changing over time or depending on circumstances, they may also identify as *genderfluid*. Polygender people can have any *gender expression*, but many prefer to be seen as *androgynous* and/or change their gender presentation to be more masculine or feminine depending on their current identity.

Polysexual: Describes someone who is capable of being attracted to multiple genders.

Queer: A term that may refer to an individual's gender identity and/or sexual orientation or may be an umbrella term inclusive of TNB and LGB folks (e.g., the queer community, queer folks). In the context of an individual identity, it is frequently used to indicate a more radical, political orientation around issues of gender identity and sexual orientation, or a more fluid identity. While there is overlap between *queer* and *transgender* identities, not all queer people are trans, and not all trans people are queer. While the term can be used in a derogatory manner, many in the TNB and LGB community have reclaimed the term.

Questioning: A term used to describe individuals who are in the process of exploring their sexual orientation and/or gender identity.

Real life experience: A guideline from the *Standards of Care for the Health of Transsexual, Transgender and Gender Nonconforming People* (see www.wpath.org) that requires individuals to live outwardly as their gender identity for a specified period of time (often one year) prior to being eligible for genital surgery. Less often referred to as the *real life test*, a term that is considered misleading and offensive and so should be avoided.

Real life test: See *real life experience*.

Romantic/affective/emotional orientation: A person's romantic and/or emotional attraction to others. Can be correlated to someone's *sexual orientation* (i.e., someone who is both heterosexual and heteroromantic, or *pansexual* and panromantic), but does not have to be (i.e., someone who is asexual and panromantic, or who is a lesbian and aromantic). *Transgender* people may be aromantic, biromantic, homoromantic, panromantic, queer, etc. just like *cisgender* people. A person's *romantic orientation* should not be assumed based on the perceived *sex* or *gender* of that person's partner(s).

Same-gender loving: A term some prefer to use instead of lesbian, gay, or bisexual, to express attraction to and love of people of the same gender. Most frequently used in the African American/Black community.

Sex: The classification of a person as male or female (typically) at birth. Infants are assigned a sex usually based on the appearance of their external anatomy. Some countries and US states allow a *gender X*, representing a *nonbinary* or third gender.

Sex assigned at birth/SAAB: The *sex* given to a child at birth, most often based on the child's external anatomy. *AMAB* is assigned male at birth, and *AFAB* is assigned female at birth. *Intersex* individuals may use CAFAB or CAMAB, to indicate being coercively assigned female at birth or coercively assigned male at birth.

Sex change/sex change operation/sex change surgery: Terms that are considered pejorative and should be avoided that represent a cluster of genital surgeries that some *transgender/nonbinary* folks get to align their body with their gender identity. See instead *gender affirmation surgery.*

Sex reassignment surgery (SRS)/Sex realignment surgery (SRS): Terms that are increasingly falling into disuse that represent a cluster of genital surgeries that some transgender/nonbinary folks get to align their body with their gender identity. See instead *gender affirmation surgery.*

Sexual behavior: Manner in which humans experience and express their sexuality. People engage in a variety of sexual acts, ranging from activities done alone to acts with another person. Sexual behaviors do not have a sexual orientation, thus terms such as "gay sex" or "lesbian sexual activity" are misleading and inaccurate.

Sexual minority: Term used to describe people whose sexual orientation is not heterosexual only. *Sexual minority* should not be used to mean *gender minority*, and the preferred term for many is LGBQ rather than sexual minority.

Sexual orientation: A person's physical, aesthetic, sexual, and/or other form of attraction to others. In Western cultures, *gender identity* and *sexual orientation* are not the same. *Transgender* people may be asexual, bisexual, gay, heterosexual, lesbian, pansexual, queer, etc. just like *cisgender* people. Can be correlated to someone's *romantic orientation* (i.e., someone who is both heterosexual and heteroromantic, or *pansexual* and panromantic), but does not have to be (i.e., someone who is asexual and panromantic, or who is a lesbian and aromantic). *Sexual orientation* is distinct from *sex*, *gender identity*, and *gender expression*. A person's *sexual orientation* should not be assumed based on the perceived *sex* of that person's partner(s), nor should an assumption be made about a person's *sexual behavior* based on their *sexual orientation*.

Sie: A non-gender specific pronoun used instead of he and she.

Standards of Care for the Health of Transsexual, Transgender, and Gender Nonconforming People/Harry Benjamin Standards of Care/WPATH Standards of Care/Standards of Care/SOC: Clinical protocols outlining recommended medical/psychological assessment and treatment of *transgender/nonbinary* individuals across the lifespan who wish to undergo social, hormonal, or surgical transition to another *sex*. The protocols are developed by *World Professional Association for Transgender Health* (formerly known as the Harry Benjamin Gender Dysphoria Association) and revised periodically to reflect a greater understanding of best practices. Were originally developed in 1979, and revised in 1980, 1981, 1990, 1998, 2001, and 2011. Criticism of the SOC have included concerns about the strictness of requirements (particularly given that the rate of post-surgical regret is very low – lower than many medically necessary and cosmetic procedures with fewer contingent requirements), the *real life experience* component which can be emotionally harmful and physically dangerous for some individuals, and for pathological language.

Stealth: When a transgender who has transitioned into a different sex or gender does not divulge the fact of transition in all or most social situations. The fear of being *outed* can be very distressing for some people who are living stealth. Some people who considered themselves *transgender* prior to *transition*, believe that after they *transition*, they are no longer *transgender*, and therefore have nothing to reveal. This term can be problematic, implying that TNB individuals have something to hide or are doing something illicit.

Surgery: Medical interventions that some *transgender/nonbinary* people seek to align their body with their gender identity. There are numerous surgical interventions that some *transgender* people seek, and as such, the term *the surgery* should be avoided as it is misleading and inaccurate. See *gender affirmation surgery*.

T: Short for testosterone.

They/Them/Theirs (singular): Gender inclusive pronouns, often used by nonbinary individuals, and can be used when someone's correct pronouns are not known, in order to not *misgender* them.

TNB: Abbreviation for *transgender* and *nonbinary*.

Top surgery: Term most often used by transmasculine individuals to refer to the removal of chest tissue, relocation and resizing of nipple complexes, and chest reconstruction to a masculine chest structure, or transfeminine individuals to refer to the addition of breast tissue/filler, and chest reconstruction to a feminine chest structure. See *gender affirmation surgery*.

Tranny: A short term for a *transgender* person. Many people consider the term derogatory, especially when used by someone who is cisgender. Do not use unless someone uses it for themselves.

Trans: Prefix or adjective used as an abbreviation for transgender.

Trans feminine: Term usually referring to someone who was assigned a male sex at birth (but not always) and who identifies and performs gender in a feminine way, but may or may not identify as a woman or trans woman.

Trans masculine: Term usually referring to someone who was assigned a female sex at birth (but not always) and who identifies and performs gender in a masculine way, but may or may not identify as a man or trans man.

Trans man/transman/man: Term usually referring to someone who was assigned a female sex at birth, but who identifies and performs gender as a man. People frequently use the term after taking some steps to express their gender as a man. See also *FTM*. Trans men are men; some may use the term trans as a descriptor, but it does not negate their status as a man.

Trans woman/transwoman/woman: Term usually referring to someone who was assigned a male sex at birth, but who identifies and performs gender as a woman. People frequently use the term after taking some steps to express their gender as a woman. See also *MTF.* Trans women are women; some may use the term trans as a descriptor, but it does not negate their status as a woman.

Trans*: An outdated term popularized in the early 2010s that signified an array of identities under the *transgender/nonbinary* umbrella. The term has been critiqued as inaccessible, binarist, and transmisogynist. It originated from search Boolean, where trans* would search for any words starting with trans (e.g., transgender, transsexual, etc.). It was used to attempt to be more inclusive; however, the term *transgender* or *trans* without an asterisk already includes all trans people.

Transgender/trans/transgender individuals: People whose gender identity differs from social and cultural assumptions connected to the gender associated with their sex assigned at birth, inclusive of nonbinary, gender diverse, and gender nonconforming individuals. The term is not indicative of *gender expression, sexual orientation,* or how one is perceived in daily life. Note that the term does not have an 'ed' at the end. The term *transgendered* should be avoided.

Transition/transitioning: The period during which a person begins to live as their true gender. It may include changing one's name or pronouns, altering their presentation, taking hormones, having surgeries or other medical interventions, and altering legal documents. Transitioning is not a one-step procedure; it is a complex process that occurs over a period of time, and looks different for different people.

Transsexual: A term that is often seen as and considered pejorative by many that indicates a person whose gender identity differs from the social and cultural assumptions connected to their sex assigned at birth. It frequently – but not always – implicates hormonal/surgical transition from one binary gender (man or woman) to the other. When speaking/writing about trans people, the term should be avoided to refer to an individual, unless it is someone who uses the term as their own identity.

Transmisogyny: A term originally coined by Julia Serano to designate the intersection of transphobia and misogyny and how they are often experienced as a form of oppression that targets trans women.

Transphobia: Systemic violence against *transgender/nonbinary* people, associated with attitudes such as fear, discomfort, distrust, or disdain.

Transvestite: Outdated term previously used to describe a cross-dresser. Now considered pejorative. See *cross-dresser.*

Trigender: Refers to those who identify as three genders. Can also identify as *multigender*.

Two Spirit/Two-Spirit: An umbrella term indicating various Indigenous gender and sexual identities among tribes in North America. The term was created by Native individuals with diverse gender identities and sexual orientations to have a non-harmful term used to describe these diverse experiences as connected to their heritage. This term should not be used or appropriated by non-Native individuals.

Variability in Sex Development (VSD)/Variation in Sex Development (VSD): See
   intersex.

Ze/Hir: A non-gender specific pronoun used instead of he or she, and him or her.

REFERENCES

Adams, C. (2017). *The gender identity terms you need to know.* Retrieved from www.cbsnews.
   com/news/transgender-gender-identity-terms-glossary/

Beemyn, G. (n.d.). *Transgender terminology.* Retrieved from https://hr.cornell.edu/sites/default/
   files/trans%20terms.pdf

Demisexual Resource Center. (2015). *Demisexuality resource center: Resources for demisexuals, partners, and allies.* Retrieved from http://demisexuality.org

Human Rights Campaign. (2020). *Glossary of terms.* Retrieved from www.hrc.org/resources/
   glossary-of-terms

Kapitan, A. (2016). *Ask a radical copyeditor: Folx.* Retreived from https://radicalcopyeditor.
   com/2016/09/12/folx/

National LGBT Health Education Center. (2010). *Fenway Health: Glossary of gender and
   transgender terms.* Retrieved from www.lgbthealtheducation.org/wp-content/uploads/
   Handout_7-C_Glossary_of_Gender_and_Transgender_Terms__fi.pdf

Pierce, C., Carew, J., Pierce-Gonzalez, D., & Willis, D. (1978). An experiment in racism: TV
   commercials. In C. Pierce (Ed.), *Television and education* (pp. 62–88). Beverly Hills, CA:
   Sage.

Riggle, E. D., & Rostosky, S. S. (2011). *A positive view of LGBTQ: Embracing identity and
   cultivating well-being.* Lanham, MD: Rowman & Littlefield Publishers.

Schulz, S. L. (2018). The informed consent model of transgender care: An alternative to
   the diagnosis of gender dysphoria. *Journal of Humanistic Psychology, 58,* 72–92.
   doi:10.1177/0022167817745217

Sue, D. W., & Constantine, M. G. (2007). Racial microaggressions as instigators of difficult
   dialogues on race: Implications for student affairs educators and students. *College Student
   Affairs Journal, 26*(2), 136–143.

Trans Student Educational Resources. (2020). *LGBTQ+ definitions.* Retrieved from www.
   transstudent.org/definitions

Transgender Hub. (2017). *Breaking down transgender terms and definitions glossary.* Retrieved
   from www.transgenderhub.com/breaking-transgender-terms-definitions-glossary/

Introduction Part 1

Introduction to social work and health care with transgender and nonbinary individuals and communities

Shanna K. Kattari, M. Killian Kinney, Leonardo Kattari, and N. Eugene Walls

RATIONALE BEHIND THIS BOOK

Transgender and nonbinary (TNB) children, youth, adults, and communities face invisibility and invalidation of their gender in numerous domains of their lives, from intake forms to bathrooms to well-intended binary-focused policies, as well as through individual and systemic violence. While there is currently unprecedented visibility and increasing levels of support and acceptance for TNB children, youth, and adults, and high levels of resistance and resilience from TNB individuals and groups, members of this population still face shockingly high rates of violence, victimization, unemployment, discrimination, and family rejection. Similarly, navigating a transphobic culture leaves many TNB individuals feeling hopeless, struggling with suicidality and self-harm impulses, and often reluctant to seek even basic health care or legal protection because of fears and anxiety about the possibility of ridicule, shaming, or outright refusal of services. They may feel wholly erased or, conversely, hyper-visible and on display. Yet, despite interpersonal and societal challenges, members of this population embody an incredible resistance and resilience to so many challenges, and their resourcefulness in not only surviving but also thriving in a society that does not always affirm their identities and existence is magnificent.

CREATION OF THIS BOOK

The intentional creation of this book in response to all of this was twofold. First, many gaps in the literature exist regarding health and wellbeing among TNB individuals and communities that are needed for improved practice, education, and research. While there have been books on counseling TNB clients, or social work practice with all lesbian, gay, bisexual, transgender, queer, intersex, asexual, and two-spirit (LGBTQIA2S+) individuals, or working specifically with TNB youth, to our knowledge, there has not been an edited volume that explores social work and related health care when it comes to this population. As both members of the TNB population and those who work with these individuals and communities regularly, we are often called upon to educate social workers, human service professionals, and health care providers. Having a volume to offer these professionals and educators as well as students being trained in these fields helped drive our intentions around this creation.

The need for the book as a tool for educators and service providers is further underscored by the reality that the major associations of mental health and health care providers currently embrace the need for culturally responsive approaches to service provision as well as the importance of educating future and current practitioners on effectively serving TNB individuals and communities. For example, the National Association of Social Workers' (2017) policy statement on TNB individuals and communities enumerates the importance of training future social workers, the need for the professional development of existing practitioners, the support for antidiscrimination policies, and the need for advocacy in public policy. The American Psychological Association (2015) has guidelines on affirmative practice with TNB individuals, which includes the need for the training of future psychologists to work competently with members of the TNB community. The American Medical Association (2017) extensively outlines general policies, physician-centered policies, and patient-centered policies underscoring support for comprehensive education and competent service delivery for TNB patients. Similar policies and guidelines can be found from the American Counseling Association (2009), the American Academy of Pediatrics (see Raffery et al., 2018), and the American Psychiatric Association (2018), among others.

Secondly, paralleling the fairly recent support for TNB individuals and communities from professional organizations outlined above, research too has become more common. Wanta and Unger (2017) reviewed all publications in the Medline database (from 1950 to mid-2016), documenting a clear trend of an increasing number of "trans-centric" articles. The body of scholarship has grown to the point where an increasing number of systematic reviews or other types of summary articles have been published, including reviews focused on mental health and gender dysphoria (Dhejne et al., 2016), gender identity in childhood (Perry et al., 2019), health care in primary care settings (Hashemi et al., 2018), cervical cancer screening (Gatos, 2017), incarceration (Glezer et al., 2013), and self-injury among children and young people (Mann et al., 2018). While increasing the knowledge about TNB individuals and communities is a welcome development, the trend is problematic in the lack of TNB authors of this scholarship, the medicalization and pathologizing of TNB individuals, and the absence of the voice of front line practitioners.

The absence of TNB authors in the literature about TNB communities is strikingly apparent. Given that peer-reviewed and professional literature are most often written by those who have access to the Academy and to medical education, it is no surprise that the very discrimination and erasure discussed earlier have prevented many TNB individuals from accessing PhDs, MDs, and other degrees that often result in conducting research and writing about TNB communities. While many research teams are now moving towards including community advisory boards in their research to ensure the voices of TNB individuals are helping guide the research enterprise, these community members are still rarely included in the resulting publications. As such, much of the research and development of best practices about this population are not written by members of the population, reinforcing the marginalization they experience, and running the risk of research that further pathologizes TNB individuals.

There have been increasingly more TNB activists, practitioners, academics, and researchers becoming visible in the past few years, and whose work we wanted to highlight. As editors of this volume, we have been committed to centering TNB voices by co-editing and co-authoring all components of this book and embodying these very tenets of empowerment, resilience, and unique experiences of intersectional identities; every chapter is co-authored by one or more TNB individuals, ensuring their voices are at the heart of this book. Brown and Strega (2005) describe *research from the margins* as research *by*, *for*, and *with* those who have been marginalized, moving those in the margins from "subject" and "object" to "author", along with the power and validity which that role entails. It is our deepest hope that this book is seen as research from the margins, and encourages others to center the voices of the marginalized, even if they do not have advanced degrees or academic positions. Recognizing individuals as experts in their own experiences is crucial to fostering equity and justice.

Relatedly, much of the research, especially in social work, is conducted by individuals in the Academy, some who have been away from their practices for decades. While this may have been how it is always done, this leaves out the voices of practitioners who are "on the front lines" in understanding practice and implementation, as well as community members, students who are bridging the community and the Academy, activists, and others. We wanted to make sure this was not just another tome from the Academy, telling practitioners what to do without actually knowing what needs might exist. As such, while many of the authors in this text are tenure-track academics, there are also clinical professors, social work practitioners, midwives, physicians, activists, PhD students, MSW students, higher education administrators, research collaborators, and community members co-authoring these chapters.

EMPOWERMENT, RESILIENCE, AND INTERSECTIONALITY

With consideration for the predominant focus of TNB literature on inequity and pathology, this book and the chapters within were created with an empowerment framework to uplift this community, emphasizing the resilience and successes already celebrated by this population. We have chosen to incorporate and highlight the incredible resourcefulness and resistance of TNB individuals and communities to challenge narratives of educators and practitioners that rely primarily on a one-dimensional perspective of risk and tragic lives. Illustrating ways in which TNB individuals successfully and effectively navigate a world that pathologizes and devalues their existence, connect to create thriving communities and relationships, and organize to find a political voice provides a counter-narrative of empowerment, and identifies potential avenues for further fostering hopefulness, power, and health.

So much of what is written about TNB people comes solely from a risk perspective: concerns about depression, anxiety, and suicidality, experiences of homelessness and murders, and experiences of discrimination. While these are all real barriers facing this population, they do not define the population. Instead of focusing only on how many TNB individuals were denied health care, we wanted to focus on ways health care professionals can create affirming interactions with their TNB patients. Beyond those dismal mental health numbers, we wanted to encourage mental health spaces to be inclusive of TNB individuals, and help them to figure out what they most want and need in their lives, rather than center solely on preventing self-harm and suicide. Changing systems requires discussion of how to empower TNB individuals to move towards leadership positions, to engage TNB communities in community-driven and engaged research, and to organize at all levels across numerous populations, including young people. This book is written with empowerment in mind, providing best practice suggestions that center on the incredible resilience of members of TNB communities, and move towards strategies for empowerment rather than just coping.

Throughout this book, you will learn how to address many of the existing gaps in services, access, and inclusion. Below are some basic best practice guidelines that will be further enumerated in the following chapters. Because the TNB community is so diverse, and each individual's experiences vary based on intersections of numerous social identities and physical locations, best practices should be thought of as a general blueprint for the work rather than as hard and fast rules. Considerations and adaptations will almost always be necessary for each individual or community. Given this, we encourage you to center the following guidelines.

1. Acknowledge the variance of experience. No two TNB persons will have the same experiences. While this book provides research and literature on a multitude of topics that give us a glimpse into the experiences of TNB people, this evidence should be used as a starting point and a broad generalization. We cannot approach our human services and health care practice with TNB people with a "one size fits all" strategy.
2. Stay educated and informed. It is our responsibility as human service professionals to stay up to date on the rapidly changing landscape of our clients' lived experiences. Gender identity and the policies and practices that influence the lives of TNB people change quickly. Do not expect TNB clients to educate you or even, at times, know themselves how policies and best practices have changed. Keep learning, keep growing, and challenge yourself to stay as informed as possible.
3. Be respectful and avoid assumptions. A theme that winds its way through many of the chapters and that parallels the best practice of acknowledging variance

of experience, this theme encourages us to avoid making assumptions about a client's experience, identities, and even the words they use to describe themselves. When appropriate, ask for more information about how an individual may identify their gender, the pronouns they use, how they define their relationships and/or sexuality, and what family means to them. When asking clarifying questions, confirm with yourself first what your intent is in asking these questions. Is this relevant to your provider/client relationship, or is this a curiosity you have for personal gain? If you're not sure if asking a direct question is appropriate, stay attuned to the words and terminology a client is using and mirror it back to them. Do not assume that all terms have the same meaning to different people. For example, one client may use the term gender diverse to describe themselves; however, another client may find that term offensive.

4. Meet individuals where they are. For some TNB people, their gender identity may be incredibly salient to their current situation and experiences. For others, they may not need support around their gender identity. If a client is not explicitly stating their need for information, resources, and support around their gender identity, proceed with caution on how you bring it up and incorporate it, if you do so at all. For example, if a client wants to discuss feeling depressed and relates it back to a recent relationship breakup, follow their lead. That should be the primary focus of your work with them. Find a balance between how gender identity may be influencing other aspects of their life if a client is not specifically bringing it up. This is especially important to consider for folks who may be questioning their gender identity.

5. Show up. There are lots of ways to show up and engage with communities. Showing up for TNB individuals is something we can do in our agencies and organizations, as well as in our interaction with external providers and organizations. We can champion efforts to change our organizational policies, update forms, and challenge anti-TNB microaggressions and explicit transphobia. Furthermore, we can do this with other agencies and organizations by working with our colleagues, joining boards, committees, and commissions, and changing how we show up and engage in meetings as facilitators or attendees. We can support TNB-focused organizations by supporting their work through in-kind and financial contributions and through building TNB leadership pipelines to bring TNB voices where they may not currently exist.

6. Use an intersectional lens. All authors in this volume were asked to be particularly intentional about writing with an intersectional lens in mind. In recognizing, for example, the disproportionately high rates of violence against transgender people of color, especially transgender women of color, a lens of intersectionality must be used (Crenshaw, 1990). Intersectionality is a theory grounded in Black feminist thought that looks at the intersection of race and gender (as well as other identities) to explore how the crossroads of multiple marginalized identities may be related to differential experiences of discrimination, victimization, and other challenging outcomes. It is crucial to use an intersectional lens when exploring the experiences of TNB individuals and communities; this concept helps to disrupt the assumption about members of this population, both who they are and what it looks like to be transgender or nonbinary.

POSITIONALITY STATEMENT OF EDITORS

We recognize the value of transparency regarding positionality, particularly around TNB populations who have been largely studied and written about by cisgender researchers. *Positionality* and *worldview* can impact one's work and can include race, gender, sexuality, disability status, social class, religious/spiritual beliefs, political values, and more (Sikes, 2004; Wellington et al., 2005). With an increasing number of TNB researchers, practitioners, and community leaders, the editors prioritized TNB inclusion with the intention of centering the perspectives, experiences, and voices of TNB individuals and communities. The structure of this edited volume was designed with TNB community members involved at all stages, along with consensus-building among the four editors, and integrating input from the 66 authors included herein. Further, the diversity of the authors' experience enriches this text with backgrounds, including artists, community organizers and activists, practitioners, researchers, and professors.

With consideration of positionality in relation to identity, the editorial team is comprised of one queer nonbinary individual, one queer trans man, one queer cisgender woman, and one gay cisgender man. Both of the cisgender editors are currently tenure-track academics (one tenured), while the trans and nonbinary editors are doctoral students. All of us have experiences with mental health challenges, one of us is disabled and experiences chronic illness/chronic pain, and two of us are neurodiverse. Additionally, all of us are White, with varying ethnicities. We have worked to include multiple authors of color, young people, those experiencing homelessness, and a few international authors throughout the book to provide viewpoints and experiences outside of our own identities and experiences.

All of us editors have been working in the field of TNB social work, health care, and wellbeing for a combined total of decades, including practice in an adolescent gender health clinic, working with non-profit wrap-around services with the TNB community, facilitating therapeutic group sessions with TNB adults, engaging health care policy specifically for TNB individuals, providing sexuality education and affirmation with TNB youth and adults, collecting state-wide data on a variety of topics including TNB youth, teaching courses on affirmative practice with TNB individuals and communities, and conducting research on TNB mental health, TNB people's health care experiences, affirming health care with TNB patients, and sexual and reproductive health care wants and desires within TNB communities.

These combined experiences speak to insider and outsider perspectives that can provide a potentially advantageous or disadvantageous perspective that may affect the process (Hammersley, 1993; Herod, 1999), especially with consideration for intersectional and differential identities. The initial choice of chapter topics was proposed by the editorial team. However, with an appreciation for varying perspectives, additional content was considered for inclusion, both on the suggestion of others we have been in dialogue with, as well as from authors themselves. One such example is the Introduction Part 2, *Place, joy, and self in trans and nonbinary justice*, which was a beautifully individual approach to the requested chapter about community organizing. As a result of the holistic framing that aligned with the intention of this book, it was decided to be placed as the opening chapter. It was with this receptiveness while writing this book that creativity and collaboration were able to thrive across different perspectives.

WHO IS THIS BOOK FOR?

Two primary categories of readership are anticipated for this text: teachers and students in higher education, and professionals in health care and social service arenas. A growing number of universities are offering electives, minors, and majors related to the LGBTQIA2S+ community. Whether focused on history, practice, theory, or policy, LGBTQIA2S+ courses may choose to utilize this book as supplemental material or as the primary text. In addition, courses that explore diversity and intersectionality could benefit from the range of chapters, including those courses in cross-professional areas such as health care, policy analysis, and community-based work.

In the changing landscape of today, people in many professions recognize the need for "cultural competence" or being culturally responsive and culturally humble in regard to a multitude of identities, including gender identity and gender expression. Professional fields that have been identified as potentially working with TNB individuals and could benefit from this book include community organizers, social workers, school-based therapists, licensed marriage and family therapists, policymakers, mental health counselors, nurses, midwives, legislators, nurses, and physicians. The chapters will include introductory to advanced information that is accessible and informative for those wanting to increase their awareness and a refresh to those currently working effectively with TNB individuals and communities. In particular, the portion of each chapter focusing on best practices will allow these portions to be used by agencies as material for internal diversity training. Beyond the two identified readerships, the potential exists for many other uses and audiences, and we welcome you as well.

ORGANIZATION OF THE BOOK

This book is designed to be used across both educational and practice settings. In this vein, each chapter includes a brief introduction, a review of existing literature (both peer-reviewed academic research and information from white papers, grey literature, and non-profits doing work with this population), information on best practices with TNB individuals and communities on the specific topic area, either a case study or an activity to apply the material in the chapter (either in class or independently), and additional resources. Some readers may choose to read the book from cover to cover, while others may focus only on specific chapters relevant to their interests. Still, others may simply want to focus on the case studies and activities to improve their knowledge and skills with this population. All of these are valid uses; this book should help meet the education and practice needs of a variety of students and professionals.

Immediately preceding this introductory chapter, we have included a glossary of terms that you might encounter in the book. While language is constantly evolving and quickly changing within the TNB community, we have attempted to provide a definition of common terms based on our current understanding of the terms' current usage. We have included this at the beginning of the book (rather than at the end) as many readers may need a foundational grounding before grappling with the content of the chapters. The second part of the introduction is written by community activists and sets a tone for the book; while there are so many interpersonal and systemic challenges facing this population, it is crucial to also recognize trans and nonbinary identities as a place of love and joy, and the incredible connection and affirmation that being in community can bring.

The **Health** section covers several areas of importance regarding the health and wellbeing of the community. Given the difference in needs between TNB young people and adults, we have separated the mental health and the medical care chapters into each of these subgroups. Additionally, two amazing midwives have co-authored a chapter on sexual and reproductive health care with this population.

The next section is on different **Areas of practice**, and how they can best serve TNB individuals. This section includes a chapter for gerontologists and those working with other adults, practitioners who focus on substance use, a chapter on homelessness for those working with shelters and in housing support, and a chapter on TNB concerns within the child welfare system.

The following section focuses on **Coming out and family**. This section includes chapters on how to support both TNB youth and TNB adults in their coming out process, how to support parents and family of TNB young people, and a chapter on parenting by TNB individuals.

In the section on **Relationships and sexuality**, there are three chapters. These chapters offer support around relationship and sex therapy with TNB individuals and couples/groups, a chapter giving a deeper dive into TNB sexuality, and a chapter on the experiences of intimate partner violence with this population and ways to support survivors.

The **Communities** section focuses on TNB communities in a variety of ways. The chapters in this section include focuses on youth empowerment with TNB young people, TNB affirming policy, conducting community-engaged research with TNB communities, supporting TNB leadership and civic engagement, and the ways through which TNB communities and individuals may use the digital age to their benefit.

The final section is on **Multiple marginalized identities and diverse communities**. While we have tried to use an intersectional approach and include information about diverse identities and communities throughout each and every chapter, we understand that some identities need an additional focus, given their unique experiences. This section includes chapters on TNB people of color, TNB disabled and chronically ill individuals, and TNB individuals who may be exploring religious, secular, and spiritual paths.

RECOGNITION AND APPRECIATION

First and foremost, we would like to take the time to thank the authors whose contributions are much appreciated. The range of perspectives represented in this book is both incredible and a point of pride. Working with so many first-time authors and those outside the Academy proved to be quite a challenge in a variety of ways, yet has made this book stronger than it ever could have been if authored solely by the editors.

The team at Routledge has been instrumental in supporting this book and bringing it from intention to fruition. As editors, we had a lot of initial concerns with this book, from worry about how the cover might look to ensuring control of language and making sure words like "transgendered" and "biological sex" did not magically appear during the publishing process. In working with numerous people in various roles, we always felt very supported that our authors' true writings would make it to the final publication.

None of this would be possible without the millions of TNB people who share their truths and their stories on a regular basis, whether through participating in research studies, showcasing their lives on social media, engaging in media of other types, helping human service and health care professionals become better, and even simply living their authentic lives. We are sorry the world has not yet been ready for all of your amazing selves and hope this is at least a drop in the pond of helping it to get there.

REFERENCES

American Counseling Association. (2009). *ALGBTIC competencies for counseling LGB-QIQA*. Retrieved from www.counseling.org/docs/default-source/competencies/algbtic-competencies-for-counseling-lgbqiqa.pdf?sfvrsn=1c9c89e_14

American Medical Association. (2017). *Policies on lesbian, gay, bisexual, transgender & queer (LGBTQ) issues*. Retrieved from www.ama-assn.org/delivering-care/population-care/policies-lesbian-gay-bisexual-transgender-queer-lgbtq-issues

American Psychiatric Association. (2018). *Position statement on discrimination against transgender and gender diverse individuals*. Retrieved from www.psychiatry.org/home/policy-finder

American Psychological Association. (2015). Guidelines for psychological practice with transgender and gender nonconforming people. *American Psychologist, 70*, 832–864. doi:10.1037/a0039906

Brown, L., & Strega, S. (2005). Transgressive possibilities. In L. Brown & S. Strega (Eds.), *Research as resistance: Critical, indigenous, and anti-oppressive approaches* (pp. 1–17). Toronto, Canada: Canadian Scholar's Press.

Crenshaw, K. (1990). Mapping the margins: Intersectionality, identity politics, and violence against women of color. *Stanford Law Review, 43*, 1241–1299.

Dhejne, C., Vlerken, R. V., Heylens, G., & Arcelus, J. (2016). Mental health and gender dysphoria: A review of the literature. *International Review of Psychiatry, 28*, 44–57. doi:10.3109/09540261.2015.1115753

Gatos, K. C. (2017). A literature review of cervical cancer screening in transgender men. *Nursing for Women's Health, 22*, 52–62. doi:10.1016/j.nwh.2017.12.008

Glezer, A., McNiel, D. E., & Binder, R. L. (2013). Transgendered and incarcerated: A review of the literature, current policies and laws, and ethics. *Journal of the American Academy of Psychiatry Law, 41*, 551–559.

Hammersley, M. (1993). On the teacher as researcher. *Educational Action Research, 1*(3), 425–445. doi:10.1080/0965079930010308

Hashemi, L., Weinreb, J., Weimer, A. K., & Weiss, R. L. (2018). Transgender care in the primary care setting: A review of guidelines and literature. *Federal Practitioner: For the Health Care Professionals of the VA, DoD, and PHS, 35*(7), 30–37.

Herod, A. (1999). Reflections on interviewing foreign elites, praxis, positionality, validity and the cult of the leader. *Geoforum, 30*(4), 313–327. doi:10.1016/S0016-7185(99)00024-X

Mann, G. E., Taylor, A., Wrenn, B., & de Graaf, N. (2018). Review of the literature on self-injurious thoughts and behaviors in gender-diverse children and young people in the United Kingdom. *Clinical Child Psychology & Psychiatry, 24*, 304–321. doi:10.1177/1359104518812724

National Association of Social Workers [NASW]. (2017). *NASW calls on President Trump to rescind plan to ban people who are transgender from the military.* Washington, DC: NASW. Retrieved from www.socialworkers.org/News/News-Releases/ID/1600/NASW-calls-on-President-Trump-to-rescind-plan-to-ban-people-who-are-transgender-from-the-military

Perry, D. G., Pauletti, R. E., & Cooper, P. J. (2019). Gender identity in childhood: A review of the literature. *International Journal of Behavioral Development, 43*, 289–304. doi:10.1177/0165025418811129

Raffery, J., AAP Committee on Psychosocial Aspects of Child and Family Health, American Academy of Pediatrics, AAP Committee on Adolescence, and AAP Section on Lesbian, Gay, Biseuxal and Transgender Health and Wellness. (2018). From the American Academy of Pediatrics policy statement: Ensuring comprehensive care and support for transgender and gender-diverse children and adolescents. *Pediatrics, 142*, e20182162.

Sikes, P. (2004). Methodology, procedures and ethical concerns. In C. Opie (Ed.), *Doing educational research: A guide for first time researchers* (pp. 15–33). Thousand Oaks, CA: Sage.

Wanta, J. W., & Unger, C. A. (2017). Review of the transgender literature: where do we go from here? *Transgender Health, 2*(1), 119–128. doi: 10.1089/trgh.2017.0004

Wellington, J., Bathmaker, A. M., Hunt, C., McCulloch, G., & Sikes, P. (2005). *Succeeding with your doctorate.* London, UK: Sage.

Introduction Part 2
Place, joy, and self in trans and nonbinary justice

Yoseñio V. Lewis, United States,
alex kime, MSW, University of Michigan,
United States

(PLACE, AN INTRODUCTION)

Where 'are' we currently? And who do we mean by we?

Greetings, reader. We, Yoseñio V. Lewis and alex kime are the authors of this chapter. To begin a conversation about justice and community organizing, we intentionally invoke a tone and tradition that may be marked as different from conventional scholarship, asking questions and giving answers full of questions. By positioning this chapter on TNB community [organizing] in conversation with the personal experiences of our two human and thus limited selves, we hope to invite a larger conversation that encompasses academia as much as it does communities and peoples who have been disenfranchised from that structure. We acknowledge the classroom, the lab, the field placement, and the conference in addition to the community center, the shelter, the reading group, the informal support network, and the chosen families where this organizing work is accomplished.

We seek to challenge the ways in which social work has itself been exclusive and (intentionally or not) supported the systems of violence it has purported to work against. The Western scientific method emphasizes the production of knowledge based on exclusionary credentials and so-called objectivity to center cisgender heterosexual White men. In numerous instances, such as intergenerational trauma, blood memory, and Ayurveda, Western science is just coming around to support what has been known in cultures that are not White, Western, and colonial. This chapter, like the rest of this book, is being written and published between 2019 and 2020. There may and/or likely will come a time when this contribution becomes outdated. As changes occur, we can only hope that the conversation has been deepened, our questions more tightly worded and complicated, and justice further fought for. We would love for our words, thoughts, and deeds to be part of the building blocks upon which a more radical and justice-revealing praxis is built.

'Where' is this chapter situated?

Beyond physical place or places, there is also the consideration of time. We (alex: White, multiethnic, neurodiverse/disabled nonbinary person from an upper-middle-class background lecturer, writer, and facilitator, and Yoseñio: Latino of African Descent, poor, disabled trans man, justice and freedom activist) are making meaning within our historical context: the stolen colonial graveyards of constructed nations, the destruction of Magnus Hirschfeld Institute for Sexual Science at the hands of the Nazis along with most of the documented Western research on sex assigned at birth and ascribed gender alignment, and so much more (Magnus Hirschfeld Society, n.d.; Meyerowitz, 2002; Stryker, 2008). A 6,000-word chapter including references is not anywhere close to 'enough' to explore the entirety of any topic, even and especially one as specific as ours. Accordingly, we are not going to try to. Instead, we hope you see our reference list as an invitation for much deeper dives into other content and perspectives. Neither of us are trans women, for example, and to engage in this work is to listen to all of us, to support all of us. We are trying to be as careful as we are limited, intentionally resisting the metaphor of Atlas, the titan solely responsible for holding up the world. If we are authentically believing in community organizing as a method of social change, we should never have to hold it alone.

Where is language currently?

The framing of this chapter would be incomplete without a note (or rather, set of notes) on language; as alex's friend Ariana Hunter said to them a few years ago, and the two of us turn to here, 'semantic difference has semantic significance' (personal communication, March 15th, 2017). The prefix-turned-noun trans and the compound word nonbinary (sometimes spelled with a hyphen) are themselves comparatively recent linguistic happenings. We know that we technically *could* (but won't) try to use the terms trans and nonbinary to describe worldwide phenomena that have existed for all of conscious memory. Without the same senses and contexts of our current moment, we find them lacking in a world where words like sodomites (Saslow, 1999) and hermaphrodites (Katz, 1976) have been seen as synonymous in the past, alongside homosexuals, transvestites, and *berdaches*, the French adaptation of the Arabic word for male prostitute (Roscoe, 1987, 1998). Another common example is the conflation of trans women, drag queens, and men in dresses, where language is far more illuminating of societal understanding than of the humans it seeks to define.

Going further, there are a number of reasons under patriarchy (e.g., employment, freedom of movement, and escaping violence) where people assigned female at birth (AFAB) would present (and perhaps to some level, identify) as cis men (Beemyn, 2014). When identifying AFAB people in the past who may have connected with manhood and masculinity beyond the immediate utility, Cromwell (1999) provides us with three criteria to understand nuance: identifying as a man, engaging in body modification, and publicly presenting as men even if concealing the complexity of their identity prevented them from life-saving medical care. Like those who have engaged this topic before us, we can point to the *Hijra* people of the Indian subcontinent, the *Fa'afaine* from the Samoan culture, and the Two Spirit people of the Indigenous Americas, regardless of whether mainstream attention was paid to these people and communities and without claiming these experiences as our own (Beemyn, 2014; Lang, 1998). In fact, the very ways that binary and incomplete constructs of sex and gender work against or with one another is something that has changed over time.

Thinking more broadly, there are so many different terms of how to identify the larger and somehow monolithic 'community' and the use of acronyms and other summative terms has been somewhat controversial. Keeping consistent with the rest of the book, we shall be using trans and nonbinary, short-handed to TNB throughout. To use just one example, the University of Michigan School of Social Work uses both TBLGQIA+ (we assume to intentionally center TNB) as well as LGBTQIA on the very same webpage, and there are a multitude of variations on this (Robertson, n.d.). It is also important to note that while language is significant, it should never be where the critical consideration ends. Labels are both useful to organize around *and* essentially limited when trying to fully describe personhood. What's more, labels change and evolve as we do, year to year and through the generations. The people they attempt to describe matter far more than the individual words themselves.

With shows like *Pose* and *RuPaul's Drag Race* in an era of digital sharing beyond physical proximity and interaction through (social) media, the slang created by the underground ballroom community is all over (largely White, moneyed, and cisgender) mainstream media without material support for the Black and Brown people across the universe of gender and attraction who created the culture at the root of those words. In our initial conversations that began to form the structure of this work, and specifically on the subject (and object) of language, Yoseñio (rightfully) kept coming back to the concept of authenticity. What does it really *mean* to be authentic? What does it mean to be 'real' in a world obsessed with rigid categories that are socially constructed around external presentation as much as they are socially enforced?

Who are we? What brought us into the work we engage in today?

Y: My 'awakening' took place in the late '80s, early '90s, upon me reading Mario Martino's 1977 book *Emergence: A transsexual autobiography*. Growing up I was vaguely aware that there were others who believed as I did … that there was some fundamental difference between how the world saw me and how I viewed myself. I'd had several significant encounters with medical personnel who not so politely let me know that my awareness was not appropriate or appreciated or even real. I did not have the language to explain the difference to people and the language that did exist did not pertain to me (e.g., transvestite). In Martino's book, I found validation as someone deemed a *girl* who desperately craved being seen and treated as a *boy*. It was not long after that reading that I found myself returning to the familiar ground of channeling my anger, frustration, and confusion into activism. I could not just complain about my circumstances and those of others like me; I needed to do something to make a positive difference. Worrying about being enough and how one should express gender not only to be seen, to be accepted and to be loved and prosper, and to also receive competent services remains a potent motivator and de-motivator for TNB people as well. We have not overcome.

There remains a rigid adherence to hierarchy, even as we blatantly demand opportunity to strip away that same hierarchy. As a Trans man, I am looked at askance because I have long locs, because I refuse to amend my birth certificate to indicate maleness at birth, because I do not consider the state of my body at birth to be a birth defect, and because I speak freely about having been pregnant. This exposes me not only to other TNB people who question my Trans identity and wish I would shut up, but also offers providers and other gatekeepers the chance to determine what, or even *if* I am worthy of receiving services. I recall coming out to a therapist about being Trans and being asked if I'd had any surgeries. When I said no, I was told, 'Then you can't be Trans.' After working so hard to open up and share the deepest secret, I felt completely invisible. How does one develop a healthy, accurate sense of self when one has just been told one does not exist? How do we seek community when there is no community for us/me? We make it for ourselves, and thus TNB community organizing.

a: I've been lucky enough to have had friends and elders (alongside participants and students younger than me!) to follow on my way towards authenticity and action. I am (and have been) trying to be as grateful as possible for the many people who have been a part of my ongoing journey, from people just being out and open around me to the friends who brought me to the meetings in my high school GSA, and out in the community in the form of Riot Youth meetings at The Neutral Zone, a multidisciplinary after-school center for teenagers where, perhaps ironically, I would eventually be supported in my questioning of neutrality itself over the six years I spent as an intern and a member of the staff after two years of involvement as a participant. I went to my first Friday afternoon meeting there with a friend, and as I looked around at the vibrant people who would later become my mentors and friends, it began to feel so right. I wasn't super present week to week, but I felt connected.

I was a newly-minted theatre kid™ trope with a developing interest in poetry slams, so when the chance came to take part in an educational skit-based performance called Gayrilla, in the tradition of Guerilla Theatre, it seemed like a perfect fit. Framed in the tradition of Augusto Boal's (1979) book *The Theatre of the Oppressed*, it explored scenarios to engage in conversations around TNB identity in addition to the broader groups of people who suffer under heteronormativity. There's this bravery in taking the stage, something I had only just begun to tap into as a young artist, and the centering of community and personal identity was a nice change. Though unnamed, I felt connected to the characters in these sketches in a way that I wasn't to the roles I had been assigned in other scripts, in no small part because the script was created with mixed methods data collected from my home community. It's worth noting that Wernick, Woodford, and Kulick (2014) took the time to develop scholarly documentation of this project and its empowerment of young people, something I can confirm from my own personal experience. In fact, it was during the Q&A after one of the performances, when I was introducing myself, that *they* as a pronoun ever slipped out of my mouth in reference to myself after the other performers had used it in their introduction. A somewhat fitting continuation of the theme, right? Being led to myself by the procession of community members; of friends.

One day, years later, after being paid to do similar theatrical work on campus and as a staff member supporting programming in the space that had benefited me so much as a younger person, I was ranting to my friend Luna Lynn about the gender binary. They responded with a simple text asking if I had accepted trans as my 'lord and savior', to which I responded that I was getting there (personal communication, May 30th, 2016). I have the privilege of having health insurance, and one day I had this catharsis at the bus stop after a particularly hard therapy session at 6:00 pm on a Wednesday. Tears in my eyes, I reflected on how access to health care is seen as a contentious issue without even getting into mental health resources. Everyone should have access to these services that I have been so lucky to access.

Writing jointly, and before we get into the organizing, what is (and/or makes) a community?

There's this persistent idea that there is this singular Community, capitalization intentional, this one single thing to be abstractly built. However, the reality is far more complex, a somewhat connected set of smaller communities based not just in identity, but also the local place and politics. As the humble and iconic elder Miss Major Griffin-Gracy put it:

> I'm not really anything special ... I'm concerned about the things that are happening to my community that've been going on ever since I realized I was not like everybody else. It becomes a matter of when those things happen, what do you do? Do you run and hide, do you let stuff go on? And it's hard to do that if you care about people. So I just want to make sure that things are better, and not just for me and my folk, but for everybody.
>
> (Nichols, 2018, para. 4)

Especially in the context of TNB communities and those emerging within them, the notion of being *enough* and societal expectations of what TNB people *should* do (by themselves, with each other, with cis and/or straight people, etc.) are things people constantly struggle with. Take, for example, the question of what it means to be TNB *enough* to fit into rigid molds. Enough for *what* exactly? To be stared at? Photographed and filmed without asking? Having a particular way you come into yourself? Who says a beard means man and long hair means woman, when we exist in a world where the straightest, most cisgender person benefits from a nonbinary analysis of gender? If all people marginalized by cisheteropatriarchy are a big broad Community, or more realistically, semi-interconnected communities, why do TNB people get disrespected in the spaces that are allegedly there to support them? If inclusion and acts of solidarity are not priorities amongst cis members of this Community, what or who exactly is holding us?

Which begs the question: What do we mean by 'community organizing'?

We must always unpack the jargon and the history behind it. To do this, it is useful to define the umbrella category of social work. U.S.-based social work (a limited frame, and also the one within which both authors exist and work) can be traced back to social service systems that existed in North America before the revolution that tried to provide aid to those who needed it the most from a certain point of view. What we might recognize today as contemporary social work is the ongoing mix of governmental systems attempting to oversee these services, being imperfect (if not willfully malicious) while attempting (or not) to do this, and the variety of groups and institutions that have stepped in to try and address inequities (Tannenbaum & Reisch, 2001). As these authors also note, as industrialization boomed in the post-Civil War era, charity organization societies and settlement houses began to form in the 1870s and 1880s. One example of this latter set is the Hull House founded by Jane Addams in Chicago. As noted by the Hull House (now a museum) website, it and other settlement houses moved away from the individualized 'get this person some aid' approach, and into employment, public health, and legal concerns, in addition to supplying what you might see in the community centers of today, like childcare, libraries, art, and educational opportunities (Jane Addams Hull-House Museum, n.d.).

As with Miss Major, it is not always the formal organization that comes first, but the critical moments of community members intervening in the status quo. Aimé Césaire warned us to 'beware of assuming the sterile attitude of a spectator, for life is not a spectacle ... a man screaming is not a dancing bear' (1939, p. 30, as cited in Césaire, Eshleman, & Arnold, 2013). Getting into TNB community organizing itself, we must pay homage to those who have come before us and likewise chose to act, in this case from Genny Beemyn's chapter in *Trans Bodies, Trans Selves*:

> For example, one night in May 1959, two Los Angeles police officers went into Cooper's Donuts—an all-night coffeehouse popular with drag queens and gay male hustlers, many of whom were Latin@ or African American—and began harassing and arresting the patrons in drag. The customers responded by fighting back, first by throwing doughnuts and ultimately by engaging in skirmishes with the officers that led the police to retreat and to call in backup. In the melee, the drag queens who had been arrested were able to escape.
>
> (2014, p. 515)

A similar incident occurred in San Francisco in 1966 at the Tenderloin location of Gene Compton's Cafeteria—a 24-hour restaurant that, like Cooper's, was frequented by drag queens and male hustlers, as well as the people looking to pick them up. As documented by historian Susan Stryker and paraphrased by Beemyn,

> ... the management called the police one August night, as it had done in the past, to get rid of a group of young drag queens who were seen as loitering. When a police officer tried to remove one of the queens forcibly, she threw

a cup of coffee in his face and a riot ensued. Patrons pelted the officers with everything at their disposal, wrecking the cafeteria in the process. Vastly outnumbered, the police ran outside to call for reinforcements, only to have the drag queens chase after them, beating the officers with their purses and kicking them with their high heels. The incident served to empower the city's drag community and motivated many to begin to organize for their rights.

(2014, p. 513)

It's worth mentioning that although Stonewall is iconic, it has also been given a contemporary spotlight in the form of multiple movies and media attention, while the Compton Cafeteria riots do not occupy that same place of cultural importance. A relatively well-known example of something comparable to the Hull House brand of comprehensive 'wraparound' services for TNB people is STAR, co-founded by Sylvia Rivera and Marsha P(ay It No Mind) Johnson that focused explicitly on TNB people, providing housing and food to those that needed it (Feinberg, 2006). As noted elsewhere in this book, the focus on TNB people *by* TNB people is essential when cis people (even those who do not fully fit the conventions of heteropatriarchy) have historically forgotten about and/or willfully excluded TNB people. As we broaden the scope of the history we pay attention to, we must learn from STAR and countless others' approach to supporting the whole person. To organize towards healthy TNB communities is to engage Maslow's (1943) Hierarchy of Needs if we are to sustainably fight for all facets of ourselves and those we love, from the foundation of safety in the form of shelter and sustenance all the way on up.

When we think about the goals of community organizing, we must think about self-actualization and distilling the best version(s) of ourselves.

To continually manifest this, we must access and distribute resources that facilitate the process. We must move beyond the physiological falsehood of the mind and body as separate into an understanding of interconnectedness, where environmental factors including but not limited to identity-based stress can have lifelong effects on the brain and entire body in the form of allostatic load (Danese & McEwen, 2012). What we might alternatively refer to as wear and tear on the body, these very serious health complications can be caused from a wide variety of accumulated stressors like air pollution, and perhaps less obviously, from social forms of discrimination and oppression (Tessum et al., 2019). Like identity itself, the structure of the brain (and accordingly, as the controller, the rest of one's body) is not static. We have to ask ourselves, moment to moment: What do we need right now? We, collectively and specifically, across the compounding systems of violence. Food, shelter (including and especially bathrooms), and safety, all forms of material support can then come firmly into focus.

Born out of necessity to impose a positive difference in the lives of their children, the work of the countercultural Latin Kings and Black Panthers to provide free, nutritious breakfasts, after-school programs and even a free ambulance service to Latinx and Black children provided the springboard for future government sanctioned programs. Studies looking at the importance of school breakfast programs (Leos-Urbel et al., 2013; Turner & Chaloupka, 2015) further reinforce the idea that attention to the most so-called basic needs (i.e., nourishment, attention, and positive support) has a profoundly positive impact on children's focus, and ability to learn and improve test scores. There are many more occasions of anecdotal evidence subsequently given legitimacy by formalized studies, legislative implementation, and policy development of the value of community organizing. As we take a contemporary look at addressing these foundational barriers to communities organizing and prospering, one noteworthy example of a project is Vision for Baltimore, a collaborative project between the local health department, public school system, Johns Hopkins University, Vision to Learn (a non-profit), and the company Warby Parker (Baltimore City Health Department, n.d.). After supplying low-SES students with glasses, they are noting positive changes in attendance and test scores (Baltimore City Health Department, n.d.; Gamard, 2017). Though of course nothing is ideal, the concept of meeting community challenges by forming a variety of coalitions across professions and sectors is essential in nurturing resilience.

Further examples include lesbians caring for themselves in regard to dismissive or non-existent care regarding breast cancer, lesbians caring for gay men diagnosed with Gay Related Immune Deficiency (GRID, Gay Cancer, later named HIV/AIDS), and LGBT persons developing medical clinics and support services to address ignored concerns (e.g., NY LGBT Community Center, Gay Men's Health Crisis, ACT-UP, Transsexual Menace, Gay Straight Alliance). Most of these efforts transformed into legitimized government-funded programs and were reflected in new laws enhancing such programs. The various communities empowered themselves to implement positive changes, not waiting for the government or other gatekeepers to notice the need they were addressing. Pointing to further worthy case studies, Leah Lakshmi Piepzna-Samarasinha and Patricia Berne are disabled women of color whose work in the disabled QTPOC care collectives amply represent the utilization of community-led community organizing.

To close out this section, we turn to the case of Camila (who also went by Aurora), a Salvadoran trans woman who fled death threats and was killed after deportation (Lavers & Valle, 2019). We indict the systems that have failed her in the style of Audre Lorde, where to care about any part of her *authentically* is to care about *all* of her, including citizenship/immigration status, race, and socioeconomic status (a term encompassing multiple forms of capital including generational wealth, income, and access to resources) in addition to her trans womanhood. Closed and exclusionary borders are another rigid dichotomy that does not serve humanity. Angela Davis reminds us 'walls turned sideways are bridges' (1974).

(JOY)

So much of the TNB context rests on tragedy and reacting to it. To an extent, this is a reasonable approach, for there is much of it in our world to survive and document. At the same time, we cannot end there. The Transgender Day of

Remembrance is both a powerful day for people to gather together to pay respects to all victims both named and unnamed for that particular year, overt and physical violence being so prevalent of an experience for communities. Likewise, there is merit to the Transgender Day of Visibility, for erasure is a powerful force in our world that props up the myth that all of this is somehow something new. At the same time, our current historical, social, and political moment cements the notion that visibility does not automatically lead to safety. We cannot organize towards the future without centering things beyond tragedy. It is too rigidly reactionary, with no articulated future one can work towards beyond the systems of oppression. Despondency is as much understandable as it is deadly, and never just to the individual. We must fiercely dream and work towards collective thriving. The short arc of this lifetime is a part of something much larger. It always has been, and always will be. The construct of scarcity (i.e., the idea that there's not enough money, food, housing, health care providers, jobs, time, people, power, empathy, etc.) is a call to reframe the rules of engagement. The elimination of this construction (a reflection of capitalism) could help eliminate the infighting that can develop when one segment of the population achieves some advancement, leaving other segments wanting.

Needless violence and defense of the marginalized are not the same thing. Assata Shakur reminds us that no one will give us the exact methods to overthrow them so therefore we must collect and filter. Toni Cade Bambara notes that 'the role of the artist is to make the revolution irresistible' (Bambara & Bonetti, 1982). Chimamanda Ngozi Adichie is, admittedly, an author who has come under fire for her public understanding of trans women. Still, Adichie, in her 'The Danger of a Single Story' TED talk (2009), reminds us that where we start and how we frame the stories we tell has a profound effect on what they tend to mean for those we share them with. Accordingly, we must use data and narrative across mediums and approaches to greatly shift the world around us. Art, research, teaching, and health care are all part of effective and ongoing community organizing that can also be enjoyable. Happily, as Emily Yoon reminds us about words themselves, 'poetry is an act of resistance against the language that governs us' (Nobile, 2019).

As we look towards solutions, we intentionally want to draw attention to the concept of biomimicry, the specific word we attribute to the late and great Otto Schmitt and a concept of learning from nature's solution that humanity has embraced or not embraced throughout the existence of the species (brown, 2017; Vincent et al., 2006). Honoring the more general concept before pushing further, adrienne maree brown's *Emergent Strategy* explicitly brings this focus on the natural world as a mindset with which to address the social ails of the world in addition to other facets of life. Where is our sense of interconnectedness amidst the individualist bootstraps and semi-shrouded oligarchy of the colonial project? Where is our understanding of herd immunity in policies around housing, insurance, and preventative health care? How can radical imagination (to think beyond our current limitations) and pleasure activism (wherein we center joy in our work) guide our way forward?

SUGGESTED ACTIVITY: CASE STUDY ANALYSIS

In a chapter about things so very much in flux, we wanted to leave you with a thought process we have found useful when considering actions and organizations that seek to build TNB communities. As we ask the questions, we shall draw upon our knowledge of two community-created organizations as examples. Take this template and use it while forming groups or planning actions, by yourself or in a group.

Example: Tenderloin **AIDS** Resource Center and AIDS Indigent Direct Services

In San Francisco in the mid-1980s, two organizations developed specifically to acknowledge particular communities devastatingly impacted by HIV/AIDS and the equally devastating indices of poverty, homelessness, active drug use, mental health issues, incarceration history, survival sex, immigration status, language capabilities, and discrimination against sexual orientation and gender identity. The **Tend**erloin **AIDS** Resource Center (TARC) and AIDS Indigent Direct Services (A.I.D.S.) were created by community members frustrated by the lack of outreach to and the skyrocketing disease-related deaths in the communities comprising the Tenderloin section of the City. Active drug using, sex working, homeless, poor queer people of color with mental health concerns started each organization because they were acutely aware of how their neighbors were being actively ignored by the more visible and palatable HIV/AIDS constituents/organizations. Pleas for help from city organizations, from private organizations, from donors quick to support other organizations fell on deliberately unhearing ears. A.I.D.S. started out of the trunk of the car of a person furious at the lack of services in the neighborhood. From that trunk, sandwiches, blankets, clean works, condoms, and love were delivered with no judgement. Memorial services were planned for clients whose bodies were rejected by families and funeral homes. Information about how to negotiate safer sex and safer use practices, directions on how to adhere to medicine regimens (if prescriptions were even available), sign-ups for emotional and practical support; that and so much more happened from that car trunk.

Eventually the work being accomplished and the difference being made was noticed by the gatekeepers, and financial support finally flowed into the neighborhood, enabling the organization to lease a building, which lent legitimacy to the work being done. A formal employment structure was created and people from the neighborhood were hired.

In the same way and with the overt support of Glide Memorial Church, TARC was the answer to the increasing needs of the neighborhood, most especially for active users, sex workers, and homeless families. TARC obtained a storefront and began providing mental health services as well as traditional emotional and practical support. Contracts were developed with medical personnel to work out of the storefront and diminish the fears some clients had at leaving the neighborhood. The organization excelled at providing services in innovative ways, such as doing outreach in the parks, bars, and street corners during the evenings. TARC purchased refrigerators to ensure clients had someplace to secure their meds when they had no refrigerators of their own, again allowing for medicine adherence. It also was open overnight for those who wanted someplace to be other than the streets and worked with city government to obtain hotel vouchers for those who needed a place to stay. The organization spearheaded a peer support program where clients could help each other attend doctor appointments, learn how to manage emotions in order to access services, ensure nutritious food was available, focus on more than just their diagnoses (by employing such activities as neighborhood clean-ups, art classes, employment training, etc.), and honor each other when people passed. Like A.I.D.S., TARC hired clients and neighborhood members to run the organization, make the rules, address issues, and deal with growth, expansion, complications, and notoriety. Each organization was unique, necessary, vital, and born of the people birthing a vibrant response to their needs instead of waiting for the gatekeepers to notice them. Inculcating a 'for us by us' ethos, each organization stepped up to fill the needs of its constituents, to restore some level of dignity and worth and to plant the seeds of advocacy in service recipients.

ACTIVITY

1. What made the organization(s) successful? How did they accomplish their goals?
2. Whose values did they embody? What creative strategies were undertaken and would they work today?
3. How do gatekeepers address organizations that are generated from the community?
4. How is the work of A.I.D.S. and TARC both similar and dissimilar to the Black Panthers? The Latin Kings? GMHC? ACT-UP? Transsexual Menace? STAR? What contributes to the success and to the downfall of such organizations?
5. If you were going to create a response to an inequity, which strategies from the various organizations would you use? Why?
6. Who/what action are you focusing on currently? What year(s) were/are they active and where?
7. How much information is readily available to you on them? How well do you trust your sources?

8. Who is the visible leadership comprised of? To your knowledge, is this representative of how things actually work?
9. Is there a manifesto or mission statement for this group? To what extent do you agree with it? To what extent do you perceive them to be embodying it? To what extent are the interlocking systems of oppression addressed in their work? How do you know this?
10. What, if anything, about this action or group stands out to you? How might you incorporate those aspects into your own practice?

(SELF)

You might be asking what the *point* of all this is. What does inclusive and material support with an emphasis on self-actualization and moving beyond the deficit-based mindset mean to the conversation on TNB Community Organizing™? Moving beyond the jargon made of diluted buzzwords, we as authors have benefited so immensely from the kinds of comprehensive, wraparound care that we reference in our home communities, and have ourselves worked to foster and sustain these efforts; we could not call ourselves honest without including those tangible, grassroots considerations when we talk about justice.

As we near the upper bound of this chapter, let us return to the self. Like Miss Major, we are not anything special as much as a product of our communities (Nichols, 2018). In humbly honoring the critical voices of the past, present, and future, we return to this concept of authenticity. The authentic self is *always* in context, and imagining anything otherwise is not useful to a critical process. Community organizing that does not consider the personal, interpersonal, community, institutional, national, and cultural/societal is not effective, and is the opposite of transformative. Capitalism, colonialism, racism, ableism, cisheteropatriarchy, and many other interlocking systems are consistent barriers to reproductive, environmental, and other forms of healing justice promoted in the kind of community organizing we emphasize. The policies and recorded history (or lack thereof) of how we got here, the bodies in the ground, the treaties that were broken, the people enslaved, the sick and hungry left to die; all connected, now and forever. Intra and inter-identity solidarity is non-negotiable in the pursuit of collective liberation beyond survival.

Let us then double down on radical inclusion, on challenging the barriers to our solidarity. Let us choose humility as the method with which we honor our mistakes, the spaces of learning people have held for us, and the ways in which we pass the tradition on. Let us always question the borders that divide us, the normalization and inertia that sap us of our hope. The dignity and worth of all persons is imperative if we are to truly progress as a world without, say, pushing our problems elsewhere. A notable example of this from environmental studies is offsetting carbon output to countries with less political power than the U.S., alongside the example from non-discrimination policy where world powers blame countries for regressive gender and attractionality (here meaning both sexual and romantic) laws left by their colonizers. The grass might seem greener in a different part of the colonial graveyard, but non-native grasses are usually water-wasting, chemically treated, and invasive.

In a reflective tweet, Mariame Kaba writes of a nun she once heard declare that 'hope is a discipline' (2018). All disciplines require practice. When we speak of and use the pronoun we, who are we including? What does it, at its core, *mean* to be transgender? To *be* nonbinary? To be resisting the inertia of the cisgender binary? What and who are we making room for, if not people who need access to surgeries as well as a lack of shame for those who don't want them? If our analysis is not working against racism, colorism, colonialism, cisheteropatriarchy, capitalism, ableism, and every other system, what is it for if not to reify what is already there? It is vital, then, to move away from the notion of 'giving voice to the voiceless', and work on amplification, supporting the work that has been ongoing across various fields.

Self-determination and self-authorship are *so* paramount to moving this work forward. The fact that the two of us are writing this chapter is in no small way related to this. *Paris Is Burning* (1992) is a compelling metaphor of this, wherein a White cis director has been criticized for barely paying the people who would become the so-called stars of a now iconic film on ball culture (Clark, 2015). Though Madonna's *Vogue* music video originally aired in 1990, it was only published to YouTube in 2009, and as of April 1st 2019 it had over 93 million views. Though this is hopefully continuing to change, these projects with White cis women as the primary facilitators and beneficiaries may well be some of the only references people have around an art form of resistance developed by Black and Brown visionaries celebrating beauty reclaimed from popular glamour; one of many examples where the powers that be have taken the labor of TNB people of color without credit or other compensation.

There is an urgent need for research, writing, and other critical work about TNB people to be conducted by and with TNB people, involving us at *every* stage of these processes. Social workers, academics, and all media producers must continually wrestle with the ways that structures have reified certain knowledge, representation, and notions of progress. It is not enough to document injustice while it runs rampant. This work must be self-determined, self-authored, non-neutral, funded, and with a grassroots foundation. Justice is (and/or should be) an urgent concern for every single person on this planet. What would the world look like if we took better care of one another with housing, health care, environmental justice, and reparations? What strategies can we use to get there? If we want expertise, what does it mean to be an expert? Who gets to be one? What does it mean for us to not be experts all the time or omnipotent ever? If it takes a village, what do we want the various villages to look and act like? If we mean all facets of TNB people, then how do we continually include and support them with the goal of collective liberation? We must think both big and small, dreaming before and after strategizing. We must share the archives, accepting that the best tools for liberation are those we have yet to develop, and that we must organize in solidarity with as many people as we can to do so.

CITATIONS AND RESOURCES

About Jane Addams and Hull-House. (n.d.). Retrieved from www.hullhousemuseum.org/about-jane-addams

Adichie, C. N. (2009, July). Retrieved from www.ted.com/talks/chimamanda_adichie_the_danger_of_a_single_story?language=en

Austin, M. J., & Betten, N. (2009). Intellectual Origins of Community Organizing, 1920–1939. *Social Service Review*, 51(1), 155–170. doi:10.1086/643478

Baltimore City Health Department. (n.d.). *Vision for Baltimore*. Retrieved May 20, 2020, from https://health.baltimorecity.gov/VisionForBaltimore

Bambara, T. C., & Bonetti, K. (1982). *Toni Cade Bambara interview with Kay Bonetti*. Columbia, MO: American Audio Prose Library.

Beemyn, G. (2014). Building our power: US history. In L. Erickson-Schroth (Ed.), *Trans bodies, trans selves: A resource for the transgender community* (pp. 501–536). Retrieved from https://ebookcentral.proquest.com

Berne, P., & Raditz, V. (2020, January). To Survive Climate Catastrophe, Look to Queer and Disabled Folks. Retrieved from https://truthout.org/authors/patty-berne/

Boal, A. (1979). *The theatre of the oppressed*. London: Pluto Press.

brown, a. m. (2017). *Emergent strategy: Shaping change, changing worlds*. Chico, CA: AK Press.

Césaire, A., Eshleman, C., & Arnold, J. (2013). *The original 1939 notebook of a return to the native land*. Bilingual Edition: Vol. Bilingual ed. Middletown, CT: Wesleyan University Press.

Chin, M. (2018). Making Queer and Trans of Color Counterpublics: Disability, Accessibility, and the Politics of Inclusion. *Affilia – Journal of Women and Social Work*, 33(1), 8–23. doi:10.1177/0886109917729666

Clark, A. (2015). Burning down the House: Why the Debate over Paris Is Burning Rages On. *The Guardian, Guardian News and Media*, 24 June 2015. Retrieved from www.theguardian.com/film/2015/jun/24/burning-down-the-house-debate-paris-is-burning

Cromwell, J. (1999). *Transmen and FTMs: Identities, bodies, genders, and sexualities*. Urbana & Chicago: University of Illinois Press.

Danese, A., & McEwen, B. S. (2012, April 12). Adverse Childhood Experiences, Allostasis, Allostatic Load, and Age-related Disease. *Physiology and Behavior*, 106, 29–39. doi:10.1016/j.physbeh.2011.08.019

Davis, A. Y. (1974). *Angela Davis: An autobiography*. New York: Random House.

Edwards, M., Post, S., & Schubeck, T. (2007). *The love that does justice*. Maryknoll, NY: Orbis Books.

Faderman, L., & Timmons, S. (2006). *Gay L.A.: A history of sexual outlaws, power politics, and lipstick lesbians*. New York, NY: Basic Books.

Feinberg, L. (1996). *Transgender warriors: Making history from Joan of Arc to RuPaul*. Boston, MA: Beacon Press.

Feinberg, L. (1998). *Trans liberation: Beyond pink or blue*. Boston, MA: Beacon Press.

Feinberg, L. (2006). Street Transvestite Action Revolutionaries. Retrieved from Workers Works website www.workers.org/2006/us/lavender-red-73/

Gamard, S. (2017, August 17). How Free Eyeglasses Are Boosting Test Scores in Baltimore. Retrieved from www.politico.com/magazine/story/2017/08/17/how-free-eyeglasses-are-boosting-test-scores-in-baltimore-215501

Hunter, A. (2017, March 15th). Personal communication.

Jane Addams Hull-House Museum. (n.d.). Retrieved May 20, 2020, from https://www.hullhousemuseum.org/

Kaba, M. (prisonculture). (2018, June 20th). "Before I log off. One thing. Many years ago, I heard a nun who was giving a speech say 'hope is a discipline.' It stuck with me and became a sort of mantra for me. I understood her to be saying that hope is a practice." [Tweet]. Retrieved from https://twitter.com/prisonculture/status/1009621164241641473?lang=en

Katz, J. N. (1976). *Gay American history: Lesbians and gay men in the U.S.A.* New York, NY: T.Y. Crowell.

Lang, S. (1998). *Men as women, women as men: Changing gender in Native American cultures.* Austin: University of Texas Press.

Lang, S. (1999). Lesbians, men-women and two-spirits: Homosexuality and gender in Native American cultures. In E. Blackwood & S. E. Wieringa (Eds.), *Female desires: Same-sex relations and transgender practices across cultures* (pp. 91–116). New York, NY: Columbia University Press.

Lavers, M. K., & Valle, E. (2019, July 26). Mother of Trans Salvadoran Woman Who Died after Leaving ICE Custody Demands Answers. Retrieved from www.washingtonblade.com/2019/07/26/mother-of-trans-salvadoran-woman-who-died-after-leaving-ice-custody-demands-answers/

Leos-Urbel, J., Schwartz, A. E., Weinstein, M., & Corcoran, S. (2013). Not Just for Poor Kids: The Impact of Universal Free School Breakfast on Meal Participation and Student Outcomes. *Economics of Education Review.* doi:10.1016/j.econedurev.2013.06.007

Livingston, J., Labeija, P., Pendavis, K., Pendavis, F., Corey, D., Xtravaganza, V., Ninja, W., St. Laurent, O. & Orion Home Video (Firm). (1992). *Paris is burning.* USA: Fox Lorber Home Video.

Lynn, L. (2016, May 30th). Personal communication.

Madonna. (2009). "Madonna – Vogue (Official Music Video)." *YouTube*, YouTube and Sire Records, 26 Oct. 2009. Retrieved from www.youtube.com/watch?v=GuJQSAiODqI

Magnus Hirschfeld Society. (n.d.). Magnus-Hirschfeld-Gesellschaft. Retrieved May 21, 2020, from https://magnus-hirschfeld.de/start-en/

Maslow, A. H. (1943). A Theory of Human Motivation. *Psychological Review.* doi:10.1037/h0054346

Meyerowitz, J. (2002). *How sex changed: A history of transsexuality in the United States.* Cambridge, MA: Harvard University Press.

Nichols, J. M. (2018, June 04). Miss Major on Rioting at Stonewall: 'That Was 3 Nights of Absolute Terror'. Retrieved from www.huffpost.com/entry/miss-major-on-rioting-at-stonewall_n_5b0c4312e4b0568a880dadbc

Nobile, T., tianabob. "'Poetry is an act of resistance against the language that governs us.'-@EmilyYoon #AWP2019" [Tweet]. Retrieved from https://twitter.com/tiananob/status/1111786296341454848

Piepzna-Samarsinha, L. (2018). *Care work: Dreaming disability justice.* Vancouver, British Columbia, Canada: Arsenal Pulp Press.

Robertson, L. A. (n.d.). Welcome prospective LGBTQIA students. Retrieved May 20, 2020, from https://ssw.umich.edu/offices/field-education/welcome-lgbtqia-students

Roscoe, W. (1987). Bibliography of Berdache and Alternative Gender Roles among North American Indians. *Journal of Homosexuality, 14*(3/4), 81–171.

Roscoe, W. (1991). *The Zuni man-woman.* Albuquerque: University of New Mexico Press.

Roscoe, W. (1998). *Changing ones: Third and fourth genders in Native North America.* New York, NY: St. Martin's Press.

Saslow, J. M. (1999). *Pictures and passions: A history of homosexuality in the visual arts.* New York, NY: Viking Press.

Silverman, V., & Stryker, S. (Directors). (2005). *Screaming queens: The riots at Compton's Cafeteria* [Motion picture]. United States: Frameline.

Stryker, S. (2008). *Transgender history.* Berkeley, CA: Seal Press.

Tannenbaum, N., & Reisch, M. (2001). From Charitable Volunteers to Architects of Social Welfare: A Brief History of Social Work. Retrieved from https://ssw.umich.edu/about/history/brief-history-of-social-work

Tessum, C. W., Apte, J. S., Goodkind, A. L., Muller, N. Z., Mullins, K. A., Paolella, D. A., … Performed, J. D. H. (2019). *Inequity in consumption of goods and services adds to racial-ethnic disparities in air pollution exposure.* doi:10.1073/pnas.1818859116

The first Institute for Sexual Science (1919–1933). (n.d.). Retrieved from https://magnus-hirschfeld.de/ausstellungen/institute/

Turner, L., & Chaloupka, F. J. (2015). Continued Promise of School Breakfast Programs for Improving Academic Outcomes: Breakfast is Still the Most Important Meal of the Day. *JAMA Pediatrics*. doi:10.1001/jamapediatrics.2014.2409

Vincent, J. F. V., Bogatyreva, O. A., Bogatyrev, N. R., Bowyer, A., & Pahl, A.-K. (2006). *Biomimetics: Its practice and theory*. doi:10.1098/rsif.2006.0127

Vision for Baltimore. (2017, August 28). Retrieved from https://health.baltimorecity.gov/VisionForBaltimore

Waters, A., & Asbill, L. (2013). Reflections on Cultural Humility. Retrieved from American Psychological Association website www.apa.org/pi/families/resources/newsletter/2013/08/cultural-humility

Wernick, L. J., Woodford, M. R., & Kulick, A. (2014). LGBTQQ youth using participatory action research and theater to effect change: Moving adult decision-makers to create youth-centered change. *Journal of Community Practice*, 22(1–2), 47–66. doi:10.1080/10705422.2014.901996

An incomplete list of relevant organizations: The Audre Lorde Project, the Sylvia Rivera Law Project, the Ruth Ellis Center, Affirmations, the Neutral Zone, the Corner Health Center, Trans Student Educational Resources, the Transgender Law Center, Trans Tech Social Enterprises, BlackTransFutures, Allied Media Projects

PART 1

Health

CHAPTER 1

Transgender and nonbinary youth and access to medical care

M. Killian Kinney, Eric T. Meininger, and Sara E. Wiener

INTRODUCTION

TNB youth and their families face unique challenges to accessing health care that impact TNB youth's psychosocial health outcomes. Challenges to health care access, including transphobic experiences with providers, have been identified as a significant threat to resilience among transgender youth (Torres et al., 2015). While a significantly higher proportion of TNB youth have mental health challenges when they are compared to their cisgender peers (Strauss et al., 2017), research has shown that affirming a young person's gender identity significantly reduces anxiety, depression, and suicidality among TNB youth, indicating the dire importance of eliminating barriers to gender-affirming medical care for TNB young people (Russell et al., 2018).

Although some youth have supportive caregivers, they may still face barriers to gender-competent and affirming providers, including the requirement of an initial mental health assessment and getting a letter for a medical referral, as well as a need to access endocrinologists and surgeons for medical transitioning. Furthermore, health insurance coverage continues to pose a significant barrier to medical care, specifically with puberty blockers, hormone replacement therapy, and gender-related surgeries despite recent improvements. While it is becoming increasingly understood that transitioning needs can differ from person to person, without a one-size-fits-all approach to transitioning (Kattari et al., 2019), some professional standards and health care policies restrict access to medical care for transgender and, particularly, nonbinary youth. In response, some professionals have called for a shift from providers as gatekeepers to providers as advocates (Aydin et al., 2016; Levine, 2019).

This chapter identifies barriers to care, gaps in the literature with this population, and ways in which health care providers can facilitate positive navigation of medical care for TNB youth and their families. Two primary approaches to clinical mental health services with TNB youth will be reviewed: The *Gender Affirmative Model* and the *Wait and See Approach*. Findings on the psychological effects of social and hormonal transition for youth are provided, while acknowledging gaps in scientific knowledge that complicate providers' and caregivers' decision-making processes regarding social and medical transitions for youth. Finally, this chapter includes a case study designed to explore some typical scenarios that may occur when working with TNB youth seeking medical care, including critical thinking focused questions intended to facilitate reflection and discussion about psychosocial support, access to medical interventions, and avenues for advocacy.

REVIEW OF THE LITERATURE

The significant frequency and degree of stigma experienced by TNB individuals in their daily lives have mental and physical health repercussions (James et al., 2016). Therefore, trans-affirming health care providers play a significant role in both physical and mental health for TNB individuals of all ages (Pitts et al., 2009). However, findings from the 2015 U.S. Transgender Survey show that a third of TNB adults reported discrimination within health care settings including physical and verbal mistreatment in the past year, and even refusal of care, all of which contribute to fear and avoidance of medical care (James et al., 2016). In a focus group of trans youth, barriers to health care identified include the lack of gender-affirming providers, lack of gender-inclusive protocols, lack of consistent use of chosen name/pronoun, gatekeeping, timeliness for accessing puberty suppression and hormone replacement therapy, and insurance exclusions (Gridley et al., 2016).

Despite a growing social presence, many practitioners are not yet informed of TNB identities and may not be prepared to address the unique needs of these patients due to lack of formal training (Rafferty, 2018). According to the Association of American Medical Colleges, cultural competence education for practitioners is one of the integral components of high-quality care for TNB youth and their caregivers (Hollenback et al., 2014). Similarly, research indicates that many primary care providers do not feel prepared to address sexual health matters with LGBQ and TNB youth (Knight et al., 2014). To further complicate these interactions, silence from mental and physical health providers may be interpreted as rejection and, as a result, gender diverse patients may withhold necessary information from providers or avoid care all together (Lewis, 2008). A recent study found that when TNB adults had access to transgender-affirming primary care providers, they were eight times more likely to have pursued a medical intervention than those without affirming PCPs (Kattari et al., 2019).

Historically, a gatekeeping model was proposed by Harry Benjamin, MD. The Benjamin Standards of Care (of the Harry Benjamin International Gender Dysphoria Association, now the World Professional Association of Transgender Health [WPATH]), as they were called, were initially designed to protect providers who were offering gender-affirming care for what was then termed gender identity disorders (Coleman et al., 2011; Harry Benjamin International Gender Dysphoria Association,

1998). The initial authors of the Standards of Care (SOC) identified two primary populations that these were applied to – "biological" males who identified as women and "biological" females who identified as men, and defined a fairly strict progression from diagnostic assessment through psychotherapy and requiring a "real-life, lived experience" before medical or surgical interventions could be offered. The SOC defined both eligibility requirements and a readiness requirement that rested upon the clinician's judgment of patient readiness. They indicated that the administration of hormones to an adolescent younger than age 18 should rarely be done. This gatekeeping model has been strongly critiqued (Aydin et al., 2016) and other, more inclusive, models have emerged.

Insurance denials for gender-related care have been identified as a significant barrier for TNB individuals (Dowshen et al., 2016; Nahata et al., 2017; Rafferty, 2018). Many insurance policies are based on the WPATH SOC, which have been critiqued for, among other things, reinforcing the gender binary, which limits access to interventions for individuals who do not identify as a man or woman (Johnson & Wassersug, 2016). For example, an analysis of policy CG-SURG-27, which is used by Blue Cross and Blue Shield among other large insurance companies, shows increased access for AFAB individuals over time as well as persistent barriers for AMAB individuals. In 2018, the language of CG-SURG-27 was updated from "the individual is a female transitioning gender to become a male" (Unicare, 2017, p. 2) to "the individual is a female desiring gender transition" (Unicare, 2018, p. 2). This simple change in language has powerful implications and serves as an example for further critical assessment of current and new policies to prioritize the elimination of barriers to care for nonbinary individuals. At the same time, breast augmentation for AMAB individuals continues to be categorized as "cosmetic" and "not medically necessary" among a lengthy list of other treatment including facial feminization procedures, hair removal, and vocal therapy (Unicare, 2019, p. 3). The most recent WPATH SOC 7 has shifted from binary to nonbinary language and includes a statement recommending that practitioners not impose the gender binary on youth (Coleman et al., 2011).

Accessing trans-related health care has been described as being divided socioeconomically between those who can afford it and those who cannot (Dowshen et al., 2016; Edwards-Leeper & Spack, 2012; Nahata et al., 2017). In addition to navigating insurance, attempting to pay out-of-pocket for gender-related treatment is a source of stress for families (Grant et al., 2011). Required documentation such as a surgical support letter from one or more mental health professionals presents financial and emotional burden to individuals. Some practitioners will not write a letter for gender affirmation surgeries until after several sessions, which, without insurance, can total in hundreds of dollars. Additionally, some TNB individuals still experience "gatekeeping" or needing to provide proof of being "trans enough" or having a valid gender identity in order to obtain the required professional letters, which fosters distrust and vulnerability with professionals (Collazo et al., 2013). Furthermore, some nonbinary individuals report feeling pressure to provide a false binary narrative in order to access necessary gender treatment (Vincent, 2016). These challenges evidence a need for increasing professional awareness of TNB individuals and establish the need for more inclusive practices (Frohard-Dourlent et al., 2017).

Psychological effects of social and hormonal transition for youth

Parental support is one of, if not the, greatest predictor of positive psychological outcomes for TNB youth. Youth whose families support their asserted gender, particularly in childhood, have more positive mental health overall and less depressive symptoms than youth with families who are unsupportive (Travers et al., 2012). There is also evidence supporting the positive impact of a social transition for TNB prepubertal youth (de Vries et al., 2014; Olson et al., 2016; Simons et al., 2013; Telfer et al., 2018). In one study of youth who socially transitioned before puberty, their rates of depression were similar to depression measures of cisgender age-matched youth (Olson et al., 2016). There is clear evidence that supporting youth in their gender identity, at any age, promotes the best mental health outcomes for them.

There is limited longitudinal data that explores the experience of youth who underwent puberty suppression, followed by hormone therapy and surgery. In the first and largest study of such a group, gender dysphoria was completely resolved (de Vries et al., 2014). In measures of psychological well-being, these youth's scores matched or exceeded the scores of cisgender, age-matched youth, and finally, none of the individuals in the sample (N =55) regretted their decision to transition (de Vries et al., 2014).

CURRENT APPROACHES TO GENDER-INCLUSIVE HEALTH CARE

There are different approaches to working with youth who assert a gender identity that differs from their sex assigned at birth, and yet a dearth of empirical data to guide interventions. At decision points such as whether to support a social transition for a young child consistently expressing a gender identity that differs from their sex assigned at birth; deciding whether to initiate hormone blockers for a TNB young person on the cusp of puberty; or considering whether to initiate cross-sex hormones for a TNB adolescent, mental health clinicians are often consulted. In 2017, the Endocrine Society released a practice guideline for treatment of TNB individuals with gender dysphoria that, despite limited research on long-term health outcomes for youth, found the current research sufficiently compelling to support the use of hormone blockers and hormone replacement therapy (Hembree et al., 2017). Virtually all providers agree that decisions should be chosen for their potential to result in the best outcome for a particular young person, but there are differing thoughts in the field of what leads to the best outcomes for TNB youth. For example, some clinician-scholars believe that due to the fact that some TNB prepubertal youth do not go on to identify with a gender that differs from their sex into adolescence and beyond, prepubertal youth expressing a gender that differs from their sex may be best served by becoming comfortable with their sex (Zucker et al., 2012).

Parents and guardians of TNB youth approach mental health clinicians with a wide variety of thoughts, feelings, and goals for treatment. Some parents and guardians reach out to mental health clinicians with the goal of changing their child's asserted or expressed identity, despite so called "conversion therapy" being harmful rather than effective, and all the major medical and mental health organizations having come out against it (see resources for a website with a comprehensive international list of professional organizations opposing conversion or reparative therapy). Other times, parents and guardians reach out to a mental health clinician for guidance and support, with the aim of providing the young person with an adult with whom they can explore their feelings and experiences. Mental health providers approach clinical practice with TNB youth in many ways. Two common approaches to the care of TNB youth include the *Gender Affirmative Model* (GAM) and the *Wait and See Approach*.

The Gender Affirmative Model

The *Gender Affirmative Model* (GAM) aims to facilitate the best mental health outcomes for youth, which, for TNB youth, involves freedom to express any gender that feels authentic without rejection or restriction. Youth who are not given the opportunity to express a gender that feels authentic are at risk of developing a host of mental health problems, including depression, suicidal ideation, suicide attempts, social anxiety, school avoidance or truancy, self-injurious behaviors, substance use and abuse, homelessness, STIs, and incarceration (Travers et al., 2012).

A central tenet of the GAM is the evidence-based idea that efforts to change a person's gender inflict harm (Keo-Meier & Ehrensaft, 2018). The GAM posits that children and adolescents should live and express a gender that feels most authentic and comfortable for them, and a young person should express their gender identity without restriction, criticism, or harassment (Keo-Meier & Ehrensaft, 2018; Olson et al., 2016). Central to this model is its belief that people who express any gender are inherently well and resilient. Another tenet of the model is a focus on the legitimacy of gender identities across a gender spectrum, and expression of these identities as a basic human right (Keo-Meier & Ehrensaft, 2018). If a child or adolescent's gender identity or expression changes over time, a clinician practicing in a gender affirmative model would remain open and affirming of these changes. Additionally, this approach takes into account various factors that shape an individual's identity, such as one's race, ethnicity, class, primary language, immigration status, ability, and religion, among other factors. This model considers that those factors fit into a larger gender picture for a given youth (American Psychological Association, 2015). Finally, the GAM considers that any pathology that is present, such as mood or behavior problems, is most often caused by cultural reactions to gender diversity (such as transphobia) rather than by internal psychological disturbances within the child (Hidalgo et al., 2013).

Proponents of the GAM point out that this treatment approach appreciates the complexities inherent in the clinical care of TNB youth. The GAM considers that childhood and adolescence is a time marked by change, growth, development, and social relationships that influence a person's identity. The model considers the role of a young person's home, family, friends, social environment, cultural context, resources, strengths, and community, and how these relate to their lived experiences. This approach involves thinking about young people in a nuanced way, considering individual characteristics such as coping skills and temperament, and environmental factors such as school and family environments, to make recommendations about next steps for a particular youth.

The Wait and See Approach

The other approach most often used with prepubertal youth asserting a gender identity that differs from their sex is known as the *Wait and See Approach*. In this approach, gendered behavior or interests are neither encouraged nor discouraged, and no action is taken to affirm a different identity. For example, a child assigned male at birth who enjoys playing with dolls and dressing as a princess would be allowed to play with dolls and dress as a princess, but adults in the child's life would neither encourage nor discourage these behaviors. In addition, there may not be efforts to provide more options of toys and clothing that deviate from what one would typically expect for youth of the child's sex assigned at birth.

People who support this approach to TNB prepubertal youth note several published studies that find a minority of prepubertal gender nonconforming youth persisted in their cross-gender identity into adolescence (Drummond et al., 2008; Steensma et al., 2013; Wallien & Cohen-Kettenis, 2008). Proponents of the *Wait and See Approach* focus on the statistics that many youths will not go on to identify with a gender that differs from their sex into adolescence and adulthood (Ehrensaft, 2014). They note that transitioning back to one's sex assigned at birth may cause more distress than waiting to make a social transition. Critics of this approach note delaying a child's ability to be known in their affirmed gender may lead to mental health problems, up to and including suicide (Keo-Meier & Ehrensaft, 2018). Critics of this approach also cite research that outlines the critical, positive impact of parental support for the mental health of TNB youth (Olson et al., 2016).

BEST PRACTICES FOR MEDICALLY SUPPORTING TNB YOUTH

Affirmative care involves considering each individual young person's feelings, experiences, culture, family, environments, beliefs, and needs. Due to limited evidence-based treatment guidelines, it is misguided to universally employ any one approach with all TNB youth, as that fails to consider the complexity of each individual child (Edwards-Leeper et al., 2016). Although more research is needed to establish best practices, some recommendations can be made for professionals:

- First of all, consider the *reversibility of interventions*. As previous research has shown, it is quite difficult to determine prepubertal children who will persist as TNB adolescents from those who will desist (Drummond et al., 2008). Most will not persist, with persistence rates of gender dysphoria to be approximately 16% across studies (Steensma & Cohen-Kettenis, 2015). Yet, there are reasonable data that a supportive family environment reduces mental health morbidity (Olson et al., 2016). Allowing children to play, dress, or present in a manner that is comfortable to them (even to the point of asking schools to use a preferred name or changing gender markers on passports for the purpose of safe travel) may brand them as different, but this has not been found to cause much, if any, harm.

- Consider involving *an interprofessional care team* early for the benefit of the caregivers. Although children will not benefit from a medical intervention during a prepubertal stage, have a full team including medicine (pediatrics or adolescent medicine), nutrition, social work, psychology, nursing, and community organizations including legal support, can provide reassurance and support to parents who are seeking to understand their child and advocate on their behalf. A lot of what causes distress for caregivers is the unknown. An interprofessional team gives caregivers a plethora of resources they can reach out to as they encounter new experiences along their child's gender journey.
- Unfortunately, many parts of the country have limited health care resources. Ideally, *training is provided to all health care practitioners* on resources and evolving best practices so they can effectively refer families or receive support in helping families navigate child development without needing to travel excessive distances.
- Interprofessional care teams that see children need to perform *resource mapping in their catchment area*. According to the Endocrine Society, multidisciplinary team of medical and mental health professionals are necessary to manage care for prepubertal TNB youth and teenagers including to confirm gender dysphoria, medical necessity, and ability to provide informed consent (Hembree et al., 2017). It is not enough to merely provide services ("build it and they will come"); rather, there needs to be a conscious needs assessment done to identify gaps in services and provide education and resources to providers (including schools and community organizations) on current best practices, training and education opportunities, and resource options.
- Lastly, *services should be designed with community involvement in mind* – both from health care practitioners and advocacy organizations, but most importantly, from family members and TNB youth and adults in the local community. Remember that TNB people have many cultural identities beyond their TNB identity.

THE ROLE OF THE MENTAL HEALTH PROFESSIONAL IN THE GENDER AFFIRMATIVE MODEL

In the *Gender Affirmative Model*, the mental health provider acts as an affirming sounding board for the child as they express their gender, support their process, and help them live a life that feels authentic and comfortable. This involves holding a judgment-free space for the youth to discuss their feelings and experiences, validating their feelings and experiences, calling the youth by the name and pronouns they wish to be called, discussing how the youth may want to share their gender with others, coping with others' reactions to their coming out, problem-solving issues that arise, and more. In the GAM, the therapist is a supportive partner for the youth in their process. The goal for therapeutic interventions with TNB youth in the *Gender Affirmative Model* is to enhance their mental, emotional, and social well-being as they navigate what it means to be trans in the world (Nealy, 2017). See Chapter 4 on supporting the mental health and well-being of TNB youth for more information.

In addition to the important role of being an individual therapist to the youth, the mental health provider in the GAM also assists parents or guardians in supporting the child in their gender identity. Keo-Meier and Ehrensaft (2018) describe the mental health provider as the "translator" who attempts to understand what the child is telling others about their gender via their words and behavior (p. 13). Many parents feel puzzled by their child's feelings and statements about their gender, and the therapist or counselor is in a unique role to educate parents and other caregivers on gender identity development and treatment options for gender dysphoria, while also helping the parents understand their particular child's feelings and experiences. The provider may help the caregivers cope with confusion, grief, loss, and anxiety about the future, and then move forward in some supportive way given the information that is known.

A critical task of the mental health provider in the GAM is identifying and managing their own feelings and beliefs about gender, which are often subconscious. Providers must recognize their biases and assumptions about gender, be forthcoming about those biases, and explore how those biases affect their ability to provide supportive treatment. Unexamined internalized beliefs about gender may interfere with the provider's ability to provide the best care (Chonody et al., 2014; Keo-Meier & Ehrensaft, 2018).

CASE STUDY

This case study describes some frequent scenarios seen among TNB youth seeking medical care. In this case study, a young person has been referred to a social worker from their school. After reading the case study, critical thinking questions can be used for individual reflection or group discussion.

Case study

Name:	Dani (Legal name: Stephanie)
Pronouns:	He/Him/His
Age:	12 years old
Sex assigned at birth:	Female
Presenting issues:	Referred for therapy due to recent disruptive behavior in school and conflict with family.

Background information:

Dani is the middle child in a middle-class, White, Midwest family. Dani is in the 7th grade at an urban public school. Recently, Dani has been getting in trouble for disruptive behavior including rudeness towards teachers, fighting with classmates, and arguing with parents. Until recently, Dani's parents reported Dani's behavior to be fairly calm and shy with current outbursts increasing over the last six months. When asked about recent behaviors, Dani describes it a response to being unhappy with themselves and everyone around them. Some exploration of this unhappiness revealed that Dani has been experiencing a growing discomfort with body parts (gender dysphoria), especially around his hips and chest areas. Dani reported increased anxiety and fear around the imminent start of menstruation and described additional feminization as "horrifying". When asked to describe his gender, Dani says that he feels mostly masculine but not entirely and shares that using he/him/his pronouns feels most comfortable but that no one actually uses them for him except for close friends.

Dani was given a diagnosis of gender dysphoria from his primary care physician and is wanting to pursue medical care, particularly postponing puberty as soon as possible. This earnest concern is persistent, and reportedly has led to much of his recent frustration. According to Dani, his parents are "as supportive as they can be". He reports that his dad is trying to understand, but he is mostly avoidant of the topic and refuses to use Dani's chosen name or male pronouns. Mom is described as making more of an effort, but also tearfully shares with Dani that it is a huge struggle for her. His brothers are both older, and do not question Dani's gender but do not defend him in family and social settings, which Dani says hurts his feelings. Dani has asked for help to convince his parents that he really is a boy, and that it is okay to stop his body from continuing to change with puberty.

In school, Dani must use his legal name due to a lack of policy for name changes, much less other support for students who are transitioning. He was consistently a B+ student until recently. His grades have been dropping, and he admits that he is less motivated to participate in school and would rather stay home. Despite a masculine gender identity and expression, he must use the women's bathroom. He used to play sports and lists some of his athletic accomplishments but has since stopped because the school will only allow him to play on the women's teams, and Dani finds the locker-room to be extremely uncomfortable. In the past, there has been a GSA; however, a faculty sponsor is required, and the last willing teacher left without a replacement. Dani also adds that he does not know if he would attend the GSA because he does not feel like he is "trans enough". When he needs help coping, Dani reports turning to his close friends who are his strongest source of support. Other times, he has resorted to cutting his thighs and restricting his diet. Dani has been told by friends and his family that he can pursue transitioning when he turns 18, but Dani states that he does not think he can wait that long, especially if he has to go through puberty.

Critical reflection questions

1. What would be your plan for working with Dani?
2. What sources of support can be identified in Dani's life as he explores his gender identity and expression?
3. What are some paths for Dani to access gender-affirming medical care?

4. What do you perceive to be the barriers for Dani in accessing medical care?
5. What options would you recommend to support Dani and his family at this time?
6. How could you advocate for Dani in related areas of his life (e.g., school environment, family, sports, etc.)?
7. What other information would you want to know to best assist Dani and his family?
8. With the lessons from this case study in mind, what changes could you implement to improve gender-affirming care in your work?

CONCLUSION

Medical care plays a significant role in the transition process for TNB youth and their caregivers. The outcomes regarding medical care and transitioning have demonstrated the need for increasing accessibility and providing affirming care for TNB youth. In moving away from a gatekeeping approach, practitioners are recommended to adopt an affirming approach that empowers TNB youth in their transition and support their caregivers. In the absence of established best practices for working with TNB youth around medical transition, two prevailing health care approaches have been reviewed, the *Gender Affirmative Model* (GAM) and the *Wait and See Approach*. In order to better support TNB youth, familiarization with multiple affirming models can allow practitioners to adapt their engagement to best fit the needs of each individual and their caregivers. Ongoing practice evaluation and research are needed to move gender-affirmative care forward towards establishing best practices that can be applied across health care settings in order to support TNB youth to ensure the healthiest outcomes possible.

RESOURCES

Websites

1. Gender Affirmative Lifespan Approach (GALA) – www.sexualhealth.umn.edu/ncgsh/gala
2. Gender Spectrums Medical (medical resources page) – www.genderspectrum.org/resources/medical-2/
3. HRC – Talking to Doctors and Medical Providers – www.hrc.org/resources/transgender-children-and-youth-talking-to-doctors-and-medical-providers
4. HRC – Coming out to your doctors – www.hrc.org/resources/coming-out-to-your-doctor
5. OutCare – www.outcarehealth.org/resources
6. WPATH SOC – www.wpath.org/publications/soc
7. List of professional organisations opposing conversion or reparative therapy targeting transgender and gender non-conforming individuals (maintained by Florence Ashley) – https://medium.com/@florence.ashley/list-of-professional-organisations-opposing-conversion-or-reparative-therapy-targeting-transgender-f700b4e02c4e

Books

Brill, S., & Kenney, L. (2016). *The transgender teen: A handbook for parents and professionals supporting transgender and non-binary teens.* Jersey City, NJ: Cleis Press.

Brill, S., & Pepper, R. (2008). *The transgender child: A handbook for families and professionals.* San Francisco, CA: Cleis Press.

Dentato, M. P. (Ed.). (2017). *Social work practice with the LGBTQ community: The intersection of history, health, mental health, and policy factors.* New York, NY: Oxford University Press.

Erickson-Schroth, L. (Ed.). (2014). *Trans bodies, trans selves: A resource for the transgender community.* New York, NY: Oxford University Press.

Keo-Meier, C., & Ehrensaft, D. (Eds.) (2018). *The Gender Affirmative Model: An interdisciplinary approach to supporting transgender and gender expansive children.* Washington, DC: American Psychological Association.

PowerPoints

Ehrensaft, D. (n.d.). *Apples, oranges, and fruit salad: Sorting out transgender, gender expansive, and gender non-binary children and youth.* Retrieved from www.transvisie.nl/wp-content/uploads/2016/12/diane-ehrensaft.pdf

REFERENCES

American Psychological Association. (2015). Guidelines for psychological practice with transgender and gender nonconforming people. *American Psychologist, 70,* 832–864.

Aydin, D., Buk, L. J., Partoft, S., Bonde, C., Thomsen, M. V., & Tos, T. (2016). Transgender surgery in Denmark from 1994 to 2015: 20-year follow-up study. *Journal of Sexual Medicine, 13*(4), 720–725. doi:10.1016/j.jsxm.2016.01.012

Chonody, J. M., Woodford, M. R., Brennan, D. J., Newman, B., & Wang, D. (2014). Attitudes toward gay men and lesbian women among heterosexual social work faculty. *Journal of Social Work Education, 50*(1), 136–152. doi:10.1080/10437797.2014.856239

Coleman, E., Bockting, W., Botzer, M., Cohen-Kettenis, P., DeCuypere, G., Feldman, J., & Zucker, K. (2011). Standards of care for the health of transsexual, transgender, and gender-nonconforming people, version 7. *International Journal of Transgenderism, 13,* 165–232. doi:10.1080/15532739.2011.700873

Collazo, A., Austin, A., & Craig, S. L. (2013). Facilitating transition among transgender clients: Components of effective clinical practice. *Clinical Social Work Journal, 41*(3), 228–237.

de Vries, A. L. C., McGuire, J. K., Steensma, T. D., Wagenaar, E. C. F., Doreleijers, T. A. H., & Cohen-Kettenis, P. (2014). Young adult psychological outcome after puberty suppression and gender reassignment. *Pediatrics, 134*(4), 696–704.

Dowshen, N., Meadows, R., Byrnes, M., Hawkins, L., Eder, J., & Noonan, K. (2016). Policy perspective: Ensuring comprehensive care and support for gender nonconforming children and adolescents. *Transgender Health, 1*(1), 75–85.

Drummond, K. D., Bradley, S. J., Peterson-Badali, M., & Zucker, K. J. (2008). A follow up study of girls with gender identity disorder. *Developmental Psychology, 44,* 34–45.

Edwards-Leeper, L., & Spack, N. P. (2012). Psychological evaluation and medical treatment of transgender youth in an interdisciplinary "Gender Management Service" (GeMS) in a major pediatric center. *Journal of Homosexuality, 59*(3), 321–336.

Edwards-Leeper, L., Leibowitz, S., & Sangganjanavanich, V. F. (2016). Affirmative practice with transgender and gender nonconforming youth: Expanding the model. *Psychology of Sexual Orientation and Gender Diversity, 3*(2), 165–172.

Ehrensaft, D. (2014). Found in transition: Our littlest transgender people. *Contemporary Psychoanalysis*, 50(4), 571–592. doi:10.1080/00107530.2014.942591

Frohard-Dourlent, H., Dobson, S., Clark, B. A., Doull, M., & Saewyc, E. M. (2017). 'I would have preferred more options': Accounting for non-binary youth in health research. *Nursing Inquiry*, 24(1), 1–9. doi:10.1111/nin.12150

Grant, J. M., Mottet, L., Tanis, J. E., Harrison, J., Herman, J., & Keisling, M. (2011). *Injustice at every turn: A report of the National Transgender Discrimination Survey*. Washington, DC: National Center for Transgender Equality.

Gridley, S. J., Crouch, J. M., Evans, Y., Eng, W., Antoon, E., Lyapustina, M., … McCarty, C. (2016). Youth and caregiver perspectives on barriers to gender-affirming health care for transgender youth. *Journal of Adolescent Health*, 59(3), 254–261.

Harry Benjamin International Gender Dysphoria Association. (1998). The standards of care for gender identity disorder. *International Journal of Transgenderism*, 2(2).

Hembree, W. C., Cohen-Kettenis, P. T., Gooren, L., Hannema, S. E., Meyer, W. J., Murad, M. H., … T'Sjoen, G. G. (2017). Endocrine treatment of gender-dysphoric/gender-incongruent persons: An Endocrine Society clinical practice guideline. *The Journal of Clinical Endocrinology & Metabolism*, 102(11), 3869–3903. doi:10.1210/jc.2017-01658

Hidalgo, M. A., Ehrensaft, D., Tishelman, A. C., Clark, L. F., Garofalo, R., Rosenthal, S. M., … Olson, J. (2013). The Gender Affirmative Model: What we know and what we aim to learn. *Human Development*, 56, 285–290.

Hollenback, A. D., Eckstrand, K. L., & Dreger, A. (Eds.) (2014). *Implementing curricular and institutional climate changes to improve health care for individuals who are LGBT, gender nonconforming, or born with DSD: A resource for medical educators*. Washington, DC: Association of American Medical Colleges. Retrieved from https://store.aamc.org/downloadable/download/sample/sample_id/129/

James, S. E., Herman, J. L., Rankin, S., Keisling, M., Mottet, L., & Anafi, M. (2016). *The report of the 2015 U.S. Transgender Survey*. Washington, DC: National Center for Transgender Equality.

Johnson, T. W., & Wassersug, R. J. (2016). Recognition of gender variants outside the binary in WPATH Standards of Care, Version 7.0. *International Journal of Transgenderism*, 17(1), 1–3. doi:10.1080/15532739.2015.1114442

Kattari, S. K., Atteberry-Ash, B., Kinney, M. K., Walls, N. E., & Kattari, L. (2019). One size does not fit all: Differential transgender health experiences by gender identity and sexual orientation. *Social Work in Health Care*, 58, 899–917. doi:10.1080/00981389.2019.1677279

Keo-Meier, C., & Ehrensaft, D. (Eds.) (2018). *The Gender Affirmative Model*. Washington, DC: American Psychological Association.

Knight, R. E., Shoveller, J. A., Carson, A. M., & Contreras-Whitney, J. G. (2014). Examining clinicians' experiences providing sexual health services for LGBTQ youth: Considering social and structural determinants of health in clinical practice. *Health Education Research*, 29, 662–670. doi:10.1093/her/cyt116

Levine, S. B. (2019). Informed consent for transgendered patients. *Journal of Sex and Marital Therapy*, 45(3), 218–229. doi:10.1080/0092623X.2018.1518885

Lewis, J. (2008). *Resilience among transgender adults who identify as genderqueer: Implications for health and mental health treatment* (Doctoral dissertation). Retrieved from ProQuest Information & Learning. (57395).

Nahata, L., Quinn, G. P., Caltabellotta, N. M., & Tishelman, A. C. (2017). Mental health concerns and insurance denials among transgender adolescents. *LGBT Health*, 4(3), 188–193.

Nealy, E. C. (2017). *Transgender children and youth: Cultivating pride and joy with families in transition*. New York, NY: W.W. Norton & Company.

Olson, K. R., Durwood, L., DeMeules, M., & McLaughlin, K. A. (2016). Mental health of transgender children who are supported in their identities. *Pediatrics*, 137(3), e20153223.

Pitts, M. K., Couch, C., Mulcare, H., Croy, S., & Mitchell, A. (2009). Transgender people in Australia and New Zealand: Health, well-being and access to health services. *Feminism & Psychology, 19*(4), 475–495. doi:10.1177/0959353509342771

Rafferty, J. (2018). Ensuring comprehensive care and support for transgender and gender-diverse children and adolescents. *American Academy of Pediatrics, 142*(4), e20182162. doi:10.1542/peds.2018-2162

Russell, S. T., Pollitt, A. M., Li, G., & Grossman, A. H. (2018). Chosen name use is linked to reduced depressive symptoms, suicidal ideation, and suicidal behavior among transgender youth. *Journal of Adolescent Health, 63*(4), 503–505. doi:10.1016/j.jadohealth.2018.02.003

Simons, L., Schrager, S. M., Clark, L. F., Belzer, M., & Olson, J. (2013). Parental support and mental health among transgender adolescents. *Journal of Adolescent Health, 53*(6), 791–793.

Steensma, T. D., & Cohen-Kettenis, P. T. (2015). More than two developmental pathways in children with gender dysphoria? *Journal of the American Academy of Child & Adolescent Psychiatry, 54*(2), 147–148. doi:10.1016/j.jaac.2014.10.016

Steensma, T. D., McGuire, J. K., Kreukels, B. P., Beekman, A. J., & Cohen-Kettenis, P. T. (2013). Factors associated with desistence and persistence of childhood gender dysphoria: A quantitative follow up study. *Journal of the American Academy of Child & Adolescent Psychiatry, 52*, 582–590.

Strauss, P., Cook, A., Winter, S., Watson, V., Wright-Toussaint, D., & Lin, A. (2017). *Trans-Pathways: The mental health experiences and care pathways of trans young people – summary of results*. Perth, Australia: Curtin University of Technology, School of Public Health.

Telfer, M. M., Tollit, M. A., Pace, C. C., & Pang, K. C. (2018). *Australian standards of care and treatment guidelines for trans and gender diverse children and adolescents (Version 1.1)*. Melbourne, Australia: The Royal Children's Hospital.

Torres, C. G., Renfrew, M., Kenst, K., Tan-McGrory, A., Betancourt, J. R., & López, L. (2015). Improving transgender health by building safe clinical environments that promote existing. *BMC Pediatrics, 15*(187). doi:10.1186/s12887-015-0505-6

Travers, R., Bauer, G., Pyne, J., Bradley, K., Gale, L., & Papadimitriou, M. (2012, October). *Impacts of strong parental support for trans youth: A report prepared for Children's Aid Society of Toronto and Delisle Youth Services*. Retrieved from http://transpulseproject.ca/wp-content/uploads/2012/10/Impacts-of-Strong-Parental-Support-for-Trans-Youth-vFINAL.pdf

Unicare. (2017, February 16). *CG-SURG-27 Sex Reassignment Surgery*. Retrieved from www.unicare.com/medicalpolicies/guidelines/gl_pw_a051166.htm

Unicare. (2018, April 25). *CG-SURG-27 Sex Reassignment Surgery*. Retrieved from www.unicare.com/medicalpolicies/guidelines/gl_pw_a051166.htm

Unicare. (2019, January 31). *CG-SURG-27 Sex Reassignment Surgery*. Retrieved from www.unicare.com/medicalpolicies/guidelines/gl_pw_a051166.htm

Vincent, B. W. (2016). *Non-binary gender identity negotiations: Interactions with queer communities and medical practice* (Doctoral dissertation). Retrieved from University of Leeds. (Accession F4399122A9BDE589).

Wallien, M. S., & Cohen-Kettenis, P. T. (2008). Psychosexual outcome of gender-dysphoric children. *Journal of the American Academy of Child & Adolescent Psychiatry, 47*, 1413–1423.

Zucker, K. J., Wood, H., Singh, D., & Bradley, S. J. (2012). A developmental, biopsychosocial model for the treatment of children with gender identity disorder. *Journal of Homosexuality, 59*(3), 369–397. doi:10.1080/00918369.2012.653309

CHAPTER 2

Transgender and nonbinary adults and access to medical care

Ashley Lacombe-Duncan, Shanna K. Kattari, and Leonardo Kattari

INTRODUCTION

Transgender and nonbinary (TNB) individuals experience a disproportionate prevalence of multiple health issues spanning physical, mental, and sexual health, among other domains. These health issues proliferate within a context of intersecting trans and other stigmas and a lack of access to the social determinants of health (e.g., employment, housing). Trans people may also interact with the health care system when accessing medical gender affirmation (e.g., hormones, gender-affirming surgeries). When interacting with the health care system, this diverse group of people faces high rates of discrimination, harassment, and even violence. While the worst case scenarios involve TNB people being explicitly denied access to medical care, many also experience being misgendered, having the wrong name used for them, and being on the receiving end of transphobic microaggressions – subtle words or phrases that signify discomfort with and/or lack of knowledge of trans experience and identities. All the while, TNB people are often forced to educate their providers in order to receive culturally responsive care.

TNB individuals often have negative experiences when accessing care and sometimes go so far as to avoid needed care altogether because of encounters ranging from misaligned paperwork (where an individual's legal name/sex marker do not match their name and gender) to welcoming and well-meaning practitioners who lack the knowledge or skill set to provide appropriate treatment. These issues may also result in TNB people being more likely to delay care. Lack of access to appropriate and timely medical care can exacerbate physical health issues, as well as cause significant psychological distress for TNB people. Discrimination and unequal treatment are also shaped by intersections of race, class, and ability.

This chapter explores the extant literature around medical access and offers suggestions regarding language, intake forms, and best practices in gender-affirming medical care. Examples will include exemplary care which has been provided to TNB people, and tips for navigating these challenges within larger health care settings, as well as dealing with insurance companies. An activity is presented that offers the reader the opportunity to reflect on practical strategies to address individual and organizational barriers to medical care access for TNB people.

HEALTH DISPARITIES AMONG TRANS AND NONBINARY PEOPLE

As mentioned, TNB individuals experience many health disparities. The majority of published studies to date have focused on sexual health disparities, addressed in Chapter 3 of this book, and in particular HIV vulnerability. A recent meta-analysis including studies from across 15 countries identified that trans women had almost 49 times the odds of laboratory-confirmed HIV infection, compared to all adults of reproductive age (Baral et al., 2013). Black trans women in the United States (US) experience HIV prevalence rates as high as 30.8% for self-reported HIV positive status and 56.3% confirmed by HIV test (Herbst et al., 2008). Many other studies have focused on mental health disparities, addressed in Chapter 4 and Chapter 5 of this book. For example, a study comparing a sample of trans and cisgender (cis) adults accessing clinical care found that trans patients were more likely to endorse a lifetime suicide attempt and ideation compared with cis patients (Reisner et al., 2014).

While fewer studies have focused on general health (Reisner et al., 2016), what does exist documents high rates of mortality, diabetes, and cancer among TNB people. Drawing on Veterans Health Administration data, one study found that past six-month health care use among trans veterans was almost triple that found in community samples of cis veterans (15.8% vs. 6.2%), suggesting higher medical care needs among this population (Mizock et al., 2012). There is an even smaller body of research comparing physical health outcomes between trans and cis people (Fredriksen-Goldsen et al., 2014). Notably, Fredriksen-Goldsen et al. (2014) found that compared to cis lesbian, gay, and bisexual adults aged 50 years and older, trans older adults are at a significantly higher risk of poor physical health. This association was partially mediated by fear of accessing health services; however, victimization and stigma explained the highest proportion of the total effect of gender identity on health outcomes.

TNB health disparities can be contextually understood through the lens of *gender minority stress theory*, which has been used to describe how trans stigma – stigma attached to having a TNB gender identity/expression – accounts for differences in physical and mental health between trans and cis people on a population level (Hendricks & Testa, 2012; White Hughto et al., 2015). *Stigma* – a social process involving labeling, stereotyping, and subsequent discrimination against a person or group of people as a form of social control (Link & Phelan, 2001) – can result in a lack of access to the social determinants of health (SDoH), defined as the immediate, social, and political context affecting one's health (e.g., income, employment, housing, health care) (Mikkonen & Raphael, 2010). Gaps in SDoH are well-documented for TNB people through community-based studies in the US (Bradford et al., 2013; Clements-Nolle et al., 2001). *Gender affirmation*, the interactive process whereby a person receives social recognition and support for their gender identity and expression (Nuttbrock et al., 2009), is a SDoH for TNB people that can also be disrupted through stigmatizing processes. Though underexplored in TNB populations, studies conducted with other groups who experience stress of a socially disadvantaged position (e.g., cis women, LGBQ people) have shown the direct physiological impact of stigma, including diastolic blood pressure reactivity, increased cortisol output, and elevated cardiovascular risk (Hatzenbuehler et al., 2014; Townsend et al., 2011).

Of equal importance is the consideration of other types of stigma which may intersect with trans stigma to further limit TNB people's access to the SDoH and subsequent health outcomes, a framework known as *intersectionality*, a critical social theory rooted in Black feminism (Hill Collins, 2000). TNB people who live at the intersection of multiple socially disadvantaged positions, including people of color and low-income people, are at a particularly high risk of experiencing both poor health outcomes and barriers to access to health care (White Hughto & Reisner, 2016).

DELAYING, DENIAL, AND AVOIDANCE OF MEDICAL CARE

Due to access barriers to care described in the next section, a significant proportion of TNB people delay necessary medical care, sometimes to the point of requiring emergency care (Grant et al., 2010), where they often face even more discrimination than in other settings. Findings from the National Transgender Discrimination Survey (NTDS) documents trans-identity-based denial of service when trying to access both ambulances/EMTs (5%) and emergency departments (13%) (Grant et al., 2010). A recent rapid review identified that 23% (range: 10%–40%) of trans people across eight studies had delayed necessary medical care (Kcomt, 2018), and rates are even higher for TNB people of color (Jaffee et al., 2016). The NTDS helps to explain why this may occur, as over one-quarter (28%) reported delaying medical care due to discrimination and almost half (48%) had delayed due to an inability to afford care (Grant et al., 2010).

Outright denial of care to TNB people is not uncommon, with over one-quarter reporting denial of care at least once in their lifetime (range: 19%–40%) (Kcomt, 2018). While 19% of the total sample of the NTDS were refused care, stark racial and ethnic differences were found. Among White TNB individuals, 17% had been denied care, while the proportion was higher for all groups of people of color, with up to 36% of Native participants having been denied care. Other research indicates that TNB individuals may even have been turned away from care in urgent and emergency situations, which may lead to the increase of health conditions and in a few extreme cases, death (Seelman et al., 2017). These negative experiences are important as they foster anticipatory stigma and can result in avoidance of health care settings altogether. These outcomes are not only situated differentially across race and ethnicity, but also across gender identity. An analysis of the impact of various components of transitioning on postponement of curative care among 4,049 TNB people found that participants who had been on hormones and had top surgery were almost twice as likely to delay care when sick or injured compared to those who had not been due to discrimination (Cruz, 2014). Both this and other studies emphasize the importance of considering the needs of sub-groups within TNB communities.

MEDICAL GENDER AFFIRMATION

TNB people have a range of medical concerns, most of which do not differ from cis people and can be addressed within primary care settings (Wylie et al., 2016). Providers tend to overestimate the extent to which TNB people's medical care needs are related to gender. However, one important area of more specialized health care for some trans people is medical gender affirmation, sometimes referred to as medical transition. This care may involve hormone therapy and/or surgery to change primary and/or secondary sex characteristics with the aim of aligning one's physical characteristics with one's gender identity (World Professional Association for Transgender Health [WPATH], 2012). Not all TNB people transition or access medical gender affirmation. However, the absence of access to this care for those who desire it has severe negative impacts on mental health and quality of life (Lindqvist et al., 2017; White Hughto & Reisner, 2016), and may increase certain health risks (Sperber et al., 2005). Alternately, access to medical gender affirmation can increase quality of life and resilience among trans people (Crosby et al., 2016; Lindqvist et al., 2017).

MULTI-LEVEL BARRIERS TO ACCESS TO MEDICAL CARE

TNB people experience many barriers to access to medical care at individual (e.g., delaying/avoiding care due to anticipated stigma; lack of knowledge about where to access care; depression or other mental health considerations), as well as interpersonal, organizational, and structural levels (Rood et al., 2016). The most pervasive barriers, and those focused on in this chapter, are those at interpersonal, organizational, and structural levels.

Cisnormativity, defined as the "sociocultural assumptions and expectations that all people are cissexual and/or have a cisgender body" (Bauer et al., 2009, p. 356), contributes to a lack of research conducted to address the health care needs of TNB people as well as the limited education of health care providers about TNB health. Combined, these result in a lack of knowledge among health care providers about providing gender-affirming care and medical gender affirmation to TNB people. LGBT-focused curriculum in medical education is sorely lacking (Obedin-Maliver et al., 2011), as it is in other allied health care professions such as social work (Erich et al., 2007). Over one-third (range: 20% to 50%) of TNB people participating across eight US-based studies had encountered health care providers who were not informed about TNB health issues (Kcomt, 2018). As a result, members of this community often spend additional energy, time, and capacity educating their providers about TNB identities, providing them with information about medical gender affirmation, and working to correct assumptions and wrong information these providers may have about these communities (Poteat et al., 2013). Knowledge gaps are even more pronounced for trans people with chronic health conditions, such as HIV infection (Lacombe-Duncan et al., 2019).

Stigmatization of TNB people by health care providers is a pervasive problem, with many experiencing verbal harassment and some even experiencing physical violence in physicians' offices (Grant et al., 2010; Kattari et al., 2015). A recent study by Kattari and Hasche (2016) found that approximately a quarter (23.4%) of TNB people reported having experienced health care discrimination, with another 26.7% reporting verbal harassment when accessing medical care. Even more concerning was that 2% had experienced physical violence that was perpetrated by a medical provider in a health care setting (Kattari & Hasche, 2016).

Discrimination is worse for TNB people in rural areas (Sperber et al., 2005), people of color (Kenagy & Bostwick, 2005), people with disabilities (Kattari et al., 2017), and those whose gender expression does not align with binary expectations of gender (i.e., feminine, masculine) (White Hughto & Reisner, 2016). Not surprisingly, these experiences of transphobic discrimination by health practitioners are correlated with poor mental health outcomes (Riggs et al., 2014). On the contrary, having a gender-affirming primary care provider is correlated with lower rates of depression and suicidal ideation among TNB individuals (Kattari et al., 2016).

Making matters worse, providers often do not listen to TNB people who stand up against discrimination. In a qualitative study of 11 trans women living with HIV infection, providers had a negative response to participants who stood up for themselves, including labeling/stereotyping trans women (e.g., calling them aggressive) and continuing to perpetuate discrimination (e.g., leaving them in the waiting room) (Lacombe-Duncan et al., 2020). Similarly, a qualitative study conducted with TNB people (*N*=55) and medical providers (*N*=12) identified how interpersonal stigma was used in the context of patient-provider relationships to affirm provider authority by positioning vocal trans patients as problematic (Poteat et al., 2013).

Organizational barriers include inappropriate electronic and written forms that do not allow for diversity in gender identity nor capture name or pronouns discordant from legal identity documentation, and gaps in the built environment, such as a lack of gender-inclusive bathrooms (Safer et al., 2016). Finally, policies can restrict access to medical transition for TNB people by reducing access to health insurance and/or coverage of various hormone therapy and/or gender-affirming surgeries (Khan, 2011), compounded by geographic differences in coverage (Gehi & Arkles, 2007). There are also many uncovered costs (e.g., transportation, post-surgical care) associated with accessing medical transition (Coronel Villalobos et al., 2018). Under-insurance is a significant access barrier to general medical care for this group as well with between 14% and 19% of TNB adults in the US lacking health insurance (Kcomt, 2018).

Most studies discuss the solutions to barriers to health care access as outside of the hands of TNB people themselves – and only in the hands of health care providers or those who organize health care. These studies overlook the substantial empowerment and activism that happens within TNB communities. Qualitative studies have shown how TNB people exhibit resilience (e.g., inner strength), actively resist stigma and discrimination (e.g., refusing care from specific types of providers), and transform discriminatory health care settings, through private self-advocacy, activism, and engagement in community-based organizations, research, and education (Lacombe-Duncan et al., 2020). These studies call for practitioners to be aware of, acknowledge, and foster TNB people's strengths through supporting their inclusion in health care spaces.

BEST PRACTICES IN PROVIDING GENDER-AFFIRMING MEDICAL CARE

Informed consent process

Much medical transition care, particularly hormone therapy, can be delivered in primary care settings, with the adoption of an informed consent model of care (Wylie et al., 2016). This model is in line with how many other non-gender-affirming-related procedures are offered (such as vaccinations, allergy testing, general medication, skin biopsies, etc.), and empowers the patient to learn about the risks and benefits of a specific medical intervention in order to make the decision for themselves about whether it is a good fit for their needs. Primary care physicians should be competent at providing medical gender affirmation, consistent with up-to-date clinical guidelines, such as those available through community health centers (e.g., Callen Lorde Community Health Center's "Protocols for the Provision of Hormone Therapy", n.d.), in addition to being able to assess other physical, mental, and sexual and reproductive health needs of TNB people.

Provider training and cultural humility in care provision

Health care provider training about basic TNB medical care and how to create gender-affirming care spaces and interactions are critically important. Evidence supports early integration of knowledge about TNB-specific clinical care into education of medical and allied health professionals (Wylie et al., 2016). *Gender-affirmative care* involves ensuring that diversity in gender identity and expression are acknowledged, affirmed, and respected (Reisner et al., 2015). The term cultural humility is preferred to cultural competence to acknowledge the ongoing, lifelong commitment to continual self-reflection and challenging of biases health professionals engage in over the course of their careers (Tervalon & Murray-Garcia, 1998). In the context of delivering gender-affirming care, a provider may be considered to show cultural humility when they: (1) have foundational knowledge about issues associated with TNB people in addition to understanding appropriate terminology; (2) continually work to reconcile personal beliefs, biases, and attitudes towards TNB people with their professional role; (3) actively work towards creating an inclusive health care environment; and (4) support patients in defining their gender and their relationship with gender (Rossi & Lopez, 2017). Studies have further stressed the importance of educating practitioners on the sociocultural context (e.g., social, legal, political landscape within which trans people live) as a critical mechanism to increase knowledge, motivation, and intention to provide culturally aware, gender-affirming care (Boroughs et al., 2015).

Providers may conduct self-assessment of trans-inclusive behaviors by utilizing validated scales, such as the Transgender Inclusive Behaviors Scale (TIBS) developed by Kattari et al. (2018). This scale assesses a range of behaviors from appropriate use of language, to keeping up-to-date regarding health and access issues affecting TNB people, to speaking out in support of trans rights both within everyday conversations and broader organizational contexts (Kattari et al., 2018). Similarly, the Transgender Inclusive Provider Scale (TIPS) offers guidance on specific things health care providers can do to offer more inclusive and affirming care to TNB patients (Kattari et al., 2020).

Some successful intervention studies have articulated processes for enhancing provider cultural competence for serving trans and gender diverse clients (Hanssmann et al., 2008; Lelutiu-Weinberger et al., 2016). These studies suggest that educational efforts to increase TNB cultural competency can increase provider awareness and understanding of TNB people (Hanssmann et al., 2008). Moreover, brief medical education interventions can improve physicians' medical knowledge and willingness to provide gender-affirming medical care (e.g., hormone administration) (Thomas & Safer, 2015). Providers and office staff should both have access to training about TNB populations and offering gender-affirmative care.

Something as easy as making sure providers are using patients' preferred names and correct pronouns has been shown to lead to more positive interactions (Aparicio-García et al., 2018). While it may be necessary to ask a patient's sex (female/male/intersex) for insurance purposes, also asking about gender and offering a blank for write-in responses is an easy way to engage patients authentically. Additionally, better care is provided when medical professionals focus on TNB patients as individuals to be treated, rather than using those interactions to ask questions about what it means to be TNB, what gender-affirming surgeries someone has had when not medically relevant, and showing off how "fine" they are with having a transgender patient ("I have met transgender people before!"). Feeling tokenized, being viewed as a spectacle, or being questioned about one's levels of "trans-ness" are also harmful to patients (Cicero & Perry Black, 2016).

Community connections

The most effective solutions to address barriers to health care for TNB people will come from the community themselves (Wylie et al., 2016). Research suggests that it is important to consider starting further up the care pipeline, and working to recruit, train, and retain members of TNB communities (and LGBQ communities) in roles such as peer educators/support staff, case managers, and with a longer-term outlook on inclusion, as members of medical professions (Mansh et al., 2015). When there are members of a community in positions of power such as a medical provider working with a patient, they can not only advocate for inclusive practices but model them for their peers. Community-based participatory research (CBPR), engages TNB community members to understand community needs and to increase the potential impact of the research on improving care (Loutfy et al., 2016; Travers et al., 2013). While used often in health care research, CBPR can be used in a variety of settings, and more can be learned about CBPR with TNB individuals and communities in Chapter 20.

Policy/advocacy

Health care providers must advocate for gender-inclusive policies and practices within health care settings, such as policies that protect against discrimination based on gender identity and expression. In addition to challenging stigma within health care and broader society, health care providers can create opportunities to receive meaningful feedback from TNB people and can create spaces for communities to connect. Medical records should use the correct pronouns of individuals, and the entire care team should know before seeing the patient what name and pronouns they use, regardless of what their legal name might be. It should be noted that this is best practice for all patients (TNB or otherwise) – using a person's preferred name helps to build rapport and strengthen the patient-provider interaction (Reisner et al., 2015).

However, advocacy should not be limited to office/hospital settings and policies. City and state policies, such as whether a person can change the gender on their birth certificate and what medical procedures may be required for them to do so, vary state to state. Health care providers can advocate with legislators towards more inclusive and affirming policies. Additionally, providers can work with local advocacy groups and non-profits to work towards more inclusive insurance policies, helping ensure that insurance covers the spectrum of TNB-related care.

ACTIVITY 1

Design an inclusive intake form

Your agency recently began seeing TNB patients. You've been tasked with developing a draft intake form that will be inclusive of gender identity and expression. Spend some time thinking about what information you might need on a health care intake form. What information is necessary for general record keeping? For insurance purposes? For connecting authentically with a patient? What is currently on intake forms that might not be affirming or inclusive? Things to consider as you design your form are: What questions do you ask? How is it laid out? Are responses given with box options, or fill in the blank options? Who will have access to the information on these forms?

Instructions

Draft an inclusive intake form that includes the following:

1. A selection of multiple gender identities and expressions
2. A selection of multiple sexualities
3. A selection for various relationship formations or structures
4. A sexual health section that does not reinforce binary gender
5. A medical history section that does not reinforce binary gender

Reflection questions

1. What are some barriers around creating inclusive intake forms?
2. Why is it important to have inclusive intake forms?
3. Who should be involved in co-creating inclusive intake forms?
4. What other identities may require inclusive intake forms?

ACTIVITY 2

Write an insurance appeal letter

Often times, TNB individuals must receive a letter from a provider for insurance coverage of transition-related (medical gender affirmation) care. Use this activity to create a template for yourself in order to write insurance appeal letters in the future.

Instructions

Draft a letter on behalf of your client that addresses the following:

1. Your licensing information or your agency's information
2. Verifies the provider/patient relationship
3. Verifies that your client has had appropriate clinical treatment for gender transition
4. States that the procedure is medically necessary
5. Declares under penalty of perjury that this information is true and correct

Reflection questions

1. What do you foresee may be barriers for TNB individuals who need a letter to get the medical services required for gender transition?
2. What risks do you take in providing a letter?
3. What risks do you take if you refuse to provide a letter?

4. What are the limitations to requiring a letter?
5. How would you support a client who was denied insurance coverage for their transition-related care?

SAMPLE

PRACTICE LETTERHEAD

I, <u>Provider's Full Name</u>, <u>Professional license or certificate number</u>, <u>Issuing U.S. State/Foreign Country of professional license/certificate</u>, am the therapist/clinician of <u>Name of Client</u>, <u>Date of Birth of Client</u>, with whom I have a provider/client relationship and whom I have treated (or with whom I have a provider/patient relationship and whose mental health history I have reviewed and evaluated).

<u>Name of Client</u> has had appropriate clinical treatment to undergo medically necessary gender transition treatment to the new gender (specify new gender male or female or nonbinary).

I declare under penalty of perjury under the laws of the United States that the foregoing is true and correct.

Signature of Provider
Typed Name
Address
Phone
Date

CONCLUSIONS

There are many health disparities and health care barriers experienced by TNB people. All providers are encouraged to take an inventory of their practice and assess areas in which they can improve access and inclusion, and to do so with an intersectional lens that recognizes how TNB individuals who hold other marginalized identities (such as TNB people of color or disabled TNB people) may experience barriers and health disparities at even higher rates. The good news is that there are also many things that providers can do when working with TNB clients and patients to improve their access to and experiences within care. From moving towards empowering informed consent models to updating policies, forms, and bathrooms to be as affirming as possible, individual providers can create change in medical settings. Additionally, continual training for all those in office or hospital spaces (i.e., not only the providers but staff as well) about TNB identities and care specific to this population, are crucial to ensuring that culturally responsive and high-quality care is available.

RESOURCES

Center of Excellence for Transgender Health
http://transhealth.ucsf.edu/
Fenway Transgender Health
https://fenwayhealth.org/care/medical/transgender-health/
National LGBT Health Education Center
https://www.lgbthealtheducation.org/resources/in/transgender-health/
Philadelphia Trans Wellness Conference
www.mazzonicenter.org/trans-wellness
Transgender Law Center Health Resources
https://transgenderlawcenter.org/resources/health
World Professional Association for Transgender Health
www.wpath.org/

REFERENCES

Aparicio-García, M. E., Díaz-Ramiro, E. M., Rubio-Valdehita, S., López-Núñez, M. I., & García-Nieto, I. (2018). Health and well-being of cisgender, transgender and non-binary young people. *International Journal of Environmental Research and Public Health*, 15(10), 2133. doi:10.3390/ijerph15102133

Baral, S. D., Poteat, T., Stromdahl, S., Wirtz, A. L., Guadamuz, T. E., & Beyrer, C. (2013). Worldwide burden of HIV in transgender women: A systematic review and meta-analysis. *Lancet Infectious Diseases*, 13(3), 214–222. doi:10.1016/s1473-3099(12)70315-8

Bauer, G. R., Hammond, R., Travers, R., Kaay, M., Hohenadel, K. M., Boyce, M. (2009). "I don't think this is theoretical; this is our lives": how erasure impacts health care for transgender people. *Journal of the Association of Nurses in AIDS Care*, 20, 348–361. doi:10.1016/j.jana.2009.07.004

Boroughs, M. S., Bedoya, C. A., O'Cleirigh, C., & Safren, S. A. (2015). Toward defining, measuring, and evaluating LGBT cultural competence for psychologists. *Clinical Psychology: Science and Practice*, 22(2), 151–171. doi:10.1111/cpsp.12098

Bradford, J., Reisner, S. L., Honnold, J. A., & Xavier, J. (2013). Experiences of transgender-related discrimination and implications for health: Results from the Virginia Transgender Health Initiative Study. *American Journal of Public Health*, 103(10), 1820–1829. doi:10.2105/AJPH.2012.300796

Callen Lorde Community Health Center. (n.d.). Protocols for the provision of hormone therapy. Retrieved July 23rd, 2019, from https://callen-lorde.org/graphics/2018/04/Callen-Lorde-TGNC-Hormone-Therapy-Protocols.pdf

Cicero, E. C., & Perry Black, B. (2016). "I was a spectacle … a freak show at the circus": A transgender person's ED experience and implications for nursing practice. *Journal of Emergency Nursing*, 42(1), 25–30.

Clements-Nolle, K., Marx, R., Guzman, R., & Katz, M. (2001). HIV prevalence, risk behaviors, health care use, and mental health status of transgender persons: Implications for public health intervention. *American Journal of Public Health*, 91(6), 915–921.

Coronel Villalobos, M., Stieler, S., Frohard-Dourlent, H., & Saewyc, E. (2018). *A survey of experiences with surgical readiness assessment and gender-affirming surgery among trans people living in Ontario*. Retrieved from http://apsc-saravyc.sites.olt.ubc.ca/files/2018/04/SARAVYC_Ontario-Surgeries-Report-Care-Survey-V4-Final-WEB.pdf

Crosby, R. A., Salazar, L. F., & Hill, B. J. (2016). Gender affirmation and resiliency among Black transgender women with and without HIV infection. *Transgender Health*, *1*(1), 86–93. doi:10.1089/trgh.2016.0005

Cruz, T. M. (2014). Assessing access to care for transgender and gender nonconforming people: A consideration of diversity in combating discrimination. *Social Science & Medicine*, *110*, 65–73. doi:10.1016/j.socscimed.2014.03.032

Erich, S. A., Boutte-Queen, N., Donnelly, S., & Tittsworth, J. (2007). Social work education: Implications for working with the transgender community. *The Journal of Baccalaureate Social Work*, *12*(2), 42–52.

Fredriksen-Goldsen, K. I., Cook-Daniels, L., Kim, H. J., Erosheva, E. A., Emlet, C. A., Hoy-Ellis, C. P., … Muraco, A. (2014). Physical and mental health of transgender older adults: An at-risk and underserved population. *Gerontologist*, *54*(3), 488–500. doi:10.1093/geront/gnt021

Gehi, P. S., & Arkles, G. (2007). Unraveling injustice: Race and class impact of medicaid exclusions of transition-related health care for transgender people. *Sexuality Research & Social Policy*, *4*(4), 7–35. doi:10.1525/srsp.2007.4.4.7

Grant, J. M., Mottet, L. A., Tanis, J., Herman, J. L., Harrison, J., & Keisling, M. (2010). *National transgender discrimination survey report on health and health care*. Retrieved from https://transequality.org/sites/default/files/docs/resources/NTDS_Report.pdf

Hanssmann, C., Morrison, D., & Russian, E. (2008). Talking, gawking, or getting it done: Provider trainings to increase cultural and clinical competence for transgender and gender-nonconforming patients and clients. *Sexuality Research & Social Policy*, *5*(1), 5–23. doi:10.1525/srsp.2008.5.1.5

Hatzenbuehler, M. L., Slopen, N., & McLaughlin, K. A. (2014). Stressful life events, sexual orientation, and cardiometabolic risk among young adults in the United States. *Health Psychology*, *33*(10), 1185–1194. doi:10.1037/hea0000126

Hendricks, M. L., & Testa, R. J. (2012). A conceptual framework for clinical work with transgender and gender nonconforming clients: An adaptation of the Minority Stress Model. *Professional Psychology: Research and Practice*, *43*(5), 460–467. doi:10.1037/a0029597

Herbst, J. H., Jacobs, E. D., Finlayson, T. J., McKleroy, V. S., Neumann, M. S., Crepaz, N., & Team, H. A. P. R. S. (2008). Estimating HIV prevalence and risk behaviors of transgender persons in the United States: A systematic review. *AIDS & Behavior*, *12*(1), 1–17. doi:10.1007/s10461-007-9299-3

Hill Collins, P. (2000). *Black feminist thought: Knowledge, consciousness, and the politics of empowerment*. New York: Routledge.

Jaffee, K. D., Shires, D. A., & Strousma, D. (2016). Discrimination and delayed health care among transgender women and men: Implications for improving medical education and health care delivery. *Medical Care*, *54*(11), 1010–1016.

Kattari, S. K., Bakko, M., Curley, K., & Misiolek, B. A. (2020). Development and vlidation of the Transgender Inclusive Provider Scale (TIPS). *American Journal of Preventative Medicine*. doi: 10.1016/j.amepre.2019.12.005 [Advance online edition].

Kattari, S. K., & Hasche, L. (2016). Differences across age groups in transgender and gender non-conforming people's experiences of health care discrimination, harassment, and victimization. *Journal of Aging and Health*, *28*(2), 285–306. doi:10.1177/0898264315590228

Kattari, S. K., O'Connor, A. A., & Kattari, L. (2018). Development and validation of the Transgender Inclusive Behavior Scale (TIBS). *Journal of Homosexuality*, *65*(2), 181–196. doi:10.1080/00918369.2017.1314160

Kattari, S. K., Walls, N. E., & Speer, S. R. (2017). Differences in experiences of discrimination in accessing social services among transgender/gender nonconforming individuals by (dis)

ability. *Journal of Social Work in Disability & Rehabilitation*, 16(2), 116–140. doi:10.10 80/1536710x.2017.1299661

Kattari, S. K., Walls, N. E., Speer, S. R., & Kattari, L. (2016). Exploring the relationship between transgender-inclusive providers and mental health outcomes among transgender/ gender variant people. *Social Work in Health Care*, 55(8), 635–650. doi:10.1080/00981 389.2016.1193099

Kattari, S. K., Walls, N. E., Whitfield, D. L., & Langenderfer-Magruder, L. (2015). Racial and ethnic differences in experiences of discrimination in accessing health services among transgender people in the United States. *International Journal of Transgenderism*, 16(2), 68–79. doi:10.1080/15532739.2015.1064336

Kcomt, L. (2018). Profound health-care discrimination experienced by transgender people: Rapid systematic review. *Social Work in Health Care*, 58(2), 201–219. doi:10.1080/0098 1389.2018.1532941

Kenagy, G. P., & Bostwick, W. B. (2005). Health and social service needs of transgender people in Chicago. *International Journal of Transgenderism*, 8(2–3), 57–66. doi:10.1300/ J485v08n02_06

Khan, L. (2011). Transgender health at the crossroads: Legal norms, insurance markets, and the threat of healthcare reform. *Yale Journal of Health Policy, Law & Ethics*, 11(2), 375–418.

Lacombe-Duncan, A., Bauer, G. R., Logie, C. H., Newman, P. A., Shokoohi, M., Kay, E. S., … Loutfy, M. (2019). The HIV care cascade among transgender women with HIV in Canada: A mixed-methods study. *AIDS Patient Care & STDs*, 33(7), 308–322.

Lacombe-Duncan, A., Logie, C. H., Newman, P. A., Bauer, G. R., & Kazemi, M. (2020). A qualitative study of resilience among transgender women living with HIV in response to stigma in healthcare. *AIDS Care*, 1–6.

Lelutiu-Weinberger, C., Pollard-Thomas, P., Pagano, W., Levitt, N., Lopez, E. I., Golub, S. A., & Radix, A. E. (2016). Implementation and evaluation of a pilot training to improve transgender competency among medical staff in an urban clinic. *Transgender Health*, 1(1), 45–53. doi:10.1089/trgh.2015.0009

Lindqvist, E. K., Sigurjonsson, H., Mollermark, C., Rinder, J., Farnebo, F., & Lundgren, T. K. (2017). Quality of life improves early after gender reassignment surgery in transgender women. *European Journal of Plastic Surg*, 40(3), 223–226. doi:10.1007/ s00238-016-1252-0

Link, B. G., & Phelan, J. C. (2001). Conceptualizing stigma. *Annual Review of Sociology*, 27(1), 363–385. doi:10.1146/annurev.soc.27.1.363

Loutfy, M., Greene, S., Kennedy, V. L., Lewis, J., Thomas-Pavanel, J., Conway, T., … Kaida, A. (2016). Establishing the Canadian HIV Women's Sexual and Reproductive Health Cohort Study (CHIWOS): Operationalizing community-based research in a large national quantitative study. *BMC Medical Research Methodology*, 16(1), 101. doi:10.1186/ s12874-016-0190-7

Mansh, M., Garcia, G., & Lunn, M. R. (2015). From patients to providers: Changing the culture in medicine toward sexual and gender minorities. *Academic Medicine*, 90(5), 574–580. doi:10.1097/acm.0000000000000656

Mikkonen, J., & Raphael, D. (2010). *Social determinants of health: The Canadian facts*. Retrieved from http://thecanadianfacts.org/The_Canadian_Facts.pdf

Mizock, L., Maguen, S., & Green, K. E. (2012). Male-to-female transgender veterans and VA health care utilization. *International Journal of Sexual Health*, 24(1), 78–87. doi:10.108 0/19317611.2011.639440

Nuttbrock, L. A., Bockting, W. O., Hwahng, S., Rosenblum, A., Mason, M., Macri, M., & Becker, J. (2009). Gender identity affirmation among male-to-female transgender persons: A life course analysis across types of relationships and cultural/lifestyle factors. *Sexual and Relationship Therapy*, 24(2), 108–125. doi:10.1080/14681990902926764

Obedin-Maliver, J., Goldsmith, E. S., Stewart, L., White, W., Tran, E., Brenman, S., ... Lunn, M. R. (2011). Lesbian, gay, bisexual, and transgender-related content in undergraduate medical education. *JAMA, 306*(9), 971–977. doi:10.1001/jama.2011.1255

Poteat, T., German, D., & Kerrigan, D. (2013). Managing uncertainty: A grounded theory of stigma in transgender health care encounters. *Social Science & Medicine, 84,* 22–29. doi:10.1016/j.socscimed.2013.02.019

Reisner, S. L., Bradford, J., Hopwood, R., Gonzalez, A., Makadon, H., Todisco, D., ... Mayer, K. (2015). Comprehensive transgender healthcare: The gender affirming clinical and public health model of Fenway Health. *Journal of Urban Health, 92*(3), 584–592. doi:10.1007/s11524-015-9947-2

Reisner, S. L., Poteat, T., Keatley, J., Cabral, M., Mothopeng, T., Dunham, E., ... Baral, S. D. (2016). Global health burden and needs of transgender populations: A review. *The Lancet, 388*(10042), 412–436. doi:10.1016/s0140-6736(16)00684-x

Reisner, S. L., White, J. M., Bradford, J. B., & Mimiaga, M. J. (2014). Transgender health disparities: Comparing full cohort and nested matched-pair study designs in a community health center. *LGBT Health, 1*(3), 177–184. doi:10.1089/lgbt.2014.0009

Riggs, D. W., Coleman, K., & Due, C. (2014). Healthcare experiences of gender diverse Australians: A mixed-methods, self-report survey. *BMC Public Health, 14,* 230. doi:10.1186/1471-2458-14-230

Rood, B. A., Reisner, S. L., Surace, F. I., Puckett, J. A., Maroney, M. R., & Pantalone, D. W. (2016). Expecting rejection: Understanding the minority stress experiences of transgender and gender-nonconforming individuals. *Transgender Health, 1*(1), 151–164. doi:10.1089/trgh.2016.0012

Rossi, A. L. P. M. M. A., & Lopez, E. J. P. (2017). Contextualizing competence: Language and LGBT-based competency in health care. *Journal of Homosexuality, 64*(10), 1330–1349. doi:10.1080/00918369.2017.1321361

Safer, J. D., Coleman, E., Feldman, J., Garofalo, R., Hembree, W., Radix, A., & Sevelius, J. (2016). Barriers to healthcare for transgender individuals. *Current Opinion in Endocrinology, Diabetes, and Obesity, 23*(2), 168–171. doi:10.1097/MED.0000000000000227

Seelman, K. L., Colon-Diaz, M. J. P., LeCroix, R. H., Xavier-Brier, M., & Kattari, L. (2017). Transgender noninclusive healthcare and delaying care because of fear: Connections to general health and mental health among transgender adults. *Transgender Health, 2*(1), 17–28. doi:10.1089/trgh.2016.0024

Sperber, J., Landers, S., & Lawrence, S. (2005). Access to health care for transgendered persons: Results of a needs assessment in Boston. *International Journal of Transgenderism, 8*(2–3), 75–91. doi:10.1300/J485v08n02_08

Tervalon, M., & Murray-Garcia, J. (1998). Cultural humility versus cultural competence: A critical distinction in defining physician training outcomes in multicultural education. *Journal of Health Care for the Poor and Underserved, 9*(2), 117–125.

Thomas, D. D., & Safer, J. D. (2015). A simple intervention raised resident-physician willingness to assist transgender patients seeking hormone therapy. *Endocrinology Practice, 21*(10), 1134–1142. doi:10.4158/ep15777.or

Townsend, S. S., Major, B., Gangi, C. E., & Mendes, W. B. (2011). From "in the air" to "under the skin": Cortisol responses to social identity threat. *Personality and Social Psychology Bulletin, 37*(2), 151–164. doi:10.1177/0146167210392384

Travers, R., Pyne, J., Bauer, G., Munro, L., Giambrone, B., Hammond, R., & Scanlon, K. (2013). 'Community control' in CBPR: Challenges experienced and questions raised from the Trans PULSE project. *Action Research, 11*(4), 403–422. doi:10.1177/1476750313507093

White Hughto, J. M., & Reisner, S. L. (2016). A systematic review of the effects of hormone therapy on psychological functioning and quality of life in transgender individuals. *Transgender Health, 1*(1), 21–31. doi:10.1089/trgh.2015.0008

White Hughto, J. M., Reisner, S. L., & Pachankis, J. E. (2015). Transgender stigma and health: A critical review of stigma determinants, mechanisms, and interventions. *Social Science & Medicine, 147*, 222–231. doi:10.1016/j.socscimed.2015.11.010

World Professional Association for Transgender Health [WPATH]. (2012). *Standards of care for the health of transsexual, transgender, and gender nonconforming people, 7th Edition.* Retrieved from www.wpath.org/publications/soc

Wylie, K., Knudson, G., Khan, S. I., Bonierbale, M., Watanyusakul, S., & Baral, S. (2016). Serving transgender people: Clinical care considerations and service delivery models in transgender health. *Lancet, 388*(10042), 401–411. doi:10.1016/s0140-6736(16)00682-6

Best practices in sexual and reproductive health care for transgender and nonbinary people

Lee Roosevelt and Simon Adriane Ellis

INTRODUCTION

The most precious and sacred form of personal information that we possess is our body. Thus, it is not surprising that visiting a health care provider and allowing for the intricate inspection and examination of our body is a source of trepidation and anxiety for most people. Perhaps the deepest level of vulnerability is an examination of the genital area. As such, sexual and reproductive health (SRH) represents one of the most vulnerable, personal, and sensitive areas of health care. For transgender and nonbinary (TNB) people this level of intimacy and sensitivity is amplified by interacting with a system that has enacted historical and current abuses at the individual and structural levels on TNB bodies. As a result, provider proficiency in the SRH needs of TNB people is an essential area of knowledge and study.

Significant structural and interpersonal barriers to SRH have been well documented among TNB people (American College of Obstetricians and Gynecologists, 2011; Hughto et al., 2018). The nature and extent of health disparities for TNB people is a rapidly expanding area of research as despite their small numbers, TNB people are a population with substantial adverse health indicators. These health inequities and disparities are likely multifactorial, with risks including structural social and economic marginalization, discrimination, and violence, including in health care settings (Reisner et al., 2016).

Allostatic load

Allostatic loads refers to how chronic life stressors, including traumatic stress, impact individuals' health via physiological responses to such chronic stressors (McEwen,

1998). The concept of allostatic load has been applied in research across various disciplines, and findings have generally confirmed that cumulative effects of social and environmental stressors increase the risk of adverse mental and physical health, particularly among vulnerable populations (Rosemberg et al., 2017). Briefly, when exposed to persistent external stressors, the endocrine system and the sympathetic nervous system are chronically stimulated, altering cardiovascular, metabolic, and inflammatory systems. The concept of allostasis is also useful when looking at outcomes related to SRH. These include increased risk for adverse pregnancy and birth outcomes, such as preterm birth (Lu et al., 2010; Wallace & Harville, 2013) and mortality from breast cancer (Parente et al., 2013).

Given that TNB people experience stigma in numerous contexts throughout their lives, it is likely that these experiences take a similarly additive toll on most aspects of their health. Many TNB people experience the cumulative allostatic load that comes with coping not only with transphobia, but also with racism, ableism, and other stigmatized identities. Despite this connection, there is a dearth of research exploring long-term physical health effects of stigma-related stress in TNB people, particularly with their SRH needs.

Health care systems and providers

One avenue in which stigma impacts TNB people is access to insurance. In the U.S., insurance access is linked almost entirely to employment (Zimlichman et al., 2013). Many TNB people lack insurance, potentially due in part to higher prevalence of unemployment among TNB people relative to the general population (James et al., 2016), likely a direct result of employment discrimination (Miller & Grollman, 2015). Even for those with access, their insurance may make assumptions of what type of care they are eligible for based on legal sex, which may or may not match their assigned sex at birth. These complex markers can create barriers to accessing necessary SRH services, such as cervical cancer screening, breast cancer screening, prostate screening, and pregnancy care, as well as accurate testing and treatment for sexually transmitted infections. As a result, TNB people are often forced to go through lengthy processes to get these services covered or pay out of pocket (Sanchez et al., 2009).

TNB individuals experience discrimination in general health care settings at rates exceeding those experienced by cisgender individuals (Hughto et al., 2018), resulting in avoiding and delaying of seeking needed medical care (James et al., 2016). For more information on general health care discrimination, see Chapters 1 and 2. One issue is lack of provider training, and this is likely even greater in the area of SRH.

Lack of training may lead to providers performing extensive health histories and unnecessary exams out of curiosity, as opposed to providing necessary SRH care to TNB patients (James et al., 2016). Despite the value of Trans 101 trainings in providing perspective on caring for TNB people, culturally responsive clinical practice with TNB people – even unrelated to gender-affirming therapies – requires knowledge that exceeds this 101 level of education. Health care providers must understand the unique experiences related to minority stress and allostatic load that TNB people encounter and how these experiences relate to both SRH vulnerability and resilience.

Resilience

Despite experiencing frequent and persistent discrimination, not all of the effects of minority stress are negative. Members of stigmatized groups may develop coping and resilience in response to stigma (Bockting et al., 2019). Resilience is not only the absence of less undesirable outcomes in the face of adversity; it is the presence of protective factors that mitigate the effects of adversity (Dyer & McGuinnes, 1996). The literature contains very few studies on coping and resilience within TNB communities. However, similar to allostatic load, what exists for other stigmatized groups likely can be extrapolated to TNB people, particularly when addressing the sensitive topic of SRH.

Rather than perpetuating the common notion of resilience as some form of intrinsic toughness endowed to a few unique individuals, resilience should be understood as a human capacity that can be developed and strengthened in all people through relationships, specifically through growth-fostering relationships (Hartling, 2008). In the area of patient-provider relationships, there is substantial data to support the influence of a strong attachment with one's provider and positive outcomes such as adherence, better communication, overall quality of life, and life satisfaction (Bennett et al., 2011). Educated and competent providers enhance the existing resilience of TNB people by using a strength-based approach that explores competencies and life skills, as opposed to placing more clinical emphasis on deficits and risks.

Sexual health history

Routine sexual health discussions between patients and health care providers are a proactive strategy for increasing SRH. They are also an important part of comprehensive quality patient care, regardless of the reason for the visit (Nusbaum & Hamilton, 2002), and have been recommended by evidence-based guidance groups such as the U.S. Preventive Services Task Force (USPSTF) (2014), and Centers for Disease Control and Prevention (CDC) (2012).

Sexuality is an important aspect of how people see themselves. According to the World Health Organization (WHO), sexual health includes physical, mental, emotional, and social well-being in all sexual behaviors and beliefs. Sexual health is not merely the absence of disease and dysfunction, but an overall balanced sense of sexual well-being (WHO, 2006). Taking a comprehensive and value-neutral health history of the TNB person is essential for providers to identify those at risk for STIs, guide risk reduction counseling, identify anatomic sites suitable for STI screening, identify functional difficulties that may be occurring during sexual activity, and answer personal questions about sexual activity and sexual functioning (Pessagno, 2013). These discussions provide an opportunity to build an alliance with TNB patients by making it explicit that their sexuality is normal, healthy, and worthy of attention and concern.

Despite the evidence supporting the importance of a comprehensive sexual health history, routine history taking is not a common practice among health care providers (Nusbaum & Hamilton, 2002; Wimberly et al., 2006), and many providers who report conducting sexual histories either do not obtain adequate sexual health information or do not document this information in the health care record (Loeb et al., 2011; Wimberly et al., 2006). Many providers feel inadequately trained to talk about sex and are reticent to encourage disclosure of sexual health concerns due to lack of expertise (Rele & Wylie, 2007; White et al., 2013), their own negative attitudes towards sex and sexuality (Gott et al., 2004), or a fear that raising the subject of sex may embarrass or offend patients (Brandenburg & Bitzer, 2009). The sensitive nature of SRH combined with historical abuses enacted on TNB people by health care providers make the sexual health history a potentially vulnerable but important moment in the health visit.

The comprehensive sexual health history: The Five Ps

Every comprehensive sexual health history needs to start with consent and the assurance of confidentiality. One way to ask consent would be to set the stage by saying you ask all people questions about their sexual health and sexual practices since they are very important to overall health, and then ask, "Is it okay with you if I ask those questions now?"

Letting the person know that you are not asking these questions out of curiosity or because you believe they are automatically at increased risk is a way to establish alliance and ease potential discomfort. Consent needs to be a primary component of all health histories and is particularly important in the context of sexual health history.

The CDC has developed a comprehensive sexual health history that may help providers remember to address all topics. These are called the Five Ps (CDC, 1996) and stand for Partners, Practices, Protection from STIs, Past history of STIs, and Prevention of pregnancy. The Fenway Institute has adapted the questions outlined in the Five Ps to be more inclusive of LGBTQ populations (2015). While the questions are not perfect and may not feel inclusive or appropriate to all people, they offer a best practice framework from which to start discussions. The language for sexual partners suggested by the Fenway Institute recommends asking if sexual partners are "men, women, or both". This language relies too heavily on the gender binary and also conflates sex and gender in a way that is not useful when taking a sexual health history. Therefore, this language has been adapted in the framework presented here.

Partners	• Who do you partner with sexually? (If needed, offer prompts: cis men? trans men? etc.) • How many people have you had sex with in the past year? • Is it possible that any of your sex partners in the past year had sex with someone else while they were still in a sexual relationship with you? • Have you experienced physical, sexual, or emotional violence from a partner?

Practices and Protection from STIs	• What kinds of sex are you having? (For example, oral sex, vaginal sex, anal sex, sharing sex toys)
	• What do you do to protect yourself from HIV and STIs?
	• Tell me about when you use condoms or other barriers.
	• When was the last time you had unprotected sex?
	• What do you know about your partner(s)' past or other sexual activities?
	• Do you have any concerns about your sex life?
	• Have you or any of your partners ever injected drugs?
	• Have you or any of your partners received or given money, shelter, or drugs for sex?
	• Have you or any of your partners ever been to jail?
	• Do you use alcohol or drugs when you have sex?
Past History of STIs	• Have you ever had a sexually transmitted infection?
	• If yes, what kind, when, and how were you treated?
	• Have you ever been tested for any STIs?
	• To your knowledge, have you ever had sex with someone who has been diagnosed with an STI?
	• Have you ever been tested for HIV?
	• To your knowledge, have you ever had sex with someone who has been diagnosed with HIV?
Pregnancy Plans	• Do you have any plans or desire to have (more) children?
	• Do you or your partner(s) ever have a need for a contraception to avoid pregnancy?
	• Do you want information on birth control?
	• Do you have any questions or concerns about pregnancy prevention?
	• What are you doing to prevent yourself or your partner from getting pregnant, or to plan for a desired pregnancy?

(Adapted from Fenway Institute, 2015)

REFLECTION ACTIVITY

Using the adapted Five Ps framework above:

1) Think about your own sexual history, and how you might answer these questions were you to be asked them by a provider.
2) Practice taking a brief sexual health history with a classmate or colleague.
3) Consider how you might integrate this into your practice.
4) Reflect on how these questions might continue to need to evolve to best serve gender diverse clients.

Fertility preservation

Family creation is a deeply personal and intimate process. When offering support or information for TNB people about family creation and fertility preservation (FP), the ultimate focus should be the empowerment of the person making the choices. An exploration of all options needs to be encouraged, recognizing that many TNB people may not have current or future access to all options available. Many TNB people wish to have a biological child and desire having the support of a clinician to discuss the impact of childbearing on quality of life, gender-affirmation process, and relationships. Access to assisted reproductive technology (ART) can be complicated by access to financial resources, physical contraindications, or previous gender-affirming therapy that may have impacted fertility. An important component of FP is a concurrent discussion on the various ways that TNB people may create families without the use of ART, including fostering, adoption. and surrogacy. There is strong evidence that a desire for biologic children is common among TNB adults and that conversations regarding fertility preservation (FP) are an acceptable and welcome topic of conversation with health care providers (Pfäfflin et al., 2002; Wierckx et al., 2012). The World Professional Association for Transgender Health (WPATH) Standards of Care and the Clinical Practice Guidelines of the Endocrine Society recommend that all mental health professionals and health care providers discuss FP options prior to initiating gender-affirming hormones or surgeries (Wallace et al., 2014).

TNB people face unique biological and social considerations that can be a challenge to navigate, especially if these conversations are happening concurrently with decisions to initiate gender-affirming interventions. It is critical for TNB people to have easy access to accurate, empowering information that can guide their thinking and inform their choices in family creation. Providers need to be skilled at presenting the limited information that is available in a way that is easy to understand while also acknowledging that there are still significant knowledge gaps. TNB people already using gender-affirming hormone therapy may need an interruption of hormone treatment for up to three months to restore possible hormone therapy-induced effects (De Roo et al., 2016). Therefore, it is important that these discussions occur prior to initiation of gender-affirming therapy. At the same time, any time is a good time to discuss parenting intention with patients who did not receive nuanced counseling before gender-affirming therapy, who were not ready at that time to fully engage in such counseling, or who have since changed their mind about FP. Routine wellness visits are an ideal opportunity to have a brief conversation about family building.

Many gender-affirming treatments may cause temporary or permanent loss of fertility (Mattawanon et al., 2018). For TNB people who are assigned male at birth (AMAB), vaginoplasty and orchidectomy lead to irreversible sterility. Additionally, prolonged estrogen treatment results in a reduction of testicular volume (Mattawanon et al., 2018). Estrogens also have a suppressive effect on sperm motility and density in a dose-dependent manner (De Roo et al., 2016). Information on success rates of each FP technique is highly patient-specific. For AMAB individuals, sperm cryopreservation is the simplest and most reliable method of preserving fertility. This method requires that the patient be pubertal. For cisgender people, it is easy, reliable, and relatively inexpensive. Some TNB people find the act of ejaculation to be dysphoric, and thus find this procedure psychologically distressing (Mattawanon et al., 2018). However, other TNB people report no discomfort with the act of harvesting sperm (Mitu, 2016).

For TNB people who are assigned female at birth (AFAB), hysterectomy with bilateral oophorectomy leads to irreversible sterility. Masculinizing hormonal therapy will, in most cases, lead to reversible amenorrhea but will likely not change ovarian reserve (Maxwell et al., 2017). In fact, hormonal interventions do not exclude possible pregnancy in TNB people using testosterone, and testosterone is not an adequate means of birth control. In a recently published report surveying TNB people who experienced pregnancy, one-third of the pregnancies were unplanned, yet pregnancy outcomes did not differ between TNB people reporting historical testosterone use and individuals who have never used testosterone (Light et al., 2014).

For AFAB TNB people, the most common methods of FP are cryopreservation of oocytes or embryos that can be used in the future to establish a pregnancy. Both techniques require the person to be pubertal and involve controlled ovarian stimulation and hormone exposure, frequent monitoring via transvaginal ultrasound, and a transvaginal surgical procedure to aspirate oocytes from follicles (Wallace et al., 2014). While embryo banking may be an appropriate option for patients with current partners or sperm donors, oocyte banking does not require fertilization at the time of banking, and provides flexibility for adolescent and single TNB people. As clinicians, it is important to recognize that the process of undergoing hormonal preparation and retrieval of eggs is challenging for everyone, but for TNB people can cause heightened dysphoria. It is important to provide support prior to, during, and after the process to reduce the emotional impact.

Many TNB people seek gender-affirming care as adults and often have a clear plan for future family planning. However, as more TNB youth gain access to puberty blockers, and an increasing number of adolescents access gender-affirming hormone therapy, it is important that these discussions happen with TNB youth and their families to ensure they are given opportunities to utilize FP technologies prior to initiation of hormone therapy (Nahata et al., 2017). It is important to note that FP techniques for pre-pubertal youth are limited to experimental procedures that are difficult to access, typically cost prohibitive, and whose future success rates are unknown (Johnson & Finlayson, 2016). For example, no human pregnancies have been achieved through testicular tissue cryopreservation and only a small number have been achieved with ovarian tissue cryopreservation (Nahata et al., 2019).

There is evidence that LGBTQ-identified youth who are affirmed by their families are more likely to be interested in parenting themselves in the future (Ryan et al., 2010). Thus, as more families are affirming and supporting TNB youth in their transition process, it may also be that more youth will be interested in the possibility of becoming parents themselves in the future (dickey et al., 2016). Currently, it is not possible for children who have not undergone natal puberty to preserve gametes. However, prolonged use of puberty blockers alone appears to be reversible and should not impair resumption of puberty upon cessation for TNB youth who are interested in discontinuing therapy in order to access FP options (Amato, n.d.).

Health promotion

Reducing and ideally eliminating health care disparities for TNB people is essential to ensuring improved health, safety, and well-being. This portion of the chapter will focus on best practices for health promotion among TNB people. The recommendations are intended to be flexible in order to meet the diverse health care needs of TNB people. Unfortunately, due to the current lack of specific research on TNB people and their SRH needs, most of the recommendations have been extrapolated from the evidence base for cisgender people or are based on limited, low-quality data, or expert opinion.

The clinical exam

The clinical exam is an intimate and vulnerable experience for all people. For TNB people the clinical exam is complicated by the often gendered nature of any SRH care visit. While competency in clinical diagnostic skills is important, learning how to provide an empowering and dignified exam is essential. Many TNB people have pre-existing trauma from previous examinations that inform their response to future exams. Providers should, therefore, be attuned to the patient's needs, communicate respectfully, and ensure that each individual's sense of dignity, agency, and control is maintained throughout the entire exam (Potter et al., 2015). Clinicians should reinforce that it is up to the person to decide if and when an examination takes place, and whether to continue or halt the exam. How this will be communicated should be decided before the onset of the exam (Potter et al., 2015).

Clinicians should query each person regarding name and pronouns they would like to be referred by, and use the person's choices throughout the clinical encounter. Since so much of the language that is used during an SRH visit is gendered, it is important to ask what anatomical terms the person prefers and to use only those terms even if they are unfamiliar or uncomfortable for the clinician. In addition, some words that are often used during these exams ("blades of the speculum", "open your legs", "stirrups") can have violent and/or sexual connotations and should be replaced with language that is more neutral ("bills of the speculum", "let your legs drop to either side", "foot rests").

There are many resources available to help clinicians learn how to perform clinical exams that promote empowerment and shared process. One simple way that this can be accomplished is by elevating the head of the bed so that eye contact can be maintained and by refraining from the use of stirrups. While the lithotomy position provides good visibility of the anatomy and easy examiner access to areas of testing, some people experience it as disempowering, abusive, and humiliating. Patients also describe metal stirrups as "cold" and "hard", and experience their use as impersonal, sterile, or degrading (Bates et al., 2011). For a visual tutorial of how to perform an exam without the use of stirrups, we recommend visiting the webpage "The Feminist Midwife" (Feminist Midwife, n.d.). For people who are taking gender-affirming testosterone, pain during pelvic examination can be minimized by using a small or even pediatric speculum, using an adequate amount of lubricant, and/or using a mixture of lubricant and topical lidocaine. A short course of vaginal estradiol can also be considered prior to exam (Potter et al., 2015).

Contraception in masculine-identified TNB people

AFAB TNB people have unintended pregnancy rates comparable to cisgender women in the U.S. (Light et al., 2014). Due to the potential teratogenic, an agent or factor that causes malformation of an embryo, effect of testosterone during pregnancy (Light et al., 2017), and the association of unintended pregnancy with adverse medical, social, and economic outcomes (Trussell, 2007), it is essential that a discussion about contraceptive practices and pregnancy desires occur. Despite the importance of this conversation, there is a lack of best practice contraceptive research for TNB people. An overly feminized SRH care environment and materials, experiences of misgendering and discrimination, and lack of clinician training have all been reported as deterrents to seeking contraceptive care. Additionally, many TNB people report difficulties locating knowledgeable and welcoming providers, insurance coverage denial because of male legal gender markers, and fertility risk misconceptions (Baum et al., 2018).

The most commonly used form of contraception used by AFAB TNB people is condoms (Light et al., 2018). This is likely due to how readily available condoms are without necessitating a visit to a health care provider. Long active reversible contraception (LARC) such as IUDs and the contraceptive implant are used less frequently, but at a higher rate than the general U.S. population (Curtis & Peipert, 2017). While there is no current research demonstrating positive or negative effects of combined hormone contraception on testosterone use, many TNB people report discontinuing their use because they "did not like the extra hormones" or thought they "interfered with hormone replacement therapy" (Light et al., 2018). This is an important gap in knowledge and one that providers should address when presenting available contraceptive options. Hysterectomy is a permanent form of birth control that may be an acceptable option for many AFAB TNB people. Given the long history of forced and coerced sterilization of TNB people in both the U.S. and around the world, care should be taken to discuss reproductive life plan before initiating a conversation about hysterectomy.

Contraception in feminine-identified TNB people

AMAB TNB people also have contraceptive needs, as those who retain their testicles can potentially produce a pregnancy in an AFAB person. While estrogens and

Spironolactone may decrease sperm counts and the viability of sperm, it is not an entirely effective form of contraception (De Roo & T'Sjoen, 2018).

The best non-permanent contraceptive choice currently available for AMAB TNB people is condoms. There are a few options available for AMAB TNB people who desire permanent contraceptive options. While vasectomy is the most common choice for cisgender men and may be a more economically accessible choice of contraception, providers should also present the option of an orchiectomy as a form of contraception. For those on feminizing hormone therapy, orchiectomy has the added benefit of simplifying hormonal regimens and may be gender-affirming (Liang & Safer, 2017). As with hysterectomy discussions, it is important to acknowledge the long history of forced and coerced sterilization of TNB people.

HIV prevention

TNB individuals have higher rates of HIV infection, but prevention efforts specifically targeting these communities have been minimal (Neumann et al., 2017). Part of the challenge of HIV prevention for TNB people is that numerous individual, interpersonal, social, and structural factors contribute to their risk. Individual and interpersonal risk factors include higher rates of condomless receptive anal intercourse, engaging in sex work, and condomless intercourse with multiple partners (Green et al., 2015). Other individual and interpersonal factors include increased rates of sexual assault, physical abuse, and lack of familial support (Grant et al., 2011). In addition to these factors, TNB people experience more social stressors such as unemployment, stigma and discrimination, and homelessness (Grant et al., 2011). These hardships, as well as economic insecurity, may lead some TNB people to engage in commercial sex work to meet their basic needs for food and housing, affirm their identity, or earn money to pay for gender-affirming care (James et al., 2016; Rowniak et al., 2011).

Because TNB people's risk of HIV infection is exacerbated by complex social determinants and intersecting social and gender identities, comprehensive HIV prevention for this population is necessary. For maximum health impact, comprehensive prevention programs that are developed by assessing the HIV prevention needs of local TNB people, prioritizing at-risk TNB groups, identifying currently available interventions and services, and determining needed resources are most likely to be effective (Neumann et al., 2017). In addition, bundling comprehensive HIV education, testing, prevention, and treatment with other SRH care services makes prevention more accessible and can influence risk behaviors, risk determinants, and overall health (Petroll et al., 2017).

The CDC recommends that persons at high risk for HIV infection be screened for HIV at least annually, although TNB people are not specified in the current recommendations (Pitasi et al., 2017). Each clinician must consider the benefits of offering more frequent screening to individuals at increased risk for acquiring HIV, weighing the persons' individual risk factors, local HIV epidemiology, and local testing policies (DiNenno et al., 2017).

Sexually transmitted infections

Screening for STIs is an important secondary prevention strategy. During STI screening and treatment, non-judgmental acknowledgement of engagement in behaviors that place people at higher risk for STIs is a critical component of communication (Miller et al., 2017). Opt-out testing for STIs, in which people are informed that everyone is routinely tested unless they decline, has increased the likelihood that a person will agree to screening as it reduces stigma associated with testing and normalizes the experience of STI screening (Glew et al., 2014). While the proportion of people tested for STIs has increased with opt-out testing, it remains unclear whether this streamlined approach to testing reduces people's awareness that the testing is voluntary and that opting-out is an option (Rosen et al., 2015). Thus, providers should take care to ensure that people know that they have autonomy and choice in what they are being screened for and when.

The 2015 STI treatment guidelines from the CDC recommend that clinicians assess STI-related risks of TNB people based on current anatomy and sexual behaviors (Workowski et al., 2015). One concern regarding the CDC screening guidelines is that the guidance lacks explicit recommendations for rectal and pharyngeal testing of STIs. One study found that less than half of surveyed young transgender women reported ever being offered screening for rectal or pharyngeal STIs (A. K. Johnson et al., 2018). This presents a missed opportunity in STI prevention efforts and a lack of adherence to currently recommended clinical guidelines. It also reinforces the importance of taking a comprehensive sexual health history to guide STI screening decision making.

Historically, clinician-collected STI swabs necessitating a genital exam have been considered the gold standard. This presents a significant barrier to some TNB people who may not otherwise need a clinical exam or be comfortable with a clinician performing the exam. A number of recent studies have found that self-collected swabs significantly increased the uptake of STI testing and were an acceptable alternative to clinician-collected swabs (Lockhart et al., 2018; Yared et al., 2017). Self-collection of STI specimens may be empowering for TNB people and should not be overlooked when providing STI testing services.

Cancer screening

Cancer screening is a key component of comprehensive SRH services and clinician recommendation is one of the strongest predictors of patient receipt of screening. The challenge is that many clinicians are unsure how to implement best practices for cancer screening for TNB people, partially due to the scarcity of research specific to this population. Providers also lack knowledge of the psychosocial, physiological, and clinical concerns unique to TNB individuals. In an effort to close these gaps, we present recommendations to guide sexual and reproductive cancer screening based on a review of the literature and guidelines set forth by professional organizations.

TABLE 3.1 Cancer screening for AFAB TNB people

Cancer Screening for AFAB TNB People		
Type of Cancer	Clinical Significance	Screening Recommendations
Breast/Chest Cancer	AFAB TNB people who have not undergone a double mastectomy likely have the same risk of breast/chest cancer as cisgender women regardless of affirming hormonal therapy. AFAB TNB people who have had a double mastectomy have a lower, but not absent, risk of breast/chest cancer but cancer may occur at younger ages (Stone et al., 2018).	AFAB TNB people without a double mastectomy should follow the U.S. Preventive Service Task Force (USPSTF) guidelines for cisgender women. The current recommendations for AFAB TNB people who have had top surgery are based on expert opinion and recommend using shared decision making to discuss the risks and benefits of mammography screening due to the challenge of performing a mammogram on a person with scant breast/chest tissue.
Cervical Cancer	The risk for AFAB TNB people is the same as for cisgender women, although AFAB TNB people generally have more risk factors than cisgender women such as smoking and a history of sexual violence (Peitzmeier et al., 2014; Wierckx et al., 2012). AFAB TNB people who have used testosterone therapy are more likely to have abnormal or insufficient pap results due to atrophic vaginal changes (Peitzmeier et al., 2014).	If a person has a cervix present, regardless of sexual partners' sex assigned at birth and even if the person has never been sexually active, the recommendation for screening is to follow the same USPSTF guidelines for cisgender women (Deutsch, 2016). The USPSTF guidelines also address the circumstances in which screening would still be appropriate when a person no longer has a cervix (U.S. Preventive Services Task Force, 2016).
Ovarian Cancer	Some guidelines on care for AFAB TNB people taking testosterone recommend surgical removal of the ovaries to prevent ovarian cancer, while others recommend following general guidelines for all people AFAB. Many of the guidelines are inconsistent and are based on theoretical risks, not actual risks seen in the literature. Affirming hormone therapy does not appear to increase the risk of ovarian cancer (Harris et al., 2017).	Routine screening for ovarian cancer is not recommended for cisgender women or AFAB TNB people (Grossman et al., 2018).

Uterine Cancer   There is a theoretical risk that exogenous testosterone can create a milieu of unopposed estrogen, which may increase a person's risk for uterine cancer. The few studies that have been done have found that affirming hormone therapy may possibly result in endometrial thinning but also demonstrate that the uterus continues to have a proliferative and secretory phase (Grimstad et al., 2018; Loverro et al., 2016).

Routine screening for uterine cancer is not recommended for cisgender women or AFAB TNB people. AFAB TNB people who experience uterine bleeding after the onset of testosterone-induced amenorrhea should have a similar work up to cisgender women experiencing abnormal uterine bleeding, which may include screening for uterine pathology (Deutsch, 2016).

TABLE 3.2 Cancer screening for AMAB TNB people

Cancer Screening for AMAB TNB People		
Type of Cancer	Clinical Significance	Screening Recommendations
Breast/Chest Cancer	AMAB TNB people who have not used affirming hormonal therapy have the same risk of breast/chest cancer as cisgender men. In the presence of hormonal affirming therapy, regardless of breast surgeries, AMAB TNB people have a higher risk than cisgender men but lower than cisgender women (Silverberg et al., 2017).	No routine screening is recommended for AMAB TNB people who have not used affirming hormone therapy. In the presence of affirming hormone therapy, AMAB TNB people who are age 50 and older AND have used affirming hormone therapy for more than ten years are recommended to utilize the USPSTF screening guidelines (Deutsch, 2016).
Prostate Cancer	There is limited data available about the risk of prostate cancer in AMAB TNB people. People who use gender-affirming hormone therapy may experience increased disease severity, however, it is uncertain if hormone therapy is a protective or aggravating factor (Deebel et al., 2017; Ingham et al., 2018). For AMAB TNB people who have had vaginoplasty surgery, digital palpation of the prostate is best achieved through the anterior vaginal wall as opposed to the rectum (Deutsch, 2016).	AMAB TNB people who are not using affirming hormone therapy should follow the same USPSTF guidelines as cisgender men. Clinicians may need to adjust the limits of PSA testing to account for the presence of gender-affirming hormone therapy.

continued . . .

TABLE 3.2 (continued)

Cancer Screening for AMAB TNB People		
Type of Cancer	Clinical Significance	Screening Recommendations
Testicular Cancer	Cases of testicular cancer are rarely reported for AMAB TNB people. There is some uncertainty of how gender-affirming hormone therapy impacts risk as estrogen may have a possible protective role as an androgen suppressor. However, there is also concern that estrogen may be a driver in the development of testicular cancer (Chandhoke et al., 2018).	Routine screening of asymptomatic people is not recommended for cisgender men or AMAB TNB people (Deutsch, 2016).

CONCLUSION

SRH is a key component of comprehensive primary health care, including for TNB individuals. Addressing SRH care needs from a social justice perspective provides a useful framework for thinking about individual health recommendations as well as the structural and systemic issues that need to be addressed. Quality SRH care is dependent upon not only good clinical care but also social and political climates that provide and ensure equity and human rights. Health is promoted through public policies and legal reforms that promote tolerance and equity for gender and sexual diversity and that eliminate prejudice, discrimination, and stigma (Coleman et al., 2012). The recommendations in this chapter are based on the evidence available at the time of writing. As there is limited research available at this time many of the recommendations for best practice are based on expert opinion as opposed to peer reviewed research. It is the hope of these authors that the next decade will see a growth of research on the SRH needs of TNB people and that this research will inform best practices for providers to provide quality, evidence-based, compassionate, and empowering care.

RESOURCES

World Professional Association for Transgender Health
www.wpath.org
Fenway Health
https://fenwayhealth.org
Callen-Lorde Community Health Center
https://callen-lorde.org
University of California, San Francisco – Center of Excellence for Transgender Health
https://transcare.ucsf.edu

Chang, S.C., Singh, A. A., dickey, l. m., & Krishnan, M. (2018). *A clinician's guide to gender-affirming care: Working with transgender and gender nonconforming clients.* Oakland, CA: Context Press.

Erickson-Schroth, L. (Ed.) (2014). *Trans bodies, trans selves.* Oxford: Oxford University Press.

Vincent, B., & Lorimer, S. (2018). *Transgender health: A practitioner's guide to binary and non-binary trans patient care.* London: Jessica Kingsley Publishers.

REFERENCES

Amato, P. (n.d.). Guidelines for the primary and gender-affirming care of transgender and gender nonbinary people: Fertility options for transgender persons. Retrieved January 27, 2019, from http://transhealth.ucsf.edu/trans?page=guidelines-fertility

American College of Obstetricians and Gynecologists. (2011). *ACOG committee opinion No. 512: Health care for transgender individuals.* Author. Retrieved from www.acog.org/Clinical-Guidance-and-Publications/Committee-Opinions/Committee-on-Health-Care-for-Underserved-Women/Health-Care-for-Transgender-Individuals

Bates, C. K., Carroll, N., & Potter, J. (2011). The challenging pelvic examination. *Journal of General Internal Medicine, 26*(6), 651–657. doi:10.1007/s11606-010-1610-8

Baum, S., Fix, L., Durden, M., Stoeffler, C., Hastings, J., Moseson, H., & Obedin-Maliver, J. (2018). Family planning needs and experiences of transgender and gender-expansive individuals in the United States: A qualitative study. *Contraception, 98*(4), 365–366. doi:10.1016/j.contraception.2018.07.112

Bennett, J. K., Fuertes, J. N., Keitel, M., & Phillips, R. (2011). The role of patient attachment and working alliance on patient adherence, satisfaction, and health-related quality of life in lupus treatment. *Patient Education and Counseling, 85*(1), 53–59. doi:10.1016/J.PEC.2010.08.005

Bockting, W., Barucco, R., LeBlanc, A., Singh, A., Mellman, W., Dolezal, C., & Ehrhardt, A. (2019). Sociopolitical change and transgender people's perceptions of vulnerability and resilience. *Sexuality Research and Social Policy.* doi:10.1007/s13178-019-00381-5

Brandenburg, U., & Bitzer, J. (2009). The challenge of talking about sex: The importance of patient–physician interaction. *Maturitas, 63*(2), 124–127. doi:10.1016/j.maturitas.2009.03.019

Centers for Disease Control and Prevention. (1996). 2.4d taking a sexual history. doi:10.1037/e502852006-001

Centers for Disease Control and Prevention. (2012). STD data and statistics. Retrieved January 22, 2019, from www.cdc.gov/std/stats/

Chandhoke, G., Shayegan, B., & Hotte, S. J. (2018). Exogenous estrogen therapy, testicular cancer, and the male to female transgender population: A case report. *Journal of Medical Case Reports, 12*(1), 373. doi:10.1186/s13256-018-1894-6

Coleman, E., Bockting, W., Botzer, M., Cohen-Kettenis, P., DeCuypere, G., Feldman, J., ... Zucker, K. (2012). Standards of care for the health of transsexual, transgender, and gender-nonconforming people, version 7. *International Journal of Transgenderism, 13*(4), 165–232. doi:10.1080/15532739.2011.700873

Curtis, K. M., & Peipert, J. F. (2017). Long-acting reversible contraception. *New England Journal of Medicine, 376*(5), 461–468. doi:10.1056/NEJMcp1608736

De Roo, C., & T'Sjoen, G. (2018). Sperm preservation in transgender patients. In A. Majzoub & A. Agarwal (Eds.), *The complete guide to male fertility preservation* (pp. 121–128). Cham: Springer International Publishing. doi:10.1007/978-3-319-42396-8_10

De Roo, C., Tilleman, K., T'Sjoen, G., & De Sutter, P. (2016). Fertility options in transgender people. *International Review of Psychiatry, 28*(1), 112–119. doi:10.3109/09540261.2015.1084275

Deebel, N. A., Morin, J. P., Autorino, R., Vince, R., Grob, B., & Hampton, L. J. (2017). Prostate cancer in transgender women: Incidence, etiopathogenesis, and management challenges. *Urology, 110,* 166–171. doi:10.1016/J.UROLOGY.2017.08.032

Deutsch, M. B. (Ed.). (2016). *Guidelines for the primary and gender-affirming care of transgender and gender nonbinary people.* San Francisco, CA: University of California.

dickey, l. m., Ducheny, K. M., & Ehrbar, R. D. (2016). Family creation options for transgender and gender nonconforming people. *Psychology of Sexual Orientation and Gender Diversity, 3*(2), 173–179. doi:10.1037/sgd0000178

DiNenno, E. A., Prejean, J., Irwin, K., Delaney, K. P., Bowles, K., Martin, T., … Lansky, A. (2017). Recommendations for HIV screening of gay, bisexual, and other men who have sex with men — United States, 2017. *MMWR. Morbidity and Mortality Weekly Report, 66*(31), 830–832. doi:10.15585/mmwr.mm6631a3

Dyer, J., & McGuinnes, T. (1996). Resilience: Analysis of the concept. *Archives of Psychiatric Nursing, 10*(5), 276–282. Retrieved from www.psychiatricnursing.org/article/S0883-9417(96)80036-7/abstract

Feminist Midwife. (n.d.). Empowering gynecologic exams: Speculum care without stirrups. Retrieved February 26, 2019, from www.feministmidwife.com/2016/11/02/empowering-gynecologic-exams-speculum-care-without-stirrups/#.XHWeHeJKjVo

Fenway Institute. (2015). *Taking routine histories of sexual health: A system-wide approach for health centers.* Retrieved from www.lgbthealtheducation.org/wp-content/uploads/COM-827-sexual-history_toolkit_2015.pdf

Glew, S., Pollard, A., Hughes, L., & Llewellyn, C. (2014). Public attitudes towards opt-out testing for HIV in primary care: A qualitative study. *British Journal of General Practice, 64*(619). doi:10.3399/bjgp14X677103

Gott, M., Hinchliff, S., & Galena, E. (2004). General practitioner attitudes to discussing sexual health issues with older people. *Social Science & Medicine, 58*(11), 2093–2103. doi:10.1016/j.socscimed.2003.08.025

Grant, J., Mottet, L., Tanis, J., & Harrison, J. (2011). Injustice at every turn: A report of the national transgender discrimination survey. Retrieved from https://www.transequality.org/sites/default/files/docs/resources/NTDS_Report.pdf

Green, N., Hoenigl, M., Morris, S., & Little, S. J. (2015). Risk behavior and sexually transmitted infections among transgender women and men undergoing community-based screening for acute and early HIV infection in San Diego. *Medicine, 94*(41), e1830. doi:10.1097/MD.0000000000001830

Grimstad, F., Fowler, K., New, E., Unger, C., Pollard, R., Chapman, G., … Gray, M. (2018). Evaluation of uterine pathology in transgender men and gender nonbinary persons on testosterone. *Journal of Pediatric and Adolescent Gynecology, 31*(2), 217. doi:10.1016/j.jpag.2018.02.009

Grossman, D. C., Curry, S. J., Owens, D. K., Barry, M. J., Davidson, K. W., Doubeni, C. A., … Tseng, C.-W. (2018). Screening for ovarian cancer. *JAMA, 319*(6), 588. doi:10.1001/jama.2017.21926

Harris, M., Kondel, L., & Dorsen, C. (2017). Pelvic pain in transgender men taking testosterone. *The Nurse Practitioner, 42*(7), 1–5. doi:10.1097/01.NPR.0000520423.83910.e2

Hartling, L. M. (2008). Strengthening resilience in a risky world: It's all about relationships. *Women & Therapy, 31*(2–4), 51–70. doi:10.1080/02703140802145870

Hughto, J. M. W., Pachankis, J. E., & Reisner, S. L. (2018). Healthcare mistreatment and avoidance in trans masculine adults: The mediating role of rejection sensitivity. *Psychology of Sexual Orientation and Gender Diversity, 5*(4), 471–481. doi:10.1037/sgd0000296

Ingham, M. D., Lee, R. J., MacDermed, D., & Olumi, A. F. (2018). Prostate cancer in transgender women. *Urologic Oncology: Seminars and Original Investigations, 36*(12), 518–525. doi:10.1016/J.UROLONC.2018.09.011

James, S. E., Herman, J. L., Rankin, S., Keisling, M., Mottet, L., & Anafi, M. (2016). *The report of the U.S. transgender survey 2015*. Washington, DC. Retrieved from https://transequality.org/sites/default/files/docs/usts/USTS-Full-Report-Dec17.pdf

Johnson, A. K., Reisner, S. L., Mimiaga, M. J., Garofalo, R., & Kuhns, L. M. (2018). Prevalence and perceived acceptability of nongenital sexually transmitted infection testing in a cohort of young transgender women. *LGBT Health*, 5(6), 381–386. doi:10.1089/lgbt.2018.0039

Johnson, E. K., & Finlayson, C. (2016). Preservation of fertility potential for gender and sex diverse individuals. *Transgender Health*, 1(1), 41–44. doi:10.1089/trgh.2015.0010

Liang, J., & Safer, J. D. (2017). Testosterone levels achieved by medically treated transgender women in a United States endocrinology clinic cohort resistance to thyroid hormone view project transgender medicine view project. doi:10.4158/EP-2017-0116

Light, A., Wang, L.-F., Zeymo, A., & Gomez-Lobo, V. (2018). Family planning and contraception use in transgender men. *Contraception*, 98(4), 266–269. doi:10.1016/J.CONTRACEPTION.2018.06.006

Light, A. D., Obedin-Maliver, J., Sevelius, J. M., & Kerns, J. L. (2014). Transgender men who experienced pregnancy after female-to-male gender transitioning. *Obstetrics & Gynecology*, 124(6), 1120–1127. doi:10.1097/AOG.0000000000000540

Light, A. D., Zimbrunes, S. E., & Gomez-Lobo, V. (2017). Reproductive and obstetrical care for transgender patients. *Current Obstetrics and Gynecology Reports*, 6(2), 149–155. doi:10.1007/s13669-017-0212-4

Lockhart, A., Psioda, M., Ting, J., Campbell, S., Mugo, N., Kwatampora, J., … Smith, J. S. (2018). Prospective evaluation of cervico-vaginal self and cervical physician-collection for the detection of chlamydia trachomatis, neisseria gonorrhoeae, trichomonas vaginalis, and mycoplasma genitalium infections. *Sexually Transmitted Diseases*, 1. doi:10.1097/OLQ.0000000000000778

Loeb, D. F., Lee, R. S., Binswanger, I. A., Ellison, M. C., & Aagaard, E. M. (2011). Patient, resident physician, and visit factors associated with documentation of sexual history in the outpatient setting. *Journal of General Internal Medicine*, 26(8), 887–893. doi:10.1007/s11606-011-1711-z

Loverro, G., Resta, L., Dellino, M., Edoardo, D. N., Cascarano, M. A., Loverro, M., & Mastrolia, S. A. (2016). Uterine and ovarian changes during testosterone administration in young female-to-male transsexuals. *Taiwanese Journal of Obstetrics and Gynecology*, 55(5), 686–691. doi:10.1016/J.TJOG.2016.03.004

Lu, M. C., Kotelchuck, M., Hogan, V., Jones, L., Wright, K., & Halfon, N. (2010). Closing the Black-White gap in birth outcomes: A life-course approach. *Ethnicity & Disease*, 20(1 Suppl 2), S2-62–76. Retrieved from www.ncbi.nlm.nih.gov/pubmed/20629248

Mattawanon, N., Spencer, J. B., Schirmer, D. A., & Tangpricha, V. (2018). Fertility preservation options in transgender people: A review. *Reviews in Endocrine and Metabolic Disorders*, 19(3), 231–242. doi:10.1007/s11154-018-9462-3

Maxwell, S., Noyes, N., Keefe, D., Berkeley, A. S., & Goldman, K. N. (2017). Pregnancy outcomes after fertility preservation in transgender men. *Obstetrics & Gynecology*, 129(6), 1031–1034. doi:10.1097/AOG.0000000000002036

McEwen, B. S. (1998). Stress, adaptation, and disease: Allostasis and allostatic load. *Annals of the New York Academy of Sciences*, 840(1), 33–44.

Miller, L. R., & Grollman, E. A. (2015). The social costs of gender nonconformity for transgender adults: Implications for discrimination and health. *Sociological Forum*, 30(3), 809–831. doi:10.1111/socf.12193

Miller, S. J., Foran-Tuller, K., Ledergerber, J., & Jandorf, L. (2017). Motivational interviewing to improve health screening uptake: A systematic review. *Patient Education and Counseling*, 100(2), 190–198. doi:10.1016/J.PEC.2016.08.027

Mitu, K. (2016). Transgender reproductive choice and fertility preservation. *The AMA Journal of Ethic*, 18(11), 1119–1125. doi:10.1001/journalofethics.2016.18.11.pfor2-1611

Nahata, L., Chen, D., Moravek, M. B., Quinn, G. P., Sutter, M. E., Taylor, J., … Gomez-Lobo, V. (2019). Understudied and under-reported: Fertility issues in transgender youth – a narrative review. *The Journal of Pediatrics*, *205*, 265–271. doi:10.1016/j.jpeds.2018.09.009

Nahata, L., Tishelman, A. C., Caltabellotta, N. M., & Quinn, G. P. (2017). Low fertility preservation utilization among transgender youth. *Journal of Adolescent Health*, *61*(1), 40–44. doi:10.1016/J.JADOHEALTH.2016.12.012

Neumann, M. S., Finlayson, T. J., Pitts, N. L., & Keatley, J. (2017). Comprehensive HIV prevention for transgender persons. *American Journal of Public Health*, *107*(2), 207–212. doi:10.2105/AJPH.2016.303509

Nusbaum, M. R., & Hamilton, C. D. (2002). *The proactive sexual health history* (Vol. 66). Retrieved from https://www.aafp.org/afp/2002/1101/p1705.html

Parente, V., Hale, L., & Palermo, T. (2013). Association between breast cancer and allostatic load by race: National health and nutrition examination survey 1999–2008. *Psycho-Oncology*, *22*(3), 621–628. doi:10.1002/pon.3044

Peitzmeier, S. M., Khullar, K., Reisner, S. L., & Potter, J. (2014). Pap test use is lower among female-to-male patients than non-transgender women. *American Journal of Preventive Medicine*, *47*(6), 808–812. doi:10.1016/J.AMEPRE.2014.07.031

Pessagno, R. A. (2013). Don't be embarrassed. *Nursing*, *43*(9), 60–64. doi:10.1097/01.NURSE.0000431139.82532.b3

Petroll, A. E., Walsh, J. L., Owczarzak, J. L., McAuliffe, T. L., Bogart, L. M., & Kelly, J. A. (2017). PrEP awareness, familiarity, comfort, and prescribing experience among US primary care providers and HIV specialists. *AIDS and Behavior*, *21*(5), 1256–1267. doi:10.1007/s10461-016-1625-1

Pfäfflin, F., Bockting, W., Coleman, E., Ekins, R., King, D., Gray, N., & Pellet, E. (2002). The desire to have children and the preservation of fertility in transsexual women: A survey. *International Journal of Transgenderism*, *6*(3), 97–103. Retrieved from www.atria.nl/ezines/web/IJT/97-03/numbers/symposion/ijtvo06no03_02.htm

Pitasi, M. A., Oraka, E., Clark, H., Town, M., & DiNenno, E. A. (2017). HIV testing among transgender women and men — 27 States and Guam, 2014–2015. *MMWR. Morbidity and Mortality Weekly Report*, *66*(33), 883–887. doi:10.15585/mmwr.mm6633a3

Potter, J., Peitzmeier, S. M., Bernstein, I., Reisner, S. L., Alizaga, N. M., Agénor, M., & Pardee, D. J. (2015). Cervical cancer screening for patients on the female-to-male spectrum: A narrative review and guide for clinicians. *Journal of General Internal Medicine*, *30*(12), 1857–1864. doi:10.1007/s11606-015-3462-8

Reisner, S., Keatley, J., & Baral, S. (2016). Transgender community voices: A participatory population perspective. *The Lancet*, *388*(10042), 327–330.

Rele, K., & Wylie, K. (2007). Management of psychosexual and relationship problems in general mental health services by psychiatry trainees. *International Journal of Clinical Practice*, *61*(10), 1701–1704. doi:10.1111/j.1742-1241.2007.01455.x

Rosemberg, M.-A. S., Li, Y., & Seng, J. (2017). Allostatic load: A useful concept for advancing nursing research. *Journal of Clinical Nursing*, *26*(23–24), 5191–5205. doi:10.1111/jocn.13753

Rosen, D. L., Golin, C. E., Grodensky, C. A., May, J., Bowling, J. M., DeVellis, R. F., … Wohl, D. A. (2015). Opt-out HIV testing in prison: Informed and voluntary? *AIDS Care*, *27*(5), 545–554. doi:10.1080/09540121.2014.989486

Rowniak, S., Chesla, C., Dawson Rose, C., & Holzemer, W. L. (2011). *Transmen: The HIV risk of gay identity. AIDS education and prevention* (Vol. 23). Retrieved from https://guilfordjournals.com/doi/pdfplus/10.1521/aeap.2011.23.6.508

Ryan, C., Russell, S. T., Huebner, D., Diaz, R., & Sanchez, J. (2010). Family acceptance in adolescence and the health of LGBT young adults. *Journal of Child and Adolescent Psychiatric Nursing*, *23*(4), 205–213. doi:10.1111/j.1744-6171.2010.00246.x

Sanchez, N. F., Sanchez, J. P., & Danoff, A. (2009). Health care utilization, barriers to care, and hormone usage among male-to-female transgender persons in New York City. *American Journal of Public Health*, *99*(4), 713–719. doi:10.2105/AJPH.2007.132035

Silverberg, M. J., Nash, R., Becerra-Culqui, T. A., Cromwell, L., Getahun, D., Hunkeler, E., ... Goodman, M. (2017). Cohort study of cancer risk among insured transgender people. *Annals of Epidemiology, 27*(8), 499–501. doi:10.1016/j.annepidem.2017.07.007

Stone, J. P., Hartley, R. L., & Temple-Oberle, C. (2018). Breast cancer in transgender patients: A systematic review. Part 2: Female to Male. *European Journal of Surgical Oncology, 44*(10), 1463–1468. doi:10.1016/J.EJSO.2018.06.021

Trussell, J. (2007). The cost of unintended pregnancy in the United States. *Contraception, 75*(3), 168–170. doi:10.1016/J.CONTRACEPTION.2006.11.009

U.S. Preventive Services Task Force. (2014). Final update summary: Sexually transmitted infections: Behavioral counseling – U.S. Preventive Services Task Force. Retrieved January 22, 2019, from www.uspreventiveservicestaskforce.org/Page/Document/UpdateSummaryFinal/sexually-transmitted-infections-behavioral-counseling1

U.S. Preventive Services Task Force. (2016). Final update summary: Cervical cancer: Screening. Retrieved from https://www.uspreventiveservicestaskforce.org/uspstf/recommendation/cervical-cancer-screening

Wallace, M. E., & Harville, E. W. (2013). Allostatic load and birth outcomes among White and Black women in New Orleans. *Maternal and Child Health Journal, 17*(6), 1025–1029. doi:10.1007/s10995-012-1083-y

Wallace, S. A., Blough, K. L., & Kondapalli, L. A. (2014). Fertility preservation in the transgender patient: Expanding oncofertility care beyond cancer. *Gynecological Endocrinology, 30*(12), 868–871. doi:10.3109/09513590.2014.920005

White, I. D., Faithfull, S., & Allan, H. (2013). The re-construction of women's sexual lives after pelvic radiotherapy: A critique of social constructionist and biomedical perspectives on the study of female sexuality after cancer treatment. *Social Science & Medicine, 76*(1), 188–196. doi:10.1016/j.socscimed.2012.10.025

Wierckx, K., Van Caenegem, E., Pennings, G., Elaut, E., Dedecker, D., Van de Peer, F., ... T'Sjoen, G. (2012). Reproductive wish in transsexual men. *Human Reproduction, 27*(2), 483–487. doi:10.1093/humrep/der406

Wierckx, K., Mueller, S., Weyers, S., Van Caenegem, E., Roef, G., Heylens, G., & T'Sjoen, G. (2012). Long-term evaluation of cross-sex hormone treatment in transsexual persons. *The Journal of Sexual Medicine, 9*(10), 2641–2651. doi:10.1111/J.1743-6109.2012.02876.X

Wimberly, Y. H., Hogben, M., Moore-Ruffin, J., Moore, S. E., & Fry-Johnson, Y. (2006). *Sexual history-taking among primary care physicians.* Retrieved from www.ncbi.nlm.nih.gov/pmc/articles/PMC2569695/pdf/jnma00199-0044.pdf

Workowski, K. A., & Bolan, G. A., & Centers for Disease Control and Prevention. (2015). Sexually transmitted diseases treatment guidelines, 2015. *MMWR. Recommendations and Reports: Morbidity and Mortality Weekly Report. Recommendations and Reports, 64*(RR-03), 1–137. Retrieved from www.ncbi.nlm.nih.gov/pubmed/26042815

World Health Organization. (2006). *Defining sexual health: Report of a technical consultation on sexual health, 28–31 January 2002, Geneva.* Geneva, Switzerland. Retrieved from https://scholar.google.com/scholar_lookup?hl=en&publication_year=2006&pages=1-35&title=Defining+sexual+health%3A+Report+of+a+technical+consultation+on+sexual+health%2C+January+28–31%2C+2002

Yared, N., Horvath, K., Fashanu, O., Zhao, R., Baker, J., & Kulasingam, S. (2017). Optimizing screening for sexually transmitted infections in men using self-collected swabs – A systematic review. *Sexually Transmitted Diseases, 1.* doi:10.1097/OLQ.0000000000000739

Zimlichman, E., Rozenblum, R., & Millenson, M. L. (2013). The road to patient experience of care measurement: Lessons from the United States. *Israel Journal of Health Policy Research, 2*(1), 35. doi:10.1186/2045-4015-2-35

Affirming and inclusive mental health care for transgender and nonbinary young people

Mere Abrams, Rachel Lynn Golden, and Jessie Rose Cohen

INTRODUCTION

As an increasing number of transgender and nonbinary (TNB) youth are present in mental health, school, and medical settings (Chen et al., 2018; de Graaf & Carmichael, 2019; Steensma et al., 2014), there is a growing need for mental health professionals to have competency and training in gender-affirming care and gender identity development. The role of mental health professionals supporting TNB youth under the age of 18 is complex and interdisciplinary. It involves fostering a non-judgmental environment, assessing for gender dysphoria alongside co-existing mental health concerns, and connecting youth with medical, mental health, and community-based support. As there is no single approach to treatment, mental health professionals must determine the most appropriate treatment plan based on each client's presenting issues and goals, and their family's concerns.

State of care

In exploring appropriate and effective models of care, mental health professionals must consider controversies such as gender dysphoria as a diagnosis, the role of professionals as gatekeepers to accessing medically necessary treatment, and the timing of medical interventions such as puberty blockers, hormone replacement therapy, and surgery. Developing an increased understanding of trauma-informed care and systems of oppression is critical. TNB young people experience harassment, discrimination, and microaggressions at a rate that is higher than their cisgender peers (James et al., 2016). As a result, many come into mental health settings with existing trauma or traumatic experiences that affect mental health, inform interactions with others, and shape their experience in the world.

Mental health professionals should approach TNB identities as naturally occurring human experiences, as opposed to a mental illness or disorder (Singh & dickey, 2017). In an effort to validate the experience of TNB individuals, the Diagnostic and Statistical Manual of Mental Disorders Fifth Edition (DSM-V) replaced the diagnosis of gender identity disorder with gender dysphoria (Drescher, 2014). The DSM-V change specifically states that someone *must* experience distress to meet criteria for a diagnosis of gender dysphoria, and notes that the experience of having a gender that differs from the sex assigned at birth is not, in and of itself, a disorder or mental health diagnosis (American Psychological Association, 2013). In addition, although many people who are TNB experience gender dysphoria and pursue medical intervention, some do not (Butler et al., 2018). The seventh edition of the Standards of Care set forth by the World Professional Association for Transgender Health (WPATH-SOC7) (Coleman et al., 2012) outlines the areas of competence and role of a mental health professional in providing care to TNB youth. Mental health professionals working with youth should gain an understanding of gender-affirming medical options, caregiver-support and family-acceptance strategies, as well as stay informed of the current research, guidelines, and policies that inform ethical, intersectional, and culturally relevant mental health and gender care (Hubach, 2017).

An expanding literature covers topics of gender related to identity development, dysphoria, and health. Advances in gender care focus less on diagnosis and, instead, center the client's experience and internal understanding of gender and self (Hidalgo et al., 2013; Lev, 2006). Shifts in access, information about gender beyond binary sex assigned at birth, and clinical observations have paved the way for emerging frameworks and specialty services such as the gender-affirmative model (Chen et al., 2018; Hidalgo et al., 2013) and gender clinics.

As more youth decide to pursue medical options to affirm their gender or reduce gender dysphoria, mental health professionals are increasingly tasked with providing introductory information about gender-affirming medical interventions. These tasks include assessing for co-occurring mental health issues, case management, and opportunities for advocacy. Given the broad scope of needs, mental health professionals should consider engaging an interdisciplinary care team that might include family members, therapists, school counselors, community allies, pediatricians, legal professionals (for name and gender marker changes), and medical specialists (e.g., endocrinologists, surgeons).

Youth seeking services

TNB youth typically seek mental health services as steps towards self-determining gender identity, coming out, and accessing gender-affirming medical care (Coleman et al., 2012). In addition, many TNB youth also struggle with depression, anxiety, trauma, self-harm, and suicidality (Edwards-Leeper et al., 2017; Katz-Wise et al., 2018). Some TNB youth may be kicked out of their homes and communities as a result of their gender identity or expression (Schmitz & Tyler, 2018). Mental health concerns are often informed by a young person's experience in their family and social environments, and the extent to which those environments and relationships are affirming or rejecting of their gender identity and gender development (Golden & Oransky, 2019).

The Minority Stress Model (Meyer, 1995, 2003) is readily applicable to experiences of TNB youth and provides a framework for gaining insight into the ways in which a young person's gender identity impacts their overall health and wellbeing. The model asserts that anti-LGBTQ prejudice or stigma is a stressor and adverse mental and physical health outcomes are associated with experiences of discrimination, rejection, and isolation related to holding an LGBT identity (Hendricks & Testa, 2012). This distress can include gender dysphoria, social anxiety, depression associated with lack of support, and trauma related to bullying or assault or chronic rejection by family or community members. As a result, clinicians serving TNB youth must be well equipped to address gender alongside mental health concerns.

The relationship between family support and mental health symptoms is an urgent area for exploration, as it has been associated with critical mental health outcomes such as suicidality and homelessness (Bauer et al., 2015). Growing evidence suggests that while anxiety remains prevalent among TNB youth, depression is less frequent in those who are supported in their gender identities (Durwood et al., 2018). Studies report that TNB youth of color (Singh, 2013) and youth in group homes or foster care are particularly vulnerable due to reported discrimination and lack of access to gender-affirming services (Beck et al., 2018).

Modalities of mental health care

Youth present for mental health services across settings (e.g., community clinics, school-based counseling centers, hospitals, and private practice), with varied systems of support, and a range of needs. Best practices with TNB youth (Coleman et al., 2012) should be informed by an intersectional approach, wherein race, culture, environment, support systems, and level of access to affirming individuals and spaces are explored and considered as factors influencing gender care and overall health and wellbeing (American Psychological Association, 2015; Burnes et al., 2010; Golden & Oransky, 2019).

Providers of gender-affirming services are tasked to consider therapy modalities that can be utilized to reduce symptoms associated with lack of gender affirmation and gender dysphoria. This requires expertise, flexibility, and critical thinking about how to best meet youth and caregiver needs. Best practices in therapy with TNB youth gives careful consideration to the impact family and social systems as well as gender dysphoria have on mental health outcomes (MacNish & Gold-Peifer, 2011; Malpas et al., 2018). In individual therapy with TNB youth, gender identity is germane as it relates to improving mental health outcomes. When psychotherapy is needed, some models appropriate for treatment of co-occurring concerns can be used. However, clinicians are tasked to modify existing modalities of therapy for use with TNB youth when modifications have not yet been made. This can include modifying structure, content, and examples to be gender-relevant and affirming.

For example, dysregulation related to chronic invalidation associated with non-affirming experiences in mental health, medical, and educational settings may be present in TNB youth, and may be associated with non-suicidal self-injury or suicidality (Arcelus et al., 2016). Thus, dialectical behavior therapy addressing emotion dysregulation, poor interpersonal relationships, and life-threatening behaviors (Linehan, 2015) may be an appropriate intervention. Notably, DBT has been modified for the treatment of TNB adults (Sloan et al., 2017), but it has not yet been tested with TNB adults or youth.

Given the prevalence of violence and abuse enacted on members of the TNB community (James et al., 2016) and the associated risk for resulting trauma symptoms (Mizock & Lewis, 2008), trauma treatment may be appropriate (Richmond et al., 2012). One such treatment is trauma focused cognitive behavioral therapy (Cohen et al., 2006), a therapy targeting trauma symptoms for youth. However, it has not been formally adapted for use with TNB youth populations to date.

Finally, transgender-affirming cognitive behavioral therapy (TA-CBT) (Austin & Craig, 2015) is a trauma-informed modification of existing cognitive behavioral therapy for use with TNB individuals. However, to date it has not been modified for use with youth, and there have not yet been randomized control trials of its efficacy.

Family and group modalities may also be appropriate in the care for TNB youth and their caregiving systems, as addressing caregiver ambivalence about support can often be an instrumental aspect of affirming TNB care. Specific adaptations of family therapy modalities do not yet exist, however intersectionally informed family therapy approaches have been explored (Golden & Oransky, 2019). Models for group supports are commonly found in community settings and include social and therapeutic supports exclusively developed for TNB teens (Oransky et al., 2018). Caregiver groups may also serve to provide social support and a place where caregivers can receive credible information and experiential knowledge from one another about supporting their TNB child (Malpas, 2011; Malpas et al., 2018).

Many treatment approaches relevant to work with TNB youth have not been tested for efficacy with this client population. Thus, clinicians often need to make adaptations to account for individual experiences connected to gender including: language used in prompts and questions, relevant examples, topics and themes covered, etc.

Providers as gatekeepers

Parental permission and/or mental health assessment are often required to gain access to gender-affirming medical interventions for TNB youth under the age of 18. These requirements vary from state to state, and from one medical clinic to another. Therefore, mental health professionals should educate themselves about their state's policies and anticipate being in the role of a gatekeeper to gender-affirming treatments. These policies may vary greatly by state and by policy (see transequality.org/know-your-rights/health-care for more information.) These requirements, along with the tensions created by gatekeeping, might prevent clients from being forthcoming with identity questions and might contribute to them feeling the need to present with certainty in order to access medically necessary gender-affirming interventions. Considerations about the pubertal development of peers alongside the identity and maturity of the young person are essential to make recommendations about the timing of gender-affirming medical interventions. Recent studies, along with the WPATH-SOC7, warn that refusing timely medical treatment for TNB adolescents can increase gender dysphoria and mental health symptoms (Nuttbrock et al., 2010). Therefore, it is crucial for mental health professionals to thoroughly understand and explore the benefits and limitations of gender-affirming medical treatment in their work with TNB youth.

CASE EXAMPLES

We have intentionally selected one case example to illustrate best practices in care, common themes observed among TNB youth, and the support systems available to them, as well as some conflicts that have arisen among youth, providers, and families. We aim to highlight the voices of TNB youth with the attention and nuance they deserve as, historically, case examples and writings about transgender youth have failed to hear from youth themselves, or to represent their story with care (Snapp et al., 2016). In selecting the case example, we have highlighted the complexity of dysphoria as well as onset of gender concerns in adolescence.

We have made an intentional decision to share a case composite rather than presenting a single case. We followed the steps outlined by Duffy (2010) to choose cases highlighting similar themes and drew representative information from each case. Next, we wove the material together to explore the common stories being told. Finally, we took all precautions to de-identify the information (Clifft, 1986).

We chose to provide composite examples for several reasons. Namely, the population of TNB individuals seeking services is small. We were concerned that with only slight modifications to obscure identity, patients would easily be able to identify their story, or their story could be identified by others. We believe that it is more difficult to eschew and invalidate patients' experience when the collective, shared narrative is told.

ROBBIE

Identifying information

Robbie (he/him) is a 15-year-old transgender male adolescent who was assigned female at birth. He identifies as multiracial, Filipino, and White. He is in the tenth grade and lives with his biological family; his mother is a teacher and his father is a sales-broker, who often travels for work. He also has a 12-year-old brother and 9-year-old sister. Robbie is a good student and a star cross-country athlete.

Presenting concerns

Robbie was referred to therapy at an outpatient mental health clinic after a psychiatric hospitalization. Robbie had revealed to a school counselor that he was experiencing suicidal ideation and was engaging in frequent non-suicidal self-injury (NSSI) by cutting on his thighs with a disassembled razor. Robbie was taken to the emergency department where he revealed to a social worker that he had struggled with sadness, hopelessness, anxiety, and NSSI since the sixth grade. The social worker learned that Robbie had disclosed his gender identity to his parents prior to the increase in mental health symptoms. He revealed increased distress since that disclosure. Safety was assessed, and at Robbie's request, his gender was not discussed at discharge.

Gender history

Robbie disclosed his male identity to his parents at age 14, after quietly questioning his sexual orientation for six months and then quitting the cross-country team. His parents became distressed and wondered if it was a phase, citing his presentation as a girl up to that time. His parents continued to use Robbie's given name and female pronouns. Though Robbie continued to maintain his grades at school, he withdrew socially and spent more time online. He also began cutting and experiencing NSSI.

Questions about gender had first arisen when he was 13 and noticed he had romantic feelings for a female friend. He felt confused and wondered if he were a lesbian. Robbie also identified distress with the onset of breast buds and menses. Though he remembered feeling anxious and having tearful episodes, he had convinced himself that it was "normal to feel awkward". As his physical development progressed, Robbie began to wear bulky sweatshirts over several sports bras. With each menses, he became distressed and often missed school, citing cramps.

Robbie began to explore gender online, where he met other TNB young people. He was able to talk about his distress related to the name given to him at birth, which he perceived to be very feminine. He received support from his online community when choosing a new name. And he was encouraged when hearing stories of adults online who identified as transgender. Though Robbie was finally able to dream of a future as a transgender adult, he continued to present as female and use his given name, going to great lengths to dispel any questioning about his gender.

Caregiver response

Robbie had been hopeful that his parents would be understanding. He had experienced them as supportive and loving about his identification with his father and clothing choices throughout his life (neutral to more masculine). However, he was met with invalidation when his mother told Robbie he was not a boy, and "I know because I raised you." She reminded him that he always liked baby dolls and wanted to be an *ina* ("mother" in Tagalog) when he was young. She prohibited

Robbie from telling his brother, sister, or grandparents. His father had tried to be supportive by saying that, "Being a lesbian was okay but you don't need to make it into something else." He also told Robbie, "You are killing your mother with this."

At the initial outpatient session, both parents expressed concern that Robbie had recently befriended LGBT-identified peers. Neither parent had noted NSSI, distress, or depression in their child prior to his hospitalization.

His parents also reported that Robbie had always "just been a tomboy", he never asked his parents to use a different name or pronoun, and had not brought gender up again after the first instance. Both parents made it clear that they would not allow any medical intervention prior to Robbie's 18th birthday.

Several identified points of intervention

Robbie began weekly individual therapy at the outpatient clinic and his parents attended monthly sessions. Robbie was referred for a psychiatric evaluation and was prescribed an antidepressant. He was also referred to the teen DBT group. The therapist met with parents alone to discuss their support of Robbie. The therapist used a harm-reduction approach to target distress around menses and chest dysphoria, recommending that Robbie purchase a chest binder and meet with a medical doctor about halting menses. As their understanding of Robbie's dysphoria progressed, they were able to support Robbie in getting his hair cut at an LGBT-affirming barbershop and allowed him to purchase more gender-affirming clothes. With these moves toward social transition, Robbie's mood notably improved.

With the therapist's support, Robbie asked that his parents use his chosen name and pronouns. His mother was ambivalent about this change and requested a "test for gender identity" to decide if she should grant this request. Ultimately, both parents were unable to agree to this and expressed concern that the therapist was "pushing an agenda".

Robbie's parents were offered information about ways to connect with other parents of TNB children. However, they declined as they believed Robbie's case was different, since the stories they had heard of about transgender children suggested that individuals gain gender awareness at a very young age. His mother also worried about the stress Robbie's gender would create for other family members. She expressed that he was disrespecting his elders and she could not imagine how her own parents would react to Robbie's identity.

The therapist worked with Robbie individually to identify settings where he could come out. He decided to tell a few school friends; their supportive response improved Robbie's mood. The therapist also introduced "vetted" online resources where other TNB teens were sharing their stories.

Outcomes

Although Robbie continued to struggle with depressive symptoms and NSSI, his symptoms had improved overall. Robbie's parents continued to struggle with accepting his gender identity but agreed not to question Robbie's authenticity directly, as it was a trigger to self-harm. Robbie felt increasingly hopeless because he could not access gender-affirming medical interventions, such as hormones or puberty blockers. Robbie reported that watching other TNB teens share stories of their experiences was both comforting and painful, feeling envious of teens who had begun medical transition. While he was relieved to not experience his monthly menses, he did admit continued frustration about taking birth control. He felt it was a "band-aid" to address his overall dysphoria rather than the interventions he felt would be affirming.

Remaining need for intervention/next steps

Robbie needs continued support and monitoring regarding acute mental health distress. A family therapy approach was indicated, with a focus on increasing understanding and affirmation. Independent parental sessions would allow his parents to privately question the legitimacy of his gender, grieve, and address their concerns and fears about medical interventions and negative consequences. Collaboration with the pediatrician and an endocrinologist would help Robbie's parents access medical expertise about interventions. Future sessions could work toward bringing the family together for Robbie to be able to share how his psychological pain was directly related to dysphoria both of his body and from his parents' response.

In addition to introducing interventions to manage Robbie's acute mental health symptoms, therapy should include exploration that supports Robbie's overall gender development and education about the non-medical gender-affirming interventions that can be introduced to mitigate dysphoria during the period of time when he cannot access gender-affirming medical care. Creating a non-judgmental space where Robbie can experience gender affirmation, discuss gender dysphoria, and openly express himself, will deepen understanding about Robbie's gender and relationship with his body.

Case study questions

Based on your understanding of Robbie's case:

1. What steps would you have taken to treat Robbie as a client?
2. How would you keep Robbie's parents engaged?
3. What might have been different if Robbie had completely supportive or completely unsupportive parents?
4. Gender euphoria is defined as a moment or series of moments when someone feels positively about one or many aspects of their gender. In what ways does Robbie experience gender euphoria? What questions might you ask Robbie to get a better sense of this?
5. How might Robbie's experiences with gender euphoria and gender dysphoria inform the approaches or interventions a therapist engages to address mental health symptoms?

IN PRACTICE

The above case includes common themes and tensions present when providing affirming and inclusive mental health and gender care to TNB youth and their families. Existing research suggests that TNB youth display symptoms of depression, anxiety, and self-harm at higher rates than their cisgender counterparts (Borgogna et al., 2019; Crissman et al., 2019). Clinicians must carefully balance addressing safety and mental health assessment alongside the existing stigma and preconceived notions that all or most TNB youth have a mental health disorder or experience mental health symptoms. Focusing on mental health when the TNB youth does not report any mental health issues can reinforce internalized shame or become a barrier to establishing rapport and a successful therapeutic relationship. Contextualizing the pain TNB youth experience due to minority stress associated with feeling unseen and misunderstood, rather than because of an internal flaw, can be validating of youth's experiences and can provide a useful frame to explore their feelings about themselves and their gender (Arcelus et al., 2016).

Similar to other parts of identity development, gender is learned and discovered over time through education and socialization. It is not uncommon for TNB youth to hide their questioning and exploration of gender from family and friends before disclosing a new gender identity (Bess & Stabb, 2009). The length of time it takes for someone to recognize their authentic gender is unique for each person. Some people explore gender by making changes to their appearance, name, and pronouns. Others simply explore gender by reading the stories and experiences of other TNB people. When appropriate, medical interventions are introduced after the exploration stage to affirm gender and help clients find congruence in their body, gender, and appearance (Milrod & Karasic, 2017).

In U.S. culture, there is a significant amount of pressure to pinpoint or identify gender with a sense of permanence. Due to this social pressure, many youths do not disclose a TNB gender until they feel confident in their identity or assured they will receive a positive response from family and peers. Thus, mental health professionals have the role of helping youth navigate and explore their identity, so they can develop a deeper understanding of self and how that self interacts with and relates to others.

While working with youth clients, mental health professionals must also provide appropriate education to parents and caregivers, so they can effectively understand how to support and affirm their young person (Katz-Wise et al., 2018). These approaches must be tailored to support both the parent who struggles to accept their child's identity as well as the parent who needs to grieve the loss of the child they thought they knew (McGuire et al., 2016; Wahlig, 2015). In cases where rejection continues to increase, providers must assess for an unsafe environment and risk related to rejection.

Research suggests that some parents have a particularly difficult time accepting and understanding their child's TNB identity, most notably when the parents perceive the onset of gender dysphoria to be sudden and at an older age (Coolhart et al., 2018). Providers must keep in mind that a parent's perception of their child's gender identity as a phase or trend is not evidence validating or invalidating a particular gender identity. Rather, it is information about what the parent is observing and experiencing, and does not provide accurate information about the TNB young person's experience of themselves. When parents are overtly rejecting or repeatedly questioning their child's assertion, mental health professionals must work with parents separately from the TNB youth. The mental health professional should provide a safe space for parents and caregivers to process their questions, concerns, and decisions related to gender affirmation (Malpas et al., 2018; Oransky et al., 2018). This intervention may reduce family rejection, exclusion, or misunderstanding while the family system develops a support plan.

Research also suggests that even when a young person has parental support, they remain vulnerable to rejection in other settings (Birnkrant & Przeworski, 2017). The mental health provider's competence in addressing cultural variables, parenting styles, and intergenerational patterns can offer parents insight leading to increased empathy and attunement (Golden & Oransky, 2019).

CONCLUSION

For TNB youth who report gender dysphoria, mental health providers are tasked with understanding the complexity of the client's experience of dysphoria. For example, does dysphoria reside in body parts, gender roles, gendered language, or external perceptions? Exploring these areas of dysphoria with TNB clients helps to inform recommended interventions. Current research suggests that chronological age is not an effective measure of mental, developmental, and emotional readiness for medical interventions such as puberty blockers, gender-affirming hormones, or gender-affirming surgery (Milrod & Karasic, 2017). For many TNB youth, gender-affirming medical intervention is an essential part of optimizing mental health and overall wellbeing, and a critical step in preventing and managing gender dysphoria.

RESOURCES

- http://transstudent.org
- www.glaad.org/transgender/resources
- https://transcare.ucsf.edu/guidelines/youth
- https://fenwayhealth.org/wp-content/uploads/TH-38-Affirming-Care-for-Gender-Diverse-Youth-Brochure-Final-Web.pdf
- www.healthline.com/health/transgender#1
- www.genderspectrum.org/resources/
- www.psychiatry.org/psychiatrists/cultural-competency/education/transgender-and-gender-nonconforming-patients

REFERENCES

American Psychiatric Association. (2013). *Diagnostic and statistical manual of mental disorders (5th ed.).* Arlington, VA: American Psychiatric Publishing.

American Psychological Association. (2015). Guidelines for psychological practice with transgender and gender nonconforming people. *American Psychologist, 70*(9), 832–864. doi:10.1037/a0039906

Arcelus, J., Claes, L., Witcomb, G. L., Marshall, E., & Bouman, W. P. (2016). Risk factors for non-suicidal self-injury among trans youth. *The Journal of Sexual Medicine, 13*(3), 402–412. doi:10.1016/j.jsxm.2016.01.003

Austin, A., & Craig, S. L. (2015). Transgender affirmative cognitive behavioral therapy: Clinical considerations and applications. *Professional Psychology: Research and Practice, 46*(1), 21–29. doi:10.1037/a0038642

Bauer, G. R., Scheim, A. I., Pyne, J., Travers, R., & Hammond, R. (2015). Intervenable factors associated with suicide risk in transgender persons: A respondent driven sampling study in Ontario, Canada. *BMC Public Health, 15*(1), 525–540. doi:10.1186/s12889-015-1867-2

Beck, M. J., Maier, C. A., Means, A., & Isaacson, L. A. (2018). Interdisciplinary collaboration for LGBTQ students in foster care: Strategies for school counselors. *Journal of LGBT Issues in Counseling, 12*(4), 248–264. doi:10.1080/15538605.2018.1526154

Bess, J., & Stabb, S. (2009). The experiences of transgendered persons in psychotherapy: Voices and recommendations. *Journal of Mental Health Counseling, 31*(3), 264–282. doi:10.17744/mehc.31.3f6241546l133w50

Birnkrant, J. M., & Przeworski, A. (2017). Communication, advocacy, and acceptance among support-seeking parents of transgender youth. *Journal of Gay & Lesbian Mental Health, 21*(2), 132–153. doi:10.1080/19359705.2016.1277173

Borgogna, N. C., McDermott, R. C., Aita, S. L., & Kridel, M. M. (2019). Anxiety and depression across gender and sexual minorities: Implications for transgender, gender nonconforming, pansexual, demisexual, asexual, queer, and questioning individuals. *Psychology of Sexual Orientation and Gender Diversity, 6*(1), 54–63. doi:10.1037/sgd0000306

Burnes, T. R., Singh, A. A., Harper, A. J., Harper, B., Maxon-Kann, W., Pickering, D. L., ... Hosea, J. (2010). American Counseling Association: Competencies for counseling with transgender clients. *Journal of LGBT Issues in Counseling, 4*(3–4), 135–159. doi:10.1080/15538605.2010.524839

Butler, G., De Graaf, N., Wren, B., & Carmichael, P. (2018). Assessment and support of children and adolescents with gender dysphoria. *Archives of Disease in Childhood, 103,* 631–636. doi:10.1136/archdischild-2018-314992

Chen, D., Edwards-Leeper, L., Stancin, T., & Tishelman, A. (2018). Advancing the practice of pediatric psychology with transgender youth: State of the science, ongoing controversies, and future directions. *Clinical Practice in Pediatric Psychology, 6*(1), 73–83. doi:10.1037/cpp0000229

Clifft, M. A. (1986). Writing about psychiatric patients: Guidelines for disguising case material. *Bulletin of the Menninger Clinic, 50*(6), 511–524.

Cohen, J. A., Debinger, E., & Mannarino, A. P. (2006). The impact of trauma and grief on children and families. In J. A. Cohen, A. P. Mannarino, & E. Deblinger (Eds.), *Treating trauma and traumatic grief in children and adolescents: A clinician's guide* (pp. 3–19). New York, NY: Guilford Press.

Coleman, E., Bockting, W., Botzer, M., Cohen-Kettenis, P., DeCuypere, G., Feldman, J., ... Zucker, K. (2012). Standards of care for the health of transsexual, transgender and gender non-conforming people, version 7. *International Journal of Transgenderism, 13,* 165–232. doi:10.1080/15532739.2011.700873

Coolhart, D., Ritenour, K., & Grodzinski, A. (2018). Experiences of ambiguous loss for parents of transgender male youth: A phenomenological exploration. *Contemporary Family Therapy, 40*(1), 28–41. doi:10.1007/s10591-017-9426-x

Crissman, H. P., Stroumsa, D., Kobernik, E. K., & Berger, M. B. (2019). Gender and frequent mental distress: Comparing transgender and non-transgender individuals' self-rated mental health. *Journal of Women's Health, 28*(2). doi:10.1089/jwh.2018.7411

de Graaf, N. M., & Carmichael, P. (2019). Reflections on emerging trends in clinical work with gender diverse children and adolescents. *Clinical Child Psychology and Psychiatry, 24*(2), 353–364. doi:10.1177/1359104518812924

Drescher, J. (2014). Controversies in gender diagnoses. *LGBT Health*, *1*(1), 10–14. doi:10.1089/lgbt.2013.1500

Duffy, M. (2010). Writing about clients: Developing composite case material and its rationale. *Counseling and Values*, *54*, 135–153. doi:10.1002/j.2161-007x.2010.tb000 11.x

Durwood, L., McLaughlin, K. A., & Olson, K. R. (2018). "Mental health and self-worth in socially transitioned transgender youth": Corrigendum. *Journal of the American Academy of Child & Adolescent Psychiatry*, *57*(11), 116–123. doi:10.1016/j.jaac.2016.10.016

Edwards-Leeper, L., Feldman, H. A., Lash, B. R., Shumer, D. E., & Tishelman, A. C. (2017). Psychological profile of the first sample of transgender youth presenting for medical intervention in a US pediatric gender center. *Psychology of Sexual Orientation and Gender Diversity*, *4*(3), 374. doi:10.1037/sgd0000239

Golden, R. L., & Oransky, M. (2019). An intersectional approach to therapy with transgender and nonbinary adolescents and their families. *Archives of Sexual Behavior. Advance online publication.* doi:10.1007/s10508-018-1354-9

Hendricks, M. L., & Testa, R. J. (2012). A conceptual framework for clinical work with transgender and gender nonconforming clients: An adaptation of the Minority Stress Model. *Professional Psychology: Research and Practice*, *43*(5), 460–467. doi:10.1037/a0029597

Hidalgo, M. A., Ehrensaft, D., Tishelman, A. C., Clark, L. F., Garofalo, R., Rosenthal, S. M., ... Olson, J. (2013). The gender affirmative model: What we know and what we aim to learn. *Human Development*, *56*(5), 285–290. doi:10.1159/000355235

Hubach, R. D. (2017). Disclosure matters: Enhancing patient-provider communication is necessary to improve the health of sexual minority adolescents. *Journal of Adolescent Health*, *61*(5), 537–538. doi:10.1016/j.jadohealth.2017.08.021

James, S. E., Herman, J. L., Rankin, S., Keisling, M., Mottet, L., & Anafi, M. (2016). *The report of the 2015 U.S. Transgender Survey.* Washington, DC: National Center for Transgender Equality.

Katz-Wise, S. L., Ehrensaft, D., Vetters, R., Forcier, M., & Austin, S. B. (2018). Family functioning and mental health of transgender and gender-nonconforming youth in the Trans Teen and Family Narratives Project. *The Journal of Sex Research*, *55*(4–5), 582–590. doi:10.1080/00224499.2017.1415291

Keo-Meier, C., & Ehrensaft, D. (2018). Introduction. In C. Keo-Meier & D. Ehrensaft (Eds.), *The gender affirmative model: An interdisciplinary approach to supporting transgender and gender expansive children* (pp. 3–20). Washington, DC: American Psychological Association.

Lev, A. I. (2006). Transgender emergence within families. In D. F. Morrow & L. Messinger (Eds.), *Sexual orientation and gender expression in social work practice: Working with gay, lesbian, bisexual, and transgender people* (pp. 263–283). New York, NY: Columbia University Press.

Linehan, M. M. (2015). *DBT skills training manual (2nd ed.).* New York, NY: Guilford Press.

MacNish, M., & Gold-Peifer, M. (2011). Families in transition: Supporting families of transgender youth. In J. Malpas & A. I. Lev (Eds.), *At the edge: Exploring gender and sexuality in couples and families* (pp. 34–42). Washington, DC: American Family Therapy Academy. doi:10.1007/978-3-319-03248-1_13

Malpas, J. (2011). Between pink and blue: A multi-dimensional family approach to gender nonconforming children and their families. *Family Process*, *50*(4), 453–470. doi:10.1111/j.1545-5300.2011.01371.x

Malpas, J., Glaeser, E., & Giammattei, S. V. (2018). Building resilience in transgender and gender expansive children, families, and communities: A multidimensional family approach. In C. Keo-Meier & D. Ehrensaft (Eds.), Perspectives on sexual orientation and diversity. *The gender affirmative model: An interdisciplinary approach to supporting transgender and gender expansive children* (pp. 141–156). Washington, DC: American Psychological Association. doi:10.1037/0000095-009

McGuire, J. K., Catalpa, J. M., Lacey, V., & Kuvalanka, K. A. (2016). Ambiguous loss as a framework for interpreting gender transitions in families. *Journal of Family Theory & Review*, 8(3), 373–385. doi:10.1111/jftr.12159

Meyer, I. H. (1995). Minority stress and mental health in gay men. *Journal of Health and Social Behavior*, 36(1), 38–56. doi:10.2307/2137286

Meyer, I. H. (2003). Prejudice as stress: Conceptual and measurement problems. *American Journal of Public Health*, 93(2), 262–265. doi:10.2105/ajph.93.2.262

Milrod, C., & Karasic, D. H. (2017). Age is just a number: WPATH-affiliated surgeons' experiences and attitudes toward vaginoplasty in transgender females under 18 years of age in the United States. *Journal of Sexual Medicine*, 14(4), 624–634. doi:10.1016/j.jsxm.2017.02.007

Mizock, L., & Lewis, T. K. (2008). Trauma in transgender populations: Risk, resilience, and clinical care. *Journal of Emotional Abuse*, 8(3), 335–354. doi:10.1080/10926790802262523

Nuttbrock, L., Hwahng, S., Bockting, W., Rosenblum, A., Mason, M., Macri, M., & Becker, J. (2010). Psychiatric impact of gender-related abuse across the life course of male-to-female transgender persons. *Journal of Sex Research*, 47(1), 12–23. doi:10.1080/00224490903062258

Oransky, M., Burke, E. Z., & Steever, J. (2018). An interdisciplinary model for meeting the mental health needs of transgender adolescents and young adults: The Mount Sinai Adolescent Health Center Approach. *Cognitive and Behavioral Practice*. doi:10.1016/j.cbpra.2018.03.002

Richmond, K. A., Burnes, T., & Carroll, K. (2012). Lost in trans-lation: Interpreting systems of trauma for transgender clients. *Traumatology*, 18(1), 45–57. doi:10.1177/1534765610396726

Schmitz, R. M., & Tyler, K. A. (2018). The complexity of family reactions to identity among homeless and college lesbian, gay, bisexual, transgender, and queer young adults. *Archives of Sexual Behavior*, 47(4), 1195–1207. doi:10.1007/s10508-017-1014-5

Singh, A. A. (2013). Transgender youth of color and resilience: Negotiating oppression and finding support. *Sex Roles*, 68(11–12), 690–702. doi:10.1007/s11199-012-0149-z

Singh, A. A., & dickey, l. m. (Eds.). (2017). *Affirmative counseling and psychological practice with Transgender and Gender Nonconforming clients*. Washington, DC: American Psychological Association.

Sloan, C. A., Berke, D. S., & Shipherd, J. C. (2017). Utilizing a dialectical framework to inform conceptualization and treatment of clinical distress in transgender individuals. *Professional Psychology: Research and Practice*, 48(5), 301–309. doi:10.1037/14957-000

Snapp, S. D., Russell, S. T., Arredondo, M., & Skiba, R. (2016). A right to disclose: LGBTQ youth representation in data, science, and policy. *Advances in Child Development and Behavior*, 50, 135–159. doi:10.1016/bs.acdb.2015.11.005

Steensma, T. D., Zucker, K. J., Kreukels, B. P., VanderLaan, D. P., Wood, H., Fuentes, A., & Cohen-Kettenis, P. T. (2014). Behavioral and emotional problems on the Teacher's Report Form: A cross-national, cross-clinic comparative analysis of gender dysphoric children and adolescents. *Journal of Abnormal Child Psychology*, 42(4), 635–647. doi:10.1007/s10802-013-9804-2

Wahlig, J. L. (2015). Losing the child they thought they had: Therapeutic suggestions for an ambiguous loss perspective with parents of a transgender child. *Journal of GLBT Family Studies*, 11(4), 305–326. doi:10.1080/1550428x.2014.945676

5

Culturally responsive mental health care for transgender and nonbinary individuals

Stephen von Merz, Brittanie Atteberry-Ash and N. Eugene Walls

MENTAL HEALTH SERVICE EXPERIENCES

Transgender and nonbinary (TNB) individuals who are seeking mental health care interface with a system that has a history of ignoring and overtly rejecting their need for support (Seelman et al., 2017). Substandard care, displays of provider discomfort, gender insensitivity, and verbal abuse have been documented (Roller et al., 2015) as leaving some individuals mistrustful of practitioners and unwilling to reach out when mental health services are needed (McCullough et al., 2017; Shipherd et al., 2010). Potentially less obvious, but still harmful, are experiences of microaggressions (Owen et al., 2019) – commonplace, everyday acts, whether intentional or not, that create hostile environments for marginalized people (Sue et al., 2008).

When TNB individuals have experiences with mental health providers that are humiliating (McCann & Sharek, 2016), or transphobic (Elder, 2016), stigma gets reinforced and experiences of marginalization can deepen (Spicer, 2010). This reinforcement of stigma is one of the most significant barriers to care and often results in disengagement with clinical services (Benson, 2013).

Provider education

Practitioners report feeling unprepared to work with TNB individuals, having had little formal or informal education regarding the population (Benson, 2013), leaving them with assumptions and biases about effective practice with TNB clients, an issue even more pronounced for TNB people of color (Noonan et al., 2018).

Frequently TNB clients have to teach providers about concerns regarding gender identity. Even basic content may be missing, such as the difference between sexual orientation and gender identity (Benson, 2013); common health concerns (Taylor et al., 2013); or the lack of legal protections (McCullough et al., 2017). Practitioners may fail to grasp the pervasive fear that can emerge as a result of transphobic experiences, including from medical providers. Further, neither practitioners nor provider educational programs are held accountable for the lack of practitioner knowledge and skills in providing competent services to TNB individuals (Shipherd et al., 2010).

It is also critical that practitioners understand what is *not* affirming for their clients. Unaware therapists are more likely to enact these behaviors, potentially rupturing the therapeutic relationship and causing harm (Mikalson et al., 2012). A well-meaning provider may erroneously believe that being kind is all that is needed to be affirming to TNB clients, failing to realize that subtle non-affirming interactions and microaggressions can be harmful.

Service approaches

Some concerns that TNB people bring to providers may be directly associated with gender identity status, transition, or life experiences as a TNB person, while other concerns may not. However, even seemingly unrelated concerns can be exacerbated by living in a transphobic world. Practitioners should neither assume that all concerns relate to the client's TNB identity, nor assume that unrelated concerns are not influenced by experiences of invalidation through lived experiences.

One approach to balancing this tension is having familiarity with common trends impacting TNB-identified individuals, and being prepared to integrate this knowledge into practice. Giving thought to the best ways of inquiring about these common concerns prior to working with TNB clients – the skill of culturally educated questioning (Rodriguez & Walls, 2000) – can help clinicians feel more confident in their abilities to embody cultural humility (Hook et al., 2017). Remembering that the client is the expert on their lived experience, supporting the clients' self-determination, and using strengths-based approaches can prevent stereotyping that may occur with familiarity of cultural trends.

Mental health concerns

As with cisgender adults, concerns that TNB adults bring to practitioners vary. Some are common issues, like mood disorders, self-esteem concerns, and trauma-related issues. Even with these more common concerns, the etiology may differ from similar concerns for cisgender clients, necessitating a different approach. Other concerns are unique to TNB clients and may include concerns about coming out or transition-related issues, requiring specialized knowledge.

Anxiety and depression

Prevalence of anxiety is two to three times higher among TNB adults than cisgender adults, with social anxiety disorder as the most common type (Harvard Medical

School, 2005; Millet et al., 2017). Similarly, depression is two to three times higher among TNB individuals (Adams et al., 2017; Reisner et al., 2016).

Factors associated with elevated rates of anxiety and depression include discrimination, violence, the stress of concealment, internalized transphobia, and fear of rejection (Bockting et al., 2013; Budge et al., 2013; Testa et al., 2015). TNB individuals in early stages of identity development may be at an increased risk for mood disorders (Testa et al., 2014), suggesting that this is an important time for involvement with affirming mental health services (Pflum et al., 2015).

For TNB individuals who desire them, gender-affirming medical interventions may act to reduce experiences of gender-related victimization by aligning one's appearance with society's binary gender norms (Butler et al., 2019). While research consistently finds a relationship between hormone therapy and reduced levels of anxiety and depression (White Hughto & Reisner, 2016), more complex patterns have emerged when examining other medical interventions such as chest surgery (Tomita et al., 2019).

Suicidality and non-suicidal self-injury (NSSI)

Elevated rates of suicidality have consistently been found among TNB populations, with approximately 32–40% of transgender adults having attempted suicide (Adams et al., 2017; James et al., 2016; Reisner et al., 2016), a rate higher than cisgender heterosexual and LGB populations (Mathy, 2002). Suicidality is particularly elevated among transgender college students with more than two-thirds reporting ideation and over one-third then reporting attempts (Liu et al., 2018).

While both suicidality and NSSI are related to physical damage to one's body, suicidality has the expressed intention to end one's life, while NSSI is undertaken to better cope (Whitlock et al., 2015). Regardless, they are strongly correlated and share similar risk factors (Nock et al., 2006). Rates of NSSI among TNB individuals is high, with 53.3% reporting lifetime rates and 22.3% reporting past year behavior (Jackman et al., 2018). NSSI among TNB people appears to be associated with body dissatisfaction, lack of family support, lower self-esteem, lower social support, perceived or anticipated rejection, and younger age (Jackman et al., 2018).

Post-traumatic stress disorder (PTSD)

Up to 61% of TNB respondents report past month PTSD symptoms (Reisner et al., 2016), compared to 7.3% of US adults (Roberts et al., 2011). Given the increased risk for acute traumatic experiences, including interpersonal and collective violence (Xavier et al., 2004), increased rates are not surprising.

Higher PTSD scores among TNB people are associated with higher rates of discrimination, childhood abuse, partner violence, nonbinary identity, unstable housing, depression, polydrug use, and living full-time in one's identified gender (Richmond et al., 2012). Transmasculine identity and younger age are also associated with lower PTSD scores. Hormones, chest surgery, and genital surgery are associated with decreased rates of PTSD symptoms for transmasculine individuals, but no relationship was found for transfeminine individuals (Tomita et al., 2019).

Eating disorders

TNB adults demonstrate elevated risks for eating disorders (Diemer et al., 2015). Unlike cisgender populations, where eating disorder pathology is associated with general affect disturbance and regulation, among TNB individuals, dissatisfaction with one's body – particularly with features incongruent with one's gender identity – may be the primary underlying mechanism (Diemer et al., 2015), suggesting that the risk of symptoms may be secondary to body dysmorphia (McClain & Peebles, 2016). Jones and colleagues (2016) found significant body image improvement after having hormone or surgical treatment, and TNB individuals who have undergone a gender-affirming medical intervention report lower levels of symptomology compared to those who wanted medical interventions but had not yet done so (Testa et al., 2017). Standard treatment approaches for eating disorder symptoms might best be addressed with strategies that ameliorate body dissatisfaction, including social transition, puberty blockers, hormone treatment, and gender-affirming medical interventions.

Coming out

The coming out process for TNB adults is explored more extensively in Chapter 11 of this text. However, given its centrality to identity development that may emerge in clinical settings, it warrants a brief mention. There are two distinct aspects of coming out: (1) coming out to one's self, and (2) disclosure to others. The process of coming out, especially to oneself, can be delayed by internalized transphobia, experiences of discrimination, stigma, and fear of other's reactions (Rood et al., 2017), issues of danger, social isolation, the importance of affirming communities, mentorship to foster healthy identity formation, and support for disclosure to others (Levitt & Ippolito, 2014). Disclosure to friends and family is often impacted by the same factors with internalized oppression, fear of rejection, stigma, and other feared consequences of publicly acknowledging one's identity hindering disclosure to others (Collazo et al., 2013). Equating complete openness about one's TNB identity with good mental health may fail to recognize contextual factors or honor client self-determination given some TNB individuals may simply identify as their gender, without a trans or nonbinary adjective, and others may be strategically open about their identity to manage safety issues and mental health energy. Finally, it is important to remember that disclosing to others is a lifelong process that exposes one to the risk of rejection repeatedly.

Transition-related concerns

Understanding guidelines regarding transition-related concerns that TNB individuals may present is helpful; however, it is critical to remember that not all TNB clients desire the same aspects of transition, if any medical transition at all (Factor & Rothblum, 2008). Because most guidelines focus on assisting clients through the identity development process toward an expected transition process (Riley et al., 2011), they may not be well-suited for those who identify as nonbinary or do not want to transition medically. TNB individuals are diverse in their desire for hormones and surgery, and it is important that therapists understand the process of transitioning for those who are interested, while also understanding the various paths to relieving gender discomfort or dysphoria for those who may not be.

While we have outlined some common mental health concerns that a clinician may find during their work with TNB clients, there are other important concerns, including substance abuse (see Chapter 6), and partner violence (see Chapter 16), that also have high rates of prevalence among TNB individuals.

Affirmative practice

Lev's (2013) book outlines practice guidelines for working with TNB clients and includes terminology, assessment guidelines, treatment recommendations, clinical vignettes, and helpful clinical documentation examples; however, intersectional approaches and work specifically with nonbinary clients is scant. Collazo and colleagues (2013) offer components of trans-affirmative practice with a focus on assessment, advocacy, and the role of practitioners in supporting transition. In 2015, the American Psychological Association released a set of 16 guidelines on working with TNB clients, organized into five clusters: (a) foundational knowledge/awareness; (b) stigma, discrimination, and barriers to care; (c) lifespan development; (d) assessment, therapy, and intervention; and (e) research, education, and training.

Creating a welcoming environment

One facilitator of trans-affirmative practice is ensuring a welcoming environment (Noonan et al., 2018), including ensuring that both practitioners and staff are knowledgeable about TNB individuals and understand the importance of using the name and pronouns that clients use (Kattari et al., 2018; McCullough et al., 2017). Indications of a welcoming environment include both aspects of the physical environment (e.g., having all-gender bathrooms) and interactional aspects. Interactional aspects include training in culturally competent care provision; provider advocacy on behalf of clients; appropriate responses when enacted stigma is experienced; and direct discussion of issues related to gender and race for TNB people of color.

Provider and staff knowledge/response

A second aspect of trans-affirmative practice is provider and staff knowledge and competence that includes education about TNB issues and people and having a nonjudgmental and supportive stance (Elder, 2016; McCullough et al., 2017; Noonan et al., 2018). Provider knowledge and sensitivity are two of the primary factors in whether or not to seek and/or remain involved in mental health care (White & Fontenot, 2019). Practitioners should obtain necessary trans-specific education rather than expect their clients to educate them (Mizock & Lewis, 2008). Additionally, providers should have working knowledge of The World Professional Associates for Transgender Health's (WPATH) Standards of Care (SOC) as well as the Informed Consent Model (Schulz, 2017).

Therapeutic alliance

One factor in mental health services is the therapeutic relationship, with a good working alliance being a strong predictor of positive affect, self-esteem, connectedness, and optimism (Nuetzel et al., 2007). Practitioners should create ongoing plans for developing and maintaining their therapeutic alliance with TNB clients (Collazo et al., 2013). Predictors of a strong therapeutic relationship include unconditional positive regard toward the client, demonstration of empathy, and building trust (Peschken & Johnson, 1997). As TNB clients often experience decreased levels of social support (Budge et al., 2013) and stigma in interpersonal relationships (Bockting et al., 2013), the therapeutic relationship can be particularly important to TNB clients and foster faster improvement (Leibert et al., 2011). To be an effective advocate, providers should be knowledgeable about unique challenges experienced by TNB clients, and willing to support clients interfacing with transphobic systems (Collazo et al., 2013; Riley et al., 2011). A non-judgmental, supportive stance is evidenced when TNB clients experience providers as affirming and not pathologizing their gender identity and demonstrating their appreciation of the client's unique experiences leading to increased interpersonal comfort and more openness during sessions (Benson, 2013; McCullough et al., 2017).

Transition-related care and support

The process of transitioning is different for each person, with some clients seeing transitioning as a long term process, preferring to identify as TNB. Conversely, many see their transition as a final event and no longer identify with being transgender, but as their identified gender or sex (Spicer, 2010). Clients may require advocacy to facilitate legal, medical, or social transitions (Collazo et al., 2013) with clinical services frequently the first step toward medical transition. As such, understanding the role of the mental health professional in both the WPATH SOC model and the Informed Consent Model is critical.

Medical transition

TNB clients face significant barriers, including expenses and limited insurance coverage, to receiving medical services related to their transition and are often reluctant to seek care due to past rejection, trauma, and fear of disclosure of their transgender status (Spicer, 2010). They may be confused, misinformed, or overwhelmed with gender dysphoria, or various dilemmas related to their decision to begin the medical transition process (Mizock & Lewis, 2008).

WPATH SOC

WPATH's SOC has evolved away from gatekeeping and continues to do so in response to the movement to humanize and depathologize transgender care (WPATH, 2012). With the diversity of needs of those seeking care (Zucker & Spitzer, 2005), there is mounting support for the use of individualized strategies. As such, SOC guidelines can be modified based on each client's situation, the clinical experiences of the practitioner, and available resources. Transition may include: (a) changes in gender expression, including living in their identified gender; (b) hormone replacement therapy to feminize or masculinize the body; (c) surgery to change primary and/or secondary sex characteristics; and (d) counseling to explore gender identity, distress caused by gender dysphoria, or to enhance support. Clinicians can facilitate informed client-driven decision-making through a comprehensive evaluation and exploration of co-occurring mental health issues and the provision of options to address gender identity (Lev, 2009).

The WPATH SOC approach relies on a gender dysphoria diagnosis, characterized by a marked incongruence between the gender one experiences, and the gender socially associated with the sex assigned at birth, manifesting in symptoms such as a strong desire to be or have the sex characteristics of a different gender (WPATH, 2012). In addition to a formal diagnosis, letters from practitioners recommending sex reassignment surgeries are required. Having a therapist who knows the process well makes the process easier, while having a co-occurring mental health diagnosis makes it more difficult (Pinto & Moleiro, 2015).

Informed Consent Model

An alternative to the WPATH SOC model and the requisite diagnosis of gender dysphoria is the Informed Consent Model of TNB care (Schulz, 2017). Historically, researchers and practitioners have viewed the transgender experience through a narrow diagnostic lens and have neglected to acknowledge the diverse experiences of those who identify as TNB. The Informed Consent Model eschews this approach, allowing clients to access hormone and surgical interventions without undergoing mental health evaluation or referral from a mental health specialist, just as cisgender people are able to consent to hormone access and surgical intervention. This model demonstrates promise for the treatment and understanding of the transgender experience outside the lens of medical pathologization.

Legal transition

Identity documents that reflect an individual's name and gender impact everything from employment applications to boarding airplanes. Practitioners should become familiar with processes and costs associated with changing one's name, legal sex on birth certificates, sex designation on driver's licenses, information on passports, and naturalization paperwork. In most states, the process varies by task and since these processes (with the exception of passports and naturalization paperwork) are under the jurisdiction of states, there is significant variation. In some states, changes depend on whether the individual has received certain cost- and health-prohibitive surgeries (Eligon, 2011). Passports and naturalization paperwork are under federal jurisdiction and are more difficult to change under the current administration. Many TNB individuals in the US report that not all of their identity documents are updated, and, presentation of an ID with a name or gender that fails to match gender presentation can result in verbal harassment, denial of benefits or services, or assault (James et al., 2016). The process of updating documents for undocumented TNB individuals is extremely difficult. Up-to-date information on legal options for modifying identity documents by state can be found on the Movement Advancement Project website (www.lgbtmap.org).

Navigating systems and social contexts

From housing, employment, and even the gender binary that society often operates under, TNB people experience microaggressions and overt discrimination in places that cisgender people generally consider harmless or even helpful. Knowing how TNB people may experience the everyday differently than their cisgender counterparts is important in order to advocate for their TNB clients effectively.

Discrimination

Approximately 23% of TNB individuals experience housing discrimination with 12% reporting experiencing homelessness due to being TNB (James et al., 2016). Housing discrimination can be experienced in several contexts, from homeownership and renting to homeless shelters, and within college dormitories (Seelman, 2014). TNB people are twice as likely to face unemployment compared to the rest of the population (Human Rights Campaign, 2013) and are more likely to report incomes below the poverty line despite having comparable or higher levels of education (Center for American Progress, 2015). Many report workplace mistreatment, hiding their gender identity, not asking for correct pronouns, and delaying transition to avoid workplace discrimination (James et al., 2016), with workplace issues a leading reason for seeking counseling (Mizock & Mueser, 2014). Anticipation of negative workplace experiences may lead some TNB people to leave work, change jobs, change career paths, and even pursue additional education in order to mediate trauma related to transitioning at work (Mizock et al., 2017). Often these experiences are driven by the lack of inclusive workplace policies at the employer, state, and national levels (Kirk & Belovics, 2008).

Daily fear and internalized transphobia

The fear of hate crimes often weighs heavily on TNB individuals. Hate crime data in the US demonstrates that TNB individuals are at a lifetime risk for violent encounters, including sexual violence, often perpetrated by known people, and many expect their lifespan to be cut short from a hate crime (Stotzer, 2009). Fears of violence and the frequent negative messages about TNB people and communities via social messages, family members, media, and governmental institutions are often internalized by TNB individuals, resulting in negative mental health (Rood et al., 2017). Understanding how one's sense of self and community plays a role in clinical interventions is needed to address societal barriers faced by the TNB community. It is important to recognize the intersectional experiences that many TNB people with other stigmatized identities face as rates of victimization may be even higher (Kattari et al., 2016).

Understanding the complexity of the experiences that TNB people face is a necessary part of understanding for mental health providers. It is also critical to be informed of the current policy context in the location in which providers are practicing. Knowing policies regarding housing, employment, identification, and health care that often impact TNB community members within the geographic area can improve a practitioner's success. In addition, addressing one's own biases that may manifest in interactions with TNB individuals is critical for practitioners to insure cultural humility and a non-judgmental approach in service provision. Finally, given the embeddedness of transphobia in many systems of care, practitioners should be prepared to advocate for fair and just treatment of their TNB clients.

ACTIVITY

Using the case study below, draft a letter recommending top surgery for your client, Miguel Doe. Your letter should be printed on professional letterhead and use affirming language without misgendering or deadnaming, noting if your client has not legally changed their name. It should include (a) client's date of birth, (b) your relationship, duration, and frequency of contact, (c) client's history of dysphoria and ways in which they are affirming their gender, (d) stability/instability in professional, academic, financial, and relational realms, (e) client's understanding of the benefits/costs of the recommended procedure (e.g., not reversible, risk of infection), (f) adequacy of aftercare plan, (g) your availability for consultation and coordination, (h) client's capacity to give consent to treatment and make fully informed decisions, and (i) history of mental health treatment and medications, including any diagnoses. The letter must state that the individual meets the criteria for Gender Dysphoria. After completing your draft letter, compare it to the sample provided in Eley (2018).

CASE STUDY

Miguel Doe (active legal name, name change in 2014) is requesting a referral letter for his surgeon, Dr. Jensen, for the following upper body/"top" surgery: subcutaneous mastectomy. He is being followed in primary care by his endocrinologist, Dr. J. Thomas. At intake, Mr. Doe self-identified as a trans man, using male pronouns, and has masculinized through prescribed hormones for two years.

Mr. Doe is a 27-year-old Latinx client born on March 20, 1992, who has maintained active participation in treatment with you since beginning services on December 17, 2018. He moved to the area in 2018 for work and currently serves as a manager for a national grocery chain. He began his physical and social transition in 2015, sought individual therapy (IT) services for himself in 2017, and saw a social worker at Family Health Services from 1/2017–11/2018. He has saved for two years and understands the permanence, costs, recovery time, and possible complications of this procedure.

Mr. Doe reports he "never ever felt like a girl." "I would always play 'house' as the dad with my friends and was only comfortable in what others considered to be 'boys' clothes." As a teenager, he became aware of his attraction to girls and came out as a lesbian; however, he "never really felt like that label fit or seemed to fit in with the lesbian community." He has had several losses in his life, including being disowned from his parents at age 22 after coming out. He has worked in therapy to address these losses while developing a strong support system, including his two younger siblings who have "always been there", his partner, and "an affirming friend group."

Mr. Doe has responded well to the medical masculinization procedures, building a productive and meaningful life as a male. He is highly revered by his co-workers and employer, and is in a relationship with someone that "gets [him] culturally and physically". He reports that his life would be "greatly improved" by having this surgery so that his body is more aligned with [his] gender identity. He meets the WPATH requirements for this referral and the DSMV criteria for Gender Dysphoria (ICD 10: F64.1). He reports no health or substance abuse problems. His pre-op appointment is scheduled in six weeks. His presentation includes a consolidated and congruent physical and psychological male gender identity and has dysphoria with his genitals.

The subcutaneous mastectomy is the next appropriate step, and he demonstrates emotional and practical readiness for the procedure. He has insurance coverage for the procedure, an aftercare plan, and is fully capable of making an informed decision about this surgery. He is aware of the potential benefits and risks, feeling that the benefits "far outweigh" the risks. He is reasonably expected to follow all pre- and post-surgical treatment recommendations responsibly.

RESOURCES

Articles

Davy, Z. (2015). The DSM-5 and the politics of diagnosing transpeople. *Archives of Sexual Behavior, 44*, 1165–1176.

Davy, Z. (2018). What is gender dysphoria? A critical systematic narrative review. *Transgender Health, 3*(1), 159–169. doi:10.1089/trgh.2018.0014

Schneider, C., Cerwenka, S., Nieder, T. O., Briken, P., Cohen-Kettenis, P. T., Cuypere, G., & Richter-Appelt, H. (2016). Measuring gender dysphoria: A multicenter examination and comparison of the Utrecht gender dysphoria scale and the gender identity/gender dysphoria questionnaire for adolescents and adults. *Archives of Sexual Behavior, 45*, 551–558.

Zeglin, R. J., Van Dam, D., & Hergenrather, K. C. (2017). An introduction to proposed human sexuality counseling competencies. *International Journal for the Advancement of Counselling, 40*(2), 105–121.

Books

Chang, S. C., Singh, A. A., & dickey, l. m. (2018). *A clinician's guide to gender-affirming care: Working with transgender and gender nonconforming clients*. Oakland, CA: Context Press.

DeBord, K. A., Fischer, A. R., Bieschke, K. J., & Perez, R. M. (2017). *Handbook of sexual orientation and gender diversity in counseling and psychotherapy*. Washington, DC: American Psychological Association.

Dentato, M. P. (Ed.). (2017). *Social work practice with the LGBTQ community: The intersection of history, health, mental health, and policy factors.* New York, NY: Oxford University Press. [See chapter 16 for relevant information].

Eckstrand, K., & Ehrenfeld, J. M. (Eds.). (2016). *Lesbian, gay, bisexual, and transgender healthcare: A clinical guide to preventive, primary, and specialist care.* New York, NY: Springer. [See chapters 5 and 13 for relevant information].

Singh, A. A. (2017). *Affirmative counseling and psychological practice with transgender and gender nonconforming clients.* Washington, DC: American Psychological Association. [See chapters 6 and 7 for relevant information].

Skinta, M. D., & Curtin, A. (Eds.). (2016). *The mindfulness and acceptance practica series. Mindfulness and acceptance for gender and sexual minorities: A clinician's guide to fostering compassion, connection, and equality using contextual strategies.* Oakland, CA: Context Press/New Harbinger Publications.

World Health Organization. (2018). *The ICD-11 classification of mental and behavioral disorders: Clinical descriptions and diagnostic guidelines.* Geneva, Switzerland: Author.

Workbooks

Singh, A. A. (2018). *The queer and transgender resilience workbook: Skills for navigating sexual orientation and gender expression.* Oakland, CA: New Harbinger Publications, Inc.

REFERENCES

Adams, N., Hitomi, M., & Moody, C. (2017). Varied reports of adult transgender suicidality: Synthesizing and describing the peer-reviewed and gray literature. *Transgender Health*, 2, 60–75. doi:10.1089/trgh.2016.0036

American Psychological Association. (2015). Guidelines for psychological practice with transgender and gender nonconforming people. *American Psychologist*, 70(9), 832–864. doi:10.1037/a0039906

Benson, K. E. (2013). Seeking support: Transgender client experiences with mental health services. *Journal of Feminist Family Therapy*, 25(1), 17–40. doi:10.1080/08952833.2013.755081

Bockting, W. O., Miner, M. H., Swinburne Romine, R. E., Hamilton, A., & Coleman, E. (2013). Stigma, mental health, and resilience in an online sample of the U.S. transgender population. *American Journal of Public Health*, 103, 943–951. doi:10.2105/AJPH.2013.301241

Budge, S. L., Adelson, J. L., & Howard, K. A. (2013). Anxiety and depression in transgender individuals: The roles of transition status, loss, social support, and coping. *Journal of Consulting and Clinical Psychology*, 81, 545–557. doi:10.1037/a0031774

Butler, R. M., Horenstein, A., Gitlin, M., Testa, R. J., Kaplan, S. C., Swee, M. B., & Heimberg, R. G. (2019). Social anxiety among transgender and gender nonconforming individuals: The role of gender-affirming medical interventions. *Journal of Abnormal Psychology*, 128, 25–31. doi:10.1037/abn0000399

Center for American Progress. (2015). *Paying an unfair price—The financial penalty for being transgender in America.* Retrieved from www.lgbtmap.org/file/paying-an-unfair-price-transgender.pdf

Collazo, A., Austin, A., & Craig, S. L. (2013). Facilitating transition among transgender clients: Components of effective clinical practice. *Clinical Social Work Journal*, 41, 228–237. doi:10.1007/s10615-013-0436-3

Diemer, E. W., Grant, J. D., Munn-Chernoff, M. A., Patterson, D. A., & Duncan, A. E. (2015). Gender identity, sexual orientation, and eating-related pathology in a national sample of college students. *Journal of Adolescent Health*, 57, 144–149. doi:10.1016/j.jadohealth.2015.03.003

Elder, A. B. (2016). Experiences of older transgender and gender nonconforming adults in psychotherapy: A qualitative study. *Psychology of Sexual Orientation and Gender Diversity*, 3(2), 180–186. doi:10.1037/sgd0000154

Eley, S. (2018). *Providing mental health assessments for gender affirming surgery referral letters*. Retrieved from https://fenwayhealth.org/wp-content/uploads/Assessments-for-gender-affirming-surgeries-Sarah-Eley-SLIDES.pdf

Eligon, J. (2011, March 11). Suits dispute city rule on recording sex changes. *The New York Times*. Retrieved from https://www.nytimes.com/2011/03/23/nyregion/23gender.html

Factor, R., & Rothblum, E. (2008). Exploring gender identity and community among three groups of transgender individuals in the United States: MTFs, FTMs, and genderqueers. *Health Sociology Review*, 17(3), 235–253. doi:10.5172/hesr.451.17.3.235

Harvard Medical School. (2005). *National Comorbidity Survey (NCS)*. Retrieved from www.hcp.med.harvard.edu/ncs/index.php

Hook, J. N., Davis, D., Owen, J., & DeBlaere, C. (2017). *Cultural humility: Engaging diverse identities in therapy*. Washington, DC: American Psychological Association.

Human Rights Campaign. (2013). *Transgender workers at greater risk for unemployment and poverty*. Retrieved from https://www.hrc.org/press/transgender-workers-at-greater-risk-for-unemployment-and-poverty

Jackman, K. B., Dolezal, C., Levin, B., Honig, J. C., & Bockting, W. O. (2018). Stigma, gender dysphoria, and nonsuicidal self-injury in a community sample of transgender individuals. *Psychiatry Research*, 269, 602–609. doi:10.1016/j.psychres.2018.08.092

James, S. E., Herman, J. L., Rankin, S., Keisling, M., Mottet, L., & Anafi, M. (2016). *The report of the 2015 US Transgender Survey*. Washington, DC: National Center for Transgender Equality.

Jones, B. A., Haycraft, E., Murjan, S., & Arcelus, J. (2016). Body dissatisfaction and disordered eating in trans people: A systematic review of the literature. *International Review of Psychiatry*, 28(1), 81–94. doi:10.3109/09540261.2015.1089217

Kattari, S., O'Connor, A., & Kattari, L. (2018). Development and validation of the transgender inclusive behavior scale (TIBS). *Journal of Homosexuality*, 65(2), 181–186. doi:10.1080/00918369.2017.1314160

Kattari, S. K., Whitfield, D. L., Walls, N. E., Langenderfer-Magruder, L., & Ramos, D. (2016). Policing gender through housing and employment discrimination: Comparison of discrimination experiences of transgender and cisgender LGBQ individuals. *Journal of the Society for Social Work and Research*, 7(3), 427–447. doi:10.1086/68692

Kirk, J., & Belovics, R. (2008). Understanding and counseling transgender clients. *Journal of Employment Counseling*, 45(1), 29–43.

Leibert, T. W., Smith, J. B., & Agaskar, V. R. (2011). Relationship between the working alliance and social support on counseling outcome. *Journal of Clinical Psychology*, 67(7), 709–719. doi:10.1002/jclp.20800

Lev, A. I. (2013). *Transgender emergence: Therapeutic guidelines for working with gender-variant people and their families*. New York, NY: Routledge.

Lev, A. (2009). The ten tasks of the mental health provider: Recommendations for revision of the world professional association for transgender health's standards of care. *International Journal of Transgenderism*, 11(2), 74–99. doi:10.1080/15532730903008032

Levitt, H. M., & Ippolito, M. R. (2014). Being transgender: The experience of transgender identity development. *Journal of Homosexuality*, 61(12), 1727–1758. doi:10.1080/00918369.2014.95126

Liu, C. H., Stevens, C., Wong, S. H. M., Yasui, M., & Chen, J. A. (2018). The prevalence and predictors of mental health diagnoses and suicide among US college students: Implications for addressing disparities in service use. *Depression and Anxiety*, 36, 8–17. doi:10.1002/da.22830

Mathy, R. M. (2002). Transgender identity and suicidality in a nonclinical sample: Sexual orientation, psychiatric history, and compulsive behaviors. *Journal of Psychology & Human Sexuality*, 14, 47–65. doi:10.1300/J056v14n04_03

McCann, E., & Sharek, D. (2016). Mental health needs of people who identify as transgender: A review of the literature. *Archives of Psychiatric Nursing*, *30*(2), 280–285. doi:10.1016/j. apnu.2015.07.003

McClain, Z., & Peebles, R. (2016). Body image and eating disorders among lesbian, gay, bisexual, and transgender youth. *Pediatric Clinics of North America*, *63*(6), 1079–1090. doi:10.1016/j.pcl.2016.07.008

McCullough, R., Dispenza, F., Parker, L. K., Viehl, C. J., Chang, C. Y., & Murphy, T. M. (2017). The counseling experiences of transgender and gender nonconforming clients. *Journal of Counseling and Development*, *95*(4), 423–434. doi:101002/jcad.12157

Mikalson, P., Pardo, S., & Green, J. (2012). *First, do no harm: Reducing disparities for lesbian, gay, bisexual, transgender, queer and questioning populations in California. The California LGBTQ Reducing Mental Health Disparities Population Report.* Retrieved from www.eqcai.org/atf/cf/%7B8cca0e2f-faec-46c1-8727-cb02a7d1b3cc%7D/FIRST_DO_NO_HARM-LGBTQ_REPORT.PDF

Millet, N., Longworth, J., & Arcelus, J. (2017). Prevalence of anxiety symptoms and disorders in the transgender population: A systematic review of the literature. *International Journal of Transgenderism*, *18*(1), 27–38. doi:10.1080/15532739.2016.1258353

Mizock, L., & Lewis, T. K. (2008). Trauma in transgender populations: Risk, resilience, and clinical care. *Journal of Emotional Abuse*, *8*(3), 335–354. doi:10.1080/10926790802262523

Mizock, L., & Mueser, K. T. (2014). Employment, mental health, internalized stigma, and coping with transphobia among transgender individuals. *Psychology of Sexual Orientation and Gender Diversity*, *1*(2), 146–158. doi:10.1037/sgd0000029

Mizock, L., Woodrum, T. D., Riley, J., Sotilleo, E. A., Yuen, N., & Ormerod, A. J. (2017). Coping with transphobia in employment: Strategies used by transgender and gender-diverse people in the United States. *International Journal of Transgenderism*, *18*(3), 282–294. doi:10.1080/15532739.2017.1304313

Nock, M. K., Joiner, T. E., Gordon, K. H., Lloyd-Richardson, E., & Prinstein, M. J. (2006). Non-suicidal self-injury among adolescents: Diagnostic correlates and relation to suicide attempts. *Psychiatry Research*, *144*, 65–72.

Noonan, E. J., Sawning, S., Combs, R., Weingartner, L. A., Martin, L. J., Jones, V. F., & Holthouser, A. (2018). Engaging the transgender community to improve medical education and prioritize healthcare initiatives. *Teaching and Learning in Medicine*, *30*(2), 119–132. doi:10.1080/10401334.2017.1365718

Nuetzel, E. J., Larsen, R. J., & Prizmic, Z. (2007). The dynamics of empirically derived factors in the therapeutic relationship. *Journal of the American Psychoanalytic Association*, *55*(4), 1321–1353. doi:10.1177/000306510705500411

Owen, J., Tao, K. W., & Drinane, J. M. (2019). Microaggressions: Clinical impact and psychological harm. In G. C. Torino, D. P. Rivera, C. M. Capodiluop, K. L. Nadal, & W. W. Sue (Eds.), *Microaggression theory: Influence and implications* (pp. 67–85). Hoboken, NJ: John Wiley & Sons.

Peschken, W., & Johnson, M. (1997). Therapist and client trust in the therapeutic relationship. *Psychotherapy Research*, *7*(4), 439–447. doi:10.1080/10503309712331332133

Pflum, S. R., Testa, R. J., Balsam, K. F., Goldblum, P. B., & Bongar, B. (2015). Social support, trans community connectedness, and mental health symptoms among transgender and gender nonconforming adults. *Psychology of Sexual Orientation and Gender Diversity*, *2*, 281–286. doi:10.1037/sgd0000122

Pinto, N., & Moleiro, C. (2015). Gender trajectories: Transsexual people coming to terms with their gender identities. *Professional Psychology: Research and Practice*, *46*(1), 12–20. doi:10.1037/a0036487

Reisner, S. L., Katz-Wise, S. L., Gordon, A. R., Corliss, H. L., & Austin, S. B. (2016). Social epidemiology of depression and anxiety by gender identity. *Journal of Adolescent Health*, *59*(2), 203–208.

Richmond, K. A., Burnes, T., & Carroll, K. (2012). Lost in trans-lation: Interpreting systems of trauma for transgender clients. *Traumatology, 18*(1), 45–57. doi:10.1177/1534765610396726

Riley, E. A., Wong, W. K., & Sitharthan, G. (2011). Counseling support for the forgotten transgender community. *Journal of Gay and Lesbian Social Services, 23*(3), 395–410.

Roberts, A. L., Gilman, S. E., Breslau, J., Breslau, N., & Koenen, K. C. (2011). Race/ethnic differences in exposure to traumatic events, development of post-traumatic stress disorder, and treatment-seeking for post-traumatic stress disorder in the United States. *Psychological Medicine, 41*, 71–83.

Rodriguez, R. R., & Walls, N. E. (2000). Culturally educated questioning: Toward a skills-based approach in multicultural counselor training. *Applied & Preventive Psychology, 9*, 89–99.

Roller, C. G., Sedlak, C., & Draucker, C. B. (2015). Navigating the system: How transgender individuals engage in health care services. *Journal of Nursing Scholarship, 47*(5), 417–424. doi:10.1111/jnu.12160

Rood, B. A., Reisner, S. L., Puckett, J. A., Surace, F. I., Berman, A. K., & Pantalone, D. W. (2017). Internalized transphobia: Exploring perceptions of social messages in transgender and gender-nonconforming adults. *International Journal of Transgenderism, 18*(4), 411–426. doi:10.1080/15532739.2017.1329048

Schulz, S. L. (2017). The informed consent model of transgender care: An alternative to the diagnosis of gender dysphoria. *Journal of Humanistic Psychology, 58*(1), 72–92. doi:10.1177/0022167817745217

Seelman, K. L. (2014). Recommendations of transgender students, staff, and faculty in the USA for improving college campuses. *Gender and Education, 26*(6), 618–635. doi:10.1080/09540253.2014.935300

Seelman, K. L., Colón-Diaz, M. J. P., LeCroix, R. H., Xavier-Brier, M., & Kattari, L. (2017). Transgender noninclusive healthcare and delaying care because of fear: Connections to general health and mental health among transgender adults. *Transgender Health, 2*(1), 17–28. doi:10.1089/trgh.2016.0024

Shipherd, J. C., Green, K. E., & Abramovitz, S. (2010). Transgender clients: Identifying and minimizing barriers to mental health treatment. *Journal of Gay & Lesbian Mental Health, 14*(2), 94–108. doi:10.1080/19359701003622875

Spicer, S. S. (2010). Healthcare needs of the transgender homeless population. *Journal of Gay & Lesbian Mental Health, 14*(4), 320–339. doi:10.1080/19359705.2010.505844

Stotzer, R. L. (2009). Violence against transgender people: A review of United States data. *Aggression and Violent Behavior, 14*(3), 170–179. doi:10.1016/j.avb.2009.01.006

Sue, D. W., Capodilupo, C. M., Nadal, K. L., & Torino, G. C. (2008). Racial microaggressions and the power to define reality. *American Psychologist, 63*(4), 277–279. doi:10.1037/0003-066x.63.4.277

Taylor, E., Jantzen, A., & Clow, B. (2013). *Rethinking LGBTQ health*. Halifax, NS, Canada: Atlantic Centre for Excellence for Women's Health.

Testa, R. J., Habarth, J., Peta, J., Balsam, K., & Bockting, W. (2015). Development of the gender minority stress and resilience measure. *Psychology of Sexual Orientation and Gender Diversity, 2*, 65–77. doi:10.1037/sgd0000081

Testa, R. J., Jimenez, C. L., & Rankin, S. (2014). Risk and resilience during transgender identity development: The effects of awareness and engagement with other transgender people on affect. *Journal of Gay & Lesbian Mental Health, 18*, 31–46. doi:10.1080/19359705.2013.805177

Testa, R. J., Rider, G. N., Haug, N. A., & Balsam, K. F. (2017). Gender confirming medical interventions and eating disorder symptoms among transgender individuals. *Health Psychology, 36*, 927–936. doi:10.1037/hea0000497

Tomita, K. K., Testa, R. J., & Balsam, K. F. (2019). Gender-affirming medical interventions and mental health in transgender adults. *Psychology of Sexual Orientation and Gender Diversity, 6*(2), 182–193. doi:10.1037/sgd0000316

White, B. P., & Fontenot, H. B. (2019). Transgender and non-conforming persons' mental healthcare experiences: An integrative review. *Archives of Psychiatric Nursing, 33*(2), 203–210. doi:10.1016/j.apnu.2019.01.005

White Hughto, J. M., & Reisner, S. L. (2016). A systematic review of the effects of hormone therapy on psychological functioning and quality of life in transgender individuals. *Transgender Health, 1*, 21–31. doi:10.1089/trgh.2015.0008

Whitlock, J., Minton, R., Babington, P., & Ernhout, C. (2015). *The relationship between nonsuicidal self-injury and suicide*. The Information Brief Series, Cornell Research Program on Self-Injury and Recovery. Ithaca, NY: Cornell University.

World Professional Association for Transgender Health. (2012). *Standards of care (7th version)*. Retrieved from https://www.wpath.org/publications/soc

Xavier, J., Hitchcock, D., Hollinshead, S., Keisling, M., Lewis, Y., Lombardi, E., ... Williams, B. (2004). *An overview of U.S. trans health priorities: A report by the Eliminating Disparities Working Group, August 2004 Update*. Washington, DC: National Coalition for LGBT Health.

Zucker, K. J., & Spitzer, R. L. (2005). Was the gender identity disorder of childhood diagnosis introduced into DSM-III as a backdoor maneuver to replace homosexuality? A Historical Note. *Journal of Sex & Marital Therapy, 31*(1), 31–42. doi:10.1080/00926230590475251

PART 2

Areas of practice

CHAPTER 6

Substance use and transgender nonbinary populations

Towards inclusive prevention and service provision

Gio Dolcecore, Isaac M. Akapnitis, G. Trey Jenkins, and Cary Leonard Klemmer

TRANSGENDER POPULATIONS AND SUBSTANCE USE

The extant research suggests that transgender and nonbinary (TNB) people are more likely to use substances. Although more study is needed, research on TNB populations has been growing in the last decade. Existing research is limited in that strong measures that assess for gender identity, sexual orientation, and gender expression have not been widely used (The GenIUSS Group, 2014). One major problem of research with TNB populations is that researchers often combine lesbian, gay, bisexual (LGB) and TNB respondents into one category. This generalized approach limits the ability to understand the unique experiences of TNB people that are different from those who are cisgender and LGB (Frohard-Dourlent et al., 2017). Furthermore, this often-used approach frequently has not taken into consideration the diversity of gender within TNB populations and other intersecting identities of TNB people, such as race, culture, and ability, to name a few.

Limited studies have been specifically designed to examine substance use within TNB populations, and important factors likely related to substance use among TNB people have not been examined (e.g., stages of transition, stigmatizing gender-based policies and practices of institutions and society). Importantly, the voices of TNB individuals themselves are sparsely included in research (for examples, see Singh, 2013; Stieglitz, 2010), and thus the ability of existing research to promote self-directed intervention and to improve the lived reality of TNB substance use has limitations (Gruskin et al., 2018).

In this chapter, the authors provide an overview of a theory used to understand substance use/misuse among TNB communities. It discusses the elevated rate of use among the TNB population, affirming prevention and intervention strategies, treatment and policy considerations, existing challenges to improving care, treatment for TNB individuals, and finally, concludes with clinical vignettes for practical understanding.

GENDER MINORITY STRESS THEORY AND SUBSTANCE USE

The numerous negative health experiences documented among LGBTQ2S+ populations as a whole have largely been attributed to the negative consequences of minority specific stigma and stress encountered in the social environment (Goldbach & Gibbs, 2017; Institute of Medicine [IOM], 2011; Klemmer et al., 2018; Meyer, 2003; Testa et al., 2015). Over the past decade, a model of gender minority stress has been adapted using Meyer's (2003) model of sexual minority stress (Testa et al., 2015). Gender minority stress theory suggests that subjection to chronic sustained stress in the form of stigma and discrimination impacts individuals' understanding of themselves (e.g., creating internalized transphobia), and the concealment of their TNB identity (Testa et al., 2015). Gender minority stress is thought to limit transgender individuals' ability to cope, and with limited social support, to lead to negative health experiences (e.g., depression, or substance use) (Goldblum et al., 2012; Testa et al., 2017).

Risk and protective factors

Many risk and protective factors for substance use among TNB populations have been identified. Table 6.1 summarizes and provides examples of many of these factors.

TRANSGENDER ADULT SUBSTANCE USE TRENDS

Substance use/misuse includes binge drinking, tobacco use, non-medical use of prescription drugs (NMUPD), marijuana use (though recent studies and surveys have not differentiated medicinal and recreational use), and additional illicit drug use. Determining prevalence of substance use/misuse and substance use disorders (SUD) among TNB populations is made difficult due to challenges such as exclusion of TNB identities within prevalence surveys, small sample sizes where TNB individuals are included, and minimal opportunities for data collection (e.g., often school or service-based locations), and limited comparison data due to lack of standardized survey tools. Despite these obstacles, research methods are broadening, and a review of the available data indicates that substance use/misuse is often higher among TNB adults and youth than their cisgender counterparts, and due to the challenges described throughout this chapter.

The 2015 U.S. Trans Survey (USTS), one of the largest survey of TNB individuals in the United States (U.S.) to date, includes questions related to substance use

TABLE 6.1 Examples of risk and protective factors for substance use/misuse among TNB populations

Micro Level Risk Factors	Micro Level Protective Factors
Microaggressions: daily verbal, behavioral, and environmental slights and indignities that send denigrating and harmful messages (Nadal, 2018; Sue, 2010):	Care, support, and affirmation of gender identity by family, friends, and other individuals (e.g., coworkers, bosses, teachers, etc.) (Walsh et al., 2016).
<ul><li>"But you're so pretty, why would you want to be a boy?"</li><li>"You're not a *real* woman."</li><li>"If you're not a boy or a girl, then what are you?"</li><li>"Have you had 'the surgery' yet?"</li></ul>	<ul><li>Do not gender clothing, apparel, or appearances. Alternative positive expressions can be "that's so beautiful" to directly compliment someone's clothing attire.</li><li>Do not gender children or family members. Instead, say "how is your sibling(s)/parent(s)" etc.</li><li>Do not place body parts on a gender hierarchy – for instance, some people have a penis/not all men have a penis.</li><li>Honor and use TNB individuals' affirmed names and gender pronouns.</li></ul>
Gender discourses that stabilize beliefs that reinforce a gender binary and that males are "masculine" and females are "feminine".	
Experiences of violence, stigma, and discrimination (Coronel-Villalobos & Saewyc, 2019; James et al., 2016; Scheim et al., 2017).	Forging meaningful connections with others (having a positive impact; being a role model; being well-liked by their community) (Moody et al., 2015).

Mezzo Level Risk Factors	Mezzo Level Protective Factors
Barriers to accessing affirming, competent, and compassionate substance use/misuse treatment providers (Movement Advancement Project [MAP] & National Center for Trans Equality [NCTE], 2018).	Gender-inclusive facilities such as bathrooms, changing rooms, sleeping quarters, and inpatient care facilities.
Limited understanding and gaps in knowledge about appropriate care for TNB communities among health care providers (Peralta & Jauk, 2011).	Inclusive client demographic forms that reflect a wide range of gender diversity and expression, as well as pronouns and chosen names.
High rates of TNB individuals being referred out of care instead of being accepted into existing substance use/misuse programming (Oberheim et al., 2017).	Use of language and treatment modalities that affirm and recognize gender diversity and excludes gender binary discourses. Access to service providers who are affirming and competent in delivering care to TNB individuals (Lyons et al., 2015; Oberheim et al., 2017).
Clinicians/providers asserting TNB individuals are "too complex" for existing programming instead of allocating funding for professional development (Oberheim et al., 2017).	

continued . . .

TABLE 6.1 (continued)

Macro Level Risk Factors	Macro Level Protective Factors
Discrimination, oppression, inequality, institutional violence, and stigma based on gender identity and expression (de Vries, 2015).	Statewide non-discrimination policies that provide protections based on gender identity and expression (MAP & NCTE, 2018).
Systems are designed in the context of oppression and privilege, and policy often does not consider diverse needs, resulting in barriers (de Vries, 2015).	

Risks that Permeate Throughout All Levels
Gender Minority Stress: Cissexism Transphobia Internalized transphobia

informed by the National Survey on Drug Use and Health. Results indicate higher prevalence among TNB than cisgender individuals in current and lifetime cannabis use (25% and 64% compared to 8% and 47% respectively), past month prescription drug misuse (7% vs. 2%), and past month illicit drug use (including marijuana, 29% vs. 10%) (James et al., 2016). This survey found slightly elevated rates of binge drinking (27% vs. 25%), while another study across three years and 120 participating college institutions found that cisgender individuals were more likely to report heavy episodic drinking than TNB individuals, but for those trans individuals who *did* engage in this behavior, they did so with greater frequency (Coulter et al., 2015). Little is currently known about tobacco use (including cigarette and e-cigarette use) among TNB populations. Thirty-six percent of USTS respondents reported using e-cigarettes or vaping products in their lifetime. USTS respondents reported lower lifetime cigarette use compared to the U.S. general population (57% vs. 63%), while reports of past month cigarette use were similar among transgender respondents and the U.S. general population (21% vs. 22% respectively) (James et al., 2016). Another national survey (N=168) found rates as high as 35.5% among TNB populations (Buchting et al., 2017).

The Canadian Pulse Project explored drug use among a transgender population and illustrated similar findings to the USTS's TNB population (Scheim et al., 2017). An estimated 12% of transgender Ontarians had used illegal drugs in the past year and were more likely to use both cocaine and amphetamines as compared to the age-standardized cisgender population. Furthermore, the prevalence of drug use among transgender people in Ontario correlated to higher rates of experiencing social exclusion, homelessness, and assaults.

The USTS and Canadian Pulse Project also inquired about intersecting factors such as age, race, and involvement in the underground economy (e.g., sex work) (James et al., 2016; Scheim et al., 2017). Native American (44%) respondents were the most likely to report consuming at least one pack of cigarettes a day, while Latinx

(32%), Middle Eastern (30%), and Black respondents (30%) reported the highest rates of binge drinking of alcohol in the last month (James et al., 2016). Canadian studies on TNB and Indigenous people illustrate them as the most vulnerable population of substance users due to the ongoing effects of colonization (Lyons et al., 2015). In another study, transgender women of color (Latinx and African Americans) were more likely to binge drink or use injectable drugs compared to the larger transgender population (Wilson et al., 2015).

Where data are available for TNB youth under the age of 18, trends indicate that substance use risk and prevalence is higher for TNB students than their cisgender peers (Day et al., 2017; Johns et al., 2019). One study suggests that prevalence is two to four times higher, with TNB youth reporting earlier drug and alcohol use than their peers (Day et al., 2017). Another study found that TNB students were more likely to report using alcohol or drugs before engaging in sexual activity, and reported higher lifetime use of all substances (27.1% cocaine; 26.1% heroin; 24.9% methamphetamines; 24.9% prescription drug issue) except for marijuana (Johns et al., 2019).

Overall, research shows that substance use among TNB individuals increases for those experiencing violence, homelessness, or living at the intersection of two or more marginalized identities, calling further attention to the need for future research (Coronel-Villalobos & Saewyc, 2019; James et al., 2016).

TREATMENT NEEDS OF TNB POPULATIONS

General treatment considerations

When creating substance use prevention, treatment, and recovery programs, the specific needs of TNB clients must be considered, including their unique risk and protective factors, barriers to accessing affirming health care providers, and their own treatment goals. Despite the fact that nearly 25 years ago groups like the San Francisco LGBT Substance Abuse Task Force identified barriers to accessing care and outlined recommendations for improving treatment facilities for TNB individuals (Oberheim et al., 2017), many challenges still exist today (Lyons et al., 2015).

In many environments, TNB individuals navigate gender binary settings that do not welcome or accommodate gender diversity. Ultimately, when TNB individuals do not feel safe or welcome in treatment settings, they are less likely to remain engaged and may terminate treatment early, or avoid seeking treatment altogether (Lyons et al., 2015). Furthermore, based on the authors' experiences working in treatment settings, individuals with a TNB identity may hide their authentic gender identity or conceal it by using a binary identity in order to access needed treatment options. Clinicians who are unable or unwilling to address their own bias towards TNB individuals also have the potential to cause more harm to their clients and prevent clients from reaching treatment or recovery goals (Oberheim et al., 2017). There is also concern about a lack of providers equipped to support the community: In *Lambda Legal's Survey of Discrimination Against LGBT People and People with HIV*, nearly two-thirds of survey respondents reported that there are not enough substance use treatment providers who have knowledge about providing affirming care to transgender populations; and over 50% reported there are not enough mental health support groups (Lambda Legal, 2010).

Affirming prevention and intervention strategies

Substance use/misuse prevention efforts include prevention education, increased community awareness, strategies that address risk and protective factors, and culturally relevant approaches (Substance Abuse and Mental Health Services Administration [SAMHSA], 2017). For example, the aggressive and exploitative tactics of corporate alcohol and tobacco marketing unduly affect LGBTQ2S+ individuals (Hunt, 2012) and must be addressed and countered within substance use/misuse prevention programming. The Network for LGBT Health Equity (2012) recommends creating marketing materials that highlight LGBTQ2S+-specific themes; using social media as a vehicle for outreach; utilizing messages that focus on overcoming challenges rather than scare tactics and going *to* the community for input and oversight of prevention activities (Gruskin et al., 2018).

It is also important to promote protective factors to prevent and reduce substance use. As outlined in Table 6.1, research has shown that LGBTQ2S+ youth who come from highly rejecting families are three times more likely to use illicit drugs than those who come from families that support their identity (Moody et al., 2015). Thus, developing parental support of their child's identity is a significant factor in preventing substance use/misuse among TNB young people. Parents can further reduce their TNB child's likelihood of substance use/misuse by maintaining open and honest communication about substance use and utilizing positive reinforcement (Harm Reduction Coalition [HRC], n.d.).

A large initiative in North America, Europe, and Australia to reduce substance use/misuse is the implementation of harm reduction, which is both an approach focused on reducing the harm associated with substance use and a movement rooted in social justice. Harm reduction centers the voices of those who use drugs and includes a range of approaches from safer or managed use to abstinence (HRC, 2019). Approaches also include connection to HIV testing, medical screenings, health and mental health services, and wound care for injection-related infections (Centers for Disease Control and Prevention, 2017). When performed correctly, harm reduction approaches can offer TNB individuals an opportunity to understand and manage the risks associated with drug use, plan for safer or reduced use, and make decisions about their readiness for treatment or other services (Robinson, 2014).

Due to the high probability of TNB individuals experiencing trauma, it is necessary that service providers implement trauma and violence-informed care. These approaches are policy and practice-driven and are considerate of histories of violence and trauma, and their impact on health outcomes. By implementing trauma and violence-informed care, a service provider is recognizing TNB individuals' relationship with substances is likely connected to a history of trauma and/or pain (Empson et al., 2017).

Using a natural supports framework can also engage TNB people with their supports, families, and chosen families. This model of practice is used throughout Canada, most often with youth experiencing homelessness (The Change Collective, 2018). However, the model fits well with TNB youth considering they have a high risk of experiencing family breakdown, homelessness, and substance use concerns (Abramovich, 2012). By using this framework, service providers can best support TNB youth by increasing a sense of community, establishing accessible support, and implementing client-driven care.

For TNB adults, being a positive role model for other TNB individuals and being respected by their community have been found to reduce suicidal ideation and attempts. In one study, participants described the importance of having a positive impact on others and creating meaningful connections as reasons for living (Moody et al., 2015). While specific to suicide, these same protective factors could be utilized in treatment settings if substance use risk factors are stemming from isolation, disconnection, or means to cope with stigma and discrimination. Prevention and intervention strategies are reviewed in Table 6.2.

TABLE 6.2 A review of prevention and intervention strategies

Strategies	Description
Client-Centered Care	Providing care that is respectful of TNB identities, and responsive to TNB stressors, preferences, needs and values, and ensuring that TNB individuals' values guide all clinical decisions.
Affirmative Programming	Programs offer all individuals access to LGBTQ2S+ psycho-education, with specific resources for gender diversity.
Professional Development and Requirements	Professionals working with TNB individuals who use substances should have the opportunity to engage in LGBTQ2S+ training that is organized and facilitated by members of the community (Dubin et al., 2018).
Harm Reduction	Harm reduction is a set of practical strategies and ideas aimed at reducing the negative consequences associated with drug use. Calls for the non-judgmental, non-coercive provision of services and resources to people who use drugs and the communities in which they live in order to assist them in reducing attendant harm.
Family Support	Family interventions and resources to support parents of TNB children and youth. Family enhancement workers and/or counselors to help parents best support TNB children and youth who use substances.
Natural Support Engagement	Support TNB individuals building needed relationships with both personal and professional supports. Align TNB individual with supports who can support with substance goals.
Community Engagement	Improve access for TNB within the larger LGBTQ2S+ community. Provide space for TNB individuals to collectively empower one another.

TREATMENT CONSIDERATIONS

Inpatient

More research is needed to document the experiences of TNB people accessing treatment though some considerations for inpatient treatment have been established (Lyons et al., 2015). From the data available, experiences while in care appear to be mixed and range from TNB people being welcomed and respected to being isolated, discriminated against, and verbally, physically, and sexually assaulted by other program participants or staff (Grant et al., 2011).

Other studies, as described previously, indicate that TNB people, especially those of color, experience high rates of harassment, abuse, and denial of care by providers (Lambda Legal, 2010). In order to remain safe, supported, and engaged in treatment, TNB individuals need to feel they are not going to be considered a disturbance or nuisance to treatment, that their presence would not make others feel unsafe or uncomfortable, or that they themselves will be harmed (Lyons et al., 2015). Additionally, providers should consider, along with patient choice/preference, placing clients in treatment based on their gender identity rather than their sex assigned at birth. Passing, the ability to be seen as the gender they identify with, is a binary construct, and for some, a concern that clients may wish to consider when being placed in treatment. Too often, TNB individuals are placed into groups or residential treatment centers without considering the patient choice and often based on sex assigned at birth, placing them at risk for treatment disengagement or discrimination (Lyons et al., 2015). Clinicians should be mindful to engage with clients using their chosen name and correct pronouns. Misgendering, outing a person's TNB identity, and use of TNB people's birth names can harm and stigmatize these clients (Oberheim et al., 2017).

Outpatient and recovery

Clinicians should continually assess for challenges to ongoing care, recovery, and sobriety, including connection to community supports and services that are TNB-affirming (Oberheim et al., 2017). TNB individuals may also need assistance in identifying spaces to socialize and build a community that do not center around alcohol. Historically, bars and nightclubs have been a safe space for LGBTQ2S+ communities to gather, and these settings continue to act as community centers, particularly in localities in which other options for socializing are limited (Hunt, 2012). Providers should be informed of this history and navigate conversations with clients to discuss community involvement in ways that are appropriate for the client's recovery. In addition to or in lieu of in-person supports, clients can also be connected to online resources, especially those who live far from metropolitan centers and lack access to LGBTQ2S+ resources.

Additional considerations should be made for care related to the client's gender transition, if desired by the client. Ongoing internal struggles to self-acceptance and living authentically may continue to impede progress toward sobriety if not addressed (Brooks & McHenry, 2014). Finally, there is a lack of consensus regarding whether LGBQ or TNB individuals should seek treatment in settings that are exclusively for LGBTQ2S+ people, or if general treatment centers should improve their ability to serve this population (Lyons et al., 2015). Regardless of the setting, TNB individuals need TNB-competent and -affirming treatment settings where they can obtain the care necessary to achieve sobriety and other positive health experiences (Lyons et al., 2015; Oberheim et al., 2017).

Provider competency

Competent and affirmative treatment settings for TNB clients are those where staff and providers have developed (a) *knowledge* on the unique needs of TNB clients seeking SUD treatment, (b) *skills* to cultivate and maintain inclusive and non-judgmental attitudes towards TNB clients and, (c) *awareness* of deep-seated personal beliefs about gender identity and transitioning (Oberheim et al., 2017). The cultivation of this body of knowledge, skills, and awareness is an ongoing responsibility of an effective and affirming substance use professional. The authors recommend the following examples as tools to assist in clinical training for staff:

- The Association of Lesbian, Gay, Bisexual, and Transgender Issues in Counseling: *Competencies for counseling with transgender clients* (Burnes et al., 2010)
- American Psychological Association: *Guidelines for psychological practice with transgender and gender nonconforming people* (2015)
- The National LGBT Health Education Center Transgender Health ECHO Program (Fenway Institute, n.d.)

POLICY AND PRACTICE RECOMMENDATIONS

In addition to the above recommendations, policy changes are needed at organizational, statewide, and national levels to prevent, reduce, and address substance use/misuse among TNB populations. These policy recommendations include but are not limited to:

- Creation and implementation of organizational practice standards that require affirming and equitable treatment of TNB individuals in care (e.g., inclusive intake forms and electronic health records; appropriate placement within treatment settings)
- Inclusion of TNB identities in state and nationwide substance use and mental health data collection efforts, such as the National Survey on Drug Use and Health, to demonstrate the existence of TNB individuals, remove stigma, document experiences and needs, and inform policies and programming (Bauer et al., 2017; Brown et al., 2017)
- National policies that allow for the legalization and expansion of harm reduction strategies such as syringe service programs and access to opioid overdose reversal medication (Girouard, 2018; HRC, 2019)

- Laws that prohibit health care providers and treatment centers from refusing care to TNB individuals based on the client's gender and gender expression (MAP & NCTE, 2018)

CLINICAL VIGNETTES

Case 1

Ava is an 18-year-old who has recently accessed walk-in counseling services for substance use. During the session, Ava discloses a history of family domestic violence and observant religiosity. This included living in a Mennonite colony that prohibits diverse gender or sexual identities and promotes a culture of strict gender role compliance. Ava discloses identifying as TNB and struggling with internalized transphobia. Ava states they have used for years to cope with depression, social isolation, and shame.

1. Identify micro, mezzo, and macro aggressions that could be affecting Ava.
2. How have these aggressions influenced a sense of shame for Ava? Consider the correlation between gender expression, religion/faith, and community identities.
3. What are three ways the clinician can support Ava and their needs?

Case 2

Fai is 46 years old and recently came out as TNB. They started hormone replacement therapy six months ago, which marked one full year of sobriety. Fai recently moved to the city from a small town five hours away. Unfortunately, they do not have many friends or family nearby. After 12 years of marriage, Fai was kicked out of the family home for being TNB. Fai has yet to change their legal gender markers and is too afraid to use the shelter system in the city in fear of being misgendered and/or misplaced. Instead, Fai has been living with an acquaintance who is actively using drugs. After bingeing on methamphetamine, Fai accidentally overdosed and was rushed to the hospital. Once stable, Fai disclosed to the social worker they need help with their addiction.

1. Considering Fai's history, what strategies should the social worker consider when supporting Fai?
2. Predict three barriers Fai may likely encounter if they accessed the hospital closest to you right now?
3. What systemic changes would be needed for Fai to feel safe and supported in your jurisdiction?

For the above, how might your answers change if given additional knowledge about the client's gender, gender expression, and additional intersecting identities? For example, how would your responses change if you knew that Ava was transmasculine? If Fai were transfeminine?

REFERENCES

Abramovich, I. (2012). No safe place to go – LGBTQ youth homelessness in Canada: Reviewing the literature. *Canadian Journal of Family and Youth/Le Journal Canadien de Famille et de La Jeunesse*, 4(1), 29–51. doi:10.29173/cjfy16579

American Psychological Association. (2015). Guidelines for psychological practice with transgender and gender nonconforming people. *American Psychologist*, 70(9), 832–864. doi:10.1037/a0039906

Bauer, G. R., Braimoh, J., Scheim, A. I., & Dharma, C. (2017). Transgender-inclusive measures of sex/gender for population surveys: Mixed-methods evaluation and recommendations. *Plos One*, 12(5), 1–28, e0178043. doi:10.1371/journal.pone.0178043.

Brooks, F., & McHenry, B. (2014). *A contemporary approach to substance use disorders and addiction counseling: A counselor's guide to application and understanding*. Alexandria, VA: American Counseling Association.

Brown, T. N. T., Herman, J. L., & Park, A. S. (2017). *Exploring international priorities and best practices for the collection of data about gender minorities, report of meeting June 17, 2016 Amsterdam, The Netherlands*. Los Angeles, CA: The Williams Institute. Retrieved from https://williamsinstitute.law.ucla.edu/wp-content/uploads/Exploring-International-Priorities-and-Best-Practices-March-2017.pdf

Buchting, F. O., Emory, K. T., Scout, Kim, Y., Fagan, P., Vera, L., & Emery, S. (2017). Transgender use of cigarettes, cigars, and e-cigarettes in a national study. *American Journal of Preventative Medicine*, 53(1), e1–e7. doi:10.1016/j.amepre.2016.11.022

Burnes, T. R., Singh, A. A., Harper, A. J., Harper, B., Maxon-Kann, W., & Pickering, D. L., ... Association for Lesbian, Gay, Bisexual and Transgender Issues in Counseling [ALGBTIC] Transgender Committee. (2010). ALGBTIC: Competencies for counseling with transgender clients. *Journal of LGBT Issues in Counseling*, 4(3–4), 135–159.

Centers for Disease Control and Prevention. (2017, August). Reducing harms from injection drug use & opioid use disorder with syringe service programs. Retrieved December 30, 2019, from www.cdc.gov/hiv/pdf/risk/cdchiv-fs-syringe-services.pdf

Coronel-Villalobos, M., & Saewyc, E. (2019). 11. Trading sex and sexual exploitation among transgender youth in Canada. *Journal of Adolescent Health*, 64(2), s6. doi:10.1016/j.jadohealth.2018.10.025

Coulter, R. W. S., Blosnich, J. R., Bukowski, L. A., Herrick, A. L., Siconolfi, D. E., & Stall, R. D. (2015). Differences in alcohol use and alcohol-related problems between transgender- and nontransgender-identified young adults. *Drug and Alcohol Dependence*, 154, 251–259. doi:10.1016/j.drugalcdep.2015.07.006

Day, J. K., Fish, J. N., Perez-Brumer, A., Hatzenbuehler, M. L., & Russell, S. T. (2017). Transgender youth substance use disparities: Results from a population-based sample. *Journal of Adolescent Health*, 61(6), 729–735. doi:10.1016/j.jadohealth.2017.06.024

de Vries, K. M. (2015). Transgender people of color at the center: Conceptualizing a new intersectional model. *Ethnicities*, 15(1), 3–27. doi:10.1177/1468796814547058

Dubin, S. N., Nolan, I. T., Streed, C. G., Jr., Greene, R. E., Radix, A. E., & Morrison, S. D. (2018). Transgender health care: Improving medical students' and residents' training and awareness. *Advances in Medical Education and Practice*, 9, 377–391. doi:10.2147/AMEP.S147183

Empson, S., Cuca, Y. P., Cocohoba, J., Dawson-Rose, C., Davis, K., & Machtinger, E. L. (2017). Seeking safety group therapy for co-occurring substance use disorder and PTSD among transgender women living with HIV: A pilot study. *Journal of Psychoactive Drugs*, 49(4), 344–351. doi:10.1080/02791072.2017.1320733

Fenway Institute. (n.d.). *Transgender health ECHO*. Retrieved January 2, 2020, from www.lgbthealtheducation.org/project-echo/trans-echo/

Frohard-Dourlent, H., Dobson, S., Clark, B. A., Doull, M., & Saewyc, E. M. (2017). "I would have preferred more options": Accounting for non-binary youth in health research. *Nursing Inquiry*, 24(1), e12150. doi:10.1111/nin.12150

Girouard, M. (2018). *Addressing opioid use disorder among LGBTQ populations.* Boston, MA: National LGBT Health Education Center. Retrieved January 6, 2020, from www. lgbthealtheducation.org/wp-content/uploads/2018/06/OpioidUseAmongLGBTQPopulations.pdf

Goldbach, J. T., & Gibbs, J. J. (2017). A developmentally informed adaptation of minority stress for sexual minority adolescents. *Journal of Adolescence, 55,* 36–50. doi:10.1016/j. adolescence.2016.12.007

Goldblum, P., Testa, R. J., Pflum, S., Hendricks, M. L., Bradford, J., & Bongar, B. (2012). The relationship between gender-based victimization and suicide attempts in transgender people. *Professional Psychology: Research and Practice, 43*(5), 468–475. doi:10.1037/ a0029605

Grant, J., Mottet, L., Tanis, J., Harrison, J., Herman, J., & Keisling, M. (2011). *Injustice at every turn: A report of the national transgender discrimination survey.* Washington, DC: National Center for Transgender Equality and National Gay and Lesbian Task Force.

Gruskin, S., Everhart, A., Olivia, D. F., Baral, S., Reisner, S. L., Kismödi, E., … Ferguson, L. (2018). In transition: Ensuring the sexual and reproductive health and rights of transgender populations. A roundtable discussion. *Reproductive Health Matters, 26*(52), 21–32. doi:10.1080/09688080.2018.1490624

Harm Reduction Coalition [HRC]. (n.d.). *Principles of harm reduction.* Retrieved January 6, 2020, from https://harmreduction.org/about-us/principles-of-harm-reduction/

Hunt, J. (2012). *Why gay and transgender population experiences higher rates of substance use.* Washington, DC: Center for American Progress.

Institute of Medicine [IOM]. (2011). *The health of lesbian, gay, bisexual, and transgender people: Building a foundation for better understanding.* Washington, DC: National Academies Press.

James, S. E., Herman, J. L., Rankin, S., Keisling, M., Mottet, L., & Anafi, M. (2016). *The report of the 2015 U.S. Transgender Survey.* Washington, DC: National Center for Transgender Equality.

Johns, M., Lowry, R., Andrzejewski, J., Barrios, L., Demissie, Z., McManus, T., … Underwood, M. (2019). Transgender identity and experiences of violence victimization, substance use, suicide risk, and sexual risk behavior among high school students – 19 states and large urban school districts, 2017. *MWMR. Morbidity and Mortality Weekly Report, 68*(3), 67–71. doi:10.15585/mmwr.mm6803a3

Klemmer, C., Arayasirikul, S., & Raymond, H. H. F. (2018). Transphobia-based violence, depression, and anxiety in transgender women: The role of body satisfaction. *Journal of Interpersonal Violence,* Mar 1: 088626051876001, 1–23. doi:10.1177/0886260518760015

Lambda Legal. (2010). *When health care isn't caring: Lambda Legal's survey of discrimination against LGBT people and people with HIV.* New York, NY: Author. Retrieved from www.lambdalegal.org/health-care-report

Lyons, T., Shannon, K., Pierre, L., Small, W., Krüsi, A., & Kerr, T. (2015). A qualitative study of transgender individuals' experiences in residential addiction treatment settings: Stigma and inclusivity. *Substance Abuse Treatment, Prevention, and Policy, 10*(1), 17. doi:10.1186/ s13011-015-0015-4

Meyer, I. H. (2003). Prejudice, social stress, and mental health in lesbian, gay, and bisexual populations: Conceptual issues and research evidence. *Psychological Bulletin, 129*(5), 674–697. doi:10.1037/0033-2909.129.5.674

Moody, C., Fuks, N., Peláez, S., & Smith, N. G. (2015). "Without this, I would for sure already be dead": A qualitative inquiry regarding suicide protective factors among adults. *Psychology of Sexual Orientation and Gender Diversity, 2*(3), 266–280. doi:10.1027/ sgd0000130

Movement Advancement Project [MAP] & National Center for Trans Equality [NCTE]. (2018, March 26). *Religious refusals in health care: A prescription for disaster.* Retrieved from www.lgbtmap.org/file/Healthcare-Religious-Exemptions.pdf

Nadal, K. L. (2018). A decade of microaggression research and LGBTQ communities: An introduction to the special issue. *Journal of Homosexuality*, 66(10), 1309–1316. doi:10.1 080/00918369.2018.1539582

Oberheim, S. T., DePue, M. K., & Hagedorn, W. B. (2017). Substance use disorders (SUDs) in transgender communities: The need for trans-competent SUD counselors and facilities. *Journal of Addictions & Offender Counseling*, 38(1), 33–47. doi:10.1002/jaoc.12027

Partnership for Drug-Free Kids. (2018). *Drug prevention tips for every age*. Retrieved December 30, 2019, from https://drugfree.org/article/prevention-tips-for-every-age/

Peralta, R. L., & Jauk, D. (2011). A brief feminist review and critique of the sociology of alcohol-use and substance-abuse treatment approaches. *Sociology Compass*, 5(10), 882–897. doi:10.1111/j.1751-9020.2011.00414.x

Queensland Health. (2009). *Community health nursing competency and skills*. Townsville Health Service District, Queensland Health.

Robinson, M. (2014). *LGBTQ people, drug use & harm reduction*. Rainbow Health Ontario. Retrieved January 6, 2020, from www.rainbow-healthontario.ca/wp-content/uploads/woocommerce_uploads/2015/06/RHO_FactSheet_LGBTDRUGUSEHARMREDUCTION_E.pdf

Scheim, A. I., Bauer, G. R., & Shokoohi, M. (2017). Drug use among transgender people in Ontario, Canada: Disparities and association with social exclusion. *Addictive Behaviors*, 72, 151–158. doi:10.1016/j.addbeh.2017.03.022

Singh, A. A. (2013). Transgender youth of color and resilience: Negotiating oppression and finding support. *Sex Roles*, 68(11–12), 690–702. doi:10.1007/s11199-012-0149-z

Stieglitz, K. (2010). Development, risk, and resilience of transgender youth. *Journal of the Association of Nurses in AIDS Care*, 21(3), 192–206. doi:10.1016/j.jana.2009.08.004

Substance Abuse and Mental Health Services Administration [SAMHSA]. (2017). *Focus on prevention. HHS Publication No. (SMA) 10–4120*. Rockville, MD: Center for Substance Abuse Prevention, Substance Abuse and Mental Health Services Administration. Retrieved from https://store.samhsa.gov/product/Focus-on-Prevention/sma10-4120

Sue, D. (2010). *Microaggressions in everyday life: Race, gender, and sexual orientation*. Hoboken, NJ: Wiley.

Testa, R. J., Habarth, J., Peta, J., Balsam, K., & Bockting, W. (2015). Development of the gender minority stress and resilience measure. *Psychology of Sexual Orientation and Gender Diversity*, 2(1), 65–77. doi:10.1037/sgd0000081

Testa, R. J., Michaels, M. S., Bliss, W., Rogers, M. L., Balsam, K. F., & Joiner, T. (2017). Suicidal ideation in transgender people: Gender minority stress and interpersonal theory factors. *Journal of Abnormal Psychology*, 126(1), 125–136. doi:10.1037/abn0000234

The Change Collective. (2018). Working with vulnerable youth to enhance their natural supports: A practice framework. Retrieved from www.burnsfund.com/wp-content/uploads/2019/01/CC-Natural-Supports-Framework_2019_FINAL_Pages.pdf

The GenIUSS Group. (2014). *Best practices for asking questions to identify transgender and other gender minority respondents on population-based surveys*. J.L. Herman (ed.). Los Angeles, CA: The Williams Institute. Retrieved from https://escholarship.org/uc/item/3qk7s1g6T

The Network for LGBT Health Equity. (2012). *MPOWERED: Best and promising practices for LGBT tobacco prevention and control*. Retrieved January 6, 2020, from www.lgbthealthlink.org/Assets/U/documents/mpowered.pdf

Walsh, C., Mulligan, C., & Dolcecore, G. (2016). Social work and sexual diversity: A review. In J. Graham, A. Al-Krenawi, & N. Habibov (Eds.), *Diversity and social work in Canada* (pp. 272–293). Don Mills, Ontario: Oxford University Press.

Wilson, E., Chen, Y., Arayasirikul, S., Wenzel, C., & Raymond, H. (2015). Connecting the dots: Examining transgender women's utilization of transition-related medical care and associations with mental health, substance use, and HIV. *Journal of Urban Health*, 92(1), 182–192. doi:10.1007/s11524-014-9921-4

CHAPTER 7

Understanding and working with transgender/ nonbinary older adults

K. Abel Knochel and Kristie L. Seelman

INTRODUCTION

Social work with TNB older adults attends to the impacts of a lifetime of gender-based oppression along with the impacts of ageism and other experiences of marginalization. Social workers who build their knowledge base, attend to their own biases, and actively advocate for anti-oppressive treatment, services, policies, and systems may effectively serve TNB older adults. This chapter highlights existing literature about the experiences, challenges, needs, and strengths of this population and identifies best practices for working with TNB older adults at the micro, mezzo, and macro levels. We also provide a case study and guiding questions to help you apply what you are learning and identify areas for additional study and training.

LITERATURE REVIEW: KEY FACTORS AFFECTING TNB OLDER ADULTS

Micro-level factors

Gender identity, transitioning, and disclosure

There are myriad experiences related to gender identity and transitioning, including whether and when one decides to transition. Older cohorts of TNB adults likely lacked social acceptability and role models when they were young, and may have felt it was untenable for them to transition (Siverskog, 2014). Other people may wait to disclose their TNB identity until later in life to avoid economic consequences while working. Some TNB older adults may not wish to transition at all, routinely changing their gender expression and/or identity and/or disrupting gender norms in other ways (Siverskog, 2015). TNB older adults who wish to transition may hesitate due to feeling that it is too late or they are "too old" (Fabbre, 2014, p. 167) or may be told that transitioning is not worthwhile in the time one has left to live (Siverskog, 2014). Chronic health conditions and other aging-related physical changes can complicate transition plans and the ability to be perceived as one's gender (Siverskog, 2014). Health conditions in later life can pose enough risk that doctors might refuse to perform gender-affirming surgeries (Siverskog, 2014, 2015).

Some aging adults may stop identifying as transgender after transitioning (Fredriksen-Goldsen et al., 2011). People who openly identified as TNB in midlife may decide to pass as cisgender in later life due to safety concerns (Siverskog, 2014). TNB older adults may not be able to pass as cisgender in settings such as nursing homes where care providers have close contact with their body; in fact, they are at increased risk of having their identity divulged by staff who are unfamiliar with TNB people's needs and bodies (Siverskog, 2014, 2015).

Physical health, disability status, and health promotion/risk behaviors

Health disparities that exist in earlier adulthood appear to persist into later life (Fredriksen-Goldsen et al., 2014). TNB older adults are more likely than their cisgender counterparts to report asthma, cardiovascular disease, diabetes, or a dental, hearing, or vision impairment, and are less likely to have HIV, hepatitis, or cataracts (Fredriksen-Goldsen et al., 2011). Some TNB older adults take hormones, so providers will need to pay attention to polypharmacy issues, including drug interactions (Finkenauer et al., 2012).

TNB older adults in the U.S. may be less likely to exercise than cisgender LGB older adults (Fredriksen-Goldsen et al., 2014). Gender identity differences in physical and mental health may be connected to a lack of exercise and obesity among TNB older adults (Fredriksen-Goldsen et al., 2014). TNB individuals may face higher rates of disability as they age than their cisgender lesbian, gay, and bisexual (LGB) counterparts (Fredriksen-Goldsen et al., 2011). Cook-Daniels and Munson (2010) found disability rates among midlife and older transgender adults "so potent that they were unable to take care of their own basic needs like food, cleanliness, and safety" (p. 174).

Mental health

TNB older adults report poorer mental health and higher rates of depression symptoms, anxiety, suicidal ideation, stress, and loneliness than their cisgender LGB peers (Fredriksen-Goldsen et al., 2011). They may struggle with unique anxieties about aging, such as a fear of forgetting that one has transitioned (Witten, 2014a). TNB older adults report greater internalized stigma than cisgender gay and lesbian older adults; such stigma is associated with poorer physical and mental health (Fredriksen-Goldsen et al., 2011). Protective factors for physical and mental health include positive feelings of belonging in a lesbian, gay, bisexual, and transgender/nonbinary (LGBTNB) community and greater social support (Fredriksen-Goldsen et al., 2014).

Legal documents and end-of-life planning

TNB people face unique considerations related to changing/updating identity documents and end-of-life planning. However, some adults avoid altering identity documents in order not to threaten their access to Social Security, veterans' benefits, or housing (Porter et al., 2016). TNB adults show very low levels of end-of-life planning, such as developing a will, durable health care power of attorney, and instructions about how to recognize the end of one's life (Fredriksen-Goldsen et al., 2011; Kcomt & Gorey, 2017). Rates are even lower among low-income TNB adults and those who are Latinx, African American, or Native American (Fredriksen-Goldsen et al., 2011).

Anticipated stigma in receiving services

TNB older adults likely anticipate continued stigma from health and social services in later life (Siverskog, 2014; Witten, 2014b), which may discourage them from seeking needed help (Witten, 2014a). Other stigmatized identities (e.g., being HIV positive) further contribute to fear of seeking services and disclosing TNB identities (Finkenauer et al., 2012; Witten, 2014b). Delaying care due to fear relates to health struggles for this population; fear of accessing health care may help account for the relationship between gender identity and health outcomes (Fredriksen-Goldsen et al., 2014). TNB older adults express concerns about institutionalized care in later life, including potential transphobia and incompetence from care providers (Witten, 2014a). Some TNB adults report they will self-euthanize if they cannot find competent care (Witten, 2014a).

Mezzo-level factors

Competency and preparedness of providers

Service providers are seldom prepared to effectively serve TNB older adults. Gerontologists are often unaware of TNB physiology or how to appropriately provide care to TNB people (Finkenauer et al., 2012). TNB older adults are more likely to report poor quality health care compared to cisgender LGB older adults (Fredriksen-Goldsen et al., 2011). TNB older adults reported a need for senior housing, transportation, social events, and support groups that are welcoming (Fredriksen-Goldsen et al., 2011). However, for such services to be offered to this population effectively, efforts are needed to increase service providers' knowledge about TNB people and ensure these services are affirming, inclusive, and responsive to TNB people's needs.

Social support network

Social support and a sense of LGBTNB community belonging are important to the health of TNB older adults (Fredriksen-Goldsen et al., 2014) and social support is often a key resource for assistance with household tasks. When TNB older adults without social support encounter significant health problems, they may ignore the problem and attempt to care for themselves or be forced to use institutionalized care (Siverskog, 2014). Fredriksen-Goldsen and colleagues (2011) found that TNB older adults have significantly less social support than their cisgender LGB peers, despite larger overall social network sizes. TNB older adults are more likely to attend spiritual or religious activities than cisgender LGB peers (Fredriksen-Goldsen et al., 2011), which may provide important social support. Siverskog (2014) notes challenges to social connectedness among rural-dwelling TNB older adults and those who do not know other TNB people. TNB adults can face a strained relationship with the larger LGBTNB community; TNB older adults are less likely to feel positive about their belonging in the LGBTNB community than cisgender LGB adults (Fredriksen-Goldsen et al., 2011).

Discrimination, harassment, victimization, and abuse

TNB older adults are more likely to experience discrimination, harassment, victimization, and abuse than cisgender LGB older adults, including discrimination in health care; verbal abuse from a partner, family member, or friend; and neglect (Fredriksen-Goldsen et al., 2011, 2014). Compared to younger cohorts, TNB older adults are less likely to report that they have experienced discrimination, which may be a result of the timing of when people transitioned, generational differences in defining discrimination, and whether participants live part-time or full-time as their authentic gender (Kattari & Hasche, 2016).

Macro-level factors

Lifetime barriers to education, employment, and savings

TNB people face significant discrimination and harassment in education and employment (James et al., 2016). These challenges likely contribute to inadequate retirement savings and income support. Sex discrimination may exacerbate this, as transgender adults who were assigned male at birth are likelier to have pensions compared to those who were assigned female at birth (Witten, 2014a).

Non-discrimination policies affecting aging-related services

Few incentives or policy mandates exist to ensure TNB inclusion and competency from the agencies, staff, and volunteers offering services to older adults. The Older Americans Act has not designated TNB people as a "greatest social need" population, a categorization that could guide federally-funded service providers to serve this population without discrimination (SAGE & NCTE, 2012, p. 31). Long-term care facilities may not understand or enforce 42 CFR 483.10, which provides rights that protect TNB residents (National Long-Term Care Ombudsman Resource Center [NORC], National Resource Center on LGBT Aging, & Lambda Legal, 2018). For instance, many institutions require a same-sex roommate (unless sharing with spouse) and assign rooms based upon sex designated at birth rather than gender identity (Porter et al., 2016).

Health insurance coverage and document-change policies

Many older adults access health care through the Veterans' Health Administration (VHA), Medicare, and/or Medicaid. VHA offers transition-related medical care (e.g., hormone replacement therapy, mental health services, pre-operative evaluation, vocal coaching, post-gender-affirming surgery care), but does not offer gender-affirming surgery (VHA Directive 1341, 2018). The VHA also directs its health centers to consistently use each person's self-identified name and pronouns, to assign rooms based on self-identified gender identity, and to enforce non-discrimination (VHA Directive 1341, 2018). Medicare covers gender-affirming surgeries and hormone replacement therapy it considers medically necessary, although it fails to cover many off-label transition-related drugs (SAGE, SHIP National Network, Justice in Aging, & Administration for Community Living [ACL], 2016). Each state determines its Medicaid coverage; currently, 19 states lack policy regarding coverage for TNB people and ten states exclude coverage (Movement Advancement Project [MAP], 2019).

Sex markers are listed on Medicare and Medicaid cards based upon Social Security records (SAGE & NCTE, 2012). To change one's sex marker with Social Security, an individual must produce a passport or birth certificate with the correct gender, a court order, or a physician letter indicating appropriate treatment related to gender transition (Social Security Administration, 2019). Eliminating the sex marker field on identity cards would remove a barrier for recognition of TNB older adults (SAGE & NCTE, 2012).

Strengths and resilience

McFadden, Frankowski, Flick, and Witten (2013) identified six "resilience repertoires" (p. 260) among TNB adults aged 61 and older that contributed to successful aging, including: (a) nurturing the spiritual self (e.g., finding peace, using positive spirituality); (b) exercise of agency (e.g., goal-setting, making decisions to promote health, transitioning when desired); (c) self-acceptance (e.g., living an active and healthy lifestyle as a means to take care of oneself, being courageous); (d) having caring relationships (e.g., caring for future generations, loving others rooted in self-acceptance); (e) advocacy and activism (e.g., educating others, deep commitment to improving the lives of trans people); and (f) enjoying an active, healthy life (e.g., living proudly and honestly, letting go of things outside of one's control, laughing, and enjoying life). Service providers can support the growth of resilience in TNB older adults by helping them strengthen their support systems, develop a positive sense of self, increase self-determination, and work for the liberation of TNB people.

Knowledge gaps

Studies of older TNB adults tend to be cross-sectional surveys using non-probability samples. Studies that include TNB older adults as part of a larger sample provide limited data about this population. We also know very little about nonbinary older adults, TNB older adults of color, those 80 and older, rural residents, and those outside of the U.S. (Finkenauer et al., 2012; Witten, 2014b).

BEST PRACTICES AT MICRO, MEZZO, AND MACRO LEVELS

Micro-level practice

Show you are trustworthy

Ageism and bias against TNB people are widespread. Social workers improve their ability to practice effectively and appropriately with TNB older adults when they understand their privilege and identify and eradicate their own biases. Be sure to seek out trainings and build lines of accountability with people who will help you identify and address biased behaviors.

TNB older adults may be wary of social workers based on past discrimination. Build trust with this population by respecting their gender identity and expression and providing a safe experience. Instead of relying on records or legal documents, ask what name they use and note this prominently in records. During intake, ask all clients, "What is your gender identity?" to avoid misgendering and to appropriately match your client to services. Collect this information out of earshot of other people or through a written form to provide safety and support for disclosure. Some TNB older adults selectively express their gender identity. For example, your client may use a different pronoun with relatives or may hide their gender identity from cisgender peers. Learn how and when your client wishes to be addressed with a particular name and pronoun and honor this wish.

TNB older adults may feel vulnerable when disclosing their legal name and sex if these differ from self-identity. They may also be reticent to discuss physical transitioning. Request this information privately and only when necessary (e.g., billing or regulations may require legal name and sex assigned a birth). Information about physical transitioning will help you match a TNB older adult with appropriate medical screenings, develop safety plans, and advocate for the most comfortable room arrangement in assisted living. A legal identity mismatch may impact your client's ability to collect retirement funds or have their wishes respected in end-of-life care. Explain why this information is needed, including who has access to it, how it will be used, and limitations on privacy or confidentiality.

Assess and bolster support networks

TNB older adults may have lost family, friends, faith community, or other supporters as they began to live in their authentic gender identity and expression. Support networks further weaken in older age as death and illness claim peers and supportive family. Screen for isolation, loneliness, and neglect. Identify existing sources of social, emotional, and material support along with gaps. Use your existing knowledge and professional networks to locate affirming sources of support, then present these to your client for consideration. If they identify with a faith or spirituality, discuss their current and desired practice and help them locate TNB-affirming options. More people need material support as they age, and TNB older adults may need more financial support than their cisgender peers. Ask your clients who helps them with needed chores, errands, or rides and who they can depend on to help with expenses.

Address impacts of past and current oppression

TNB older adults who have experienced employment discrimination or paid out-of-pocket for gender-affirming medical care may have debt and/or paltry savings. Assess their financial situation and connect them with financial supports. Help identify free or inexpensive ways to meet their needs. For example, local Area Agencies on Aging offer congregate dining programs, Meals on Wheels, transportation, chore assistance, and other support. Screen potential resources to understand their capacity to be TNB-affirming and share with your client so they can make an informed choice.

TNB older adults may need part-time or full-time employment, but age discrimination and TNB bias create challenges. Work together to write a resume that deemphasizes employment gaps. Practice answers to questions about such gaps that honor their wishes about disclosing their TNB identity. Strategize together about how to handle reference checks for jobs performed under a different name or gender identity. Help your client apply for positions with TNB-affirming employers.

Screen for mental health concerns

Cumulative impacts of oppression may affect the mental health of TNB older adults. Social workers gatekeep access to gender-affirming health care and legal recognition. Your client may have had negative or controlling experiences with previous mental health providers. Assure your client that you will not use mental health diagnoses to deny them access to gender-affirming care. Disclose any limits on this so they can decide what to share in their work with you.

Help your TNB older adult client address unresolved grief and the impacts of trauma. They may grieve losses from waiting until later life to express their authentic gender or from rejection experienced in past attempts at self-expression. They may have experienced violence and other trauma related to their gender identity and expression. Grief and trauma may be activated by stories of TNB youth who are well-supported. TNB people may benefit from storying their gender journey and reframing traumatic experiences as they approach the end of life.

Plan for end of life

Among older adults, end-of-life planning can contribute to a sense of agency, increase the likelihood that one's wishes will be respected, and reduce stress and uncertainty among loved ones. Assist TNB older adults to prepare for a safe end of life that is lived on their own terms. People who are legally entitled to make financial and medical decisions for your client and to inherit from them may not be who your client trusts or chooses. Develop with your client a durable financial power of attorney that names a trusted person to handle their finances. Help your client outline expectations for gender presentation, name, and pronoun in their advance care directive. Identify with your client a person to make medical decisions and advocate for respectful gender recognition, then name this person in a health care power of attorney and advance care directive. Help your client create a legal will naming those they wish to provide with an inheritance.

Make a plan with your client to receive care from a person or service that is likely to be TNB-affirming and competent. Identify assisted living facilities that train their staff to provide affirming care to TNB residents and actively enforce non-discrimination policies based on gender identity and expression. Ask administrators how they identify and address bullying. Help your client consider their options if a TNB-affirming facility or caregiver cannot be identified or afforded.

Mezzo-level practice

Explore family relationships and safe opportunities to strengthen ties

TNB older adults may have lost relatives when they embraced their authentic gender identity and expression. They may fear such losses if they are beginning their gender journey. They may wish to rekindle lost family connections or challenge compromises they made to preserve relationships. Explore family counseling with your TNB older adult client if they wish to maintain or strengthen relationships with their family of origin.

Develop a group with transgender/nonbinary older adults

Establishing a group for TNB older adults can build their support networks and improve mental health. TNB older adults may have gaps in their support systems stemming from their emergence into their gender identity and expression. Strong peer relationships can help them stave off loneliness, build and maintain a positive self-identity, and develop ways to navigate older adulthood and oppression. Establishing a group for TNB older adults is also a precursor to organizing against the oppression they face based on age, gender identity, and gender expression. Creating opportunities for TNB older adults to gather and build connections with one another is the first step toward creating a collective identity and sense of shared power.

Eliminate age and gender bias in older adult and TNB communities

Older adult communities may exhibit bias toward TNB peers. Train cisgender older adults about gender identity and expression. Offer such training to all participants and staff in aging programming, such as congregate dining, grief and caregiver support groups, senior centers, and assisted living facilities. Help aging programs develop and enforce non-discrimination policies. Work with the community to offer programming for all genders instead of separating by men and women.

Existing TNB communities, often populated by young people, may exhibit age bias toward older adults. Work with existing TNB communities to address ageism and develop welcoming, useful programming before referring TNB older adults into those spaces. A TNB community space could establish congregate dining or offer a speaker on end-of-life planning. Hold TNB groups and events during the day in well-lit areas on public transportation routes and in settings that are physically accessible to make them more feasible and comfortable for older TNB people. Undertake this training and advocacy work in partnership and consultation with willing TNB older adults whenever they can be located. The social worker can draw on existing training and advocacy models.

Ensure affirming, appropriate practice by aging services organizations

It is important to train the entire workforce, adopt non-discrimination policies, and enforce those policies to provide an oppression-free experience for TNB older adults at all points of contact. Best practices for organizational policies and practices are covered in Chapter 18 as well as being noted in other chapters and can be applied to aging services. SAGE Care offers training and consultation on providing welcoming, appropriate services to LGBTNB older adults, including a module on TNB aging. Your state or local area may provide its own training. If your organization provides residential care or senior group programming, orient all residents or participants at the point of intake and prominently display and enforce non-discrimination policies.

Macro-level practice

Seek culture change through social movements

Social movements that work for gender liberation or that target ageism are not new, yet there has not been a social movement that addresses liberation among TNB older adults. Mezzo-level work that brings TNB older adults together is a precursor; once collective identity is formed, a social movement can launch. Social workers can help TNB older adults build a movement if they are invited to do so. Social workers who are involved in TNB social movements or aging social movements can also build awareness of TNB older adults, foster understanding of interconnected issues, and gain commitment to work for shared liberation.

Seek change in local and state aging services

State Units on Aging (SUA) and Area Agencies on Aging (AAA) have the right to designate TNB older adults as "a population of greatest social need" in their plans, per the Administration on Aging (Movement Advancement Project & SAGE, 2017, p. 31). Work with your SUA to make this designation and direct AAAs to assess the needs of TNB older adults in their area, following Massachusetts' model (National Resource Center on LGBT Aging, 2017).

You can work with your AAA to include TNB older adults as an underserved population. Help your AAA establish an external advisory group, inclusive of TNB older adults and their allies, to help develop plan objectives, action steps, and outcome measures and assist in implementation and evaluation. The National Resource Center on LGBT Aging (2017) provides detailed advice. AAAs contract out many aging services. Advocate for your AAA to require contractors to serve TNB older adults according to the plan (MAP and SAGE, 2017) and participate in training.

Gather data to show need and create and enforce supportive public policy

Advocate for including gender identity questions in the demographic portion of surveys, forms, and assessments used by aging services in your state and require those collecting the data to receive training (National Resource Center on LGBT Aging, 2017). Massachusetts, California, and New York require aging services to collect gender identity data (National Resource Center on LGBT Aging, 2016). Gather TNB older adults and their trusted community partners to help monitor data collection. Next, collaboratively analyze collected data and disseminate recommendations for practice and policy change.

Improve care and quality of life for TNB older adults through state and federal policy. Work with your governor and state legislature to establish a statewide commission, following Massachusetts' lead (National Resource Center on LGBT Aging, 2017), that includes TNB older adults and recommends changes in laws and regulations to protect them. Advocate for your state to require long-term care and senior housing facilities to create and enforce non-discrimination policies, educate residents, and train staff to serve TNB older adults in a welcoming, appropriate manner (MAP and SAGE, 2017). Lobby your state to cover gender-affirming surgeries under Medicaid. Advocate with the Department of Veteran Affairs to cover gender-affirming surgeries and train personnel.

Work to enforce existing legal protections for TNB older adults. Medicare covers gender-affirming surgery, hormone replacement therapy, and medically necessary, sex-specific procedures. Coverage frequently requires an appeal. Advocate to maintain the regulation and appeal process for Medicare under the U.S. Department of Health and Human Services (SAGE, SHIP National Network, Justice in Aging, & Administration for Community Living [ACL], 2016). Section 1557 of the Affordable Care Act (ACA) prohibits TNB discrimination by federally-funded and federally-administered health care providers, including those with Medicaid or Medicare patients. However, much of this has been rolled back by the Trump administration. Educate health care providers and monitor their compliance (SAGE, SHIP, Justice in Aging, & ACL, 2016).

Federal nursing home regulations, 42 CFR 483 (483.10 Residents' Rights), protect TNB older adults at all facilities that receive Medicaid or Medicare funding. Protections include:

- Freedom from harassment and other abuse
- Privacy about bodies and gender identity
- Visits without regard to gender identity
- Right to participate in TNB-affirming activities without repercussion
- Right to be addressed by self-identified name and pronoun
- Self-chosen clothing and grooming
- Involvement in care planning and health care treatment, including transition-related
- Advance notice of a room or roommate change
- Right to remain housed absent a legally permissible reason to move or discharge (NORC, National Resource Center on LGBT Aging, & Lambda Legal, 2018)

Long-Term Care Ombudspersons (LTCO) advocate for the rights of nursing homes and assisted living residents. Locate your state's LTCO through the National Long-Term Care Ombudsman Resource Center (NORC). Advocate for enforcement through your state's nursing home licensing, certification, and regulation agency. The National Consumer Voice for Quality Long-Term Care supports political advocacy on behalf of long-term care residents (NORC, National Resource Center on LGBT Aging, & Lambda Legal, 2018).

CASE STUDY

Sandra, a 75-year-old Latina trans woman, began a physical, legal, and social transition when she was 47. She lost her salaried job at the start of her transition and was underemployed until she began to collect Social Security at age 62.

Sandra and her wife divorced when Sandra was 49. They maintain regular contact. Sandra has three children and has contact with her youngest child, who calls her Dad. Sandra has not met her grandchildren.

Sandra moved to a mobile home community when she was 52. While she is friendly with the neighbors, she is not out to them as transgender. Sandra self-maintains her mobile home, which is showing signs of neglect.

Sandra has never received preventive health screenings. She ended hormone replacement therapy (and her primary care provider relationship) when she was 60. Sandra attended therapy during transition and expresses negative feelings about this experience. She shows symptoms of depression and anxiety. Sandra says she will do "whatever it takes" to avoid long-term care and home health care. She fears mistreatment and being outed.

Sandra's Social Security records and driver's license carry her correct name and gender marker, but her birth certificate remains under her former name and identifies her as male.

Sandra is concerned that somebody could discover her transgender identity if she uses senior services. Sandra attended a free lunch at the senior center once, but sat alone and found the other adults to be unfriendly.

Sandra is intrigued but anxious about meeting other transgender people. Sandra identified a local TNB group through social media but finds the terms they use for themselves and their "militancy about small things" bewildering. She wonders how she can relate to people the age of her grandchildren.

Questions – micro level

1. Identify Sandra's needs for healthy aging. What resources does she possess? What resources might you connect her with?

	Needs	Resources (Has)	Resources (Connect)
Physical			
Mental			
Emotional			
Financial			

2. What can you do to locate safe, welcoming, and appropriate resources for Sandra? How will you talk with Sandra about her wishes around gender identity disclosure and any limits on this?
3. How might individual biases play out in Sandra's relationships with family? Friends? Neighbors? Providers? What impact(s) might these experiences have on Sandra's well-being? In planning for the future?

Questions – mezzo level

4. How might you strengthen Sandra's ties to her family of origin? How would you gauge the appropriateness of this?
5. How might you build Sandra's connection to other transgender people? Other older adults?
6. What can you do to help these groups/communities become safe, welcoming support spaces for Sandra?
7. How else might you try to build her support system? What questions might you ask Sandra to learn more?

Questions – macro level

8. What do you imagine Sandra's experiences were with oppression leading up to her transition, during her transition, and in the years since her transition? How might she have experienced bias in public spaces? In health care? How do you imagine structural bias played out at her job? In the health care system?
9. What policies might have been at play then? What policies might be at play now? What policy change(s) are needed?
10. Why do you think Sandra does not know TNB people her age?
11. What can be done to make senior services more welcoming for Sandra and other TNB older adults?

Intersectionality

12. Imagine *one* of the following differences in Sandra's story. How does this change what she has experienced? Consider potential limitations and potential advantages. Consider physical, mental, social, emotional, and financial implications. How does this change your plans for working with Sandra?
    a. Sandra is Sandy, a nonbinary person.
    b. Sandra is Steve, a transgender man.
    c. Sandra is White.
    d. Sandra is an undocumented immigrant.
    e. Sandra began transitioning after retirement (2005).
    f. Sandra began transitioning in her early 20s (1965).
    g. Sandra's state of residence does not protect civil rights based on gender identity and gender expression.

Strengths

13. Review the "resilience repertoires" earlier in this chapter.
    a. How can you identify Sandra's existing resilience repertoires?
    b. How can you build up Sandra's resilience repertoires?
    c. What might overwhelm Sandra's ability to enact resilience? What are some ways to mitigate these risks (policy, practice, etc.)?

CONCLUSION

While TNB people are aging in greater, more visible numbers, our understanding of this population and our social work practices to serve them are underdeveloped. By partnering with TNB older adults to transform oppressive systems, policies, and practices, we will improve their ability to age well. By working with TNB older adults to identify and meet their current needs, we can lessen the cumulative effects of bias on their later years. By building our profession's knowledge base and skills to serve TNB older adults and addressing our gender-based biases, we will develop the capacity to practice in an anti-oppressive manner across lines of age, gender identity, and gender expression.

RESOURCES

National Resource Center on LGBT Aging – Transgender Aging Resources
www.lgbtagingcenter.org/resources/resources.cfm?s=27
FORGE's Transgender Aging Network https://forge-forward.org/aging/
SAGE: Advocacy and Services for LGBT Elders www.sageusa.org/
To Survive on this Shore Website and book by Jess T. Dugan and Vanessa Fabbre offer first-person narratives from TNB elders. www.tosurviveonthisshore.com/
MAJOR! Documentary film about Miss Major Griffin-Gracy. www.missmajorfilm.com/

- Short excerpt of Miss Major's recounting of Stonewall Riots: https://vimeo.com/222884639

Lambda Legal Legal support and resources, including particular attention to aging and to transgender people. www.lambdalegal.org/issues/seniors
National Center for Transgender Equality Provides advocacy, including aging advocacy. https://transequality.org/issues/aging
Stryker, S. (2017). *Transgender history: The roots of today's revolution* (2nd ed.). New York, NY: Seal Press.

REFERENCES

Cook-Daniels, L., & Munson, M. (2010). Sexual violence, elder abuse, and sexuality of transgender adults, age 50+: Results of three surveys. *Journal of GLBT Family Studies*, 6(2), 142–177. doi:1080/15504281003705238

Fabbre, V. D. (2014). Gender transitions in later life: The significance of time in queer aging. *Journal of Gerontological Social Work*, 57(2–4), 161–175. doi:10.1080/01634372.2013.855287

Finkenauer, S., Sherratt, J., Marlow, J., & Brodey, A. (2012). When injustice gets old: A systematic review of trans aging. *Journal of Gay and Lesbian Social Services*, 24(4), 311–330. doi:10.1080/10538720.2012.722497

Fredriksen-Goldsen, K. I., Cook-Daniels, L., Kim, H.-J., Erosheva, E. A., Emlet, C. A., Hoy-Ellis, C. P., … Muraco, A. (2014). Physical and mental health of transgender older adults: An at-risk and underserved population. *The Gerontologist*, 54(3), 488–500. doi:10.1093/geront/gnt021

Fredriksen-Goldsen, K. I., Kim, H., Emlet, C. A., Muraco, A., Erosheva, E. A., Hoy-Ellis, C. P., … Petry, H. (2011). *The aging and health report: Disparities and resilience among lesbian, gay, bisexual, and transgender older adults*. Seattle, WA: Institute for Multigenerational Health. Retrieved from http://caringandaging.org

James, S. E., Herman, J. L., Rankin, S., Keisling, M., Mottet, L., & Anafi, M. (2016). *The report of the 2015 U.S. transgender survey*. Washington, DC: National Center for Transgender Equality. Retrieved from www.transequality.org/sites/default/files/docs/USTS-Full-Report-FINAL.PDF

Kattari, S. K., & Hasche, L. (2016). Differences across age groups in transgender and gender non-conforming people's experiences of health care discrimination, harassment, and victimization. *Journal of Aging and Health, 28*(2), 285–306. doi:10.1177/0898264315590228

Kcomt, L., & Gorey, K. M. (2017). End-of-life preparations among lesbian, gay, bisexual, and transgender people: Integrative review of prevalent behaviors. *Journal of Social Work in End-of-Life and Palliative Care, 13*(4), 284–301. doi:10.1080/15524256.2017.1387214

McFadden, S. H., Frankowski, S., Flick, H., & Witten, T. M. (2013). Resilience and multiple stigmatized identities: Lessons from transgender persons' reflections on aging. In J. D. Sinnott (Ed.), *Positive psychology: Advances in understanding adult motivation* (pp. 247–267). New York, NY: Springer. doi:10.1007/978-1-4614-7282-7

Movement Advancement Project. (2019). *Healthcare laws and policies*. Denver, CO: Author. Retrieved from www.lgbtmap.org/equality-maps/healthcare_laws_and_policies/medicaid

Movement Advancement Project, & SAGE. (2017). *Understanding issues facing LGBT older adults*. Boulder, CO: Movement Advancement Project. Retrieved from https://www.lgbtmap.org/understanding-issues-facing-lgbt-older-adults

National Long-Term Care Ombudsman Resource Center, National Resource Center on LGBT Aging, & Lambda Legal. (2018). *Residents' rights and the LGBT community: Know your rights as a nursing home resident*. Retrieved from https://ltcombudsman.org/uploads/files/issues/lgbt-rr-factsheet.pdf

National Resource Center on LGBT Aging. (2016). *Inclusive questions for older adults: A practical guide to collecting data on sexual orientation and gender identity*. New York, NY: SAGE.

National Resource Center on LGBT Aging. (2017). *Strengthen your state and local aging plan: A practical guide for expanding the inclusion of LGBT older adults*. New York, NY: SAGE.

Porter, K. E., Brennan-Ing, M., Chang, S. C., dickey, l. m., Singh, A. A., Bower, K. L., & Witten, T. M. (2016). Providing competent and affirming services for transgender and gender nonconforming older adults. *Clinical Gerontologist, 39*(5), 366–388. doi:10.1080/07317115.2016.1203383

SAGE, & National Center for Transgender Equality. (2012). *Improving the lives of transgender older adults: Recommendations for policy and practice*. Retrieved from www.lgbtagingcenter.org/resources/pdfs/TransAgingPolicyReportFull.pdf

SAGE, SHIP National Network, Justice in Aging, & Administration for Community Living. (2016). *Medicare changes for transgender older adults: A time of change*. Retrieved from www.nasuad.org/sites/nasuad/files/SAGE%20SHIP%20Sheet%20Medicare%20Transgender%20FINAL%20Web.pdf

Siverskog, A. (2014). "They just don't have a clue": Transgender aging and implications for social work. *Journal of Gerontological Social Work, 57*(2–4), 386–406. doi:10.1080/01634372.2014.895472

Siverskog, A. (2015). Ageing bodies that matter: Age, gender and embodiment in older transgender people's life stories. *NORA – Nordic Journal of Feminist and Gender Research, 23*(1), 4–19. doi:10.1080/08038740.2014.979869

Social Security Administration. (2019). How do I change my gender on Social Security's records? Retrieved from https://faq.ssa.gov/en-us/Topic/article/KA-01453

Veterans Health Administration (2018). VHA directive 1341: Providing health care for transgender and intersex veterans. Retrieved from www.va.gov/vhapublications/ViewPublication.asp?pub_ID=6431

Witten, T. M. (2014a). End of life, chronic illness, and trans-identities. *Journal of Social Work in End-of-Life and Palliative Care, 10*(1), 34–58. doi:10.1080/15524256.2013.877864

Witten, T. M. (2014b). It's not all darkness: Robustness, resilience, and successful transgender aging. *LGBT Health, 1*(1), 24–33. doi:10.1089/lgbt.2013.0017

CHAPTER 8

Trans/nonbinary individuals and homelessness

Jama Shelton and Twiggy Pucci Garcon

INTRODUCTION

Homelessness is a form of discrimination and social exclusion. In addition to lacking a fixed and stable residence, people experiencing homelessness are forced into the socially constructed identity of "the homeless" and as a group are subjected to victimization, discrimination, and criminalization (Canada without Poverty, 2016). It is important to remember that homelessness is an experience and that the experience does not define the entirety of the individual experiencing it. Individuals who belong to a group forced to the margins of society are often overrepresented in the population of people experiencing homelessness and are further marginalized as a result of this experience. This is the case for TNB people.

Framework/macro context

Though their specific experiences will vary depending on a combination of sociodemographic factors, TNB people share experiences of bias and cisgenderism as they navigate their daily lives. TNB people do not exist within a vacuum; they operate within and are impacted by social systems that may or may not affirm who they are, much less celebrate them. Therefore, when preparing people to work with TNB people experiencing homelessness, it is imperative to contextualize homelessness among TNB people within the larger social context and the oppressive structures that produce and maintain the marginalization of TNB people in society at large, and specifically within the housing market and homeless serving systems.

Cisgenderism shapes the U.S. social context, from the micro level of interpersonal interactions to the establishment of institutions and the policies and procedures that govern them (Bauer et al., 2009). Social systems in the U.S. often render TNB people invisible through marginalizing policies and practices that assume universal identification with the gender binary (Grossman & D'Augelli, 2006; Shelley, 2009; Shelton, 2015). For example, within the U.S. homelessness system, the majority of programs segregate people based on their sex. Sex is often linked to genitalia or the sex designation on an individual's birth certificate. These types of exclusionary policies lead to exclusionary programs and practices that deny people's understanding of their genders. While some transgender people may indeed identify within the gender binary, the utilization of a binary classification is problematic when the classification is externally imposed and does not align with an individual's self-designated gender (Ansara & Hegarty, 2012). It is also problematic when access to social services is dependent upon a binary gender classification.

Racism is also inextricably linked to housing access and homelessness. The U.S. is built upon centuries of racist housing policy that has disadvantaged people of color, particularly Black people, for generations. Black TNB people experiencing homelessness not only face challenges rooted in cisgenderism, they also must contend with systemic racism and its effects, such as racial profiling, police and community harassment, and racial microaggressions (Gattis & Larson, 2017). Many service systems and settings (such as housing, health care, education, employment) often lack the ability to recognize and respond to the needs of individuals whose lives are impacted by the multiple and layered stigmas resulting from racism, classism, cisgenderism, and transbias (Olivet & Dones, 2016).

Prevalence rates

TNB people are thought to be overrepresented in the population of people experiencing homelessness. However, it is difficult to say exactly how many TNB people experience homelessness due to several methodological limitations in enumerating their prevalence. For example, questions about gender do not always include comprehensive options that would allow TNB people to self-identify accurately. If comprehensive gender options do exist on intake forms or in surveys, individuals may not feel comfortable disclosing this information for fear of harassment or service denial. When utilizing administrative-level data to estimate the prevalence of homelessness among TNB people, it is important to remember that many TNB people may not be actively engaged in homeless serving organizations due to prior experiences of discrimination. Therefore, TNB people may not be captured by social service administrative data, leading to underreporting. In research, the experiences of TNB people are often grouped with lesbian, gay, and bisexual people, making it difficult to determine the percentage of TNB people within the aggregated "LGBT" group data. In studies of people experiencing homelessness, different age categories further complicate estimates of youth and adult homelessness. While adults are often measured from age 18 and older, sometimes the category youth includes young adults up to the age 18; other times the category of youth goes up to age 21, other up to 24 or 25.

Despite the challenges in enumerating the population of TNB people experiencing homelessness, it is evident that homelessness is a critical issue for TNB people. The United States Transgender Survey (USTS) found that 30% of the 27,715 respondents experienced homelessness at some point in their lives (James et al., 2016). TNB adults comprise approximately 0.6% of the U.S. population (Flores et al., 2016); in studies of homelessness, TNB people make up between 1% and 9% of study samples (Center for Innovation through Data Intelligence, 2015; Shelton et al., 2018; Whitbeck, Lazoritz, Crawford, & Hautala, 2014). The range is due to the aforementioned methodological challenges, as well as differences in sampling strategies, methodologies, and geographic locations.

One way in which prevalence rates of people experiencing homelessness are monitored is through the annual Point-in-Time (PIT) count, required by communities that are funded by the U.S. Department of Housing and Urban Development (HUD) to provide homelessness assistance. The PIT count details the census of people experiencing homelessness on one night in January each year. In 2018, TNB people made up approximately 1% of the 372,417 individuals experiencing homelessness – that is, in households without children. Though on the low end of the estimated prevalence of homelessness among TNB people, at 1% TNB people are overrepresented in the homeless population compared to their representation in the general population. And the problem appears to be getting worse. The number of TNB people experiencing homelessness increased by 22% from 2017 to 2018 (U.S. Department of Housing and Urban Development, 2018). The 22% increase in the number of TNB people experiencing homelessness from 2017 to 2018 was primarily of unsheltered individuals (U.S. Department of Housing and Urban Development, 2018). Also, it is likely that this is an under-estimate. Because PIT counts rely largely on street and shelter-based identification, individuals who are more hidden, such as those who are couch-surfing or sleeping in discreet places, who actively avoid services (Morton et al., 2018), or for whom it is not safe to disclose their gender, are not reflected in the count.

Several recent studies have focused on homelessness among TNB youth and young adults. An examination of youth homelessness in New York City revealed that 9% of unstably housed young people surveyed (N=317) identified as TNB (Center for Innovation through Data Intelligence, 2015). In a multi-city survey of street outreach programs for youth (N=656), 7% identified as transgender (Whitbeck et al., 2014). The Homeless Youth Risk and Resiliency Study surveyed 1,427 young adults experiencing homelessness in seven U.S. cities; 7.5% identified as TNB (Realyst, 2019). Though the sample sizes, geographic locations, methods of data collection, and reported prevalence rates of these studies vary, one thing is consistent – that TNB people are disproportionately represented in the population of young people experiencing homelessness.

TNB people of color are more likely to experience homelessness than their White counterparts. Specifically, TNB people who identify as Black or African American, American Indian or Alaskan Native, Biracial or Multiracial have been found to be significantly more likely than their White counterparts to experience homelessness or seek temporary sleeping arrangements due to their gender identity (Begun & Kattari, 2016). This is not surprising, given the overrepresentation of Black people in the population of people experiencing homelessness. Whereas Black people made up 13.4% of the U.S. population in 2018, they accounted for 40% of the population of people experiencing homelessness (National Alliance to End Homelessness, 2018).

Pathways into homelessness

There is no single cause of homelessness for any population. Multiple, interacting factors are often at play and must be considered when thinking about pathways into homelessness for TNB people. Some of these factors are structural, such as racism, cisgenderism, and heterosexism (Shelton et al., 2018). Systemic inequity, including unequal treatment under the law, can be a contributing factor (Jones, 2016). Family conflict is frequently cited as a reason for homelessness (Choi, Wilson, Shelton, & Gates, 2015). System involvement, mental health challenges, and poverty have also been noted as potential pathways into homelessness (Choi et al., 2015; Ecker, Aubry, & Sylvestre, 2019; Shelton et al., 2018).

A salient factor contributing to homelessness among TNB people is widespread discrimination and transbias – in their homes of origin, in their communities, in the housing sector, in their educational pursuits, and in the workplace – all of which make TNB people more vulnerable to poverty and homelessness (Mottet & Ohle, 2006). Additionally, TNB people have lower homeownership rates (16%) compared to the U.S. population (63%) and they are four times less likely to own a home than cisgender individuals (James et al., 2016).

Much of the literature about homelessness among TNB young people focuses on identity-based family rejection as the leading cause of homelessness (Choi et al., 2015; Shelton & Bond, 2017). Identity-based family rejection and being kicked out of one's home has a lasting impact on TNB people during adolescence and through-out their lives. The experience of family rejection heightens the risk of homelessness and increases the likelihood of suicide attempts (James et al., 2016). Family rejection sometimes leads to expulsion from the home, an experience that also leads to negative outcomes related to financial stability, homelessness, and physical and mental health (James et al., 2016). As a result of family rejection, TNB adults at risk of or experiencing homelessness may not have access to familial support during a housing crisis. This lack of economic and/or residential support may render TNB individuals even more vulnerable to experiencing homelessness (Ecker et al., 2019). While identity-based family rejection is an important contributing factor to homelessness among TNB people, it is also important to consider additional factors at play. To focus solely on family characteristics and individual risk ignores the systematic oppression and stigmatization TNB people face. Additional reasons for homelessness among TNB young people noted in the literature include domestic violence, parental substance use, aging out of child welfare systems, and a lack of affordable housing (Choi et al., 2015; Gangamma, Slesnick, Toviessi, & Serovich, 2008; Shelton et al., 2018).

Challenges

TNB young adults have been found to experience longer durations of homeless-ness than their heterosexual and cisgender counterparts (Choi et al., 2015) and TNB adults report experiencing episodic homelessness more frequently than their cisgen-der counterparts (Montgomery, Szymkowiak, & Culhane, 2017). Longer durations of homelessness negatively impact resilience among TNB young adults (Cleverley &

Kidd, 2011), and are associated with higher rates of sexual risk behaviors, including the less consistent use of contraceptives and engaging in sex while under the influence of substances. Likewise, motivation to adopt and maintain HIV-protecting behaviors are negatively impacted by longer durations of homelessness (Collins & Slesnick, 2011; Rew, Grady, Whittaker, & Bowman, 2008). Additionally, longer durations of homelessness may result in greater difficulty exiting homelessness, as was found among a sample (N=1,677) of Australian people who first experienced homelessness when they were 18 years old or younger (Johnson & Chamberlain, 2008).

What causes longer durations of homelessness for TNB people? A combination of structural barriers to care and increased exposure to violence and victimization, in addition to widespread discrimination in employment and housing, contribute to the extended duration of homelessness for TNB people. This is more pronounced for TNB people of color. TNB people lack universal protection from employment and housing discrimination, and people of color frequently encounter racial discrimination in the housing market. Approximately a quarter of transgender people surveyed (N=27,715) report experiencing housing discrimination related to their gender identity, with transgender women of color most likely to report housing discrimination (James et al., 2016).

Risk/victimization

Minority stress theory posits that discrimination, prejudice, and stigma experienced by minority populations contribute to unique and chronic psychosocial stressors that negatively impact health outcomes (Meyer, 2003). Such stressors may result in psychological distress and/or influence an individual's health behaviors (e.g., substance use) and health care utilization (Meyer, 2003). TNB people experience health and mental health disparities, regardless of their housing status. For TNB people who experience homelessness, these disparities are even greater. Past illicit drug use and lifetime suicide attempts are higher among TNB people who have experienced homelessness compared to those who have not (James et al., 2016). Service providers working with youth and young adults experiencing homelessness report that the physical and mental health status of the TNB youth and young adults they serve are worse than those of their cisgender counterparts (Choi et al., 2015).

Violence towards TNB people, particularly transgender women of color, is a significant social problem. The hypervisibility that often accompanies homelessness places TNB people experiencing homelessness in danger. Furthermore, because emergency shelters are often gender-segregated (Mottet & Ohle, 2006; Sakamoto, Chin, Chapra, & Ricciardi, 2009), TNB individuals are forced into living situations outside of the shelter system, which may heighten their risk of experiencing violence (Spicer, 2010). In a recent study comparing gender differences among individuals experiencing homelessness (N=25,481), TNB people were more likely than their cisgender counterparts to report experiencing a violent attack while homeless (Montgomery et al., 2017). Seeking help from the police is often not an option, due to the harassment and violence many TNB people and people of color routinely face when encountering the police (James et al., 2016; Spicer, 2010).

Service barriers

Despite the increased vulnerability of TNB people experiencing homelessness, TNB people may be less likely to engage in and remain connected to services meant to transition people out of homelessness and into stable housing. Transbias is a pervasive part of the lives of TNB people; it shapes their interactions with individuals, communities, and systems such that rejection and discrimination become the norm. TNB people experiencing homelessness constantly navigate an oppressive society that frequently disregards or denies their self-designated genders. This disregard/denial occurs across a range of settings, and manifests in the form of binary-gendered bathrooms and sex-segregated facilities, to exclusionary paperwork, frequent questioning, misgendering, transbias, and discrimination (Shelton, 2015). Navigating binary-gendered spaces can cause marked distress for TNB individuals (Herman, 2013), due to the frequent failure on the part of programs to respect how people would like to be classified within the gendered space.

When considering service provision and the engagement of TNB people experiencing homelessness with homeless serving organizations, it is important to recognize that most homeless service systems were created with the cisgender service user in mind. As a result, homeless systems in the U.S. are not designed to accommodate nonbinary genders or anyone whose self-designated gender is different from their assigned sex at birth; thus, organizational policies and procedures may not apply to or include TNB people (Abramovich, 2017; Mallon, 2009; McGuire & Conover-Williams, 2010; Pyne, 2011; Shelton, 2015). Consequently, TNB people face barriers to care and experience negative and sometimes violent interactions when attempting to access care. When accessing shelter, TNB people report being harassed, forced out of the shelter, and/or physically attacked. These negative experiences sometimes lead to TNB people leaving shelters due to a lack of safety and poor treatment, even when they have nowhere else to stay (James et al., 2016). Alternatively, some TNB people may make the difficult choice to present as the wrong gender in order to be safe within a shelter or be forced to do so in order to remain in the shelter (Begun & Kattari, 2016; James et al., 2016).

Experiences of discrimination in the shelter system may leave TNB people experiencing homelessness without access to services, driving many to survival sex as a way to obtain basic necessities. Multiple negative outcomes are associated with engagement in survival sex, such as suicide attempts, HIV transmission, exposure to violence, and potential involvement in the criminal legal system (James et al., 2016; Kattari & Begun, 2016). Mirroring racial disparities identified elsewhere in relation to TNB homelessness, Black TNB individuals were found to be four times more likely to engage in survival sex than their White counterparts (Kattari & Begun, 2016). Although negative outcomes related to survival sex are commonly reported, it is important to note that some individuals may experience engagement in sex work as an empowering choice towards financial stability, and therefore may not view sex work as entirely negative (Kattari & Begun, 2016).

THE WAY FORWARD

Structural competence: A both/and approach

Structural discrimination concerns:

> the policies of dominant race/ethnic/gender institutions and the behavior of the individuals who implement these policies and control these institutions, which are race/ethnic/gender neutral in intent but which have a differential and/or harmful effect on minority race/ethnic/gender groups.
>
> (Pincus, 2000, p. 4)

To adequately address the overrepresentation of TNB people in the population of people experiencing homelessness, we must intervene on all levels – micro, macro, and structural – to ensure adequate and affirming care is being provided and to eliminate the conditions that produce and maintain the marginalization of TNB people. Structural competence provides a framework for this dual focus, as it seeks to identify, examine, and take action toward the causes of oppression (George & Marlowe, 2005). A structural competence framework thus indicates that engagement with the systemic causes of oppression is not only a macro practice, but also imperative when working to effectively support individuals.

Housing is a human right

In addition to engaging with the structural causes of homelessness among TNB people, another helpful paradigmatic shift is to adopt a human rights framework with regard to housing. Too often, homelessness is conceptualized as an individual failure to secure and maintain housing when it is actually a structural and often political problem (Canada without Poverty, 2016). This is perhaps no more evident than in the laws that criminalize people experiencing homelessness, which furthers social exclusion and often adds to the difficulty TNB people may have in exiting homelessness. A human rights approach recognizes homelessness as the result of structural inequity and a failure of states to ensure the human rights of all citizens. The oppressive structural dynamics of cisgenderism and racism that inform the daily experiences of TNB people experiencing homelessness are a human rights violation. It is incumbent upon elected officials, policymakers, homelessness advocates, and organizational leaders to extend their intervention efforts beyond supporting individual TNB people to include structural interventions to dismantle systems and institutions rooted in the historical pathologization of TNB identities and centuries of racist housing policy (Shelton et al., 2018).

Include TNB individuals

One way to help ensure the needs of TNB people experiencing homelessness are being met within the organizations meant to assist them is to involve TNB people directly in the creation and recreation of program structures. Who is an expert on the experiences of homelessness among TNB people? TNB people who have experienced homelessness! Unique needs exist among TNB people experiencing homelessness (Abramovich, 2017; Mottet & Ohle, 2006; Shelton, 2015); it would be irresponsible to not consider these unique needs when developing programs geared towards supporting individuals experiencing homelessness in obtaining housing stability. TNB people who have experienced homelessness can be included in a range of ways. Below are just a few examples:

1. Hire TNB people who have experienced homelessness as consultants.
2. Form a community advisory board including TNB people.
3. Conduct a needs assessment of the TNB individuals in your community.
4. Hire TNB people to conduct ongoing assessment and training within the organization to ensure the organization is providing a safe, inclusive, and affirming environment for TNB people.
5. Create pathways for TNB people to become credentialed social workers to address the underrepresentation of TNB people in the profession of social work.

Creating a safe and affirming program

Connection to a safe and identity-affirming program has been noted as critically important for TNB young people experiencing homelessness. An identity-affirming program can be understood as one that supports the self-stated genders of program participants without question and does not pathologize TNB genders. Affirming the genders of program participants is an integrated part of the organizational structure, from the types of services offered, to the language used in documentation and speaking (Shelton, 2015). There are specific actions an organization can take to become safer for and affirming of TNB people in the areas of organizational policy, training, documentation, intake/screening, placement, physical space, and community engagement. The following recommendations are based on existing best practice recommendations for working with TNB people experiencing homelessness and in other service-oriented systems of care (Massachusetts Transgender Political Coalition, 2020; Mottet & Ohle, 2003; True Colors United Learning Community, n.d.; Wilber, Ryan, & Marksamer, 2006).

The above recommendations can be implemented to help ensure TNB people experiencing homelessness have access to safe and affirming services. These are imperative if we are to adequately address homelessness among TNB people, as research indicates that only about half of TNB individuals who have experienced homelessness in their lifetimes have ever accessed a shelter (Grant et al., 2011; Kattari & Begun, 2017). In addition to these recommendations, the literature points to several interventions that may further assist TNB people in exiting homelessness into stable living situations. For instance, given the reported prevalence of TNB young people who experience family rejection and/or are kicked out of their homes, prevention strategies that target the families of TNB people and the systems in

TABLE 8.1 Recommendations for specific actions an organization can take to become safer for and affirming of TNB people in the areas of organizational policy, training, documentation, intake/screening, placement, physical space, and community engagement

Organizational policy	• Add gender identity and expression as protected attributes in non-discrimination policies. • Create a grievance policy with clear procedures to follow if someone has been harassed or mistreated within the program. • Review organizational policies and documents for binary-gendered language and replace such language with more inclusive terminology. For instance, he or she could be replaced with he, she, or they.
Training	• Ensure all employees who interact with service users receive ongoing training on TNB-affirming practices. • Provide employees an opportunity to practice using affirming language that may not be a part of their daily speech (i.e., using they/them as a pronoun). • Partner with a local TNB-led organization and/or TNB people who have experienced homelessness to design and deliver trainings.
Documentation	• Provide a space on paperwork for people to self-identify their gender. • Ensure service users' names and pronouns are clearly documented for staff to avoid misgendering.
Intake/Screening	• If possible, eliminate check-in areas that are separated by gender. • Service users should be able to indicate their name, rather than providing an ID card that is used to gather this information. An individual's name may not be the same as what is on the government-issued ID. • Only the name an individual indicates as the name they use should be called out in a public space. An individual's government name (or "dead name") should never be used. • The employee conducting the intake or screening should introduce themselves to all service users with their name and pronoun, modeling how this is done and setting a standard for TNB inclusion. • Be mindful of questions that may be triggering to TNB people and consider the utility of such questions. If the information is necessary to know for programmatic purposes, approach the questions in a sensitive manner. For instance, some trans men or nonbinary people may not wish to discuss questions related to menstruation.
Placement	• TNB individuals should be allowed to access sex-segregated programs that correlate with the gender with which they identify. • In sex-segregated programs, TNB individuals should be placed in the place in which they feel the safest. • When creating a new program, consider individual sleeping rooms, which better ensures safety and privacy for all, while also offering a more humane form of shelter than the traditional warehouse model.

Physical Space	• Ensure your organization has at least one designated all-gender restroom. • When creating a new program, design it such that all restrooms are individual, ADA accessible restrooms, which better ensures privacy, accessibility, and safety for all. • Post welcoming messages in the physical space, such as "People of all races, gender identities, gender expressions, sexual orientations, religions, and abilities are welcome here." • Post the TNB inclusive non-discrimination policy in clear sight of all who enter.
Community Engagement	• Establish relationships with local TNB organizations. • Participate in community-based activities related to TNB people and communities (i.e., Transgender Day of Remembrance). • Engage in structural change efforts to address the inequities faced by TNB people, particularly TNB people of color, in your community. • Discuss how partnering organizations ensure the safety and inclusion of TNB service users and include these terms in any MOUs outlining organizational partnerships. • Ensure that any third parties associated with the organization are aware of your organizational policies regarding the safety and inclusion of TNB people, and do not do business with outside vendors or others who do not share the same values. • Be a visible and vocal ally to TNB people.

which TNB people are involved (i.e., education, health care) are needed (Gattis & Larson, 2017; Shelton et al., 2018).

Additionally, the role of poverty in homelessness among TNB cannot be overlooked. TNB people are more likely to live in poverty, be un- or underemployed, and less likely to own homes, all of which make TNB people more vulnerable to experiencing homelessness (James et al., 2016). Employment discrimination undoubtedly contributes to the high poverty levels among TNB people as their unemployment rate is three times that of the general population (James et al., 2016). Unemployment and underemployment can make obtaining and maintaining stable housing nearly impossible for TNB people, who may also experience discrimination from landlords. From a practice perspective, many programs designed to assist TNB people experiencing homelessness presume they are in need of a range of micro-level interventions related to mental health symptom management, individual skill building, or job "readiness". This is likely true for some TNB people and is only a part of what is needed for others. However, some TNB people may be experiencing homelessness due to a financial crisis. In these cases, resources may be better utilized by providing short-term rental assistance, universal basic income, or affordable housing options for TNB people experiencing homelessness.

CONCLUSION

Homelessness among TNB people is, in part, a manifestation of the oppressive structural dynamics of cisgenderism, classism, and racism that permeate U.S. society. While it is imperative that those working with people experiencing homelessness are able to provide safe and affirming care to TNB people, that is simply not enough. A holistic approach to addressing the problem of homelessness for any population, and especially for TNB people, must include a conceptual reorganization of the idea of housing as a privilege to be earned to housing as a human right, as well as a commitment to addressing the conditions that produce and maintain the marginalization of TNB people.

CASE STUDY

Name: Star
Pronouns: She/Her/Hers
Age: 21 years old

Background information:

Star was living with her mother and three siblings prior to coming out as trans. A single mom, Star's mother ran a day care center out of their home. The business was not lucrative, and the family was living paycheck to paycheck. A fashion design student, Star worked a late shift at a locally owned retail store to pay for her education. She traveled to school each morning with an outfit and makeup, arriving an hour before classes started and getting ready for the day in the bathroom. After classes, she would change back into her "boy's clothes" before going to work. Star was accepted by her classmates and professors and excelled in school. On several occasions, Star lost track of time and was late for work. Her boss warned her if she was late once more, she would be fired. For this reason, she went to work one day without changing back into her "boy's clothes". She was hoping she could sneak into the bathroom at work before anyone saw her. Most people she saw each day knew her and her family, and she didn't want them to tell her mother she wore a skirt. Things didn't work out as planned. Her boss was waiting on her when she arrived, since she was already five minutes late. He took one look at her and told her to leave and not return. By the time she got home, her boss had already called her mother, and Star walked in the house to find her secret stash of women's clothing in a pile on the floor. Her mother said:

> I love you, but I can't have you in this house being this way. It's not that I care, I'm your mother and I've known about this. But now it's no longer a secret. No one will bring their kids to my day care if you are here. So if this is who you are, you're going to need to find somewhere else to live.

Star put the pile of women's clothes into a garbage bag, kissed her mother and siblings, and left. Star's mother gave her $40 before leaving, all the cash she had left. Star crashed for a few weeks in a friend's dorm room before being discovered and asked to leave. With no job, no one to help her pay for school, and nowhere to live, Star took a leave of absence. This was a devastating decision – Star saw fashion as her way out of poverty and an opportunity for her to be celebrated for who she is.

Critical reflection questions

- What would be your plan for working with Star?
- What strengths/internal resources do you see in Star?
- What external resources might be leveraged in your work with Star?
- What are potential barriers to Star obtaining housing? Finding employment? Re-enrolling in school?
- How would you address those barriers?

RESOURCES

Massachusetts Transgender Political Coalition (2020): https://www.masstpc.org/
True Colors United Learning Community: https://learn.truecolorsunited.org/
US Department of Housing & Urban Development LGBTQ Resources: www.hud.gov/ LGBT_resources
Transitioning our Shelters: A guide for making homeless shelters safe for transgender people: https://srlp.org/wp-content/uploads/2012/08/TransitioningOurShelters.pdf
Where am I going to go? Intersectional approaches to ending LGBTQ2S youth homelessness in Canada and the U.S. (a free e-book): www.homelesshub.ca/WhereAmIGoingtoGo

REFERENCES

Abramovich, A. (2017). Understanding how policy and culture create oppressive conditions for LGBTQ2S youth in the shelter system. *Journal of Homosexuality, 64*(11), 1484–1501. doi:10.1080/00918369.2016.1244449

Ansara, Y. G., & Hegarty, P. (2012). Cisgenderism in psychology: Pathologizing and misgendering children from 1999 to 2008. *Psychology & Sexuality, 3,* 137–160. doi:10.1080/1 9419899.2011.576696

Bauer, G., Hammond, R., Travers, R., Kaay, M., Hohenadel, K., & Boyce, M. (2009). "I don't think this is theoretical; this is our lives": How erasure impacts health care for transgender people. *Journal of the Association of Nurses in AIDS Care, 20*(5), 348–361. doi:10.1016/j.jana.2009.07.004

Begun, S., & Kattari, S. K. (2016). Conforming for survival: Associations between transgender visual conformity/passing and homelessness experiences. *Journal of Gay & Lesbian Social Services, 28*(1), 54–66. doi:10.1080/10538720.2016.1125821

Canada without Poverty. (2016). *Youth rights! Right now! Ending youth homelessness: A human rights guide.* Retrieved from www.homelesshub.ca/sites/default/files/attachments/ YouthRightsRightNow-final.pdf

Center for Innovation through Data Intelligence. (2015). *2015 NYC youth count report.* Retrieved from www.nyc.gov/html/cidi/downloads/pdf/youth-count-report-2015.pdf

Choi, S. K., Wilson, B. D. M., Shelton, J., & Gates, G. (2015). *Serving our youth 2015: The needs and experiences of lesbian, gay, bisexual, transgender, and questioning youth experiencing homelessness.* Los Angeles, CA: The Williams Institute with the True Colors Fund.

Cleverley, K., & Kidd, S. (2011). Resilience and suicidality among homeless youth. *Journal of Adolescence, 34*(5), 1049–1054. doi:10.1016/j.adolescence.2010.11.003

Collins, J., & Slesnick, N. (2011). Factors associated with motivation to change HIV risk and substance use behaviors among homeless youth. *Journal of Social Work Practice in the Addictions, 11*(2), 163–180. doi:10.1080/1533256X.2011.570219

Ecker, J., Aubry, T., & Sylvestre, J. (2019). A review of the literature on LGBTQ adults who experience homelessness. *Journal of Homosexuality, 66*(3), 297–323. doi:10.1080/0091 8369.2017.1413277

Flores, A., Herman, J., Gates, G., & Brown, T. (2016). *How many adults identify as transgender in the United States?* Los Angeles, CA: The Williams Institute. Retrieved from https://williamsinstitute.law.ucla.edu/wp-content/uploads/How-Many-Adults-Identify-as-Transgender-in-the-United-States.pdf

Gangamma, R., Slesnick, N., Toviessi, P., & Serovich, J. (2008). Comparison of HIV risks among gay, lesbian, bisexual and heterosexual homeless youth." *Journal of Youth and Adolescence, 37,* 456–464. doi:10.1007/s10964-007-9171-9

Gattis, M., & Larson, A. (2017). Perceived microaggressions and mental health in a sample of Black youths experiencing homelessness. *Social Work Research, 41*(1), 7–17. doi:10.1093/swr/svw030

George, P., & Marlowe, S. (2005). Structural social work in action: Experiences from rural India. *Journal of Progressive Human Services,16*(1), 5–24. https://doi.org/10.1300/J059v16n01_02

Grant, J. M., Mottet, L. A., Tanis, J., Harrison, J., Herman, J. L., & Keisling, M. (2011). *Injustice at every turn: A report of the National Transgender Discrimination Survey.* Washington, DC: National Center for Transgender Equality and National Gay and Lesbian Task Force.

Grossman, A., & D'Augelli, A. (2006). Transgender youth: Invisible and vulnerable. *Journal of Homosexuality, 51*(1), 111–128. doi:10.1300/J082v51n01_06

Herman, J. (2013). Gendered restrooms and minority stress: The public regulation of gender and its impact on transgender people's lives. *Journal of Public Management and Social Policy, 19*(1), 65–80.

James, S., Herman, J., Rankin, S., Keisling, M., Mottet, L., & Anafi, M. (2016). *The report of the 2015 U.S. Transgender Survey.* Washington, DC: National Center for Transgender Equality.

Johnson, G., & Chamberlain, C. (2008). From youth to adult homelessness. *Australian Journal of Social Issues, 43*(4), 563–582. doi:10.1002/j.1839-4655.2008.tb00119.x

Jones, M. (2016). Does race matter in addressing homelessness? A review of the literature. *World Health & Medical Policy,* 139–156. doi:10.1002/wmh3.189

Kattari, S., & Begun, S. (2016). On the margins of the marginalized: Transgender homelessness and survival sex. *Affilia: Journal of Women and Social Work, 32*(1), 92–103. doi:10.1177/0886109916651904

Mallon, G. (2009). Knowledge for practice with transgender and gender variant youth. In G. Mallon (Ed.), *Social work practice with transgender and gender variant youth* (pp. 22–37). London, UK and New York, NY: Routledge.

McGuire, J., & Conover-Williams, M. (2010). Creating spaces to support transgender youth. *The Prevention Researcher, 17*(4), 17–20.

Meyer, I. H. (2003). Prejudice, social stress, and mental health in lesbian, gay, and bisexual populations: Conceptual issues and research evidence. *Psychological Bulletin, 129*(5), 674–697. doi:10.1037/0033-2909.129.5.674

Montgomery, A., Szymkowiak, D., & Culhane, D. (2017). Gender differences in factors associated with unsheltered status and increased risk of premature mortality among individuals experiencing homelessness. *Women's Health Issues, 27*(3), 256–263. doi:10.1016/j.whi.2017.03.014

Morton, M. H., Dworsky, A., Matjasko, J., Curry, S., Schleuter, D., Chavez, R., & Farrell, A. (2018). Prevalence and correlates of youth homelessness in the United States. *Journal of Adolescent Health, 62*(1), 14–21. doi:10.1016/j.jadohealth.2017.10.006

Mottet, L., & Ohle, J. M. (2003). Transitioning Our Shelters. *Washington, DC: National Gay and Lesbian Task Force Policy Institute and National Coalition for the Homeless.*Retrieved from https://srlp.org/wp-content/uploads/2012/08/TransitioningOurShelters.pdf

Mottet, L., & Ohle, J. (2006). Transitioning our shelters: Making homeless shelters safe for transgender people. *Journal of Poverty, 10*(2), 77–101. doi:10.1300/J134v10n02_05

National Alliance to End Homelessness. (2018). *Racial inequities in homelessness, by the numbers.* Retrieved from https://endhomelessness.org/resource/racial-inequalities-homelessness-numbers/

Olivet, J., & Dones, M. (2016). Intersectionality and race: How racism and discrimination contribute to homelessness among LGBTQ youth. In C. Price, C. Wheeler, J. Shelton, & M. Maury (Eds.), *At the intersections: A collaborative report on LGBTQ youth homelessness* (pp. 56–59). New York: True Colors Fund and the National LGBTQ Task Force.

Pincus, F. (2000). Discrimination comes in many forms: Individual, institutional, and structural. In M. Adams, W. Blumenfeld, R. Casteneda, H. Hackman, M. Peters, & X. Zuniga (Eds.), *Readings for social justice and social change* (pp. 31–35). New York, NY: Routledge.

Pyne, J. (2011). Unsuitable bodies: Trans people and cisnormativity in shelter services. *Canadian Social Work Journal, 28*(1), 129–138.

Realyst. (2019). *Homeless Youth Risk and Resilience Survey.* Retrieved from https://www.realyst.org/hyrrs

Rew, L., Grady, M., Whittaker, T., & Bowman, K. (2008). Interaction of duration of homelessness and gender on adolescent sexual health indicators. *Journal of Nursing Scholarship, 40*(2), 109–115. doi:10.1111/j.1547-5069.2008.00214.x

Sakamoto, I., Chin, M., Chapra, A., & Ricciardi, J. (2009). A "normative" homeless woman? Marginalisation, emotional injury, and social support of transwomen experiencing homelessness. *Gay and Lesbian Issues and Psychology Review, 5*(1), 2–19.

Shelley, C. (2009). Transgender people and social justice. *The Journal of Individual Psychology, 65*(4), 386–396.

Shelton, J. (2015). Transgender youth homelessness: Understanding programmatic barriers through the lens of cisgenderism. *Children and Youth Services Review, 59*, 10–18. doi:10.1016/j.childyouth.2015.10.006

Shelton, J., & Bond, L. (2017). "It just never worked out": How transgender and gender expansive youth understand their pathways into homelessness. *Families in Society, 98*(4), 235–242. doi:10.1606/1044-3894.2017.98.33

Shelton, J., DeChants, J., Bender, K., Hsu, H., Narendorf, S., Ferguson, K., ... Santa Maria, D. (2018). Homelessness and housing experiences among LGBTQ youth and young adults: An intersectional examination across seven U.S. cities. *Cityscape, 20*(3), 9–33.

Spicer, S. S. (2010). Healthcare needs of the transgender homeless population. *Journal of Gay & Lesbian Mental Health, 14*, 320–339. doi:10.1080/19359705.2010.505844

U.S. Department of Housing and Urban Development. (2018). *Homelessness in the United States: The 2018 annual homeless assessment report to Congress.* Retrieved from www.hudexchange.info/resources/documents/2018-AHAR-Part-1.pdf

Whitbeck, L., Lazoritz, M., Crawford, D., & Hautala, D. (2014). *Street outreach program: Data collection project executive summary.* Retrieved from www.acf.hhs.gov/sites/default/files/fysb/fysb_sop_summary_final.pdf

Wilber, S., Ryan, C., & Marksamer, J. (2006). *Best practice guidelines: Serving LGBT youth in out-of-home care.* Washington, DC: Child Welfare League of America. Retrieved from www.nclrights.org/wp-content/uploads/2013/07/bestpracticeslgbtyouth.pdf

CHAPTER 9

Working with transgender and nonbinary youth in the child welfare system

Richard A. Brandon-Friedman, Ryan Karnoski, and Seventy F. Hall

INTRODUCTION

Transgender and nonbinary (TNB) youth make up a small but substantial portion of youth in the child welfare system (CWS). These youth are not homogenous and each face different challenges per their membership in one of four different subgroups: (1) those who enter the CWS directly and partially due to familial conflict regarding their gender identities; (2) those who enter the CWS for reasons unrelated to their gender identities and for whom their gender identities were not a significant source of strain within their families of origin, (3) those who enter the CWS for reasons other than their gender identities, come out when they are in the CWS, and their gender identities become a significant source of strain within their families of origin; and (4) those who enter the CWS for reasons unrelated to their gender identities, come out while in care, and for whom their gender identities are not a source of strain within their families of origin. Each set of youth faces different challenges in their lives and within the CWS but have similarities in how they are treated within the CWS.

TNB youth are often treated poorly by child welfare workers, service providers, and caregivers within the CWS. Efforts to understand their experiences typically rely on behavioral frameworks that attribute blame to the youth by emphasizing their gender-expansive identities and difficulties with social functioning instead of focusing on care and affirmation. A more informed lens would acknowledge and foreground the significant stress and trauma the youth have experienced and recognize the need for specialized services and individualized treatment plans that address their unique life situations. The development of supportive, affirming environments that are designed to assist TNB youth with navigating their identities requires explicit attention to how professionals and caregivers interact with these youth. The intent of this chapter is to summarize the existing body of research on the experiences of

TNB youth in the CWS, provide recommendations for policy change, and offer best practice guidelines, so individuals who work with TNB youth in the CWS can better serve this population.

LITERATURE REVIEW

Few studies have explored the experiences of TNB youth in foster care. However, preliminary analyses suggest that these youth become involved with the CWS at disproportionately high rates and face additional concerns relative to their cisgender peers throughout their time in out-of-home care. Among a random sample of LA County foster youth between the ages of 12 and 21, 5.6% identified as trans [sic] despite transgender youth making up only approximately 1–2% of the general youth population (Herman et al., 2017; Johns et al., 2019; Wilson & Kastanis, 2015). Few studies have explored the rate of nonbinary individuals among the general youth population. TNB youth also have greater crossover involvement with the juvenile justice system than cisgender youth, with one study showing 3.5 times as many trans and gender-nonconforming [sic] youth in the juvenile justice system had previously been involved with the CWS and five times as many had been placed with foster families or in group home facilities (Irvine & Canfield, 2016).

Even though sexual orientation and gender identity are distinct concepts, it is worth noting that studies indicate that over three-quarters of TNB individuals have lesbian, gay, bisexual, queer, pansexual, asexual, or other sexual orientation identities that are not heterosexual (James et al., 2016). Sexual minority youth in the CWS experience disparities relative to heterosexual youth, such as reduced self-sufficiency, lower levels of sexual health wellbeing, worse sexual health outcomes, and lower quality of foster parent and peer relationships (Brandon-Friedman, 2019; The Annie E. Casey Foundation, 2016). For instance, LGBQ youth report histories of physical abuse and TNB youth report being kicked out of the house or running away at approximately four and six times the rates of heterosexual and cisgender youth, respectively (Irvine & Canfield, 2016; Wilson & Kastanis, 2015).

TNB foster youth also suffer disparities across a wide range of risk domains, including abuse history at home and in the community, ongoing conflicts with members of their families of origin, mistreatment by child welfare workers and system-based caregivers, rates of mental health hospitalization and congregate care placements, housing insecurity, placement instability, academic achievement, and odds of aging out of foster care (Irvine & Canfield, 2016; McCormick, Schmidt, & Terrazas, 2016; Wilson & Kastanis, 2015). Furthermore, many of these youth experience additional harassment and/or abuse while in care, contradicting the CWS's goals of achieving safety and permanency for youth (Matarese, Greeno, & Betsinger, 2017; McCormick et al., 2016).

TNB youth are also at increased risk of exposure to *identity abuse* while in care (Woulfe & Goodman, 2018). According to Woulfe and Goodman, identity abuse may entail disclosure of an individual's gender identity without their consent (i.e., outing), use of homophobic or transphobic slurs, attempts to shame the individual about their gender identity, refusal to allow the individual to express their gender identity, and/ or efforts to bar contact with the LGBTQ+ community altogether. Within the context of foster care, identity abuse may manifest as harassment from caregivers, staff, and peers; failure to use gender pronouns and names that align with youths' gender identities; or outright discrimination against TNB youth.

Scholars have hypothesized that the limited number of families willing to foster who have experience caring for TNB youth, as well as transphobia or discrimination within the CWS, contribute to placement instability and insecurity among TNB youth (Barnett, 2018; McCormick et al., 2016). Other pertinent areas of consideration include the strong religious foundations of many child welfare agencies, the legal ability of social service agencies to refuse to place a sexual or gender minority youth, misconceptions about sexual minority youth (e.g., they are more likely to sexually offend against other youth), and state policies that do not require social service agencies to consider sexual orientation and/or gender identity when making placement decisions (Bucchio, 2012; Clements & Rosenwald, 2008; Martin, Down, & Erney, 2016).

POLICY CONSIDERATIONS

Several organizations and agencies have developed policies and best practice guidelines to assist professional providers and caregivers with working with TNB youth. While some focus on LGBQ+ individuals as well, this chapter will only explore guidelines for working with TNB youth. What follows is a synthesis of recommendations from the National Resource Center for Adoption, National Resource Center for Permanency and Family Connections, and National Resource Center for Recruitment and Retention of Foster and Adoptive Parents at AdoptUSKids (n.d.); Children's Rights, Lambda Legal, and the Center for the Study of Social Policy (Remlin, Cook, Erney, Cherepon, & Gentile, 2017); the Putting Pride Into Practice Project of Family Builders by Adoption (Wilber, 2013); New York City's Administration for Children's Services (Ryan, 2016); the National Center for Lesbian Rights (Marksamer, Spade, & Arkles, 2011); the Capacity Building Center for States (n.d.); the Child Welfare League of America (2012); the Walter S. Johnson Foundation (Perron, 2015); Mallon (2011); McCormick et al. (2016); the Human Rights Campaign (n.d.); the University of Maryland School of Social Work's Institute for Innovation & Implementation (Matarese et al., 2017); and the California getR.E.A.L. Initiative (getR.E.A.L., n.d.). Agencies not familiar with the needs of TNB youth would benefit from having a consultant attuned to these youths' needs available when making treatment and placement decisions.

Regulations

State regulations are often unclear on differentiating gender and sex, so many agencies have adopted conservative policies based on a young person's sex assigned at birth (generally limited to males and females). State statutes are needed that distinguish between sex and gender and allow for recognition of youths' gender identities. Written policies should also require accommodations related to dress codes, sleeping arrangements, and attendance at gender-segregated activities. For example, inclusive regulations would ensure that TNB youth are permitted to wear clothing that corresponds with their gender identities.

Documentation

A lack of well-established standards for collecting data on the sexual orientations and/or gender identities of youth in the CWS likely contributes to their visibility (Barnett, 2018; Wilson & Kastanis, 2015). Wilber (2013) developed a comprehensive set of guidelines for documentation of youths' sexual orientations and gender identities in state and clinical records. The guidelines suggest that these areas of youths' lives should only be noted when pertinent, such as in therapy referrals, but should otherwise be minimized to prevent an invasion of privacy. Further, records that include this information should document the reasons for its inclusion. Finally, due to the inherent fluidity of gender identity and expression, those who work with youth in the CWS should continually reassess the impacts of these factors on the youths' placement and service needs.

Use of names and pronouns

Although court and medical records must have youths' legal names documented in them, these standards need not apply to everyday interactions with youth (Marksamer et al., 2011). Failure to use TNB youths' chosen names and identified pronouns can harm their mental health and psychosocial functioning, especially as others in the youths' lives may have displayed this behavior in an attempt to demean them and/or negate their identities previously (Marksamer et al., 2011; Matarese et al., 2017; Woronoff, Estrada, & Sommer, 2006). Child service agencies should implement written policies that require professional providers and caregivers to use the names and pronouns specified by youth when addressing them directly and in communications that do not require legal name usage.

Placement decisions

All youth have equal rights to placement decisions and treatment protocols, yet, even though doing so is illegal, the CWS often isolates TNB youth from other youth under the pretext of "ensuring their safety" (Marksamer et al., 2011). It is incumbent on the CWS to prescreen prospective placement settings for safety to eliminate the need for such measures. Preferably, a multidisciplinary team experienced in working with TNB youth would explore the options available and make individualized placement decisions according to the youths' specific needs. A youth-driven approach that gives youth the opportunity to identify individuals with whom they feel safe and affirmed might be advantageous in these cases, though child welfare agencies must ensure that such a placement would meet state standards. Moreover, youth should have the authority to determine how out they want to be to their caregivers and to what degree their gender identities should play a role in placement decisions. In some circumstances, youth may choose to background their gender identities in order to maintain or enter a placement they feel will be in their best interests (Stoessel, 2013). Doing so should only be done per a youth's choice.

BEST PRACTICES

Wilber (2013) suggested four principles to guide services for LGBTQ+ youth in the CWS: (1) All children deserve safety and acceptance; (2) Children need support and nurturance to explore and develop positive identities, including their sexual orientations and gender identities; (3) Children thrive when caregivers affirm and respect their sexual orientations and gender identities and expressions; and (4) Children perceived as LGBTQ+ experience the same risks as those who are LGBTQ+. An additional consideration is what the Capacity Building Center for States (n.d.) refers to as the principle of "normalcy". In upholding this principle, the CWS must place TNB youth in environments that are as close to the standards and healthy as possible and ensure that they feel as "normal" as their peers. TNB youth must receive the same degree of safety, freedom from abuse, and ability to explore themselves and their identities as do all other youth, whether that be with supportive professionals, socially with peers, or in relationships. The remainder of this section will note common concerns TNB youth in the CWS face and suggest ways to address them.

Affirming environments

TNB youth are accustomed to seeking out indications that they are in affirming environments. Displaying symbols used by lesbian, gay, bisexual, transgender, queer, and other sexual and gender minority communities (e.g., rainbow, transgender flags, pink triangles), safe space indicators, non-discrimination policies, and books or reading materials that celebrate diversity and let TNB youth know they are in places that recognize and affirm them. Caregivers and service providers should also be knowledgeable about local and national service agencies that work with TNB youth so youth can access them as needed.

Evaluating caregivers

Before placing TNB youth, the CWS must assess placements for safety and the caregivers' and service providers' abilities to provide affirmative environments. This conversation should take place before making a placement decision to minimize the risk of harassment, abuse, and/or subsequent placement disruptions. Areas to assess include the caregivers' and service providers': (1) knowledge of gender identity and expression; (2) willingness to accept and affirm the youth; (3) ability to discuss gender identity and expression openly and in a positive, respectful manner; (4) strategies for addressing gender identity and expression with others to whom the youth is exposed, including their ability to exercise discretion in disclosing a youth's gender identity and intention to confront harassment and/or abuse directed towards the youth; and (5) willingness and ability to connect the youth with other TNB youth and organizations serving these populations.

Lack of caregiver and service provider education regarding gender identity

It is essential that all caregivers and service providers that work with youth in the CWS receive comprehensive training on gender identity, gender diversity, and gender fluidity, as many feel unprepared to discuss these topics with youth in their care. Even those who feel they are reasonably familiar with these issues may feel uncomfortable broaching them with youth if they do not know how to initiate the conversation or lack an understanding of what is considered appropriate for discussion. In addition to a basic foundation in sex, gender identity, gender expression, and gender fluidity, training curricula should cover other frequently misunderstood areas such as the differences between these terms, their relationships to sexual orientation and sexual behavior, and various nonbinary gender identities (e.g., enby, genderqueer, agender). Many trainings fail to address these other gender identities, leaving youth who identify as gender minorities but not as transgender misunderstood.

Abuse and harassment

Among the factors identified as contributing to elevated levels of harassment and/or victimization among TNB youth in the CWS are inadequate caregiver and provider training, high professionals and caregivers turnover, lack of policies that explicitly forbid harassment related to sexual orientation and gender identity, failure to enforce existing policies, inadequate staff oversight, the tendency to frame such actions as representing professionals' and caregivers' personal or religious beliefs and therefore not subject to discipline, and the number of religiously-affiliated social service agencies that are legally able to exclude LGBTQ+ adults from their agencies. Anti-harassment policies and oversight are essential to addressing the needs of TNB youth in the CWS and should remain applicable to all perpetrators, whether they be caregivers, providers, staff members, peers, foster siblings, mentors, or others with whom the youth interact. Agencies should establish procedures for reporting harassment and abuse safely and confidentially and must ensure that all caregivers and service providers are aware of these procedures and their responsibility to utilize them.

When considering placements with religiously-affiliated agencies or with caregivers who hold strong religious beliefs, service providers must carefully evaluate the environment. While many of these organizations are welcoming, affirming, and supportive, others can be hostile for TNB youth. For example, some caregivers and agency personnel try to force youth to attend therapy to change their gender identities, despite the proven ineffectiveness and danger of reparative practices (Bucchio, 2012; Matarese et al., 2017; McCormick et al., 2016). Caregivers and professionals must address their own biases and remember the guiding principles of safety, youth affirmation, positive support, and normalcy, as well as ethical and legal standards that prohibit conducting or advocating for conversion or reparative therapies (e.g., American Psychiatric Association, 2018; National Association of Social Workers, 2015).

Furthermore, agencies, caregivers, and service providers must be in tune with aspects of youths' environments that are outside of their direct control. When youth experience abuse or harassment offsite, such as in an educational facility or community location, it is incumbent on those who have legal responsibility or who are serving as caregivers for the youth to intervene and advocate on their behalf. Caregivers can mitigate concerns ahead of time by approaching the school or other social organizations to discuss accommodations for the TNB youth before they arrive.

Privacy

Privacy and discretion regarding gender identity and body are concerns for many TNB youth. In home environments, TNB youth should be treated according to their gender identities and not forced to share rooms with youth with different gender identities against their will. When a single room is unavailable, youth should be placed with someone of their asserted gender unless doing so would pose safety risks. In particular, caregivers and providers should be aware that it may not be safe to place adolescents who were assigned female at birth with cisgender males due to concerns about sexual assault.

Within congregate care settings, attention must be paid to multi-person restrooms, shower facilities, and policies regarding bodily searches. TNB youth should have access to facilities that match their asserted genders or, where more appropriate, single-user facilities. A youth's decision to use a multi-person restroom that corresponds with their asserted gender should be respected as long as safety can be maintained (e.g., keeping other residents out of the multi-person restroom when the youth is using it). During mandatory body searches, TNB youth should be provided a location separate from other residents and be permitted to choose the gender of the person conducting the search.

Gender policing and sexualization

LGBTQ+ youth in the CWS often experience more oversight of their peer interactions and social engagements than those who are cisgender and heterosexual. Examples include banning the youth from dating, attending social events, or having peers over to visit and excessive monitoring of communications and clothing choices (McCormick et al., 2016; Woronoff et al., 2006). Furthermore, caregivers of TNB youth are more likely to misread the youths' actions as sexualized and, thus, to restrict their rights and privileges, despite the lack of empirical evidence indicating they are more sexually motivated than other youth (McCormick et al., 2016). Such practices are discriminatory and hamper youths' intrapersonal and interpersonal development. While it may be necessary to consider a youth's gender when evaluating sleeping arrangements, social events, and other activities when relevant, such evaluations should not subject TNB youth to additional scrutiny relative to their cisgender peers.

Access to community resources

TNB youth should have access to community agencies and organizations that serve LGBTQ+ individuals. Affirming environments and the ability to socialize with others who identify as LGBTQ+ positively impact youths' intrapsychic and social development and afford them opportunities to grow and establish autonomy (Brandon-Friedman & Kim, 2016; Matarese et al., 2017). TNB youth should be granted access to these programs, including through facilitated transportation per the same policies that allow any youth to attend any other social events.

Access to mental health care and health care

As a consequence of harassment, abuse, stigma, and discrimination, many TNB youth experience significant social-emotional concerns and require clinical therapeutic services. While being TNB is not directly associated with mental health needs, TNB youth may experience psychosocial difficulties related to the incongruence between their self-image and their bodily presentation and the gendered ways they are treated (Connolly, Zervos, Barone, Johnson, & Joseph, 2016). Clinicians who provide therapeutic services to TNB youth should have experience working with this population and understand the trauma many have experienced.

Regulations regarding access to gender-affirming medical treatments for youth in the CWS vary widely by state, with several states providing little guidance. Medical associations recommend that TNB youth be permitted to receive gender-affirming care from a young age and advocate that youth should have access to age-appropriate information about gender-affirming medical treatments. Medical treatment options range from puberty suppression for prepubertal youth to gender-affirming hormones for pubertal youth to surgical interventions for late teens and older individuals. Many larger cities have multidisciplinary clinics that provide TNB youth with comprehensive mental and physical health care as well as access to fertility resources, care for eating disorders, and additional psychological services. Caregivers and service providers should be knowledgeable about these specialty clinics and include professionals from such clinics or other mental health providers attuned to the unique needs of TNB youth during care planning. These resources are especially important during placement changes, as this is when TNB youth often experience disruptions in gender-related care (Karnoski, 2017). For more information on medical care and mental health care for TNB youth, please see Chapter 1 and Chapter 4 in this volume.

Role models

LGBTQ+ youth often emphasize the importance of positive adults as role models in their lives. Unfortunately, LGBTQ+ adults face considerable barriers when attempting to become foster or adoptive parents. For instance, some states do not permit members of these populations to be licensed or do not allow individuals in a same-sex relationship to adopt, and many social service providers hold negative views of LGBTQ+ individuals. As a result, LGBTQ+ adults may begin to doubt their own abilities to serve as positive role models for youth (All Children – All Families, 2012; Mallon, 2011). Recommendations to counteract these difficulties include targeted recruitment of LGBTQ+ adults, modification of discriminatory state licensing and adoption laws, efforts to increase knowledge about sexual and gender minorities and reduce prejudice among social service providers, and integration of sexual orientation and gender identity into agency non-discrimination policies (All Children – All Families, 2012; Mallon, 2011). As suggested previously, connecting youth to community-based agencies serving TNB individuals can provide access to these resources.

Relationships with families of origin

Specific attention to TNB youths' prior home environments is crucial, as LGBTQ+ youth experience higher levels of adverse childhood experiences, enter the child welfare system due to direct conflict with family members more often (for reasons that are frequently related to sexual orientation and/or gender identity), and are more likely to have been physically, sexually, or emotionally abused by their parents (Brandon-Friedman, 2019; Friedman et al., 2011; McCormick et al., 2016). The assessment tool noted previously for evaluating affirming environments can be used with families of origin, as can other toolkits such as that from the Child Welfare League of America (2012). Regardless of the reasons that TNB youth enter the CWS, services should address the home environment if it was not affirming of the youth's gender identity. Strategies that could improve the home environment include family member education, family member support groups, and family therapy. For further information on working with parents and families of TNB youth, please see Chapter 12 in this volume.

CONCLUSION

TNB youth in the CWS system face interpersonal, familial, and systemic challenges that exceed those of their cisgender peers. They often experience harassment and/or discrimination from those charged with their care and have significantly worse psychosocial and educational outcomes. Organizations have developed guidelines CWS agencies can use to evaluate their current practices and modify them to best serve TNB youth, many of which have been synthesized in this chapter. Ultimately, service decisions for TNB youth in the CWS should adhere to the principles of normalcy, safety, and acceptance; support and nurturance for identity exploration and development; and respect and affirmation. Appropriate service provider and caregiver education, adherence to stated non-discrimination policies, and conscious attention to the development of positive and affirming environments can ensure TNB youth in the CWS receive the care needed to thrive.

CASE STUDIES

General reflection questions for both case studies

1. What are the largest challenges currently facing the client?
2. What do you think the client would identify as their greatest need at this time?
3. What are the client's strengths?
4. What are the most important considerations for the state caseworker?
5. How is the client's gender identity impacting their current situation?
6. As the client's social worker, what would be your treatment foci be with the client?
7. As the client's social worker, how might you best advocate for your client?

Case study 1

Jasmine (she/her/hers) is a 7-year-old trans girl living in a therapeutic group home for foster children. She entered foster care at age 3 after being found wandering on the street with her siblings. She was placed into foster care, later diagnosed with gender dysphoria and oppositional defiant behaviors, and separated from her siblings. Jasmine's original foster placement disrupted after Jasmine broke a window and she moved between several other foster placements before moving into the group home at age 6. Jasmine attends school in her community, has several friends there, and is at grade level academically. Jasmine's mom Brandi reported that Jasmine's father died before she was born. A termination of parental rights petition may soon be filed against Brandi after two disrupted trial returns home for her children, and there is a concurrent permanency plan with a primary plan of adoption.

Brandi is in recovery for addiction and has recently begun participating in extrajudicial visits with her children to rebuild relationships with them. Brandi credits her substance abuse recovery to her Christian faith and believes gender must correspond to sex. Brandi and Jasmine's siblings refuse to use Jasmine's chosen name and use he/him pronouns despite protestation from Jasmine. During family visits, Brandi frequently makes disparaging comments about Jasmine being allowed to wear girl clothes, noting she gave birth to a boy. A trans-affirming employee in the group home overheard these comments, and Brandi is no longer allowed to visit at the group home. Jasmine has told her therapist that while the comments upset her, she still wants to visit her mom and siblings regularly.

Six months ago, a couple with two other children in the home began having pre-adoptive visits with Jasmine. After multiple visits per week in the community, Jasmine began to have overnight visits in the couple's home. During a lengthy visit, the couple unexpectedly returned Jasmine to the group home early, yelling that Jasmine had exposed her genitals to their two other children explaining to them, "I'm a girl with a penis." The on-call case manager at the group home wrote a case note about this incident, labeling Jasmine a "sexually aggressive youth." Jasmine's new state caseworker is struggling to find Jasmine an adoptive home and is considering moving her to a group home that offers long-term placements for youth sexual offenders.

Case study 1 reflection questions

1. How do you think Jasmine may feel in this situation?
2. What do you think are the priorities of Jasmine, her mother, the group home case manager, the state caseworker, and the prospective adoptive family?
3. How might Jasmine's gender identity impact others' interpretation of the events in the couple's home?
4. If you were Jasmine's therapist, how would you process her experience with the adoptive couple with her?
5. If you were a visit supervisor, how would you coach Brandi on using language that reflects her commitment to Jasmine without disrespecting Jasmine's gender identity?

Case study 2

Quintin (they/them/theirs), a 14-year-old nonbinary teenager assigned female at birth, is currently in a kinship care placement with their grandparents after their parents were incarcerated for felony burglary. Quintin's current permanency plan is relative guardianship to be finalized in the next few months. Quintin regularly dresses in ties, top hats, tutus, and tights. Quintin recently began ninth grade and has been bullied at school, primarily around their clothing choices, changing in the women's locker room, and using the women's bathroom. During a meeting with Quintin, their grandparents, and the school principal, the principal "outed" Quintin as nonbinary to their grandparents, who did not know Quintin had been using they/them pronouns or requesting use of a single-stall bathroom. After this meeting, Quintin ran away from their grandparents' home and stayed in a teen shelter for two nights, before being returned to their grandparents' home by their state caseworker. Quintin's grades began to suffer and it was discovered that Quintin had been skipping class to use the bathroom at a nearby coffee shop where there was an all-gender bathroom they could use.

Quintin's grandparents are concerned about the amount of time Quintin spends online and on their cell phone and recently threatened to restrict Quintin's access to the internet. Later that night, Quintin superficially cut themselves with a razor blade and posted online that they had taken a handful of pills. An online friend called 911 and Quintin was taken to an inpatient behavioral health unit where they remained for one week. While there, Quintin stated that they were suicidal because of their severe gender dysphoria related to their body. A psychiatrist diagnosed Quintin with major depressive disorder and gender dysphoria and recommended an antidepressant, but Quintin refused the prescription. At the end of the hospital stay, Quintin stated that they would not return home unless they could begin taking testosterone. Quintin's grandfather refused, stating that although he would support Quintin identifying as nonbinary, he would not allow Quintin to make any permanent changes to their appearance. Quintin was discharged from the hospital to their grandparents' care despite Quintin's objections.

Quintin currently receives weekly outpatient counseling, but the therapist told Quintin that she had never had a transgender client before and that it might be a good opportunity for her to learn something new through Quintin. Quintin has not come out to their parents and is worried that their grandparents will "out" them when discussing Quintin's mental health care and hospital stay. Recently Quintin's grandparents have begun threatening to disrupt the placement as they feel too overwhelmed by Quintin's difficulties and gender "problems". This would result in Quintin being placed into foster care. Yesterday, Quintin told a teacher at their school that they plan to run away to live with a 19-year-old boyfriend they met through school friends and who supports their gender identity.

Case study 2 reflection questions

1. How do you think Quintin is feeling in this situation?
2. How do you think Quintin's grandfather is feeling in this situation?
3. If you were Quintin's state caseworker, what would you do to try to stabilize Quintin's placement with their grandparents? Would you seek an alternative placement for Quintin? Why or why not?
4. What do you think of Quintin's therapist's comment? How do you think Quintin would feel after hearing their therapist say that?
5. How do you think being in kinship care impacts Quintin's experience of coming out as nonbinary? How might this be different than being in foster care with an unrelated family?

RESOURCES

A Place of Respect: A guide for Group Care Facilities Serving Transgender and Gender Non-Conforming Youth (2011)
Guide developed by the National Center for Lesbian Rights
Safe Havens: Closing the Gap Between Recommended Practice and Reality for Transgender and Gender-Expansive Youth in Out-of-Home Care (2017)
Guide developed by Children's Rights, Lambda Legal, and the Center for the Study of Social Policy
Guidelines for Managing Information Related to the Sexual Orientation & Gender Identity and Expression of Children in Child Welfare Systems (2013)
Guidelines developed by Family Builders, Legal Services for Children, National Center for Lesbian Rights, and the Center for the Study of Social Policy
Caring for LGBTQ Children & Youth: A Guide for Child Welfare Providers
Guide developed by the Human Rights Campaign
beFierce: A Toolkit for Providers Working with LGBTQ Foster Youth
Toolkit developed with support from the Walter S. Johnson Foundation

REFERENCES

All Children – All Families. (2012). *Promising practices in adoption and foster care: A comprehensive guide to policies and practices that welcome, affirm, and support lesbian, gay, bisexual and transgender foster and adoptive parents.* Washington, DC: Human Rights Campaign Foundation.

American Psychiatric Association. (2018). *Position statement on conversion therapy and LGBTQ patients.* Washington, DC: Author.

Barnett, L. E. (2018). *A phenomenological look at the lived experiences of lesbian, gay, bisexual, transgender, and questioning foster youth in the Fresno, CA area.* (Masters Thesis), Retrieved from www.fresnostate.edu/chhs/ccassc/documents/LaurelBARNETT.pdf

Brandon-Friedman, R. A. (2019). *The impact of sexual identity development on the sexual health of youth formerly in the child welfare system.* (Doctoral dissertation), Retrieved from http://hdl.handle.net/1805/18599

Brandon-Friedman, R. A., & Kim, H.-W. (2016). Using social support levels to predict sexual identity development among college students who identify as a sexual minority. *Journal of Gay & Lesbian Social Services, 28*(4), 1–25. doi:10.1080/10538720.2016.1221784

Bucchio, J. D. (2012). *Characteristics of foster parents willing to care for sexual minority youth.* (Doctoral dissertation), Retrieved from http://trace.tennessee.edu/cgi/viewcontent.cgi?article=2687&context=utk_graddiss

Capacity Building Center for States. (n.d.). Considerations for LGBTQ children and youth in foster care: Exploring normalcy as it relates to P.L. 113–183. Retrieved from https://library.childwelfare.gov/cwig/ws/library/docs/capacity/Blob/105738.pdf?r=1&rpp=10&upp=0&w=±NATIVE%28%27recno%3D105738%27%29&m=1

Child Welfare League of America. (2012). *Recommended practices to promote the safety and well-being of lesbian, gay, bisexual, transgender and questioning (LGBTQ) youth and youth at risk of or living with HIV in child welfare settings.* Washington, DC: Author.

Clements, J. A., & Rosenwald, M. (2008). Foster parents' perspectives on LGB youth in the child welfare system. *Journal of Gay & Lesbian Social Services, 19*(1), 57–69. doi:10.1300/J041v19n01_04

Connolly, M. D., Zervos, M. J., Barone, C. J., 2nd, Johnson, C. C., & Joseph, C. L. (2016). The mental health of transgender youth: Advances in understanding. *Journal of Adolescent Health, 59*(5), 489–495. doi:10.1016/j.jadohealth.2016.06.012

Friedman, M. S., Marshal, M. P., Guadamuz, T. E., Wei, C., Wong, C. F., Saewyc, E. M., & Stall, R. (2011). A meta-analysis of disparities in childhood sexual abuse, parental physical abuse, and peer victimization among sexual minority and sexual nonminority individuals. *American Journal of Public Health, 101*(8), 1481–1494. doi:10.2105/AJPH.2009.190009

getR.E.A.L. (n.d.). *Transgender and gender nonconforming children in California foster care.* Washington, DC: Center for the Study of Social Policy.

Herman, J. L., Flores, A. R., Brown, T. N. T., Wilson, B. D. M., & Conron, K. J. (2017). *Age of individuals who identify as transgender in the United States.* Los Angeles, CA: The Williams Institute.

Human Rights Campaign. (n.d.). *Caring for LGBTQ children & youth: A guide for child welfare providers.* Washington, DC: Author.

Irvine, A., & Canfield, A. (2016). The overrepresentation of lesbian, gay, bisexual, questioning, gender nonconforming and transgender youth within the child welfare to juvenile justice crossover population. *Journal of Gender, Social Policy & the Law, 24*(2). Retrieved from http://digitalcommons.wcl.american.edu/jgspl/vol24/iss2/2

James, S. E., Herman, J. L., Rankin, S., Keisling, M., Mottet, L., & Anafi, M. (2016). *The report of the 2015 U.S. Transgender Survey.* Washington, DC: National Center for Transgender Equality.

Johns, M. M., Lowry, R., Andrzejewski, J., Barrios, L. C., Demissie, Z., McManus, T., & Underwood, J. M. (2019). Transgender identity and experiences of violence victimization, substance use, suicide risk, and sexual risk behaviors among high school students – 19 states and large urban school districts, 2017. *MMWR. Morbidity and Mortality Weekly Report, 68*(3), 67–71. doi:10.15585/mmwr.mm6803a3

Karnoski, R. (2017). *Experiences of healthcare providers of lesbian, gay, bisexual, and transgender foster youth*. (Masters Thesis), Retrieved from https://digital.lib.washington. edu/researchworks/bitstream/handle/1773/39874/Karnoski_washington_0250O_17019. pdf?sequence=1&isAllowed=yf

Mallon, G. P. (2011). The home study assessment process for gay, lesbian, bisexual, and transgender prospective foster and adoptive families. *Journal of GLBT Family Studies, 7*(1–2), 9–29. doi:10.1080/1550428x.2011.537229

Marksamer, J., Spade, D., & Arkles, G. (2011). *A place of respect: A guide for group care facilities serving transgender and gender non-conforming youth*. San Francisco, CA: National Center for Lesbian Rights.

Martin, M., Down, L., & Erney, R. (2016). *Out of the shadows: Supporting LGBTQ youth in child welfare through cross-system collaboration*. Washington, DC: Center for the Study of Social Policy.

Matarese, M., Greeno, E., & Betsinger, A. (2017). *Youth with diverse sexual orientation, gender identity and expression in child welfare: A review of best practices*. Baltimore, MD: Institute for Innovation & Implementation, University of Maryland School of Social Work.

McCormick, A., Schmidt, K., & Terrazas, S. (2016). LGBTQ youth in the child welfare system: An overview of research, practice, and policy. *Journal of Public Child Welfare, 11*(1), 27–39. doi:10.1080/15548732.2016.1221368

National Association of Social Workers. (2015). *Sexual orientation change efforts (SOCE) and conversion therapy with lesbians, gay men, bisexuals, and transgender persons*. Washington, DC: NASW Press.

National Resource Center for Adoption, National Resource Center for Permanency and Family Connections, & National Resource Center for Recruitment and Retention of Foster and Adoptive Parents at AdoptUSKids. (n.d.). *Strategies for recruiting lesbian, gay, bisexual, and transgender foster, adoptive, and kinship families*. Washington, DC: U.S. Department of Health and Human Services, Children's Bureau.

Perron, S. (2015). *beFIERCE! A toolkit for providers working with LGBTQ foster youth*. San Francisco, CA: Walter S. Johnson Foundation.

Remlin, C. W., Cook, M. C., Erney, R., Cherepon, H., & Gentile, K. (2017). *Safe havens: Closing the gap between recommended practice and reality for transgender and gender-expansive youth in out-of-home care*. New York, NY: Children's Rights.

Ryan, C. (2016). *Identifying LGBTQ affirming homes*. New York, NY: New York City's Administration for Children's Services.

Stoessel, T. Y. (2013). Addressing the harm of silence and assumptions of mutability: Implementing effective non-discrimination policies for lesbian, gay, bisexual, transgender, and queer youth in foster care. *UC Davis Journal of Juvenile Law & Policy, 17*(1), 79–124.

The Annie E. Casey Foundation. (2016). *LGBTQ in child welfare: A systematic review of the literature*. Retrieved from www.aecf.org/m/resourcedoc/aecf-LGBTQ2inChildWelfare-2016.pdf

Wilber, S. (2013). *Guidelines for managing information related to the sexual orientation and gender identity and expression of children in child welfare systems*. Oakland, CA: Putting Pride Into Practice Project, Family Builders by Adoption.

Wilson, B. D. M., & Kastanis, A. A. (2015). Sexual and gender minority disproportionality and disparities in child welfare: A population-based study. *Children and Youth Services Review, 58*, 11–17. doi:10.1016/j.childyouth.2015.08.016

Woronoff, R., Estrada, R., & Sommer, S. (2006). *OUT of the margins: A report on the regional listening forums highlighting the experiences of lesbian, gay, bisexual, transgender and questioning youth in care*. Washington, DC: Child Welfare League of America.

Woulfe, J. M., & Goodman, L. A. (2018). Identity abuse as a tactic of violence in LGBTQ communities: Initial validation of the identity abuse measure. *Journal of Interpersonal Violence* (Advance online publication). doi:10.1177/0886260518760018

PART 3

Coming out
and family

CHAPTER 10

Supporting transgender and nonbinary youth in their coming out process

M. Killian Kinney and Finneran K. Muzzey

INTRODUCTION

In addition to the typical stressors of childhood and adolescence, gender-expansive or transgender and nonbinary (TNB) youth face additional challenges related to social and medical transitioning that are unique from their LGBQ peers (e.g., chosen name, pronouns, bathrooms). TNB individuals have to overcome rejection, stigma, discrimination, and victimization at rates higher than their LGBQ peers (Harrison et al., 2012; Su et al., 2016); these obstacles may come from sources intended to function as support systems for youth (e.g., families, friends, school administration) which further complicates the process of transitioning. Families of origin may struggle with grief related to the perceived loss of their child and aspirations they had based on sex assigned at birth (such as motherhood) (McNeilly, 2019). In particular, parents often struggle with understanding nonbinary gender identities and gender-neutral pronouns like they/them or ze/zir, and may even pressure nonbinary individuals to transition to a binary gender (Lewis, 2008). Teachers and school administrators may struggle with understanding gender-expansive identities and how to best accommodate the needs of TNB youth (Schindel, 2008).

Despite these potential difficulties, there is a growing acceptance of TNB youth identities in society and even small amounts of support can set forth a path of resilience for TNB youth. Social media support sources (e.g., Facebook, Tumblr, Instagram) may set an important foundation of resilience, even if that support is not experienced in person. In addition, many peers, school administrators, and family of origin members desire to be supportive of TNB youth during transitional periods, although they may be misinformed about gender identity and expression and unsure of how to best provide that support. Creating accessible clinical environments which foster support and validation for those that play important relational roles in the lives of TNB youth is paramount.

This chapter will examine the process of coming out for TNB youth, the role of caregivers, schools, and social media in the coming out process, and factors for resilience and thriving for TNB youth. Best practices for providing support and validation for youth and their families during the coming out process also will be discussed. The chapter ends with an activity designed to facilitate self-reflection, critical thinking, and empathy with regards to the coming out process for TNB youth.

WHAT WE KNOW

To date, much less is known about TNB identity development than about LGBQ identity development, of which coming out (the act of internally and socially announcing one's sexual and/or gender identity) is an essential developmental stage for wellbeing among LGBQ and TNB people (Asakura & Craig, 2014; Kosciw, Palmer, & Kull, 2015).

Being out in one's gender has been correlated with better wellbeing (Kosciw, Greytak, Diaz, & Bartkiewicz, 2010). However, fear of victimization and loss of social support lead some people to delay coming out (Beemyn & Rankin, 2011; Kosciw, Greytak, Bartkiewicz, Boesen, & Palmer, 2012), especially when weighing multiple marginalized identities (Nicolazzo, 2016). In some cases, being outed by others may remove choices around coming out (Budge, Tebber, & Howard, 2010; Kosciw et al., 2015). Interestingly, a longitudinal study of stigma management found that gay men and lesbian women reported higher wellbeing (as measured by depression, self-esteem, and life-satisfaction) on days when they decided not to disclose their sexual orientation when given an opportunity (Beals, Peplau, & Gable, 2009).

The process of coming out plays a pivotal point in identity development for TNB youth, one which is strongly influenced by the level of supportive caregivers as well as the environment (Baiocco et al., 2015; Kinney, 2018b). Safer, more affirming environments (e.g., support from parents and schools) have been attributed to a growing number of youth and young adults coming out as TNB (Budge et al., 2013). However, concerns regarding coming out persist, including rejection and bullying.

School environments are primary social environments that have the potential to bolster or hinder wellbeing in TNB youth with opportunity for: (1) experiences of discrimination, bullying, and victimization; and/or (2) experiences of support, community, and friendship (Kosciw et al., 2012; Kosciw, Greytak, Palmer, & Boesen, 2014). The interpersonal and structural discrimination of TNB youth is well-documented with findings indicating high levels of aggressiveness from peers and school administrators (Abreu, Black, Mosley, & Fedewa, 2016), as well as through the collectively named "bathroom bills", which target TNB youth's ability to use their correct gender's bathroom (Beese & Martin, 2018). Hostile school environments have been found to severely compromise the psychosocial wellbeing of LGBTQ youth (Asakura & Craig, 2014). Studies have confirmed reports of verbal harassment and feeling unsafe in school among TNB individuals (Harrison et al., 2012; Kosciw, Greytak, Giga, Villenas, & Danischewski, 2016). In response to hostile school environments, TNB youth report resorting to isolation by distancing themselves from school to counteract victimization (Grossman et al., 2009). Such environments inhibit the coming out process with potentially long-lasting repercussions regarding identity development. On the other hand, school environments can also provide valuable opportunities for TNB youth to gain acceptance and validation of their gender identity. Peers who are similar to them may be found, and a sense of community and kinship can begin to be established (Marx & Kettrey, 2016).

TNB youth are at a higher risk of losing or ending their relationships to their families of origin than their cisgender heterosexual or lesbian, gay, and bisexual peers (Durso & Gates, 2012). Parents of LGBQ youth often cite their fear of never having grandchildren, of their child having a normal life, of their child being aggressively bullied, and a general lack of misunderstanding of the identity of their child (Fuller & Riggs, 2018). These things hold true for TNB youth, with an important addition: the parental grief of losing a child (Wahlig, 2015). TNB young adults often describe having to combat and console their parents through feeling as if their child has died (Kinney, Muzzey, & McCauley, 2019). These factors, combined with structural stigma and discrimination, work to contribute to the increased likelihood of losing relationships to families of origin for TNB youth (McConnell, Birkett, & Mustanski, 2016). Conversely, when parents are more accepting, youth report experiencing lower psychological distress and behavioral problems than those whose parents rejected their gender nonconformity (Bradley, 2009).

Gender identity development is normal among all youth, regardless of cisgender, transgender, or nonbinary gender identities. Further, sexual and gender identity development follow similar developmental trajectories. The implications of the type of identity are what shapes the social experiences of the youth. Cisgender heterosexual identities are what are considered "normal" in our society, and deviations from those identities may be fraught with stigmatization, discrimination, and victimization experiences (Worthen, 2016). It is not that TNB youth develop differently or erroneously as compared to their cisgender peers; rather, it is that their identity is considered different/non-normative and is treated as such by society at large. For TNB youth, coming out is a process that they will continue to navigate, and one which can be improved by creating affirming environments and providing support.

There are similarities between the gender identity developmental trajectory of TNB youth and LGBQ youth. For instance, gender identity development tends to begin early, with many youth noticing a bothersome difference between their gender identity and gender norms based on their assigned sex at birth (ASAB), a phenomenon known as gender dysphoria (Olson-Kennedy et al., 2016). The DSM-5 describes gender dysphoria as referring to distress that arises from an incongruence between one's ASAB and gender identity and recognizes that not all TNB individuals experience dysphoria (American Psychiatric Association, 2013). At a young age, some TNB youth may begin to make announcements about their genitalia, suggesting that it does not belong on their body (Olson, Schrager, Belzer, Simons, & Clark, 2015). TNB youth may also remark that they are not the gender that has been assigned to them at birth and may ask to be referred to by a different name (Kinney, 2018a). As puberty approaches and the body physically begins to manifest secondary sex characteristics in line with the sex assigned at birth, these dysphoric feelings often intensify (Olson et al., 2015).

Research has shown that the average age of awareness of LGBQ identity is 10 years of age, and the average age of disclosure to others is 14 (D'Augelli, Grossman, & Starks, 2005). One study showed the average age for self-awareness of gender identity for binary transgender youth (trans boys and trans girls) to be around 11 years old and nonbinary youth slightly older around 13 years old (Grossman, Park, & Russell, 2016). The average age of coming out for TNB youth has yet to be well established; however, one study found the average age for TNB coming out to family and socially transitioning to be approximately 17 years old. Although, recent research indicates that coming out among nonbinary individuals has been linked to the emergence of gender identity language, regardless of age (Kinney, 2018a).

It is important to note that there is no "typical" path of intervention for TNB youth. Gender dysphoria occurs at different levels and in different ways; some youth may desire some interventions (e.g., puberty blockers) but not others (e.g., surgery) (Hidalgo et al., 2013). Additionally, these desires for the type of intervention may change across time and are also contingent on several other contextual factors (e.g., support of their family, having access to medical insurance, and knowledgeable medical professionals). Among TNB youth, the onset of puberty (generally within the early teenage years or pre-teenage years) may mark a need to begin medical interventions to align the physical body with their gender (Hidalgo et al., 2013). Puberty blockers, hormone therapy, and interventions to change the physical body (e.g., hair removal, surgery) may all be necessary for some TNB youth (Olson & Garofalo, 2014). Some youth may delay these interventions because they do not want to have them, may not realize that they exist, or do not have the access or support to reach them (Kinney et al., 2019; Muzzey, Kinney, & McCauley, 2019).

TNB youth face a unique set of barriers when progressing through their identity development process. In addition to requiring or desiring medical interventions (Hidalgo et al., 2013), TNB youth may also consider things such as changing their name, clothing, hairstyles, and legal documents (such as changing the sex marker on their birth certificate) (Kinney et al., 2019; Muzzey et al., 2019). These additional challenges often require supportive and affirming family, friends, mentors, community members, and/or therapeutic professionals to complete (Cavalcante, 2016; McConnell et al., 2016). Without that support system, these developmental and transitioning milestones may not be completed, or they may be delayed (Kinney et al., 2019; Muzzey et al., 2019).

HOW TO CREATE AFFIRMING ENVIRONMENTS

Successful navigation of the process of coming out has consistently been shown to be linked with improved psychosocial functioning (Mustanski, Newcomb, & Garofalo, 2011). There are four sources of crucial support for TNB youth: (1) family of origin, (2) friends and/or chosen family, (3) TNB community centers and groups; and 4) mental health professionals (Muzzey et al., 2019). The school environment is also an important source of support or lack of support for TNB youth (Abreu et al., 2016). Each one of these sources of support has the potential to be beneficial for TNB youth, even though these are complex relationships. Families of origin relationships are complicated, with TNB often having some desire to maintain these relationships while also feeling the need to hide pieces of their identity (e.g., their pronouns or chosen name) or to educate their family member about it (Muzzey et al., 2019). Community groups are also complicated in that they are often dominated by people who are White and do not meet the needs of TNB of color (Muzzey et al., 2019). Support from family, school environments, community/peers, and practitioners significantly reduce the difficulties youth face when navigating the coming out process (Brandon-Friedman & Kim, 2016; Mustanski et al., 2011). Therefore, these may be some of the simplest ways to bolster wellbeing among TNB youth.

Family of origin

Supportive families have been shown to contribute to the successful navigation of the sexual identity development process (Brandon-Friedman & Kim, 2016; Bregman, Malik, Page, Makynen, & Lindahl, 2013; Shilo & Savaya, 2011). Youth with support for socially transitioning show no difference in rates of depression, mental health, and self-worth than their cisgender counterparts (Durwood, McLaughlin, & Olson, 2017). The integral role of family support in the wellbeing of TNB youth highlights the importance of providing support for their caregivers. Family acceptance can offer protection for youth's safety and ability to thrive and may be "a parent's best insurance policy" (Ehrensaft, 2016, p. 137).

LGBTQ youth continue to experience high rates of familial rejections, leading to adverse psychosocial outcomes (Bregman et al., 2013; Shilo & Savaya, 2011). However, it should be noted that the loss of families of origin relationships is not an inherently negative outcome for some TNB youth and these relationships may not need to be reconciled. Indeed, relationships to those within the family of origin generally protect against potentially detrimental outcomes such as substance use and homelessness for most youth (Fuller & Riggs, 2018; McConnell et al., 2016), but this is not necessarily the case for TNB youth. TNB youth experience exponentially higher rates of familial abuse than both their cisgender heterosexual and LGBQ peers (Choi, Wilson, & Shelton, 2015). Reconnecting TNB youth to their families of origin may prove to be dangerous for them. In fact, some TNB youth also describe intentionally severing or distancing themselves from these relationships because they are often forced to live non-authentic lives in those spaces, a factor that has been shown to contribute to increased suicidal ideation, self-harm, and suicide attempts (Shelton, 2016; Taliaferro, McMorris, & Eisenberg, 2018). These concerns are important considerations for understanding the potential risks and finding the safest circumstances for TNB youth.

School environment

Despite increasing potential victimization, the benefits of being out at school to the wellbeing of TNB young people have been found to mitigate adverse effects as well as promote resilience (Kosciw et al., 2015). School-related protective factors against adverse mental health outcomes (e.g., depression and suicidality) include perceived school safety and other caring adults and teachers (Eisenberg & Resnick, 2006;

Kosciw et al., 2010). Teachers and school administrators, when supportive and acting as advocates, can be valuable natural mentors, which are shown to provide a salient bolster to TNB wellbeing (Taliaferro et al., 2018). However, TNB youth have reported significantly lower quality student-teacher relationships compared to their cisgender counterparts (Eisenberg et al., 2017).

Policies that protect TNB youth and create spaces for them to thrive (e.g., bathrooms, sports, transitioning, enumerated anti-bullying policies) are integral to creating a more supportive school environment. In particular, gender and sexuality (formerly gay-straight) alliance/equality alliance (GSA/EA) student groups have been shown to have a tremendous impact on the overall culture of acceptance for TNB youth (Marx & Kettrey, 2016). GSA/EA student groups have been consistently shown to reduce the poor mental health outcomes that many TNB youth face and improve the school experiences of LGBTQ+ students, regardless of participation in the program (Poteat, Sinclair, DiGiovanni, Koenig, & Russell, 2013; Walls, Wisneski, & Kane, 2013). This suggests that the mere presence of an administratively supported advocacy, awareness, or support-driven student group begins to shift the entire culture of acceptance for TNB youth. Despite the identified need, LGBTQ youth often lack access to such supportive resources (Asakura & Craig, 2014), indicating the importance of advocating for affirming and inclusive programming and policies.

Community of friends and chosen family

There is limited research on the effectiveness of social support as a protective factor for TNB youth, but the existing literature suggests that higher levels of social support can provide a buffering effect against poor health outcomes such as suicidal ideation, suicide, self-harm, and depression (Russell, Pollitt, Li, & Grossman, 2018). Connecting with other gender-expansive peers may be particularly important when embracing one's gender (Saltzburg & Davis, 2010), particularly during the transitioning process (Budge et al., 2013). Additionally, community and peer connectedness can be an escape from stigmatizing environments and provide reciprocal support from those with shared experiences (Meyer & Frost, 2013). Community centers that serve LGBTQ+ youth often provide opportunities for socialization, support groups, educational assistance, and mentoring, and have been linked with increased positive psychosocial functioning (Asakura, 2010). However, some TNB individuals feel isolated and unsupported even among LGBTQ communities and may desire to create their own community, often composed of other TNB individuals with shared experiences (Rankin & Beemyn, 2012). Friends and/or chosen family have been demonstrated as one of the most valuable sources of support for TNB youth, providing unconditional emotional support and a space that has been described as "home" (Muzzey et al., 2019).

Mental health professionals and organizations

Practitioners can play a crucial role in enhancing or hindering the wellbeing of TNB youth, as they are often described as the first sources of support sought out during the coming out process (Kinney, 2018b). Mental health professionals have been shown to be an important source of support for TNB youth by providing a space for validation (Muzzey et al., 2019). Mental health professionals can provide a relatively unique role in offering a safe space where TNB youth could explore their identity without fear of retaliation or victimization (Kinney, 2018b). Practitioners, particularly mental health professionals, are uniquely positioned to support TNB youth during their coming out process, in part, because of the World Professional Association for Transgender Health (WPATH) Standards of Care. WPATH requires a diagnosis for TNB youth to seek medical interventions and this diagnosis often comes from a mental health care professional (WPATH, 2019). Thus, practitioners may be some of the first people to whom TNB youth disclose their gender identity.

Affirmative practices, such as using the correct names and pronouns, as well as validating gender identities can ameliorate suicide and depression among TNB youth (Russell et al., 2018) and even buffer other areas in which the young person is not receiving support (Hidalgo et al., 2013). Therapist offices may be one of the first places that TNB youth begin to "try on" their gender, using the safe and non-judgmental space to test out different names, discuss aesthetic concerns, and learn the language of their gender (Kinney, 2018b). Practitioners can also act as a conduit for connecting TNB youth to their community; providing access to support groups and community organizations, advice on how to proceed with legal and medical changes, and other necessary resources that the youth may not yet be aware of (Kinney et al., 2019; Muzzey et al., 2019). Even more than addressing marginalization and processing coming out, practitioners can assist clients through learning how to promote positive transgender and nonbinary identities (Riggle, Rostosky, McCants, & Pascale-Hague, 2011).

However, if a transgender or nonbinary young person seeks out a mental health professional that is not supportive or affirming, that can have a lasting and harmful impact on the development of their gender (Knutson, Koch, Arthur, Mitchell, & Martyr, 2016; Porter et al., 2016). Misunderstandings by clinicians about gender identity through non-affirmation of identity, harmful practices, and inadequate training, can hinder the wellbeing of TNB youth while coming out. Conversion therapy, which has been presented as credible therapeutic practice, has led to suicide, post-traumatic stress disorder, and long-lasting effects on mental health (SAMHSA, 2015).[1] To prevent the perpetuation of microaggressions and harmful practice, culturally responsive and trans-affirming practice across all mental health professions is essential.

CLASSROOM ACTIVITY

This activity is intended to increase understanding and empathy regarding the coming out process, as well as to increase self-awareness of one's gender identity.

Participants should break out into groups of two. In these dyads, individual time should be devoted to self-reflecting on the questions provided followed by roleplaying, with each member taking turns as the sharer and the responder. Finally, a group discussion or individual reflection paper can help to synthesize the experience.

Reflection questions

- How would you currently describe your gender?
- What does your gender mean to you?
- When did you first realize your gender?
- How has your gender changed over time?
- When did you first share your gender with someone?
- How is your gender affirmed or challenged (excluded, invalidated, etc.) on an ongoing basis?
  - Interpersonal interactions (friends, family, co-workers, place of worship, etc.)
  - Within society (social media, advertisements, entertainment, etc.)
  - Within policy (insurance, bathrooms, nondiscrimination, etc.)

Roleplay

Now that you have reflected on your gender, think about how you would share your gender with a new person. You will alternate and play both the sharer and the responder. As the sharer, roleplay coming out or sharing your gender identity. As the responder, roleplay how to respond in an affirming way. Imagine you are meeting someone new who may not know about your name or pronouns and you want to be fully seen as yourself.

Tips for sharing:

Some things you might share include name, pronouns, and gender identity label(s). You may even choose to share part of your experience about how you came to know your gender identity. Consider the context and what information you may strategically select to share depending on the circumstances and person with whom you are sharing. It may be helpful to select a specific scenario when you might be sharing your gender identity.

Tips for responding:

How might a professional in a variety of roles and settings respond? What information do you need to know in order to be affirming of this individual? How much would you share about yourself? These questions may vary according to settings and context (ex. "What names and pronouns would you be most comfortable with me sharing outside of our therapy sessions?").

Group discussion or reflection paper

- How did it feel to reflect on your gender?
- Did you learn anything new about yourself by reflecting about your gender?

- How did it feel to share your gender identity?
- Was the roleplay easy/challenging/awkward/other?
- Did it make you feel vulnerable sharing this part of yourself?
- Would the information you shared change by individual, context, or personal factors at that moment?
- How did responses to your roleplay feel?
- Which responses felt invasive, motivated by curiosity, inappropriate? Which responses felt affirming?
- How will you apply the lessons from this activity in the future?

CONCLUSION

For TNB youth, the coming out process can be fraught with challenges as well as opportunities for bolstering wellbeing. The more supportive and affirming an environment, the greater the chance for positive outcomes for TNB youth. In general, TNB youth benefit from affirming environments that offer support throughout all areas of their lives. In addition to providing support in each of the settings discussed, TNB youth could benefit from a general normalization of gender diversity (e.g., all-gender bathrooms, pronoun introductions) and increased representation of TNB individuals in leadership and mentorship roles. The practice recommendations provided in this chapter are intended to assist families/caregivers, schools, community agencies, and practitioners with ways to support and affirm TNB youth, particularly through their coming out process.

NOTE

1   To all of those affected by the disastrous effects of "conversion therapy"; we love, support, and see you. You are valid and perfect as you are. To those who have lost their lives, rest peacefully.

RESOURCES

Hotlines

- Trans Lifeline (hotline) US: 877-565-8860 Canada: 877-330-6366
- The Trevor Project (24/7 hotline) 1-866-488-7386

Guides

- The Trevor Project: Coming out as you! – www.thetrevorproject.org/about/programs-services/ coming-out-as-you

- LGBT Youth Scotland: Coming Out: A Coming Out Guide for Trans Young People – www.lgbtyouth.org.uk/media/1054/coming-out-guide-for-t-people.pdf
- HRC – Trans Gender Visibility: A guide to being you – assets2.hrc.org/files/assets/resources/trans_guide_april_2014.pdf?_ga=2.222194008.1348453748.1551144191-1558130908.1551144191

Websites

- Gender Spectrums – www.genderspectrum.org
- GLSEN – www.glsen.org
- Youth Pride Inc – www.youthprideri.org

Caregiver support

- Family Acceptance Project – familyproject.sfsu.edu
- PFLAG – pflag.org
- Trans Youth Family Allies – www.imatyfa.org

Coming out day

America and internationally – National Coming Out Day (NCOD) – Oct 11th
  New Zealand – Big Gay Out – the Sunday closest to Valentine's Day

Books

Brill, S. A., & Kenney, L. (2016). *The transgender teen: A handbook for parents and professionals supporting transgender and non-binary teens.* San Francisco, CA: Cleis Press Inc.
Brill, S. A., & Pepper, R. (2008). *The transgender child: A handbook for families and professionals.* San Francisco, CA: Cleis Press Inc.
Testa, R. J., Coolhart, D., & Peta, J. (2015). *The gender quest workbook: A guide for teens and young adults exploring gender identity.* Oakland, CA: New Harbinger Publications, Inc.

REFERENCES

Abreu, R. L., Black, W. W., Mosley, D. V., & Fedewa, A. L. (2016). LGBTQ youth bullying experiences in schools: The role of school counselors within a system of oppression. *Journal of Creativity in Mental Health*, 11(3–4), 325–342. doi:10.1080/15401383.2016.1214092
American Psychiatric Association. (2013). *Diagnostic and statistical manual of mental disorders: DSM-5 (5th Edition)*. Washington, DC: Author.
Asakura, K. (2010). Queer youth space: A protective factor for sexual minority youth. *Smith College Studies in Social Work*, 80(4), 361–376. doi:10.1080/00377317.2010.516716
Asakura, K., & Craig, S. L. (2014). "It gets better" … but how? Exploring resilience development in the accounts of LGBTQ adults. *Journal of Human Behavior in the Social Environment*, 24(3), 253–266. doi:10.1080/10911359.2013.808971
Baiocco, R., Fontanesi, L., Santamaria, F., Ioverno, S., Marasco, B., Baumgartner, E., … Laghi, F. (2015). Negative parental responses to coming out and family functioning in a sample

of lesbian and gay young adults. *Journal of Child and Family Studies*, 24(5), 1490–1500. doi:10.1007/s10826-014-9954-z

Beals, K. P., Peplau, L. A., & Gable, S. L. (2009). Stigma management and well-being: The role of perceived social support, emotional processing, and suppression. *Personality and Social Psychology Bulletin*, 35(7), 867–879. doi:10.1177/0146167209334783

Bradley, H. A. (2009). *Transgender children and their families: Acceptance and its impact on well-being* (Doctoral dissertation). Retrieved from PsycINFO. (2010-99140-414).

Brandon-Friedman, R. A., & Kim, H.-W. (2016). Using social support levels to predict sexual identity development among college students who identify as a sexual minority. *Journal of Gay & Lesbian Social Services*, 28(4), 292–316. doi:10.1080/10538720.2016.1221784

Bregman, H. R., Malik, N. M., Page, M. J., Makynen, E., & Lindahl, K. M. (2013). Identity profiles in lesbian, gay, and bisexual youth: The role of family influences. *Journal of Youth & Adolescence*, 42(3), 417–430. doi:10.1007/s10964-012-9798-z

Beemyn, G., & Rankin, S. (2011). *The lives of transgender people*. New York, NY: Columbia University Press.

Beese, J. A., & Martin, J. L. (2018). The bathroom case: Creating a supportive school environment for transgender and gender nonconforming students. *Journal of Cases in Educational Leadership*, 21(2), 65–76.

Budge, S. L., Katz-Wise, S. L., Tebbe, E., Howard, K. A. S., Schneider, C. L., & Rodriguez, A. (2013). Transgender emotional and coping processes: Use of facilitative and avoidant coping throughout the gender transition. *The Counseling Psychologist*, 41(4), 601–647. doi:10.1177/0011000011432753

Budge, S. L., Tebber, E. N., & Howard, K. A. S. (2010). The work experiences of transgender individuals: Negotiating the transition and career decision-making processes. *Journal of Counseling Psychology*, 57(4), 377–393. doi:10.1037/a0020472

Cavalcante, A. (2016). "I did it all online": Transgender identity and the management of everyday life. *Critical Studies in Media Communication*, 33(1), 109–122. doi:10.1080/1529 5036.2015.1129065

Choi, S. K., Wilson, B. D. M., & Shelton, J. (2015). *Serving our youth 2015: The needs and experiences of lesbian, gay, bisexual, transgender, and questioning youth experiencing homelessness*. Los Angeles, CA: The Williams Institute with True Colors Fund.

D'Augelli, A. R., Grossman, A. H., & Starks, M. T. (2005). Parents' awareness of lesbian, gay, and bisexual youths' sexual orientation. *Journal of Marriage and Family*, 67(2), 474–482.

Durso, L. E., & Gates, G. J. (2012). *Serving our youth: Findings from a national survey of service providers who work with lesbian, gay, bisexual, and transgender youth who are homeless or at risk of becoming homeless*. Los Angeles, CA: The Williams Institute with True Colors Fund and The Palette Fund.

Durwood, L., McLaughlin, K. A., & Olson, K. R. (2017). Mental health and self-worth in socially transitioned transgender youth. *Journal of the American Academy of Child & Adolescent Psychiatry*, 56(2), 116–123. doi:10.1016/j.jaac.2016.10.016

Ehrensaft, D. (2016). *The gender creative child: Pathways for nurturing and supporting children who live outside gender boxes*. New York, NY: The Experiment.

Eisenberg, M. E., & Resnick, M. D. (2006). Suicidality among gay, lesbian and bisexual youth: The role of protective factors. *Journal of Adolescent Health*, 39(5), 662–668. doi:10.1016/j.jadohealth.2006.04.024

Eisenberg, M. E., Gower, A. L., McMorris, B. J., Rider, G. N., Shea, G., & Coleman, E. (2017). Risk and protective factors in the lives of transgender/gender nonconforming adolescents. *Journal of Adolescent Health*, 61(4), 521–526. doi:10.1016/j.jadohealth.2017.04.014

Fuller, K. A., & Riggs, D. W. (2018). Family support and discrimination and their relationship to psychological distress and resilience amongst transgender people. *International Journal of Transgenderism*, 19(4), 379–388. doi:10.1080/15532739.2018.1500966

Grossman, A. H., Haney, A. P., Edwards, P., Alessi, E. J., Ardon, M., & Howell, T. J. (2009). Lesbian, gay, bisexual and transgender youth talk about experiencing and coping with school violence: A qualitative study. *Journal of LGBT Youth*, 6, 24–46. doi:10.1080/19361650802379748

Grossman, A. H., Park, J. Y., & Russell, S. T. (2016). Transgender youth and suicidal behaviors: Applying the interpersonal psychological theory of suicide. *Journal of Gay & Lesbian Mental Health*, 20(4), 329–349. doi:10.1080/19359705.2016.1207581

Harrison, J., Grant, J., & Herman, J. L. (2012). A gender not listed here: Genderqueers, gender rebels, and otherwise in the national transgender discrimination survey. *LGBTQ Policy Journal at the Harvard Kennedy School*, 2(1), 13–24.

Hidalgo, M. A., Ehrensaft, D., Tishelman, A. C., Clark, L. F., Garofalo, R., Rosenthal, S. M., … Olson, J. (2013). The gender affirmative model: What we know and what we aim to learn. *Human Development*, 56, 285–290. doi:10.1159/000355235

Kinney, M. K. (2018a, January). *A resilience based approach to exploring non-binary identities*. Poster session at the 22nd Annual Conference of the Society for Social Work and Research, Washington, DC. doi:10.13140/RG.2.2.34467.35365

Kinney, M. K. (2018b). "The first line of acceptance": Bolstering resilience among non-binary clients through affirming health care practice. *Journal of Adolescent Health*, 62(2), S48–S49. doi:10.1016/j.jadohealth.2017.11.098

Kinney, M. K., Muzzey, M. F., & McCauley, H. (2019). Identity development through chosen names among nonbinary young adults. *Journal of Adolescent Health*, 64(2), S105–S106. doi:10.1016/j.jadohealth.2018.10.224

Knutson, D., Koch, J. M., Arthur, T., Mitchell, T. A., & Martyr, M. A. (2016). "Trans broken arm": Health care stories from transgender people in rural areas. *Journal of Research on Women and Gender*, 7, 30–46.

Kosciw, J. G., Greytak, E. A., Bartkiewicz, M. J., Boesen, M. J., & Palmer, N. A. (2012). *The 2011 National School Climate Survey: The experiences of lesbian, gay, bisexual, and transgender youth in our nation's schools*. New York, NY: GLSEN.

Kosciw, J. G., Greytak, E. A., Diaz, E. M., & Bartkiewicz, M. J. (2010). *The 2009 National School Climate Survey: The experiences of lesbian, gay, bisexual, and transgender youth in our nation's schools*. New York, NY: GLSEN.

Kosciw, J. G., Greytak, E. A., Palmer, N. A., & Boesen, M. J. (2014). *The 2013 National School Climate Survey: The experiences of lesbian, gay, bisexual and transgender youth in our nation's schools*. New York, NY: GLSEN.

Kosciw, J. G., Palmer, N. A., & Kull, R. M. (2015). Reflecting resiliency: Openness about sexual orientation and/or gender identity and its relationship to well-being and educational outcomes for LGBT students. *American Journal of Community Psychology*, 55(1–2), 167–178. doi:10.1007/s10464-014-9642-6

Kosciw, J. G., Greytak, E. A., Giga, N. M., Villenas, C., & Danischewski, D. J. (2016). *The 2015 national school climate survey: The experiences of lesbian, gay, bisexual, transgender, and queer youth in our nation's schools*. New York, NY: GLSEN.

Lewis, J. (2008). *Resilience among transgender adults who identify as genderqueer: Implications for health and mental health treatment* (Doctoral dissertation). Retrieved from ProQuest Information & Learning. (Accession 57395).

Marx, R. A., & Kettrey, H. H. (2016). Gay-straight alliances are associated with lower levels of school-based victimization of LGBTQ+ youth: A systematic review and meta-analysis. *Journal of Youth and Adolescence*, 45(7), 1269–1282. doi:10.1007/s10964-016-0501-7

McConnell, E. A., Birkett, M., & Mustanski, B. (2016). Families matter: Social support and mental health trajectories among lesbian, gay, bisexual, and transgender youth. *Journal of Adolescent Health*, 59, 674–680. doi:10.1016/j.jadohealth.2016.07.026

McNeilly, E. (2019). Disrupting cisnormativity: Decentering gender in families. *Emerging Perspectives: Interdisciplinary Graduate Research in Education and Psychology*, 3(2), 35–41.

Meyer, I. H., & Frost, D. M. (2013). Minority stress and the health of sexual minorities. In C. J. Patterson & A. R. D'Augelli (Eds.), *Handbook of psychology and sexual orientation* (pp. 252–266). New York, NY: Ford University Press.

Mustanski, B. S., Newcomb, M., & Garofalo, R. (2011). Mental health of lesbian, gay, and bisexual youth: A developmental resiliency perspective. *Journal of Gay & Lesbian Social Services*, 23(2), 204–225. doi:10.1080/10538720.2011.561474

Muzzey, F. K., Kinney, M. K., & McCauley, H. L. (2019). Support networks of transmasculine and non-binary young adults during chosen name transition. *Journal of Adolescent Health*, 64(2), S107. doi:10.1016/j.jadohealth.2018.10.227

Nicolazzo, Z. (2016). 'It's a hard line to walk': Black non-binary trans* collegians' perspectives on passing, realness, and trans*-normativity. *International Journal of Qualitative Studies in Education*, 29(9), 1173–1188. doi:10.1080/09518398.2016.1201612

Olson, J., & Garofalo, R. (2014). The peripubertal gender-dysphoric child: Puberty suppression and treatment paradigms. *Pediatric Annals*, 43(6), e132–e137.

Olson, J., Schrager, S. M., Belzer, M., Simons, L. K., & Clark, L. F. (2015). Baseline physiologic and psychosocial characteristics of transgender youth seeking care for gender dysphoria. *Journal of Adolescent Health*, 57(4), 374–380. doi:10.1016/j.jadohealth.2015.04.027

Olson-Kennedy, J., Cohen-Kettenis, P. T., Kreukels, B. P. C., Meyer-Bahlburg, H. F. L., Garofalo, R., Meyer, W., & Rosenthal, S. M. (2016). Research priorities for gender nonconforming/transgender youth: Gender identity development and biopsychosocial outcomes. *Current Opinion in Endocrinology, Diabetes, and Obesity*, 23(2), 172–179. doi:10.1097/MED.0000000000000236

Porter, K. E., Brennan-Ing, M., Chang, S. C., dickey, l. m., Singh, A. A., Bower, K. L., & Witten, T. M. (2016). Providing competent and affirming services for transgender and gender nonconforming older adults. *Clinical Gerontologist*, 39(5), 366–388. doi:10.1080/0731 7115.2016.1203383

Poteat, V. P., Sinclair, K. O., DiGiovanni, C. D., Koenig, B. W., & Russell, S. T. (2013). Gay-straight alliances are associated with student health: A multischool comparison of LGBTQ and heterosexual youth. *Journal of Research on Adolescence*, 23(2), 319–330. doi:10.1111/j.1532-7795.2012.00832.x

Rankin, S., & Beemyn, G. (2012). Beyond a binary: The lives of gender-nonconforming youth. *About Campus*, 17(4), 2–10. doi:10.1002/abc.21086

Riggle, E. D., Rostosky, S. S., McCants, L. E., & Pascale-Hague, D. (2011). The positive aspects of a transgender self-identification. *Psychology & Sexuality*, 2(2), 147–158. doi:10.1002/abc.21086

Russell, S. T., Pollitt, A. M., Li, G., & Grossman, A. H. (2018). Chosen name use is linked to reduced depressive symptoms, suicidal ideation, and suicidal behavior among transgender youth. *Journal of Adolescent Health*, 63(4), 503–505. doi:10.1016/j.jadohealth.2018.02.003

Saltzburg, S., & Davis, T. S. (2010). Co-authoring gender-queer youth identities: Discursive tellings and retellings. *Journal of Ethnic & Cultural Diversity in Social Work*, 19(2), 87–108. doi:10.1080/15313200903124028

Schindel, J. E. (2008). Gender 101—beyond the binary: Gay-straight alliances and gender activism. *Sexuality Research & Social Policy*, 5(2), 56–70.

Shelton, J. (2016). Reframing risk for transgender and gender-expansive young people experiencing homelessness. *Journal of Gay & Lesbian Social Services*, 28(4), 277–291. doi:10.1 080/10538720.2016.1221786

Shilo, G., & Savaya, R. (2011). Effects of family and friend support on LGB youths' mental health and sexual orientation milestones. *Family Relations*, 60(3), 318–330. doi:10.1111/j.1741-3729.2011.00648.x

Su, D., Irwin, J. A., Fisher, C., Ramos, A., Kelley, M., Mendoza, D. A. R., & Coleman, J. D. (2016). Mental health disparities within the LGBT population: A comparison between transgender and nontransgender individuals. *Transgender Health*, 1(1), 12–20. doi:10.1089/trgh.2015.0001

Substance Abuse and Mental Health Services Administration. (SAMHSA). (2015). *Ending conversion therapy: Supporting and affirming LGBTQ youth*. HHS Publication

No. (SMA) 15-4928. Rockville, MD: Substance Abuse and Mental Health Services Administration.

Taliaferro, L. A., McMorris, B. J., & Eisenberg, M. E. (2018). Connections that moderate risk of non-suicidal self-injury among transgender and gender non-conforming youth. *Psychiatry Research*, *268*, 65–67. doi:10.1016/j.psychres.2018.06.068

Wahlig, J. L. (2015). Losing the child they thought they had: Therapeutic suggestions for an ambiguous loss perspective with parents of a transgender child. *Journal of GLBT Family Studies*, *11*(4), 305–326. doi:10.1080/1550428X.2014.945676

Walls, N. E., Wisneski, H., & Kane, S. B. (2013). School climate, individual support or both? Gay-straight alliances and the mental health of sexual minority youth. *School Social Work Journal*, *37*(2), 88–111. doi:10.1177/0044118X09334957

World Professional Association for Transgender Health (WPATH). (2019). *Standards of Care, Version 7*. Retrieved from www.wpath.org/publications/soc

Worthen, M. G. (2016). Hetero-cis–normativity and the gendering of transphobia. *International Journal of Transgenderism*, *17*(1), 31–57. doi:10.1080/15532739.2016.1149538

CHAPTER 11

Supporting trans and nonbinary adults in their coming out processes

Jessie Read and Will R. Logan

INTRODUCTION

"Coming out" is a term typically used to describe the process of disclosing any sexuality other than heterosexual or gender identity other than cisgender. Trans and/or nonbinary (TNB) people encounter a variety of coming out experiences, often navigating sexual and gender identity disclosure throughout their lifetime. Options for TNB people in coming out vary widely, and can include choosing not to come out or to come out selectively. Coming out processes are typically non-linear and highly dependent on the historical, social, cultural, and political contexts of the client and their communities.

Much of what we know in society about coming out is in relation to disclosing sexual identity, such as queer, bisexual, pansexual, lesbian, gay, or same-gender loving. It is important as a practitioner to know that while there are some similarities for coming out related to gender, the experience can differ in a variety of ways. Some of these ways will become clear in this chapter, although we will not address them directly.

In this chapter, we examine current knowledge related to supporting TNB adults navigating coming out processes and experiences. We combine this knowledge with our experience as trans individuals and clinicians to provide what we believe to be the current best practices for supporting TNB clients with these experiences. Finally, we provide a classroom activity with important considerations for self-reflection for both cisgender and TNB clinicians.

Many people support TNB people in their coming out processes, such as social workers, case managers, therapeutic group facilitators, therapists, etc. For consistency, we will use the term "clinician" throughout this chapter to encompass any or all of these roles. We use the terms trans, nonbinary, and TNB throughout this chapter as is consistent with the rest of the book, although we do acknowledge that these terms may not be the best fit to encompass all gender-expansive and agender identities. In addition, language is always changing and there is no doubt that, at some point, the connotations of the terms used here may shift significantly.

In recognition of the personal and political significance of being or expressing identities targeted by white supremacy, we honor the capitalization of Black along with all other targeted racial identities and choose to not capitalize white as an identity, despite the American Psychological Association's guidelines to do so. We believe that it is essential for all white people to locate ourselves within experiences of whiteness and white supremacy without further centering whiteness as a dominant identity, especially contrasted with the intentional claiming of Black identities by those who cannot otherwise trace their ethnic heritage due to colonization and slavery.

We are acutely aware that this short chapter is imperfect and incomplete. We welcome feedback and seek to be accountable to our mistakes and omissions. Our knowledge and writing have been influenced greatly by non-academic sources, especially by our partners, friends, clients, and TNB communities, including those of which we are a part and those from whom we have had the immense privilege of learning. We specifically want to thank and acknowledge the fierce wisdom and knowledge of so many trans and otherwise gender-defiant people past and present, especially those who live at the margins and intersections of targeted identities.

A message to fellow TNB clinicians

As two trans clinicians, we have often struggled to find professional resources written both by and for TNB psychotherapists working with TNB communities. With this in mind, we have written this chapter with special attention to including our fellow TNB clinicians as the intended audience. We hope that it is equally applicable and useful to TNB clinicians as well as our cisgender colleagues.

LITERATURE REVIEW

Historical context of coming out

People have been sharing experiences of "non-normative" sexuality and gender for as long as there have been sexual and gender norms. In addition to the pathologizing of gender-expansiveness, historical perspectives of TNB experiences are often ignored, resulting in the misconception that TNB identities are new (Singh & Burnes, 2010). It is necessary to challenge these perspectives when working with TNB clients, connecting both the clients and our work to historical and varied genders. We can apply this when working with a client who is considering or in the process of coming out by actively working to understand the context of the coming out narrative, including where the ideas of coming out derive from and what impact they might have on a person's life.

Prior to the 1960s, "coming into" gay communities was more common than the idea of "coming out" (Bronski, 2011). In the social climate of the time, people were less likely to be open about "deviant" or non-normative experiences than they were to find separate spaces in which they could live as themselves part or all of the time. White males who cross-dressed in private and wanted to maintain their daily reality of privilege often resisted the idea of coming out—something that was not an option for their peers who sought to live "full-time" or did not experience maximum privilege in other realms of identity (Stryker, 2017). The gay liberation movement of the 1960s was one shift away from assimilation-focused gay rights activism, changing the norm of coming into towards a norm of coming out (Bronski, 2011). During this time, people began coming out as a political movement to gain access to equal rights and protections.

Social constructionism and coming out

It may be of more use to consider the social construction of the closet than to examine the process of coming out, as binaohan notes that the concept of a closet is dependent on the "public/private distinction so crucial to whiteness" (2014, p. 39). This distinction between public and private is especially troublesome for people whose embodied experiences have historically been under the assumed jurisdiction of white people and systems of white supremacy. With this in mind, binaohan also critiques the assumption that coming out is obligatory and states that "it is never wrong to prioritize your safety" (binohan, 2014, p. 41).

Because the experience of living outside of the socially-constructed gender binary often leads to experiences of stigmatization and ostracization, coming out may involve a process of "crossing over" from one binary gender category to another, regardless of if this is reflective of one's authentic identity (Gagné et al., 1997). From this perspective, the gender binary not only forces disclosure on TNB people, it also creates pressure for gender-expansive people to adopt binary gender identities as a way to minimize social erasure. This phenomenon is heightened within the medical system, where individuals seeking medical transition must disclose their identity in a way that gains them access to the care they need (Gagné et al., 1997). In recent years, nonbinary identities have been selectively legitimized through certain means, such as the addition of an "X" option on legal documentation in some states. However, the social, medical, and legal pressure to elect a binary gender identity remains for most TNB people.

"Strategic essentialism", in which creating discrete categories of identity is a political strategy that creates the ability for specific political protection within a politically violent system, has often played a role in narratives about coming out (Barker & Scheele, 2016). This often looks like separating sexuality from gender, so that appropriate measures can be taken against oppression. However, within the lived experience of TNB individuals, sexuality is an intertwined and often inseparable aspect of identity related to the coming out process (Gagné et al., 1997), and there are colonialist underpinnings in viewing sexuality as separate from gender (binaohan, 2014).

Types and processes of coming out

Chang, Singh, and dickey describe supporting clients in finding a balance between coming out to others and "clue-ing in" to their own identity exploration (2018). Individual coming out processes are described as nonlinear and fluctuating over time. Indeed, the concept of coming out can limit our understanding of a person's process, particularly in the way it is often viewed as a one-time event in a person's life (Chang et al., 2018). In the context of intimate relationships, coming out often involves a long-term negotiation and fluctuation of identity.

Coming out can happen proactively or reactively (Vanderburgh, 2014). When choosing to come out proactively, a person might feel excited or pressured to share their experience. They may also anticipate a time when others might be able to tell that something is changing or has changed physically, emotionally, or socially. No matter the reason, coming out proactively refers to when a person comes out to others before they think others might know. Coming out reactively refers to disclosing after something happens that makes it clear to others that their gender is different than what they have thought before. This might include being seen in different clothing or being addressed differently by friends. Vanderburgh describes each of these as useful in different contexts and does not suggest that either is the "right" or "better" way to come out (2014).

BEST PRACTICES

Now that we have examined some of the historical context and current literature related to coming out, we will discuss what we believe to be the best practices when working with clients navigating a coming out process. We explore these practices in the areas of the personal work of the clinician, the need for an affirming relationship, and the specifics of supporting a client in their coming out process. These steps are not linear and should be revisited as often as is appropriate. Coming out is rarely ever completely done, and this may be a conversation to which we as clinicians will often return with our clients.

Do your personal work

Commit to ongoing learning

Knowledge about TNB identities and our coming out experiences requires an ongoing commitment to learning. There is never a point at which "competency" is reached, even for TNB clinicians. As clinicians, we should have enough education about gender and TNB identities not to need our clients to educate us, and we should seek ongoing education and information. We want to stress that seeking sources of information and education about coming out created *by* TNB people, especially non-academic sources, is essential. Consider TNB-created blogs, videos, social media groups and chat or forum threads, performance art, podcasts, and self-published books or zines as potential sources of shared wisdom. Our communities are under-researched, and much of the research and academic information available is either not by TNB people, and/or is not representative of broader TNB experiences, especially those with multiple marginalized identities. Language, terminology, values, and perspectives change frequently, and often differ between communities and identities.

The resources you access through your learning will likely be important to share with your clients as well. TNB people often encounter the expectation that they will have all the information about what it means to be TNB. However, it may be the case that your client does not have a vast knowledge of TNB identity and will want or need some more information. The American Counseling Association Competencies for Working with Transgender Clients describes that an aspect of competency is offering resources and opportunities for clients to access a variety of options related to coming out and transitioning (Burnes et al., 2010).

Challenge your own stereotypes and biases about gender and coming out

As clinicians, it is not possible to ever be truly neutral in our work. Instead, we must know enough about our identities, beliefs, values, and biases to recognize when and how they show up with clients, challenge ourselves, and get supervision and support when needed. We have included a self-reflection activity at the end of the chapter with important questions for both cisgender and TNB clinicians to consider.

Get supervision, consultation, and support

In challenging your own stereotypes and biases about gender and coming out, discuss and explore your responses with supervisors and consultants. Seek support with experiences of transference and countertransference that arise with clients, including your own reactions to a client's coming out processes, and any parallel experiences that are arising for the client while sharing their identities with you. Remember that transference and countertransference are not inherently bad; recognizing the role they play can strengthen your relationships with your clients.

When working with any client, it is essential to understand the ethical guidelines of your specific profession. When working with TNB clients coming out, unique ethical concerns may arise. Review your specific professional guidelines and check in with your own needs when considering your work in this capacity. Always seek supervision or consultation when considering referring out TNB clients who have just come out to you. Each therapeutic relationship is different and there is potential for great harm in referring out clients, especially someone who has just come out.

If you are working with TNB clients, seek supervision and consultation from clinicians who are knowledgeable and experienced in supporting TNB clients with coming out processes. In particular, if you are a cisgender clinician, consider seeking paid supervision or consultation from TNB professionals. It may also be helpful to process your work with other cisgender clinicians to create space to speak freely about your personal process without concern for your TNB supervisor's experience. For TNB clinicians, seeking supervision from other TNB professionals can be a powerful and relieving option. Regardless of your identity, if you are located in a small community with limited TNB clinicians, there are many options for consultation via video conferencing from TNB clinicians in other areas of your state, country, or the world.

An often forgotten aspect of supporting clients who are coming out is seeking support for yourself as a clinician (of any gender) if your client's process does not go well. You may experience frustration, impatience, disappointment, protectiveness, or fear as you witness your client come up against obstacles because of their gender. Self-disclosure of your experience may support a client in understanding their importance to you, so long as the intention is therapeutic and does not center your feelings. There will be many times, however, when self-disclosure in this sense is not appropriate. Participating in advocacy and activism can be a way to maintain a sense of your own agency while also making the world a better place for your clients. Regardless, allowing your support system to hold some of your distress will create space for you to do that for your clients.

Develop an affirming therapeutic relationship

As with any client and any therapeutic process, building trust and having a strong relationship is foundational. For many TNB people, important factors in developing a strong therapeutic alliance include the identity of the therapist and knowledge of a therapist's active participation in community and advocacy (McCullough et al., 2017). Singh and Burnes note that "embrac[ing] genderqueerness and resisting gender dichotomies" are necessary next steps in creating a trans-affirmative counseling field (2010, p. 251). It is also important to be able to separate gender theory from the practice of therapy, recognizing the limitations of the binary while fully supporting people with trans binary identities. Above all, McCullough and colleagues found that TNB clients want mental health professionals who are caring, supportive, and respectful, which can be expressed in a variety of ways (2017).

Create an affirming experience for all clients

Safety for clients is often determined by whether they can bring their own selves to their therapeutic work. As we actively work to be people whom our clients can trust, it is our responsibility to ensure that the space we hold is always affirming. It is essential to acknowledge and explore the multiplicity and intersectionality of the identities that our clients hold. Intersections of gender, race, class, sexuality, neurodiversity, disability, religion, and other relevant and meaningful identities are present for all of our clients. We as clinicians are responsible for making space in our sessions early on to explore these experiences and to challenge relevant dominant narratives. Specifically, who we are as TNB-affirming therapists should permeate every session with every client, regardless of their identities.

You may have TNB clients who come to you specifically for support with navigating their coming out process. It is also highly likely that you will begin working with clients before they even choose to disclose—or perhaps even explore for themselves—aspects of their TNB gender identity to you. As a clinician, you may be in the position of receiving someone's early "coming out" disclosure. Ideally, if a client chooses to "come out" to you after working together for a period of time, this should not be the first time that you have opened the space up to discuss or explore gender as a topic. You may also work with clients who choose not to share their gender identity at all; coming out does not need to be the focus of any professional relationship in order to create a TNB-affirming space for all clients.

Utilize self-disclosure

One way to build trust in a therapeutic relationship with TNB clients is to model self-disclosure. Disclosing your gender, pronouns, and other identities in your initial introduction to a client can signal to them that they are welcome to do the same with you. If a client has just come out to you and you have not shared your gender with them, this may be an appropriate time to share about yourself. Especially for cisgender clinicians, it will be important to do this in a way that does not center your experience or come with an expectation for your client to react in a particular way. For TNB clinicians, it may be helpful to have clarity about why you may not have shared with a client yet and to share this as appropriate for your relationship with them. Be sure to seek any necessary support you might need in your own process of coming out to your clients.

Believe your clients

If a client has trusted you with information about their gender identity, the first step is to believe them. Our clients will share their selves with us at their own pace and it is not our job to decide whether a client's identity or experience is valid or true. If a client's disclosure is surprising to you, they may not have shared with you all of the information that makes their identity clear for them. Believing them creates more space for them to share openly about their identity.

Be flexible and adaptable

Having a safe space to explore options for gender identity supports clients in figuring out what makes the most sense for them. This may include trying things out, having second thoughts, or changing their mind in a way that appears contradictory to what they have disclosed. For many people exploring a new gender identity, societal pressure can limit the spaces available to talk about or explore their identity. The therapeutic relationship should have the capacity to hold contradiction and uncertainty that may not be safe or accepted in other settings, creating opportunities for a client to continually change and disclose as is appropriate for them.

As a clinician, flexibility and willingness to use new language is a non-negotiable element of competent support. Many TNB people try out or choose new pronouns and names simultaneously with coming out. This process often includes periods of time in which a client is unsure about what name or pronouns they would like for people to use for them. If a client has shared with you that they are considering or have decided to use a new name, you can ask them if that is a name they would like you to use for them as well. If a client who is newly coming out has given you a range of pronouns, you might ask if they have any preference or if one feels more challenging and exciting than another. When you offer to try out new names and pronouns with clients, you should be confident in your ability to fluidly adjust to new language quickly in a session.

Adjusting how you think about a client outside of a session will support your ability to be flexible and use correct language with clients as it evolves. This applies to all aspects of your work, including how you talk about them in supervision or consultation, as well as in your paperwork, filing system, and note-writing.

Follow your client's lead

As you support your client in their coming out process, following their lead can support them in recognizing and using their agency. Ideally, this process will also decenter your expectations and allow your client to develop or enhance a sense of their own authenticity. This may include developing patience with a client who is not ready or does not want to come out to others as well as adjusting our expectations of what it means to be *ready* for those who come out more quickly. The vast majority of each client's life happens outside of sessions and your work should allow your client to decide what experiences are most authentic for them.

Support the client throughout their unique process

Explore dominant stories, power dynamics, and systems of oppression

The idea of a dominant narrative can be useful in any therapeutic framework seeking to implement social justice perspectives of client experience. Dominant narratives are those that are widely culturally-accepted and maintain the status quo. Narratives related to gender normativity are inextricable from all other forms of systems of oppression and social normativity. Oftentimes, the dominant narratives encountered by TNB people are also embedded in beliefs that are influenced by racism and white supremacy, sexism, heterosexism, ageism, classism, sizeism, ableism, and myriad other forms of oppression.

As discussed in our review of the existing literature above, dominant narratives about coming out are strongly connected to the historical context of coming out. These narratives, for various reasons, often align with a view that coming out is compulsory. One implication of the historical coming out narrative is the assumption that TNB identities require disclosure due to difference or non-normativity, such as the belief that "passing" TNB people who do not disclose their TNB identity are "tricking" others (see Stryker, 2017 for more information about this, including the so-called "panic defense").

A similarly influential narrative includes having to prove the existence of TNB identity from childhood to obtain validity. For many TNB clients, the presence or absence of this historical experience can permeate the coming out process. This may show up as questions such as: "Am I really nonbinary?" or "Have I known about my identity long enough to justify coming out?"

Some other dominant narratives that we have encountered that may influence our clients' coming out stories are:

- "You are not trans/nonbinary if you are not out."
- "You are not proud of being trans/nonbinary if you are not out."

- "You must come out to impact politics."
- "You are obligated to come out to be a role model for others."
- "To really be trans/nonbinary, you have to have known since you were young."
- "You are not trans/nonbinary enough to come out."

These are just some of the examples of influential narratives, but there are many more. A search of TNB-created media may provide further insight into the impact of these and other dominant narratives. As a clinician, take time to examine your personal stances of these narratives and how this might limit or support your clients. Additional questions for reflection are included in the activity at the end of the chapter.

The pressure felt by TNB people related to coming out does not exclusively come from cisgender people. For some clients, the greatest pressure they experience comes from other TNB people. Regardless of the origin of the message, helping clients identify the influence of these expectations on their own lives can support them in creating a coming out process that is authentic for them.

When supporting clients in recognizing dominant narratives, it may be helpful to offer the perspective that these narratives are not stories that they made up or that come from within them. Dominant narratives can often trick us into isolation, believing that there is something inherently off about ourselves that de-legitimizes our TNB identities. Recognizing that these narratives impact others, including cisgender people, can remove this myth of isolation and allow our clients to start deciding whether these narratives are working for them or not.

It is important to mention that just because a narrative is a dominant one, it does not mean it is inauthentic or harmful for an individual. For many TNB people, coming out in support of political progress and becoming a role model for others is empowering and desired. For some, having a history of gender-variant experience to draw upon creates a foundation for a strong sense of certainty moving forward. These narratives become problematic when they co-opt a person's authenticity and become the "only" or "right" way to be trans and/or nonbinary.

In addition to highlighting dominant narratives related to gender, it is essential to consider how dominant narratives intersect with all of a client's identities, both in areas of privilege and areas of marginalization. As in all of your work, explore intersections of gender, race, class, sexuality, neurodiversity, disability, religion, and other relevant and meaningful identities. Clients who hold multiple marginalized experiences are likely to be more or differently impacted by dominant narratives.

Support the creation of an authentic coming out and disclosure process

In the context of a strong therapeutic alliance and with awareness of dominant narratives, co-creation of an authentic coming out process can take place. This includes exploring various disclosure options and navigating context-specific decisions, including those impacting their closest relationships and extended networks. Extended networks may include families, work environments, colleges or universities, places of worship, government bodies, and other similarly complex systems.

When considering how to come out, it may be helpful for clients to be connected to others who have gone through or are going through a similar process so they can explore what works or does not work for their own process. This will include exploring what kind of transition, if any, feels right for them. Increasing access to the variety of TNB identities and bodies in the world can empower clients to find authenticity while mitigating the threat of isolation. In addition to providing educational materials like books and handouts, having a strong understanding of the local community, including centers, clubs, social media groups, and individuals willing to share their experience can be an important way to support TNB clients in their process.

Coming out is not a binary process in that it is never as simple as "out" or "not out". Options for coming out include disclosure, non-disclosure, and selective or partial disclosure. Selective disclosure refers to coming out only to certain people, whereas partial disclosure refers to only sharing part of their identity. Each of these possibilities will be context-specific and informed by the client's knowledge of their networks. Throughout this process, it may be helpful to remind yourself and your client that authenticity is contextual and that they are always themself even if they choose not to disclose or to disclose only some information. As your client moves towards coming out to others, it will be important to allow them to change their mind about coming out decisions and try out different options without having to commit.

There are as many ways to come out as there are people who are coming out. For some, the process may look like coming out as a different gender and moving quickly to have that become their daily reality. For others, their daily reality may be incredibly fluid in a way that would be impossible to conceptualize within our binary gender system. This often changes throughout a person's life, although many TNB people may feel hesitant to share this for fear of not being taken seriously. For example, a person who initially came out as a woman and transitioned her body may circle back to explore nonbinary masculinity years later. Someone who came out as nonbinary and firmly against hormones years ago may decide that xe would like to reconsider hormones and remain nonbinary. A man who was assigned female at birth may feel pressured to start hormones early on in coming out but realize later that he loves his body as it is. All of these are real, valid, and beautiful, and should be taken with the same amount of seriousness.

Explore the relationship between transition and coming out

If a TNB client is considering medical transition, it will be important to support them in understanding how the timing of medical transition relates to their disclosure process. This will include exploring their current and anticipated experiences of safety related to how others view them. For TNB people who are starting testosterone, physical changes that cannot be hidden can occur quite quickly, depending on dosage and method of administration. This includes having a deeper voice, growing facial hair, and body fat redistribution (Coleman et al., 2012). For TNB people who are starting estrogen, the changes may be slower and subtler, but the rate of change and level of noticeability will depend on the client. Similar considerations need to be made for clients pursuing procedures such as gender-affirming surgeries, laser hair removal, etc.

Choices around social transition will also impact a client's coming out experiences. Clients who were designated female at birth may have a relatively easier time adapting more "gender neutral" or "masculine" aspects of presentation, if applicable. However, TNB people designated male at birth may experience transmisogyny when presenting in ways viewed by others as more "feminine". As always, these experiences are complex and contextual.

Consider safety and stability related to coming out

Coming out can influence major aspects of a client's life, including relationships, financial security, housing, employment, health and medical care, and interactions with law enforcement and police. Within these experiences, the conflict between safety and authenticity impacts every TNB person's coming out process in some way. Important topics to address to assess safety prior to coming out include race, religion, age, class, disability status, living situation, financial resources, employment, and your client's specific gender. These discussions should center and explore the meaning and importance that they assign to their own identities, rather than the clinician's assumptions about them. For some clients, they may need support in recognizing that the privileges they embody actually provide relative safety for them. For others, the concerns for safety are incredibly real and it would be unwise and unsafe to push disclosure before they are ready or to neglect to talk about the possible impacts.

TNB people seeking congruent legal identification face unique barriers that do not exist in the same way for those who are disclosing sexuality or sexual orientation. There are sometimes legal and financial concerns that prevent TNB people from completing this process in a way that maintains the integrity of their identity. Conversations with clients preparing for this unique context of coming out should include how much and what kind of information will be necessary to disclose to get their needs met. Becoming familiar with the logistics of these processes, including specific policies in your city and/ or state, can let your clients know that you not only understand the emotional impact, but are in solidarity with them against the structural barriers put in their way.

With recent additions of a nonbinary, "X", or third gender option for legal identification in many places, it may be relevant to have conversations with TNB clients about the practical considerations of this option. This will include the impact of having identification that may regularly "out" them as TNB when it is presented to other people (from police and security guards to bartenders and cashiers). This is especially true for those with a nonbinary gender marker with which others may not be familiar, or when traveling to locations where that gender marker is not in use. In general, having a nonbinary or "X" gender marker may increase the number of "coming out" experiences a client needs to navigate regularly. A similar conversation will be relevant for any individual whose perceived gender does not match the gender of their identification.

For every client, we must at least consider the option that coming out will not go well and be prepared to support in whatever way is needed. It may end up being necessary to connect clients with case management, legal resources, alternative medical providers, employment resources, and alternative housing options, among others. We strongly recommend familiarizing yourself with these kinds of local resources before they are needed.

When considering aspects of safety regarding coming out, it is also essential for us to note the very serious impacts that the possibility—but certainly not inevitability—of rejection may have on a client's well-being. Directly discussing with a client whether fear of or experiences of rejection may lead them to consider suicide could be an important aspect of support in their coming out process. Appropriate safety planning, if applicable, will help to ensure that more TNB people live their fullest, most authentic, most beautiful gender-expansive lives.

Explore the relational and attachment significance of coming out

In supporting your client in all of the above coming out processes, remember that coming out is always a relational process, involving interactions between your client and others in their life. Throughout these experiences, it is important to explore both the relational and attachment significances of each coming out interaction for your client.

Fear of losing close relationships may have a significant impact on a person's coming out process. Attachment-related fears of rejection or abandonment by family, friends, partners, and other significant relationships may lead to high levels of distress or emotional dysregulation (Chang et al., 2018). It may be useful to explore a client's typical relational patterns and attachment strategies, including the ways they typically seek connection or self-protection.

The therapeutic relationship can be a place for clients to experience preparatory or reparative coming out experiences and to explore the relational process of coming out. The ways that clients chose to share with us may or may not mirror how our clients choose to approach disclosure with others in their lives. How you respond to a client's disclosure may help them develop a sense of what it will feel like for them in other settings.

It is rarely the case that the impacts of coming out are limited to a single significant relationship, even if a person only comes out to one person and the recipient agrees to keep this information private. Maintaining relationships where non-disclosure is or feels like a necessity also has relational impacts on TNB people, possibly including the hurt or pain of isolation or lack of support. Hurt and pain may also arise if a client's disclosure is rejected or dismissed.

Narratives of coming out often contain biases towards individualism. This is noticeable in the common expectation that a person should leave unsupportive families or communities completely and find a new support system. This expectation discounts practical limitations such as finances and housing, as well as the importance of remaining within families and communities because of cultural expectations, personal values, or because of the attachment significance of those relationships. These are just some of the reasons that a client may decide to stay within unsupportive or minimally supportive communities or family systems. This is not to say that TNB people must stay in unsupportive relationships, but rather to emphasize that this is a valid, and often more likely, option as compared to complete distancing from those systems. It may be appropriate with a client's consent to offer educational resources, including support groups, for families or significant relationships who are struggling to support their TNB loved one.

Religion can act as a major barrier to acceptance in families and communities, but can also be a powerful support, depending on the beliefs of the specific tradition.

It may be helpful to connect clients and their families with trans-affirming resources specific to their religious traditions. It may also be necessary to help clients sort through their own spiritual beliefs and determine to what degree and how they would like to continue participating in their spiritual practices in support of their process.

Of course, regardless of a client's identity and context, people in their lives may surprise them with acceptance or rejection. It is our role as clinicians to explore all of these possibilities with clients and support them with their decisions and related outcomes. Many of our clients will experience rejection or loss of relationships, and many will have coming out stories that end in closer relationships.

We may be able to use the significance of the therapeutic relationship to support a client in receiving validation and regaining agency if they have had difficult or traumatic coming out experiences, or to celebrate if their process has gone well. It is possible that your client will navigate coming out in a way that ultimately supports their well-being. They may experience stronger relationships, enhanced spiritual practices, deeper intimacy, and an infinite number of other new experiences. Celebrating this with your client might be as simple as having a conversation, or as elaborate as a dedicated event involving their communities.

CONCLUSION

Coming out is a highly contextual and relational process that will appear throughout a person's life. There are many important and unique considerations when working with a client navigating this process. The best practices that we have identified in our work, with support from resources created by others, include doing your own personal work related to coming out and gender, developing a strong and affirming therapeutic relationship, and supporting a unique and authentic process for each client. This list is incomplete, and we encourage continued learning by all clinicians, both cisgender and TNB, throughout professional careers to best support gender-expansive clients of all identities.

SELF-REFLECTION ACTIVITY

As emphasized in the best practices above, we must know enough about our identities, beliefs, values, and biases to recognize when and how they show up with clients and challenge ourselves to counter them as needed. Whether in a classroom or on your own time, we encourage you to write down your reflections to the following questions. After writing, share your writing or reflections with your professor, peers, colleagues, and supervisors as desired.

   Note: As trans clinicians and lifetime learners, we encourage self-reflection, but caution against expectations of sharing personal reflections in group settings. Group sharing experiences may have consequences such as undesired outing of TNB participants and unnecessary exposure of TNB participants to hurtful, harmful, and oppressive opinions or statements by their peers.

- What is your relationship to and history with your gender identity and gender presentation?
- Where do you hold rigidity or fluidity around gender, whether your own or other people's?
- What gender standards, biases, or stereotypes do you hold?
- What assumptions or expectations do you have about coming out?
- How do your assumptions, expectations, or standards about coming out potentially differ in relation to various TNB identities?
- In what ways do you actively challenge your own stereotypes and biases about gender in order to make it safer for all clients, both cisgender and TNB, to deviate from societal expectations of gender identity, presentation, and gendered behavior?
- In what ways do you actively challenge your own stereotypes and biases about coming out in order to make it safer for all clients to choose their own unique processes of coming out, or not coming out?
- What dominant narratives have you learned about coming out?
  - What is your personal stance on them?
  - How might these narratives limit or support your clients?
- Additionally, if you are a TNB clinician:
  - What has your relationship been to coming out?
  - How do your clients' identities and experiences differ from your own?
  - What barriers or privileges do they hold that are different from your own?

RESOURCES

Brown Boi Project: www.brownboiproject.org/
Desi LGBTQ Helpline for South Asians: www.deqh.org/
My Trans Health: http://mytranshealth.com/
National Black Justice Coalition: http://nbjc.org
National Queer and Trans Therapists of Color Network: www.nqttcn.com/
The Queer and Transgender Resilience Workbook: Skills for Navigating Sexual Orientation and Gender Expression by Anneliese A. Singh
T-Buddy: https://tbuddy.us/
To Survive on This Shore, photographs and interviews with transgender and gender nonconforming older adults by Jess Dugan: www.tosurviveonthisshore.com
Trans in the South, a resource directory by the Campaign for Southern Equality: https://southernequality.org/resources/transinthesouth/

Trans Latin@ Coalition: www.translatinacoalition.org/
Trans Lifeline: www.translifeline.org/
Transgender Law Center: https://transgenderlawcenter.org/
Transgender Professional Association for Transgender Health: http://tpathealth.org/

REFERENCES

Barker, M., & Scheele, J. (2016). *Queer: A graphic history*. London: Icon Books.

binaohan, b. (2014). *Decolonizing trans/gender 101*. Toronto: Biyuti Publishing.

Bronski, M. (2011). *A queer history of the United States*. Boston, MA: Beacon Press.

Burnes, T. R., Singh, A. A., Harper, A. J., Harper, B., Maxon-Kann, W., Pickering, D. L., & Hosea, J. (2010). American Counseling Association: Competencies for counseling with transgender clients. *Journal of LGBT Issues in Counseling*, 4(3–4), 135–159. doi:10.108 0/15538605.2010.524839

Chang, S. C., Singh, A. A., & dickey, l. m. (2018). *A clinician's guide to gender-affirming care: Working with transgender and gender nonconforming clients*. Oakland, CA: Context Press.

Coleman, E., Bockting, W., Botzer, M., Cohen-Kettenis, P., DeCuypere, G., Feldman, J., … Monstrey, S. (2012). Standards of care for the health of transsexual, transgender, and gender-nonconforming people, version 7. *International Journal of Transgenderism*, 13(4), 165–232. doi:10.1080/15532739.2011.700873

Gagné, P., Tewksbury, R., & McGaughey, D. (1997). Coming out and crossing over: Identity formation and proclamation in a transgender community. *Gender & Society*, 11(4), 478–508.

McCullough, R., Dispenza, F., Parker, L. K., Viehl, C. J., Chang, C. Y., & Murphy, T. M. (2017). The counseling experiences of transgender and gender nonconforming clients. *Journal of Counseling & Development*, 95(4), 423–434. doi:10.1002/jcad.12157

Singh, A. A., & Burnes, T. R. (2010). Shifting the counselor role from gatekeeping to advocacy: Ten strategies for using the competencies for counseling with transgender clients for individual and social change. *Journal of LGBT Issues in Counseling*, 4(3–4), 241–255. doi:1 0.1080/15538605.2010.525455

Stryker, S. (2017). *Transgender history*. Berkeley, CA: Seal Press.

Vanderburgh, R. (2014). Coming out. In L. Erickson-Schroth (Ed.), *Trans bodies, trans selves: A resource for the transgender community* (pp. 105–123). New York, NY: Oxford University Press.

CHAPTER 12

Supporting caregivers and families of transgender and nonbinary youth

Richard A. Brandon-Friedman, Rand Warden, Rebecca Waletich, and Kelly L. Donahue

INTRODUCTION

Support from the family and social environment are strong protective factors for transgender and nonbinary (TNB) youth, mitigating the impact of other negative experiences and reducing mental health and substance use concerns (Gower et al., 2018). However, achieving an affirmative family environment is not always easy; family members often experience a complex range of emotions, thoughts, and concerns when a TNB youth first comes out, and these may require social support or professional assistance to process. This chapter reviews the literature on the importance of affirmative family environments for TNB young people, common concerns raised by family members, and how providers can help families to create positive, affirmative, and safer spaces for TNB youth.

FAMILY SUPPORT DURING THE COMING OUT PROCESS

TNB youth are more likely to experience parental and familial rejection than their cisgender or lesbian, gay, bisexual, or queer peers (Gower et al., 2018). Family support is crucial for the wellbeing of TNB youth in almost every aspect of their lives, including their transition into adulthood. TNB youth who lack parental or family support experience increased psychological distress, including depression, anxiety, and suicidal ideation and attempts; lower self-esteem; higher rates of substance use; and higher likelihood of experiencing homelessness (Gower et al., 2018; James et al., 2016). In contrast, TNB youth supported in their social transition by family members show no difference in depressive symptomology and only slightly elevated levels of anxiety relative to cisgender youth (Olson et al., 2016).

Supportive families have a greater capacity for impacting social environments, as they can advocate on behalf of TNB youth to resolve issues of feeling unsafe and other types of harm (Chan, 2018). TNB youth in affirmative environments can flourish and express themselves openly (Aramburu Alegría, 2018; Bull & D'Arrigo-Patrick, 2018). Supportive families can also serve as catalysts for change by challenging non-affirmative public dialogue and inequity and advocating for legislation that protects TNB individuals (Chan, 2018). In helping TNB youth navigate the web of discrimination and oppression they are likely to encounter, supportive families serve as sources of resilience, equipping the youth with the skills to not only survive but truly thrive in their environment (Ehrensaft, 2016; Gower et al., 2018).

PUTTING KNOWLEDGE INTO PRACTICE

Family reactions to disclosure

Family members may react in different ways when TNB youth come out. Responses depend upon the unique constellation of family members' experiences, beliefs, understandings of gender and gender identities, exposures to TNB individuals, and their relationships with the youth (Hill & Menvielle, 2009). Lev (2004) described four stages family members often experience following the disclosure of an individual's TNB identity. The first stage, *discovery and disclosure*, encompasses the initial revelation to family members and their reactions. Family members may express shock and/or feel betrayed as they seek to understand the disclosure and its impact on their own lives. They may question how long this information has been concealed and why, or, alternatively, why it needs to be discussed now. This stage can be traumatic for the entire family, and it often consists of non-affirming statements and reactions from family members that may be painful for the TNB youth and others.

During the second stage, *turmoil*, families often seek support. They are processing the disclosure in a more nuanced manner and seeking information on how to best engage with the TNB youth. A completely unsupportive family may desire services to "change" the youth's gender identity. Such forms of treatment, often referred to as "reparative" or "conversion" therapies, are ineffective, unethical, harmful, and should not be offered or considered (National Association of Social Workers, 2015). Instead, services should focus on educating family members about gender identity and helping them process their reactions, fears, and emotions regarding the youth's disclosure. For professionals working with families in the stage of turmoil, the best practices outlined later in this chapter will be highly pertinent.

Families within the third stage, *negotiation*, are working to establish boundaries both within and outside of the family. This stage involves discussions about the youth's desired goals for social, medical, and/or legal affirmation, and how the family will discuss the youth's gender identity with others. Service goals during this stage should focus on resolving conflicts between the youth and family members and seeking agreements and shared goals. If some family members or associates are unsupportive and/or rejecting of the youth, more supportive family members may need assistance with renegotiating how, when, and whether to interact with these less affirming individuals.

Families in the final stage, *finding balance*, have reached a new equilibrium in which the youth's gender identity is well understood and incorporated into the family's life. Family members' views and roles have adjusted, as discussed below, and the family can discuss the youth's gender identity without significant strain. During this time, many family members become advocates, actively seeking to counteract discrimination the youth may face.

The timeline for progressing through these stages varies considerably, with some people moving quickly and others spending years in each stage. While not reflective of all youths' experiences, this framework is a useful guide for understanding shifting considerations. Still, services must be tailored to unique familial needs. The next section reviews questions and concerns commonly encountered by providers working with caregivers and family members of TNB youth and provides recommendations for addressing and resolving them.

Gender identity influences

Caregivers' first reactions to disclosure may be to seek "causes" for the youth's TNB identity. Gender is an extremely complex aspect of a youth's development that consists of several dimensions. Gender identity, expression, and perception exist as parts of a broader *gender web* in which each person inhabits a unique space or position (Ehrensaft, 2016). For everyone, whether cisgender or TNB, this space has many influences, including, but not limited to, culture, social learning, familial norms, genetics, prenatal hormonal exposure, and early parental attachment patterns (Shumer, Nokoff, & Spack, 2016). The interactions between social factors, nature, and nurture in youths' lives lead to their understandings of their own and others' genders.

When inquiring about "causes" of the youth's gender identity, family members are generally seeking to understand its development. They may experience guilt, believing they did something they perceive as wrong, as societal messaging pathologizing gender diversity often seeks to blame caregivers despite no scientific evidence that child-rearing practices, trauma, or other stressors "cause" TNB identities (Brill & Kenney, 2016; Shumer et al., 2016). Parental openness to diversity in gendered play and expression and providing exposure to others whose gender may not fit societal norms may allow children to explore their gender identity safely and may create a nurturing environment in which TNB youth may come out earlier, but there is no evidence that such practices contribute to a youth "becoming" TNB who otherwise would not have identified as such. Bringing family members' attention to the fact that there have always been a vast array of genders and gender expressions, but systems of power have erased these from history through attempts to impose a strict gender binary, can also be affirming and assist in building solidarity with those TNB youth who are resistant to others' insistence on defining their genders (Lugones, 2007). Ultimately, family members should be educated about gender diversity and helped to move beyond asking why and toward processing the impact of the youth's gender identity on the youth and themselves.

Gender identity and mental illness

Research on the intersection between gender identity and mental health is often misunderstood. The presence of gender dysphoria as a diagnosis in the 5th edition of the Diagnostic and Statistical Manual of Mental Disorders (DSM; American Psychiatric Association, 2013) complicates many people's understanding of the mental health of TNB individuals. The 4th edition of the DSM included a diagnosis of gender identity disorder, suggesting that individuals receiving the diagnosis were "disordered"; this was updated in the 5th edition to emphasize that individuals receiving a gender dysphoria diagnosis are not themselves disordered, but rather, are experiencing a dysphoric reaction to aspects of their body or gendered social expectations that do not align with their experiences of their own genders.

While this change was intended to reduce the stigmatization of individuals so diagnosed, the continuing presence of a gender-related diagnosis in the DSM is a source of controversy. The diagnosis is generally required to access gender-affirming care, but in the process assigns a diagnosis to a person whose distress is largely due to the perceptions and expectations of others rather than intrapersonal dysfunction. Providers must help family members and TNB youth understand the place of gender dysphoria within the DSM while processing the implications of the diagnosis.

At the same time, professionals and family members must be attuned to the increased risk for mental health concerns experienced by TNB youth. TNB individuals experience disproportionately high levels of depression, anxiety, self-harming behaviors, suicidality, and substance use (Shumer et al., 2016). Being TNB does not inherently lead to problems in psychosocial functioning; in contrast, research suggests struggles are more often a consequence of the individuals' dysphoria and the continuous negative societal responses to their gender identities (Hendricks & Testa, 2012; Shumer et al., 2016). Family members and professionals should monitor TNB youth for psychosocial distress and address it using affirmative interventions such as those outlined in Chapter 4 in this volume.

Addressing family reactions and supporting adjustment

When youth come out as TNB, family members go through a period of adjustment. Caregivers often experience a multifaceted sense of loss, as many children are gendered from birth (or prior to birth via ultrasound), suggesting a life narrative to which many family members attach (Aramburu Alegría, 2018; Norwood, 2013). Even those who are supportive of their youth's TNB gender identity must reimagine aspects of future social interactions (e.g., events such as prom, dating and marriage, future child-rearing, etc.). Family members often describe this experience as grieving the loss of the previously-known youth while simultaneously grappling with the idea of having a "new" family member and the formation of a new projective narrative (Bull & D'Arrigo-Patrick, 2018). When addressing these concerns, many family members and providers find benefit from exploring Kübler-Ross' five stages of grieving and/or attention to models of ambiguous loss (Wahlig, 2014).

Family members of TNB youth must also develop a new sense of their own identity (Wahlig, 2014). When confronted with their own limited knowledge about gender or lack of reflection on the role gender plays in society, many family members engage in an intense process of introspection and social re-evaluation of their own gender expression. This often includes the gendered ways in which they were raised and the manners in which gender norms are enforced on partners, family members, and youth (Bull & D'Arrigo-Patrick, 2018; Hill & Menvielle, 2009). Furthermore, familial roles are often gendered, with parents viewing themselves as the parent of a daughter or son. For example, a mother of a transmasculine youth may struggle to now see herself as a mother to a son, questioning how to act in this new role. Gendered social activities such as Scouts or sports also may be affected, requiring family members to alter their social circles. Attention to gender's place in familial interactions may be especially important for TNB youth of color, as some cultures may emphasize gender roles in different manners (Bull & D'Arrigo-Patrick, 2018).

As familial roles shift, it is not uncommon for family members to feel their life is centered on the youth's gender identity. The continuous attention to gender in social interactions, serving as an educator and advocate, worrying about the youth's mental health, and intervening in social situations can leave families feeling as if they are enveloped by an exhausting, all-encompassing "trans filter" (Aramburu Alegría, 2018). Furthermore, reoccurring discussions with others regarding gender transitions and addressing social needs can lead to familial conflicts and require modifications in relationship structures and interaction patterns. These readjustments can be stressful and foster resentment toward the youth, which also can contribute to intense feelings of guilt among family members.

Guilt is often experienced by family members in other forms as well. Family members of TNB youth who transition later in adolescence may question how they could have "missed" earlier signs of the youth's gender identity. This is especially the case when they learn about the intense dysphoria the youth has been experiencing or come to understand that post-pubertal transitions can be less cosmetically impactful. They may also recall previously-made disparaging comments about gender diversity or attempts they had made to force the youth to conform to socially-designated gender roles and feel remorse that is hard to process and express.

Providers must be attuned to family members' complex experiences of emotions and introspection and their effects on familial relationships. Family members often need to process their feelings of confusion, loss, and guilt experiences without the youth present. These services should be framed as an opportunity to explore feelings and experiences in a safe place so that they can give voice to concerns or fears without risk of offending or negatively impacting their TNB youth.

TNB youth need to understand these sessions are not intended to be secretive or exclusive, but rather to help their family members proceed through their own identity development stages and become more affirming. Youth often need to be reminded that while they have had time to process their own TNB identity, family members' developmental clocks have just begun. Other more in-depth therapeutic interventions to address TNB youth's mental health and/or family interactions may also be needed; please see Chapter 4 on affirmative mental health care with TNB youth for best-practice suggestions.

Supporting youth through the process of social and/or medical affirmation

Family members often report that some of their most difficult decisions involve how to best support the youth's desire to present and live as their asserted gender (Aramburu Alegría, 2018; Gray, Sweeney, Randazzo, & Levitt, 2016). Family members often question the likely longevity of such desires and whether allowing the youth to live in their asserted gender may be developmentally or socially harmful (Sharek, Huntley-Moore, & McCann, 2018). As such, many acknowledge their first reactions to the youth's gender-expansive behaviors and desires were to attempt to suppress or counteract them. Often, these concerns stem from fears for the youth's social, physical, and emotional safety, whereas others develop based on questionable research that has suggested that most youth "desist" or return to identifying with their birth-assigned sex.

Such research has been criticized due to methodological concerns and for promoting harmful interactions with service providers who encourage attempts to force youth to comply with gendered social standards (Temple-Newhook et al., 2018). While some youth who initially identify as TNB do later find this identity no longer fits their experience, there is no research evidence to suggest their first gender-affirming social transition caused them harm (Ehrensaft, 2016). Instead, existing research consistently documents families' attempts to counteract youths' asserted gender identities are associated with poorer psychosocial outcomes (Travers, Bauer, Pyne, Gale, & Papadimitriou, 2012). When family members are supported in shifting their focus from fears of social judgment and uncertainty toward the youth's wellbeing, progress is more likely. In fact, some family members report that recognizing the toll their own actions were having on the TNB youth was an important catalyst for them starting to support the youth (Hill & Menvielle, 2009; Ryan, 2016).

It is impossible to project youths' future gender journeys, but research provides some guidance. Concerns that youth are too young to know their gender is often alleviated when family members learn that individuals' senses of their gender develop early in life, often by age 3; among older youth, those who identify as TNB during puberty and after are more likely to maintain their gender identity (Shumer et al., 2016). Youth who experience very intense signs of gender dysphoria and/or who express their gender identity in concrete, explicit ways such as "I am a girl" are also more likely to identify as TNB later in life (Temple-Newhook et al., 2018). When youth are persistent in their gender identity, resistant to being referred to as a different gender, and insistent that they be referred to as their self-identified gender, the youth's gender identities are more likely to remain consistent as they age.

Decisions regarding gender-affirming medical treatment are also of significant concern to family members (Sharek et al., 2018). When accessing gender-related care, youth are often anxious to start gender-affirming hormone treatment, and many have researched gender-affirming surgical interventions. Family members' concerns regarding these treatments are not necessarily solely rooted in resistance to the youth's identity but also in fear of making semi-permanent or permanent changes to the youth's body. Discussions regarding gender-affirming medical care must be tailored to the youth's specific desires and should involve only pertinent family members. Chapter 1 in this volume provides further discussion of medical care for TNB youth.

Services for family members should provide space to examine these fears and explore concerns. Expressions of confusion, resistance to disclosing to others for fear of "making it real", and concerns regarding making wrong choices should be normalized. Family members may be unaware of the roots of their fears and concerns. Receiving accurate information from a trusted source and having space to verbalize and analyze thoughts and emotions are important steps to becoming affirmative (Sharek et al., 2018). Once the youth and family members are comfortable with their identities and those of the others in the family, they can more easily move toward determining the level of disclosure to others that they desire.

Considerations for disclosure and safety

Coming out as a TNB individual is not a singular event but rather an ongoing lifelong process. In many ways, family members of TNB youth undergo a similar continuous coming out process. Once family members learn about the youth's identity, they must also begin a dialogue about how and when to discuss this information with others (Ehrensaft, 2016). Unfortunately, extended family members' and friends' reactions are not always positive, and many schools, community organizations, and health care providers are not trained to work with TNB youth. As a result, family members are likely to find themselves thrown into the role of educator and advocate for TNB youth, which they may experience as daunting and exhausting. This may be particularly true for families of TNB youth of color as they negotiate multiple stigmatized identities across environments, so connecting them to resources targeted to TNB youth of color and their families is beneficial.

The family environment

The broader familial environment can pose a particular difficulty, as extended family members are typically aware of a youth's birth-assigned sex. These family members often require education about gender identity and how to interact appropriately with the TNB youth. While many extended family members are supportive of TNB youth, negative responses from other family members may include rejection of the TNB youth and their immediate family unit, criticism of the youth's primary caregivers for their parenting practices, blaming family members for the youth's gender diversity, and attempts to push the youth's primary caregivers to pursue conversion therapies (Brill & Kenney, 2016; Ehrensaft, 2016).

TNB youth and their immediate family must choose how to respond to such negative reactions. When disclosing the youth's gender identity to extended family members, many caregivers report expressing clear support for the youth and a refusal to tolerate harassment (Birnkrant & Przeworski, 2017). When this is not successful, primary caregivers often report feeling forced to cut ties with extended family members and/or not attempt to re-engage family members who choose to avoid them.

In this way, the TNB youth's immediate families serve as buffers against extended family rejection and harassment. Both the youth and their immediate family may need assistance in processing this rejection; support from others who have faced similar circumstances through support groups and community organizations can be quite helpful.

The school environment

TNB youth often report that the school environment is one of the most difficult settings to navigate. Schools have a legal requirement to provide all youth, regardless of gender identity, with a safe environment free from harassment and discrimination, but many school policies lack specific protections from bullying by peers, teachers, and school staff for TNB youth (Kosciw, Greytak, Zongrone, Clark, & Truong, 2018). When school policies include specific protections for TNB youth, the youth feel safer, have improved attendance, have greater intention to complete school, and experience lower levels of victimization (Kosciw et al., 2018). Family members of TNB youth report often having to serve as educators, advocates, and intermediaries between the youth and school personnel when trying to develop affirmative school environments and should be supported when doing so.

Specific school personnel should be made aware of the youth's sex assigned at birth, as the legal documents required for school registration may not match the youth's gender presentation and school personnel may have to treat medical conditions. As this information is considered part of the youth's medical and educational records, school personnel cannot ethically or legally reveal it to others, providing privacy protection for the youth and family (Orr et al., n.d.). A full discussion of school advocacy is beyond the scope of this chapter, but additional guidance for families can be found in the resource list at the end of this chapter.

The social environment

Community-based activities or organizations can create challenges for privacy, as their leaders are not similarly bound by confidentiality or non-discrimination laws and may uphold policies that negatively impact TNB youth. When a youth comes out as TNB at a very young age, they often begin school and first enter into social groups as their asserted gender. In these cases, many individuals in the social environment may remain unaware of the youth's sex assigned at birth unless disclosure of such information is needed. For example, a caregiver may feel it is appropriate for transfeminine youth to join a gender-segregated organization such as a girls' club, but depending on the information requested by the organization, the youth's sex assigned at birth cannot be withheld. For example, if documentation such as a birth certificate is required, this may involuntarily "out" the youth and/or prevent them from joining the group.

Gender-segregated activities pose unique difficulties for TNB youth. Sports participation can be contentious due to concerns about sex-based physiological differences and navigating locker room environments. Currently, legal guidance and protections regarding participation in gender-segregated activities are inconsistent; policies vary by state, and courts are divided on this issue. If organizations are unwilling to work with the family or insist on adhering to the youth's sex assigned at birth, family members should work with their TNB youth to understand this at an age-appropriate level while also recognizing that if an environment is not supportive it may also be unsafe.

Informal gender-segregated social interactions, such as sleepovers, also pose challenges for TNB youth and their families. Peers and their parents may be uncomfortable, for example, about a transmasculine youth attending a boys' sleepover party. TNB youth may struggle to understand these situations and feel rejected. In these situations, family members of TNB youth are often forced to take on the role of educator/advocate in addition to consoling the youth. Support groups for family members and TNB youth can be helpful for processing these experiences and learning to cope with them.

Youth who come out as TNB at a later age often experience additional social difficulties related to transitioning. While strangers or new acquaintances may not know a youth's sex assigned at birth, those in the family's existing social environment will notice changes in gender presentation, names, and/or pronouns. Some families choose to move to a new location or have the youth change schools so that they may start anew in their asserted gender. When this is not possible, families must choose how to address questions about the youth's gender transition with others. Families are generally advised to address any questions openly when it is safe to do so (Brill & Kenney, 2016; Ehrensaft, 2016).

When faced with unsupportive individuals, families can either disengage or act as advocates for the youth. Such experiences may lead family members to question their own decisions or activate a sense of protectionism and spur social action. These choices are often guided by the context of the social interaction and their level of comfort with the youth's gender identity, perception of the youth's needs and level of resilience, and degree of comfort with being an advocate (Gray et al., 2016). Providers can help family members improve their sense of efficacy in these roles.

Addressing mistakes

Because gender roles and gendered language are highly engrained into contemporary society, family members are bound to make mistakes regarding a youth's chosen name and pronouns. These mistakes can be painful for both the youth and family members, who may feel guilty after making an error, but they can be readily addressed. TNB youth can be astutely aware of a mistake versus an individual's conscious choice, and they tend to be forgiving when mistakes are made and addressed sincerely. When a mistake is made, family members should briefly apologize and then move forward in their dialogue.

Individuals making such an error may be prone to overcompensate by "over-apologizing", turning a small, honest mistake into a prolonged and negative social interaction. While an extended apology may be well-intended, it places the onus to respond on the misgendered or misnamed youth, who then often feels pressure to minimize the felt impact or to reassure or comfort the individual who made the error.

Depending on the family, conjoint youth/family sessions may be needed to process hurt feelings or anger over such mistakes.

CONCLUSION

A youth coming out as TNB affects their entire family system. Within many families, roles, interaction patterns, and projections about the future must shift. Feelings of loss, guilt, and anger may need to be processed, often leading to intra- and interpersonal strain and conflict. Both the youth and their family members may need support in becoming attuned to each other's needs and recognizing each other's struggles. Providers must be prepared to assist them in the complex process of creating affirmative environments in which TNB youth can thrive.

CASE STUDIES

General reflection questions for case studies 1–3

1. What emotions, thoughts, biases, or curiosities of your own did you notice arise as you read the case study? Why are these important to note?
2. What are the largest challenges currently facing the youth?
3. What are the youth's strengths? The family's?
4. What do you think the youth would identify as their greatest need at this time?
5. How is the youth's gender identity impacting the current situation?
6. As the youth's social worker, what would be your treatment focus?
7. As the youth's social worker, how might you best advocate for your client?

Case study 1: Parent of Jayce, age 14

"I have a daughter—well … son, I guess. I don't know … That's why I'm here. Jayce wants to be called Jayce. She was Jessica, so I'll probably say Jessica, too. I'm sorry. This is all so new. Jess—Jayce—came out to us as a lesbian about a year ago. My husband and I were a little bit surprised because she—he—just had a boyfriend, but I talked to my older daughter about it and she wasn't surprised in the least! I have several gay friends and my brother-in-law is gay also, so it's fine with us. I took her to the LGBTQ youth center, and he really loved it there. He went to groups and met friends and seemed to be really happy.

"Then, one night after I picked her, um, him, up from the center, he tells me in the car that he is not Jessica and does not want us to refer to him with feminine pronouns. He wants to be called Jayce and for everyone to refer to him with masculine pronouns. Well, if I thought I was surprised by the lesbian thing, this just *absolutely floored me*! I mean, is this some kind of fad or something? Should I not let my child go to that youth center anymore? Is this what happens? Do they start out as gay and then decide they're transgender or whatever? I just don't understand it. I mean, Jess even loves wearing make-up sometimes! And my husband is just dead set on the fact that he has two daughters and that is that. There's no talking to him about it at all. He won't even engage in a conversation if he thinks it's going to go there.

"Also, one night after Wednesday night bible study, I get a call from my pastor. He's been my pastor for more than ten years. He says he wants me to come in and meet about something that Jess—sorry, Jayce—said at youth group. Well, I knew it was about this. My husband … again … wouldn't even go with me because he knew it was about 'the transgender thing.' I go in, and sure enough, Jayce had asked his friends in youth group to call him Jayce and use he/him and the youth pastor and our senior pastor have 'serious concerns' about it all. They don't want Jayce to come back as long as he's 'going to do this transgender thing.' I just don't know what to do. I don't want to lose my kid, but I don't know."

Specific reflection questions

1. What support or information do you think might be important for you to provide to this mother at this point in her journey?
2. At what point would you try to engage with Jayce's father, if at all?

Case study 2: Parent of Lisa, age 6

"When my child started 'playing' as a boy, at first it was cute. She was 4, and who does not make-believe to be all sorts of things when you are little? Then when this 'game' lasted two years, 24 hours a day, seven days a week, I could not help but take notice, though it was mostly subconsciously. Denial is strong. Then one day, when she was out with the neighborhood kids playing superheroes, I overheard one of the boys say, 'You have to be Wonder Woman! You are a girl.' My child burst out in tears. She came over to me sobbing, guttural sobs of deep pain, and said to me between sobs, 'Mommy, I am not a girl! I am not a girl!' I held my baby as tightly as I could as he screamed. Then I knew … my denial was shattered. My beautiful daughter … child … son … needed help. I researched, then took *him* to see a specialist, who told me the work was more with me than with him. He knew who he was and what he needed. I needed to learn to support and advocate for him in a world that will not always understand him as well as he understands himself."

Specific reflection questions

1. Denial is often an early stage in a parent's journey towards acceptance. What other experiences might you need to prepare this mother for in her personal journey towards acceptance?
2. Caregivers must often engage with various systems in order to find support and advocate for their child. With what systems might this mother need to be prepared to engage?

Case study 3: Jaymi, age 12, and father Larry

Jaymi: "I have known who I am for as long as I can remember. This should be no surprise to anyone. I was always 'mom' when I played house with my friends. I have a pink bedspread. All my friends are girls. Dad, even my teachers know I am a girl."

Larry: "That's just not true. Science says you have a penis, so you are a boy. Period. I won't put up with this liberal bull you get from your friends at school. Look, I did not bring him here for you to teach him how to be a girl, I brought him here for you to figure out what is wrong with him that he cannot accept who he is."

Specific reflection questions

1. As a professional, how can you balance the need to help Jaymi feel supported while also meeting the father where he is?
2. How might you respond to the father's assertion that science "says" his child is a boy?

RESOURCES

Brill, S., & Kenney, L. (2016). *The transgender teen: A handbook for parents and professionals supporting transgender and non-binary teens.* Jersey City, NJ: Cleis Press.

Brill, S., & Pepper, R. (2008). *The transgender child: A handbook for families and professionals.* San Francisco, CA: Cleis Press.

Ehrensaft, D. (2016). *The gender creative child: Pathways for nurturing and supporting children who live outside gender boxes.* New York, NY: The Experiment.

Nealy, E. C. (2017). *Transgender children and youth: Cultivating pride and joy with families in transition.* New York, NY: W. W. Norton & Company.

Orr, A., Baum, J., Brown, J., Gill, E., Kahn, E., & Salem, A. (n.d.). *Schools in transition: A guide for supporting transgender students in K-12 schools.* Retrieved from www.hrc.org/resources/schools-in-transition-a-guide-for-supporting-transgender-students-in-k-12-s

REFERENCES

American Psychiatric Association. (2013). *Diagnostic and statistical manual of mental disorders* (5th ed.). Arlington, VA: American Psychiatric Publishing.

Aramburu Alegría, C. (2018). Supporting families of transgender children/youth: Parents speak on their experiences, identity, and views. *International Journal of Transgenderism, 19*(2), 132–143. doi:10.1080/15532739.2018.1450798

Birnkrant, J. M., & Przeworski, A. (2017). Communication, advocacy, and acceptance among support-seeking parents of transgender youth. *Journal of Gay & Lesbian Mental Health, 21*(2), 132–153. doi:10.1080/19359705.2016.1277173

Brill, S., & Kenney, L. (2016). *The transgender teen: A handbook for parents and professionals supporting transgender and non-binary teens.* Jersey City, NJ: Cleis Press.

Bull, B., & D'Arrigo-Patrick, J. (2018). Parent experiences of a child's social transition: Moving beyond the loss narrative. *Journal of Feminist Family Therapy*, *30*(3), 170–190. doi:10.1080/08952833.2018.1448965

Chan, C. D. (2018). Families as transformative allies to trans youth of color: Positioning intersectionality as analysis to demarginalize political systems of oppression. *Journal of GLBT Family Studies*, *14*(1–2), 43–60. doi:10.1080/1550428x.2017.1421336

Ehrensaft, D. (2016). *The gender creative child: Pathways for nurturing and supporting children who live outside gender boxes*. New York, NY: The Experiment.

Gower, A. L., Rider, G. N., Brown, C., McMorris, B. J., Coleman, E., Taliaferro, L. A., & Eisenberg, M. E. (2018). Supporting transgender and gender diverse youth: Protection against emotional distress and substance use. *American Journal of Preventive Medicine*, *55*(6), 787–794. doi:10.1016/j.amepre.2018.06.030

Gray, S. A., Sweeney, K. K., Randazzo, R., & Levitt, H. M. (2016). "Am I doing the right thing?": Pathways to parenting a gender variant child. *Family Process*, *55*(1), 123–138. doi:10.1111/famp.12128

Hendricks, M. L., & Testa, R. J. (2012). A conceptual framework for clinical work with transgender and gender nonconforming clients: An adaptation of the Minority Stress Model. *Professional Psychology: Research and Practice*, *43*(5), 460–467. doi:10.1037/a0029597

Hill, D. B., & Menvielle, E. (2009). "You have to give them a place where they feel protected and safe and loved": The views of parents who have gender-variant children and adolescents. *Journal of LGBT Youth*, *6*(2–3), 243–271.

James, S. E., Herman, J. L., Rankin, S., Keisling, M., Mottet, L., & Anafi, M. (2016). *The report of the 2015 U.S. transgender survey*. Washington, DC: National Center for Transgender Equality.

Kosciw, J. G., Greytak, E. A., Zongrone, A. D., Clark, C. M., & Truong, N. L. (2018). *The 2017 National School Climate Survey: The experiences of lesbian, gay, bisexual, transgender, and queer youth in our nation's schools*. New York, NY: GLSEN.

Lev, A. I. (2004). *Transgender emergence: Therapeutic guidelines for working with gender-variant people and their families*. Binghamton, NY: Haworth Clinical Practice Press.

Lugones, M. (2007). Heterosexualism and the colonial/modern gender system. *Hypatia*, *22*(1), 186–209.

National Association of Social Workers. (2015). *Sexual orientation change efforts (SOCE) and conversion therapy with lesbians, gay men, bisexuals, and transgender persons*. Washington, DC: NASW Press.

Norwood, K. (2013). Grieving gender: Trans-identities, transition, and ambiguous loss. *Communication Monographs*, *80*(1), 24–45. doi:10.1080/03637751.2012.739705

Olson, K. R., Durwood, L., DeMeules, M., & McLaughlin, K. A. (2016). Mental health of transgender children who are supported in their identities. *Pediatrics*, *137*(3), e20153223. doi:10.1542/peds.2015-3223

Orr, A., Baum, J., Brown, J., Gill, E., Kahn, E., & Salem, A. (n.d.). Schools in transition: A guide for supporting transgender students in K-12 schools. Retrieved from www.hrc.org/resources/schools-in-transition-a-guide-for-supporting-transgender-students-in-k-12-s

Ryan, K. (2016). *Examining the family transition: How parents of gender-diverse youth develop trans-affirming attitudes*. Unpublished manuscript.

Sharek, D., Huntley-Moore, S., & McCann, E. (2018). Education needs of families of transgender young people: A narrative review of international literature. *Issues in Mental Health Nursing*, *39*(1), 59–72. doi:10.1080/01612840.2017.1395500

Shumer, D. E., Nokoff, N. J., & Spack, N. P. (2016). Advances in the care of transgender children and adolescents. *Advances in Pediatrics*, *63*(1), 79–102. doi:10.1016/j.yapd.2016.04.018

Temple-Newhook, J., Pyne, J., Winters, K., Feder, S., Holmes, C., Tosh, J., & Pickett, S. (2018). A critical commentary on follow-up studies and "desistance" theories about transgender and gender-nonconforming children. *International Journal of Transgenderism, 19*(2), 212–224. doi:10.1080/15532739.2018.1456390

Travers, R., Bauer, G., Pyne, J., Gale, L., & Papadimitriou, M. (2012). *Impacts of strong parental support for trans youth: A report prepared for Children's Aid Society of Toronto and Delisle Youth Services.* Toronto, Canada: Trans Pulse.

Wahlig, J. L. (2014). Losing the child they thought they had: Therapeutic suggestions for an ambiguous loss perspective with parents of a transgender child. *Journal of GLBT Family Studies, 11*(4), 305–326. doi:10.1080/1550428x.2014.945676

13

Trans and nonbinary parenting

Trish Hafford-Letchfield, Christine Cocker, Rebecca Manning, and Keira McCormack

INTRODUCTION

This chapter focuses on the practices and meanings given to 'parenting', 'caring', and 'family' when working with transgender or nonbinary (TNB) people within social work. Our understanding of gender identities has increased exponentially through legislative and policy changes, and in response to political, cultural, and social contexts (Council of Europe, 2015). These changes require practitioners in public sector services to take an active role in acquiring knowledge and skills to ensure that these transformations towards equality for TNB populations directly benefit the individuals and families involved. Despite this changing context, TNB issues remain relatively under-explored within social work, and TNB rights are marginalised within mainstream professional practice (Hudson-Sharp, 2018; McPhail, 2004; Siverskog, 2014). The experience of gender transition can have a profound impact on the lives of individuals and their family members (Dierckx & Platero, 2018). Integrating research findings and reaching out to those impacted, combined with the use of critical reflection, should ensure that decision-making and support for families is underpinned by the best practice possible.

This chapter integrates selected evidence on TNB parenting from a published systematic review of the international, empirical literature on TNB parenting (Hafford-Letchfield et al., 2019) combined with the authors' own experiences as trans activists and social work professionals with research, practice, and personal experience in LGB family care (Cocker, 2011; Cocker, Hafford-Letchfield, Ryan, & Barran, 2018; Hafford-Letchfield, Cocker, Ryan, & Melonowska, 2016). We draw on this evidence to aid understanding of some of the challenges arising in practice. Furthermore, we have highlighted a legal case study from the UK in order to illustrate some of the practical implications of working with families with parents that identify as gender-diverse. We conclude with pointers on how to best support TNB families using a critical lens to analyse practice.

BACKGROUND

International collaborations to improve recognition of lesbian, gay, bisexual, transgender, and queer (LGBTQ) families have influenced efforts to eliminate discrimination in law, policies, and practices relating to forms of partnership or parenting (including marriage, partnership, reproductive rights, adoption, and parental responsibility) (ILGA, 2015). Some of these collaborations have focused on the elimination of restrictions on the rights and responsibilities of parents based on their sexual orientation, gender identity, and gender expression. The rights of the child remain a core and guiding principle in this recognition.

The developing body of literature on lesbian and gay parenting (Cocker, 2011; Golombok et al., 2014; Golombok & Tasker, 1996) has taken a social constructionist position to challenge heteronormative parenting. Social constructionism sees knowledge and meaning as socially created and located within particular historical and cultural contexts. Therefore, meaning is not fixed, rather it is constructed using dominant discourses. Using a social constructionist position has provided positive research evidence on outcomes for childrens', familial, and social relationships (Hicks, 2011) and the quality of parenting in families of choice (Hicks, 2011; Hicks & McDermott, 2018). In contrast, research on TNB parenting is scarce and often subsumed with the LGBTQ parenting with significantly less or, at times, no discussion or identification of the 'B', 'Q', or 'T' in this acronym (Hines, 2017). Failure to adequately differentiate the 'T' in research reinforces the invisibility of gendered experiences (Lane & Seelman, 2018; Siverskog, 2014).

In addition, support to manage the intersection of TNB identity and parenting requires intentional services that are rare (Haines, Ajayi, & Boyd, 2014), given the multiple stressors resulting from transphobia (Pyne, Bauer, & Bradley, 2015). There may also be stress personally for parents who are searching for their authentic selves (Veldorale-Griffin & Darling, 2016). These differentiations remain marginal to social work, despite discourses on sexuality and gender politics in families having attracted academic debate and theorising of queer parenting (Hicks, 2011). Whilst changing concepts of family forms can affirm those seen as 'relationship innovators', families with individuals identifying as TNB still experience a hostile environment. Further, due to conceptual and practical issues surrounding the collection of data on gender identities, there are currently no official estimates of the size or growth of the TNB population. This is true for the UK (Office for National Statistics, 2017) where there are few examples of robust evidence on TNB experiences (see reviews by Communities Analytical Review, 2013; Hudson-Sharp & Metcalf, 2016; Mitchell & Howarth, 2009), as well as the United States, where the census does not collect gender identity.

Evidence from a report commissioned by the British Government (House of Commons Women and Equalities Committee, 2016) on TNB equality confirmed significant levels of inequality across a wide range of policy areas and in the provision of public services. This included discrimination and transphobia in schools, social services, the

National Health Service (NHS), prisons and probation services, and the police. A subsequent rapid evidence review and limited empirical work (Hudson-Sharp, 2018) sought to ascertain the adequacy and consistency of child and family social work education in regard to gender identities. Findings revealed a significant lack of TNB-specific social work research on this topic, resulting in poor experiences of TNB individuals and families within social work and social care settings, as well as everyday discrimination and gaps in services (Alleyn & Jones, 2010; Government Equalities Office, 2016). Very few social workers receive specific education or training in relation to TNB issues, at qualifying BA/MA or MSW or post-qualifying/post MA/MSW levels. This lack of specificity and inclusivity for families with TNB individuals, and the tendency to work with deficit models, are further undermined by a lack of resources regarding TNB issues and the lack of networking by TNB families or practitioners working with TNB families. The presence of TNB service users actively campaigning for better services and the potential for social work researchers and practitioners with particular expertise in LGBQ and/or TNB equality have also been noted (Miles, 2018).

What do we know about trans and nonbinary parenting?

Our previous systematic review on the empirical evidence on TNB parenting (Hafford-Letchfield et al., 2019) sought to: (1) evaluate existing findings on how TNB people negotiate their relationships with partners, children, and grandchildren following transition, across the life course; and (2) consider the implications for professional practice with TNB people in relation to how best support TNB individuals with their family caring roles.

These questions were addressed through a synthesis of the findings of 26 existing studies conducted between 1990 and 2017, with the goal of assessing the strength of the reported evidence, making it available to inform social workers, and helping to identify future research, education, and practice priorities in this area. Taking a life course approach by including grandparenting acknowledges the tendency of individuals to come out or transition in later life, many of whom are more likely to already be in parenting roles (Pyne et al., 2015; Rosser, Oakes, Bockting, & Miner, 2007; Stotzer, Herman, & Hasenbush, 2014; Tornello, Riskind, & Babić, 2019).

Pyne and colleagues (2015) highlighted that whilst the majority of TNB parents might be biological parents to their children, a sizeable minority can be step-parents or partners of biological parents, or intentional non-biological parents, indicating that they were parents to their child(ren) since birth, yet not through biological relationships. This points to the diversity of TNB parenting. It also includes Indigenous or First Nation perspectives (Evans-Campbell, Fredriksen-Goldsen, Walters, & Stately, 2007) such as the special role that 'Two-Spirit' people play in their communities as caregivers. Consideration also needs to be given to those who aspire or wish to be parents through family planning (Pyne et al., 2015), fertility choices (Ellis, Danuta, & Pettinato, 2015; Riggs & Bartholomaeus, 2018; von Doussa, Power, & Riggs, 2015), assisted reproduction (James-Abra et al., 2015), and other pathways to parenthood (Riggs, Fraser, Taylor, Signal, & Donovan, 2016).

The summative findings from this review demonstrate that people who identify as TNB are as invested and committed to their loved ones as any other persons, but fear that knowledge of their authentic selves may alienate and destroy their familial bonds (Hafford-Letchfield et al., 2019). Findings confirmed that ongoing barriers, both personal, interfamilial, and systemic in the lives of TNB parents are reinforced through a transphobic context, and a lack of appropriate services, targeted support, and advocacy. The literature confirmed that TNB experiences are indeed distinct from LGB experiences, and in the ways in which TNB parents reconcile their parenting. Further, people with TNB identities may be best conceptualised within an intersectional framework, which explores how multiple axes of identity or social location interact to influence people's experiences, perceptions, and enactments of self in different contexts. Participants in many of the research studies demonstrate heightened degrees of personal agency, which helped to create equitable and caring social networks within their patterns of partnering and parenting. Parents and carers identifying as TNB were highly excluded from mainstream as well as same sex-specific parenting resources. Given that TNB parents tend to transition within the community where they are already living, with the goal of retaining all that is good in their lives, their transition has to be reflexively negotiated alongside complex commitments to family and work.

Selected themes from the review relevant to social work

We expand on two themes from the systematic review to elaborate on findings specifically relevant for social work. Firstly, the impact on family members where a parent transitions; and secondly, what is needed from professionals who are in a position to support them.

Impact on or within the family

TNB parents were more concerned about what being a good parent entailed and its relational aspects, than they were about their gender or their parenting capabilities during or following transition. In a study of fathers, trans parents tied their role closely to the love they had for their children and less to how they functioned as a parent within their couple relationship (Faccio, Bordin, & Cipolletta, 2013). When talking about themselves as parents, for example, they focused on their individual qualities, rather than on any specific gendered ones (Walls, Kattari, & DeChants, 2018).

Other findings revealed that there are many ways in which families responded to parental disclosure, and many of these can be positive (Dierckx & Platero, 2018). Whilst there may be conflict within family relationships in the short term, the effect on a child depends on a range of variables such as how each parent or carer copes with the situation and the age and gender of the child. Adolescents whose own sexual development can predispose them to being hypersensitive can be exceptionally challenging (Veldorale-Griffin, 2014). White and Ettner (2004) suggested that pre-adolescents and young adult sons may have an easier time adjusting to their parent's transition. In one study (Pyne et al., 2015), just under half of survey participants indicated that they had strong support from their children towards their gender identity. However, Haines et al. (2014) found that disclosure to children may also invite increased parent–child conflict. The processes related to transition may force members of the family to confront complex emotions and issues previously unsurfaced within their familial relationships.

There are a number of risk and protective factors for children with a parent undergoing a gender transition. Risk factors included abrupt separation from either parent, extreme opposition from partners and parental conflict, and poor mental health in either the transitioning or non-transitioning parent (White & Ettner, 2007). Protective factors include close emotional ties for the child to either parent, support from extended family, and co-operation and ongoing contact with both parents (White & Ettner, 2007). For some children, resulting family conflict outweighed the stress of having a parent transition although there was some evidence that children may hide their feelings. Haines et al.'s (2014) findings echoed many of these themes of high levels of family and relationship conflict in TNB households. Increased level of conflict between parents was associated with increased level of conflict between the trans parent and the child (White & Ettner, 2007).

For many of Haines, Ajayi, and Boyd's participants, the conflict between partners/former partners was a result of the shift in gender roles and partnering dynamics that transition necessitates (2014). Many reported that their co-parents (usually, former partners) could not handle the transition and this served as the basis of irresolvable differences that often lead to relationship dissolution (Walls, Kattari, Speer, & Kinney, 2019). Clarke and Demetriou's small study reported how one 'dad' experienced major long-lasting depression and came out after his wife left the marital home (2016). Children in their study drew on normalising discourses to minimise the differences associated with their trans parents within their LGT participant sample. They went to great lengths to neutralise insinuations of 'parental selfishness' by giving accounts that were both protective of their parents and which challenged heterosexist, homophobic, and transphobic assumptions about their families. Their research aimed to show how shifting focus on the damaging effects of transphobia should be a key focus in concerns for children's wellbeing. rather than them having a non-traditional family structure. These effects of transphobia are compounded further by the negative social and cultural associations that TNB parents experience, with no positive images to counter these negatives (Faccio et al., 2013).

Hines' (2006) study also revealed how TNB parents often reflexively negotiated their transition alongside commitments to family and work, and how this negotiation involved complex navigation around timing of disclosure to maximise emotional care for children. One parent reported de-transitioning specifically and temporarily for the sake of their family (Haines et al., 2014). Openness, honesty, and trust were cited as key values in enabling children to understand and adapt to the changes including explaining procedures involved in gender reassignment. Having an open dialogue allowed parents and children to emotionally support each other. Transitioning after becoming a parent was seen as a risk to maintaining positive relationships with their children or losing them. In contrast, Evans-Campbell et al.'s (2007) study of Native caregiving in the two-spirit community found that there were many benefits to transitioning, because these changes were contextualised within cultural norms and cultural values. Here, community-based parenting in and with communities overrode any perspectives about the individuals' own lives. Barnes et al.'s (2006) wider study of trans and two-spirit people in Canada, conversely, described people having hidden their trans identity out of fear of losing access to the children in their lives.

Von Doussa and colleagues speak to the positive influence family and friends can have on how adults who identified themselves as trans with one participant as intersex considered possibilities for parenthood (2015). Questions like, 'When are you going to start a family?', or 'You'd be great with kids', enabled trans adults to see beyond their own internalised transphobia around parenting and consider this as an option for their future. For some significant others/partners, transition can challenge the non-transitioning partner's perceptions of their own sexual orientation: 'their perceived sexual orientation was relationally connected to their partner's transgender status' (Whitely, 2013, p. 608). Some identified a fear of community rejection and talked about other family members questioning why they decided to stay in a relationship with their partner during and after transition. Other influences, such as religion, also have a part to play in how the 'undoing' and 'redoing' influences decision-making. For some individuals, a religious identity is important and can be a source of support and strength.

One study suggested that for parents of young children, the school environment and particularly the reaction of teachers, parents, and other children, were important factors that impacted a child's adaptation to parental gender transition (Hines, 2006). One parent reported how the head teacher played a significant role in addressing schoolchildren when people had started questioning that parent's identity, which made it easier for the family.

What is needed from professionals?

Themes from the review demonstrated a range of needs that TNB parents may have in accessing professional support in both the short and long term. Besides issues associated with increased family conflict, having to manage and balance one's own needs with those of others can be compounded and clouded by discrimination and disadvantage faced by TNB parents (Walls et al., 2019), notwithstanding managing their own internal oppression and self-censorship. Some gave highly detailed descriptions of other people's opinions and included terms such as 'perversion' and 'paedophilia' to describe other people's opinions about their identities (Faccio et al., 2013). Moreover, they were aware that they were considered 'sick', 'crazy', 'confused', and 'incapable of raising a child' by others, which reflects their feelings of social marginalisation. This requires extreme sensitivity in offering support and balancing the needs of the individuals involved in a family.

Gender identity and expression are often used against parents in child custody proceedings (Green, 2007), and courts are more likely to be involved in Black, Asian, and Multiracial families than in White families. There are distressing implications for those who require costly legal counsel during child custody disputes for those living in poverty (Pyne, 2012). Cumulative losses through family rejection and loss of friends, community relationships, and contacts were a large concern for people (Veldorale-Griffin, 2014). Many studies confirm that TNB-identifying parents have limited contact with their children (Grant et al., 2011). Living with the fear of transphobia led some parents to avoid public spaces or travel (Pyne et al., 2015). Some parents were anxious about being turned down for a job, or losing employment. One study found that respondents were more likely to be living in poverty or near-poverty; often unemployed, underemployed, or unhappily employed where they were unable to be their authentic self in the workplace (Barnes et al., 2006). Many participants gave up their jobs in order to transition, and others were restricted in their employment opportunities, particularly where there was a complete absence of guidance on employment rights. These findings highlight many issues for social workers in supporting families.

Children may also experience TNB-related bullying. Parents in one study identified three major ways of managing transphobia and bullying experiences; by discussing them with authorities; by processing these situations directly with their children; and through discussion of how the family managed disclosure as a preventative strategy (Haines et al., 2014). TNB parents conveyed a sense of carefully judging whether it was wise to be out in particular parenting settings but took on transphobia and bullying directly and immediately if it occurred. This is another area relevant to social work intervention and support.

Having access to therapy and support groups was beneficial (Veldorale-Griffin, 2014). Adult children said that individual therapy was also useful (just under half the sample had used therapeutic services and reported positive experiences), but they did not have access to support groups, and adult children reported that these groups might have been useful. Online information, including YouTube videos, was seen as enabling for transgender parents to talk with and hear stories about other parents. Ensuring that therapists were TNB-friendly and knowledgeable was also important.

Valdorale-Griffin and Darling suggest that therapists and other human service professionals need to have good skills in helping parents to prepare for disclosing their TNB status to their families, in particular to their children (2016). Discussing feelings of loss related to parental gender transition is also important in terms of the impact this may have on family roles and the family system as a whole, and in so doing, to lessen the 'boundary ambiguity' experienced by the transgender parent. Their research suggests that assisting the parent's sense of coherence serves as a protective factor for the TNB individual, but developing ways of evaluating this in practice is required. The role of a therapist in this process could potentially be supportive/transformative, with a considerable number of parents and adult children commenting that therapy was useful to them.

The probable lack of education and understanding of service providers is also an issue in relation to caring practices and cultures in Indigenous communities (Evans-Campbell et al., 2007). This is about the role of the organisation in terms of the values it should have, for example, carer support and implications for alternative family care which is usually limited to those who are caring for relations, rather than other community members.

What can we learn?

These findings bring into clear focus the pervasiveness and overwhelming collective weight of discrimination that TNB people endure and how these can negatively impact families in so many different ways (Grant et al., 2011; Hafford-Letchfield et al., 2019). Yet professionals are woefully ill-equipped to provide services due to lack of training and skills, and potential biases to advocate for equitable treatment of TNB members in their communities. Access and availability of appropriate, sensitive services are yet to be developed in many places, particularly those which enable family members to receive psychosocial support and strengthen the resilience and self-worth among TNB parents (Pyne, 2012). Evans-Campbell and colleagues further suggest that service providers need to be cognisant of the cultural diversity reflected in some populations, particularly around help-seeking where there may be intercultural differences (2007).

There are gaps in the literature; for example, the scholarship on domestic abuse in families has a dominant narrative which focuses solely on heterosexual, cisgender men and women leaving service providers ill-equipped to provide inclusive services (Donovan & Hester, 2010). Amongst TNB people, high levels of intimate partner violence and other forms of abuse in families are routinely reported with dire consequences (Riggs et al., 2016; Seelman, 2015). TNB individuals may also experience threats to out them to other families or friends, or threats and/or the actual withholding of medicine and/or money to pay for transition-related medicines or surgery. One study reminds us that it is paramount that services acknowledge the different array of potential abuses that sit alongside abuses more traditionally conceived (Riggs et al., 2016). Another study reports of TNB people who experienced IPV who found their gender identity being problematised by practitioners, rather than focusing on the abuse they had experienced within their intimate relationships (Rogers, 2016).

A further gap in the literature is the absence of research into the experiences of TNB grandparenting, which potentially reflects ageism in TNB lives (Siverskog, 2014). For social workers, an effective service needs to be able to work with all parties involved, to understand their different perspectives and to broker negotiations which keep the interests of children at the forefront of any decision-making and support (Freeman, Tasker, & DiCeglie, 2002). Service providers need to consider the implications for involvement of any new partners, step-siblings, and/or half-siblings who may be on the margins of the family.

TRANSGENDER PARENTING AND RELIGION: A CASE STUDY FROM UK CASE LAW

We illustrate some contemporary issues for good practice through a legal case study in the UK. Over the past few years, there have been a small number of cases involving TNB parents that have made their way through the British legal system to the higher courts. Cases have involved TNB parents' gender status on their children's birth certificates, and issues of contact between TNB parents and their children. These cases have generated debates about TNB people's rights and women's rights that raise fundamental questions about transphobia, sex, gender, and gender identity, as well as the need for urgent legislative review (Government Equalities Office, 2016).

One legal case, *Re M (Children) [2017] EWCA Civ 2164*, involved a judge from the Appeals Court overturning a decision made by a judge sitting at a lesser court, where direct contact had been originally refused between a transgender woman and her five children, from an ultra-orthodox Jewish community. The original private law proceedings were between the father and the mother of five children, aged between 3 and 13 years old. The father had left the family home to live as a woman. She was shunned by the Charedi Jewish community in which the children had always been brought up, and the children faced ostracism by the community if they had direct contact with her. The reason given by the judge for his original decision was that despite there being many reasons in favour of direct contact, the risk of psychological harm to the children was considered too great as contact with their transgender parent ran the risk of ostracising the children from their community.

Upon review, the Court of Appeal found for the transgender woman, on the basis that the original judge had failed to:

(i) Ask a number of important questions about how his conclusion could follow from his role as a judicial responsible parent applying the standards of reasonable men and women in 2017, in circumstances where the community focus was as much on itself and the adults as it was on concern for the children [77].
(ii) Suitably deal with the children's and parent's human rights [78].
(iii) Provide clear reasons for preferring indirect contact over direct contact, in circumstances where the concern was the role of the community.
(iv) Grapple with all efforts to make contact work.

In the Court of Appeal judgement, the court emphasised that:

> [T]he judge in a case like this is to act as the 'judicial reasonable parent', judging the child's welfare by the standards of reasonable men and women today, 2017, having regard to ever changing nature of our world including, crucially for present purposes, changes in social attitudes, and always remembering that the reasonable man or woman is receptive to change, broadminded, tolerant, easy going and slow to condemn. We live or strive to live, in a tolerant society. We live in a democratic society subject to the rule of law. We live in a society whose law requires people to be treated equally and their human rights are respected. We live in a plural society, in which the family takes many forms, some of which would have thought inconceivable well within living memory.
>
> (Re M (Children), 2017, p. 60)

In stating that direct contact was in the children's best interests the Court of Appeal concluded:

> [I]n our judgment the best interests of these children seen in the medium to longer term is in more contact with their father if that can be achieved. So

strong are the interests of the children in the eyes of the law that the court must, with respect to the learned judge, persevere. As the law says in other contexts, 'never say never'. To repeat, the doors should not be closed at this early stage in their lives.

(Re M (Children), 2017, p. 138)

Critical commentary

This case study is complex because it involves the issue of contact between a parent identifying as transgender and their children from an orthodox religious community. The Court of Appeal's interpretation of the paramountcy of the children in decision-making to have an ongoing direct relationship with their transgender parent, even with the challenges that this would mean for the mother and the children within their closed community, was significant in their decision to overturn the decision of the previous judge. It asserts the role that religious belief, practice, or observance should have in influencing the decisions of the courts. The Court of Appeal also commented that it was unfortunate that the judge had not addressed the plain human rights issues and issues of discrimination arising in this case. In this complex intersectional situation, it is the children's needs that are paramount. A child needs to know both their parents when possible and not experience significant harm in the doing.

Questions

1. If you were the social worker for these children, how would you approach this situation?
2. What about if you were the social worker for the transgender woman? What issues would need to be taken into consideration?
3. In what way do these positions differ from each other? Why?
4. How could policies be changed to support children's and parents' rights in situations like the one described?

Our commentary also draws on lived experiences from within our authorship. The judges remind us of the creativity required to support family relationships. Further, the whole process for parents achieving their authentic selves involves a lot of different aspects at different times. There may be a natural grieving process for the individual, their family, and close networks, thus adding more emotion to an already emotional situation. Further, the transition process will likely continue throughout life. People may, however, feel punished for asserting their own needs, be seen as selfish for persevering against all odds, particularly during any experimental phase, be blamed for losing compassion, or be accused of not giving priority to their family members. Not only can this be unsettling but may involve having to stop caring what other people think, so as to survive the process. Many will have fought hard to meet their needs and desires and when this is realised, may find that transition was not a single event, but requires insight into a longer-term future. The parent's journey to be their true selves can be used as a weapon against them, which mirrors battles between society, the larger community, their family, and their internal narrative. These are important aspects that can be missed or misinterpreted by professionals who need to appreciate the whole picture and not make judgements or assumptions on engagement.

Promoting affirming practice with TNB parents and carers

There are several points from the evidence reviewed that can be used to improve social work and social care practice. Further, Lane and Seelman (2018) argue that the identity categories we address or neglect in our work, and the ways in which we analyse social problems, can potentially reinforce hegemonic discourses that maintain exploitative, oppressive, social relationships. They suggest that our professional voice has an influence on this process. Social workers can highlight and utilise an analysis of exploitation and identity construction through critical theoretical lenses that help us assess our profession in a way that problematises and denaturalises how we speak or do not speak about the families and individuals we work with. There is a need to address TNB-supportive practices, staff training, and guidance in the caring professions. These need to include improving the capabilities of social work with gender-diverse populations, and provide accessible evidence-based practice guidelines on legal, ethical, and human rights issues impacting the community. We are reminded that the social work profession has potential to impact provision, but without a sophisticated understanding of identity and its work, will continue to contribute to the exploitation of service users and overlook practice areas in need of intervention (Lane & Seelman, 2018). There needs to be greater engagement with critical theory in social work practice, research, and education to counteract this and make good social work's commitment to social justice as a key tenet of the profession.

Social workers need to take responsibility for making themselves aware of the debates on gender diversity, and have a nuanced understanding of LGBTQ+ oppression as part of their practice. Through education and training, they need opportunities to develop the confidence to challenge gender-normative and heteronormative assumptions and prejudices, such as the widespread assumption of binary gender 'normality' (Miles, 2018). A survey of 311 transgender and gender nonbinary parents about how they became parents (Tornello et al., 2019) found that pathways to parenthood are very diverse within marginalised gender groups, further highlighting the need for individualised advice and support. Having a nuanced and ethical understanding of the associations between the different factors impacting on different parents and carers, and understanding their experiences, can help professionals and support staff to work more effectively and in serving TNB parents, prospective parents, and their families.

There are several practice pointers emerging from the literature (see Veldorale-Griffin, 2014; White & Ettner, 2004). The emphasis for the social worker is on the potential complexity of support that individual family members may require around parental transition, and the impact of this for individual family members and on family dynamics as a whole. These may involve expressed or unexpressed feelings of grief and loss for both parents and their children or partners. Working with family members to strengthen and support relationships where this is possible is of course paramount, but there may well be issues and challenges where strong emotions are expressed and need to be aired, recognising that these feelings can and will change over time. The research suggests that it is the strength of the parents' relationship that is key and critical to positive outcomes for children, and for the mental health of parents themselves, who may experience many challenges in relation to their feelings of self-worth and self-esteem. Acrimonious parental relationships can be harmful for children, so working with parents to minimise this is important.

Practical support for children and families is also important, including issues like what children should call their transitioning parent in public and private. Social workers have the skills to be able to offer an environment where these conversations can occur. Creating a non-judgemental and safe environment in which these conversations can take place is key and critical. Adolescents may require additional support, and group work with other young people may be a strategy to help children experiencing similar changes in their families. Finally, it is essential to be able to recognise and actively address transphobia alongside the provision of advocacy to promote the human rights of people being impacted by it and helping them deal with and combat discrimination. This suggests that professionals are in a strong position to use their roles, own agency, and place of employment to be an ally and to promote TNB awareness and equality.

CONCLUSION

This chapter has provided insights into some of the complex issues involved in working with families with gender-diverse parents or carers. By drawing on a combination of selected evidence from a systematic review, current research, and from a legal case study and scoping report on practice issues from the UK, we were able to demonstrate several key issues. People who are TNB are as invested and committed to their loved ones as any other persons, but many fear that knowledge of their authentic selves may alienate and destroy their familial bonds. Ongoing barriers, both personal, interfamilial, and systemic in the lives of trans parents are reinforced through a transphobic context, and a lack of appropriate services, targeted support, and advocacy. Whilst LGBQ families have pioneered new family forms, this emerging body of literature reveals that the TNB experience is distinct from the LGBQ experience, and there are differences in how parents who are TNB reconcile their parenting (Tornello et al., 2019). Many parents and carers who are TNB are also excluded from existing mainstream and LGBQ parenting resources, furthering the need for resources specifically tailored to their experiences.

Social work professionals should provide support and advocacy to LGBTQA+ families in the same way they provide support to all families – focusing on human rights, tailoring work to the specific needs of individuals and families, and affirming the diversity of family life. They have a responsibility and accountability in educating themselves and others on these rights and to reach out to the community to include them in improving services as well as being active in their own organisations to ensure these are inclusive and responsive.

ACKNOWLEDGEMENTS

The authors wish to acknowledge the contributions of Deborah Rutter and Moreblessing Tinarwo to the published systematic review, referenced and discussed in this chapter.

RESOURCES

CORAMBAAF https://corambaaf.org.uk/ – an independent membership organisation for professionals, foster carers, and adopters, and anyone else working with or looking after children in or from care, or adults who have been affected by adoption. They have produced a Practice Note to assist practitioners who are assessing transgender applicants in the UK who wish to foster or adopt, and to help fostering services and adoption agencies to work in a way that encourages and values applications from this group of people.

Gender Essence Support Services www.genderessence.org.uk/ – a specialist professional counselling organisation, aimed at providing emotional and therapeutic support to those who identify within the Trans* spectrum, including Gender Fluid, Nonbinary, Intersex, Asexual.

Gender Identity Research & Education Society (GIRES) www.gires.org.uk/ – a UK-wide organisation whose purpose is to improve the lives of trans and gender non-conforming people of all ages, including those who are nonbinary and non-gender.

Gendered Intelligence http://genderedintelligence.co.uk/ – a charity whose mission is to increase understandings of gender diversity and particularly specialise in supporting young trans people.

Mermaids www.mermaidsuk.org.uk/parents/ – raises awareness about gender non-conformity in children and young people amongst professionals and the general public. Mermaids campaign for the recognition of gender dysphoria in young people and call for improvements in professional services.

Stonewall www.stonewall.org.uk/search/Trans – a national campaigning organisation which works with institutions to create inclusive and accepting cultures and to empower LGBT people as advocates and agents of change in wider society.

REFERENCES

Alleyn, C., & Jones, R. L. (2010). Queerying care: Dissident trans identities in health and social care settings. In R. L. Jones & R. Ward (Eds.), *LGBT issues: Looking beyond categories. Policy and practice in health and social care (10)* (pp. 56–68). Edinburgh: Dunedin Academic Press.

Barnes, J., Breckon, M. R., Houle, K., Morgan, R., Paquette, M., & Taylor, C. (2006). *Nowhere near enough: A needs assessment of health and safety services for transgender and two spirit people in Manitoba and Northwestern Ontario.* Winipeg, Manitoba: Crime Prevention Branch Public Safety and Emergency Preparedness Canada.

Clarke, V., & Demetriou, E. (2016). 'Not a big deal'? Exploring the accounts of adult children of lesbian, gay and trans parents. *Psychology & Sexuality*, 7(2), 131–148. doi:10.1080/1 9419899.2015.1110195

Cocker, C. (2011). Sexuality before ability? The assessment of lesbians as adopters. In P. Dunk-West & T. Hafford-Letchfield (Eds.), *Sexual identities and sexuality in social work: Research and reflections from women in the field* (pp. 141–162). Farnham, Surrey: Ashgate.

Cocker, C., Hafford-Letchfield, T., Ryan, P., & Barran, C. (2018). Positioning discourse on homophobia in schools: What have lesbian and gay families got to say? *Qualitative Social Work*, 1–18. doi:10.1177/1473325018767720

Communities Analytical Services. (2013). *Scottish government equality outcomes: Lesbian, gay, bisexual and transgender (LGB&T) evidence review. The Scottish Government [Online]*. Retrieved from www.scotland.gov.uk/Publications/2013/04/7520

Council of Europe. (2015). *Protecting human rights of transgender persons: A short guide to legal gender recognition*. Strasbourg, France: Author.

Dierckx, M., & Platero, R. L. (2018). The meaning of trans* in a family context. *Critical Social Policy*, 38(1), 79–98. doi:10.1177/0261018317731953

Donovan, C., & Hester, M. (2010). "I hate the word 'victim'": An exploration of recognition of domestic violence in same sex relationships. *Social Policy and Society*, 9(2), 279–289.

Ellis, S. A., Danuta, M. W., & Pettinato, M. (2015). Conception, pregnancy, and birth experiences of male and gender variant gestational parents: It's how we could have a family. *Journal of Midwifery and Women's Health*, 60(1), 62–69. doi:10.1111/jmwh.12213

Evans-Campbell, T., Fredriksen-Goldsen, K. I., Walters, K. L., & Stately, A. (2007). Caregiving experiences among American Indian Two-Spirit men and women: Contemporary and historical roles. *Journal of Gay & Lesbian Social Services*, 18(3–4), 75–92.

Faccio, E., Bordin, E., & Cipolletta, S. (2013). Transsexual parenthood and new role assumptions. *Culture Health & Sexuality*, 15(9), 1055–1070. doi:10.1080/13691058.2013. 806676

Freeman, D., Tasker, F., & DiCeglie, D. (2002). Children and adolescents with transsexual parents referred to a specialist gender identity development service: A brief report of key developmental features. *Clinical Child Psychology and Psychiatry*, 7(3), 423–432. doi:10.1177/1359104502007003009

Golombok, S., Mellish, L., Jennings, S., Casey, P., Tasker, F., & Lamb, M. E. (2014). Adoptive gay father families: Parent–child relationships and children's psychological adjustment. *Child Development*, 85, 456–468. doi:10.1111/cdev.12155

Golombok, S., & Tasker, F. (1996). Do parents influence the sexual orientation of their children? Findings from a longitudinal study of lesbian families. *Developmental Psychology*, 32, 3–11.

Government Equalities Office. (2016). *Government response to the women and equalities committee report on transgender equality*. London: HMSO.

Grant, J. M., Mottet, L., Tanis, J. E., Harrison, J., Herman, J., & Keisling, M. (2011). *Injustice at every turn: A report of the National Transgender Discrimination Survey*. Washington, DC: National Center for Transgender Equality and National Gay and Lesbian Task Force.

Green, R. (2007). Sexual identity of 37 children raised by homosexual or transsexual parents. *American Journal of Psychiatry*, 135(6), 692–697.

Hafford-Letchfield, T., Cocker, C., Rutter, D., Tinarwo, M., Manning, R., & McCormack, K. (2019). What do we know about transgender parenting? Findings from a systematic review. *Health and Social Care in the Community*. doi:10.1111/hsc.12759

Hafford-Letchfield, T., Cocker, C., Ryan, P., & Melonowska, J. (2016). Rights through alliances: Findings from a European project tackling homophobic and transphobic bullying in schools through the engagement of families and young people. *British Journal of Social Work*, 46(8), 2338–2356. doi:10.1093/bjsw/bcw104

Haines, B. A., Ajayi, A. A., & Boyd, H. (2014). Making trans parents visible: Intersectionality of trans and parenting identities. *Feminism & Psychology*, 24(2), 238–247. doi: org/10.1177/0959353514526219

Hicks, S. (2011). *Lesbian, gay and queer parenting: Families, intimacies, genealogies*. Basingstoke: Palgrave Macmillan.

Hicks, S., & McDermott, J. (2018). *Lesbian and gay foster care and adoption* (2nd ed.). London: Jessica Kingsley Publishers.

Hines, S. (2006). Intimate transitions: Transgender practices of partnering and parenting. *Sociology*, 40(2), 353–371. doi:10.1177/0038038506062037

Hines, S. (2017). Transgendering care: Practices of care within transgender communities. *Critical Social Policy*, 27(4), 462–486. doi:10.1177/0261018307081808

House of Commons Women and Equalities Committee. (2016). *Transgender equality, first report of session 2015–16: Report*. Retrieved from https://publications.parliament.uk/pa/cm201516/cmselect/cmwomeq/390/390.pdf

Hudson-Sharp, N. (2018). *Transgender awareness in child and family social work education: Research report*. National Institute of Economic and Social Research. London: Department of Education. Retrieved from https://www.scie-socialcareonline.org.uk/transgender-awareness-in-child-and-family-social-work-education-research-report/r/a110f00000NXp4QAAT

Hudson-Sharp, N., & Metcalf, H. (2016) *Inequality amongst lesbian, gay, bisexual and transgender groups in the UK: An evidence review*. London: NIESR [Online]. Retrieved from www.gov.uk/government/publications/inequality-among-lgbt-groups-in-the-uk-a-review-of-evidence

ILGA. (2015). *Annual review of the human rights situation of lesbian, gay, bisexual, trans and intersex people in Europe*. Brussels, Belgium: Author.

James-Abra, S., Tarasoff, L. A., Green, D., Epstein, R., Anderson, S., Marvel, S., & Ross, L. E. (2015). Trans people's experiences with assisted reproduction services: A qualitative study. *Human Reproduction*, 30, 1365–1374. doi:10.1093/humrep/dev087

Lane, W. A., & Seelman, K. L. (2018). The apparatus of social reproduction: Uncovering the work functions of transgender women. *Affilia: Journal of Women and Social Work*, 33(2), 154–163. doi:10.1177/0886109917747614

McPhail, B. A. (2004). Questioning gender and sexuality binaries: What queer theorists, transgendered individuals, and sex researchers can teach social work. *Journal of Gay & Lesbian Social Services*, 17(1), 3–21.

Miles, L. (2018). Updating the Gender Recognition Act: Trans oppression, moral panics and implications for social work. *Critical and Radical Social Work*, 6(1), 93–106. doi:10.1332/204986018X15199226335105

Mitchell, M., & Howarth, C. (2009). *Trans research review*. Manchester, England: Equality and Human Rights Commission.

Office for National Statistics. (2017). *Gender identity update* [Online]. Retrieved from www.ons.gov.uk/methodology/classificationsandstandards/measuringequality/genderidentity/genderidentityupdate

Pyne, J. (2012). *Transforming family: The struggles, strategies and strengths of trans parents*. Toronto, Ontario: Sherbourne Health Centre.

Pyne, J., Bauer, G., & Bradley, K. (2015). Transphobia and other stressors impacting trans parents. *Journal of GLBT Family Studies*, 11(2), 107–126. doi:10.1080/1550428X.2014.941127

Re M (Children). (2017). EWCA Civ 2164 [Online]. Retrieved from www.familylawweek.co.uk/site.aspx?i=ed189596

Riggs, D. W., & Bartholomaeus, C. (2018). Fertility preservation decision making amongst Australian transgender and non-binary adults. *Reproductive Health*, 15(1), 181. doi:10.1186/s12978-018-0627-z

Riggs, D. W., Fraser, H., Taylor, N., Signal, T., & Donovan, C. (2016). Domestic violence service providers' capacity for supporting transgender women: Findings from an Australian workshop. *British Journal of Social Work*, 46(8), 2374–2392. doi:10.1093/bjsw/bcw110

Rogers, M. (2016). Breaking down barriers: Exploring the potential for social care practice with trans survivors of domestic abuse. *Health & Social Care in the Community*, 24(1), 68–76. doi:10.1111/hsc.12193

Rosser, B. R. S., Oakes, J. M., Bockting, W. O., & Miner, M. (2007). Capturing the social demographics of hidden sexual minorities: An internet study of the transgender population in the United States. *Sexuality Research and Social Policy*, 4(3), 50–64.

Seelman, K. L. (2015). Unequal treatment of transgender individuals in domestic violence and rape crisis programs. *Journal of Social Service Research*, 41(3), 307–325. doi:10.1080/01488376.2914.987943

Siverskog, A. (2014). "They just don't have a clue": Transgender aging and implications for social work. *Journal of Gerontological Social Work*, 57(2–4), 386–406. doi:10.1080/01634372.2014.895472

Stotzer, R. L., Herman, J. L., & Hasenbush, A. (2014). *Transgender parenting: A review of existing research*. Los Angeles, CA: Williams Institute.

Tornello, S. L., Riskind, R. G., & Babi´c, A. (2019). Transgender and gender non-binary parents' pathways to parenthood. *Psychology of Sexual Orientation and Gender Diversity*, 6(2), 232–241. doi:10.1037/sgd0000323

Veldorale-Griffin, A. (2014). Transgender parents and their adult children's experiences of disclosure and transition. *Journal of GLBT Family Studies*, 10(5), 475–501. doi:10.1080/1550428X.2013.866063

Veldorale-Griffin, A., & Darling, C. A. (2016). Adaptation to parental gender transition: Stress and resilience among transgender parents. *Archives of Sexual Behavior*, 45(3), 607–617. doi:10.1007/s10508-015-0657-3

von Doussa, H., Power, J., & Riggs, D. (2015). Imagining parenthood: The possibilities and experiences of parenthood among transgender people. *Culture Health & Sexuality*, 17(9), 1119–1131. doi:10.1080/13691058.2015.1042919

Walls, N. E., Kattari, S. K., & DeChants, J. (2018). Transmasculine spectrum parenting: Beyond a gendered fatherhood. *Social Work Research*, 42(3), 223–235.

Walls, N. E., Kattari, S. K., Speer, S. R., & Kinney, M. K. (2019). Transfeminne spectrum parenting: Evidence from the National Transgender Discrimination Survey. *Social Work Research*, 1–12. doi:10.1093/swr/syz005

White, T., & Ettner, R. (2004). Children of parents who make a gender transition: Disclosure, risks and protective. *Journal of Gay & Lesbian Psychotherapy*, 8, 129–145.

White, T., & Ettner, R. (2007). Adaption and adjustment of children of transsexual parents. *Euro Child Adolescent Psychiatry*, 16, 215–221. doi:10.1007/s00787-006-0591-y

Whitely, C. T. (2013). Trans-kin undoing and redoing gender: Negotiating relational identity among friends and family of transgender persons. *Sociological Perspectives*, 56(4), 597–621. doi:10.1525/sop.2013.56.4.597

PART 4

Relationships and sexuality

CHAPTER 14

Sex and relationship therapy with trans and nonbinary individuals

Jennifer A. Vencill, Leonardo Candelario-Pérez, Ejay Jack, and G. Nic Rider

INTRODUCTION

Sexual and relationship health is a critical, albeit often overlooked, aspect of over-all health and well-being (Nusbaum, Gamble, Skinner, & Heiman, 2000; Robinson, Bockting, Rosser, Miner, & Coleman, 2002; World Health Organization [WHO], 2006, 2010). Many specialty health care providers – most notably, sex therapists, marriage and family therapists, and other relationally-focused providers – have worked to champion sexual and relationship health. Traditionally, however, sex and relationship therapy has focused on serving White, heterosexual, cisgender, upper middle-class individuals and couples (Spencer, Iantaffi, & Bockting, 2017; Spencer & Vencill, 2017). Only recently have we started to witness a shift in sexual and relation-ship health care toward a more diverse and inclusive practice (e.g., Rider et al., 2019).

In general, trans/nonbinary (TNB) people face significant challenges in accessing competent and affirming health care (Bauer et al., 2009; Grant et al., 2010; Safer et al., 2016). This difficulty is exacerbated when specialty health care focused on sexual and relationship health is needed or desired (Spencer & Vencill, 2017). In this chapter, we cover the limited, but growing, body of knowledge available regarding sexual and relationship health and therapy for TNB people. We will also review and discuss current best practices for providing competent sex and relationship therapy that is both gender-affirming and inclusive.

WHAT WE KNOW: A REVIEW OF THE LITERATURE

Sexuality is an integral part of our humanity. Yet, research on sex and sexuality typi-cally goes under- or unfunded unless focused on sexually transmitted infections (STIs) and disease prevention (Canada is a notable exception; Bielski, 2017). This scientific funding climate, in which sexual topics are largely overlooked, has resulted in an overall dearth of evidence-based literature focused on sexual and relationship therapy. While this is true for all populations, it is particularly insidious when considering the needs of the TNB community. At present, we are not aware of any published research focused on clinical outcomes or intervention efficacy for sex therapy with gender diverse people. That being said, work in the area of TNB sexual health is beginning to receive greater recognition. In this section, we summarize the limited empirical literature focused on sex and relationship health and therapy with TNB people. We also review critical knowledge that has emerged from the community itself, recognizing that most scholarship on TNB sexual health (and health, in general) is produced by cisgender scholars about transgender experiences (Levy, 2013). This is highly problematic, and we aim to better center the voices and lived experiences of TNB people.

Outside of research on STI prevention, the bulk of currently published literature on trans sexual health has focused on sexual functioning following gender-affirming genital surgeries (for a thorough review, see Wylie, Wootton, & Carlson, 2016). This research tends to demonstrate increased overall health following gender-affirming surgeries, with significant improvements in sexual functioning outcomes as surgical techniques have become more sophisticated. Post-surgical difficulties with sexual/genital pain, arousal, and lubrication, however, remain common and can be very difficult for clients and their partners (Holmberg, Arver, & Dhejne, 2018; Wylie et al., 2016). Focusing sexual health research primarily on post-surgical outcomes is critical for continuing to refine surgical techniques and care, but can be limiting as, despite the prevailing cultural narrative, many TNB folks do not desire or are unable to pursue such interventions (Bauer & Hammond, 2015).

Researchers have published calls to address sexual health and functioning among patients seeking gender-affirming medical care (e.g., Holmberg et al., 2018; Lev, 2014). However, research specifically focused on sex and relationship therapy with TNB people remains scarce. Spencer and Vencill (2017) argue that the challenge of accessing sex and relationship therapy for TNB folks is related to two major barriers: (1) limited formal research on the specific sexual and relationship health needs of TNB people (outside of surgical outcomes), and (2) a lack of health care providers well-trained in this specialized area of care. Their paper is unique in that it outlines a group therapy framework for transfeminine people focused on a variety of sex therapy topics (e.g., dating, gaining sexual self-esteem, self-pleasure, and exploration). Book chapters have also been written about sexual health and sex therapy with TNB people (e.g., Hill-Meyer & Scarborough, 2014; Lev & Sennott, 2012; Spencer et al., 2017), including Lev's (2014) chapter which traces shifting historical perspectives about trans sexuality in Western culture.

Overall, couples and family therapy journals tend to ignore gender diversity, providing little guidance for clinicians (Blumer, Green, Knowles, & Williams, 2012), yet publications regarding general couples/family or relationship therapy for "couples in transition"[1] do appear to be on the rise (Bischof, Stone, Mustafa, & Wampuszyc, 2016). Such work generally focuses on relationships in which one partner has come out as TNB and may be considering, or in the process of, social and/or medical transition (Malpas, 2012; Platt & Bolland, 2018). Unfortunately, a great deal of early literature in this area approached coming out as a relational trauma and focused largely on whether relationships could be "saved" in light of a partner coming out as trans (Samons, 2009). This trend has shifted toward more affirming and gender-competent relationship research and therapy, led by pioneers in the field (e.g., Lev, 2004) who increasingly encourage an intersectional (Addison & Coolhart, 2015) and dyadic (Gamarel, Reisner, Laurenceau, Nemoto, & Operario, 2014; Gamarel et al., 2018) lens. In addition, empirical work has emerged documenting the difficulties, including cisgenderism and transmisogyny,[2] that TNB people often face within the dating world (e.g., Blair & Hoskin, 2018).

Outside academic literature, a number of resources on sexual and relationship functioning have emerged from within the TNB community, highlighting the voices and experiences of TNB people and their sexual partners. Such resources tend to be books or zines that are self-published or printed by smaller publishing firms. For example, in their book, *The Trans Partner Handbook: A Guide for When Your Partner Transitions*, Green (2017) outlines a number of important themes regarding sex and sexuality that tend to arise for couples in transition. These may include shifts in preferred sexual activities, feelings of dysphoria that impact sex, or changes in libido. Other authors have focused on sexual exploration and achieving pleasure with a range of diverse anatomy, navigating dating situations, addressing transphobia during sex and dating, and finding gender-affirming language for one's body and sexual activities (e.g., Bellwether, 2010; DeWitt & Gass, 2017; Erickson-Schroth, 2014; Roche, 2018). We include some publications in our resources section and believe they are important for clinicians to be familiar with, in an ongoing effort to challenge cisnormative narratives created about – but not for or with – the TNB community.

SO WHAT? IDENTIFYING BEST PRACTICES

Despite the lack of research, there is much that can be done to provide supportive, affirming, and therapeutic care around sexual and relationship concerns. Below, we detail several ways in which you can begin to incorporate these skills into your practice with TNB clients.

Seek out specialty training for specialized care

Sexuality and gender topics should be an integral part of all mental health provider training programs. At this point in time, however, most training programs do not routinely cover such topics, and many providers report feeling inadequately trained to address sexuality concerns in a clinical context (Miller & Byers, 2010; Wittenberg & Gerber, 2009). For better or worse, sex and relationship therapy and gender-affirming clinical care currently represent specialty areas of practice, and it is incumbent upon mental health professionals (and those in training) to seek additional knowledge and experience in order to provide competent care. Spencer and Vencill

(2017) appropriately note that while programmatic training in both gender and sexual health is not yet widespread, there are currently several advanced training mechanisms available for increasing competency in these areas:

- Global Education Initiatives (GEIs) offered by the World Professional Association for Transgender Health (WPATH)
- Certification in sexual counseling or therapy by the American Association for Sex Educators, Counselors and Therapists (AASECT), including clinical supervision from AASECT-certified mental health providers
- Postdoctoral training and/or certificate programs in human sexuality and gender health offered by an increasing number of universities (e.g., the University of Minnesota's Program in Human Sexuality, Widener University's Center for Human Sexuality Studies, the Sexual Health Certificate Program at the University of Michigan)
- Specialized training experiences and courses focused on gender and sexual health (e.g., The Transgender Training Institute, Modern Sex Therapy Institutes)

It is important to note that increasing one's competence around sex and relationship therapy with TNB clients may require a piecemeal approach. Many formal training programs in sex and relationship therapy, or those on gender-affirming clinical care, do not necessarily integrate these two topics together well. As an emerging area of practice, it is still unfortunately common that sex therapy specific to the needs of TNB clients may not be an explicit focus of training. Those seeking additional knowledge and skills via a specific training program are encouraged to inquire with said program about whether their sex and relationship therapy training covers gender diverse clients, or in parallel, whether a program on transgender health care will cover skills related to sex and relationship therapy.

Check your biases

Though research supports that many clients want their providers to initiate conversations related to sexual and gender health, clinicians tend to avoid these topics due to poor training, discomfort about sexuality and gender topics, and/or a mistaken belief that sexuality and relationship information is not clinically relevant (Haider et al., 2017; Maragh-Bass et al., 2017). A critical aspect of any therapeutic provider's work is to grow aware of potential thoughts, feelings, and biases that may impact the care of clients. We ask you to consider the following:

- How might you feel, or have felt, when explicitly discussing sexual and gender identity, sexual behaviors, and sexual functioning with therapy clients?
- What is your comfort level with discussing topics such as gender dysphoria, sexual frequency, specific sexual acts (e.g., masturbation habits, oral sex, anal sex, bondage, sex toy use), erotica/pornography use, genital lubrication, erectile functioning, orgasm, ejaculation, sexual attractions, fidelity, sex work, nonmonogamy, and so on?

- What particular areas of sex and sexuality are you most comfortable discussing with clients? Least comfortable?
- What stereotypes might you hold about sex, gender, and sexual identity? How do these intersect with other stereotypes (e.g., regarding race, age, or ability status)?
- During your own development, what messages were you given (implicit or explicit) about gender, sexual orientation, reproduction, and sexual activity?
- How might you begin to work on increasing your comfort with sexuality and gender topics?

In order to provide gender-affirming sex and relationship therapy, it is critical to address internalized biases and messages that stem from sexism, heteronormativity, cisgenderism, transphobia, and transmisogynoir,[3] to name a few. It will be difficult, if not impossible, to assist therapy clients with these tasks if we, as providers, are not also actively working to uproot and challenge oppressive narratives related to gender and sexuality.

Utilize an intersectional lens

According to the Black feminist theory of intersectionality (Crenshaw, 1989), one's lived experience may be shaped by multiple interlocking oppressions related to race, gender, socioeconomic status, sexual orientation, and other characteristics (Moradi & Grzanka, 2017; Rosenthal, 2016). In working with TNB clients (indeed, we would argue, all therapy clients!), it is important to understand the potential interactive effects of multiple oppressions and how this experience can impact sexual and relationship health (Burnes & Chen, 2012; de Vries, 2015). For example, TNB individuals are already culturally stigmatized when it comes to sexuality – often viewed as sexually deviant or as fetishized objects (Bradford & Syed, 2019). Considering other identity aspects, which may actually involve conflicting sexual stereotypes (e.g., older adults as asexual or uninterested in sex), is critical to competent clinical care. We particularly appreciate the Gender Affirmative Lifespan Approach (GALA) presented by Rider and colleagues (2019), which outlines aspects of trans-affirmative and intersectional mental health care, including the foundational tenet that transgender is an identity – not a disease.

Utilizing an intersectional lens in clinical practice focused on sexual health also involves challenging your own narratives, assumptions, and/or beliefs around what a TNB person may sexually want or need. This may involve interrogating general misconceptions about sexuality and sexual scripts (e.g., a penis must be rock hard to reach climax; anything other than penile-vaginal penetration is strange/wrong/not "real" sex), and recognizing the many pleasurable and affirming ways to engage with one's body that are different from cisgender and heterosexual norms and assumptions. Additionally, this might involve engaging clients in exploring affirming language for anatomy (e.g., a transmasculine individual who refers to his penis instead of a clitoris and uses "front hole" as affirming language for vagina). Identifying such language is typically a collaborative therapeutic process by which sex and relationship therapists can support individuals in exploring how they refer to their bodies in a manner consistent with all aspects of their identity, including gender and sexual orientation. Finally, as clinicians working with the TNB community, we believe it is important to be transparent about historical and current oppressions related to gender and sexual health (e.g., forced sterilization), and how these may interact with identities such as race, nationality, and age cohort.

Recognize the biopsychosocial nature (and implications) of sexual health

Sexual health is perhaps best understood through the lens of the biopsychosocial model (Berry & Berry, 2013; Engel, 1980), as it involves a complex interaction of physiology, psychological functioning, sociocultural factors, and, often, interpersonal relationships. Disruption of one or more of these components can negatively impact both sexual and overall well-being (WHO, 2006, 2010). Biological factors in sexual health might include general health status, the presence of illness/disease, or the use of various medications or other drugs that impact physiological processes (including hormone therapy). Psychological factors may include mental health concerns such as depression and anxiety, as well as negative body image, gender dysphoria, minority stress, or a history of trauma. Regarding sociocultural factors: experiences with prejudice and discrimination, faith-based or cultural beliefs, relationship factors, and life stage stressors (e.g., changes in family structure) can all play a role in sexual health. Which factors are most relevant to one's sexual health varies on a case-by-case basis and can certainly change over time and with age.

Given the biopsychosocial nature of sexual functioning and health, multidisciplinary care that involves a collaborative team of providers is considered best practice. Mental health providers, particularly those who specialize in sexual and relationship therapy, have an important role to play in helping clients navigate medical systems that are historically pathologizing of TNB people and bodies. Medical providers, however, are also critical to assessing the biological and physiological aspects of sexual health concerns (e.g., providers who may be assisting clients with hormone therapy). Other types of health care providers, such as pelvic floor physical therapists, can also be a critical part of a multidisciplinary sexual health team (Jiang, Gallagher, Burchill, Berli, & Dugi, 2019). It is important to remember that sexual health is not just defined as the absence of disease or dysfunction (American Sexual Health Association, 2017; Office of the Surgeon General (US), 2001; WHO, 2006, 2010), but includes pleasure and satisfaction. As such, providing sexual health care that supports the overall well-being and individual, biopsychosocial needs of each client is a critical and ethical part of care.

CASE STUDY

The following case represents a composite of many clients with whom we have had the pleasure and privilege to work in the context of sex and relationship therapy. Following the case description, we have included several discussion questions for further thought and exploration.

Cassidy is a 28-year-old, White, *transfeminine* and *nonbinary* person whose pronouns are they/them or she/her.[4] They have a full-time job and access to supportive medical care and insurance. Cassidy currently lives with their partner of four years, Alexandra. Alexandra is a 26-year-old Latina cisgender woman who uses she/her pronouns and identifies as straight.

When they started dating Alexandra, Cassidy was open about identifying as nonbinary, and Alexandra was "OK" with this fact. Over the past year, Cassidy started to publicly express their gender in a more feminine manner, and throughout that time, Alexandra was supportive and affirming. She attended several family therapy sessions with Cassidy and had come to better understand their gender identity. While Alexandra was accepting of Cassidy's feminine gender expression (which was not new to her), she felt concerned when Cassidy expressed interest in hormone therapy (HT). Alexandra asked Cassidy whether they also planned on pursuing other gender-affirming medical interventions, such as surgeries. Cassidy revealed experiencing recent dysphoria about their genitals, but uncertainty about their desire to pursue surgery. Given these potential medical interventions, both partners had concerns about sexual health and satisfaction moving forward.

Alexandra experienced insecurities about her own sexual identity after learning that Cassidy was interested in feminizing their body; specifically, Alexandra felt she would be viewed by others as a lesbian. This became a point of tension for the couple, as Cassidy understood Alexandra's sexual identity struggles to be a sign of misunderstanding about their nonbinary gender identity. Cassidy's therapist, Ace, suggested that the couple seek help from a qualified sex therapist, competent in TNB identities, to help the couple navigate differences and concerns regarding sexual well-being and satisfaction. Ace directed the couple to different search tools for finding qualified sex therapists (e.g., AASECT.org) and encouraged the couple to ask potential providers about their level of training and experience with TNB people.

The couple eventually started sex therapy services with a provider named Sam. Sam began treatment by gathering background information about each partner, including individual sexual and relationship histories. Sam used the initial session to develop an understanding of each partner's gender identity and sexual orientation, and how Cassidy and Alexandra related to those two identities. Sam learned that, before Cassidy revealed they were interested in pursuing gender-affirming medical interventions, both partners felt satisfied with their sexual lives. This initial phase of therapy revealed that, for Alexandra, her personal identity as a woman was strongly enmeshed with her sexual orientation. More specifically, she found that her sense of womanhood was tied to being in a relationship with a partner who has a penis and being the penetrated partner during sexual activity. For Cassidy, their gender identity and sexual orientation were not as strongly enmeshed. Cassidy had historically been attracted to feminine presenting people but chose to label their sexual orientation as queer. Guided by supportive exploratory questions from Sam, Cassidy was able to express that for them, sexual identity was based more on how they were treated during sexual activity, and on their own internal visual imagery of two feminine individuals having sex.

As sex therapy progressed, Sam encouraged and taught the couple to use assertive communication skills about their sexual needs, wonders, and worries. Cassidy was able to express worries about Alexandra reducing their gender identity to their penis. Alexandra came to the realization that she had actually viewed Cassidy as a man who was feminine, and that it was not until finding out that they were considering gender-affirming medical interventions that she truly understood Cassidy's dysphoria. Sam subsequently began working with the couple on addressing narratives on what "sex should be" as understood by their own individual realities. The topics of replicating cisnormative behaviors, the impact of gender dysphoria on sexuality, comfort with one's own body, and sexual behaviors that evoke gender identity were introduced.

Through their individual counseling, Cassidy came to understand and later shared a desire for some of the feminizing effects of hormone therapy, though they continued to express uncertainty about gender-affirming genital surgery. In fact, Cassidy identified that although they experienced dysphoria around their genitals, they also enjoyed the pleasure they felt from their genitals during partnered sex. This led to a deeper conversation with Alexandra about how Cassidy related to their genitals and sexual behavior. Sam assisted the couple in further exploring the notion that a penetrative partner is not necessarily a masculine one. Alexandra then felt comfortable asking Cassidy if medical feminization of any kind would have an impact on how they interacted sexually, in addition to expressing fear about her own attraction towards Cassidy if their body were to change with medical interventions. Cassidy shared that they did not foresee their relationship dynamics changing, and reiterated their satisfaction with Alexandra as a sexual partner. Noting a need for greater understanding about the impact of hormone therapy, Sam provided a list of local physicians offering gender-related medical services and suggested that the couple attend a consultation to discuss what to expect.

After consulting with a physician, the couple returned for a sex therapy session with Sam to discuss two important aspects of sexuality: (a) sexuality for the purposes of reproduction, and (b) their sexual wellness as a couple. Cassidy informed Sam that they had decided to pursue low dose HT but had not yet started. The couple learned from the physician that while estrogen might impact Cassidy's fertility, it was not exactly known to what extent. Sam helped the couple explore and develop a plan for addressing reproduction as well as considering pregnancy prevention, given that HT should not be considered a method for preventing pregnancy. After much discussion and thought, Cassidy and Alexandra decided to follow through with HT and opt out of sperm banking for fertility. This decision was reached for practical and value-based reasons. Both partners agreed that sperm banking was not financially practical, nor did they feel strongly about having biological children. Given the uncertainty about the impact of HT on Cassidy's sperm production, Alexandra opted to continue use of her intrauterine device (IUD) for pregnancy prevention.

Cassidy began hormones and, after about a month, the couple returned to sex therapy with Sam. Sam explored where each individual was at regarding sexual well-being since the last visit. The couple shared that, although they still had concerns about their sexual future, both agreed that the relationship was important enough that it would not cause a separation. Sam revisited discussion from previous sessions about each partner's sexual identities. She introduced the notion of avoiding replicating cisnormative ideas of sexuality and sexual behavior (e.g., the person with the penis initiates sexual activity) and invited Cassidy and Alexandra to be more creative about behaviors, concepts, names, and ideas relating to their sexual lives. Alexandra was openly baffled at first, stating: "I never really thought about creating my own sexuality in this way." Cassidy looked at her and said, "Love, welcome to my world! I never realized how much I assumed you knew because you've been so accepting, but there's a lot more to share." They smiled and held Alexandra's hand. Sam used this space of vulnerability and trust and asked Alexandra: "So, what about your partner having a penis is important to your gender identity and to your sexual identity?" Alexandra paused and realized that Cassidy having a penis still allowed her to retain a mental image of her relationship as conforming to one that is cisnormative and reinforcing of her straight identity. Additionally, Alexandra noted that she was erotically attracted to the idea of her partner having a penis.

Sam reflected that throughout the relationship, both partners appeared to differ in how their individual and sexual identities related to the relationship as a whole. Sam recalled that before Cassidy started HT, both partners reported being satisfied with their sexual lives. This would suggest a disconnect between identities and their lived sexual experiences as a couple, or sexual behaviors that lead to sexual satisfaction. Cassidy sat back in their chair, took a deep breath, and looked at Alexandra. They said, "Well, now that I think about it, what we do sexually with each other has never relied heavily on me penetrating you." Alexandra nodded her head and responded, "Yeah, now that I think about it, that has never been our go-to thing." Both chuckled and looked at Sam, who commented, "Cassidy, I remember you saying that your sexual identity was based on the way you were treated during sex and your own mental imagery when having sex. Do you find that has been your experience with Alexandra?" Cassidy replied, "Well…yes!" They looked at Alexandra and said, "Whether you realize it or not, you are very affirming when you have sex with me. There is a delicateness in the way you touch me that makes me feel very feminine and affirmed."

Over the next couple of sessions, the couple continued to work on bridging the disconnect between their sexual and gender identities, and what they found sexually satisfying. Sam helped Cassidy to be more communicative with Alexandra about how they experienced changes in their body, both sexually and non-sexually, on HT. While they were still able to achieve an erection with psychological and physiological stimulation, the erections were not as firm as prior to starting hormones. This was not bothersome to Cassidy, but did cause Alexandra to worry about Cassidy's sexual satisfaction. Sam emphasized trusting what each partner expressed about their satisfaction. Since the couples' sexuality did not historically rely heavily on penile-vaginal penetration, sexual exploration was focused on expanding behaviors that were satisfying and validating for both partners. While Cassidy continued to experience some dysphoria around their genitals, they recognized the erotic importance of their penis for Alexandra and decided to not pursue more feminizing surgical genital interventions. In turn, Alexandra gained greater awareness of how she treated Cassidy during sex, and what was validating to Cassidy's gender.

Case study questions

After reviewing the case, take some time to contemplate the following questions, which reflect therapeutic considerations demonstrated throughout the case study.

1. How do gender identity, sexual identity, and sexual behavior differ from one another?
2. Why is it important to understand how a person relates to their gender identity, sexual identity, and sexual behavior?
3. What have you been taught regarding the gender binary or gender spectrum? How might that impact your clinical work with a TNB client?
4. Why is being aware of cis- and heteronormativity important when working with gender diverse clients and their sexual wellness?
5. Take a moment to engage in self-reflection. What feelings arose for you while you were reading or after you read the case study? How comfortable do you think you would be as the therapist discussing topics from this case?
6. Why is it important to challenge potential assumptions that because a person experiences dysphoria with regard to their genitals, they do not value or want to engage with this area of their body?
7. Why is it important to challenge the idea that identity (both gender and sexual) is fixed or concrete?
8. What resources do you have in your community and/or online that would allow you to support a couple like this one if they presented to you for therapy? Would you feel comfortable working with them, or decide to refer out? If the latter, do you know to whom you would refer?

CONCLUSION

Transgender and gender diverse people continue to face significant barriers in their access to quality health care with competent providers. For clients who seek specialty care related to their sexual and relationship health, these barriers can seem even more daunting as research is scarce, and mental health professionals often lack training and experience addressing both gender and sexuality concerns with clients. The best practices described in this chapter, while somewhat general in nature, are also foundational for learning to provide gender-affirming and inclusive sexual and relationship therapy. These practices are derived from both the empirical literature on trans sexual health as well as emerging resources written by and for TNB people, which speak to the unique sexual and relationship needs of this community.

NOTES

1   "Couples in transition" is a phrase used within the TNB community, and increasingly in scholarship, that refers not only to the TNB individual but also to their partner(s), who may undergo a parallel transition of their own, and to overall changes in relationship dynamics during gender transition.
2   Cisgenderism refers to the prejudicial preference and favoring of cisgender individuals, and stigmatizing, devaluing, and invalidating of TNB individuals. Transmisogyny is the confluence of transphobia and misogyny, demonstrated by prejudice and discrimination toward TNB individuals, especially trans women and other transfeminine individuals, who fall along the feminine spectrum of gender identity and/or expression.
3   Transmisogynoir refers to the intersection of transmisogyny (see above) and misogynoir, demonstrated by prejudice and discrimination toward transfeminine people of color.
4   As the reader can see, Cassidy has multiple pronouns. For the sake of brevity, the authors chose to use they/them throughout the remainder of this case study.

RESOURCES

Literature relevant to sex and relationship health for TNB individuals is sorely lacking but highly needed. Below is a list of resources that may be helpful to students, practitioners, and clients.

Books/Chapters

- Airton, L. (2018). *Gender: Your guide: A gender-friendly primer on what to know, what to say, and what to do in the new gender culture*. Adams Media.
- Barker, M. J., & Hancock, J. (2018). *Finally, helpful sex advice!* Icon Books Ltd.
- Erickson-Schroth, L. (Ed.). (2014). *Trans bodies, trans selves: A resource for the transgender community* (1st ed.). Oxford University Press.
- Moon, A. (2014). *Girl Sex 101*. Lunatic Ink.
- Nagoski, E. (2015). *Come as you are*. Simon & Schuster Paperbacks.
- Roche, J. (2018). *Queer sex: A trans and non-binary guide to intimacy, pleasure, and relationships*. Jessica Kingsley Publishers.
- Tannehill, B. (2019). Dating and sex. *Everything you ever wanted to know about trans (but were afraid to ask)* (pp. 46–63). Jessica Kingsley Publishers.

Zines (note: most have a fee)

- Bellwether, M. (2010). *Fucking trans women: A zine about the sex lives of trans women (FTW) (Volume 1)*. CreateSpace Independent Publishing Platform.
- DeWitt, V., & Gass, B. (Eds.). *Trans Sex Zine* (Volumes 1 & 2). https://transsexzine.com
- Mac, A., & Kayiatos, R. *Original Plumbing*. https://originalplumbing.bigcartel.com

Erotica and Pornography

- Bonus Hole Boys [from the website: "the web's hottest hardcore gay FTM porn exclusively featuring trans men and cis men fucking"]: www.bonusholeboys.com
- Hill-Meyer, T. (Ed.). (2017). *Nerve endings: The new trans erotic*. Instar Books.

- Pink and White/CrashPadSeries.com (co-run by nonbinary porn star Jiz Lee)
- Taromino, T. (Ed.). (2011). *Take me there: Transgender and genderqueer erotica*. Cleis Press.

Poems and plays

- Moses, G. (2011). How to make love to a trans person. www.genderqueerchicago.org/2011/02/how-to-make-love-to-a-trans-person/
- The Naked I: Monologues from Beyond the Binary by Tobia D. Davis: https://tobiaskdavis.com/plays/the-naked-i/

For cisgender partners

- Aaron, E. (2011). *Transcending anatomy: A guide to bodies and sexuality for partners of trans people*. https://drive.google.com/viewerng/viewer?url=https://azinelibrary.org/approved/transcending-anatomy-1-guide-bodies-and-sexuality-partners-trans-people-1.pdf
- Green, J. (2017). *The trans partner handbook: A guide for when your partner transitions*. Jessica Kingsley Publishers.
- Johnson, J., & Garrison, B. (Eds.). (2015). *Love, always: Partners of trans people on intimacy, challenge, and resilience*. Transgress Press.
- Maynard, D. M. (2019). *The reflective workbook for partners of transgender people: Your transition as your partner transitions*. Jessica Kingsley Publishers.
- Newman, L. (2012). *A love less ordinary: Sharing life, laughter, and handbags with my transgender partner*. Bramley Press.

REFERENCES

Addison, S. M., & Coolhart, D. (2015). Expanding the therapy paradigm with queer couples: A relational intersectional lens. *Family Process*, 54(3), 435–453. doi:10.1111/famp.12171

American Sexual Health Association. (2017). Understanding sexual health. Retrieved from http://www.ashasexualhealth.org/sexual-health/.

Bauer, G. R., & Hammond, R. (2015). Toward a broader conceptualization of trans women's sexual health. *The Canadian Journal of Human Sexuality*, 24(1), 1–11. doi:10.3138/cjhs.24.1-CO1

Bauer, G. R., Hammond, R., Travers, R., Kaay, M., Hohenadel, K. M., & Boyce, M. (2009). "I don't think this is theoretical; this is our lives": How erasure impacts health care for transgender people. *Journal of the Association of Nurses in AIDS Care*, 20(5), 348–361. doi:10.1016/j.jana.2009.07.004

Bellwether, M. (2010). *Fucking trans women: A zine about the sex lives of trans women (FTW) (Volume 1)*. CreateSpace Independent Publishing Platform.

Berry, M. D., & Berry, P. D. (2013). Contemporary treatment of sexual dysfunction: Reexamining the biopsychosocial model. *The Journal of Sexual Medicine*, 10(11), 2627–2643. doi:10.1111/jsm.12273

Bielski, Z. (2017, November 23). How Canada is dominating the field of sexuality research: The big brains behind Canada's good sex. *The Globe and Mail*. Retrieved from www.theglobeandmail.com/life/relationships/the-big-brains-behind-canadas-goodsex/article37056097/

Bischof, G., Stone, C., Mustafa, M. M., & Wampuszyc, T. J. (2016). Couple relationships of transgender individuals and their partners: A 2017 update. *Michigan Family Review*, 20(1), 37–47. doi:10.3998/mfr.4919087.0020.106

Blair, K. L., & Hoskin, R. A. (2018). Transgender exclusion from the world of dating: Patterns of acceptance and rejection of hypothetical trans dating partners as a function of sexual and gender identity. *Journal of Social and Personal Relationships, 36*(7), 2074–2095. doi:10.1177/0265407518779139

Blumer, M. L., Green, M. S., Knowles, S. J., & Williams, A. (2012). Shedding light on thirteen years of darkness: Content analysis of articles pertaining to transgender issues in marriage/couple and family therapy journals. *Journal of Marital and Family Therapy, 38,* 244–256. doi:10.1111/j.1752-0606.2012.00317.x

Bradford, N. J., & Syed, M. (2019). Transnormativity and transgender identity development: A master narrative approach. *Sex Roles, 81,* 306–325. doi:10.1007/s11199-018-0992-7

Burnes, T. R., & Chen, M. M. (2012). The multiple identities of transgender individuals: Incorporating a framework of intersectionality to gender crossing. In R. Josselson & M. Harway (Eds.), *Navigating multiple identities: Race, gender, culture, nationality, and roles* (pp. 113–128). Oxford University Press.

Crenshaw, K. (1989). Demarginalizing the intersection of race and sex: A Black feminist critique of antidiscrimination doctrine, feminist theory and antiracist politics. *University of Chicago Legal Forum, 1989,* 139–167. http://chicagounbound.uchicago.edu/uclf/vol1989/iss1/8

de Vries, K. M. (2015). Transgender people of color at the center: Conceptualizing a new intersectional model. *Ethnicities, 15,* 3–27. doi:10.1177/1468796814547058

DeWitt, V. & Gass, B. (2017). Trans sex zine. Retrieved from https://transsexzine.com/.

Engel, G. L. (1980). The clinical application of the biopsychosocial model. *The American Journal of Psychiatry, 137,* 535–544.

Erickson-Schroth, L. (Ed.). (2014). *Trans bodies, trans selves: A resource for the transgender community.* Oxford University Press.

Gamarel, K. E., Reisner, S. L., Laurenceau, J. P., Nemoto, T., & Operario, D. (2014). Gender minority stress, mental health, and relationship quality: A dyadic investigation of transgender women and their cisgender male partners. *Journal of Family Psychology, 28*(4), 437–447. doi:10.1037/a0037171

Gamarel, K. E., Sevelius, J. M., Reisner, S. L., Coats, C. S., Nemoto, T., & Operario, D. (2018). Commitment, interpersonal stigma, and mental health in romantic relationships between transgender women and cisgender male partners. *Journal of Social and Personal Relationships, 36*(7), 2180–2201. doi:10.1177/0265407518785768

Grant, J. M. M. L., Mottet, L., Tanis, J., Herman, J. L., Harrison, J., & Keisling, M. (2010). *National Transgender Discrimination Survey report on health and health care.* National Center for Transgender Equality.

Green, J. (2017). *The Trans Partner Handbook: A Guide for when Your Partner Transitions.* Philadelphia: Jessica Kingsley Publishers.

Haider, A. H., Schneider, E. B., Kodadek, L. M., Adler, R. R., Ranjit, A., Torain, M., ... & German, D. (2017). Emergency department query for patient-centered approaches to sexual orientation and gender identity: the EQUALITY study. *JAMA internal medicine, 177*(6), 819–828.

Hill-Meyer, T., & Scarborough, D. (2014). Sexuality. In L. Erickson-Schroth (Ed.), *Trans bodies, trans selves: A resource for the transgender community* (pp. 355–389). Oxford University Press.

Holmberg, M., Arver, S., & Dhejne, C. (2018). Supporting sexuality and improving sexual function in transgender persons. *Nature Reviews Urology, 16,* 121–139. doi:10.1038/s41585-018-0108-8

Jiang, D. D., Gallagher, S., Burchill, L., Berli, J., & Dugi, D., III. (2019). Implementation of a pelvic floor physical therapy program for transgender women undergoing gender-affirming vaginoplasty. *Obstetrics & Gynecology, 133*(5), 1003–1011. doi:10.1097/AOG.0000000000003236

Lev, A. I. (2004). *Transgender emergence: Therapeutic guidelines for working with gender-variant people and their families*. London: Routledge.

Lev, A. I. (2014). Understanding transgender identities and exploring sexuality and desire. In G. H. Allez (Ed.), *Sexual diversity and sexual offending: Research, assessment, and clinical treatment in psychosexual therapy* (pp. 45–64). Routledge.

Lev, A. I., & Sennott, S. (2012). Understanding gender nonconformity and transgender identity: A sex positive approach. In P. Kleinplatz (Ed.), *New directions in sex therapy* (2nd ed., pp. 321–336). Routledge.

Levy, D. L. (2013). On the outside looking in? The experience of being a straight, cisgender qualitative researcher. *Journal of Gay & Lesbian Social Services*, 25(2), 197–209. doi:10.1080/10538720.2013.782833

Malpas, J. (2012). Can couples change gender?: Couple therapy with transgender people and their partners. In J. J. Bigner & J. Wetchler (Eds.), *Handbook of LGBT-affirmative couple and family therapy* (pp. 69–85). Taylor and Francis.

Maragh-Bass, A. C., Torain, M., Adler, R., Ranjit, A., Schneider, E., Shields, R. Y., ... & Schuur, J. (2017). Is it okay to ask: Transgender patient perspectives on sexual orientation and gender identity collection in healthcare. *Academic Emergency Medicine*, 24(6), 655–667.

Miller, A. S., & Byers, S. E. (2010). Psychologists' sexual education and training in graduate school. *Canadian Journal of Behavioural Science*, 42, 93–100. doi:10.1037/a0018571

Moradi, B., & Grzanka, P. R. (2017). Using intersectionality responsibly: Toward critical epistemology, structural analysis, and social justice activism. *Journal of Counseling Psychology*, 64, 500–513. doi:10.1037/cou0000203

Nusbaum, M. R., Gamble, G., Skinner, B., & Heiman, J. (2000). The high prevalence of sexual concerns among women seeking routine gynecological care. *Journal of Family Practice*, 49(3), 229–229.

Office of the Surgeon General (US). (2001). The Surgeon General's call to action to promote sexual health and responsible sexual behavior. Retrieved from https://www-ncbi-nlm-nih-gov.proxy.lib.umich.edu/books/NBK44216/

Platt, L. F., & Bolland, K. S. (2018). Relationship partners of transgender individuals: A qualitative exploration. *Journal of Social and Personal Relationships*, 35(9), 1251–1272. doi:10.1177/0265407517709360

Rider, G. N., Vencill, J. A., Berg, D. R., Becker-Warner, R., Candelario-Pérez, L., & Spencer, K. G. (2019). The gender affirmative lifespan approach (GALA): A framework for competent clinical care with nonbinary clients. *International Journal of Transgenderism*, 20(2–3), 275–288. doi:10.1080/15532739.2018.1485069

Robinson, B. E., Bockting, W. O., Rosser, B. R., Miner, M., & Coleman, E. (2002). The sexual health model: Application of a sexological approach to HIV prevention. *Health Education Research*, 17(1), 43–57. doi:10.1093/her/17.1.43

Roche, J. (2018). *Queer sex: A trans and non-binary guide to intimacy, pleasure, and relationships*. Jessica Kingsley Publishers.

Rosenthal, L. (2016). Incorporating intersectionality into psychology: An opportunity to promote social justice and equity. *American Psychologist*, 71(6), 474.

Safer, J. D., Coleman, E., Feldman, J., Garofalo, R., Hembree, W., Radix, A., & Sevelius, J. (2016). Barriers to health care for transgender individuals. *Current Opinion in Endocrinology, Diabetes, and Obesity*, 23(2), 168–171. doi:10.1097/MED.0000000000000227

Samons, S. L. (2009). Can this marriage be saved? Addressing male-to-female transgender issues in couples therapy. *Sexual and Relationship Therapy*, 24(2), 152–162. doi:10.1080/14681990903002748

Spencer, K. G., Iantaffi, A., & Bockting, W. O. (2017). Treating sexual problems in transgender clients. In Z. D. Peterson (Ed.), *The Wiley handbook of sex therapy* (pp. 291–305). Wiley Blackwell. doi:10.1002/9781118510384.ch18

Spencer, K. G., & Vencill, J. A. (2017). Body beyond: A pleasure-based, sex-positive group therapy curriculum for transfeminine adults. *Psychology of Sexual Orientation and Gender Diversity*, 4(4), 392–402. doi:10.1037/sgd0000248

Wittenberg, A., & Gerber, J. (2009). Recommendations for improving sexual health curricula in medical schools: Results from a two-arm study collecting data from patients and medical students. *Journal of Sexual Medicine*, 6(2), 362–368. doi:10.1111/j.1743-6109.2008.01046.x

World Health Organization. (2006). *Defining sexual health: Report of a technical consultation on sexual health 28–31 January 2002, Geneva*. Retrieved from www.who.int/reproductivehealth/topics/gender_rights/defining_sexual_health.pdf

World Health Organization. (2010). *Developing sexual health programmes: A framework for actions*. Retrieved from https://apps.who.int/iris/bitstream/handle/10665/70501/WHO_RHR_HRP_10.22_eng.pdf

Wylie, K., Wootton, E., & Carlson, S. (2016). Sexual function in the transgender population. In R. Ettner, S. Monstrey, & E. Coleman (Eds.), *Principles of transgender medicine and surgery* (2nd ed., pp. 173–177). Routledge.

CHAPTER 15

Trans/nonbinary sexualities and prioritizing pleasure

Cassie Withey-Rila, Megan S. Paceley, Jennifer J. Schwartz, and Lynne M. Alexander

DEDICATION

Our communities are vast and heterogeneous, we have many genders in our communities, whereas cisgender people have only two (Pasley, Hamilton, & Veale, 2019). In this chapter, we intentionally use a wide range of language to reflect the wide range of our communities. While there is no way to consolidate so many experiences and variations into a single umbrella term (e.g., gender diverse, gender expansive), we hope that we can convey that these terms are intended to include all the people at all the fuzzy edges. This chapter is dedicated to those who have gone through a transition, identify as transgender, transsexual/transexual; those that have gone through any amount of social, medical, or legal transition, or none at all. This chapter is for trans women, trans men, nonbinary, genderqueer, agender, and any combination of any of these identities. This chapter is for, and in solidarity with, our Two Spirit, sistergirls, brotherboys, takatāpui, mak nyah, and hijra siblings. This chapter is for those of us in the closet, stealth, birth stealth, out, selectively out, questioning, re-transitioned, putting off transition, or any combination thereof. This chapter is for people that do not feel any attachment to existing Western terms, those that are of a gender outside the realm of all of these gender understandings. This chapter is for clinicians that care about equity and justice. This chapter is for people that love us. This chapter is for all of us.

INTRODUCTION

Working with gender diverse communities ethically requires a commitment to understanding the lack of structural support and the societal barriers TNB communities face. Supporting TNB communities depends not only upon centering individual experiences and recognizing community resilience, but collectively celebrating moments of defiance and pleasure in a world that seeks to negate them. TNB narratives are negatively impacted by dominant discourses around medicalization, binary thinking, and transmisia (anti-transgender sentiment and systems, an alternative to "transphobia" coined by Simmons University library). This chapter provides tangible ways to reframe and challenge these normative assumptions, as well as ways in which individuals can support TNB people, personally and professionally. Using an intersectional, anti-oppressive lens, this chapter explores the complexities of sexuality and gender in a broadly accessible way, filling a gap in the existing literature. The language and interventions identified are intended to be accessible to a non-academic audience, with the intention of being widely useful to providers and laypersons, whether TNB-identified or those working in solidarity. By focusing on lived experiences of pleasure in love and sex, this text will more fully and authentically inform clinicians working with TNB communities. Macro-level interventions, as well as clinical models will be discussed.

Gender euphoria

The desire to be seen and loved for who we are is a basic human need, widely required, but rarely provided by society to those targeted for oppression. Acceptance and positive social integration are particularly conditional on socially normative presentation, both in gender and gender expression, as well as sexuality, leaving many TNB people ostracized and isolated. Gender nonconformity with social (and cisgender) standards, whether or not one identifies as TNB, has historically and contemporarily been medicalized and pathologized in Western society. This focus on deficit, ailment, and pathologizing of human variation has very real impacts on marginalized communities, including TNB populations. For example, access to transition services often requires "persistent, well-documented gender dysphoria" in order to be legitimized and treated (WPATH, 2012, pp. 34, 59). This widely accepted framework of diagnosis of discomfort implies that the TNB experience is inherently pathological and requires "treatment". The Western biomechanical model of health tells us that sickness is a failing to be remedied; if we require diagnosis and treatment, there must be something inherently wrong with us.

Pearce (2018) articulates a wide range of conceptualizations of Western trans identities over the years. She names two dominant framings of transgender existence that were observed in her work: trans as a diagnosis and trans as a movement. The former is easily seen in the previous paragraph; the latter is quite a departure from that negative, pathologizing view of gender diversity. Trans as a movement addresses how "transgender" is both an adjective and also, potentially, a verb: how do we DO trans? Is it the action of transitioning? Or is it performing gender? While there is very limited research on positive aspects or experiences of transgender people, it does show that people experience positivity around sense of self and relation to their larger communities (Riggle, 2011). Finding community is hugely important for TNB people, and is being explored as a protective factor for health and wellbeing (Paceley, Okrey-Anderson, & Heumann, 2017).

This chapter purposes that TNB communities would be better defined by **gender euphoria** – the affirming ways that gender experiences and presentations can be joyful and actualized positively. Benestad (2010) elaborates, suggesting that "[b]elonging is to be perceived by others the same way as one perceives oneself. Gender belonging is positive when the gender perceived is given a positive value, both by the individuals and by the others" (p. 226). We purpose that positive manifestations of TNB sexualities often involve gender euphoria. There can be an ecstatic quality to being truly seen as the gender that you are, and when your partner(s) not only recognizes this but also experiences pleasure from it. It may emerge, in part, by knowing that your partner does not expect societal standards, and does not attach normative social meanings to body parts, acts, or positions. Perhaps it is in hearing the right words used to describe your body, perhaps it is in additions – toys, prosthetics, other aids – being respected and loved as part of yourself. Gender euphoria can develop from being recognized and desired – not in spite of, but because of your sense of self. It is in some ways, an unconditional love, a sacred act, of knowing and owning one's self. Gender euphoria can be seen in trans-specific spaces, like Trans Twitter, as well as in the validation one receives from feeling seen as their gender in social contexts. This sense of place, of positive positionality, can be seen in studies on the positive experiences of transgender identity, in the individual, interpersonal, and in larger social connections like activism and the wider LGBTQIA+ community (Paceley, 2016; Paceley et al., 2017; Riggle, 2011).

Narrative: Tiffany, a 27-year-old Black pansexual trans woman from Detroit writes:

As a trans woman, sexual pleasure has proven to be only the tip of the iceberg [regarding] the depth of the connection sex has to who I am as a person. In my early twenties, sexual pleasure was the dominant factor in my engagement with and selection of partners. Over time that has drastically changed. I find myself now, a 27-year-old Black trans woman who once identified as heterosexual, now pansexual, embarking on what sex and its pleasurable benefits really mean to me holistically. I view sex so differently now in this point in my life. I see sexual engagement not only as a physical satisfier (which I support 100%) but [also] as a conduit to a deeper understanding of self. As a trans woman, I am aware of the obsession that society has over my body and its functions, and that has [inspired] me to explore my own body and sexual desires and its connections to my greater self. Using my "God given" parts any way I see fit is empowering as a trans woman, especially in a patriarchal world. To be quite frank, I personally find it empowering to be a woman with a penis. Right now, in my sex life, what is going unbelievably well for me is the feeling of control I feel I have over my body. There was a point in my life in which I questioned the control I had over my sexual urges. Now, my partner, a transgender man, and I have a connection that encompasses very healthy and transparent communication surrounding our sexual practices and desires. As a trans woman, sexual pleasure for me is a teacher, a declaration, and conduit for communication, and I love every bit of it!

Suggestion for clinicians

Language is an incredibly powerful tool in constructing realities and understanding of one's self. It is the primary method for communication and collaboration, and a key to community building. Language is integral for developing affirming, positive spaces for individuals. By being intentional in language use, gender euphoria and self-actualization can be supported for people along their journeys. Language can encourage and evoke pleasure; by discussing pleasure openly and centering it in practice, it can become more attainable to those whose pleasure is erased or denied. Examples can range from bathroom signage and intake forms being inclusive and accessible to a wide variety of genders, to using proper names and pronouns in notes or files, to normalizing providing pronouns in introductions or in professional correspondence.

"You cannot be what you cannot see" to "possibility models"

Without visible narratives, interpersonal interactions, and media representation, can humans conceptualize or embody their potential? It is meaningful for people, especially socially marginalized people, to see modeled ways of doing, being, or performing positive existence. Laverne Cox (2014) refers to "possibility models", as an alternative to the traditional concept of role models, giving a further feel of self-determination and autonomy. For years, transgender characters and celebrities simply did not exist in movies and the news, and while there is an increase in visibility and awareness, media sources often would suggest that gender diversity is limited to trans women who all live short, sad lives. This increased visibility of TNB people is not, in and of itself, a win. Depictions of TNB communities in movies, TV, and news coverage being limited to tragic ends, medical mishaps, and abuse (as victim or perpetrator) does a disservice to TNB communities. These dominant narratives of what it means to be TNB in Western culture implies that TNB people do not deserve, or even have the capability of, attaining pleasure. As a marginalized group, it can take a degree of normalization and social acceptance before media is produced about, or by, TNB people, without the gaze of the cisnormative voyeur.

Within social work and social science research, there is a notable absence of community involvement in scholarship on gender diverse populations. A lack of participatory research, involvement of community organizations, or advisory groups is found throughout academia. The longstanding activist adage "nothing about us without us" demands no policies, research, or social justice work should be done without input from the marginalized populations most affected (Golding, 2015). A cursory review of existing literature concerning TNB individuals and pleasure shows very little research done on this aspect of TNB people's existence (Gibson et al., 2016; Riggle, 2011; Toomistu, 2018) and even fewer that clearly involve TNB authors (Benestad, 2010; Hill-Meyer, 2017). Searching for literature on TNB sexuality/sexual pleasure reveals many gaps, and a significant number of the articles we would repudiate as in conflict with any TNB-affirming framing or content. The research ranges from studies that misgender TNB participants by labeling their sexuality based upon sex assigned at birth, to studies that center cisgender sexual partners, rather than include TNB voices (Bishop, 2012; Brown, 2009; Chivers & Bailey, 2000; Sojka, 2017). Greater dedication is necessary to locate research that is both gender-affirming and centers the needs and desires of TNB people. TNB people deserve to be the primary informants in all aspects of their lives, including experiences of pleasure, and the ethics of social work support that approach.

Holistic beings

TNB communities' identities and ways of being have been pathologized; additionally, pleasure, especially sexual pleasure, has been deemed inherently inappropriate by normative societies. Generally, the mention of pleasure in context of LGBTQIA+ communities is assumed to be a sexual pleasure, which is a limiting assumption about how TNB people exist in their bodies and communities.

The move to discourage "identity politics", coupled with the shift to separate gender and sexuality in the current LGBTQIA+ categorization, may have left communities with a fragmented sense of self. This requires TNB people to see themselves as gendered, and as having a discrete sense of sexuality, ethnicity, and culture: all separate from one another, just coincidentally inhabiting one person. That sexuality and gender have been so definitively separated in modern LGBTQIA+ activist discourse does a disservice; while they are not the same concept, they are often intertwined. McPhail (2004) articulates that "failure to recognize the complexities of sexualities is more than a theoretical or semantic dispute, but can have life and death consequences as well" (p. 11). Allowing TNB people to integrate all aspects of themselves is essential. Practitioners, family, and compassionate humans must keep these needs on the forefront when addressing the complex sexualities of gender diverse communities.

Narrative: LaMar, a 32-year-old Black, queer, nonbinary, fat-identified person from Brooklyn writes:

Sexual pleasure describes the feelings of pleasure during sex, whether before, during, or after. For me, that can be so many things. First, the sound of breath, the smell of it. The faster and shorter it is, the better. The feeling of touch. It can be painful. It can be calm. But, to get to that point, I must have a mutual emotional connection. I wouldn't call [myself] demi-sexual because I'm always DTF ["down to fuck"]. "Semi-demi" because my [sexual] attraction [is only toward] people who identify as men or masculine. As a nonbinary person, this is the hardest part of sexual pleasure for me. I finally feel like there is a group I can relate to regarding sexuality and romance, but I am worried it will keep me from finding someone. I don't really date or have sex, but would like to with the right person.

It's just so hard to explain that I would rather be alone 95% of the time and wait for someone I connect with, than have a meaningless relationship and sex with a person I kind of get along with.

I typically date people who are more masculine, cis or trans, although I love feminine cis guys. My sexual practices tend to [reflect] what[role] the other person is not. But, I'd rather be the submissive role in bed. I like condoms. I use them more now than I did when I was young. I'm on PrEP. I use lube. I know the proper way to put on a condom. Although I'm an outspoken, fat, queer person (I identify as unapologetically loud), in bed or during sexual experiences, I like to be told what to do. I think of myself like a cat. I do what I want, unless you're doing something that I like. I ignore you as a form of foreplay. I let you get interested. Then, I make you beg for more attention. The game of cat and mouse, or dog and cat. I like them both.

I finally got to the point when I'm happy in my fatness. And I want the person who I'm with to love my fat too. Kiss my stretch marks, hold my body, and worship my size. Here's to getting that. Here's to waiting for it to come to. I'm a patient kitty that knows what the long haul looks like.

As seen in this narrative, TNB individuals' pleasure connections can be complicated, conditional, and contextual. Some people's experience of gender euphoria and pleasure are based on their trans-ness and gender concept, and some not.

(Re)Claiming pleasure

Using the framing presented in this chapter, the concept of TNB pleasure can be seen for what it is: potentially attainable, but suppressed by the common narratives of singular sadness. Irrespective of dominant narratives, TNB pleasure can manifest in many ways, inclusive of and beyond sexual pleasure. One way that TNB people experience pleasure is through chosen families, the individuals and communities with whom they feel supported, affirmed, and validated (Croghan, Moone, & Olson, 2013; Goffnett & Paceley, under review). Emphasizing the ways in which TNB communities build themselves up together highlights the ways in which TNB people are resilient and enacting their own pleasurable experiences. Additionally, embracing and encouraging connections with chosen family aligns well with the social work value of self-determination. Research illustrates the importance of trans-specific spaces in providing safety and comfort for TNB people (Paceley, 2016; Paceley et al., 2017). Being surrounded by people that understand gender on a similar level can decrease the fears associated with navigating potentially hostile spaces and affirm gender identities and expressions across a spectrum.

For TNB people, pleasure can also manifest via affirmations of gender, across a spectrum of identities and expressions. TNB people may experience gender affirmation when their families of origin express support and acceptance of their gender identities (Simmons, Schrager, Clark, Belzer, & Olson, 2013). Affirmation may also manifest with TNB people's environments, for example, when bathroom signage reflects genders beyond a binary and holds space for their gender experience. Gender affirmation may also be transition-related, whether the TNB person experiences a social transition (e.g., affirming a name/pronoun consistent with their gender; expressing their gender in a way that feels comfortable and affirming) or a medical transition (e.g., hormones or surgical interventions). Socially marginalized people often are left with less secure forms of employment, along various forms of marginalization, including transgender or gender diverse experiences (Cecilia Benoit, Jansson, Smith, & Flagg, 2018). While sex work stigma, and the intersecting stigma of being transgender and a sex worker, has huge impacts on health and wellbeing (Cecilia Benoit et al., 2018), some transgender people find that sex work is a positive way to affirm their gender experience (Gibson et al., 2016; Hill-Meyer, 2017; Toomistu, 2018).

Finally, pleasure may be reclaimed by media and visible content that shows TNB people as more than a punchline, abuse victim, or facilitators of "emotional transformation" of cisgender characters (Macintosh, 2018). Although images of TNB people have increased in popular media, their depictions still remain predominantly negative. Media, including news stories, movies, books, and television shows, that depict TNB people as people, who may face challenges, but are also whole people inclusive of and beyond their gender, can go a long way in TNB experiencing pleasure.

Narrative: Chase, a 32-year-old White, queer, nonbinary individual who identifies as a relationship anarchist, and as part of the BDSM and Leather communities in Chicago, writes:

So much of the trans narrative that is portrayed [in the media] is focused on the very real tragedies that we face. It focuses on dysphoria. There is value in those stories, but there is very little joy shown. There is rarely portrayal of pleasure that isn't fetishized. I feel like sexual pleasure is my birthright as a trans person. It's a political act to enjoy my body, both as it is currently, and as it changes. I fight to be seen outside the binary and I fight to be seen as more than my body. Yet, I also am my body and I want to be valued for all the things my body is capable of experiencing. Sex for me is about power and energy exchanged between myself and others. It exists beyond gender, but I use it as a means to explore gender as well. I get to be my truest self when I have sex.

I got into Leather right around the time that I came out as nonbinary and I feel like there was a link for me to being both a gender outlaw and a sexual outlaw. Pushing my limits and enjoying my body is probably the biggest fuck you to the world. I fought for this body. I sure as fuck am going to enjoy the fruits of my labor, loudly and unapologetically. I enjoy my body and gender because of who I am, and not in spite of it.

As Chase's narrative illustrates, the experiences, unique worldview, and resourcefulness of TNB communities are not defined by the institutional and interpersonal discrimination endured, but by the resistance and joy found in authentic existence. Centering pleasure in the discussion of TNB sexualities offers a radical alternative to dominant narratives. Pleasure can be a physical manifestation of bodily autonomy, empowerment, and self-determination. It represents an active rejection of normative Western cisgender/heterosexual/patriarchal standards of what pleasure can and should be. Prioritizing pleasure undermines the negative dominant discourses and subverts a cultural understanding that perpetuates the otherness of TNB communities.

Perhaps pleasure will always exist in the same world as pain, with one contextualizing the other. Is it affirming to remember how far one has come from all the transantagonistic abuse to trans-affirming pleasure? Can one condemn the defining of self through wretched experiences or existences, but also acknowledge the legitimacy of cobbling together a positive or even just functional sexuality with what one has on hand? There is no wrong way to experience gender, and there is no wrong way to experience gender euphoria.

Clinical and professional applications

The oppressive status quo and harmful dominant discourses must be actively undermined and dismantled. Passivity and inaction allow these systems to be maintained, and actively contributes to harm they may be inflicting. The ethical foundation of social work requires clinicians to actively work towards social equity and justice. Centering TNB pleasure, be that a queer sexuality or gender euphoria, is a radical act that practitioners can bring to all aspects of client engagement.

Suggestions for clinicians

Current best practices in the field of sexual health include assessment of an individual's comprehensive sexual health history. One tool recommended by the Centers for Disease Control, incorporates the "Five Ps", as a way to organize this information. The Five Ps include partners, practices, protection from STDs, past history of STDs, and prevention of pregnancy (CDC, n.d.). Some providers advocate for the inclusion of a sixth P – "Pleasure" – as a strength-based component, to assess what is going well for a client sexually, whether in the context of partnered sex or masturbation. Inclusion of pleasure as a health measure may seem unusual, but proponents of its use suggest that increasing positive regard for one's body results in better adherence to health maintenance, health screenings, etc.

While it is beneficial to mention pleasure when working with a person's sexual health, clinicians must be sure they avoid superficially expanding the assessment, while failing to address underlying issues. They must ensure the structural issues or overarching themes that are causing larger sexual health issues are explored. This chapter encourages practitioners to reframe their perception of a client's or patient's engagement with their sexuality to improve clinician insights, build relationships, and center TNB communities' ability to have pleasurable experiences. Currently, the criteria outlining diagnoses of sexual dysfunction in the 5th edition of the Diagnostic and Statistical Manual of the American Psychiatric Association, are predicated upon heteronormative, "penis in vagina" sex practices, occurring between cisgender men and cisgender women. More inclusive criteria would need to be considered if these diagnoses and their corresponding treatments are to serve TNB clients in an effective and socially just way. By opening up the conversation to include attributes beyond functionality and fertility, the clinician can gain insight into other potential concerns. This is more in line with the intent and purpose of both holistic medicine and social work. The focus on pleasure can give clients opportunities to disclose sexual practices they might not otherwise feel inclined to share (e.g., BDSM/kink, anal sex, non-monogamy/polyamory) due to social stigma. Engaging with a client should not be a list of the ways a person has engaged in risky practices, but indicators of a larger practice of humanity and connection. Building trust so clients can share their ways of existing can be facilitated and eased by centering pleasure, especially pertaining to sexuality.

Framing

As previously addressed, pleasure has a relationship to identity, as identity is used by society to justify and allot access to resources. Gender expansive identities endure policing by society, as well as interpersonal and systemic gatekeeping. This catches TNB, and other gender diverse people, in a position where they are both obligated to declare an identity and also are punished for "choosing the incorrect path" (i.e., assumptions that it is an active choice to be TNB and electing to act upon it). Nowhere in this narrative is there space for someone to innately be TNB and believed, nor space for someone to simply choose to be that way. Regardless of how innate being TNB is experienced by a client, policing a person's concept of self is always oppressive. Freedom of self-expression can be, and is, a way to foster and support gender euphoria. When society makes social policy or medical policy that limits access to social expressions of identity, like name change or affirming medical care, TNB clients are being sentenced to an existence without authenticity and, therefore, potentially limiting their access to autonomy, self-actualization, and pleasure. There are many ways social workers and health care providers can engage with TNB individuals and communities. The following sections outline the ways people with a social work background or an interest in social equity and justice can enact change, as well as tools for clinical work with TNB populations.

Macro-level implications

It is essential that social workers and health providers consider how to use their positions and power to advocate for changes in TNB people's communities, culture, and politics that shift away from pathology and dysphoria toward pleasure and euphoria. Advocacy work in institutional, organizational, and legal policies can improve access and participation for TNB people – see Chapter 18 for more information. Assurance of basic physiological and safety needs (Maslow, 1999) is necessary for the attainment of pleasure in the form of love/belonging, esteem, and self-actualization. Policies that include name and gender marker changes, inclusive restrooms, medical, housing, and educational policy, are essential and directly in line with social work values of promoting social justice.

As self-determination is vital for improving wellbeing of socially marginalized communities, ensuring opportunities for leadership roles and development is important to keep in mind in all social work and health care contexts (see Chapter 19 on leadership). From informing policy-making to co-research and community advisory groups, centering and giving platform to the voices of the communities is essential. Advocating for and supporting institutions that allow TNB people to access paid positions and leadership roles is a way to support and uplift TNB people.

Additionally, social workers and health providers can promote the development and sustainability of community-based organizations that are TNB-specific and affirming. Community-based organizations provide TNB people with the ability to access a local TNB community, build chosen family, access resources, and obtain support (Paceley, 2016; Paceley et al., 2017). Social workers and health providers can create the programs, organizations, or groups; support current groups; or ensure existing organizations have TNB-specific and inclusive programming – see the third part of the introduction on community organizing. Within schools, social workers and health providers can also advocate for sex-positive TNB-inclusive sex education. Tompkins (2014) argues that any sex-positive movement must include a focus on diverse TNB identities in order to promote sexual health and, we would argue, a reclaiming of pleasure. Riggs and Bartholomaeus (2018) extend this perspective and indicate that ignoring or pathologizing TNB identities in sex education is rooted in cisgenderism (Ansara's concept of cisgenderism describes "systemic and individual acts that occur in a variety of cultural contexts, including those that are hostile or benevolent and those that are intentional or unintentional" (p. 1)). Resources are provided at the end of this chapter that can act as guides or resources for creating TNB-inclusive, sex-positive sex education programs.

Micro interventions

Many therapeutic interventions have the potential to reduce emotional and physical pain in TNB individuals, as well as increase the awareness of existing pleasure and build individuals' capacity to experience more pleasure. Behavioral models, such as cognitive behavioral therapy (CBT) and dialectical behavioral therapy (DBT), encourage personal interrogation of social and internalized messages of judgment, freeing TNB individuals to better explore identity and desires, as well as providing skills to increase the communication and negotiation necessary for fulfilling relationships and sexual encounters. Additionally, DBT interventions focus on somatic practice, such as mindfulness, and attention to sensory experiences, both of which have the potential to provide pleasure. Further, a schedule of pleasurable activities is offered as an alternative to individuals' existing painful or maladaptive coping processes. Both modalities are undergirded by a humanistic perspective, which emphasizes the goodness inherent in all people, regardless of identity or affiliation, a perspective that encourages radical acceptance of the self, and which is led by clinicians enacting Rogers' (1961) technique of unconditional positive regard.

Techniques that emphasize the integration of the body into emotional wellness can assist TNB individuals in exploring the physical experiences of gender and sexuality and more fully embody those identities. For example, Gestalt therapy (Perls, 1978) provides opportunities for bodywork and mindfulness that can help TNB people connect past experiences with present physiological and emotional feelings. Similarly, holistic practices, like yoga, encourage participants to bring increased awareness to their bodies, while discouraging self-judgment and social comparisons that have the potential to diminish self-love and personal satisfaction in TNB individuals.

The following sections provide additional tools and resources for assisting gender diverse clients in the exploration of pleasure. As with any social work practice, social workers should work with clients and meet them where they are as they engage in these practices.

Social Interactionism/Cooley's "Looking-glass Self" conceptualization is an interdisciplinary tool drawing from sociology and psychology, which posits that the construction of an individual's self is a product of social interaction (Cooley, 1902). Therapists serving TNB individuals may utilize this framework to assist clients with understanding the ways in which their own perceptions of their identity have been shaped via their experiences with others. This may allow TNB clients to reflect upon the relationships and social interactions responsible for self-concept, esteem, desire, and experiences of pleasure.

Integration of queer theory into therapeutic practice can provide TNB individuals a powerful framework from which to critically examine the messages they receive about gender, sexuality, and pleasure. Acknowledging intersectionality via the exploration of an individual's various salient identities, eschewing labels, and rejecting cisheteropatriarchal roles, standards of beauty, and messages about desire, supports the acceptance of radicalized bodies, non-normative relationships, and sex acts, and frees individuals to pursue what is pleasurable, rather than adhere to what is normative. Social workers may integrate queer theory into their practice in a number of ways (Burdge, 2007). Social workers can avoid pathologizing clients, advocating for change to diagnostic criteria requiring a diagnosis for transition-related support and promote acceptance of a diverse array of gender identities and expressions. Normalizing TNB and diverse gender identities and expressions beyond a binary cisgender male/female is a way of integrating queer theory into practice. TNB clients have heard from many sources that their gender and/or expression is invalid, wrong, or sinful. By embracing and supporting the development of gender, while rejecting gender norms and binaries, social workers can promote pleasure in the process of discovering gender.

Adapt identity development models to TNB experiences. Various models of identity development have emerged to articulate and normalize common TNB experiences of self-discovery. The Cass (1984) Model of Homosexual Identity Development, while focused upon sexual orientation, is an extremely accessible and adaptable tool for TNB clients to express awareness, acceptance, and integration of nearly any pleasure-related sexual identity – for example, a kink identity or BDSM orientation. D'Augelli's (1994) Homosexual Lifespan Model, can be similarly adapted, and has the advantage of a non-linear framework, which may allow TNB individuals further freedom in sex exploration. The Transgender Emergence Model (Lev, 2013) may be of particular utility, not only to TNB individuals, but also to therapists serving these clients, as it is writing from a counseling perspective.

Finally, the PLISSIT Model of Addressing Sexual Functioning has promise for adapting to provide affirmation and support of TNB sexuality. The PLISSIT Model provides direction for clinicians to discuss sexual health with clients and stands for: Permission, Limited Information, Specific Suggestions, and Intensive Therapy (Annon, 1976). Dunk (2007) suggests that most social work clients never go further than the "P" which is feeling as if their social worker is a person in which they can discuss sexuality. In adapting the model for affirming work with TNB people, the social work might not just make space for the TNB client to discuss sexuality, but demonstrate their awareness and affirmation of TNB sexualities as normal, healthy, and pleasurable. Additionally, they can actively work to move through the other stages with TNB people. In this context, "Limited Information" would include providing just enough information to support a TNB client's sexuality or sexual development (e.g., one of the resources provided at the end of this chapter). "Specific Suggestions" can be developed alongside a TNB client to promote empowerment and self-determination. The final stage, "Intensive Therapy", may only be necessary for some TNB clients who express sexuality or sexual health needs that go beyond providing affirming information and support. In this way, we can avoid pathologizing TNB identities and sexualities.

The second stage involves providing "Limited Information" in a targeted manner toward any concerns or questions raised by the TNB person, again in an affirming and knowledgeable manner (e.g., not shaming sex work or sexual pleasure).

CONCLUSION

Gender euphoria, as a new model for conceptualizing gender diversity, is achievable, but the lack of visible pleasure and space to integrate all aspects of one's identity are barriers to attainment. By (re)claiming pleasure, individuals and communities can improve their sense of self and increase positivity. Social workers have an ethical obligation to promote social equity and justice. The tools and concepts outlined in this chapter are widely applicable for in and out groups engaged in advocacy for TNB and other gender expansive identities.

RESOURCES

TNB-inclusive sex education

Cortes, N., Eisler, A., & Desiderio, G. (2016). Tip sheet: Gender, sexuality, and inclusive sex education. Baltimore: Healthy Teen Network. www.healthyteennetwork.org/wp-content/uploads/TipSheetGenderSexualityInclusiveSexEd.pdf

Guide on Implementing Queer- and Trans-Inclusive Sex Education in Michigan. The Michigan Radical Sex Ed Initiative. www.thetaskforce.org/wp-content/uploads/2019/04/Guide-on-Implementing-Queer-and-Trans-Inclusive-Sex-Education-in-Michigan.pdf

Trans Sex Ed. Trans Student Educational Resources. www.transstudent.org/health

Our Whole Lives: a secular holistic lifespan sexual health curriculum through the Unitarian Universalist or United Church of Christ. www.uua.org/re/owl

Scarlet Teen: Sex education for the real world. www.scarleteen.com/

TNB sex and sexuality

Erickson-Schroth, L. (2014). *Trans bodies, trans selves*. Oxford University Press.

Gittelman, M. (2019). 3 Steps toward Good Sex beyond the Binary: Having Sex with A Non-Binary Person, Even When That Person is You. https://thebodyisnotanapology.com/magazine/sex-with-the-non-binary-person-even-when-that-person-is-you-maya/

Bellweather, M. (2010). Fucking Trans Women. Zine available for purchase digitally here: https://payhip.com/b/hRtK

Hill-Meyer, T. (Ed.). (2017). *Nerve endings: The new trans erotic*. New York, NY: Instar Books.

The Trans Language Primer: A guide to the language of gender, sexuality, accessibility, and acceptance. www.translanguageprimer.org/

REFERENCES

Annon, J. S. (1976). The PLISSIT Model: A proposed conceptual scheme for the behavioral treatment of sexual problems. *Journal of Sex Education and Therapy*, 2(1), 1–15. doi:10.1080/01614576.1976.11074483

Benestad, E. E. P. (2010). From gender dysphoria to gender euphoria: An assisted journey. *Sexologies, 19*, 225–231. doi:10.1016/j.sexol.2010.09.003

Bishop, K. C. (2012). Moments of transformation: Gender, sexuality, and desire among partners of trans men (Unpublished dissertation).

Brown, N. R. (2009). The sexual relationships of sexual-minority women partnered with trans men: A qualitative study. *Archives of Sexual Behavior, 39*, 561–572. doi:10.1007/s10508-009-9511-9

Burdge, B. J. (2007). Bending gender, ending gender. Theoretical foundations for social work practice with the transgender community. *Social Work, 52*, 243–250.

Cass, V. C. (1984). Homosexual identity formation: Testing a theoretical model. *The Journal of Sex Research, 20*(2), 143–167.

Cecilia Benoit, S., Jansson, M., Smith, M., & Flagg, J. (2018) Prostitution stigma and its effect on the working conditions, personal lives, and health of sex workers. *The Journal of Sex Research, 55*(4–5), 457–471. doi:10.1080/00224499.2017.1393652

Centers for Disease Control and Prevention. (n.d.). A guide to taking a sexual history. Retrieved from www.cdc.gov/std/treatment/sexualhistory.pdf

Chivers, M. L., & Bailey, J. M. (2000). Sexual orientation of female-to-male transsexuals: A comparison of homosexual and nonhomo-sexual types. *Archives of Sexual Behavior, 29*, 259–278.

Cooley, C. H. (1902). *Human nature and the social order*. New York, NY: Scribner's.

Cox, L., [Laverncox]. (2014, October 15). .@MTVact I prefer "possibility model". Some of my p. models: Leontyne Price and Eartha Kitt to name a few. #AskLaverne [tweet]. Retrieved from https://twitter.com/Lavernecox/status/522072765336416256?s=20

Croghan, C. F., Moone, R. P., & Olson, A. M. (2013). Friends, family, and caregiving among midlife and older lesbian, gay, bisexual, and transgender adults. *Journal of Homosexuality, 61*, 79–102. doi:10.1080/00918369.2013.835238

D'Augelli, A. R. (1994). Identity development and sexual orientation: Toward a model of lesbian, gay, and bisexual development. In E. J. Trickett, R. J. Watts, & D. Birman (Eds.), *The Fossey-Bass social and behavioral science series. Human diversity: Perspectives on people in context* (pp. 312–333). San Francisco, CA: Jossey-Bass.

Dunk, P. (2007). Everyday sexuality and social work: Locating sexuality in professional practice and education. *Social Work and Society: International Online Journal, 5*(2), 135–142.

Gibson, B. A., Brown, S., Rutledge, R., Wickersham, J. A., Kamarulzaman, A., & Altice, F. L. (2016). Gender identity, healthcare access, and risk reduction among Malaysia's mak nyah community. *Global Public Health, 11*, 1010–1025. doi:10.1080/17441692.2015.1134614

Goffnett, J., & Paceley, M. S. (under review). Challenges, pride, and connection: A qualitative exploration of advice transgender youth have for other youth.

Golding, F. (2015) *Nothing about us without us*. Retrieved from http://frankgolding.com/nothing-about-us-without-us/

Hill-Meyer, T. (Ed.). (2017). *Nerve endings: The new trans erotic*. New York, NY: Instar Books.

Lev, A. I. (2013). *Transgender emergence: Therapeutic guidelines for working with gender-variant people and their families*. New York: Routledge.

Macintosh, P. (2018). *Queer capital: Transgender representation in contemporary American cinema* (Unpublished master's thesis). Victoria University of Wellington, Wellington, New Zealand.

Maslow, A. H. (1999). *Towards a psychology of being* (3rd ed.). New York, NY: John Wiley & Sons.

McPhail, B. A. (2004) Questioning gender and sexuality binaries. *Journal of Gay & Lesbian Social Services, 17*(1), 3–21.

Paceley, M. S. (2016). Gender and sexual minority youth in nonmetropolitan communities: Individual- and community-level needs for support. *Families in Society, 97*, 77–85. doi:10.1606/1044-3894.2016.97.11

Paceley, M. S., Okrey-Anderson, S., & Heumann, M. (2017). Transgender youth in small towns: Perceptions of community size, climate, and support. *Journal of Youth Studies, 20*, 822–840. doi:10.1080/13676261.2016.1273514

Pasley, A., Hamilton, T., & Veale, J. (2019, February 16). *Transnormativities [Video file]*. Retrieved from www.youtube.com/watch?v=dBNR_VJ6FwU&t=5s&fbclid=IwAR1bGC C6gfQbAETPcmj0Yykcwwtck5aOV4nDJbe8PMDqhnZL_KibNiC9lvs

Pearce, R. (2018) *Understanding trans health*. Bristol, UK: Policy Press.

Perls, F. S. (1978). Cooper Union Forum-Lecture Series. "The self" and "Finding self through gestalt therapy". *Gestalt Journal, 1*(1), 54–73.

Riggle, D. B. (2011). The positive aspects of a transgender self-identification. *Psychology & Sexuality, 2*(2), 147–158. doi:10.1080/19419899.2010.534490

Riggs, D. W., & Bartholomaeus, C. (2018). Transgender young people's narratives of intimacy and sexual health: Implications for sexuality education. *Sex Education, 18*(4), 376–390. doi:10.1080/14681811.2017.1355299

Rogers, C. (1961). *On becoming a person: A therapist's view of psychotherapy*. New York, NY: Houghton-Mifflin.

Simmons, L., Schrager, S. M., Clark, L. F., Belzer, M., & Olson, J. (2013). Parental support and mental health among transgender adolescents. *Journal of Adolescent Health, 53*, 791–792. doi:10.1016/j.jadohealth.2013.07.019

Sojka, C. J. (2017). *The partners of transgender people: Gender, sexuality, and embodiment in relationships through transition* (Unpublished dissertation).

Tompkins, A. B. (2014). "There's no chasing involved": Cis/trans relationships, 'tranny chasers', and the future of a sex-positive trans politics. *Journal of Homosexuality, 61*(5), 766–780. doi:10.1080/00918369.2014.870448

Toomistu, T. (2018). Playground love: Sex work, pleasure, and self-affirmation in the urban nightlife of Indonesian waria. *Culture, Health & Sexuality, 21*, 205–218. doi:10.1080/1 3691058.2018.1459847

World Professional Association for Transgender Health [WPATH]. (2012). *Standards of care for the health of transsexual, transgender, and gender-nonconforming people*. Minneapolis, MN: WPATH.

CHAPTER 16

Exploring trans/nonbinary intimate partner violence

What to know to create inclusive spaces and services

Lisa Langenderfer-Magruder and Andrew Seeber

DEFINING INTIMATE PARTNER VIOLENCE

Intimate partner violence (IPV) has been defined in different ways by organizations and agencies over time. For the purposes of this chapter, IPV is defined as "physical violence, sexual violence, threats of physical or sexual violence, stalking, and psychological aggression (including coercive tactics) by a current or former intimate partner" (Black et al., 2011, p. 37). An intimate partnership can be characterized in several ways, and is not limited to identifying as being or having been in a romantic relationship. Intimate partners can include current or former legal or common-law spouses or domestic partners, boyfriends or girlfriends, dating partners, or ongoing sexual partners (Breiding, Basile, Smith, Black, & Mahendra, 2015). Further, regardless of current relationship status, victims and perpetrators with a child in common are considered intimate partners (Breiding et al., 2015).

IPV is often conceived of in its physical form, including various tactics ranging from slapping or shoving to beating, choking, and burning (Centers for Disease Control and Prevention [CDC], 2018a). Sexual partner violence can also occur, involving physical or non-physical tactics ranging from unwanted sexual verbalizations (e.g., harassment) to sexual coercion to rape (CDC, 2018a). Stalking is patterned victimization wherein the perpetrator causes fear in the victim through unwanted contact, including harassment or threats (CDC, 2018a). Finally, psychological abuse involves aggressive verbalizations, such as name-calling, insults, and humiliation, as well as coercive controlling behaviors that make the victimized partner feel threatened, monitored, or controlled (CDC, 2018a).

There are two linguistic matters of note in discussing IPV. First, though often used interchangeably, IPV and domestic violence are distinct. Legally, domestic violence can encompass relationships beyond romantic or intimate partnerships (e.g., sibling violence). Intimate partner violence is both a narrower and broader term. It narrows the violence to that between intimate partners, but broadens our conceptualization of who can be impacted by removing the married or shared living space connotation of the word "domestic". For consistency, the present chapter uses the term "intimate partner violence", however, linguistic adaptations may be necessary based on the area of practice.

Second, those who have experienced IPV may identify as a "victim" or a "survivor" of violence. There are varying personal and political perspectives on which term is more appropriate and in what contexts. Much of the discussion around these distinctions occur in sexual violence research, specifically, with the Rape, Abuse & Incest National Network (2019) noting that an appropriate approach is to ask preferences on an individual basis. To honor both choices, the terms "victim" and "survivor" are used interchangeably throughout this chapter.

A brief history of the systemic response

Historically, IPV was considered a familial, rather than a social problem, and enforcement of relevant laws was lacking until the second wave of feminism in the 1970s and 1980s (Pleck, 1989). At that time, the narrative of patriarchy progressively took hold, and IPV (or domestic violence, as it was more commonly called) was increasingly viewed as a means men used to gain and maintain power over women (Schecter, 1982). The "battered women's movement" prioritized victim safety and gave rise to the community-coordinated response to IPV (Pence & Shepard, 1999).

Additional efforts were made in the 1990s to curb these systemic problems, most notably, the Violence Against Women Act (VAWA) in 1994. VAWA provided funding at state and local levels to address gender-based violence (e.g., domestic violence, stalking, rape) through improved criminal justice response (Rosenthal, 2012). Despite its name, VAWA protects people of all genders (National Task Force to End Sexual and Domestic Violence Against Women [NTF], 2006). Since its initial passage, VAWA has been reauthorized in 2000, 2005, and 2013 (Modi, Palmer, & Armstrong, 2014). Notably, while VAWA typically received bipartisan support (Holder, 2012), the 2013 reauthorization was contested, in part due to the explicit inclusion of service provision for lesbian, gay, bisexual, transgender, and queer (LGBTQ) individuals (Ortega & Rusch-Armendariz, 2013). Eventually, the House passed the Senate's LGBTQ-inclusive bill, and it was signed into law (Modi et al., 2014).

As of this writing, VAWA has expired, partly due to the impact of the January 2019 government shutdown, as well as Democrats' desire to expand the Act (Tatum, Mattingly, & Killough, 2019). In March 2019, Senator Karen Bass (D-CA) introduced H.R. 1585, which included several TNB-relevant provisions. In addition to explicit direction that grant recipients can use funds for training on identifying and ending LGBT discrimination, several additions were included for better protection of federally-incarcerated

TNB individuals: (1) the inclusion of LGBT and intersex individuals in the definition of "vulnerable" prisoners (p. 169); (2) direction that decisions regarding housing or programming assignments of transgender or intersex prisoners take into consideration, on a case-specific basis, if the assignment ensures the prisoner's safety and health, with "serious consideration of the prisoner's own views with respect to their safety", as well as if and how the placement presents challenges (e.g., management, security; p. 171); (3) regulation that a transgender prisoner's sex is determined by the sex with which the prisoner identifies; and (4) regulation that "a correctional officer may not search or physically examine a prisoner for the sole purpose of determining the prisoner's genital status or sex" (p. 171) (H.R. 1585, 2019). On April 4, 2019, the House of Representatives passed the Violence Against Women Reauthorization Act of 2019 (H.R. 1585), though the Senate did not immediately follow. In November 2019, Senator Dianne Feinstein (D-CA) introduced S. 2843 as a companion bill to H.R. 1585; however, later in the month, Senator Joni Ernst (R-IA) introduced an alternative version (S. 2920), which advocacy groups have denounced, in part, for its rollback of existing LGBTQ protections (National Coalition Against Domestic Violence, 2019; NTF, 2019).

While these efforts have been significant and helped countless victims of violence, the history of the systemic response illuminates its limited narrative scope. IPV has been framed as a cisgender, heterosexual problem, with men as perpetrators and women as victims—particularly cisgender White women (Aspani, 2018). Members of the LGBQ community and trans/nonbinary (TNB) people, in particular, have been rendered invisible in conversations around sex and gender-based violence. More recent research with the LGBTQ community has amassed and is disputing the singular narrative of male perpetrator/female victim. Given the high prevalence of IPV against TNB people, scholars have called for an overhaul in how IPV is conceptualized—including those who identify outside the binary (Yerke & DeFeo, 2016).

TRANS/NONBINARY EXPERIENCES OF INTIMATE PARTNER VIOLENCE

When explored binarily, both one in three women and men report lifetime IPV, though more women (25%) report an IPV-related impact than men (10%) (Smith et al., 2018). Lifetime prevalence is higher for psychological (36.4% women, 34.2% men) and physical violence (30.6% women, 31.0% men) than for sexual violence (5.5% women, 8.2% men) and stalking (18.3% women, 2.2% men) (Smith et al., 2018). Research with LGBTQ participants has indicated an elevated prevalence of IPV compared to their cisgender, heterosexual peers (Brown & Herman, 2015). Like much of the research on LGBTQ people, IPV research has focused on this population generally, rarely teasing apart differences between sexual orientation and gender identity. In some instances, this may be an extension of cis, heteronormative thinking in the conceptualization of IPV. In other instances, there are practical considerations of research, such as lack of adequate TNB sample sizes for analyses. More recent scholarship has called attention to this problem, underscoring the need to attend to intersecting identities (Barrett & Sheridan, 2017; Walls et al., 2019).

Obtaining a comprehensive understanding of the scope of IPV against TNB people is further complicated since TNB IPV victims are often misgendered and misnamed in media reports, furthering the erasure of TNB people within the IPV conversation (National Coalition of Anti-Violence Programs [NCAVP], 2017). Additionally, much extant IPV research with TNB participants captures lifetime IPV prevalence, not accounting for when the violence occurred and making it challenging to determine if TNB identities were associated with the violence (Henry, Perrin, Coston, & Calton, 2018). However, research is beginning to address this: in the 2015 United States Transgender Survey (USTS), participants were asked if their experiences of IPV were related to their gender identity (James et al., 2016). As more is known about the IPV experiences of TNB people, it is essential to keep in mind that, in addition to IPV being underreported overall (Tjaden & Thoennes, 2000), it is likely reported even less within LGBTQ populations (Brown, 2008). It is possible and probable that violence is much more extensive than what is published in research or seen in the media.

Though there is limited research on the IPV experiences of TNB people, lifetime prevalence is as high as 72% (Brown & Herman, 2015; Garthe et al., 2018; Henry et al., 2018; James et al., 2016), with research indicating TNB persons report a higher lifetime prevalence of IPV than cisgender peers (Langenderfer-Magruder, Whitfield, Walls, Kattari, & Ramos, 2016). In examining specific forms of violence, a national sample of 78 transgender/gender nonconforming adults found high prevalence for psychological IPV (71%), physical IPV (42%), sexual IPV (32%), and IPV assault with injury (29%; Henry et al., 2018). Notably, this pattern of descending prevalence—psychological, physical, and sexual IPV—mirrors that seen in broader IPV research (e.g., Coker, Smith, McKeown, & King, 2000).

As with any group, TNB individuals likely experience unequal risk for IPV based on their intersecting identities. LGBTQ biases in IPV incidents are vast and include, but are not limited to, heterosexist or homophobic, transphobic, HIV/AIDS-related, anti-immigrant, and anti-sex worker biases (NCAVP, 2018). Limited evidence shows these intersecting identities, and others, result in a higher prevalence of IPV victimization for specific TNB persons. While research indicates that TNB people experience IPV more frequently than cis people, trans women appear to be at especially high risk. A large study of primary care patients' reports of exposure to IPV found trans women were five times more likely than cis women to have experienced physical or sexual IPV in the last year (Valentine et al., 2017). This is compared to lower, but still elevated odds for trans men, gender nonbinary, and gender unidentified/not reported individuals (Valentine et al., 2017). The NCAVP (2017) similarly found that, within an LGBTQ sample, trans women were two-and-a-half times more likely than all others to be stalked or experience financial violence, and twice as likely to experience online harassment by an intimate partner.

As with sex assigned at birth and gender identity, documented differences in IPV exist along other demographic variables. For example, the 2015 USTS data indicate a high prevalence of IPV among TNB people of color, particularly among American Indian (73%), Multiracial (62%), and Middle Eastern (62%) people (James et al., 2016). In 2016, of 15 IPV-related homicides of LGBTQ people, two were trans women and one was gender nonconforming; all three were people of color (NCAVP,

2017). High IPV prevalence rates are also observed in TNB people across age groups, including youth (Goldenberg, Jadwin-Cakmak, & Harper, 2018) and young adults (Whitfield, Coulter, Langenderfer-Magruder, & Jacobson, 2018), though research is lacking with older adults. Concerning sexual orientation, among the general population, bisexual individuals experience unusually high rates of IPV (Walters, Chen, & Breiding, 2013), though a recent intersectional analysis of college students' IPV experiences found no elevated odds for TNB bisexual individuals (Whitfield et al., 2018), indicating a need for further examination. Additional identities that make TNB people vulnerable to violence in general also demonstrate elevated prevalence of IPV, including those with disabilities (61%), undocumented individuals (68%), those experiencing homelessness (72%), and those who have engaged in income-based sex work (77%) (James et al., 2016).

Intersecting identities and social problems may further elevate IPV prevalence for TNB people. The prevailing theory for heightened IPV among LGBQ and TNB populations draws on the concept of minority stress, suggesting that the stress of a marginalized identity can make an individual more vulnerable to additional stressors (Meyer, 2003), such as victimizations. For example, LGBTQ research broadly has demonstrated associations between IPV and internalized homophobia or homonegativity (Balsam & Szymanski, 2005; Edwards & Sylaska, 2013). Vulnerabilities often seen in TNB populations such as family rejection and employment discrimination (e.g., Bradford, Reisner, Honnold, & Xavier, 2013), could create further oppression. A study of young trans women in Chicago and Boston found that minority stressors (i.e., discrimination, day-to-day unfair treatment) were associated with higher rates of IPV, including trans-related victimization (Garthe et al., 2018). These stressors may push TNB people to rely on others for support (e.g., financial, emotional), thus increasing opportunity for potential abuse.

As researchers have primarily examined TNB IPV experiences within the broader context of LGBTQ IPV, consequences resulting from IPV specific to this population are lacking. Studies of TNB victimization, generally, indicate significant negative correlates, such as suicidality (Testa et al., 2012). Some recent scholarship specific to TNB consequences following IPV exists. For example, among TNB youth, Goldenberg et al. (2018) found participants were eight times more likely to report IPV if they reported depressive symptoms. Among adults, Henry et al.'s (2018) survey of 78 TNB people found that while IPV had no relationship with life satisfaction, significant correlations emerged between IPV and anxiety and depression. Specifically, all four types of IPV (e.g., physical, psychological, sexual, IPV with injury) were positively associated with anxiety and all but physical IPV were positively associated with depression (Henry et al., 2018).

Tactics of abuse

As understanding evolves regarding the dynamics of IPV (e.g., females can perpetrate, IPV occurs outside of the heterosexual context), the focus shifts from gendered language about male violence and female suffering toward a gender-neutral focus on perpetrators exerting power and control over victims. In some regards, IPV experiences look similar for TNB and cis, heterosexual individuals. For example, overarching tactics (e.g., emotional abuse, coercion, economic abuse; Domestic Abuse Intervention Programs, 2017) are applicable regardless of identity; however, TNB identity-specific tactics exist. FORGE (2013) summarizes these tactics into six categories used against or by TNB partners:

1. safety, outing, disclosure (e.g., threatening to "out", threatening to take children);
2. community attitudes (e.g., telling a victim they will harm LGBT communities if abuse is exposed);
3. gender stereotypes and transphobia (e.g., telling victim they are not a real man/woman, claiming abuse is a result of hormones or being "butch");
4. undermining identity (e.g., using incorrect pronouns or "it", ridiculing their body);
5. violating boundaries (e.g., non-consensual fetishizing of victim's body, touching areas of the victim's body they do not want to be touched); and
6. restricting access (e.g., hiding hormones or prosthetics, denying access to medical care).

Researchers have suggested a lack of sexual scripts or relationship role models may play a part in elevated prevalence of IPV in LGBTQ communities (Kubicek, 2018; Whitfield et al., 2018). Partners of TNB individuals, regardless of their own gender, may try to normalize IPV, and given the lack of sexual or relational scripts, victims may be more susceptible to the normalizing. Guadalupe-Diaz and Jasinksi's (2017) qualitative work with TNB IPV survivors seems to support this as participants reported struggling to identify and address abuse given the gendered notions of victimization. While survivors feel disempowered by victimization regardless of gender, TNB people additionally struggled with how to "navigate the gender tightrope" (Guadalupe-Diaz & Jasinksi, 2017, p. 782). For example, one MTF participant felt that a friend did not understand why they did not overpower their abuser because they were larger than their partner; conversely, one FTM participant felt that part of being masculine meant not reaching out for help (Guadalupe-Diaz & Jasinksi, 2017).

Accessing services

Based on their review of available literature, Calton, Cattaneo, and Gebhard (2016) suggest that there are three primary barriers to IPV help-seeking within the LGBTQ population:

1. limited understanding of the problem;
2. stigma; and
3. systemic inequities.

Issues such as homophobia, transphobia, and heterosexism not only introduce unique IPV tactics, they increase structural barriers to help-seeking (Guadalupe-Diaz & Jasinksi, 2017). For a topic with research spanning decades, scholars are only beginning to scratch the surface of IPV in the LGBTQ population—even more so for TNB-specific work. Valentine et al. (2017) concluded from their study of transgender,

gender nonconforming, and sexual minority IPV that there is a general need for increased visibility surrounding IPV.

Some of this invisibility could be due to a lack of IPV reporting by TNB people. In a community sample of 122 TNB people in Colorado, nearly one-third experienced IPV, though only 18.4% of those reported the violence to the police (Langenderfer-Magruder et al., 2016). Interviews with domestic violence service providers and researchers indicate professional perceptions that law enforcement response to TNB IPV is ineffective, due to lack of training and a history of TNB mistrust of police (Tesch & Bekerian, 2015). The 2015 USTS showed that 58% of participants experienced past-year harassment by police and 57% would feel uncomfortable seeking police assistance if needed (James et al., 2016). Further, 11% of transgender women who interacted with police were assumed to be sex workers; this was particularly true for transgender women of color (James et al., 2016). Qualitative work with TNB people corroborates this; previous negative interactions with law enforcement can make reaching out for help following IPV an undesirable option, particularly for survivors of color who, in addition to homophobia and transphobia, fear racism (Guadalupe-Diaz & Jasinksi, 2017).

Though TNB survivors need health, mental health, and social services, as with law enforcement, they may be reluctant to seek assistance. Henry et al. (2018) suggest TNB victims may be hesitant to seek mental health services given how they have been historically pathologized. IPV shelters, in particular, can be problematic, as many TNB people are denied access since they are often framed as "women-only" spaces (Aspani, 2018). Among the participants in Guadalupe-Diaz and Jasinksi's (2017) qualitative study of TNB IPV survivors, few even discussed shelters as a potential option and only one had utilized shelter services. Indeed, research supports that TNB victims face barriers when attempting to access help. NCAVP (2017) data shows that 43% of LGBTQ people who sought IPV shelter were refused, including 32% because of their gender identity. Certain sociodemographic and psychosocial factors result in further discrimination. In a sample of transgender participants who had attempted to access domestic violence shelter services while presenting as transgender, Seelman (2015) found several risk factors for unequal treatment: low socioeconomic status, having a disability, suicidality, history of sex work, loss of family due to gender identity, and frequency of being perceived as transgender or gender-nonconforming. Additionally, other research has found that TNB people of color report a significantly higher prevalence of discrimination when attempting to access domestic violence shelters compared to their White peers (Kattari, Walls, Whitfield, & Langenderfer-Magruder, 2017).

CREATING TRANS/NONBINARY-INCLUSIVE IPV SPACES

The Transgender Law Center (2019) found that much of the LGBT population lives in states with low or negative (anti-) gender identity policy protections. Concerning IPV, the Violence Against Women Act (VAWA) protects help-seekers from discrimination based on sex, sexual orientation, or gender identity since its reauthorization in 2013 (U.S. Department of Justice [DOJ], 2014). This means any program that receives VAWA funds cannot legally turn away a TNB client (NCTE, 2019), though caveats remain. For example, VAWA-funded programs can continue "sex-segregated" or "sex-specific" services that they deem vital to the program's operation (DOJ, 2014). Still, even segregated programs must provide comparable services (i.e., quality, duration) to TNB clients (DOJ, 2014). Though not all programs are VAWA-funded, other TNB protections may exist (National Center for Transgender Equality, 2019). FORGE (2015) suggests TNB persons who have experienced discrimination file a complaint with the DOJ, even if they are unsure which entities fund the program.

Using Calton et al.'s (2016) findings as a guide, providers should focus efforts on:

1. education and training around TNB survivors and their needs;
2. engaging potential and current TNB clients by making them "visible" to the agency; and
3. working together to promote the overall visibility of the needs of TNB IPV victims in an effort to influence larger systemic change.

Previous research has found that IPV agency staff want to provide more culturally competent LGBTQ services, but feel unprepared to do so due to lack of knowledge and skills (e.g., Helfrich & Simpson, 2006). As such, the first step toward inclusion is committing to better understanding IPV in the TNB community, both globally and locally. Agency leaders must ensure culturally responsive, ongoing training opportunities for both themselves and staff, including an awareness of the unique forms of IPV TNB survivors may face. Additionally, training must address how other intersecting identities (e.g., sexual orientation, race, ethnicity, disability status) may impact experiences of IPV. Further, staff must be educated on how to address TNB-specific needs following victimization. This will likely necessitate relationships with other TNB-inclusive providers and services. Ford, Slavin, Hilton, and Holt (2013) similarly suggest that LGBT IPV training should be conducted in diverse agencies; target all staff members (e.g., administration, service providers, management); address needs of both clients and staff; and include regular "booster" sessions (p. 87). In continuing education efforts, agencies must ensure they are engaging in monitoring and evaluation efforts that are inclusive of their TNB clients to help identify specific gaps in services.

Services that target TNB survivors must actively reduce stigmatizing practices to help encourage TNB people's reporting and service utilization. To increase visibility, providers should include LGBQ and TNB language and visuals in promotional materials to indicate an inclusive space (Ard & Makadon, 2011). Providers should avoid unnecessarily gendered language on paperwork (e.g., intake forms) that might insinuate a TNB survivor is unwelcome. Ideally, agencies should offer various gender options, including the ability to self-specify, or simply include open-ended questions, such as, "How do you identify your gender?" and "What pronouns would you like me to use in our communication?" This language should be used across clientele so as not to make assumptions about anyone's identity. Further, shelters or other services where survivors interact with one another should enact and enforce a policy that fellow clients respect and utilize each other's self-defined names and pronouns.

As noted above, relational scripts for LGBQ survivors to compare their partnerships to are lacking (Whitfield et al., 2018). Similarly challenging is the lack of visibility of TNB people in general (Valentine et al., 2017), including what healthy relationships look like when one or more partners identify as TNB. This, coupled with TNB people's self-reported challenges to identifying abusive behaviors (Guadalupe-Diaz & Jasinksi, 2017), indicates that service providers need to validate the victimization experiences of TNB people while stressing the unacceptability of abuse. Using tools that are relevant to TNB clients' lives is essential for communicating to them that their experiences are valid and resources exist to help them. For example, The New York City Gay & Lesbian Anti-Violence Project (2003) adapted the traditional power and control wheel often used in IPV practice to be inclusive of LGBT relationships and the specific abuse tactics LGBT survivors may have encountered. As previously discussed in this chapter, FORGE (2013) more narrowly presents TNB power and control tactics—those used both against and by TNB individuals—in a brief guide.

As a cautionary note, service providers should be conscious not to overstress gender identity. The American Psychological Association's (2015) practice guidelines for working with TNB people suggest that because gender intersects with other identities, the salience of particular identities might evolve, given an individual's psychosocial development, regardless of transition. In this vein, Ard and Makadon (2011) suggest IPV clinicians avoid labeling patients as TNB unless prompted by the client.

CLASSROOM ACTIVITY: ADVOCACY SKILLS

According to the National Association of Social Workers' (NASW, 2017) Code of Ethics, "social workers should advocate for living conditions conducive to the fulfillment of basic human needs and should promote social, economic, political, and cultural values and institutions that are compatible with the realization of social justice." This includes public participation and taking social and political action, particularly when it comes to advocating for historically marginalized or oppressed groups (NASW, 2017). Social work educators should help students develop these advocacy skills in various realms. Given the ubiquity of IPV in diverse communities, it is a social problem that many educators might find accessible for use as an exemplar for building advocacy skills in research, practice, and policy. Before beginning, the instructor should understand IPV, the TNB population, and the intersection of the two. This knowledge should be conveyed to students ahead of the activity (e.g., through lecture and/or discussion).

The following activity is intended for students to complete as a group work assignment that stretches multiple course sessions. It is possible to conduct in a single class session as a critical thinking exercise, though with adaptations, instructors should be mindful of the amount of background research students can do within a particular time frame. If, for example, students are to complete this in one session as an in-class activity, the instructor should consider providing essential information or specific prompts and documents to each group. However, if students complete this as an assignment over multiple sessions, they can be expected to do the background research. Though instructors can adapt this to be an individual assignment, the authors suggest a group format as much advocacy requires the input and viewpoints of multiple stakeholders.

Instructors should begin by placing students in three topical groups: *research*, *policy*, and *practice*. They should provide broad instructions to students that their task is to advocate for TNB inclusion as it relates to IPV. Students will need to take the following steps:

1. **Assess the state of trans/nonbinary inclusion related to IPV**. This could be at the federal, state, and/or local level. Students should review the available evidence, which, depending on the group, could come in varying forms (e.g., peer-reviewed literature, laws and statutes, internal documentation of agency policy).
2. **Identify specific gaps for trans/nonbinary people (e.g., protections, services)**. Again, this will likely vary based on the group. The research group might do a mini systematic review on IPV among TNB people, identifying gaps in the literature. The policy group might conduct a policy analysis of a particular law as it relates to TNB IPV survivors. The practice group might examine local shelter policies for TNB inclusionary or exclusionary language.
3. **Create a plan for advocacy to address one or more gaps**. Students should create an advocacy plan based on their findings in steps one and two.
4. **Optional: Implementation of an advocacy plan**. In this optional phase, the instructor can ask students to implement their advocacy plan. Ideally, a concluding reflection paper would be assigned to allow students to critically assess their experiences, noting any particular challenges or successes.

This activity can not only help enhance social work students' advocacy skills and knowledge of community-based practice content, but also help engage other stakeholders in understanding the importance of promoting TNB visibility in IPV research, policy, and practice.

CONCLUSION

Those working in the field of IPV—regardless of role—are called to reduce systemic inequities for TNB survivors. Providers should be well-educated in TNB IPV and enacting inclusive policies in their workplaces. Researchers should be inclusive of and specifically recruit TNB survivors when exploring IPV victimization (Ard & Makadon, 2011). Legal scholars should be exploring ways to fight TNB discrimination for survivors trying to access services (e.g., Aspani, 2018). Ensuring that TNB victims of IPV are receiving culturally competent and inclusive care and services requires social work on all levels.

RESOURCES

To learn more about this topic, readers are encouraged to explore the FORGE (https://forge-forward.org/) and Anti-Violence Project's Training and Technical Assistance Center (https://avp.org/ncavp/tta-center/) websites. In addition to the aforementioned New York City Gay & Lesbian Anti-Violence Project's (2003) adapted LGBT power and control wheel, readers might also be interested in the Gay, Lesbian, Bisexual, and Trans Power and Control Wheel adapted by Roe and Jagodinksy (Texas Council on Family Violence, n.d.), available at www.ncdsv.org/images/TCFV_glbt_wheel.pdf. To access FORGE's (2013) guide to TNB-specific power and control tactics, visit: http://forge-forward.org/wp-content/docs/power-control-tactics-categories_FINAL.pdf. Additionally, Adam Messinger's (2017) book, *LGBTQ Intimate Partner Violence: Lessons for Policy, Practice, and Research*, contains further trans/nonbinary-specific content throughout.

REFERENCES

American Psychological Association. (2015). *Guidelines for psychological practice with transgender and gender nonconforming people.* Retrieved from www.apa.org/practice/guidelines/transgender.pdf

Ard, K. L., & Makadon, H. J. (2011). Addressing intimate partner violence in lesbian, gay, bisexual, and transgender patients. *Journal of General Internal Medicine, 26*(8), 930–933. doi:10.1007/s11606-011-1697-6

Aspani, R. (2018). Are women's spaces transgender spaces: Single sex domestic violence shelters, transgender inclusion, and the equal protection clause. *California Law Review, 106,* 1689–1753.

Balsam, K. F., & Szymanski, D. M. (2005). Relationship quality and domestic violence in women's same-sex relationships: The role of minority stress. *Psychology of Women Quarterly, 29*(3), 258–269. doi:10.1111/j.1471-6402.2005.00220.x

Barrett, B. J., & Sheridan, D. V. (2017). Partner violence in transgender communities: What helping professionals need to know. *Journal of GLBT Family Studies, 13*(2), 137–162. doi:10.1080/1550428X.2016.1187104

Black, M. C., Basile, K. C., Breiding, M. J., Smith, S. G., Walters, M. L., Merrick, M. T., … Stevens, M. R. (2011). *The National Intimate Partner and Sexual Violence Survey (NISVS): 2010: Summary report.* Atlanta, GA: National Center for Injury Prevention and Control, Centers for Disease Control and Prevention. Retrieved from www.cdc.gov/ViolencePrevention/pdf/NISVS_Executive_Summary-a.pdf

Bradford, J., Reisner, S. L., Honnold, J. A., & Xavier, J. (2013). Experiences of transgender-related discrimination and implications for health: Results from the Virginia Transgender Health Initiative study. *American Journal of Public Health, 103*(10), 1820–1829. doi:10.2105/AJPH.2012.300796

Breiding, M., Basile, K. C., Smith, S. G., Black, M. C., & Mahendra, R. R. (2015). *Intimate partner violence surveillance: Uniform definitions and recommended data elements. Version 2.0.* Atlanta, GA: National Center for Injury Prevention and Control, Centers for Disease Control and Prevention. Retrieved from https://stacks.cdc.gov/view/cdc/31292

Brown, C. (2008). Gender-role implications on same-sex intimate partner abuse. *Journal of Family Violence, 23,* 457–462. doi:10.1007/s10896-008-9172-9

Brown, T. N. T., & Herman, J. L. (2015). *Intimate partner violence and sexual abuse among LGBT people: A review of existing research.* Retrieved from The Williams Institute website https://williamsinstitute.law.ucla.edu/wp-content/uploads/Intimate-Partner-Violence-and-Sexual-Abuse-among-LGBT-People.pdf

Calton, J. M., Cattaneo, L. B., & Gebhard, K. T. (2016). Barriers to help seeking for lesbian, gay, bisexual, transgender, and queer survivors of intimate partner violence. *Trauma, Violence, & Abuse, 17*(5), 585–600. doi:10.1177/1524838015585318

Centers for Disease Control and Prevention [CDC]. (2018a). *Intimate partner violence: Definitions.* Retrieved from www.cdc.gov/violenceprevention/intimatepartnerviolence/definitions.html

Coker, A. L., Smith, P. H., McKeown, R. E., & King, M. J. (2000). Frequency and correlates of intimate partner violence by type: Physical, sexual, and psychological battering. *American Journal of Public Health, 90*(4), 553–559.

Domestic Abuse Intervention Programs. (2017). *Wheel gallery: Power and control.* Retrieved from www.theduluthmodel.org/wheel-gallery/

Edwards, K. M., & Sylaska, K. M. (2013). The perpetration of intimate partner violence among LGBTQ college youth: The role of minority stress. *Journal of Youth and Adolescence, 42*(11), 1721–1731.

Ford, C. L., Slavin, T., Hilton, K. L., & Holt, S. L. (2013). Intimate partner violence prevention services and resources in Los Angeles: Issues, needs, and challenges for assisting lesbian, gay, bisexual, and transgender clients. *Health Promotion Practice, 14*(6), 841–849. doi:10.1177/1524839912467645

FORGE. (2013). *Trans-specific power and control tactics.* Retrieved from http://forge-forward.org/wp-content/docs/power-control-tactics-categories_FINAL.pdf

FORGE. (2015). *Trans survivors of domestic and sexual violence.* Retrieved from http://forge-forward.org/wp-content/docs/know-your-rights-VAWA-fact-sheet.pdf

Garthe, R. C., Hidalgo, M. A., Hereth, J., Garofalo, R., Reisner, S. L., Mimiaga, M. J., & Kuhns, L. (2018). Prevalence and risk correlates of intimate partner violence among a multisite cohort of young transgender women. *LGBT Health, 5*(6), 333–340. doi:10.1089/lgbt.2018.0034

Goldenberg, T., Jadwin-Cakmak, L., & Harper, G. W. (2018). Intimate partner violence among transgender youth: Associations with intrapersonal and structural factors. *Violence and Gender, 5*(1), 19–25. doi:10.1089/vio.2017.0041

Guadalupe-Diaz, X. L., & Jasinksi, J. (2017). "I wasn't a priority, I wasn't a victim": Challenges in help seeking for transgender survivors of intimate partner violence. *Violence Against Women, 23*(6), 772–792. doi:10.1177/1077801216650288

Helfrich, C. A., & Simpson, E. K. (2006). Improving services for lesbian clients: What do domestic violence agencies need to do? *Health Care for Women International, 27*(4), 344–361. doi:10.1080/07399330500511725

Henry, R. S., Perrin, P. B., Coston, B. M., & Calton, J. M. (2018). Intimate partner violence and mental health among transgender/gender nonconforming adults. *Journal of Interpersonal Violence.* doi:10.1177/0886260518775148

Holder, E. (2012). *Statement from Attorney General Eric Holder on the 18th anniversary of the Violence Against Women Act.* Department of Justice: Office of Public Affairs. Retrieved from www.justice.gov/opa/pr/2012/September/12-ag-1109.html

James, S. E., Herman, J. L., Rankin, S., Keisling, M., Mottet, L., & Ana, M. (2016). *The Report of the 2015 U.S. Transgender Survey.* Washington, DC: National Center for Transgender Equality.

Kattari, S. K., Walls, N. E., Whitfield, D. L., & Langenderfer Magruder, L. (2017). Racial and ethnic differences in experiences of discrimination in accessing social services among transgender/gender-nonconforming people. *Journal of Ethnic & Cultural Diversity in Social Work, 26*(3), 217–235. doi:10.1080/15532739.2015.1064336

Kubicek, K. (2018). Setting an agenda to address intimate partner violence among young men who have sex with men: A conceptual model and review. *Trauma, Violence, & Abuse, 19*(4), 473–487. doi:10.1177/1524838016673599

Langenderfer-Magruder, L., Whitfield, D. L., Walls, N. E., Kattari, S. K., & Ramos, D. (2016). Experiences of intimate partner violence and subsequent police reporting among lesbian, gay, bisexual, transgender, and queer adults in Colorado: Comparing rates of cisgender and transgender victimization. *Journal of Interpersonal Violence, 31*(5), 855–871. doi:10.1177/0886260514556767

Messinger, A. M. (2017). *LGBTQ intimate partner violence: Lessons for policy, practice, and research*. Oakland, CA: University of California Press.

Meyer, I. H. (2003). Prejudice, social stress, and mental health in lesbian, gay, and bisexual populations: Conceptual issues and research evidence. *Psychological Bulletin, 129*, 674–697. doi:10.1037/0033-2909.129.5.674

Modi, M. N., Palmer, S., & Armstrong, A. (2014). The role of Violence against Women Act in addressing violence: A public health issue. *Journal of Women's Health, 23*(3), 253–259. doi:10.1089/jwh.2013.4387

National Association of Social Workers [NASW]. (2017). Code of ethics: Ethical standards. Retrieved from www.socialworkers.org/about/ethics/code-of-ethics/code-of-ethics-english

National Center for Transgender Equality [NCTE]. (2019). *Know your rights: Survivors of violence*. Retrieved from https://transequality.org/know-your-rights/survivors-violence

National Coalition against Domestic Violence. (2019). Action alert: Call your senators and ask them to support S. 2843 and NOT Senator Ernst's VAWA reauthorization bill. Retrieved January 20, 2020, from https://ncadv.org/blog/posts/action-alert-call-your-senators-and-ask-them-to-support-s-2843-and-not-senator-ernsts-vawa-reauthori

National Coalition of Anti-Violence Programs [NCAVP]. (2017). *Lesbian, gay, bisexual, transgender, queer, and HIV-affected intimate partner violence in 2016*. Retrieved from http://avp.org/wp-content/uploads/2017/11/NCAVP-IPV-Report-2016.pdf

National Coalition of Anti-Violence Programs [NCAVP]. (2018). *Lesbian, gay, bisexual, transgender, queer, and HIV-affected hate and intimate partner violence in 2017*. Retrieved from http://avp.org/wp-content/uploads/2019/01/NCAVP-HV-IPV-2017-report.pdf

National Task Force to End Sexual and Domestic Violence against Women [NTF]. (2006). *Frequently asked questions about VAWA and gender*. Retrieved from www.ncdsv.org/images/FAQ_VAWA%20and%20Gender.pdf

National Task Force to End Sexual and Domestic Violence against Women [NTF]. (2019). NTF statement on S.2920, Senator Ernst's VAWA reauthorization bill. Retrieved January 20, 2020, from www.4vawa.org/ntf-action-alerts-and-news/2019/11/22/ntf-statement-on-s2920-senator-ernsts-vawa-reauthorization-bill

New York City Gay & Lesbian Anti-Violence Project. (2003). *Power & control in lesbian, gay, transgender & bisexual relationships*. Retrieved from http://forge-forward.org/wp-content/docs/NY-AVP-LGBT-power-and-control-wheel.pdf

Ortega, D., & Rusch-Armendariz, N. (2013). In the name of VAWA. *Affilia, 28*(3), 225–228. doi:10.1177/0886109913495644

Pence, E. L., & Shepard, M. F. (1999). An introduction: Developing a coordinated community response. In M. F. Shepard & E. L. Pence (Eds.), *Coordinating community responses to domestic violence: Lessons from Duluth and beyond* (pp. 3–23). Thousand Oaks, CA: Sage Publications, Inc.

Pleck, E. (1989). Criminal approaches to family violence, 1640–1980. *Crime and Justice, 11*, 19–57.

Rape, Abuse & Incest National Network. (2019). *Key terms and phrases*. Retrieved from www.rainn.org/articles/key-terms-and-phrases

Rosenthal, L. (2012). *Strengthening the Violence against Women Act*. Retrieved from www.whitehouse.gov/blog/2012/04/25/strengthening-violence-against-women-act

Schecter, S. (1982). *Women and male violence: The visions and struggles of the battered women's movement*. Boston, MA: South End Press.

Seelman, K. L. (2015). Unequal treatment of transgender individuals in domestic violence and rape crisis programs. *Journal of Social Service Research, 41*(3), 307–325. doi:10.1080/01488376.2014.987943

Smith, S. G., Zhang, X., Basile, K. C., Merrick, M. T., Wang, J., Kresnow, M., & Chen, J. (2018). *The National Intimate Partner and Sexual Violence Survey (NISVS): 2015 data brief – Updated release*. Atlanta, GA: National Center for Injury Prevention and Control, Centers for Disease Control and Prevention. Retrieved from www.cdc.gov/violenceprevention/pdf/2015data-brief508.pdf

Tatum, S., Mattingly, P., & Killough, A. (2019, February 15). *Funding bill leaves out Violence against Women Act extension*. Retrieved from www.cnn.com/2019/02/15/politics/violence-against-women-act-spending-bill/index.html

Tesch, B. P., & Bekerian, D. A. (2015). Hidden in the margins: A qualitative examination of what professionals in the domestic violence field know about transgender domestic violence. *Journal of Gay & Lesbian Social Services, 27*(4), 391–411. doi:10.1080/1053872 0.2015.1087267

Testa, R. J., Sciacca, L. M., Wang, F., Hendricks, M. L., Goldblum, P., Bradford, J., & Bongar, B. (2012). Effects of violence on transgender people. *Professional Psychology: Research and Practice, 43*(5), 452–459. doi:10.1037/a0029604

Texas Council on Family Violence. (n.d.). *Gay, lesbian, bisexual and trans power and control wheel*. Retrieved from the National Center on Domestic and Sexual Violence website www.ncdsv.org/images/TCFV_glbt_wheel.pdf

Tjaden, P., & Thoennes, N. (2000). *Full report of the prevalence incidence, and consequences of violence against women: Findings from the National Violence against Women Survey*. U.S. Department of Justice, Office of Justice Programs: National Institute of Justice. Retrieved from www.ncjrs.gov/pdffiles1/nij/183781.pdf

Transgender Law Center. (2019). *National equality map*. Retrieved from https://transgenderlawcenter.org/equalitymap

U.S. Department of Justice [DOJ]. (2014). *Frequently asked questions, April 9, 2014: Non-discrimination grant condition in the Violence against Women Reauthorization Act of 2014*. Retrieved from www.justice.gov/sites/default/files/ovw/legacy/2014/06/20/faqs-ngc-vawa.pdf

Valentine, S. E., Peitzmeier, S. M., King, D. S., O'Cleirigh, C., Marquez, S. M., Presley, C., & Potter, J. (2017). Disparities in exposure to intimate partner violence among transgender/gender nonconforming and sexual minority primary care patients. *LGBT Health, 4*(4), 260–267. doi:10.1089/lgbt.2016.0113

Violence against Women Reauthorization Act of 2019, H.R. 1585, 116th Cong. (2019–2020).

Violence against Women Reauthorization Act of 2019, S. 2843, 116th Cong. (2019–2020).

Violence against Women Reauthorization Act of 2019, S. 2920, 116th Cong. (2019–2020).

Walls, N. E., Atteberry-Ash, B., Kattari, S. K., Peitzmeier, S., Kattari, L., & Langenderfer-Magruder, L. (2019). Gender identity, sexual orientation, mental health, and bullying as predictors of partner violence in a representative sample of youth. *Journal of Adolescent Health, 64*(1), 86–92. doi:10.1016/j.jadohealth.2018.08.011

Walters, M. L., Chen, J., & Breiding, M. J. (2013). *The National Intimate Partner and Sexual Violence Survey (NISVS): 2010 findings on victimization by sexual orientation*. Atlanta, GA: National Center for Injury Prevention and Control, Centers for Disease Control and Prevention. Retrieved from www.cdc.gov/violenceprevention/pdf/nisvs_sofindings.pdf

Whitfield, D. L., Coulter, R. W., Langenderfer-Magruder, L., & Jacobson, D. (2018). Experiences of intimate partner violence among lesbian, gay, bisexual, and transgender college students: The intersection of gender, race, and sexual orientation. *Journal of Interpersonal Violence*. doi:10.1177/0886260518812071

Yerke, A. F., & DeFeo, J. (2016). Redefining intimate partner violence beyond the binary to include transgender people. *Journal of Family Violence, 31*(8), 975–979. doi:10.1007/s10896-016-9887-y

PART 5

Communities

CHAPTER 17

Transgender and nonbinary youth empowerment

M. Alex Wagaman and Aaron Kemmerer

I feel powerful when my voice and my authentic self are being lifted up and listened to.

– Jae, age 24, multiracial, pansexual, genderfluid person.
From an interview conducted by M. Alex Wagaman

INTRODUCTION

Transgender and nonbinary (TNB) youth specifically *desire* and *require* social environments that foster healthy physical, psychological, social, and spiritual development. To say the lives of TNB youth are negatively influenced by a host of social injustices is a severe understatement; this is reflected in the experiences of many TNB youth in their families and schools. The systemic violence, oppression, and marginalization TNB youth endure do not leave youth devoid of hope or willingness to live proudly in their identities and in community. Resilience in the face of marginalization is the transformational magic of TNB youth.

This chapter will briefly discuss socio-political realities faced by TNB youth and introduce the current knowledge base on TNB youth resilience. Understanding the context restricting the power of TNB youth proves essential to understanding how to utilize an empowerment framework. We will then introduce an approach to empowerment, which can be practiced by service providers. This approach to empowerment extends beyond accessing personal power, and into promoting collective power through engagement in leadership and decision-making around issues impacting TNB youth.

WHO ARE TRANSGENDER AND NONBINARY YOUTH?

TNB individuals do not fit neatly into categories. TNB youth are young people whose gender identity is different from the sex they were assigned at birth. Although some TNB youth identify with more traditional categories, they often create new linguistic categories – gender-expansive identities – which push social boundaries to better express gender as they experience it (Miranda et al., 2018). For a more detailed exploration of definitions of terms surrounding TNB identity, revisit the introduction of this text. Historically, youth is a socio-developmental category implying a minor person under age 18; however, definitive boundaries around youth are ever-changing and political (Finn, Nybell, & Shook, 2013). Some youth-serving organizations offer services well beyond age 18 into the mid-twenties, recognizing the unique developmental needs of youth unmet by adult-focused programs and services. Socially and physiologically, we know youth continue to develop well into their twenties (Arnett, 2014). We suggest *youth* means people between the ages of 14 and 25.

TNB youth are represented among all races, disability statuses, economic groups, sexual orientations, geographic regions, communities, and sub-populations. As such, we must recognize that youth experiences are shaped by the many intersecting identities they hold, creating unique lived realities that are neither additive nor comparable. For example, a young trans woman of color experiences a confluence of racism, misogyny, and transphobia as she navigates her environments (Singh, 2013). Her experience is unique and cannot be compared to that of her peers. We ask readers to keep this in mind throughout the chapter, and considered in the intersectional application of the empowerment framework presented herein.

WHAT WE KNOW ABOUT TNB YOUTH

The landscape

Examining the political landscape for transgender people of all ages can be a harrowing experience. TNB people of all ages face state violence and hate violence (Stanley & Smith, 2015); alarming rates of fatal intimate partner violence and sexual assault, especially against transgender women (Lee, Miranda, Hadfield, Mazeitis, & Winger, 2018); disproportionate rates of mental health crises, substance abuse, and suicidal ideation (James et al., 2016); rampant discrimination in education (Greytak, Kosciw, & Diaz, 2009), employment, and housing (Shelton, 2016); and lack of sensitivity toward TNB individuals in health care systems (Makadon, Mayer, Potter, & Goldhammer, 2015). These conditions of structural violence are compounded by and likely connected to significant economic struggle (James et al., 2016). TNB youth living at the intersections of multiple marginalized identities, such as TNB youth of color and TNB youth living in poverty, face compounding adverse experiences, including criminalization, economic disadvantage, and housing discrimination (Singh, 2013; Stanley & Smith, 2015). A few key areas that significantly impact TNB youth, specifically, are educational environments and family acceptance. Each affects the overall health and wellbeing of TNB youth in the U.S. Some of the negative outcomes associated with experiencing oppression and rejection in these key areas can be mediated by empowering environments at youth-serving organizations (Lepischak, 2004).

Educational environments

TNB youth are vulnerable to bullying and discrimination in K-12 school environments. Seventy-seven percent of surveyed TNB adults who were out in school reported adverse experiences, "such as being verbally harassed, prohibited from dressing according to their gender identity, or physically or sexually assaulted" (James et al., 2016). Within the larger cohort of LGBTQ+ youth, TNB youth experience specific challenges around gender-segregated social spaces, such as bathrooms and locker rooms, and family acceptance situations (Greytak et al., 2009; Miranda et al., 2018).

Family acceptance

Family acceptance is a vital factor in TNB youth wellbeing (Miranda et al., 2018). The support of one trusted adult in the life of a young person can significantly alter their life's trajectory, particularly if they have experienced trauma (Salanoa-Ogbechie, 2018). This rings true for TNB youth who are vulnerable to the harmful social patterns detailed above. TNB youth experience more positive health outcomes when they are in "supportive, safe, and affirming homes" (Miranda et al., 2018). Accepting family environments can help TNB youth embrace their own identities and develop positive and healthy coping mechanisms (Simons, Schrager, Clark, Belzer, & Olson, 2013). If the family is a toxic transphobic environment, then TNB youth are at high risk of facing situations of housing instability (Shelton, 2016) and engagement with criminalized economies like sex work and drug trade (Stanley & Smith, 2015).

TNB youth resilience

Oppressive social norms and hostile environments which reinforce these norms via policy and practice are detrimental to the wellbeing of TNB youth (Greytak et al., 2009; Grossman, D'Augelli, & Frank, 2011). Research provides significant insight into the need for supports, which nurture resilience and empowerment among TNB youth. Approaching resilience through a social-ecological lens shifts the focus onto the environment (Ungar, 2011). For example, if a TNB youth suffers from serious mental health challenges as a result of unchecked harassment at school, an individually-focused approach to resilience asks how their capacity to cope may be strengthened rather than examine their circumstances in a broader context including school policy, teacher awareness, and peer support. This shift creates a collective sense of accountability among stakeholders who have the power to change the environment, increasing access to the resources needed to bounce back from adversity (Asakura, 2016). There is no doubt TNB youth are incredibly resourceful, tending to minimize their involvement in systems that reinforce systematic discrimination (Singh, 2013). Instead, they seek out affirming and supportive systems, spaces, and relationships (Wagaman, Shelton, Carter, Stewart, & Cavaliere, 2019).

The social-ecological approach to understanding resilience honors the power of community and connection, important resilience factors among transgender youth (Barr, Budge, & Adelson, 2016; Wagaman et al., 2019). It also provides an important framework for assessing the behavioral responses of TNB youth to their environments, as suggested by Shelton (2016) in their study of transgender youth and young adults with experiences of homelessness. If we view TNB youth only through the lens of their behaviors (i.e., leaving home, dropping out of school), then we are likely to only see the associated risks. However, if we view youth in the context of their environments, leaving a traumatizing home or school may actually be an act of resilience. In the context of understanding empowerment, this conceptual shift is crucial.

The research on resilience among TNB youth is limited. Several significant studies have highlighted resilience-promoting factors, many of which are linked to empowerment. Research suggests the ability to define oneself and to theorize about gender, particularly with supportive others, is important for resilience (Johnson, Singh, & Gonzalez, 2014; Singh, 2013; Singh, Meng, & Hansen, 2014). TNB youth recognize their unique gender journeys require opportunities to engage and reflect (Wagaman et al., 2019). Developing a strong sense of identity – or identities in the case of youth who live at the intersections of multiple marginalized identities – is an individual process requiring time and support. Finding spaces of belonging where youth see themselves represented is another important factor associated with resilience (Singh, 2013). When TNB youth do not have ready access to physical community spaces, they find them online (Singh, 2013). This aligns with research on TNB youth resilience, which suggests connections to others who share a TNB identity are important to a young person's ability to overcome adversity (Wagaman et al., 2019).

Self-advocacy and a sense of personal agency in relation to transphobic institutions and systems are important to resilience among TNB youth (Singh et al., 2014). Youth who have access to resources and self-advocacy skills use them to combat a sense of powerlessness in the face of adversity. In the following section, we will explore the term empowerment, including the theoretical framework we propose using when approaching TNB youth empowerment.

EMPOWERMENT: A FRAMEWORK FOR PRACTICE

Freire as guide

A transformative approach to the empowerment of TNB youth comes from legendary Brazilian educator and philosopher, Paulo Freire. Freire's (2000) *Pedagogy of the Oppressed* examines concepts of liberation, oppression, and revolutionary critical consciousness through his popular education methodology. Popular education views liberation as a mutual process practiced in collective spaces. Prioritizing people most directly impacted is the underlying principle of Freirean popular education pedagogy: those who feel the weight of the societal structures of oppression already know what is required for changing structures; the lived experience is inherently expertise.

The role of a service provider working with TNB youth in a Freirean pedagogical process is not to educate youth, but to facilitate empowering spaces and programs for youth to raise their own and each other's consciousness about all forms of oppression and gender-based oppression specifically. Freire's (2000) concepts can be applied to one of the most pervasive issues among TNB youth – mental health concerns connected to self-harm and suicidality – which result from the dehumanizing transphobia found rampant in dominant gender-binary culture. The daily compounding effects of living as an oppressed class in the U.S. wear on the spirits of TNB youth. The process of building capacity among TNB youth towards resilience is linked to Freire's concept of oppressed people's struggle toward *life-affirming humanization*. Ultimately, the lives and narratives of TNB youth are shaped by their personal and collective efforts towards being celebrated as more fully human.

Building on Freire: A framework for empowerment

In 1990, social work scholar Lorraine Gutierrez wrote about the impact of systemic oppression on women of color and proposed a framework for working from an empowerment perspective. Gutierrez's framework calls for a shift from focus on the stressors women of color experience as a result of their social location – or position in society based on constructed hierarchies – to a focus instead on the ways in which their power has been limited through controls placed on personal agency, the development of stigma and negative stereotypes, and denial of access to social and material resources (Gutierrez, 1990). Like Freire, Gutierrez shifts the gaze from individual to collective, from personal to systemic. Gutierrez calls on practitioners to work with people to increase their power with an understanding of the systemic context within which the person is located – a process of empowerment involving efforts to increase power at the personal, interpersonal, and political levels (Gutierrez, 1990).

We find this approach to empowerment particularly helpful for thinking about empowerment practice with TNB youth. As previously described, TNB youth experience structural violence and systemic oppression rooted in cisgenderism and transphobia – in many ways questioning their very right to exist. Singh (2013) notes the importance of addressing issues of powerlessness in the lives of TNB youth. This leads us to ask, *How might service providers – assuming that power and powerlessness are key factors in the issues faced by TNB youth – seek to work with youth to increase their power at each level while simultaneously working toward the life-affirming humanization described by Freire?*

A queering of empowerment

Drawing from the work of Freire and Gutierrez, we propose a queering of empowerment for use in social work practice with TNB youth. Empowerment as a practice has been criticized based on the implication that the service provider somehow bestows or transfers power to a client or patient. Without an explicit naming of the power that exists between a provider and a young person receiving services or care, this unidirectional sense of control can become a disempowering reality (Pease, 2002). Queer theory provides useful principles to challenge this weakened notion of empower-ment. First, queer theory acknowledges each of us has personal agency in our social contexts, even when those contexts are oppressive (Jagose, 1996). If our society is based on socially constructed categories – such as gender – then they can also be deconstructed (Foucault, 1990). Second, queer theory – like all critical theories – calls attention to power and its unequal distribution, particularly related to people whose existence challenges established hierarchies of power (McRuer, 2006). Third, queer theory questions the existence of binary categorizations (Jagose, 1996). In this sense, the notion that there is someone doing the empowering and someone being empow-ered is a false binary. When we challenge binaristic thinking and embrace fluidity, we begin to see the ways in which empowerment is multidirectional. Further, if we extend beyond two individuals, empowerment is a collective process, rooted in the very community connection, which contributes to the wellbeing of TNB youth.

This approach to TNB youth empowerment helps to bridge the connection emphasized by Gutierrez (1990) – that empowerment is a simultaneous engagement of increasing personal power with the wellness that emerges from that process, and engagement in activities that shift the structural context that initially created a condi-tion of powerlessness. In the following section, we offer specific principles that pro-mote empowerment in settings where practitioners interact with and serve TNB youth.

BEST PRACTICES FOR TNB YOUTH EMPOWERMENT

Seven key principles in health and social work practice can guide practitioners in making conscious shifts toward supporting and nurturing empowering environments. In the descriptions below, we offer specific practice examples for each. Given the breadth of environments within which practitioners might be working, we encourage you to consider additional ways these might apply in practice or action for the setting in which you are or will be working.

Shifting the power to self-define

A primary and often consistent way TNB youth experience their power being con-strained is the limitation of their capacity to self-define. This could be in the form of denying name and pronoun assertion or limiting the gender options with which one can identify on an intake form. While this may seem obvious, TNB youth are empow-ered by interactions that shift the power to define themselves, including how they are addressed by others, to their control. Practitioners should examine the paperwork and forms used at their organizations, as well as their standard protocol for making introductions with a new client or patient. *Are youth asked what name they would like for people at your agency to use for them? Are they asked for their pronouns?*

To put this principle into practice requires practitioners to resist preemptively categorizing youth either on paper or in one's mind. Exploring one's assumptions about a person's identity is important internal work to do, and may require supervi-sory support. The power to self-define also means youth may assert their identities differently in different settings. This is important to pay attention to and respect as a practitioner working with TNB youth. It may even require a private conversation with the young person. For example, a young person may ask you to use one set of pronouns for them when engaging with them one-on-one, and another set of pronouns when engaging with them around others. Honoring the youth's wishes is important. The power to self-define in service settings is a form of validation beyond names and identity labels. The practice affirms the humanity of a young person, enhances the clinical relationship, and establishes a level of trust that cannot be gained without it.

Engaging in critical consciousness-raising

In Singh's research on transgender youth resilience (2013), she recognizes the empowering process of unlearning social norms about race and gender. In many ways, this reflects the Freirean concept of critical consciousness-raising as a part of the empowerment process (2000). All youth, including TNB youth, have been socialized into cultural norms about their identities. Critical consciousness often develops and is nurtured in the community with others who share similar identities. Using a Freirean approach, TNB youth can learn about the social context of their experiences by talking with others, learning about their history, and exploring ideas that challenge existing social norms. Practitioners can (1) *work to learn about these topics themselves,* (2) *create spaces in their agencies where critical consciousness-raising activities can occur, and* (3) *connect youth to resources in the community where they can engage in unlearning social norms and putting their experiences in a broader socio-historical context.*

Practitioners can also bring resources into their organizations that examine society's treatment of TNB people. Accessible resources, and the spaces to explore them, offer TNB youth opportunities to connect across generations and locations with those who paved the way for TNB people, placing their lives in a historical context and providing a sense of connection to something bigger than themselves (Wagaman, 2016).

Creating and facilitating spaces for peer support

In many health and social work settings, the primary interaction occurs between adult providers and youth receiving care or services. However, TNB youth need to be encouraged to build relationships and a sense of community with other TNB youth; nothing can replace the power in knowing that you are not alone in your experience. There is power in the implicit message that there is something to be gained from another TNB young person, rather than focusing solely on receiving care and/or services from a provider. *Peer support can be implemented in a variety of ways*: through support groups, which meet regularly and are ideally peer-facilitated; or through the establishment of peer support or peer navigation staff positions, in which TNB youth are hired and trained to provide peer support as part of the care the organization provides. When organizations decide to formally invest in peer support services, leaders should be intentional in how they train and support TNB youth to serve in facilitation and/or peer navigation roles.

Using a harm reduction perspective

Taking a harm reduction approach when working with TNB youth is a way to practice with critical consciousness, and to honor choice and control. Harm reduction, at a basic level, acknowledges TNB youth are living in a society structured to limit access and opportunity for TNB people. Such an environment can put TNB youth in positions to make choices appearing – from the outside – to be unhealthy or high risk. Instead of judging or shaming youth for these choices, harm reduction meets them where they are, providing access to resources that may lower the risk of high-risk behaviors (Hawk et al., 2017). For example, we know transgender women of color face high rates of employment discrimination and other forms of violence. This does not, however, take away their need for housing and food in order to live. In some cases, young trans women of color engage in sex work as a means of taking care of their needs. This can put them at greater risk for violence and other negative health outcomes (Nadal, Davidoff, & Fujii-Doe, 2014). A practitioner working from a harm reduction standpoint would acknowledge the barriers this client has faced, and work with her to identify strategies to support her safety if she decides to engage in sex work. This may be as simple as making sure she has access to safer sex items, or it may include working together to identify a network of support with whom she can communicate when she feels in danger and needs help.

Working from a harm reduction standpoint puts individual experiences and choices in a broader social context, recognizing we make decisions based on the opportunities available to us. Such an approach helps providers move away from approaches to service provision involving shame and blame of TNB youth, and instead create spaces for forming trusting relationships. Within these kinds of relationships, youth have the space to consider all of their options without judgment and to set their own timeframe for accessing care or making different choices.

Honoring choice and control

In a society with limited choices for TNB youth, creating environments where choices are opened up and where youth are given control over the things they can determine for themselves is crucial for empowerment practice. Often, in service settings, it is easier for the provider to create a menu of options or categories from which the client or patient makes a choice. When possible, providers should ask themselves if the ease of having a menu of options is worth the harm of re-creating categorical options limiting a young person's choice and control. This shift in a service relationship can open up opportunities for TNB youth to practice asking questions related to their care, helping them use their power in other roles and settings.

As an example, when making a referral to another provider, consider taking the time to offer the young person all their options, including transparently communicating your knowledge about previous experiences TNB people have had with each. Then ask, *"What is important to you when you are making a decision like this?"* The young person might identify proximity to public transportation as the most important factor when choosing a referral provider. They might only choose a provider who has an established reputation of serving TNB people well. An important distinction reflected in this example is the decision-making power of the young person *and* their benefit from your knowledge as a provider. That way, they are able to make an informed choice. If there are things that they want to know about the provider that you can't answer, you can work together to find out the answers. This power-shifting, collaborative approach has benefits well beyond the referral itself.

Challenging adultism

Adultism is a form of bias valuing the ideas and contributions of adults over children and youth (LeFrançois, 2014). It plays out in daily interactions, as well as policies and practices that make blanket assumptions about youths' capacity. As a provider serving TNB youth, it is essential to recognize the ways in which adultism manifests in your daily interactions with youth, in your organization, and in the broader communities where youth live. TNB youth are often told their identity is "just a phase" or they are "too young to know" who they are. Similarly, TNB youth often have to obtain parental consent for care or treatment, even if they have already been caring for their own basic needs. These are all forms of adultism. Adultist ideas and beliefs minimize and invalidate youth, so challenging them can create spaces where TNB youth can access their power and thrive on an individual level. *Working to unlearn adultism in ourselves as practitioners can also open up spaces to encourage youth to step into leadership roles, share their ideas, and view themselves and each other as having important contributions to make now – not just in the future.*

Challenging adultism also must happen at organizational and systemic levels. Often times, programs and services are developed for TNB youth without having TNB youth at the table. Asking *"Where are the youth?"* at these tables is a first step in opening up these dialogues and challenging the taken-for-granted assumptions about youth participation. These same strategies can often be employed when systems, institutions, and governments limit access to youth based on adultist beliefs.

Engaging youth as decision-makers and action-takers

As youth begin to feel empowered at individual and interpersonal levels, they need opportunities to step into roles as decision-makers and action-takers. While youth can and will create their own opportunities, providers can support TNB youth by connecting them to existing opportunities, initiating or reinforcing youth advisory boards in their organizations, and encouraging youth to give voice to their ideas and concerns. Be wary of youth voice or leadership opportunities that do not prepare youth and the adults involved to come to the table as equal partners. Collaboration is often a new experience for both youth and adults. All people need preparation. Be wary, also, of opportunities tokenizing TNB youth. *Are youth being asked to come to the table but not really being listened to? Work with the youth you serve to be able to identify these kinds of experiences for what they are and make decisions about the kinds of involvement that make them feel honored and valued.*

If a TNB young person is going to participate in a youth leadership opportunity that is not solely for TNB youth, talk with the young person about how they can assess before and during the experience if it is a TNB-affirming space. If it is not, how do they intend to handle that? What resources do they need to feel supported? Providers who are competent in working with TNB people and communities can also offer to provide support and training to other organizations as they seek to include the voices of TNB youth in their work.

APPLYING THE PRINCIPLES TO PRACTICE

Use the case study of Ashleigh below to begin to apply the principles of empowerment practice with TNB youth. After reading about Ashleigh, engage with the guiding questions to consider the opportunities and barriers to engaging in empowerment practice.

CASE STUDY: ASHLEIGH

Ashleigh is a 17-year-old multiracial (African American and Puerto Rican) transgender woman who was born and raised in the mid-sized city where she receives services at a free community health clinic where you work, which was originally founded to help community members who are high risk for HIV/AIDS. Coming out to her small family one year ago has strained Ashleigh's relationship with her mother. Her mother immigrated to the U.S. shortly before becoming pregnant with Ashleigh. Her father has been uninvolved with the family since that time. Ashleigh has two siblings who support her transition. Although her mother does not approve of Ashleigh's "lifestyle", she allows Ashleigh to stay at the family house. Some nights, Ashleigh stays with boyfriends or friends, but mostly she stays at her mother's house. While she is in her mother's house, she is not permitted to wear gender-affirming styles, such as dresses or makeup.

Ashleigh is seeking hormone replacement therapy (HRT). Normally, when a minor (under age 18) presents at the clinic, staff are required to complete parental consent forms before providing services. Ashleigh expresses that her mother cannot be notified of the HRT process. She first presented at the clinic two years ago for mental health services as part of her care plan following hospitalization due to a suicide attempt by overdosing on prescription medication. Ashleigh has regularly kept appointments with the clinic's therapist and has indicated that HRT would help her cope better with mental health struggles.

Guiding questions

- What are the intersecting issues that are impacting Ashleigh in this case?
- Considering that your agency has a policy that limits Ashleigh's access to HRT without parental consent, what are some ways that you can maximize her choice and control in this situation?

- What role might Ashleigh play in the agency to advocate for changes that could increase access to HRT (and other services) for herself and other young TNB people? In what ways could you support her in this?

CONCLUSION

TNB youth experience restrictions on their use of power across the settings within which they must navigate. Their bodies and lives are controlled by systems that are complicit in enacting violence. Despite these oppressive experiences, TNB youth find spaces and opportunities to support their resilience. Empowerment practice with TNB youth nurtures their resilience and enhances their capacity to engage in advocacy and collective action. Using the guiding principles of empowerment practice, practitioners can shift their interactions, services, and organizations in ways that increase opportunities for TNB youth to use their power to increase our capacity to support the life-affirming humanization that they desire and deserve.

RESOURCES: A PLACE TO BEGIN

Critical consciousness-raising resources

Feinberg, L. (1996). *Transgender warriors: Making history from Joan of Arc to Dennis Rodman*. Boston, MA: Beacon Press.

Grant, J. M., Mottet, L. A., Tanis, J., Harrison, J., Herman, J. L., & Keisling, M. (2011). *Injustice at every turn: A report of the National Transgender Discrimination Survey*. Washington, DC: National Center for Transgender Equality and National Gay and Lesbian Task Force.

Stryker, S. (2017). *Transgender history: The roots of today's revolution*. Emeryville, CA: Seal Press.

Self-advocacy

National Center for Transgender Equality – Know Your Rights
https://transequality.org/know-your-rights

Harm reduction

Harm Reduction Coalition
https://harmreduction.org/
The Steady Collective (harm reduction in action at a community level)
www.thesteadycollective.org/

Community-based & national organizations (putting the principles into practice)

Soy Toronto
https://soytoronto.com/about/
True Colors
https://truecolorsfund.org/

REFERENCES

Arnett, J. J. (2014). *Adolescence and emerging adulthood*. Boston, MA: Pearson.

Asakura, K. (2016). It takes a village: Applying a social ecological framework of resilience in working with LGBTQ youth. *Families in Society: The Journal of Contemporary Social Services*, 97(1), 15–22. doi:10.1606/1044-3894.2016.97.4

Barr, S. M., Budge, S. L., & Adelson, J. L. (2016). Transgender community belongingness as a mediator between strength of transgender identity and well-being. *Journal of Counseling Psychology*, 63(1), 87–97. doi:10.1037/cou0000127

Foucault, M. (1990). *The history of sexuality: An introduction*. New York, NY: Vintage Books.

Finn, J. L., Nybell, L. M., & Shook, J. J. (2013). Place, power, and possibility: Remaking social work with children and youth. *Children and Youth Services Review*, 35(8), 1159–1165. doi:10.1016/j.childyouth.2013.04.002

Friere, P. (2000). *Pedagogy of the oppressed* (30th anniversary ed.). New York, NY: Continuum. Original work published in 1970.

Greytak, E. A., Kosciw, J. G., & Diaz, E. M. (2009) *Harsh realities: The experiences of transgender youth in our nation's schools*. New York, NY: GLSEN.

Grossman, A. H., D'Augelli, A. R., & Frank, J. A. (2011). Aspects of psychological resilience among transgender youth. *Journal of LGBT Youth*, 8(2), 103–115. doi:10.1080/19361653.2011.541347

Gutierrez, L. M. (1990). Working with women of color: An empowerment perspective. *Social Work*, 35(2), 149–153.

Hawk, M., Coulter, R. W., Egan, J. E., Fisk, S., Friedman, M. R., Tula, M., & Kinsky, S. (2017). Harm reduction principles for healthcare settings. *Harm Reduction Journal*, 14(70), 1–9. doi:10.1186/s12954-017-0196-4

Jagose, A. (1996). *Queer theory: An introduction*. New York, NY: New York University Press.

James, S. E., Herman, J. L., Rankin, S., Keisling, M., Mottet, L., & Anafi, M. (2016). *The report of the 2015 U.S. Transgender Survey*. Washington, DC: National Center for Transgender Equality. Retrieved from www.transequality.org/sites/default/files/docs/USTS-Full-Report-FINAL.PDF

Johnson, C. W., Singh, A. A., & Gonzalez, M. (2014). "It's complicated": Collective memories of transgender, queer, and questioning youth in high school. *Journal of Homosexuality*, 61(3), 419–434. doi:10.1080/00918369.2013.842436

Lee, M., Miranda, L., Hadfield, K., Mazeitis, J., & Winger, G. (2018). *A national epidemic: Fatal anti-transgender violence in 2018*. Retrieved from Human Rights Campaign Foundation, Public Education & Research Program at www.hrc.org/resources/a-national-epidemic-fatal-anti-transgender-violence-in-america-in-2018

LeFrançois, B. A. (2014). Adultism. *Encyclopedia of Critical Psychology*, 47–49.

Lepischak, B. (2004). Building community for Toronto's lesbian, gay, bisexual, transsexual and transgender youth. *Journal of Gay & Lesbian Social Services*, 16(3–4), 81–98.

Makadon, H., Mayer, K., Potter, J., & Goldhammer, H. (2015). *The Fenway guide to lesbian, gay, bisexual, and transgender health*. Retrieved from https://www.lgbthealtheducation.org/publication/textbook/

McRuer, R. (2006). *Crip theory: Cultural signs of queerness and disability* (Vol. 9). New York, NY: NYU Press.

Miranda, L., Lee, M., Whittington, C., Kahn, E., Brown, J., Watson, R., & Winger, G. (2018). *Gender-expansive youth report*. Retrieved from Human Rights Campaign Foundation, Public Education & Research Program at https://assets2.hrc.org/files/assets/resources/GEreport1.pdf?_ga=2.99654999.879204248.1548717160-1826604160.1548717160

Nadal, K. L., Davidoff, K. C., & Fujii-Doe, W. (2014). Transgender women and the sex work industry: Roots in systemic, institutional, and interpersonal discrimination. *Journal of Trauma & Dissociation, 15*(2), 169–183. doi:10.1080/15299732.2014.867572

Pease, B. (2002). Rethinking empowerment: A postmodern reappraisal for emancipatory practice. *British Journal of Social Work, 32*, 135–147.

Russell, S. T., & McGuire, J. (2008). The school climate for lesbian, gay, bisexual, and transgender (LGBT) students. In M. Shinn & H. Yoshikawa (Eds.), *Toward positive youth development: Transforming schools and community programs* (pp. 133–149). Oxford: Oxford University Press.

Salanoa-Ogbechie, H. J. (2018). *Promoting Resilience in Children with Trauma* (Doctoral dissertation, Alliant International University).

Shelton, J. (2016). Reframing risk for transgender and gender-expansive youth experiencing homelessness. *Journal of Gay & Lesbian Social Services, 28*(4), 277–291. doi.org/10.1080/10538720.2016.1221786

Simons, L., Schrager, S. M., Clark, L. F., Belzer, M., & Olson, J. (2013). Parental support and mental health among transgender adolescents. *Journal of Adolescent Health, 53*(6), 791–793. doi:10.1016/j.jadohealth.2013.07.019

Singh, A. A. (2013). Transgender youth of color and resilience: Negotiating oppression and finding support. *Sex Roles, 68*(11–12), 690–702. doi:10.1007/s11199-012-0149-z

Singh, A. A., Meng, S. E., & Hansen, A. W. (2014). "I am my own gender": Resilience strategies of trans youth. *Journal of Counseling & Development, 92*(2), 208–218. doi:10.1002/j.1556-6676.2014.00150.x

Stanley, E. A. & Smith, N. (2015). *Captive genders: Trans embodiment and the prison industrial complex*. Chico, CA: AK Press.

Ungar, M. (2011). The social ecology of resilience: Addressing contextual and cultural ambiguity of a nascent construct. *American Journal of Orthopsychiatry, 81*(1), 1–17. doi:10.1111/j.1939-0025.2010.01067.x

Wagaman, M. A. (2016). Promoting empowerment among LGBTQ youth: A social justice youth development approach. *Child and Adolescent Social Work Journal, 33*(5), 395–405. doi.org/10.1007/s10560-016-0435-7

Wagaman, M. A., Shelton, J., Carter, R., Stewart, K., & Cavaliere, S. J. (2019). "*I'm totally transariffic*": Exploring how transgender and gender-expansive youth and young adults make sense of their challenges and successes. *Child & Youth Services, 40*(1), 43–64. doi: 10.1080/0145935X.2018.1551058

CHAPTER 18

TNB-affirming policy

Current landscape, issues, and change practices

Matthew Bakko, Leonardo Kattari, and Rory P. O'Brien

INTRODUCTION

TNB people navigate their lives around policies that often act as barriers to living a happy and healthy life. Policies can take place at multiple levels: from the halls of Congress to local organizations, including places of employment and service providers. This chapter provides an overview of TNB-relevant policy issues enacted at multiple levels – national, state, local, and organizational – that can both marginalize or empower TNB people. While not an exhaustive list, policy domains covered here include employment and housing, public accommodations, health care, identity documents, and organizational policy. This chapter then provides readers with a framework for policy analysis and action they can utilize to empower themselves and others towards policy change. The chapter concludes with case scenarios and a TNB policy resource toolkit for both educational and advocacy purposes. This chapter is not intended to replace other introductions to policy, policy-making, or policy practice. Rather, it highlights important policy issues and considerations relevant to TNB populations within the contemporary United States.

While multiple theories are available to help understand policy formation and implementation processes, including rationalism, institutionalism, and elite-focused theory (Anderson, 2014), this chapter views policy through a lens familiar to social workers and public health professionals: ecological systems theory (Bronfenbrenner, 2009). Ecological systems theory allows practitioners to view TNB individuals and communities as embedded within a larger policy environment at both macro-political and mezzo-organizational levels. The connections between these levels help us understand how policy affects the lived experience of TNB populations. Indeed, in highlighting TNB-specific policy issues, this chapter stresses different policy's effects on the micro-level experiences of TNB individuals. However, caution must be exercised in relying too heavily upon systems theory to effect policy change. To combat the cisgenderism rooted in harmful policies, systems theory must be combined with an anti-oppressive theoretical framework (Payne, 2015). In doing so, the explicit values of the social work and public health professions can guide practitioners towards socially-just policy outcomes.

REVIEW OF TNB-SPECIFIC POLICIES

This section briefly highlights policy issues integral to the experience of TNB populations across the United States. Existing policies vary depending on the state, city, or other jurisdiction (Green, 2017), and many jurisdictions have enacted trans-affirming policies in multiple policy domains. As the TNB policy domain is dynamic, policies and change priorities may shift over time and across locale from what is discussed in this chapter. Additionally, TNB policy is frequently decided by judicial or executive branch interpretations, which may result in a rapid change in the policy landscape. Advocates looking to enact policy change may wish to look at successful efforts in neighboring localities and states as potential models. Research has shown that states that have already enacted a trans-affirming policy are more likely to enact more in the future (Taylor, Lewis, Jacobsmeier, & DiSarro, 2012). Additionally, policy resources, such as those provided by the Movement Advancement Project (2019a, 2019b), can provide readers with an updated state-by-state understanding of TNB-specific policy. Readers are invited to use the many scholarly and organizational references cited here to further their understanding.

Employment and housing

Employment is critical for most adults but is far from guaranteed for TNB individuals. According to the 2015 United States Transgender Survey (USTS), 30% of employed TNB respondents were either fired, refused promotion, or mistreated due to their gender, while 77% either hid or delayed gender transition, or quit their job, to avoid discriminatory treatment (James et al., 2016). This is despite Title VII of the federal 1964 Civil Rights Act, which contains sex discrimination laws interpreted by courts and the U.S. Equal Employment Opportunity Commission (EEOC) to include employment and hiring protections for TNB individuals. These anti-discrimination protections apply to hiring, promotion, firing, and the right to be free from harassment. Discrimination-based complaints can be filed with the EEOC, or comparable state-based agency, prior to filing legal suits (NCTE, 2014a). Additionally, 23 U.S. states either expressly prohibit employment-based discrimination against TNB individuals or interpret existing laws as doing so (MAP, 2019b). A federal law to extend and unify non-discrimination laws across the United States, the Employment Non-Discrimination Act (ENDA), has been introduced repeatedly in Congress but has ultimately failed to pass (NCTE, 2014b).

Housing is also a basic human need, yet gender identity is not protected by federal housing law, including the Fair Housing Act (Esses, 2008). Just under half of all U.S. states prohibit housing-based discrimination against TNB individuals (MAP, 2019b). However, the 2012 and 2016 Equal Access to Housing Rules by the US Department of Housing and Urban Development (2016) expressly provide protections for gender identity and sexual orientation in all of its core programs and funded shelter facilities. This policy covers both TNB individuals and their families, such that low-income or homeless TNB individuals and families should not face discrimination when accessing or utilizing the largest and most crucial housing programs in the United States. This is critical as housing-based discrimination is prevalent among the TNB population. The USTS found that nearly one-fourth of TNB people experienced housing-based discrimination in a one-year period, including evictions or housing denials based upon gender identity. Further, among homeless TNB people, 70% experienced some form of discrimination in a shelter setting (James et al., 2016).

Research has shown that TNB individuals report higher rates of employment-based and housing-based discrimination than cisgender individuals in the LGBTQ community (Kattari, Whitfield, Walls, Langenderfer-Magruder, & Ramos, 2016). These rates are further stratified along the lines of race and ethnicity (Kattari et al., 2016). TNB individuals living in states without non-discrimination laws report higher experiences of stigma and discrimination. These experiences are linked to negative mental health outcomes, including increased rates of anxiety and suicide (Gleason et al., 2016). Conversely, TNB individuals who reside in states with non-discrimination laws report lower experiences of stigma, discrimination, and related mental health concerns (Gleason et al., 2016). While state-based non-discrimination policies have been increasingly enacted in recent years, research shows that state legislatures may prove difficult ground for TNB policy advocacy efforts; judicial and regulatory policy advocacy have shown to be more favorable to TNB non-discrimination policy change efforts (Flores, Herman, & Mallory, 2015). However, claims of a TNB-friendly judiciary may soon be inaccurate as the current federal administration appoints judges with "a demonstrated history of anti-LGBT bias" (Lambda Legal, 2018).

Public accommodations

Public accommodations include settings such as restaurants and stores, transportation, and, perhaps most well-known from recent political battles – restrooms. There is no federal law that provides protections for TNB individuals in public accommodations (NCTE, 2014d). However, 22 states currently have such protections in place (MAP, 2019b). Public accommodation rights include the right to entry, participation, services, to dress in accordance with one's gender identity, and to not be harassed (NCTE, 2014d).

TNB individuals face discrimination in public accommodations frequently. The USTS reports that 31% of respondents faced discrimination in the previous one-year period, while 59% avoided a public restroom due to the anticipated discrimination or harassment that might be experienced within (James et al., 2016). Other research confirms frequent discrimination in public accommodations (Reisner et al., 2015;

Seelman, 2014), a form of discrimination that has been linked to negative health outcomes (Reisner et al., 2015), including physical health problems from avoiding restrooms (Herman, 2013) and increased rates of suicide (Seelman, 2016). Individuals who have transitioned their gender have been found less likely to experience discrimination in restrooms, which suggests that socially normative binary gender expression is disciplined less in public accommodations (Herman, 2013). TNB activists have conducted campaigns to educate their own communities on safe restroom use, provided resources to other activists interested in restroom safety, and advocated for gender-inclusive policies in which people are allowed to use restrooms that correspond to their gender identity (TLC, 2005). Due in part to advocacy efforts, the International Building Code has been recently updated to improve restroom accessibility for TNB people (NCTE, 2019).

Health care

All individuals require access to affordable and safe health care, but TNB individuals may also need transgender-specific services such as gender-affirming surgery or hormone therapy. TNB individuals are also at increased risk for disability and mental health issues, including depression and suicide, than their cisgender counterparts (Downing & Przedworski, 2018; Streed, McCarthy, & Haas, 2017). However, TNB individuals are less likely than cisgender individuals to have health insurance, a primary care physician, or access to health care facilities (dickey, Budge, Katz-Wise, & Garza, 2016; Gonzales & Henning-smith, 2017). Even when seeing a health care professional, TNB individuals face obstacles, including substandard treatment, lack of provider knowledge of TNB health needs and treatment, and refusals to provide care (James et al., 2016; Stotzer, Silverschanz, & Wilson, 2013). The USTS reports that one-third of respondents who accessed a health care provider faced such discriminatory experiences. Research shows these experiences are further stratified along the lines of race, ethnicity, disability, and age (James et al., 2016; Kattari & Hasche, 2016; Kattari, Walls, Whitfield, & Langenderfer-Magruder, 2015). Such discrimination may lead TNB individuals to delay seeking future care (Cruz, 2014).

The health insurance policy landscape is complex. An Obama-era regulatory interpretation extended the Affordable Care Act's (ACA) sex discrimination protections to protect gender identity. As such, transgender status is no longer considered a pre-existing condition (Stroumsa, 2014). The current federal administration, generally understood to be hostile to transgender rights, is reconsidering this interpretation of ACA's sex discrimination protections (Underhill, 2018). On the federal level, Medicare has provided coverage for gender-affirming surgery and hormone therapy since 2014 (NCTE, 2014c). State-based insurance coverage is even more fragmented. States have different, and sometimes contradictory, non-discrimination laws for private insurance, Medicaid, and state employee benefits; a state may have a non-discrimination policy for one form of insurance, but not others (MAP, 2019a). Among USTS respondents, 55% who tried to access transition-related surgery, and 25% who sought hormones, were denied insurance coverage (James et al., 2016).

However, research has shown that insurance for transgender-affirming care is ultimately cost-effective (Padula & Baker, 2017). With such a complex landscape that fosters disparate TNB health care experiences, practitioners are advised to examine how their local and state policy is or is not reflected by current standards of care (Coleman et al., 2012).

Identity documents

Identity documents (ID) are needed to access many domains of life, including financial institutions and employment. IDs with gender markers include state-issued identification, such as a driver's license, U.S. passport, social security card, and immigration documents (NCTE, 2018a). Possessing documents that have gender identifiers incongruent with one's gender identity can make access to these domains difficult (NTCE, n.d.). Among USTS respondents, 68% had no ID indicating their preferred name or gender. Additionally, when showing others an ID that indicated a gender incongruent with their gender presentation, one-third of respondents faced repercussions, such as denial of benefits or harassment (James et al., 2016).

ID laws vary by state, with many requiring a court order or physician's letter, and some requiring surgical procedures, prior to allowing for changes to an ID's gender marker (TLC, 2017b). Both the World Professional Association for Transgender Health (WPATH) and the American Medical Association (AMA) have asked governments to eliminate such requirements (Lambda Legal, 2016). Fortunately, states are increasingly removing the need for physician letters, which are often difficult or expensive to obtain. Some are also implementing a nonbinary or gender-neutral option (NCTE, 2018b). California's Gender Recognition Act of 2017 provides a model for other states seeking to standardize gender marker changes to state documents, eliminate physician letter or court order requirements, and add nonbinary options (TLC, 2017a).

Organizational policy

While the macro policy issues outlined above are important, it is crucial to consider mezzo-organizational policies that affect TNB individuals. Indeed, issues such as employment discrimination and health care access are just as salient to organizational policy. It has been argued that organizations have a responsibility to support their LGBTQ workers and communities in which they are situated (Barron & Hebl, 2010; King & Cortina, 2010). The American Public Health Association (2016) advocates for inclusive organizational environments, citing that non-inclusive policies can lead to negative health outcomes. Conversely, research has shown that the perception of transgender supportive organizational policies and coworkers can lead to a decrease in perceived discrimination (Ruggs, Martinez, Hebl, & Law, 2015). Organizations, including those that both employ and provide services to TNB individuals, can enact formal policies, anti-discrimination statements, trans-inclusive benefit packages, and diversity training initiatives to foster an inclusive environment (King & Cortina, 2010).

The Transgender Law Center has helpful organizational policy models for places of employment, as well as housing and shelter programs. These models can be applied to other organizational and service settings. These policy models are guided by gender-affirming goals, while being sensitive to the organizational environment. Employment policy areas include names/pronouns, transitioning while employed, sex-segregated job assignments, restrooms, dress codes, and insurance benefits (TLC, 2013). Housing policy areas include establishing client gender identity, confidentiality, restrooms, service eligibility and provision, pronouns, dress code, harassment, and managing concerns of other clients (TLC, 2016). To illustrate, a sample organizational *name and gender pronoun policy* might read:

> An employee has the right to be addressed by the name and pronoun that correspond to the employee's gender identity, upon request. A court-ordered name or gender change is not required. The intentional or persistent refusal to respect an employee's gender identity (for example, intentionally referring to the employee by a name or pronoun that does not correspond to the employee's gender identity) can constitute harassment and is a violation of this policy. If you are unsure what pronoun a transitioning coworker might prefer, you can politely ask your coworker how they would like to be addressed.
>
> (TLC, 2013, p. 5)

The Human Rights Campaign (2019) and Out and Equal Workplace Advocates (2016, 2018) also have helpful workplace-related policy resources.

POLICY ANALYSIS ACTIVITY

If you identify a problem that affects TNB people in your organization, county, region, state, or country, you will need to fully understand the problem to respond effectively. Through policy analysis, you can build a complete picture of the problem. What is the problem? What policies created and sustain it? Who has power in shaping and enforcing those policies? This analysis should consider how the problem is created across levels of the socio-ecological model – by organizational, local, state, and national policies.

What is the problem?

Your first task is to identify the problem. It may be that you have noticed something in your organization that feels unjust and discriminatory toward TNB people. For example, your nonbinary colleague was reprimanded by a supervisor for not following the company dress code. While most organizations have a dress code and exercise some liberty in designing those codes, they can restrict the self-expression of TNB people, women, people of color, disabled individuals, and religious communities like Muslims and Sikhs. You first want to reach out to people affected by the incident – your nonbinary colleague in this example – to learn what happened, understand the scope of the problem, and offer your support.

What policies create the problem?

Effective policy change requires knowledge of what policies already govern the problem. A problem can be an effect of multiple policies, one specific policy, or a lack of needed policy. For example, insurance coverage for medical gender-transition services often depends on the alignment of employer, insurance company, state, and federal policies. Identifying what policies shape a problem requires looking at layers of organizational, local, state, and national policy.

A lack of needed policy, as has often been the case in TNB non-discrimination, allows organizations, local jurisdictions, and states to create their own to fill in the gaps in higher-level policy. In many organizations, the policy solution in the dress code example may be simple – a request to a friendly human resources staff member may be enough to rewrite the policy. However, imagine that your organization is embedded in county services where organizational policy reflects county policy. In such a case, there may be several layers of policy governing what can be worn to work and there may be many key players in shifting those policies. Gather the information necessary to understand these policy layers.

Who is affected by the problem?

Policies govern populations and have import on the experiences of all people in that population, but it differentially confers specific privileges or acts as an oppressive force in the lives of particular people. It is, therefore, important to ask how a policy affects various groups differently, and who might share in a policy-based experience. As mentioned previously, dress codes often disproportionately restrict the self-expression of women, people of color, disabled individuals, and religious minorities, as well as TNB people. Identifying and reaching out to those affected by a policy issue can build momentum toward policy change and expand an argument to the civil rights of many groups of people.

Who has power in this situation?

Within any particular organization or government system, power is typically distributed such that specific people or groups are tasked with creating and enforcing policy. By asking *who has power*, you can identify decision-makers, allies, and opponents to your policy change proposal. Take the example of your colleague reprimanded with a dress code violation. Depending on the structure of your organization, the supervisor in question may have some power but may not be a decision-maker. By power-mapping key players, such as the supervisor, human resources staff, coworkers, and executive leadership at the organization, you can gain a clear picture of where people stand on an issue and how much clout they hold. A power map is a simple x-y grid with support to opposition on the x-axis and influential to non-influential on the y-axis (see "Power Mapping Methodology" in this chapter's resource section) and can be a particularly useful tool in guiding this exercise.

Is the problem systemic and enforceable through policy?

Where social work and public health professionals are trained to think about systems and population levels, it can be all too easy to individualize experiences. Contextualizing discrimination is an important step in identifying policy solutions. Your colleague may feel unseen, unjustly criticized, or dysphoric at their supervisor's demand to fit a gendered dress code. However, they may not link their individual experience to a larger oppression of TNB people, or to the work of women, disabled individuals, and people of color in fighting for the right to dress as themselves at work. By looking to resources, like narratives written by TNB people and others affected by the issue, you may discover that the problem you have identified is not individual, but rather systemic and in need of a systems-level solution.

Responding to the problem on a policy level

How do I build power to support my strategy for policy change?

Many of the questions above provide opportunities to build power in the community. By researching the issue, creating your power map, and identifying the problem as systemic in nature, you can build a list of allies, including colleagues, community members, advocates, and policymakers, whom you could reach out to for support. Bring them in to help shape your arguments and your strategies for policy change. Building relationships, especially through one-on-one interactions, with others affected by and responding to this issue together, can lend more capacity to your efforts, strengthen and broaden your arguments for policy change, and give your proposal for policy change greater institutional power. It may be helpful to reach out to national, state, and local organizations and advocates to support your efforts. Many such organizations offer technical assistance, lessons learned, public and media attention, or members who can fill a room and call for change, depending on your needs and strategies.

How will I frame my argument?

The framing of your argument can make or break your policy proposal. Proposals for the good of all people addressing a common struggle may more likely garner the interest and support of decision-makers. Unfortunately, many decision-makers are unaware of, unsympathetic to, or antagonistic toward TNB people. Therefore, TNB advocates may choose to take a problem like dress codes and emphasize the effect of the policy not on an individual TNB person's workplace mental health, but on the mental health of the workplace as a whole and the implications of this issue for workplace relationships and job satisfaction (Badgett, Durso, Kastanis, & Mallory, 2013). Individual stories can be emotionally persuasive and should certainly supplement a policy change proposal, but arguments speaking to the institutional or population-level effect of a form of oppression can often carry more weight and give the decision-maker a more personal reason (such as funding, re-election, or prestige) to support your cause.

How do I want to address the problem?

Choosing a strategy depends on your capacity, the political structure you're engaging, and the intransigence of decision-makers. If allies within a system hold discrete power, as the human resources staff's power over dress codes, then policy change can be as simple as a conversation. More formal approaches may involve requesting meetings with decision-makers, attending executive or public meetings, writing letters, and making a public comment.

Some decision-makers outright oppose policies that promote TNB health and wellbeing. When engaging with oppositional decision-makers, first return to your power map. You want to look at your map for points of leverage that can push the decision-maker to support your proposal. Do you have allies who supervise or hold power over that decision-maker, and who could support your cause? Does the oppositional decision-maker depend on funding from trans-affirming corporations? Enlist the support of powerful people to support your agenda.

If you face strong resistance to your proposal, stronger methods may be considered to place greater pressure on decision-makers. Public voice and media should be on your map and have been highly effective at raising TNB civil rights to the national dialogue. Involve local and national TNB and civil rights organizations. With greater community involvement, policies can be shifted by engaging in multiple public simultaneous strategies – such as culture jamming, disruptive tactics, hashtag campaigns, petitioning, and strikes. When engaging in these tactics, be sure to offer your demands to decision-makers so that they have a clear path to resolution with their stakeholders.

How do I keep decision-makers accountable afterward?

The work does not end with policy change. Policy implementation is a frequently forgotten step, but it is extremely important to ensure that the new policy is used effectively. Policy implementation should be tracked at every step. To return to our example, if a policy to amend the dress code is adopted, then:

- Was the dress code rewritten in a trans-affirming way?
- Were managers trained in the use and purpose of the dress code change?
- Have TNB people noticed a positive shift in their environment because of the policy change?
- Have TNB people experienced a backlash, or did unintended consequences of the policy change disproportionately affect TNB people, people of color, women, disabled individuals, or other structurally disempowered groups?

Oppositional decision-makers may try to not implement the policy, or they may implement it badly or incorrectly. Furthermore, a transphobic public may pressure supportive decision-makers to regress or not enforce the policy. As an advocate, you need to continue the conversation, remind decision-makers that they have made an important ethical commitment to TNB civil rights, and maintain pressure to ensure that promises are kept.

POLICY CHANGE CASE EXAMPLE: GENDER EXPRESSION NON-DISCRIMINATION ACT (GENDA)

While many think of New York's (NY) politics as progressive because of New York City, the NY State Legislature is a politically complex system reminiscent of many states in its election-by-election vacillation between conservative, moderate, and liberal control. With historically conservative communities like the suburbs of Long Island and rural post-industrial and farmlands of upstate NY, GENDA failed to pass through legislative committees and floor votes for more than a decade and a half (Allen, 2019). The bill was introduced every year since 2003; however, the strategy began years earlier in the late 1990s by trans activist Sylvia Rivera. This story reflects the history of TNB policy advocacy being pushed to the sidelines during the fight to secure marriage equality (Schindler, 2019).

Most laws do not pass on their first attempt. However, most bills do not take two decades to pass, and it becomes disheartening for members of the TNB community to engage in advocacy to justify their own existence year after year. While lawmakers usually get the praise and recognition when historic bills like GENDA pass through state legislatures or city councils, as it eventually did in NY, the years-long battle in NY exemplifies the reality of ongoing, and oftentimes, exhausting and resource-draining individual and community engagement processes. Multiple organizations formed coalitions, trained hundreds of volunteers, and prepared testimony for people to share their voices year after year. During that time, organizations went defunct, new TNB-focused organizations emerged, and more allied organizations championed the effort as TNB issues have become more mainstream (Schindler, 2019).

INSTRUCTIONAL CASE STUDY

You are employed as a case manager by a mid-size not-for-profit organization in a small Midwestern city. This organization provides wrap-around services for children and adolescent clients – including physical health, behavioral health, food access, transportation services, and after-school programming.

A 15-year-old transgender client, Kegan, who you have been seeing for eight months, misses their session scheduled with you without notification. Knowing this is not typical behavior for them, you go to the after-school program where Kegan goes most days when they are not meeting with you to see if they may have forgotten about your session. You do not see Kegan in the crowd, so you ask the after-school program manager about Kegan's whereabouts.

The program manager responds and shares with you that Kegan was told not to return to the organization because it does not serve transgender clients. Parents of other youth had complained that Kegan was making them uncomfortable and that they did not want their child to be influenced by Kegan. The program manager shares that Kegan was well-liked by and supportive of the younger children in the after-school program, and that staff have seen a big improvement in Kegan's social interactions since they started receiving services.

Shocked that the organization you work for could blatantly refuse services to a young person solely for their gender identity, you ask your supervisor if this is true. They confirm the program manager's story and sympathize that it is a terrible situation for a well-liked client, but that it is just the way it is. Your supervisor then mentions that one of the organization's board members has a transgender child and speculates whether or not that board member will remain on the board.

After doing some initial research, you learn that there is no non-discrimination policy protecting transgender clients in your state, city, or organization. You are determined to make sure that gender identity is included in your organization's non-discrimination policy, so future clients and employees do not experience what Kegan has at your organization.

Case scenario questions

1. What additional research on federal, state, local laws, and organizational policies needs to be done? Where might you find this research?
2. Who might be potential allies, opponents, or neutral parties at your organization? How do you approach those allies? How might your approach differ if the ultimate policy decision-maker(s) is an ally, opponent, or neutral party?
3. How could you go about engaging the TNB community or TNB individuals in the process?
4. If you were to give a presentation to the organization's board of directors, what would you include to convince them of the benefit of updating the organization's non-discrimination policy?
5. What does success look like beyond the policy change itself?

RESOURCES

Talking about transgender-inclusive non-discrimination laws: An Ally's guide:

A guide for framing and discussing your non-discrimination policy efforts: www.lgbtmap.org/allys-guide-talking-about-transgender-inclusive-nondiscrimination-laws

Re:Power

A leading organization in political training and inclusive politics: https://repower.org/

Storytelling for social change

A free course to develop storytelling skills for social change: www.edx.org/course/storytelling-for-social-change

Power mapping methodology

Beautiful Rising offers a power mapping tool, focused on key power relationships, to assist in your own social and policy change efforts: https://beautifulrising.org/tool/power-mapping

Sample policies

- **Model Transgender Employment Policy:** https://transgenderlawcenter.org/wp-content/uploads/2013/12/model-workplace-employment-policy-Updated.pdf
- **Model Transgender Shelter Policy:** http://transgenderlawcenter.org/wp-content/uploads/2016/02/03.09.2016-Model-Homeless-Shelter-TG-Policy-single-pages.pdf
- **Model Restroom Access Policy:** www.lambdalegal.org/know-your-rights/article/trans-model-restroom-policies
- **Model School District Policy for Transgender and Non-Binary Students:** www.glsen.org/article/transgender-model-district-policy
- **Best Practices for Non-Binary Inclusion in the Workplace** http://outandequal.org/app/uploads/2018/11/OE-Non-Binary-Best-Practices.pdf
- **Guidelines for Workplace Gender Identity and Transition** http://outandequal.org/app/uploads/2016/09/Transition-Guidelines-Full-Edition.pdf

REFERENCES

Allen, S. (2019, January 15). New York passes historic transgender anti-discrimination law. *The Daily Beast.* Retrieved from www.thedailybeast.com/new-york-passes-historic-transgender-anti-discrimination-law?ref=scroll

American Public Health Association. (2016). Promoting transgender and gender minority health through inclusive policies and practices (Policy No. 20169). Retrieved from https://apha.org/policies-and-advocacy/public-health-policystatements/policy-database/2017/01/26/promoting-transgender-and-genderminority-health-through-inclusive-policies-and-practices

Anderson, J. E. (2014). *Public policymaking.* Stamford, CT: Cengage Learning.

Badgett, M. V. L., Durso, L. E., Kastanis, A., & Mallory, C. (2013). *The business impact of LGBT-supportive workplace policies.* UCLA School of Law. Los Angeles, CA: The Williams Institute.

Barron, L. G., & Hebl, M. R. (2010). Extending lesbian, gay, bisexual, and transgendered supportive organizational policies: Communities matter too. *Industrial and Organizational Psychology, 3*(1), 79–81.

Bronfenbrenner, U. (2009). *The ecology of human development: Experiments by nature and design.* Cambridge, MA: Harvard University Press.

Coleman, E., Bockting, W., Botzer, M., Cohen-Kettenis, P., DeCuypere, G., Feldman, J., … Monstrey, S. (2012). Standards of care for the health of transsexual, transgender, and gender-nonconforming people, version 7. *International Journal of Transgenderism, 13*(4), 165–232.

Cruz, T. M. (2014). Assessing access to care for transgender and gender nonconforming people: A consideration of diversity in combating discrimination. *Social Science & Medicine, 110,* 65–73. doi:10.1016/j.socscimed.2014.03.032

dickey, l. m., Budge, S. L., Katz-Wise, S. L., & Garza, M. V. (2016). Health disparities in the transgender community: Exploring differences in insurance coverage. *Psychology of Sexual Orientation and Gender Diversity, 3*(3), 275–282. doi:10.1037/sgd0000169

Downing, J. M., & Przedworski, J. M. (2018). Health of transgender adults in the US, 2014–2016. *American Journal of Preventive Medicine, 55*(3), 336–344. doi:10.1016/j.amepre.2018.04.045

Esses, D. L. (2008). Afraid to be myself, even at home: A transgender cause of action under the Fair Housing Act. *Columbia Journal of Law and Social Problems, 42,* 465–509.

Flores, A. R., Herman, J. L., & Mallory, C. (2015). Transgender inclusion in state non-discrimination policies: The democratic deficit and political powerlessness. *Research & Politics, 2*(4), 1–8. doi:10.1177/2053168015612246

Gleason, H. A., Livingston, N. A., Peters, M. M., Oost, K. M., Reely, E., & Cochran, B. N. (2016). Effects of state nondiscrimination laws on transgender and gender-nonconforming individuals' perceived community stigma and mental health. *Journal of Gay & Lesbian Mental Health, 20*(4), 350–362. doi:10.1080/19359705.2016.1207582

Gonzales, G., & Henning-smith, C. (2017). Barriers to care among transgender and gender nonconforming adults. *The Milbank Quarterly, 95*(4), 726–748. doi:10.1111/1468-0009.12297

Green, J. (2017). Legal issues for transgender people: A review of persistent threats. *Sexual Health, 14*(5), 431–435. doi:10.1071/SH17104

Herman, J. L. (2013). Gendered restrooms and minority stress: The public regulation of gender and its impact on transgender people's lives. *Journal of Public Management & Social Policy, 19*(1), 65–80.

Human Rights Campaign. (2019). *Transgender inclusion in the workplace: Recommended policies and practices.* Retrieved from www.hrc.org/resources/transgender-inclusion-in-the-workplace-recommended-policies-and-practices

James, S. E., Herman, J. L., Rankin, S., Keisling, M., Mottet, L., & Anafi, M. (2016). *The report of the 2015 U.S. transgender survey.* Washington, DC: National Center for Transgender Equality.

Kattari, S. K., & Hasche, L. (2016). Differences across age groups in transgender and gender nonconforming people's experiences of health care discrimination, harassment, and victimization. *Journal of Aging and Health, 28*(2), 285–306. doi:10.1177/0898264315590228

Kattari, S. K., Walls, N. E., Whitfield, D. L., & Langenderfer-Magruder, L. (2015). Racial and ethnic differences in experiences of discrimination in accessing health services among transgender people in the United States. *International Journal of Transgenderism, 16*(2), 68–79. doi:10.1080/15532739.2015.1064336

Kattari, S. K., Whitfield, D. L., Walls, N. E., Langenderfer-Magruder, L., & Ramos, D. (2016). Policing gender through housing and employment discrimination: Comparison of discrimination experiences of transgender and cisgender LGBQ individuals. *Journal of the Society for Social Work and Research, 7*(3), 427–447. doi:10.1086/686920

King, E. B., & Cortina, J. M. (2010). The social and economic imperative of lesbian, gay, bisexual, and transgendered supportive organizational policies. *Industrial and Organizational Psychology, 3*(1), 69–78. doi:10.1111/j.1754-9434.2009.01201.x

Lambda Legal. (2016). *Identity documents.* Retrieved from www.lambdalegal.org/sites/default/files/transgender_booklet_-_documents.pdf

Lambda Legal. (2018). *Trump's judicial assault on LGBT rights.* Retrieved from www.lambdalegal.org/sites/default/files/publications/downloads/2018_eoy_judicial_report.pdf

Movement Advancement Project (MAP). (2019a). *Healthcare laws and policies.* Retrieved from www.lgbtmap.org/equality-maps/healthcare_laws_and_policies

Movement Advancement Project (MAP). (2019b). *Non-discrimination laws.* Retrieved from www.lgbtmap.org/equality-maps/non_discrimination_laws

National Center for Transgender Equality (NCTE). (2014a). *Employment discrimination and transgender people.* Retrieved from https://transequality.org/sites/default/files/docs/kyr/EmploymentKnowYourRights_July2014.pdf

National Center for Transgender Equality (NCTE). (2014b). *Fact sheet: Employment Non-Discrimination Act*. Retrieved from https://transequality.org/issues/resources/fact-sheet-employment-non-discrimination-act

National Center for Transgender Equality (NCTE). (2014c). *Medicare and transgender people*. Retrieved from https://transequality.org/sites/default/files/docs/kyr/MedicareAndTrans-People.pdf

National Center for Transgender Equality (NCTE). (2014d). *Transgender people and access to public accommodations*. Retrieved from https://transequality.org/sites/default/files/docs/kyr/PublicAccommodations_September2014.pdf

National Center for Transgender Equality (NCTE). (2018a). *ID documents center*. Retrieved from https://transequality.org/documents

National Center for Transgender Equality (NCTE). (2018b). *The shifting landscape of IDs for trans people*. Retrieved from https://medium.com/transequalitynow/the-shifting-landscape-of-ids-for-trans-people-97834478701a

National Center for Transgender Equality (NCTE). (2019). *Recent amendments to International Building Code address gender-neutral public bathroom design*. Retrieved from https://transequality.org/press/releases/recent-amendments-to-international-building-code-address-gender-neutral-public

National Center for Transgender Equality (NCTE). (n.d.). *Identity documents and privacy*. Retrieved from https://transequality.org/issues/identity-documents-privacy

Out and Equal Workplace Advocates. (2016). *Workplace gender identity and transition guidelines*. Retrieved from http://outandequal.org/app/uploads/2016/09/Transition-Guidelines-Full-Edition.pdf

Out and Equal Workplace Advocates. (2018). *Best practices for non-binary inclusion in the workplace*. Retrieved from http://outandequal.org/app/uploads/2018/11/OE-Non-Binary-Best-Practices.pdf

Padula, W. V., & Baker, K. (2017). Coverage for gender-affirming care: Making health insurance work for transgender Americans. *LGBT Health*, 4(4), 244–247. doi:10.1089/lgbt.2016.0099

Payne, M. (2015). *Modern social work theory* (6th ed.). New York City, NY: Oxford University Press.

Reisner, S. L., Hughto, J. M. W., Dunham, E. E., Heflin, K. J., Begenyi, J. B. G., Coffey-Esquivel, J., & Cahill, S. (2015). Legal protections in public accommodations settings: A critical public health issue for transgender and gender-nonconforming people. *The Milbank Quarterly*, 93(3), 484–515. doi:10.1111/1468-0009.12127

Ruggs, E. N., Martinez, L. R., Hebl, M. R., & Law, C. L. (2015). Workplace "trans"-actions: How organizations, coworkers, and individual openness influence perceived gender identity discrimination. *Psychology of Sexual Orientation and Gender Diversity*, 2(4), 404–412. doi:10.1037/sgd0000112

Schindler, P. (2019, January 15). Legislature approves trans rights, ban on conversion therapy. *Gay City News*. Retrieved from www.gaycitynews.nyc/stories/2019/2/genda-politics-2019-01-17-gcn.html

Seelman, K. L. (2014). Transgender individuals' access to college housing and bathrooms: Findings from the National Transgender Discrimination Survey. *Journal of Gay & Lesbian Social Services*, 26(2), 186–206. doi:10.1080/10538720.2014.891091

Seelman, K. L. (2016). Transgender adults' access to college bathrooms and housing and the relationship to suicidality. *Journal of Homosexuality*, 63(10), 1378–1399. doi:10.1080/00918369.2016.1157998

Stotzer, R. L., Silverschanz, P., & Wilson, A. (2013). Gender identity and social services: Barriers to care. *Journal of Social Service Research*, 39(1), 63–77. doi:10.1080/01488376.2011.637858

Streed, C. G., McCarthy, E. P., & Haas, J. S. (2017). Association between gender minority status and self-reported physical and mental health in the United States. *JAMA Internal Medicine, 177*(8), 1210–1212. doi:10.1001/jamainternmed.2017.1460

Stroumsa, D. (2014). The state of transgender health care: Policy, law, and medical frameworks. *American Journal of Public Health, 104*(3), e31–e38. doi:10.2105/AJPH.2013.301789

Taylor, J. K., Lewis, D. C., Jacobsmeier, M. L., & DiSarro, B. (2012). Content and complexity in policy reinvention and diffusion: Gay and transgender-inclusive laws against discrimination. *State Politics & Policy Quarterly, 12*(1), 75–98. doi:10.1177/1532440011433589

Transgender Law Center (TLC). (2005). *Peeing in peace: A resource guide for transgender activists and allies.* Retrieved from https://transgenderlawcenter.org/resources/public-accommodations/peeing-in-peace

Transgender Law Center (TLC). (2013). *Model transgender employment policy: Negotiating for inclusive workplaces.* Retrieved from https://transgenderlawcenter.org/wp-content/uploads/2013/12/model-workplace-employment-policy-Updated.pdf

Transgender Law Center (TLC). (2016). *Model policy and legal guidelines for homeless shelters and housing programs.* Retrieved from http://transgenderlawcenter.org/wp-content/uploads/2016/02/03.09.2016-Model-Homeless-Shelter-TG-Policy-single-pages.pdf

Transgender Law Center (TLC). (2017a). *California's Gender Recognition Act of 2017 (SB 179).* Retrieved from https://transgenderlawcenter.org/resources/id/ca-sb179

Transgender Law Center (TLC). (2017b). *State-by-state overview: Rules for changing gender markers on birth certificates.* Retrieved from https://transgenderlawcenter.org/resources/id/state-by-state-overview-changing-gender-markers-on-birth-certificates

Underhill, K. (2018). Raising the stakes for nondiscrimination protections in the ACA. *Hastings Center Report, 48*(1), 8–9. doi:10.1002/hast.805

US Department of Housing and Urban Development. (2016). *Equal access to housing final rule.* Retrieved from www.hudexchange.info/resource/1991/equal-access-to-housing-final-rule/

19

Trans and nonbinary leadership and civic engagement

Heather Arnold-Renicker, Kyle Inselman, Jennifer Rivera, and Cameron T. Whitley

INTRODUCTION

The National Association of Social Workers [NASW] Code of Ethics (2017) discusses social workers' ethical responsibility to society. Ethical standard number six states:

> Social workers should promote the general welfare of society, from local to global levels, and the development of people, their communities, and their environments. Social workers should advocate for living conditions conducive to the fulfillment of basic human needs and should promote social, economic, political, and cultural values and institutions that are compatible with the realization of social justice.
>
> (Social Workers' Ethical Responsibilities to the Broader Society section, para. 1)

In this chapter, we discuss the practice of civic engagement and leadership with TNB communities, share examples of civic engagement and leadership, and offer case studies for students to practice applying social work values and leadership skills to a particular situation.

BACKGROUND OF LEADERSHIP AND CIVIC ENGAGEMENT

Civic engagement is the process of promoting social change in an attempt to increase the quality of life in a community (Ehrlich, 2000). Civic engagement takes many forms, including volunteerism, community involvement, organizational work, and engaging in civic political processes like participating in elections. Rome and

Hoechstetter (2010) assert that civic engagement hinges on using the political process to promote social good and also highlight the dearth of literature on the topic of civic engagement amongst social work professionals. In many instances, leadership is an extension of civic engagement.

Although leadership can take many forms, we argue that leadership for TNB people is a radical act of civic engagement. Theories of leadership have historically neglected to address how having an underrepresented status factors into development (Chin, 2010). Scholars that include leadership among LGBTQ individuals recognize the unique stigma and marginalization that these populations face, the unique platform of using one's identity as a leadership tactic, and having one's identity become tied to leadership performance (Fassinger, Shullman, & Stevenson, 2010). Because of these unique challenges, some assert that LGBTQ people often engage in leadership from an authentic position, not necessarily because of choice, but because of obligation (Hernandez & Fraynd, 2014). Research shows that increased leadership for TNB people leads to an increased public LGBTQ identity (Renn, 2007). Similar to how TNB people engage in emotional labor as a broad civic engagement exercise, TNB leaders are often forced to come out as spokespeople for their identity group, regardless of whether they are leaders for this group or have chosen leadership positions in relation to another identity, cause, or service (Renn & Bilodeau, 2005; Watson & Johnson, 2013).

One theoretical approach that has gained traction within leadership development circles is authentic leadership, which is an approach that emphasizes the individual's legitimacy through openness, honesty, and full disclosure of self (Watson & Johnson, 2013). Scholars have readily identified numerous ways in which authentic leadership can be applied. Some scholars argue that TNB people may face challenges in engaging in authentic leadership. Specifically, Fine (2017) outlines three barriers that TNB individuals might face. First, being fully authentic, or open about one's identity, could place an individual in emotional and/or physical risk. Second, norms of leadership that coincide with heterosexual and gender normativity, such as the gendered mannerisms associated with conveying authority and confidence, may make it difficult for a TNB leader's authenticity to be interpreted as leaderly if their expression is incongruent with the expected norms of a cisgender person. Lastly, the entire idea of authenticity is inherently problematic because it hinges on the evaluation and interpretation of the observer. In discussing leadership development among student populations, Jourian (2014) highlights how binary understandings of gender privilege gender conformity over genderqueer identity/expression, speaking to the challenges in observational dependent authenticity policing. In order to engage in authentic leadership, TNB leaders inherently question the way we show up, perform, and talk about gender and sexuality while also critiquing the concept of authenticity.

Additionally, Shields (2010) focuses on the theory of transformative leadership as a practice for social justice, equity acknowledgement of dynamics of power and privilege, and activism. This theory in application can help leaders problematize, deconstruct, and then reconstruct the ways we think about the world and, for the sake of this chapter, gender expectations and leadership for people who are TNB. Keddie (2006) takes transformative leadership and applies it specifically to the idea of gender justice; how we think about the learning and leadership of boys and men through a feminist lens and challenging gender roles and expectations using transformative concepts. All of these approaches are useful when analyzing how TNB people can and have shown up as leaders in civic engagement spaces. Below, we look at what current literature says about the motivations for civic engagement and leadership and what this specifically looks like for TNB individuals.

Civic engagement among LGBTQ people

Given that there is limited research on civic engagement among TNB people, we have looked at what we know about civic engagement among underrepresented populations and LGBTQ people broadly, and how this may or may not be relevant for TNB people. It should come as no surprise that political acumen and grassroots organizing become a natural space to express professional ambition for people who are TNB, due to the politicized nature of gender identity and sexuality in today's society. *Activation* of special populations is a common political goal for campaigns looking to bolster their base—speaking directly to issues prioritized by those target populations. TNB communities have recognized this mode of operation as an opportunity to extend their rights and protections, and to shape the narrative of their stories in the public policy sphere. At the same time, with the world's information at their fingertips and social media platforms readily accessible, TNB people are elevating a first-person narrative, personalizing their experiences for the world to see, providing a TNB-centered alternative to the framing used by cis people in news reports and entertainment.

James et al. (2016) find that more than three-quarters (76%) of TNB U.S. citizens of voting age report that they were registered to vote in the November 2014 midterm election, compared to 65% of the U.S. population. More than half (54%) of TNB U.S. citizens of voting age report that they voted in the midterm election, compared to 42% of the U.S. population. Half (50%) of respondents identified as Democrats, 48% identified as Independents, and 2% identified as Republicans, compared to 27%, 43%, and 27% of the U.S. population, respectively. When asked what they believed were the most important policy priorities for people who are transgender, respondents most often identified addressing violence against transgender people (25%), health insurance coverage (15%), and racism (11%) as their top priorities. TNB people are participating in civic life and demanding that their representation be TNB-inclusive. Elected officials, social workers, and advocacy organizations will need to respond in kind to effectively meet the needs of this community.

Social drivers of civic engagement

People become civically engaged for a variety of reasons that may or may not be unique to having an LGBTQ identity, such as a personal interest in an issue or because they feel that they could have a particular influence on an issue (Lilleker & Koc-Michalska, 2017). What *is* unique for TNB people is that becoming civically engaged is often based on necessity in order to maintain or obtain basic human rights. Although the research on why and how TNB people get involved in civic engagement is sparse, there is research that suggests marginalized populations may have higher rates of civic engagement largely due to a culture of engagement that has been reinforced through technology, community organizing, and necessity over several decades (Bowers & Whitley, 2018).

TNB people have historically used a variety of technological tools to establish community, formulate identities, and develop a sense of belonging (Cavalcante, 2016; Hill, 2005; Nicolazzo, 2017). While these virtual environments have been important in identity development, they have also served another purpose: to create a culture of civic engagement. Research shows that online connective environments for TNB people have been effectively used to distribute information about how to be civically engaged for TNB people, as well as LGBTQ people more broadly (Becker & Copeland, 2016). The nature of civic engagement in TNB communities is not surprising, as it builds on the history of the LGBTQ Rights Movement, which was solidified into a major movement with the Stonewall riots in 1969. These riots were led by transgender women of color and self-described street queens (Arriola, 1995; Stein, 2019). However, until recently, the LGBTQ movement—including Pride celebrations—centered on cis/White identities, negating the history, diversity, and vibrancy of the community (Jones, 2019). Furthermore, the likely elevated civic engagement of TNB people is not surprising when compared with engagement levels among other underrepresented communities. Research shows that women (Malin, Tirri, & Liauw, 2015), people of color (Bañales, Mathews, Hayat, Anyiwo, & Diemer, 2019; Wong, 2017), undocumented individuals (Suárez-Orozco, Hernández, & Casanova, 2015), older adults (Gonzales, Matz-Costa, & Morrow-Howell, 2015), and those with disabilities (Kimball, Moore, Vaccaro, Troiano, & Newman, 2016) often engage in higher rates of identity-based civic engagement.

Forced civic engagement as emotional labor

It is no secret that TNB populations face higher rates of depression, anxiety, and suicide ideation than their cisgender counterparts (James et al., 2016). Research shows that these rates are related to social exclusion and marginalization (Cyrus, 2017). While educating the public is important in reducing stigma and associated rates, the public often turns to TNB people to provide this education as a form of civic responsibility leadership (see Inselman, 2017). This means that many TNB people feel forced to publicly explain their identities, engage in educational discussions, and field questions that may be extremely personal or deeply painful in order to secure social tolerance. This is a form of forced emotional labor.

Applying the concept to women, Hochschild (2012) described emotional labor as the regulation of one's emotions in order to support the emotional process of another or a group. The concept is most often applied to emotional management in paid work environments. Although individuals may enjoy this form of engagement, it can also be emotionally draining. In this case, TNB people are often asked to suppress their emotions when faced with transphobic remarks or challenging questions from those around them, such as coworkers or community members, in order to facilitate discussion and promote acceptance. Most often, this emotional labor is unpaid. Once again, there has been little work done to assess the emotional management and labor

TNB people select to, or are forced to, participate in. Of the few studies that have been done, there is evidence that transgender women (at least in the Philippines) are recruited for certain positions for their emotional labor (David, 2015). Beyond the lack of recognition for TNB emotional labor, most of the work applying this concept has looked at paid labor, and not assessed the impact of unpaid identity-based engagement.

Promoting civic engagement for positive identity development

While there are negatives to forced civic engagement, voluntary civic engagement can assist in positive identity development. The theory of positive youth development (PYD) focuses on optimizing positive identity and behaviors by creating an environment with affirming adults who can highlight youth assets and show them how they can contribute to positive change among each other and within their broader communities, while rejecting the idea of trying to "correct" what is deemed "wrong" with the individual (Catalano, Berglund, Ryan, Lonczak, & Hawkins, 2004; Larson, 2000; Lerner, Phelps, Forman, & Bowers, 2009). Although not broadly applied to LGBTQ people (Poteat et al., 2015), PYD may be particularly important for TNB identity development for all regardless of age because it attempts to eliminate or minimize the focus on a deficit while refocusing on an individual's potential (Johns, Beltran, Armstrong, Jayne, & Barrios, 2018).

Foundational theories such as empowerment theory are also helpful in positive identity development and may be applied when working with TNB communities, particularly TNB communities of color. Gutierrez (1990) describes the theory as a process by which an individual or group increases power at multiple levels (individual, political, institutional) to improve upon their experiences in the world. With roots in community organizing, empowerment theory seeks to shift power relations and change social institutions. The empowerment lies in having a sense of agency and control over what happens and the ability to make changes for an individual or community. More recently, Turner and Maschi (2015) discuss feminist and empowerment theory in the context of social work practice, helping clients see that their struggles are a function of institutional, political, and economic structures that are disempowering.

Given that many TNB youth are criticized, scrutinized, and harassed about their identities, outward presentations, and general engagements with society (Kosciw, Greytak, Palmer, & Boesen, 2014), such an approach could have a powerful impact on supporting positive identity development, likely reducing negative perceptions of the self. A 2018 study showed TNB youth reported attempting suicide at an almost 300% higher rate than their cisgender peers, with transgender boys experiencing the highest rate of attempt at 50.9% (Toomey, Syvertsen, & Shramko, 2018). Broadly, research in the realm of PYD shows that when youth are given opportunities or even directives to be civically engaged, beneficial developments transpire. Mentoring LGBTQ youth to be actively engaged has many positives. Not only does it inform positive identity development, but when constructed under a PYD format, it can show TNB youth that may otherwise feel excluded from society that they have valuable contributions. It can also be a place where adult TNB individuals can mentor youth into active political engagement, which can be confidence-building (see Bruce et al., 2015).

EXAMPLES OF LEADERSHIP IN CIVIC ENGAGEMENT FOR TRANS AND NONBINARY PEOPLE

Although the examples below of TNB civic engagement are not extensive, this section serves to highlight a few arenas where TNB leadership has emerged. However, this section also documents the challenges that individuals may face in these spaces.

Leadership in politics

There is a growing body of literature showing the diverse ways in which TNB people are actively engaged in politics (Bowers & Whitley, 2018). Beyond voting and volunteering for campaigns, TNB individuals also seek to be political leaders, but can face a series of hurdles in pursuing this leadership (Haider-Markel et al., 2017). As with all candidates, TNB individuals engage around issues and values with a hesitancy to center any one aspect of their identities. Additionally, funding for TNB candidates is limited, and both the media and political contenders often center attacks on their opponent's TNB status (Beachum, 2019). For example, Representative Brianna Titone, a transgender woman from House District 27 in Arvada, Colorado, states that her focus is on making sure she adequately represents her constituency, and to not be seen as someone solely focused on furthering policy that is in her own best interest. Representative Titone states,

> I told the people in my district I was going to do the things important to them and I wanted to keep my promise ... The last thing I want people to do is, is pigeonhole me to have an agenda to help myself.
>
> (Birkeland, 2019, para 7–9)

Additionally, Andrea Jenkins, a Black trans woman elected to represent Ward 8 on Minneapolis City Council states, "We didn't shy away from my identity as a Black woman, as a trans woman," Jenkins said. "I have lived firsthand the oppressions that others only talk about, only think about. But that is not what we led with. That's not what won us this race" (Collins, 2017, para 7). Often, when someone holds an identity that is of an oppressed status, even simply speaking up about an issue related to their oppression is seen by those representing the dominant culture as furthering a self-interested "agenda". When people who are TNB are engaged in civic life, this is something that is at the forefront.

Leadership in business

While most of the literature on TNB experiences in business and the workplace focus on discrimination or transitioning on the job (Bender-Baird, 2011; McFadden & Crowley-Henry, 2016; Schilt, 2010), increasingly corporations are looking for TNB leaders. An article featured in Forbes suggests that now is the time for TNB leaders, especially in business and finance (Schneider & Auten, 2018). Interestingly, in this article, as well as other narratives regarding transition in the workplace, transitioning on the job or being out as transgender at work are considered acts of leadership in and of themselves, perhaps hinting at more opportunities for authentic leadership for TNB individuals in business sectors. Whereas gender transition used to be seen as a distraction from worker productivity (Irving, 2008), it now appears to be recognized as a gateway to increased engagement and productivity for companies with TNB-inclusive policies and practices. Another way that TNB people lead in business is through entrepreneurship, including social enterprise projects that give back to the community. Dr. Kortney Ryan Ziegler is a Black trans man who has founded film and tech projects, including Trans*H4CK, which provides opportunities for transgender people in tech (Bonney, 2017). Since 2013, Trans*H4CK has had over 600 trans people attend its hackathons and helped 50 of them to secure jobs in the tech industry (Trans*H4CK, n.d.).

Leadership in health care

Much of the literature shows that the health care needs of TNB people have been neglected. In order to remedy this situation, TNB people have become leaders and advocates for their communities. In some cases, this involves taking on health care leadership positions, like doctors Marci Bowers and Christine McGinn have done by founding their own surgical practices serving the TNB community (Bowers, 2019; Papillon Center, 2015). In other cases, TNB people are researching and writing about their own health care needs to raise awareness. For instance, when experiencing sudden kidney failure, one of us (Cameron Whitley) partnered with leading clinical chemist Dina Greene to write a peer-reviewed journal article about how the current kidney transplant waiting list did not adequately account for variation in transgender bodies, which unintentionally placed transgender men at a higher risk of not being placed on the transplant list, or receiving a lifesaving kidney in an appropriate time frame (Whitley & Greene, 2017). These are the places where activism is about survival—not just for the community, but for the self as well.

Leadership in faith and spirituality

Like the general population, TNB people have varied ways of relating to spirituality and religion. Many (especially transgender women) report experiencing hostility and conflict with church leadership over their transgender status (Yarhouse & Carrs, 2012), which can limit their ability to feel included or engage in their congregations. However, some TNB people feel called to become ordained, though the reality is that not all denominations will ordain TNB individuals. Shay Kearns, the first trans ordained priest in the Old Catholic Church, described this experience in his own path to ordination:

> Two years after seminary I was floundering in my search for a denomination that would ordain me. It wasn't that I experienced outright rejection, but I saw friends who had gone through the process, been approved, and then not been able to find any church that would hire them. Or the process to ordination involved lengthy and expensive psychological testing (from the 1950's) that was designed to fail transgender people.
>
> (Kearns, n.d., para 11)

While controversy remains among many Christian denominations regarding this issue, some, like the Evangelical Lutheran Church in America (ELCA), have made formal statements about the importance of recognizing people of various gender and sexual identities in their membership and through ordination.

Other forms of TNB leadership in religious spaces have taken the form of civic engagement by adherents seeking to make more inclusive spaces in their faiths. Examples of this work include the development of the online resource Trans Torah, developed by TNB rabbis and Jewish practitioners, as well as the 2019 "Creating Joy in Community" Buddhist meditation retreat organized by TNB Buddhist leaders, and taught and staffed by TNB people. In developing the retreat as the first TNB-only residential meditation retreat, retreat manager Martin Vitorino, a trans man, said:

> The idea of being in the majority feels exciting. I hope that people feel that they can let their guard down on some level, and feel that little bit safer to just be who they are without the added thoughts, considerations, insecurities, and fears that can come up when you're the only one.
>
> (Greenblatt, 2019, para 19)

These examples highlight that leadership in religious spaces can take form not only by becoming a traditional leader, but also by creating new spaces and imagining new opportunities for inclusion.

BEST PRACTICES

Drawing from organizational programming, current research, and therapeutic practice guides, we aim to highlight examples of practice at the macro and mezzo levels as it relates to leadership, civic engagement, and TNB people. Best practices at the micro level are covered more extensively in other chapters within this book. The following are examples of how the engagement of TNB people is and could be supported, encouraged, and developed, with an eye towards the complex identities and contextual factors at play.

Best practices at the macro level

One of the most prevalent strategies for bringing TNB people into civic engagement spaces is leadership development programs. Organizations across the country from the Transgender Law Center, AIDS United, Center for LGBTQ and Gender Studies in Religion, The Gay and Lesbian Victory Fund, and many more are focusing their efforts on supporting the leadership of TNB people. Many of these programs offer training to develop the leadership skills of those seeking to engage in civic life, such as the National LGBTQ Task Force's *Trans Leadership Exchange*, Basic Rights Oregon's *Catalyst Trans Leadership Program*, and *Emerge*. Often, these trainings consist of skill development around fundraising, messaging and communications, organizing, policy, running for office or running an electoral campaign, as well as personal leadership skills. An essential component of these programs is the inclusion of people who are TNB, not just in the programming but in the visioning, development, and implementation of the programming as curriculum developers, trainers, coaches, program managers, and program directors.

These programs attempt to create a "leadership pipeline", (Ginwright, 2010; Kezar & Carducci, 2007; Peters, 2011), which considers the lack of representation of people from marginalized communities in positions of power and offers leadership development opportunities to create pathways to leadership roles for those traditionally underrepresented. Often, these programs partner with other organizations involved in civic engagement, legal, and political action work to give program participants access to jobs while also receiving this leadership training. The idea is that, in offering both these positions as well as the training, TNB people will have resume-building experiences that allow more leadership opportunities down the road—in elected office, as executive directors, campaign managers, organizers, and other civic engagement positions.

Best practices at the mezzo level

An example of best practices at the mezzo level can be found in higher education. Marine (2011) notes that, in contrast to activists of the past who focused on larger social movements, present-day LGBTQ student activists are focusing on their own personal sphere—that is, on creating more inclusive college and university campuses. Renn (2007) describes that this involvement can take on an "involvement-identification cycle" (p. 318), in which involvement in the campus LGBTQ community leads to students taking on leadership roles, which in turn leads to increased salience or outness as LGBTQ, and thence further involvement in leadership. Leadership thus becomes "inseparable" from the students' identities, which evolve over time as their involvement grows. This "involvement-identification cycle" could theoretically be applied to the creation of a leadership pipeline; by providing supportive space for emerging TNB leaders to feel supported in being open about their identity, these leaders could feel motivated to increase the scope or level of their leadership.

In the most positive sense, this involvement strengthens identity. On the other hand, this leadership can sometimes be taken on by TNB students out of necessity rather than choice. Some trans student respondents in Inselman's (2017) study of campus resource use noted that not only did their leadership roles lead to burnout or a "pressure to be 'on call'" (p. 68), but it also could lead to the spread of misinformation. A best practice suggestion is to shift the role of educating to outside consultants or university staff. To strike a balance with this shift, it is important to note Nicolazzo's (2017) suggestion that organizations hesitate to turn exclusively to administrative policies, and instead, encourage "trickle-up" approaches to leadership taken on by trans students, staff, and faculty. This "trickle-up" approach, which centers the leadership of trans people, can be supported by staff and faculty who integrate trans education into student leadership development (Jourian, 2014).

CASE STUDIES

The following are case studies to help students consider the varied implications of civic engagement and leadership amongst TNB communities as social workers.

Case study 1

Aidan is an Asian-American trans man in his early 20s attending a small liberal arts college in the rural Midwest. He is an officer in his college's Gender and Sexualities Alliance and attends peer support meetings for TNB people at an LGBTQ center in a nearby city. He publicly identifies as pansexual but does not tell many people that he is trans, sharing that part of his identity only with close friends and a few staff at his college. He was recently approached by a diversity and inclusion coordinator, who knows about his trans identity, and asked to join an educational committee to work with different departments on the campus to incorporate gender identity non-discrimination and other policies or procedures to better include TNB students. The idea was that if he could share his personal experiences with these policies, that it may help others to understand the issues in a more familiar way, as well as would make available a trans person to go to with questions instead of relying on cisgender staff. Aidan is debating if he wants to join this committee. On the one hand, he has been interested in learning more about policy, especially after he had to advocate for himself to change his student records to reflect his gender identity. On the other hand, he has enjoyed being able to be seen as "just" Aiden rather than "the trans guy". As he considers joining this committee, he thinks about other trans students who may enroll at the college in the future, and wonders if he could make it easier for them by coming out and doing this work.

Questions

1. What are some of the outcomes—positive, neutral, or negative—that Aidan may be considering as he thinks about this decision?
2. What are some ways you might approach helping Aidan with his decision?
3. What are some opportunities that may be available to Aidan if he chooses to join this committee? What about if he chooses not to join?
4. What are some other resources or opportunities that the college may use? What are some other approaches that the college could take?

Case study 2

Pamela is a transfeminine Latinx nonbinary person and lives in a major metropolitan city. They coordinate an online social group for nonbinary people of color and are also involved with their local drag community, frequently performing in clubs around the city where they have raised money for local LGBTQ nonprofits. After the 2016 election, they were inspired to learn more about politics and decided to start with city politics. They began attending city council meetings, school board meetings, and townhalls co-sponsored by a statewide LGBTQ political advocacy organization. Online, they started a page to share links to petitions and fundraisers and soon they started to informally connect people from across the country with each other to find support and resources. In the coming year, one of the city council seats will become open, and they are determined to be elected. They reached out to one of their mentors in their political party, an older gay man named Tom. He said they were not yet ready because they did not have any "real" leadership experience. "Also," Tom said, "You're gonna have to tone down the drag. I was a queen too when I was your age, but that doesn't get you elected." Though Pamela respects Tom as a mentor, this advice didn't sit right. Pamela is now uncertain if the party will support their run and is looking at the next steps that they can take to get onto the ballot.

Questions

1. Why might the party not consider Pamela's experience to be "real" leadership experience? Is the party right or wrong?
2. What are some of the thoughts and feelings that Pamela may be having? What are some approaches that could be taken to support Pamela?
3. What experiences may have been similar or different between Pamela and Tom as LGBTQ leaders in this party?
4. What are some options and resources available to Pamela?

CONCLUSION

As demonstrated in this chapter, there are many varieties of leadership and civic engagement within and among TNB communities. Considering useful theories of leadership and civic engagement, as well as looking to examples of TNB leaders in politics, business, health, and religion, allow practitioners to build on engagement strategies that are working well to create even more opportunities for TNB communities to advance social change. While having a marginalized identity creates unique challenges in public life, there is a myriad of opportunities for people who are TNB to take on leadership roles and lead the charge for social justice. For social workers, the Code of Ethics (NASW, 2017) is a cornerstone for ethical practice, and connecting these values and ethical standards to TNB leadership and civic engagement practices and impact is essential to effectively engage people who are TNB in civic life.

RESOURCES

The National LGBTQ Task Force: www.thetaskforce.org/get-trained/trans-leadership-exchange.
    html
Offers a six-month leadership development program for transgender and genderqueer leaders
Basic Rights Education Fund, Catalyst: www.basicrights.org/wp-content/uploads/2017/09/
    Catalyst-Web-Packet-1.pdf
Year-long cohort style leadership development program in Oregon

Transgender Law Center: https://transgenderlawcenter.org/events/leadershipworkshops
Hosts an annual transgender leadership summit
Aids United: www.aidsunited.org/Programs-0024-Grantmaking/Transgender-Leadership-Initiative.aspx
Transgender Leadership Initiative focuses on leadership development in the field of HIV/AIDS advocacy
Center for LGBTQ and Gender Studies in Religion: https://clgs.org/our-work/transgender-religious-roundtable/trans-seminarians-cohort/
Hosts a year-round leadership development program for transgender and genderqueer seminarians
Victory Fund: https://victoryfund.org/about/
Organization dedicated to electing LGBTQ officials at all levels of government

REFERENCES

Arriola, E. R. (1995). Faeries, marimachas, queens, and lezzies: The construction of homosexuality before the 1969 stonewall riots. *Columbia Journal of Gender & Law, 5*(1), 33. doi:10.7916/cjgl.v5i1.2378

Bañales, J., Mathews, C., Hayat, N., Anyiwo, N., & Diemer, M. (2019). Latinx and Black young adults' pathways to civic/political engagement. *Cultural Diversity & Ethnic Minority Psychology.* Advance online publication. doi:10.1037/cdp0000271

Beachum, L. (2019, March 6). Transgender political candidates are increasingly common. The money backing them is not. *The Center for Political Integrity.* Retrieved from https://publicintegrity.org/federal-politics/elections/transgender-political-candidates-are-increasingly-common-the-money-backing-them-is-not/

Becker, A. B., & Copeland, L. (2016). Networked publics: How connective social media use facilitates political consumerism among LGBT Americans. *Journal of Information Technology & Politics, 13*(1), 22–36. doi:10.1080/19331681.2015.1131655

Bender-Baird, K. (2011). *Transgender employment experiences: Gendered perceptions and the law.* Albany, NY: SUNY Press.

Birkeland, B. (2019, February 18). *Rep. Brianna Titone sees her first year as a balance between her district and her identity.* Retrieved from www.cpr.org/news/story/rep-brianna-titone-sees-her-first-year-as-a-balance-between-her-district-and-her-identity

Bonney, L. (2017, August 31). 40 under 40. *Diablo Magazine.* Retrieved from www.diablomag.com/September-2017/Forty-Under-Forty/

Bowers, M. L. (2019). *Serve patients, have fun, change the world.* Retrieved from http://marcibowers.com/dr-bowers/

Bowers, M. M., & Whitley, C. T. (2018). Assessing voter registration among transgender and gender non-conforming individuals. *Political Behavior.* doi:10.1080/19331681.2015.1131655

Bruce, D., Harper, G. W., & Bauermeister, J. A. (2015). Minority stress, positive identity development, and depressive symptoms: Implications for resilience among sexual minority male youth. *Psychology of sexual orientation and gender diversity, 2*(3), 287–296.

Catalano, R. F., Berglund, M. L., Ryan, J. A., Lonczak, H. S., & Hawkins, J. D. (2004). Positive youth development in the United States: Research findings on evaluations of positive youth development programs. *The Annals of the American Academy of Political and Social Science, 591*(1), 98–124. doi:10.1177/0002716203260102

Cavalcante, A. (2016). "I did it all online": Transgender identity and the management of everyday life. *Critical Studies in Media Communication, 33*(1), 109–122. doi:10.1080/15295036.2015.1129065

Chin, J. L. (2010). Introduction to the special issue on diversity and leadership. *American Psychologist, 65*(3), 150–156. doi:10.1037/a0018716

Collins, J. (2017, November 8). *Transgender candidates win Mpls. City Council seats, make history.* Retrieved from www.mprnews.org/story/2017/11/08/minneapolis-elects-transgender-candidates-to-city-council

Cyrus, K. (2017). Multiple minorities as multiply marginalized: Applying the minority stress theory to LGBTQ people of color. *Journal of Gay & Lesbian Mental Health, 21*(3), 194–202. doi:10.1080/19359705.2017.1320739

David, E. (2015). Purple-collar labor: Transgender workers and queer value at global call centers in the Philippines. *Gender & Society, 29*(2), 169–194. doi:10.1177/0891243214558868

Ehrlich, T. (2000). *Civic responsibility and higher education.* Westport, CT: Greenwood Publishing Group.

Fassinger, R. E., Shullman, S. L., & Stevenson, M. R. (2010). Toward an affirmative lesbian, gay, bisexual, and transgender leadership paradigm. *American Psychologist, 65*(3), 201–215. doi:10.1037/a0018597

Fine, L. E. (2017). Gender and sexual minorities' practice and embodiment of authentic leadership: Challenges and opportunities. *Advances in Developing Human Resources, 19*(4), 378–392. doi:10.1177/1523422317728734

Ginwright, S. (2010). *Building a pipeline for justice: Understanding youth organizing and the leadership pipeline.* Funders' Collaborative on Youth Organizing, OPS 10. Retrieved from https://fcyo.org/uploads/resources/6252_FCYO_OPS_10_ScreenVersion.pdf

Gonzales, E., Matz-Costa, C., & Morrow-Howell, N. (2015). Increasing opportunities for the productive engagement of older adults: A response to population aging. *The Gerontologist, 55*(2), 252–261. doi:10.1093/geront/gnu176

Greenblatt, L. (2019, July 25). InsightLA to hold first residential meditation retreat for transgender community. *Lion's Roar.* Retrieved from www.lionsroar.com/insightla-to-hold-first-residential-meditation-retreat-for-transgender-community/

Gutierrez, L. M. (1990). Working with women of color: An empowerment perspective. *Social Work, 35*(2), 149–153. doi:10.1093/sw/35.2.149

Haider-Markel, D., Miller, P., Flores, A., Lewis, D. C., Tadlock, B., & Taylor, J. (2017). Bringing "T" to the table: Understanding individual support of transgender candidates for public office. *Politics, Groups, and Identities, 5*(3), 399–417. doi:10.1080/21565503.2016.1272472

Hernandez, F., & Fraynd, D. J. (2014). Leadership's role in inclusive LGBTQ-supportive schools. *Theory into Practice, 53*(2), 115–122. doi:10.1080/00405841.2014.885811

Hill, D. B. (2005). Coming to terms: Using technology to know identity. *Sexuality and Culture, 9*(3), 24–52. doi:10.1007/s12119-005-1013-x

Hochschild, A. R. (2012). *The managed heart: Commercialization of human feeling.* Berkeley, California: University of California Press.

Inselman, K. (2017). *Differences in use of campus resources for gender transition and support by trans college students: A mixed-methods study.* Master's thesis. University of Utah, Salt Lake City, UT.

Irving, D. (2008). Normalized transgressions: Legitimizing the transsexual body as productive. *Radical History Review, 2008*(100), 38–59.

James, S. E., Herman, J. L., Rankin, S., Keisling, M., Mottet, L., & Anafi, M. (2016). *The Report of the 2015 U.S. Transgender Survey.* Washington, DC: National Center for Transgender Equality.

Johns, M. M., Beltran, O., Armstrong, H. L., Jayne, P. E., & Barrios, L. C. (2018). Protective factors among transgender and gender variant youth: A systematic review by socioecological level. *The Journal of Primary Prevention, 39,* 263–301. doi:10.1007/s10935-018-0508-9

Jones, J. D. (2019). Finding home: Black queer historical scholarship in the United States Part II. *History Compass, 17*(5), 1–9. doi:10.1111/hic3.12533

Jourian, T. J. (2014). Trans*forming authentic leadership: A conceptual framework. *Journal of Critical Thought and Praxis, 2*(2), 1–15. doi:10.31274/jctp-180810-78

Kearns, K. (n.d.). A strange calling – The 1st Old Catholic transgender priest. *The Salt Collective*. Retrieved from http://thesaltcollective.org/strange-calling-1st-old-catholic-transgender-priest/

Keddie, A. (2006). Pedagogies and critical reflection: Key understandings for transformative gender justice. *Gender and Education, 18*, 99–114. doi: 10.1080/09540250500195184

Kezar, A., & Carducci, R. (2007). Cultivating revolutionary educational leaders: Translating emerging theories into action. *Journal of Research on Leadership Education, 2*(1), 1–46. doi:10.1177/194277510700200104

Kimball, E. W., Moore, A., Vaccaro, A., Troiano, P. F., & Newman, B. M. (2016). College students with disabilities redefine activism: Self-advocacy, storytelling, and collective action. *Journal of Diversity in Higher Education, 9*(3), 245–260. doi:10.1037/dhe0000031

Kosciw, J. G., Greytak, E. A., Palmer, N. A., & Boesen, M. J. (2014). *The 2013 National School Climate Survey: The experiences of lesbian, gay, bisexual and transgender youth in our nation's schools*. New York, NY: GLSEN.

Larson, R. W. (2000). Toward a psychology of positive youth development. *American Psychologist, 55*(1), 170–183. doi:10.1037/0003-066X.55.1.170

Lerner, J. V., Phelps, E., Forman, Y. E., & Bowers, E. P. (2009). Positive youth development. *Handbook of Adolescent Psychology, 1*. doi:10.1002/9780470479193

Lilleker, D. G., & Koc-Michalska, K. (2017). What drives political participation? Motivations and mobilization in a digital age. *Political Communication, 34*(1), 21–43. doi:10.1080/10584609.2016.1225235

Malin, H., Tirri, K., & Liauw, I. (2015). Adolescent moral motivations for civic engagement: Clues to the political gender gap? *Journal of Moral Education, 44*(1), 34–50. doi:10.1080/03057240.2015.1014324

Marine, S. B. (2011). Stonewall's legacy: Bisexual, gay, lesbian, and transgender students in higher education [Monograph]. *ASHE Higher Education Report, 37*(4), 1–145. doi:10.1002/aehe.3704

McFadden, C., & Crowley-Henry, M. (2016). A systematic literature review on trans* careers and workplace experiences. In T. Köllen (Ed.), *Sexual orientation and transgender issues in organizations* (pp. 63–81). Switzerland: Springer.

National Association of Social Workers. (2017). *NASW code of ethics*. Retrieved from www.socialworkers.org/About/Ethics/Code-of-Ethics/Code-of-Ethics-English

Nicolazzo, Z. (2017). *Trans* in college*. Sterling, VA: Stylus Publishing.

Papillon Center. (2015). *About us*. Retrieved from www.drchristinemcginn.com/aboutus/

Peters, J. L. (2011). The pipeline and women practitioners. In M. J. D'Agostino & H. Levine (Eds.), *Women in public administration: Theory and practice* (pp. 231–235). Sudbury, MA: Jones & Bartlett Publishers.

Poteat, V. P., Yoshikawa, H., Calzo, J. P., Gray, M. L., DiGiovanni, C. D., Lipkin, A., ... Shaw, M. P. (2015). Contextualizing gay-straight alliances: Student, advisor, and structural factors related to positive youth development among members. *Child Development, 86*(1), 176–193. doi:10.1111/cdev.12289

Renn, K. A. (2007). LGBT student leaders and queer activists: Identities of lesbian, gay, bisexual, transgender, and queer identified college student leaders and activists. *Journal of College Student Development, 48*(3), 311–330. doi:10.1353/csd.2007.0029

Renn, K. A., & Bilodeau, B. L. (2005). Leadership identity development among lesbian, gay, bisexual, and transgender student leaders. *NASPA Journal, 42*(3), 342–367. doi:10.2202/1949-6605.1512

Rome, S. H., & Hoechstetter, S. (2010). Social work and civic engagement: The political participation of professional social workers. *The Journal of Sociology & Social Welfare, 37*, Article 6. Retrieved from https://scholarworks.wmich.edu/jssw/vol37/iss3/7

Schilt, K. (2010). *Just one of the guys? Transgender men and the persistence of gender inequality*. Chicago, IL: University of Chicago Press.

Schneider, J., & Auten, D. (2018, June 17). Apply now: Thousands of transgender job opportunities in financial services. *Forbes*. Retrieved from www.forbes.com/sites/debt-freeguys/2018/06/17/apply-now-thousands-of-transgender-job-opportunities-in-financial-services/#21f293e4d967

Shields, C. M. (2010). Transformative leadership: Working for equity in diverse contexts. *Educational Administration Quarterly, 46,* 558–589. https://doi.org/10.1177/0013161X10375609

Stein, M. (2019). *The stonewall riots: A documentary history*. New York, NY: NYU Press.

Suárez-Orozco, C., Hernández, M. G., & Casanova, S. (2015). "It's sort of my calling": The civic engagement and social responsibility of Latino immigrant-origin young adults. *Research in Human Development, 12*(1–2), 84–99. doi:10.1080/15427609.2015.1010350

Toomey, R. B., Syvertsen, A. K., & Shramko, M. (2018). Transgender adolescent suicide behavior. *Pediatrics, 142*(4), e20174218. doi:10.1542/peds.2017-4218

Trans*H4CK. (n.d.). *Our mission*. Retrieved from www.transhack.org/mission

Turner, G., & Maschi, M. (2015). Feminist and empowerment theory and social work practice. *Journal of Social Work Practice, 29*(2), 151–162. doi:10.1080/02650533.2014.941282

Watson, L. W., & Johnson, J. M. (Eds.). (2013). *Authentic leadership: An engaged discussion of LGBTQ work as culturally relevant*. Charlotte, NC: IAP.

Whitley, C. T., & Greene, D. N. (2017). Transgender man being evaluated for a kidney transplant. *Clinical Chemistry, 63*(11), 1680–1683. doi:10.1373/clinchem.2016.268839

Wong, C. (2017). *Voting together: Intergenerational politics and civic engagement among Hmong Americans*. Redwood City, CA: Stanford University Press.

Yarhouse, M. A., & Carrs, T. L. (2012). MTF transgender Christians' experiences: A qualitative study. *Journal of LGBT Issues in Counseling, 6*(1), 18–33. doi:10.1080/15538605.2012.649405

Conducting community-based participatory research with transgender/nonbinary individuals and communities

Jonah P. DeChants, Jaime M. Grant, and Shanna K. Kattari

INTRODUCTION

Community-based participatory research, often referred to as CBPR (sometimes Community Action Research/CAR or Community-Based Participatory Action Research/CBPAR), is an umbrella term for research methodologies which prioritize the participation of community in research design, execution, and analysis. This style of research works to center the needs, experiences, and voices of the participants at every stage of the research process, viewing them as collaborators rather than simply as subjects in a researcher's project. CBPR has been used in a variety of topic areas, from discussions on social justice and groups (Jacobson & Rugeley, 2007) to engaging issues of health disparities (Baffour, 2011; Berge, Mendenhall, & Doherty, 2009), and has even been used as a social work intervention itself rather than simply a research method (Branom, 2012). There has also been a call for health practitioners to integrate CBPR into their practice setting as a way to gain skills and knowledge, and better serve their communities of practice (Spector, 2012).

CBPR has found to be particularly effective as a health care intervention strategy, as it helps to ensure that the interventions are designed to fits the needs of and have accessibility for the communities and populations of focus (Guttmacher, Kelly, & Ruiz-Janecko, 2010). Using CBPR in tandem with patients, community advisory boards, and other existing groups can help to strengthen the cultural responsive ness of health care provision, especially for marginalized populations (Guttmacher et al., 2010; Spector, 2012). Given that TNB individuals have unique health needs, as well as differential barriers to care from their cisgender counterparts, participating in CBPR methods and interventions can be not only empowering, but can also support providers and researchers in understanding these needs, and creating more effective interventions.

WHAT ARE CBPR METHODS?

Research, like any other social interaction, is fraught with power imbalances. These imbalances stem from the divide between the *researcher* and the *researched*. Tuhiwai Smith (1999) and other Indigenous scholars (Crazy Bull, 2004; Wallerstein & Duran, 2008) have documented how research has historically been conducted as a process of extraction from Indigenous and other marginalized communities. The researcher, who may be considered an expert on a social problem or phenomenon which they have never personally experienced, extracts information from their research subjects, analyzes that information to create meaning, and publishes that meaning as scientific truth. CBPR methods attempt to disrupt this power differential, blur the lines between researcher and researched, and develop a more democratic process for approaching social problems and determining scientific truth.

The term CBPR includes many different research methods and epistemologies. But what they hold in common is that research about a social problem or phenomenon should include the people and communities who are impacted by that problem or phenomenon. Like the "nothing about us without us" principles of community organizing, CBPR methods endeavor to democratize the research process, include voices who have traditionally been excluded from the research process, and create knowledge which empowers marginalized communities.

Historical origins

CBPR methods emerged from the political and social tumult of the 1960s. Traditional notions of power, knowledge, and authority were being questioned both in the academy and in society at large (Wallerstein & Duran, 2008). Contemporary CBPR methods are influenced by two schools of thought challenging traditional academic notions of creating knowledge: the Northern tradition and the Southern tradition. Thinkers of the Northern tradition challenged the dominant positivist paradigm of the time, asserting that knowledge is not discovered as an objective truth, but rather found in subjective experiences of both researchers and research participants. They emphasized the inclusion of community members and articulated a consensus model of decision-making, hoping to share power equally among all research team members. Kurt Lewin was an influential member of the Northern tradition, coining the term *action research* and arguing that research can be used to solve practical problems (Wallerstein & Duran, 2008).

The Southern School of participatory research emerged in Latin America, Asia, and Africa in the 1970s (Wallerstein & Duran, 2008). This tradition, influenced by both Marxist critique and liberation theology, adopted a more radical, emancipatory approach to research. Philosophers such as José Ortega y Gasset and Paolo Freire emphasized the importance of common people's lived experiences and expertise. These communities' experiences of marginalization and oppression give them expert knowledge about the systems which marginalize them. Researchers, therefore, should facilitate participatory research projects which allow communities to explore their own knowledge and use it to inform action and social change (Freire, 1970; Wallerstein & Duran, 2010). Research should not aim to be neutral but should serve as a vehicle for people to speak truth to power, to examine their own experiences, create meaning, and collectively work toward liberation.

Contemporary CBPR methods are influenced by both traditions, with some scholars focusing on incremental improvements to existing systems and others advocating for widescale societal transformation. When examining CBPR studies, it may be helpful to think of these traditions as two ends of a continuum. When planning CBPR projects, research teams should consider the needs and aspirations of their community. Does that community need improvements to an existing system? For example, do TNB people in your community need better access to existing health care providers? Or, is the community interested in radical social change? For example, do TNB in your community want to examine how strict gender binaries marginalize them from your community and society more broadly? Considering these questions will help you determine the scope of desired change, and whether a pragmatic or emancipatory approach is appropriate.

Core concepts

Wallerstein and Duran (2008) have argued that there are three core concepts of CBPR: participation, theories and use of knowledge, and power relations. Each of these core concepts is important, but also hard to define. Ambiguity is a common theme for CBPR methods, both in theory and in practice. In comparison with other research methodologies, CBPR methods are messier, less linear, and less strictly planned. This messiness is both a challenge and a strength. It can be difficult to write a proposal to your institution's Internal Review Board (IRB) when you are unsure about the methods your research team will select for your project. Researchers wishing to use CBPR methods, therefore, should anticipate some ambiguity and messiness.

Participation

The first core concept of CBPR is participation. This contrasts CBPR methods from other research methods, where the line between researcher and participant is strict and immutable. In CBPR, there are no research participants, only co-investigators who come from the community which the research aims to benefit. Academic researchers, however, must be mindful and reflective about the power and privilege which comes from being affiliated with a university or research institution. While academic researchers can bring many resources in the form of expertise, information, and funding, it is imperative to remember that academic research can seem like simply another system which serves to marginalize or exclude community. This is of special importance when working with TNB communities. TNB people frequently are treated poorly by societal institutions, such as hospitals or schools, and may be justifiably wary of working with research scientists. This wariness may be compounded when working with TNB people who have multiple marginalized identities.

It is important to remember that both researchers and community partners come to the work with their own interests and agendas (Wallerstein & Duran, 2008). Sometimes these interests will align and sometimes they will diverge. Research teams should establish explicit agreements about what participation in the research project entails and should be transparent about converging or diverging interests. Who gets to participate? What elements of the project will they get to contribute to? What are barriers to participation and how can they be eliminated? The working environment of the research team should be collaborative and transparent; each member should understand how they can contribute to the collective goal. Finally, researchers must practice reflexivity throughout the course of any CBPR project in order to consider how their own identities or positions give them power and how to share that power among the CBPR team (Wallerstein & Duran, 2008).

Theories and use of knowledge

All research methods endeavor to create knowledge. CBRP methods are unique in their attention to why knowledge is created and how it is used. Given CBPR's emphasis on action, CBPR researchers must be extra attentive to the purpose of their research. Indigenous scholars have argued that there is a difference between knowing simply for the sake of knowing versus knowing for the sake of decolonizing, transforming, mobilizing, or healing (Crazy Bull, 2004; Tuhiwai Smith, 1999; Wallerstein & Duran, 2008). CBPR researchers, therefore, should be intentional and explicit about the purpose of their inquiry. Why are we attempting to answer this research question? Who will benefit from answering this question? Is there a practical reason, a system which to be improved? Or is there a critical or emancipatory reason, a desire to better understand how power and hierarchies impact the community (Habermas, 1971; Wallerstein & Duran, 2008)? Attending to these questions prior to the start of the research project allows researchers to be transparent and explicit about the purpose of their research with their community partners and research team. It also allows researchers to anticipate and minimize harmful consequences.

Power relations

Researchers engaging in CBPR projects must be mindful of who in the research team holds power and how they use it (Wallerstein & Duran, 2008). This can be difficult, however, since there are many different types of power. Foucault (1977, 1979) describes power as both repressive and productive. Repressive power is power used to directly or indirectly control other people or communities. We see repressive power in the hierarchies of systematic cisgenderism that marginalize TNB people, preventing them from having the same opportunities as cisgender people (Ansara & Hegarty, 2011). Productive power, in contrast, is power which marginalized individuals and communities can generate through their resistance to the repressive power used against them. For example, TNB people may build power against repressive systems when they create community spaces where they can feel safe and connect with others. CBPR can be a useful tool to both examine the repressive power experienced and build productive power for social change.

CBPR researchers, however, must be mindful that there will never be a perfect balance of power (Wallerstein & Duran, 2008) and that repressive and productive power also exist *within* the CBPR research and team (Mason et al., 2013). Researchers from academic backgrounds must attend to the power they hold due to their proximity to powerful institutions, such as universities and agencies. They should also be aware of how their own identities (e.g., racial, gender, sexual orientation, class, ability) may impact their power. One important way of thinking about power is to consider accountability. While academic scholars are held accountable to their research institutions by nature of their roles, that is not the same as being accountable to the community with which they are working. CBPR research teams must decide how they will be accountable to the community – how will community members hold decision-making power throughout the duration of the project and how will researchers report to them, similar to how they report to academic supervisors or authorities?

BEST PRACTICES FOR USING CBPR METHODS WITH TNB COMMUNITIES

Given the unique needs of each community and the complexity of conducting CBPR projects, there is no handbook which can tell you exactly how to plan and implement your CBPR study. Hacker (2013), however, presents nine broad steps for engaging in CBPR methods. These steps are not intended to be exhaustive, mutually exclusive, or linear. However, amidst the messiness of CBPR, attending to these steps can help you plan and implement your study and disseminate your findings for social action. This section discusses these steps, with special attention to engaging TNB individuals and communities.

Define the community

The first step of any CBPR project is to define the community with which you hope to work. There should be clear boundaries defining the make-up of the community and of the problem which you will investigate (Hacker, 2013). These boundaries may be geographic (e.g., a neighborhood) or may be characteristics which the community shares (e.g., a common gender identity). This may seem simple as you may already have a community in mind. However, it is important to consider that every community has subgroups within the community. Are you interested in working with members of all of these subgroups? Or would your exploration be richer if you focused on a group within the community? CBPR researchers must attend to how intersections of identities can create unique experiences. For example, Latinx members of your community of interest may have completely different experiences and needs than White or African American members.

The question of defining your community of interest is especially important when we consider the tremendous diversity within TNB communities. This diversity includes a variety of gender identities, races, sexual orientations, socio-economic statuses, abilities, and other forms of difference. As a research team, it is extremely important to consider who is affected by the issue which you hope to investigate. For example, if you are examining how family conflict around gender identity impacts TNB people, you may want to include all different kinds of gender identities. Family conflict is a phenomenon which impacts TNB people across race, class, sexual orientation. Therefore, it may make sense to include transfeminine, transmasculine, and nonbinary people in your defined community. Conversely, if you are interested in investigating how intimate partner violence impacts TNB people in your community, it may be helpful to be more specific in defining a subgroup among TNB people. Intimate partner violence may manifest very differently for TNB people with different identities and you may find it helpful to narrow your investigation to a specific subgroup such as transfeminine people. As a research team, it will be important to discuss how you collectively define the community in question and the language you will use to describe the study to community members. For example, if your project is focused on nonbinary people, how will you collectively understand and define nonbinary identities? You must be thoughtful and intentional when defining your community and the problem or phenomenon under investigation.

Engage the community

Next, you will want to engage with the community with which you hope to partner, because it is crucial for community members to be engaged at every level of the research process (Satcher, 2005). Do your homework. Read about the experiences of TNB people in your community through local media or social media. Acquaint yourself with the resources in your community and the people they serve. What is the current climate like for TNB people? After learning about the situation in your local community, you can start reaching out to agencies and community leaders. Ask for the opportunity to sit down and have an informational interview with leaders of your local LGBTQ community center or media outlets. Ask them what they perceive to be the most pressing needs for TNB people. Have an open mind and be prepared to shed your own assumptions about TNB people and their needs (Hacker, 2013). Practice cultural humility and be reflective about your own identities and perspective (Hacker, 2013; Tervalon & Murray-Garcia, 1998). The most effective CBPR projects arise when the researcher approaches the community with openness and is not already committed to a specific research topic or question. When approaching community agencies, be mindful of with whom you are speaking. Do they hold power within the agency and therefore represent one perspective on the problem? Are they TNB people, or are they cisgender people who work with TNB people? Work on having conversations with diverse representatives to broaden your view and perspective of the issues being examined by your research project.

It may take you a long time to build relationships with partners in your community of interest. You may find it helpful to become more involved in the community outside of your research role, volunteering your time or attending community events. You may also contact people through social media in order to include community members who are not connected to an agency or program. From these conversations, build your research team. Ask people if they are interested in participating in a CBPR project, explaining their potential role, and benefits of participating. As you build your research team, you may consider offering community members different levels of involvement. Some members may become part of your community advisory board, whom you check in with regularly for accountability and guidance. Others may join your research team and take on more responsibility. It is important to be transparent and upfront with potential community partners about what you are hoping to achieve with the project and how you imagine their role looking.

Assess community needs

Next, you will assess the needs of the community. This can take place at the same time as your initial community engagement. As you meet with community members and learn more about what they perceive the needs to be, you will naturally be assessing community needs. You may also find it helpful to meet with key community stakeholders who can speak to the community's needs, even if they are not interested or able to be a part of the research team. The important component of your community needs assessment is to organize and prioritize the needs that you are learning about from the community; what is the most urgent or pressing need for TNB people? The needs identified by the community may differ from the needs you have assumed. As a CBPR researcher, it is important to be flexible and willing to change direction based on the needs and views of the community – you may need to let go of the question or topic that you initially wanted to investigate. Which of the needs identified can you feasibly investigate and take action on? Ensure that community partners know that CBPR is not an "add-on" but should be integrated to support the work they are already doing (Mason et al., 2013).

Identify research question

Identifying your research question is one of the trickiest parts of any research project. This difficulty stems from finding the right balance between breadth and specificity. You want your research question to be broad enough that you have adequate data, but you also want to be specific enough that you can examine one phenomenon thoroughly. This difficulty may be intensified in a CBPR project because there will be multiple stakeholders on the research team who need to agree on the question. While community members bring expertise in identifying a research topic, an academic researcher may have more training and experience in determining the scope and feasibility (Hacker, 2013). While all CBPR projects should endeavor to share power and be mindful of the power which academic researchers hold, there are certainly situations where it is appropriate for a researcher to share their skills, expertise, or knowledge of the existing literature. The research question should be of interest to all members of the research team, to ensure that stakeholders remain engaged in the research project. Some examples of research questions include: What kinds of discrimination do TNB people in our community encounter when accessing medical care? What are community-generated best practices for asking patients for their name and pronouns? How can we increase access to gender-affirming health care for TNB people in our community?

Research design and methods

Similar to determining the research question, developing the study design is a process where an academic researcher and the community members must work together in their complementary capacities. An academic researcher may have expertise in specific research methods or access to new methods through their training or academic literature. Community partners on the research team can speak to the feasibility of conducting using those methods with the chosen community (Hacker, 2013). For example, a researcher may want to measure TNB people's experiences of discrimination in employment and wish to talk to employers about their attitudes in hiring TNB employees. TNB community partners on the research team might note that employers have incomplete understandings of transphobic discrimination and, therefore, it would be more effective to speak to TNB workers about their experiences of discrimination.

It is important that the study methods complement the research questions. If you seek to establish the prevalence of a given phenomenon, quantitative methods such as a survey or field observation can count the incidents of that phenomenon. If you want to understand how a particular phenomenon occurs from the perspective of a person impacted by that phenomenon, qualitative methods such as in-depth interviews or focus groups can capture their narrative. Many CBPR projects use mixed methods designs because they ask complex, multifaceted research questions. Before selecting your research methods, ask yourself and your research team, with whom you are hoping to share these findings and how your methods can establish credibility with that audience? It is also important to discuss and negotiate data ownership (Hacker, 2013). Who owns the data? A university or agency? What can they use the data for? This is consistent with the CBPR core principle of use of knowledge (Wallerstein & Duran, 2008), as previously discussed in this chapter.

Roles and responsibilities

It is extremely important to explicitly discuss and negotiate roles and responsibilities for all members of the research team. Roles should ideally be determined based on team members' skills, interest, and time (Hacker, 2013). You may also need to consider the financial costs of participating in your project. Your community partners are devoting their time and expertise and, whenever possible, should be compensated for their labor. Ideally, community members should be involved in all parts of the research process. Community members are uniquely well-positioned for certain roles, including recruiting other community members to participate in the study and conducting interviews, surveys, or focus groups. Their proximity to the issue being explored, as well as their shared identity with the community, may allow study participants to feel more comfortable and share more accurate information about their experiences. For example, if you are studying TNB people's satisfaction with gender-affirming surgeries, you should consider having TNB interviewers conduct the data collection. There is still much misinformation about gender-affirming surgeries among cisgender people and it is likely that TNB people will feel more comfortable discussing intimate parts of their bodies and medical histories with people who share their identity. You should ensure that all members of the team are trained to conduct research procedures, such as obtaining consent, interviews, and focus groups; many community partners have identified this as capacity and skill-building that they appreciate (Mason et al., 2013). The most important element of this step is to ensure that each member of the team has a clear understanding of how they are contributing to the project.

Sometimes the hardest part of CBPR is balancing the time and energy of the different members of the research team. For a university-affiliated researcher, it is important to remember that this work is part of our professional roles, while our colleagues from the community are likely doing this work in addition to the time they spend on their own jobs, with their families, and on other responsibilities. One technique to address this issue is to ask everyone on the research team to estimate the amount of time that they are able to dedicate to the project and assign tasks accordingly. The university-affiliated researcher may have more time to dedicate to things like IRB paperwork or grant submission, while community members' time may be more suited for action tasks such as conducting interviews or coding data. It is important to check in periodically with everyone on the team to see if their time availability has changed and how tasks should be shifted. Open communication about each member's time can help everyone be on the same page.

Conduct of research

Throughout this process, it remains imperative for all team members to be clear about who is responsible for all tasks and the timeline of when they should be completed. There will, inevitably, be setbacks or bumps in the road. You may struggle to find study participants and need to brainstorm new methods of recruitment. You may find that your survey or interview is too long and need to refine your questions. As these difficulties arise, do not panic. Remain in communication with your community partners and research team. Make decisions as a group about how to respond to setbacks. Maintain a sense of collaborative accountability to keep everyone on the team on track (Hacker, 2013).

Analysis and interpretation

Participation by community members in data analysis varies widely across CBPR projects. In some projects, academic researchers do the analysis and bring it back to the team members, although that can feel very othering to community members (Mason et al., 2013). This is particularly relevant for studies using advanced statistical methods which require expertise and access to software. Even in these cases, community members can still be very helpful in thinking about which variables are useful in the analysis. Other projects do collaborative data analysis with researchers and community members working together to explore variables or themes. Qualitative analysis lends itself to inclusivity; themes can be developed and refined as a team.

Community members play an especially important role in interpreting the findings and presenting them to a larger audience (Hacker, 2013). They understand the context of the findings in ways that an outside academic researcher cannot. It is also important to lean on community members' expertise when strategizing about how to talk or write about your findings. It is important to ensure that findings, which may reveal problems or challenges, are not presented in a way which reflects poorly on the community. For example, you and your research team may find that TNB youth in your city are much more likely to have attempted suicide than their cisgender peers. Simply reporting this finding is not sufficient or helpful, it may cause people to mistakenly believe that TNB youth are inherently more likely to experience depression or have fewer coping skills than cisgender youth. Working with your research team, you can think how to share and contextualize these findings in a way which highlights the tremendous stress that transphobia places on TNB youth and how that oppression contributes to their mental health outcomes.

Dissemination

It is important to remember that different members of the research team have different interest and needs in terms of dissemination (Hacker, 2013). An academic researcher may be primarily interested in publishing in peer-reviewed journals or presenting at academic conferences. Community members, on the other hand, may be interested in using the study findings to engage in advocacy and taking action. These interests are not mutually exclusive; it is possible and advantageous to do both.

Simply writing up a report of your findings, whether it is in a journal or other document, is not likely to create lasting change. Your research team will need to be proactive in sharing your findings, whether in a written report, a formal presentation, or more creative forms of expression, with the stakeholders in your larger community. When planning your advocacy, it is imperative to be strategic. Consider these questions together: Who would benefit from learning about these findings? What change is necessary to address the problem examined in this project? Who has the power to create that kind of change? Take your findings to decision-makers. Ask for clear and specific change. For example, if your team has found that TNB people would benefit from more efficient procedures for updating their identification documents, take those findings to your state's Secretary of State or Department of Vital Records. Let them know about the negative impact of the existing policies and tell them what new policies would benefit TNB people in your state.

CASE STUDY: THE POWER OF COMMUNITY-BASED RESEARCH: THE 2011 NATIONAL TRANSGENDER DISCRIMINATION SURVEY

by Jaime M. Grant

In 2007, in the aftermath of the excision of transgender protections from the Employment Non-Discrimination Act, the betraying actions of the Human Rights Campaign and Congressman Barney Frank exposed a fault line within the LGBTQ community: many gay people saw transgender people and trans issues as tangential to sexual orientation, and frankly, as less than. Several transgender researchers believed that the lack of national data on the breadth of discrimination faced by TNB people was a key factor in this devastating defeat. This group of grassroots researchers created the first national study of discrimination against transgender people in the U.S., the National Transgender Discrimination Study (NTDS).

Despite our grief, this was a thrilling project. None of us could have anticipated the seismic shift the study would create. After its publication, every watershed TV interview, news article, legislative campaign, and movement offensive drew on the data to make its point. The study changed attitudes, policy, and law. It shifted funding. It changed movements. Many individual TNB people won fellowships, jobs, and leadership positions because of it. While the picture of discrimination and violence that the data presented was truly appalling – as an advocacy tool, it mounted resistance of equal, far-reaching power.

WHO

Like many out lesbians of the 80s generation, my life has been an often-costly exercise in gender transgression. I've lost jobs, health, and family to rejection of my life as "inappropriate" to my gender. As a mom with trans and genderqueer partners and kids, and a researcher with a PhD in gender and sexuality studies, my hope was to craft a "big tent" study on transgender discrimination, and my grounding was feminist research methods.

Other key actors had crucial roles: Mara Keisling[1], intrepid founding executive director of the National Center for Transgender Equality, had been a political pollster in her former life, and she carried into that room the weight of the trans community and movement; Lisa Mottet, the Task Force's Trans Civil Rights Director was a tremendously successful strategist on legal protections for TNB people; at that table she was a lawyer, an ardent ally, and a lobbyist who thought foremost about the tools that advocates needed to move the opposition. As the three of us (primarily) crafted the survey instrument for the study, we were visited by dozens of additional contributors to the process – Justin Tanis, a staffer at NCTE who drew on his life as a trans man and divinity school training; Somjen Frazer, a queer stats geek who has gone on to undertake many other important quantitative studies of discrimination; Susan Rankin, a Penn State lesbian faculty member who held the data on servers and helped them through the all-important IRB process. We drew on the expertise of many trans activists as reviewers, including Marsha Boetzer,

Hawk Stone, Diego Sanchez, Dr. Scout, and others. Many LGBTQ Task Force and NCTE interns also took part in the work of refining the survey, including Eli Vitulli, Morgan Goode, Amanda Harris, Jack Harrison-Quintana, and Stephen Wiseman.

The *Who* matters. As we devised language and methodology for a first-of-its-kind study, the people who led the effort held a dynamic mix of embodied strengths:

- Many were living the crosshairs of the violence they were attempting to confront.
- A significant number identified as activists, accountable to the community first and foremost.
- Many would be end-users of this data as lobbyists, drafters of legislation, and campaign strategists – knowing what data could move the dial.
- We were a vibrant mix of revolutionaries, rule-makers, and bean-counters.
- We had enough connection to the academy to create a study that would be credible.

The HOW

The crafting of the survey took almost a year. We needed the data desperately, and completing the questionnaire seemed insurmountable. The strengths of the research team made deliberations fractious; a lawyer's point of view about what matters most was quite different from a feminist researcher plotting gender revolution. In the end, each lost battles, yet got to a stunning finish line.

We eschewed public health and sociological language ("populations"); we deleted the language of oppressors ("criminal", "passing", "prostitute"). We made up new words to describe phenomena that had never been studied ("visual non-conformers" for people who could be identified as trans by total strangers from a distance). We included many terms that came from inside the communities (genderqueer, two-spirit, aggressive, queen, androgynous). Above all, we wanted the language of the survey to form an extravagant welcome to the respondents. We presented the opposite of the pathologizing research frameworks every trans survey-taker knew too well, and in doing so, signaled that we understood the precious value of the respondents' lives and stories.

During the year crafting survey, intern Eli Vitulli was on the phone, talking with tiny trans-led groups and established programs, letting them know that we wanted to create a 360-degree portrait of trans life in the U.S. In the first week, 3,500 respondents answered what mainstream and LGB researchers had termed a "ridiculous" survey of 70 questions. In week one, we had gathered the largest sample of trans experience in history.

In the ensuing weeks, we spent $3,000 in funding wisely – sending paper surveys in English and Spanish to front-line workers at shelters, legal clinics, roving health vans for people living on the street, among others. Years later, trans researcher Sari Reisner would look closely at these respondents' experiences and conclude that all trans survey work must include paper as well as online outreach, or it will fail (Reisner et al., 2014).

The WHAT

We posed the following four key, qualifying questions at the start of the NTDS:

Q1: "Transgender/gender nonconforming" describes people whose gender identity or expression is different, at least part of the time, from their sex assigned to them at birth. Do you consider yourself to be transgender/ gender nonconforming in any way? ❑ Yes ❑ No

If no, do NOT continue.

Q2: What sex were you assigned at birth, on your original birth certificate? ❑ Male ❑ Female

Q3: What is your primary gender identity today?
❑ Male/man
❑ Female/woman
❑ Part-time as one gender, part-time as another
❑ A gender not listed here, please specify _____

Q4: For each term listed, please select to what degree it applies to you (not at all, somewhat, strongly).
❑ Transgender
❑ Transsexual
❑ FTM (female to male)
❑ MTF (male to female)
❑ Intersex
❑ Gender nonconforming or gender variant
❑ Genderqueer
❑ Androgynous
❑ Feminine male
❑ Masculine female or butch
❑ A.G. or Aggressive
❑ Third gender
❑ Cross-dresser
❑ Drag performer (King/Queen)
❑ Two-spirit
❑ Other, please specify _____

Coming to an agreement on these four questions was perhaps the most pivotal accomplishment. *Do you consider yourself to be transgender/gender nonconforming in any way?* created that the big tent desired. At the time, many theorized that genderqueer people were doing better than binary-identified transgender people within current gender-penalizing hierarchies. But our findings showed a more complex picture.

Open-ended questions were another very important decision. With almost no money and little paid labor, open-ended questions meant more work. The Q3 option, *A gender not listed here, please specify:_____* illuminated the truth that genders are constantly unfolding, forever under construction. In the NTDS, 840 of the 6,500 respondents wrote in *500 distinct terms* for their genders, firmly laying to rest the idea that there are "only two".

Discussion questions

- How did this survey engage TNB people at every level?
- What were some of the challenges and successes of CBPR in this case study?
- What do you think some of the lasting impacts might be from this study for TNB communities?
- What can you learn from this case study regarding how you engage CBPR in your own practice?

CONCLUSION

This chapter presents the historical origins and core concepts of CBPR methods and identifies steps for planning and implementing CBPR projects. Special attention has been paid to the potential benefits of using CBPR methods with TNB individuals and communities and tips have been offered for issues to consider when working with TNB people and communities. Whether you are a social work researcher, or a social worker conducting a needs assessment or evaluation for your agency, we hope that you have a renewed understanding of the importance of working with TNB people to create knowledge which combats transphobia and promotes TNB equality.

NOTE

1   This chapter is being written during a period where NCTE's role in trans advocacy work is being called into question around a failure to center trans people of color in their leadership. The current crisis reflects a long-standing issue for the organization; it is notable that only one of the six contributors listed as authors of the study is a gay man of color. No trans people of color are primary authors, although many trans people of color contributed to the development of and fielding of the survey. (The 2015 follow-up to the NTDS, the USTS, was helmed by Sandy James, a Black trans man.) Additionally, many people of color-led organizations created mini reports on findings of the NTDS in partnership with the National LGBTQ Task Force and NCTE, including the National Black Justice Coalition, the League of United Latin American Citizens (LULAC), and the National Queer Asian Pacific Islander Alliance (NQAPIA).

RESOURCES

Books

Cammarota, J., & Fine, M. (Eds.). (2010). *Revolutionizing education: Youth participatory action research in motion*. New York, NY: Routledge.

Smith, L. T. (2013). *Decolonizing methodologies: Research and Indigenous peoples*. London, UK: Zed Books Ltd.

Wallerstein, N., Duran, B., Oetzel, J. G., & Minkler, M. (Eds.). (2017). *Community based participatory research for health: Advancing social and health equity*. San Francisco, CA: John Wiley & Sons.

Organizations

The Public Science Project
http://publicscienceproject.org/

REFERENCES

Ansara, Y. G., & Hegarty, P. (2011). Cisgenderism in psychology: Pathologising and misgendering children from 1999 to 2008. *Psychology & Sexuality*, 3(2), 137–160.

Baffour, T. D. (2011). Addressing health and social disparities through community-based participatory research in rural communities: Challenges and opportunities for social work. *Contemporary Rural Social Work Journal*, 3(1), 3.

Berge, J. M., Mendenhall, T. J., & Doherty, W. J. (2009). Using community-based participatory research (CBPR) to target health disparities in families. *Family Relations*, 58(4), 475–488.

Branom, C. (2012). Community-based participatory research as a social work research and intervention approach. *Journal of Community Practice*, 20(3), 260–273. doi:10.1080/10 705422.2012.699871

Crazy Bull, C. (2004). Decolonizing research: Indigenous scholars can take over the research process. *Tribal College*, 16(2), 14.

Freire, P. (1970). *Pedagogy of the oppressed*. New York, NY: Seabury Press.

Foucault, M. (1977). *Discipline and punish: The birth of the prison*. London, UK: Allen Lane.

Foucault, M. (1979). *The history of sexuality*. London, UK: Allen Lane.

Guttmacher, S., Kelly, P. J., & Ruiz-Janecko, Y. (2010). *Community-based health interventions*. San Francisco, CA: John Wiley & Sons.

Habermas, J. (1971). *Knowledge and human interests* (J. Shapiro, Trans.). Boston, MA: Beacon Press.

Hacker, K. (2013). *Community-based participatory research*. London, UK: Sage Publications.

Jacobson, M., & Rugeley, C. (2007). Community-based participatory research: Group work for social justice and community change. *Social Work with Groups*, 30(4), 21–39.

Mason, M., Rucker, B., Reed, M., Morhardt, D., Healy, W., Curry, G., … Dunford, C. (2013). "I know what CBPR is, now what do I do?": Community perspectives on CBPR capacity building. *Progress in Community Health Partnerships*, 7(3), 235.

Reisner, S. L., Conron, K., Scout, N., Mimiaga, M. J., Haneuse, S., & Austin, S. B. (2014). Comparing in-person and online survey respondents in the US National Transgender Discrimination Survey: Implications for transgender health research. *LGBT Health*, 1(2), 98–106. doi:10.1089/lgbt.2013.0018

Satcher, D. (2005). *Methods in community-based participatory research for health*. Hoboken, NJ: John Wiley & Sons.

Smith, L. T. (1999). *Decolonizing methodologies: Research and Indigenous people*. London, UK: Zed Books Ltd.

Spector, A. Y. (2012). CBPR with service providers: Arguing a case for engaging practitioners in all phases of research. *Health Promotion Practice*, 13(2), 252–258. doi:10.1177/1524839910382081

Tervalon, M., & Murray-Garcia, J. (1998). Cultural humility versus cultural competence: A critical distinction in defining physician training outcomes in multicultural education. *Journal of Health Care for the Poor and Underserved*, 9(2), 117–125.

Wallerstein, N., & Duran, B. (2008). The theoretical, historical and practice roots of CBPR. In M. Minnkler & N. Wallerstein (Eds.), *Community based participatory research for health: Advancing social and health equity* (pp. 27–52). San Francisco, CA: Jossey-Bass.

Wallerstein, N., & Duran, B. (2010). Community-based participatory research contributions to intervention research: the intersection of science and practice to improve health equity. *American Journal of Public Health*, 100(S1), S40–S46. doi: 10.2105/AJPH.2009.184036

CHAPTER 21

Creating safe spaces

Digital as an enabling environment for TNB people

Nyx McLean

INTRODUCTION

Like all people, transgender and nonbinary (TNB) people need spaces where they are safe and feel that they belong. TNB people need safe spaces of belonging, even more so in light of the violence and exclusion they face in offline communities. Digital environments are key to creating space for marginalised and vulnerable groups, such as those with TNB identities, to share their experiences, especially when offline spaces do not always make this possible (McLean & Mugo, 2015; O'Rourke, 2018; Prinsloo et al., 2012). This chapter explores how online spaces can create supportive environments and a sense of community, including using the case study of an online support group for nonbinary people based in South Africa.

Violence against transgender people has increased worldwide, with a significant spike in hate-crime-related murders in the last five years, and with many TNB people experiencing some form of hate-based physical violence (Human Rights Campaign, 2019). We see this occurring with the rise of conservative and right-wing politics globally. In light of this increasing violence, safe spaces, be they offline or online, become crucial. In a world where offline spaces do not guarantee safety, we are seeing more marginalised and vulnerable people turning to digital environments for this safety and sense of community. As Vincent and Manzano (2017) write, "stigma and discrimination can drive gender and sexuality minorities underground," (p. 25) or in this case, online.

The internet is often viewed as a safer space, one that can be used for both communication and identity formation, especially in specific contexts, such as in many African countries, where offline spaces may be hostile or dangerous for TNB people (McLean & Mugo, 2015). The nonbinary online support group in South Africa, which is a focus of this chapter, is just one example of such a space.

First, this chapter discusses online communities, inclusion, and belonging. It is then followed by a discussion of recommendations for the formation of digital spaces of support and belonging, a discussion of a South African case study, and guiding questions before concluding the chapter.

DIGITAL AS ENABLING COMMUNITY

In response to the violence and prejudice experienced by TNB people, a number of organisations have been established to protect and advocate for TNB people who face such prejudice and violence, as well as advocate for inclusive schools, and better access to health care. These groups primarily have an offline presence in predominantly major cities. While some of them do have an online presence, their pages are more for information related to their organisation, and less about creating a space of support for TNB people (Miller, 2017).

There is limited research and knowledge produced about TNB experiences of online spaces in the African context. Prinsloo and colleagues (2012) presented how primarily binary transgender South Africans made use of a forum on a transgender organisation's website in order to share their experiences with regards to transitioning, as well as discrimination they faced. This chapter is informed by the work of Prinsloo et al.'s (2012) EROTICS project study on transgender use of the internet. In addition, it draws on Dahlberg's (2007) proposition that the internet makes it possible for counter-publics to exist, as well as Warner (2005) and Fraser's (2007) discussions on publics and counter-publics, and McLean and Mugo's (2015) work on queer digital counter-publics.

The internet can provide TNB people with crucial information, and online forums help to create a sense of belonging and community (Prinsloo et al., 2012). The Association for Progressive Communications' study entitled the EROTICS project (Exploratory Research on Sexuality and ICTs) focused on how marginalised people in Brazil, Lebanon, India, South Africa, and the USA made use of the internet "in the exercise of their sexual rights" (Tagnay & Kee, 2013, p. 117). This research was conducted between 2008 and 2011 before Facebook groups were being widely used as a means of creating communities of support. This chapter aims to extend this study's findings to include TNB digital support groups such as the Facebook group for non-binary people in South Africa.

The internet is home to multiple publics and counter-publics (McLean, 2014). A public is an ideological concept that is sustained through discourse, of which it cannot exist outside of (Dahlberg, 2007; Warner, 2005). When a public is in conflict with a larger public, this breaches the status quo and can be considered to be a counter-public (Warner, 2005). Dahlberg (2007) proposes that the internet makes it possible for counter-publics to exist. Fraser (2007), too, speaks to the notion of counter-publics in relation to vulnerable or marginalised people. They state that it is in the interest of marginalised people experiencing discrimination and violence, such as TNB people, to organise themselves into a counter-public. Counter-publics may serve the purpose of being spaces of safety, reorganising, and renewal (Fraser, 2007). These counter-publics are environments in which vulnerable or marginalised people can produce counter-discourses, which allow them to determine and declare their identities, and their understandings of their identities and related interests (McLean & Mugo, 2015).

A counter-public, with regards to gender and sexuality, may do more than simply "represent the interests of gendered or sexualised persons in a public sphere" (Warner, 2005, p. 57). It also serves to make possible new social and cultural means for lived gender and sexual realities (Warner, 2005). Online support groups may act as a safe space where members share their experiences among peers, and it is in this sharing that they are able to garner a sense for a world in which their identities can be experienced, validated, and affirmed; and through this, conceive "new forms of gendered or sexual citizenship" (Warner, 2005, p. 57).

African queer womxn's experiences of online spaces found that these digital spaces provided womxn with the space to speak freely of their experiences without fearing for their safety (McLean & Mugo, 2015). Womxn is written with an "x" here to ensure that the term is intersectional and inclusive of all people who identify as womxn. They were also afforded protection by these spaces from homophobic and transphobic laws as well as able to access information and resources, access health care, and a space to organise in order to establish autonomy over their bodies and identities (McLean & Mugo, 2015). Online spaces create new possibilities for marginalised identities, such as queer womxn, to access information, health care, as well as creating spaces that are free from discrimination and violence. These spaces may make it possible for marginalised identities to own their identities and their experiences in a safe way outside of the fear and threat of persecution. This is relevant to the experiences of TNB people who, too, face discrimination and violence on the basis of their gender identity, and are in need of safe spaces to express and experience their identities (McLean & Mugo, 2015).

Early internet researchers theorised cyberethnography in terms of online spaces as alternative realities where people were able to imagine and create other lives for themselves (Turkle, 1995). The internet not only houses information but is considered a social space in and of itself (McLelland, 2002). Online and offline experiences cannot be thought of as separate from each other but rather as complementary (Robinson & Schulz, 2009). Online identities came to be understood as not separate from the offline self but rather as an extension of the self (Robinson & Schulz, 2009). The relevance of this is that while TNB people may turn to digital spaces to gain a sense of belonging that they may not have offline, it is precisely because of their experiences offline that they do so. And for some, the support and information they receive in online spaces may assist them to make changes in their offline spaces (McLean & Mugo, 2015; Miller, 2017).

It is important to note though, that the internet – while removed from geographic boundaries – is still accessed by people located in physically geographical spaces (McLelland, 2002). And these digital spaces may be governed by the geographic spaces that the individuals accessing the internet find themselves in. This brings with it a need to consider who may be monitoring who in these spaces (e.g., governments or groups specifically targeting TNB and queer people).

Digital spaces provide TNB people with a sense of community, inclusion, and belonging; context-specific advice; and a sense of safety from risks and challenges they may face offline and in other digital spaces. These themes are elaborated below.

Sense of community, inclusion, and belonging

In a world where many TNB people experience discrimination, violence, and threats to their lives, the internet creates a space for respite from these overwhelmingly negative experiences (Miller, 2017). In digital communities, TNB people may interact with and relate to others who share similar experiences because of their gender identity; and, thus, gain a sense of belonging (Reed, 2019).

Community, as a concept, originally referred to a particular geographic or shared physical space. Communities were thus understood as geographically bound (Cosson, 2010). Over time, with the introduction of modernity and the ability to travel beyond one's geographic community, the definition came to be extended to a network or organisation of long-standing and constant relationships among people who share a foundation of common values (Cosson, 2010). The introduction of the internet has made it possible for the formation of online communities, which allow for essential ties to be formed between TNB people and TNB communities divided socially and geographically (Psihopaidas, 2017).

A sense of belonging as part of a collective identity is essential for the affirmation of LGBTIAQ identities who are discriminated against by broader society on the basis of their gender and sexual identity (McLean, 2017). Collective identity has the ability to shape the reality that members share; and their sense of unity, solidarity, and belonging (David & Bar-Tal, 2009). Due to the potentially violent and hostile nature of offline spaces, TNB people require the digital space for a sense of safety and community. It is here that they are able to share their stories, experiences, and challenges with people who have experienced similar journeys and may be able to offer support, advice, or simply bear witness to their journey.

Digital spaces make it possible for people to connect. While "liking", sharing, and tagging on Facebook "may seem like the merest nods", they are acts of recognition because ultimately all "people are hungry for recognition" (Evans, 2014, p. 155). For marginalised people, simply knowing that there are others like them and that they are not alone with their experiences is enormously reassuring and liberating (McLean & Mugo, 2015). This affirmation of identity and validation of experience is helpful for other members of the community to witness because they then see that their experiences, too, are valid. They may recognise their own experiences in the sharings of others, or be able to relate to someone sharing an experience, and be affirmed by this. This affirming practice may help create a shared sense of community and a celebration of identities. In many instances, some members of online communities may become friends with other members of their group and go on to establish a relationship that they feel they can take offline, having established a sense of belonging, kinship, and trust (McLean & Mugo, 2015).

As well as gaining community and sense of belonging, members may use online spaces to access information on identity and experiences, such as seeking information regarding gender-affirming treatment or health care. Members crowdsource information about treatment that is context-specific, local, and trusted, such as that relating to gender-affirming surgeries in a specific city. The majority of TNB people use the internet to search for information, including information about experiences of TNB, access to health care, the availability of offline support groups, and potential meet-ups (Miller, 2017). TNB people also share information around global developments such as recent developments in other countries around gender markers on birth certificates and drivers licenses (Miller, 2017). While this may not yet occur in some countries, members can engage with the content, discuss ways to consider this as a possibility, and ultimately imagine a world where this is possible. They may even be moved to mobilise to lobby for the same or similar policy changes (Miller, 2017).

A sense of safety

Offline spaces are more often than not unsafe for TNB people to gather in due to socio-political responses to gender and sexual identities that are outside of cis- and heteronormative understandings of identity. Violence against TNB people are considered hate crimes and are cruel forms of violence (Swiebel & Van Der Veur, 2009). Hate crimes can take the form of physical and sexual assault and murder and are considered to be driven by transphobia (Meer et al., 2017; Swiebel & Van Der Veur, 2009). It is because of this threat of violence that digital spaces are often safer for TNB people to seek out safe spaces to "re-energise, collaborate and gather in" (McLean & Mugo, 2015, p. 99).

TNB people are also at risk of violence and discrimination in other online communities. While these experiences are negative and can be harmful to TNB people, they may find that people within their digital community will come to their aid, support them, and/or take on their harassers. The risk is then, to some degree, taken on by the community and those that feel strongly and up to the challenge may confront harassers on behalf of the person targeted, and thus come to share the burden.

While some online groups may be closed (a group that is visible and requires sending a join request and waiting for it to be approved) or secret (the group is not visible and members are added by association through invitations from existing members), as is the case with some on Facebook, trolls and transphobic people may gain access by presenting themselves initially as TNB people. Once their membership has been approved, they then target members in the comments of their posts or via direct messaging. Not only is this expression about the safety of members, but it is also about drawing a clear line about who does and who does not belong in the community. The inclusion or exclusion of people from a community "not only defines their social positioning, but also constructs the collective itself" (Gal et al., 2016, p. 1699).

A call for an intersectional approach

Intersections of sexuality, race, class, and disability, etc. must emerge as central, given the diverse lived experiences of TNB people. Intersectionality, as coined by Crenshaw (1989), was developed from the notion of intersecting roads to show and explicate how discrimination based on gender and race exacerbate each other. The argument of intersectionality is that by focusing on one social relation, such as race or gender, one would not account for how, for instance, marginalised Black womxn are vulnerable to discrimination on the basis of both their race and gender and often also their class and sexuality (Crenshaw, 1989). An intersectional approach, with particular emphasis on gender, race, class, and disability, would allow for difficult yet necessary discussions on exclusion within TNB digital communities and the ways in which these spaces may come to replicate or mimic oppressive behaviours on the basis of race, class, gender, and disability (Iantaffi, 2017).

Many LGBTIAQ and TNB spaces are dominated by middle-class, White, and able-bodied people (Burns, 2012; Cruz-Malave & Manalansan, 2002; McLean, 2017). The exclusion of other aspects of identity in a community space, although not necessarily an active decision, is an oversight given that TNB identities "are cut through with multiple variables such as gender, sexuality, 'race' and ethnicity, class, age, transitional time span and geographical location" (Hines, 2007, p. 49). TNB identities are but one aspect of an individual's identity, and they should not be considered as separate or removed from other aspects of the individual's identity (Iantaffi, 2017). Koyama (2006) advocates for transgender people to engage with feminist issues of power and privilege in order to understand the full range of prejudice and oppression that many members of TNB communities face. Such an approach would make the space equally safe and supportive of all its TNB members.

In summary, the internet makes it possible for the formation of online communities by TNB people in order to create a sense of community, inclusivity, and belonging, as well as a sense of safety in a world that remains largely transphobic and violent towards TNB people.

CASE STUDY: FACEBOOK GROUP FOR NONBINARY AND GENDER NONCONFORMING PEOPLE IN SOUTH AFRICA

This case study explores an online support group on Facebook for TNB people in South Africa. This case study attempted to explore an all-inclusive understanding of "how participants relate and interact with each other", and how they make sense of the digital space that is the online support group (Nieuwenhuis, 2011, p. 75). Only administrators of the group were included as research subjects. All research participants' identities remain anonymous in order to protect their privacy and to continue to keep the space safe for members. The group's name is not disclosed here in order to protect its members.

South Africa has one of the most progressive constitutions globally due to its protection of rights relating to gender and sexual orientation in the Equality Clause (Constitution of the Republic of South Africa, 1996). Despite having a progressive constitution, identities that fall outside of heteronormative ideals continue to face prejudice and violence (Prinsloo, 2011; Tagnay & Kee, 2013). In South Africa, there are a few organisations that cater to the needs of transgender people, such as GenderDynamiX and Iranti.org, which are found in Cape Town and Johannesburg, two of South Africa's largest cities.

A Facebook group was created for nonbinary people in South African because there "were no existing spaces online for this particular group/demographic." The group was formed in 2015 in order to create "a safe space for gendernauts." A participant explains that "gendernaut" refers to:

> gender astronauts space-walking in the space of free gender expression (because of the connotations of being an explorer, conquering fear, moving in the exciting realms of gender beyond the cis het binary, doing and discovering, treated with respect and recognised for the bravery they have, acknowledging the risks existing in the space of free gender expression and the responses one can get from bigots).

While another participant described it as "a virtual space for South African nonbinary folk to share experiences in a safe space." The founding member, in one of the first posts in the group in 2015, explained that the group was specifically for people who do not "identify as 'binary/FTM/MTF'" but as "gender non-conforming" or "non-binary of some flavour" and then lists these possible "flavours" as "genderfluid, genderqueer, agender and undefined transness." They go on to explain that the group was created in order to provide "a safe space to explore their identities in which they can feel unconditionally supported and accepted."

The group identifies as a "support" group with regards to "type" on Facebook, and uses the following tags: "genderqueer", "genderfluid", "gender non-conforming", "agender", and "transgender". At the time of writing this chapter, the group consisted of 1330 members (including the ten administrative members). Members from South Africa accounted for 86% of the group's membership, of which the majority of members being from Cape Town (556 members) and Johannesburg (117 members), two of the country's biggest cities. The group is dispersed over 62 other South African cities with membership ranging from one to 45 people per city. Of the members, 43% are between the ages of 25 and 34 years of age. These data do not include South Africans or members of the group located in cities outside of South Africa which include countries such as the Netherlands, USA, Canada, United Kingdom, Germany, or China, as it is a case study of nonbinary people residing in South Africa making use of the online support group.

The group is managed by ten administrators who share responsibility in managing incoming member screening and moderation of posts before they are approved. The administrators interact and make decisions collectively but also have the authority to act individually. Decision-making occurs through a Facebook chat in Messenger where members flag, debate, and decide on responses to issues. When one of the administrators makes an individual decision, they note it in the chat in order to keep the other administrators informed.

Several themes emerged from administrators of the digital support group interview responses. The content was predominantly positive in nature except for reference made to violence experienced by TNB people of colour in offline spaces, and the presence of people seeking to gain access to the group in order to harass members (i.e., "trolls").

Sense of community, inclusion, and belonging

Research participants described the online space as giving members "access to a community" and "a space in which they can feel safe in." They explained that members come to the space in order to share and draw experiences and insights from other members. The online support group provides the environment for members to "seek allyship, advice and support from other members with similar experiences." They shared that they felt that a community existed and described it as providing "the feeling of belonging."

Facebook group members shared that they felt a sense of "connection" and inclusion from the group explaining that because their "identity is extremely complex" that they "often feel alienated" and felt in some spaces outside of the group that they were "not trans enough or not gay enough or not cis enough". However, in the support group, they "feel accepted and at home", going on to share that "no matter where I am on the spectrum, I'm accepted". This may be due to the nature of the space, as well as how administrative members interact with members. For instance, one member had asked the group if their gender identity was included in this group. An admin member responded assuring them they were welcome, and that the group was "quite an encompassing and welcoming group" that placed "emphasis on the beauty of the diversity of human experience rather than being too category-focused." They continued to explain to the member that in the group they would not find that someone would "tell you that you aren't [something]-enough to be here."

The group has been described as providing an environment of "kindness, acceptance, non-judgement" for members. Online support spaces are, as with offline spaces, "a key source of care within transgender communities" (Hines, 2007, p. 180). An example of this, and tied to information sharing, is how in Cape Town some TNB people showed concern around a surgeon's behaviour and interactions with them, and when sharing this, other members offered up information regarding trusted surgeons who were respectful of their experiences, were kind, and concerned not only with results but also the person's emotional well-being. This is a form of problem-solving by hearing out members' negative experiences and sharing experiences in order to provide people with alternative options. A participant said that they found the information being shared in the group with this regard to be "insightful".

A sense of safety

The group manages the challenges and risks it faces through distributing the care or management of the group across ten administrators. In sharing the responsibility, they are able to "facilitat[e] a healthy online environment." One of the challenges the administrators face include the presence of trolls who harass members. This was described by a research participant as an "infiltration of evil cishet" people who were "not a gendernaut." The research participant continued to explain that they were not sure if they were there to "harass", "report", or "share personal information about members." They continued to share that they were "tired of racists, homophobes, and transphobes" and that "the vileness spewed online is something that sickens me." They strongly expressed that "They have no space here in OUR space."

This strong reaction makes sense when a safe space like that of the nonbinary support group comes under threat by transphobic individuals who wish to harass members. Research participants explained that this is one of the key reasons for the group being a closed one that requires members to request membership, and for administrators to monitor their responses to the membership or join request questions. The group makes use of join request questions to mitigate against the risk of harassment, questions like "what do you think gender is?", "why do you want to be part of [this group]?", and "how can you tell if someone is a transgender person?" These questions help administrators determine whose requests to approve.

Challenges and recommendations for online TNB community groups

The discussion now turns to challenges, recommendations, and lessons learned by the online support group. These are helpful for those who are considering forming online support groups for TNB people and other marginalised and vulnerable people.

The Facebook group fields "10 to 30 join requests a day" from people or accounts outside of South Africa. Members explain that they believe these people to be potential trolls due to the fact that they do not complete the join request questions, do not have any peers in the group, and do not appear to have any membership in other transgender or LGBTIAQ groups on Facebook – this information is provided by Facebook when members ask to join. Administrative members are shown whether they have any peers in the space or belong to any other relevant groups.

Some research participants were concerned that they might "deny someone entry that really should be in the group" because they had not completed the questions or did not appear to be a member of other transgender or LGBTIAQ online groups. As mentioned above, in order to add another level to the approval process, when someone has not provided answers to the join request questions, administrators will approve a request if the person appears to be in other transgender or LGBTIAQ groups on Facebook. If they are truly unsure, they will send a message to the member requesting access to ask them to complete the questions so that they may make a decision regarding their join request. This is a form of gatekeeping that, in other circumstances, could be considered exclusionary, but in this case, it is used to ensure the safety of current and future TNB members of the digital community. More information on gatekeeping can be found in Chapter 1 on access to health care for TNB youth.

Another challenge faced by the group's administrators is that of posts made by vulnerable members. The administrators do sometimes receive posts that have self-harm or suicide ideation content. Vulnerable members turn to the group to share their distress because they do not have another safe space available to them. Administrators of the group manage this by making use of the setting, which requires admins to approve a post from a non-administrative member of the group. It is in this space that members can identify a vulnerable member and engage them, and then direct them towards practitioners trained to manage and assist people in a time of crisis. This post-approval aspect of the group also enables administrators to identify hate-related content being posted by a troll, they can then block the content, and then the member who has posted this content.

The above has shown how TNB people make use of an online space in order to establish a sense of community, inclusion, and belonging, as well as a sense of safety. However, it must be noted that very little attention was given to intersectionality by administrators. The only brief mention of identity factors, other than gender and sexual identity, was with regards to hate crimes when one research participant shared that "Black trans and queer people have some of the toughest lives on the planet", that "when outed they could be harassed, raped and even killed." They felt that "White trans, queer, or gender non-conforming people have it slightly better because of White privilege." No reflection on the role the group could play in addressing this was shared. As Meer et al. (2017) write, unpacking gender and sexual identity within post-apartheid South Africa must include "parallel analyses race, class, ethnicity, culture, and gender" (Meer et al., 2017, p. 40). This is not limited to South Africa, but in the South African context one would anticipate a particular degree of focus on intersecting and diverse lived experiences.

Based on this case study, recommendations for creating a similar online community group include:

- Make use of closed or secret groups;
- Include join request questions to ensure that only TNB people join;
- Post weekly questions to maintain discussion;
- Moderate posts to ensure that group members are not being harassed by trolls;
- Have clear duties, process, and distribution of responsibilities for group administrators;
- Adopt an intersectional and social justice approach to ensure that members feel that (all aspects of) their identity is (are) valid and that the community can support them;
- Regularly request feedback from the community to ask if there are aspects of the group that can be improved.

Guiding questions

1. When establishing an online community for TNB people, what are some of the key issues to consider?
2. What are some of the potential risks that an online community for TNB people may face?
3. How would you mitigate these potential risks?
4. How can you cater to a diverse group of people with different lived experiences?

CONCLUSION

Digital communities provide the sort of environment where TNB people can gather safely within the means or structures of digital spaces like Facebook, and express themselves in as safe a way as possible as they come to terms with their gender identity and expression. They can then gather support online that can then transform into offline support such as meeting up with other local TNB people they have met online. A level of comfort is provided to TNB people in knowing that there exists an online community that they can turn to in order to celebrate, or commiserate with, their experiences in offline spaces.

As always, when researching communities online, it is important to point out that not all people have access or "digital social capital" and that this impacts on who does and does not engage in digital environments (Murthy, 2008).

REFERENCES

Burns, K. (2012). Cosmopolitan sexual citizenship and the project of queer world-making at the Sydney 2002 Gay Games. *Sexualities, 15*(3/4), 314–335.

Constitution of the Republic of South Africa. (1996). *The Constitution of the Republic of South Africa, Act 108 of 1996*. Pretoria, South Africa: Government Printers.

Cosson, F. (2010). Voice of the community? Reflections on accessing, working with and representing communities. *Oral History, 38*, 95–101.

Crenshaw, K. (1989). Demarginalizing the intersection of race and sex: A Black feminist critique of antidiscrimination doctrine, feminist theory and antiracist politics. *University of Chicago Legal Forum, 140*, 139–167.

Cruz-Malave, A., & Manalansan, M. F. (2002). Introduction: Dissident sexualities/alternative globalisms. In A. Cruz-Malave & M. F. Manalansan (Eds.), *Queer globalisations: Citizenship and the afterlife of Colonialism* (pp. 1–10). New York, NY: New York University Press.

Dahlberg, L. (2007). The internet, deliberative democracy, and power: Radicalizing the public sphere. *International Journal of Media & Cultural Politics, 3*(1), 47–64. doi:10.1386/macp.3.1.47_1

David, O., & Bar-Tal, D. (2009). A sociopsychological conception of collective identity: The case of national identity as an example. *Personality and Social Psychology Review, 13*(4), 354–379. doi:10.1177/1088868309344412

Evans, S. (2014). The challenge and potential of the digital age: Young people and the internet. *Transactional Analysis Journal, 44*(2), 153–166. doi:10.1177/0362153714545312

Fraser, N. (2007). Transnationalizing the public sphere, on the legitimacy and efficacy of public opinion in a post-Westphalian world. *Theory, Culture and Society, 24*(4), 7–30. doi:10.1177/0263276407080090

Gal, N., Shifman, L., & Kampf, Z. (2016). "It Gets Better": Internet memes and the construction of collective identity. *New Media & Society, 18*(8), 1698–1714. doi:10.1177/1461444814568784

Hines, S. (2007). *TransForming gender: Transgender practices of identity, intimacy and care*. Bristol, UK: Policy Press.

Human Rights Campaign. (2019). *Violence against the transgender community in 2018*. Retrieved from www.hrc.org/resources/violence-against-the-transgender-community-in-2018

Iantaffi, A. (2017). Future directions. In C. Richards, W. P. Bouman, & M.-J. Barker (Eds.), *Genderqueer and non-binary genders* (pp. 283–296). London, UK: Palgrave Macmillan.

Koyama, E. (2006). Whose feminism is it anyway? The unspoken racism of the trans inclusion debate. In S. Stryker & S. Whittle (Eds.), *The transgender studies reader* (pp. 698–705). New York, NY: Routledge.

McLean, N. (2014). Considering the Internet as enabling queer publics/counter publics. *Spheres Journal for Digital Cultures, 1*. Retrieved from http://spheres-journal.org/considering-the-internet-as-enabling-queer-publicscounter-publics/

McLean, N. (2017). *The rupture in the rainbow: An exploration of Joburg Pride's fragmentation, 1990 to 2013* (Doctoral dissertation). Retrieved from Rhodes University, Grahamstown. (Identifier http://hdl.handle.net/10962/63822).

McLean, N., & Mugo, T. K. (2015). The digital age: A feminist future for the queer African woman. *IDS Bulletin, 46*(4), 97–100. doi:10.1111/1759-5436.12163

McLelland, M. J. (2002). Virtual ethnography: Using the internet to study gay culture in Japan. *Sexualities, 5*(4), 387–406. doi:10.1177/1363460702005004001

Meer, T., Lunau, M., Oberth, G., Daskilewicz, K., & Muller, A. (2017). *Lesbian, gay, bisexual, transgender and intersex human rights in Southern Africa: A contemporary literature review*. Johannesburg, South Africa: HIVOS. Retrieved from https://open.uct.ac.za/handle/11427/28329

Miller, B. (2017). YouTube as educator: A content analysis of issues, themes, and the educational value of transgender-created online videos. *Social Media+ Society, 3*(2). doi:10.1177/2056305117716271

Murthy, D. (2008). Digital ethnography: An examination of the use of new technologies for social research. *Sociology, 42*(5), 837–855. doi:10.1177/0038038508094565

Nieuwenhuis, J. (2011). Qualitative research designs and data gathering techniques. In K. Maree (Ed.), *First steps in research* (pp. 70–97). Pretoria, South Africa: Van Schaik Publishers.

O'Rourke, S. (2018). Seeking space and place: Experiences of online engagement among queer women in Cape Town. *Journal of Visual and Media Anthropology, 4*(1), 36–51.

Prinsloo, J. (2011). Negotiating transgender identities on the internet – A South African study. *Agenda, 25*, 30–41. doi:10.1080/10130950.2011.630527

Prinsloo, J., Moletsane, R., & McLean, N. (2012). Cyberqueer SA: Reflections on internet usage by some transgender and lesbian South Africans. *Gender and Media Diversity Journal, 10*, 139–146.

Psihopaidas, D. (2017). Intimate standards: Medical knowledge and self-making in digital transgender groups. *Sexualities, 20*(4), 412–427. doi:10.1177/1363460716651415

Reed, T. V. (2019). *Digitized lives: Culture, power and social change in the Internet era*. New York, NY: Routledge.

Robinson, L., & Schulz, J. (2009). New avenues for sociological inquiry: Evolving forms of ethnographic practice. *Sociology, 43*(4), 685–698. doi:10.1177/0038038509105415

Swiebel, J., & Van Der Veur, D. (2009). Hate crimes against lesbian, gay, bisexual and transgender persons and the policy response of international governmental organisations. *Netherlands Quarterly of Human Rights, 27*(4), 485–524. doi:10.1177/016934410902700403

Tagnay, C., & Kee, J. S. M. (2013). Erotics: Sexuality, freedom of expression and online censorship. *Feminist Africa, 18*, 117–123.

Turkle, S. (1995). *Life on the screen: Identity in the age of the internet*. New York, NY: Simon & Schuster.

Vincent, B., & Manzano, A. (2017). History and cultural diversity. In C. Richards, W. P. Bouman, & M.-J. Barker (Eds.), *Genderqueer and non-binary genders* (pp. 11–30). London, UK: Palgrave Macmillan.

Warner, M. (2005). *Publics and counterpublics*. New York, NY: Zone Books.

PART 6

Multiply marginalized identities and populations

CHAPTER 22

Centering trans/nonbinary people of color

Health disparities, resiliency, and opportunities for affirmative clinical practice

Darren L. Whitfield, T.J. Jourian, and K. Tajhi Claybren

INTRODUCTION

Historically, trans/nonbinary (TNB) people of color (POC) have experienced greater health disparities, discrimination, harassment, and violence compared to TNB White people. However, social work education and awareness about the experiences of TNB POC are lacking. Research on TNB communities often misses the mark when it comes to collecting accurate and reliable information about the experiences of TNB people of color – especially Indigenous, Middle Eastern, Native Hawaiian, and Multiracial TNB people. The chapter describes the current research literature on the health of TNB POC, illustrating the gaps in service provisions, and critically examining culturally responsive practices to build authentic, collaborative, trans*formative relationships with TNB people/communities of color. The chapter concludes with a call to action for the social work profession to use its resources, power, and privilege to assist these communities in not only surviving, but thriving in an unjust transphobic/racist society.

WHAT WE KNOW

Harassment and violence

TNB POC experience significantly higher levels of harassment and violence as compared to White TNB people (James et al., 2016). A recent report found that 58% of TNB persons experienced unequal treatment, verbal harassment, and/or physical violence in the past year. However, American Indians, Middle Eastern, and Multi-racial TNB persons were more likely to report these experiences compared to TNB persons of other races/ethnicities (James et al., 2016). TNB POC were more likely to report being denied equal treatment because of their racial/ethnic identity, with Black TNB persons in particular reporting greater unequal treatment than TNB people of other races (James et al., 2016). Similarly, TNB POC were more likely to report verbal harassment compared to White TNB persons, with Black and Asian TNB persons reporting greater experiences of verbal harassment compared to all other TNB persons (James et al., 2016). Furthermore, TNB POC are more likely to report physical assault compared to White TNB persons, with American Indian and Middle Eastern individuals more likely to report physical assault as compared with all other TNB persons (James et al., 2016).

The intersection of cissexism and racism is a contributing factor in the rate of murder among TNB people. Among all anti-LGBTQ and HIV-affected murder victims, there has been a dramatic increase in report of TNB women of color being murdered, with 16 murders occurring among TNB women in the first six months of 2017 compared to a total of 17 in 2016 (National Coalition of Anti-Violence Programs [NCAVP], 2017). From 1995 to 2005, it was estimated 91% of TNB murder victims were TNB POC and 92% were TNB women (Wilchins & Taylor, 2006). However, several structural and institutional barriers prohibit systematic collection of murder rates among TNB people including definitions of transgender in national criminal data systems, voluntary nature of reporting to the Federal Bureau of Investigations (FBI), and exclusion of gender identity in the existing Uniform Crime Reports system (Stotzer, 2017).

TNB POC experience higher rates of sexual assault than White TNB people (Nemoto, Operario, & Keatley, 2005; Xavier, Bobbin, Singer, & Budd, 2005). More than 50% of TNB POC reported being sexually assaulted in 2016, compared to 45% of White TNB persons, with Indigenous TNB persons experiencing the highest rates (James et al., 2016). Experiences of sexual assault were higher for trans men and non-binary people assigned female at birth, and among trans men, Indigenous, Middle Eastern, and Multiracial trans men were more likely to report sexual assault compared to other racial/ethnic groups of trans men (Nemoto et al., 2005). Among non-binary people assigned female at birth, Indigenous, Multiracial, Black, and Middle Eastern people were more likely to report sexual assault than their White counterparts. Of the TNB POC who needed related services, 29% reported not receiving them (Nemoto et al., 2005).

TNB POC have a higher risk of experiencing partner violence than White TNB people (NCAVP, 2013). Indigenous, Multiracial, and Middle Eastern TNB people had the highest rates of reporting intimate partner violence when compared to all other TNB persons (James et al., 2016). Estimates suggest more than half of TNB women report lifetime experiences of physical abuse by an intimate partner, and more than two-thirds of these women report lifetime experiences of emotional partner violence (Nuttbrock et al., 2010) – for more in intimate partner violence, please see Chapter 16. Hwahng and Nuttbrock (2014) found that the perpetrators of physical and psychological abuse during adolescence were usually family members; while during post-adolescence the perpetrators were most often strangers and acquaintances, neighbors, or police officers (Hwahng & Nuttbrock, 2014). Noteworthy, studies suggest police officers were 2.5 times more likely to be violent towards TNB POC than White TNB people (Chang & Singh, 2016). Simultaneously, when attempting to access domestic violence programs and rape crisis centers, TNB POC were twice as likely to experience discrimination than White TNB individuals (Kattari, Walls, Whitfield, & Langenderfer Magruder, 2017; Seelman, 2015).

Mental and physical wellbeing

Experiences of oppression function as significant barriers to the mental and physical wellbeing of TNB POC (James et al., 2016; NCAVP, 2014; Saffin, 2011). Sutter and Perrin (2016) found that the interaction between racism and anti-LGBTQ discrimination had an effect on mental health and increased the risk for suicidal ideation for LGBTQ POC. Compared to 7% of all TNB people and 0.6% of the general U.S. population, 10% each of Indigenous and Multiracial, and 9% each of Black and Latinx TNB individuals reported having attempted suicide in the past year (James et al., 2016). When reporting on lifetime suicide attempts, TNB POC again reported higher rates than White TNB people (37% as compared to 57% of Indigenous, 50% of Multiracial, 47% of Black, 45% of Latinx, 44% of Middle Eastern, and 40% of Asian people).

Experiences of fetishization, racialized sexual objectification, genital and transition-based comments, body policing, sexualized gaze and body objectification, and sexual violence have adverse psychological effects on TNB POC (Flores et al., 2018). This included general distress, hypervigilance and physical safety anxiety, self-doubt and expectation of rejection, gender incongruence, and self-objectification. Those who had been targets of sexual objectification named varied ways of coping, such as asserting one's self and establishing boundaries, social support, self-advocacy and self-care, educating others, accessing counseling, avoidant or survival responses, protective measures, (re)defining gender, and self-harming. The study also found that the frequency of sexual objectifications differed based on others' perception of the TNB person's race and gender, with some TNB POC reporting less sexual objectifications when they were situationally perceived as White and/or as men, and more when they were not (Flores et al., 2018).

TNB POC experience higher rates of discrimination at mental health clinics than White TNB; 14.1% v. 9.1% respectively (James et al., 2016; Kattari et al., 2017). Similarly, TNB POC report high rates of negative experiences with doctors and health care providers. Kattari et al. (2017) found that Multiracial and Latinx TNB people experienced higher rates of discrimination than White TNB people across service providers in mental and physiological health care, substance-abuse services, HIV care, and homeless shelters. The realities of these experiences exacerbate concerns that TNB POC have about not finding culturally competent health care providers, and therefore delaying or avoiding seeking needed health care, which can further aggravate health concerns (Bith-Melander et al., 2010). This is particularly true for

Indigenous and Middle Eastern TNB people who often avoid seeing health care providers due to fear of mistreatment (James et al., 2016). Access to care is further complicated by insurance coverage and cost. Due to systemic barriers to health insurance, TNB people are more likely to be uninsured than cisgender individuals, with Black, Indigenous, Latinx, and Multiracial TNB people being more likely to be uninsured than White, Asian, and Middle Eastern TNB people (James et al., 2016). This has led TNB POC to forgo seeking medical attention when needed.

Substance abuse

The combination of racism and anti-trans antagonism intensifies the likelihood of TNB POC internalizing the systemic oppression they experience, leading to high rates of drug abuse (Drazdowski et al., 2016). TNB women of color sex workers report clients forcing them to take drugs or paying them more for having sex under the influence of drugs (Bith-Melander et al., 2010). TNB women of color also report using drugs to meet people and to self-medicate due to mental health concerns, heightened when dealing with both gender identity and poverty (Bith-Melander et al., 2010). When accounting for binge drinking (five or more drinks within a couple of hours), Latinx (32%), Middle Eastern (30%), and Black (30%) TNB people were more likely to report binge drinking than their White counterparts (James et al., 2016). As with other service providers identified thus far, TNB POC also reported experiencing discrimination at higher rates than White TNB people when accessing substance abuse related services (5.6% v. 1.9%) (Kattari et al., 2017).

HIV

TNB people are living with HIV at nearly five times the overall U.S. population rate (1.4% v. 0.3%), a difference primarily reflective of HIV prevalence among TNB POC. While some White TNB people are living with HIV, Black, Indigenous, and Latinx TNB people experience disproportionate rates of HIV infection, in particular, Black, Indigenous, and Latina trans women (James et al., 2016). At the same time, more than two-thirds of Black and Indigenous TNB people report testing for HIV, much higher than 34% of the general U.S. population.

In a San Francisco-based study, participants pointed to the pressures faced by some trans women of color in sex work to have unprotected sex with clients as one of the causes of these high rates (Bith-Melander et al., 2010). Historical trauma and racial social inequality play significant roles here. Hwahng and Nuttbrock (2014) point to studies showing Two Spirit people,

> experiencing disproportionately burdensome stressors not only from their own lifetime victimization experiences [of childhood physical abuse, sexual abuse, and intimate partner violence] but also because of the greater extent to which they were affected by the intergenerational transmission of historical trauma through their memory/experience of said trauma.
>
> (p. 694)

This compounding effect has led to higher participation in sexual activities with high HIV risk, in addition to substance abuse and deteriorating mental health.

The historical trauma of colonialism, genocide, and slavery that particularly impact Indigenous, Black, and Latinx communities is transmitted intergeneration-ally through within-family homophobic and transphobic violence (Hwahng & Nutt-brock, 2014). In turn, this violence heightens individual trauma, depression, and suicidality, which are all connected to increased HIV risk (Garofalo, Deleon, Osmer, Doll, & Harper, 2006; Sugano, Nemoto, & Operario, 2006). Additionally, the effects of racist discrimination and social cissexism mean that TNB POC have less access to community resources, which in turn also contributes to increased HIV risk.

Health disparities and societal factors

Although this chapter cannot provide adequate attention to the experiences of TNB POC beyond health disparities, we would like to emphasize that these disparities can-not be eradicated without addressing the economic and social factors that produce them. Whether we examine unemployment and underemployment, homelessness, food insecurity, and/or poverty, TNB POC are exposed to higher rates across these economic indicators than White TNB people, as well as higher rates of discrimination from respective service providers (James et al., 2016). These realities have significant effects on TNB POC's health and health-seeking; e.g., homelessness, increased likeli-hood of HIV transmission, etc. (Siembida, Eaton, Maksut, Driffin, & Baldwin, 2016), as well as increased rates of sex work participation as compared to White TNB peo-ple (Fitzgerald, Elspeth Patterson, & Hickey, 2015). These are further exacerbated by significantly higher rates of criminalization and mistreatment by police that TNB POC (particularly women of color and immigrants) face, perpetuated by so-called "quality of life" laws (Amnesty International, 2006; Daum, 2015; Edelman, 2014; Galvan & Bazargan, 2012; Human Rights Watch, 2012; Ritchie, 2013).

Resilience and kinship

Far less scholarship exists on how TNB POC survive and even thrive at the nexus of multiple intersecting institutional and sociocultural barriers. This imbalance maintains a deficit-formed outlook on TNB POC, suggesting that improvement of their/our livelihoods depends on others' (individual and organizational) char-ity and desire to save the downtrodden. On the contrary, TNB POC are necessar-ily resourceful, resilient, and creative in accessing and creating support systems for each other (Bith-Melander et al., 2010; Hwahng & Nuttbrock, 2014; Jourian, 2017; Piepzna-Samarasinha, 2018; Singh, 2013; Singh & McKleroy, 2011). Resil-iency practices and experiences include building both gender-diverse and gender-alike social networks of color (such as immigrant Latina social networks, the Ball community, Black and brown masculine of center communities), pride in one's iden-tities, recognition of oppression systems, accessing health and financial resources, connecting with activist TNB communities of color, and nurturing spiritual suste-nance and critical hope.

Social support and interpersonal relationships

Several scholars highlight the utility of social support and interpersonal relationships as essential to resilience within TNB communities of color. (Cerezo, Morales, Quintero, & Rothman, 2014; Crosby, Salazar, & Hill, 2016; Graham et al., 2014; Loza, Beltran, & Mangadu, 2017; Singh, 2013). In one study of transgender youth of color and resilience, participants identified connecting to other transgender youth of color through social media as both empowering and providing resistance strategies against racism and cissexism (Singh, 2013). Similarly, studies of interpersonal relationships and social support of Black transgender women (Crosby et al., 2016; Graham et al., 2014), and another study focused on immigrant transgender Latinx (Cerezo et al., 2014), showed that social and financial support, as well as connections with other trans women of color, was affirming and countered the impact of being rejected by given families. According to Graham and colleagues (2014), Black transgender women's sense of value and worth does not rest in being tokenized or different, but rather in having their identities celebrated by those who shared their cultural orientation.

Passing

Within literature for TNB communities of color, participants often shared their experience of passing in relationship to their ability to navigate life. Passing can be understood as the alignment between a TNB person's gender expression and cultural expectations of how either masculinity or femininity is performed. In a study of Black transgender women navigating community institutions, concerns about safety, lack of community and companionship, and experiencing disrespect led to conforming to traditional expressions of womanhood (Graham, 2014). Similarly, Sun et al. (2016) highlight that for transgender Latina women, "passing may be a coping strategy that decreases direct discrimination experience; on the other hand, it may serve to hide or conceal one's identity, which can lead to stress and depression" (p. 4). Similarly, TNB POC who had survived traumatic life events identified that passing translated to higher-paying jobs and careers, less employment discrimination, and a higher degree of comfort in their gender identity (Singh & McKleroy, 2011). As such, for some TNB communities of color, the necessity to pass was simultaneously connected to greater access to stability and comfort in their gender identity while possibly creating pressure to adhere to binary gender roles.

GAPS IN THE LITERATURE

The literature leaves a number of gaps both in content and conceptualization. No studies were found, for example, regarding TNB POC and aging, reproductive health and justice, and chronic health conditions, to name a few. Similarly, the extant literature does not include nuanced analyses of the experiences of disabled TNB POC. Broader conceptualizations of wellbeing, such as access to affirming gyms and athletic communities, nutritional health, and food justice, are necessary to have more holistic perspectives of TNB POC's health.

Within research, better efforts need to be made to disaggregate racial categories, such as ethnic specificity within Latinx and Asian Pacific Islander (API) populations. This is particularly important with the latter, as there are vast disparities in economic and social determinants of health among different API communities (Edlagan & Vaghul, 2016; John, de Guia, Chang, & Dinh, 2016). An aggregated approach to understanding the experiences of API TNB people inadvertently minimizes structural barriers that impact some API communities more than others. A disaggregated approach makes more room to understand intra-community disconnections, including across linguistic and cultural distinctions (Bith-Melander et al., 2010).

More research is also needed focusing on and inclusive of Indigenous and Middle Eastern TNB people. Both communities are often either missing entirely from studies of TNB POC, or dropped from analyses due to lack of statistical power. It is important to note that depending on what racial demographic options are available on surveys, some Middle Eastern people may be selecting White, given no other viable options. Due to the complex understanding of gender and sexuality within Indigenous communities, the literature focused on Two Spirit communities is difficult to incorporate because the term Two Spirit can refer to an individual's sexual orientation, gender identity, or both, depending on the Indigenous community and background. Thus, highlighting the challenge of utilizing a non-Western concept, Two Spirit, within a Western understanding/context (Epple, 1998; Thomas & Jacobs, 1999). In regard to Multiracial TNB people, it is unclear if studies allow for identification as such when their perspectives are missing.

Similar limitations exist in understanding how gender is operationalized in research. Reflective of professional practice and service provision, one is likely to find scholarship where trans means trans women, with trans men, transmasculine, and nonbinary individuals either missing or not clearly identified. There is also a need to disaggregate information by gender, particularly in studies focused on gender-based violence, such as sexual assault, intimate partner violence, and harassment, to better understand these experiences and tailor interventions accordingly.

BEST PRACTICES

Despite TNB POC's, particularly trans women of color's, historical and contemporary leadership and organizing for gender liberation (Gossett & Wortzel, 2017; Stryker, 2017), visibility of and engagement with TNB people has been predominantly geared towards White TNB people. This is evident in research about TNB people and communities, dominated by the perspectives and experiences of White TNB individuals, constructing a perception of White homogeneity in TNB communities (Sarfaty, 2016; Tompkins, 2011; Vidal-Ortiz, 2014). The dearth of research on TNB POC, and the prioritizing of White TNB perspectives. impacts community and societal resources made available to TNB communities of color. Additionally, the aggregating of TNB communities of color into one analytic category further deters service providers' ability to deliver culturally competent care and advocacy. As such, it is important for clinicians and health providers to implement affirmative approaches to clinical practice responsive to the needs of TNB communities of color. This section highlights TNB affirmative practice approaches specifically designed to be responsive to TNB communities of color.

Chang and Singh (2016) offer a set of practices to enhance the provision of affirmative care for TNB communities of color. Many of these suggestions are based on the American Psychological Association's (2015) *Guidelines for Psychological Practice with Transgender and Gender Nonconforming Clients.* These provisions of practice include interrogating intersectional identities, challenging assumptions about TNB communities of color, building rapport and acknowledging differences, as well as accompanying power dynamics and assumptions about the experiences, capabilities, and resilience of TNB POC, in order to build trust-based rapport and provide a variety of affirming resources (Chang & Singh, 2016).

In addition to the provisions outlined above for affirmative therapeutic practice with TNB communities of color, social workers should also refer to the National Association of Social Worker (NASW)'s *Standards and Indicators for Cultural Competence in Social Work Practice* to establish TNB affirmative practice. Specifically, clinicians should focus on cross-cultural skills, service delivery, and empowerment and advocacy to address the institutional racism and anti-trans practices in the mental health profession.

This necessitates awareness of racism within TNB communities, acknowledging the legitimacy of TNB POC's distrust of institutional agents, and challenging the centering of White and/or Western notions of masculinity and femininity that leave out or dismiss culturally-specific ways of navigating gender (Beauchamp & D'Harlingue, 2012). Gender creativity in communities of color, especially in regards to nonbinary gender identities, includes terms different from TNB, such as Two Spirit or masculine of center, that may or may not integrate gender and sexual identities. White people's colonizing of Indigenous communities globally, including the U.S. (known as Turtle Island by its original inhabitants), relied on the violent imposition of the gender binary, resulting in the intentional erasure of language and traditions connected to gender diversity across nations and communities of color (Hamer, Wilson, & Florez, 2014; Hunt, 2018; Lugones, 2007). Re-adoption of historical terms and the creation of new ones for some TNB POC is a form of resistance to and decolonization of identities and language disconnected from ancestors.

The institutional and sociopolitical barriers that place TNB POC in precarious economic and social realities necessitate social workers' move beyond service provision and into advocacy. Rather than aid the "war on solicitation" that criminalizes TNB bodies of color, social workers ought to advocate for the removal of "quality-of-life" policing practices (Daum, 2015), while simultaneously expanding service provision and outreach beyond the public sphere into online and private spaces, where TNB POC's safety can be centered. Advocacy efforts can be bolstered through coalitional work and increasing TNB POC's access to economic opportunities (e.g., through jobs and paid internships, compensated consulting) (Lerner & Robles, 2016). Attention ought to be paid to region-specific racial demographics within TNB communities to inform varied approaches to outreach and service provision, including how aggregated/disaggregated these approaches ought to be (e.g., for TNB POC as a whole, race-specific, ethnicity-specific) (Bith-Melander et al., 2010).

Given the diversity in racial identification and experiences among TNB communities as a whole and the TNB community of color particularly, we caution against uncritical adoptions of best practices, often positioned as tick-boxes (Ahmed, 2012; Nicolazzo, 2016a). Although, practices and recommendations offered as best practices when working with TNB POC are necessary to attend to interpersonal and structural barriers to care, they are not "a panacea to confronting, resisting, and otherwise dismantling the complex imbrications of trans* oppression and other forms of systemic oppression" (Nicolazzo, 2016a, p. 1185). A move away from tick-box practices would challenge educators and practitioners alike to "see our work as being about practice, process, reflection, and self-evaluation" (Nicolazzo, 2016b, p. 554) and "promot[e] the type of deep unlearning of gender that would proliferate possibilities" (Nicolazzo, 2016a, p. 1185) for how TNB POC can show up and navigate a variety of institutions.

CONCLUSION

This chapter outlines key health and wellbeing issues facing TNB POC in the United States. TNB POC experience disproportionate rates of harassment, violence, and health disparities due to institutional and sociopolitical barriers and intersecting issues of transphobia and racism within society. While these disparities exist, the communities are resilient and find ways to overcome challenges to achieve health and wellbeing. As practitioners, it is important to understand the social context impacting the experiences of TNB POC when seeking health services, and provide adequate, culturally responsive services that address individuals' whole experience. Furthermore, as clinicians, it is important to not only seek to eradicate social injustices impacting TNB POC but also work to bolster evidence-based practices specific to these communities.

DISCUSSION QUESTIONS AND EXERCISES

1. Read the American Psychological Association's (2015) *Affirmative Counseling* guide and the National Association for Social Worker's (Hunter & Hickerson, 2003) *Affirmative Practice Understanding and Working with Lesbian, Gay, Bisexual, and Transgender Persons* guide. What similarities and differences do you notice in the two approaches to practice? Do they distinguish practice with White TNB persons from TNB POC and, if so, how?
2. Using your own practice setting, what are areas where you notice strengths and opportunities for making your organization more TNB affirmative for TNB POC?
3. Cognitive-based, psychodynamic, and systems theory are three major branches of therapeutic practice. How might these major approaches to clinical practice be made more affirmative for TNB POC? What components can be adapted to fit the needs of TNB POC?

4. Jai is a 35-year-old TNB person of color who was referred to your office for mental health concerns. They are currently living with their friends and working part-time at a fast-food chain. They have a history of depression, substance use, and intimate partner violence victimization. The client was referred to you after being discharged from two other therapists for non-compliance with treatment. How will you build rapport with the client? Using the principles of affirmative practice, how will you develop a treatment plan with the client?

5. You are facilitating a psychotherapy group for individuals who are in recovery from substance abuse. After the group, a client mentions they identify as gender-expansive. They indicate they do not feel safe in the group because of some of the statements made by other group members but insist they find the group beneficial for their sobriety. How can you use affirmative practice skills to address the group issues?

RESOURCES

Internet

1. National Center for Transgender Equality – https://transequality.org
2. Black Trans Advocacy – www.blacktrans.org/
3. National Queer and Trans Therapists of Color Network – www.nqttcn.com
4. QTPoC Mental Health online support group – www.facebook.com/QTPOCsupport/
5. Trans Latin@ Coalition – www.translatinacoalition.org/
6. Transgender Professional Association for Transgender Health – http://tpathealth.org/
7. World Professional Association for Transgender Health (WPATH) – www.wpath.org

ADDITIONAL READINGS

Cole, B., & Han, L. (Eds.). (2011). *Freeing ourselves: A guide to health and self love for brown bois*. Oakland, CA: The Brown Boi Project.

Erickson-Schroth, L. (Ed.). (2014). *Trans bodies, trans selves: A resource for the transgender community*. New York, NY: Oxford University Press.

Singh, A. A., & dickey, l. m. (Eds.). (2017). *Affirmative counseling and psychological practice with transgender and gender nonconforming clients*. American Psychological Association. Washington, DC: APA Press.

World Professional Association for Transgender Health (WPATH). (2011). *Standards of care for the health of transsexual, transgender, and gender nonconforming people* (7th ed.). Atlanta, GA: WPATH.

REFERENCES

Ahmed, S. (2012). *On being included: Racism and diversity in institutional life*. Durham, NC: Duke University Press.

American Psychological Association. (2015). Guidelines for psychological practice with transgender and gender nonconforming people. *American Psychologist*, 70(9), 832–864. doi:10.1037/a0039906

Amnesty International. (2006). *Stonewalled – Still demanding respect: Police abuses against lesbian, gay, bisexual, and transgender people in the USA*. London, UK: Author. Retrieved from www.amnesty.org

Beauchamp, T., & D'Harlingue, B. (2012). Beyond additions and exceptions: The category of transgender and new pedagogical approaches for women's studies. *Feminist Formations*, 24, 25–51. doi:10.1353/ff.2012.0020

Bith-Melander, P., Sheoran, B., Sheth, L., Bermudez, C., Drone, J., Wood, W., & Schroeder, K. (2010). Understanding sociocultural and psychological factors affecting transgender people of color in San Francisco. *Journal of the Association of Nurses in AIDS Care*, 21(3), 207–220. doi:10.1016/j.jana.2010.01.008

Cerezo, A., Morales, A., Quintero, D., & Rothman, S. (2014). Trans migrations: Exploring life at the intersection of transgender identity and immigration. *Psychology of Sexual Orientation and Gender Diversity*, 1(2), 170–180. doi:10.1037/sgd0000031

Chang, S. C., & Singh, A. A. (2016). Affirming psychological practice with transgender and gender nonconforming people of color. *Psychology of Sexual Orientation and Gender Diversity*, 3(2), 140–147. doi:10.1037/sgd0000153

Crosby, R. A., Salazar, L. F., & Hill, B. J. (2016). Gender affirmation and resiliency among Black transgender women with and without HIV infection. *Transgender Health*, 1(1), 86–93. doi:10.1089/trgh.2016.0005

Daum, C. W. (2015). The war on solicitation and intersectional subjection: Quality-of-life policing as a tool to control transgender populations. *New Political Science*, 37(4), 562–581. doi:10.1080/07393148.2015.1089030

Drazdowski, T. K., Perrin, P. B., Trujillo, M., Sutter, M., Benotsch, E. G., & Snipes, D. J. (2016). Structural equation modeling of the effects of racism, LGBTQ discrimination, and internalized oppression on illicit drug use in LGBTQ people of color. *Drug and Alcohol Dependence*, 159, 255–262. doi:10.1016/j.drugalcdep.2015.12.029

Edelman, E. A. (2014). 'Walking while transgender': Necropolitical regulations of transfeminine bodies of color. In J. Haritaworn, A. Kuntsman, & S. Posocco (Eds.), *Queer necropolitics* (pp. 172–190). New York, NY: Routledge.

Edlagan, C., & Vaghul, K. (2016, December 14). *How data disaggregation matters for Asian Americans and Pacific Islanders*. Washington Center for Equitable Growth. Retrieved from https://equitablegrowth.org/how-data-disaggregation-matters-for-asian-americans-and-pacific-islanders/

Epple, C. (1998). Coming to terms with Navajo Nádleehí: A critique of Berdache, "Gay," "Alternate Gender," and "Two-spirit". *American Ethnologist*, 25(2), 267–290. doi:https://doi.org/10.1525/ae.1998.25.2.267

Fitzgerald, E., Elspeth Patterson, S., & Hickey, D. (2015, December). *Meaningful work: Transgender experiences in the sex trade*. Washington, DC: National Center for Transgender Equality.

Flores, M. J., Watson, L. B., Allen, L. R., Ford, M., Serpe, C. R., Choo, P. Y., & Farrell, M. (2018). Transgender people of color's experiences of sexual objectification: Locating sexual objectification within a matrix of domination. *Journal of Counseling Psychology*, 65(3), 308–323. doi:10.1037/cou0000279

Galvan, F. H., & Bazargan, M. (2012, April). *Interactions of Latina transgender women with law enforcement* [Report]. Los Angeles, CA: Bienestar Human Services. Retrieved from https://escholarship.org/uc/item/62p795s3

Garofalo, R., Deleon, J., Osmer, E., Doll, M., & Harper, G. W. (2006). Overlooked, misunderstood and at-risk: Exploring the lives and HIV risk of ethnic minority male-to-female transgender youth. *Journal of Adolescent Health*, 38(3), 230–236. doi:https://doi.org/10.1016/j.jadohealth.2005.03.023

Gossett, R. (Producer & Director), & Wortzel, S., (Producer & Director). (2017). *Happy birthday, Marsha!* [Motion Picture]. United States: Star People.

Graham, L. F. (2014). Navigating community institutions: Black transgender women's experiences in schools, the criminal justice system, and churches. *Sexuality Research and Social Policy*, 11(4), 274–287. doi:10.1007/s13178-014-0144-y

Graham, L. F., Crissman, H. P., Tocco, J., Hughes, L. A., Snow, R. C., & Padilla, M. B. (2014). Interpersonal relationships and social support in transitioning narratives of Black transgender women in Detroit. *International Journal of Transgenderism*, 15(2), 100–113. doi:10.1080/15532739.2014.937042

Hamer, D., Wilson, J., & Florez, C. M. (2014). *Kumu Hina* [Documentary]. U.S.A.: ITVS.

Human Rights Watch. (2012, July 19). *Sex workers at risk: Condoms as evidence of prostitution in four cities*. Retrieved from www.hrw.org/report/2012/07/19/sex-workers-risk/condoms-evidence-prostitution-four-us-cities

Hunter, S., & Hickerson, J. C. (2003). *Affirmative Practice: Understanding and working with lesbian, gay, bisexual, and transgender persons*. Washington, DC: National Association of Social Worker Press.

Hunt, S. (2018). Embodying self-determination: Beyond the gender binary. In M. Greenwood, S. de Leeuw, & N. M. Lindsay (Eds.), *Determinants of Indigenous people's health: Beyond the social* (2nd ed., pp. 22–39). Toronto, ON: Canadian Scholars' Press.

Hwahng, S. J., & Nuttbrock, L. (2014). Adolescent gender-related abuse, androphilia, and HIV risk among transfeminine people of color in New York City. *Journal of Homosexuality*, 61(5), 691–713. doi:10.1080/00918369.2014.870439

James, S. E., Herman, J. L., Rankin, S., Keisling, M., Mottet, L., & Anafi, M. (2016). *The Report of the 2015 U.S. Transgender Survey*. Washington, DC: National Center for Transgender Equality.

John, I., de Guia, S., Chang, R., & Dinh, Q. (2016, August 17). *AANHPI communities stand in solidarity with movement for racial justice through data equity*. California Pan-Ethnic Health Network. Retrieved from https://cpehn.org/blog/201608/aanhpi-communities-stand-solidarity-movement-racial-justice-through-data-equity

Jourian, T. J. (2017). "Fun and carefree like my polka dot bowtie": Disidentifications of trans*masculine students of color. In J. M. Johnson & G. C. Javier (Eds.), *Queer people of color in higher education* (pp. 123–143). Charlotte, NC: Information Age Publishing.

Kattari, S. K., Walls, N. E., Whitfield, D. L., & Langenderfer Magruder, L. (2017). Racial and ethnic differences in experiences of discrimination in accessing social services among transgender/gender-nonconforming people. *Journal of Ethnic & Cultural Diversity in Social Work*, 26(3), 217–235. doi:10.1080/15313204.2016.1242102

Lerner, J., & Robles, G. (2016). The need for social work advocacy to create social justice for transgender people: A call to action. *The Journal of Sociology & Social Welfare*, 43(1), 3–18. Retrieved from https://scholarworks.wmich.edu/jssw/vol43/iss1/2/

Loza, O., Beltran, O., & Mangadu, T. (2017). A qualitative exploratory study on gender identity and the health risks and barriers to care for transgender women living in a US–Mexico border city. *International Journal of Transgenderism*, 18(1), 104–118. doi:10.1080/1553 2739.2016.1255868

Lugones, M. (2007). Heterosexualism and the colonial/modern gender system. *Hypatia*, 22(1), 186–219. doi:10.1111/j.1527-2001.2007.tb01156.x

NCAVP. (2013). *Lesbian, gay, bisexual, transgender, queer, and HIV-affected intimate partner violence in 2012.* Retrieved from https://avp.org/wp-content/uploads/2017/04/ncavp_2012_ipvreport.final_.pdf

NCAVP. (2014). *Lesbian, gay, bisexual, transgender, queer, and HIV-affected hate violence in 2013.* Retrieved from http://avp.org/wp-content/uploads/2017/04/2013_ncavp_hvreport_final.pdf

NCAVP. (2017). *A crisis of hate: A mid-year report on homicides against lesbian, gay, bisexual and transgender people.* Retrieved from http://avp.org/wp-content/uploads/2017/08/NCAVP-A-Crisis-of-Hate-Final.pdf

Nemoto, T., Operario, D., & Keatley, J. (2005). Health and social services for male-to-female transgender persons of color in San Francisco. *International Journal of Transgenderism*, 8(2–3), 5–19. doi:10.1300/J485v08n02_02

Nicolazzo, Z. (2016a). "It's a hard line to walk": Black non-binary trans collegians' perspectives on passing, realness, and trans*-normativity. *International Journal of Qualitative Studies in Education*, 29(9), 1173–1188. doi:10.1080/09518398.2016.1201612

Nicolazzo, Z. (2016b). "Just go in looking good": The resilience, resistance, and kinship-building of trans* college students. *Journal of College Student Development*, 57(5), 538–556. doi:10.1353/csd.2016.0057

Nuttbrock, L., Hwahng, S., Bockting, W., Rosenblum, A., Mason, M., Macri, M., & Becker, J. (2010). Psychiatric impact of gender-related abuse across the life course of male-to-female transgender persons. *Journal of Sex Research*, 47(1), 12–23. doi:10.1080/00224490903062258

Piepzna-Samarasinha, L. L. (2018). *Care work: Dreaming disability justice.* Vancouver, British Columbia, Canada.arsenal pulp press.

Ritchie, A. (2013). Crimes against nature: Challenging criminalization of queerness and Black women's sexuality. *Loyola Journal of Public Interest Law*, 14(2), 355–374. Retrieved from https://home.heinonline.org/titles/Law-Journal-Library/Loyola-Journal-of-Public-Interest-Law/?letter=L

Saffin, L. A. (2011). Identities under siege: Violence against transpersons of color. In E. A. Stanley & N. Smith (Eds.), *Captive genders: Trans embodiment and the prison industrial complex* (pp. 141–162). Oakland, CA: AK Press.

Sarfaty, A. N. (2016). *Not trans enough: The intersections of whiteness and nonbinary gender identity* (Unpublished undergraduate honors thesis). University of Colorado, Boulder, CO.

Seelman, K. L. (2015). Unequal treatment of transgender individuals in domestic violence and rape crisis programs. *Journal of Social Service Research*, 41, 307–325. doi:10.1080/0148 8376.2014.987943

Siembida, E. J., Eaton, L. A., Maksut, J. L., Driffin, D. D., & Baldwin, R. (2016). A comparison of HIV-related risk factors between Black transgender women and Black men who have sex with men. *Transgender Health*, 1(1), 172–180. doi:10.1089/trgh.2016.0003

Singh, A. A. (2013). Transgender youth of color and resilience: Negotiating oppression, finding support. *Sex Roles*, 68, 690–702. doi:10.1007/s11199-012-0149-z

Singh, A. A., & McKleroy, V. S. (2011). "Just getting out of bed is a revolutionary act": The resilience of transgender people of color who have survived traumatic life events. *Traumatology*, 20, 34–44. doi:10.1177/1534765610369261

Stotzer, R. L. (2017). Data sources hinder our understanding of Transgender murders. *American Journal of Public Health*, 107(9), 1362–1363. doi:10.2105/AJPH.2017.303973

Sugano, E., Nemoto, T., & Operario, D. (2006). The impact of exposure to transphobia on HIV risk behavior in a sample of transgendered women of color in San Francisco. *AIDS and Behavior, 10*(217). doi:10.1007/s10461-005-9040-z

Sun, C. J., Ma, A., Tanner, A. E., Mann, L., Reboussin, B. A., Garcia, M., ... Rhodes, S. D. (2016). Depressive symptoms among Latino sexual minority men and Latina transgender women in a new settlement state: The role of perceived discrimination. *Depression Research and Treatment, 2016.* doi:10.1155/2016/4972854

Stryker, S. (2017). *Transgender history: The roots of today's revolution* (2nd ed.). New York, NY: Seal Press.

Sutter, M., & Perrin, P. B. (2016). Discrimination, mental health, and suicidal ideation among LGBTQ people of color. *Journal of Counseling Psychology, 63*(1), 98–105. doi:10.1037/cou0000126

Thomas, W., & Jacobs, S. E. (1999). "... And we are still here": From Berdache to two-spirit people. *American Indian Culture and Research Journal, 23*(2), 91–107. doi:https://doi.org/10.17953/aicr.23.2.k5255571240t5650

Tompkins, A. (2011). *Intimate allies: Identity, community, and everyday activism among cisgender people with trans-identified partners* (Unpublished doctoral dissertation). Syracuse University, Syracuse, NY.

Vidal-Ortiz, S. (2014). Whiteness. *TSQ: Transgender Studies Quarterly, 1*(1–2), 264–266. doi:10.1215/23289252-2400217

Wilchins, R. A., & Taylor, T. (2006). *50 under 30: Masculinity and the war on America's youth – A human rights report.* Washington, DC: GenderPAC. Retrieved from https://static1.squarespace.com/static/599e3a20be659497eb249098/t/59a6aeae7131a53fb428a00c/1504095933569/50+under+30.pdf

Xavier, J. M., Bobbin, M., Singer, B., & Budd, E. (2005). A needs assessment of transgendered people of color living in Washington, DC. *International Journal of Transgenderism, 8,* 31–47. doi:10.1300/J485v08n02_04

CHAPTER 23

At the intersection of trans and disabled

Vern Harner and Ian M. Johnson

INTRODUCTION

Individuals with disabilities and/or chronic illness experience elevated rates of discrimination in our society (Krahn, Walker, & Correa-De-Araujo, 2015; Luo, Xu, Granberg, & Wentworth, 2012), with trans/nonbinary (TNB) individuals experiencing disparities at even higher rates (James et al., 2016; United States Census Bureau, 2015). Moreover, people with disabilities are often seen as not experiencing gender; some have been told that they cannot be TNB or have control over their transition due to their disabilities, or are asked to focus on one identity at the expense of another (Iantaffi, 2010). As social workers, we must be prepared to work with TNB disabled clients in ways that are competent and affirming.

This chapter explores the scant research on the intersections between being TNB and disabled while offering suggestions on how to ensure social work practice is as accessible, inclusive, and welcoming to TNB people with disabilities as possible. Major themes include parallels in the experience of being TNB and disabled. Additionally, calls to action regarding systemic shifts to increase accessibility within social work are made. Because of the breadth of experiences related to both disability and transness, it is not possible to discuss the impact of all of these – however, an introduction and overview of considerations for social work practice with those living at this intersection will be provided.

This chapter will use "trans" and "disabled" to encapsulate an array of identities and experiences while recognizing that not everyone impacted by what is discussed uses this language to refer to themselves. Identity-first language ("disabled person") will be used interchangeably with person-first language ("person/people with disabilities"), acknowledging the movement among disability scholars and activists to embrace disability identity and push back against erasure (Andrews et al., 2019). Identity-first language is used to describe a variety of people (e.g., lower-income family, Black man, trans woman) (Kattari, Lavery, & Hasche, 2017). We also acknowledge that there is a preference among others in the community to use person-first language and continued efforts within the health care industry to use language that centers the human experience (Crocker & Smith, 2019).

While these sentiments around language are just starting to reach academia, disabled individuals have created a large body of work around this issue. Literature around the stigma-inducing impact of person-first language has just begun to emerge in academia, as well (Collier, 2012; Dunn, Andrews, & Anderson, 2015; Gernsbacher, 2017). However, it is important to recognize that many people with disabilities do prefer person-first language. Terms such as "differently-abled" should only be used for individuals who explicitly state that is their identity. Some disabled scholars argue that "the loss of the term 'disability' risks diminished visibility, which results in waning services and opportunities" (Andrews et al., 2019, p. 5) and that replacing "disability" with euphemisms "reveal[s] discomfort with disability and reinforce[s] the implication that disability is a negative and undesirable state" (Andrews et al., 2019, p. 5).

WHAT WE KNOW

Introducing disability

There are many definitions of disability in both academic and non-academic literature, each one offering its own perspective and nuance. The International Classification of Functioning, Health, and Disability (ICF) provides a definition that has been adopted by many, including the World Health Organization. The ICF (World Health Organization, 2006) defines disability as "a difficulty in functioning at the body, person, or societal levels, in one or more life domains, as experienced by an individual with a health condition in interaction with contextual factors" (p. 1,220).

With 15–20% of individuals ages 15 and older having a disability (United States Census Bureau, 2012, 2015), social workers must be prepared to engage with disabled clients. Disability is an expansive category that can include physical (e.g., being being blind and/or d/Deaf or hard of hearing, chronic pain, paralysis, amputation), developmental (e.g., Downs syndrome, autism, spina bifida, cerebral palsy), neurological (e.g., epilepsy, multiple sclerosis, traumatic brain injury), learning (e.g., dyslexia, ADHD), mental health (e.g., PTSD, bipolar disorder), and more. Disabilities may be chronic or temporary, and they may be something someone is born with (congenital) or acquired during the life span (Smart, 2011).

Disabilities are not always visible. For example, the impact and symptoms of conditions can include chronic or intermittent pain or fatigue. Impairments can also be covered by clothing (e.g., a sleeve covering a prosthetic arm), masked by behavior (e.g., staying seated), or alleviated by accommodation (e.g., hearing aid). Invisible disabilities may sometimes become "visible" through disclosure, intermittent visibility of symptoms, or occasional use of an assistive device. Disability erasure may have both positive and negative consequences. For example, an individual may be offered an employment position they would have been denied if their disability status were known, but then feel unable to respond to microaggressions or expected to perform tasks they are unable to.

The degree to which a disability affects a person's ability to engage in life activities, communicate with others, and live independently varies greatly. Some disabilities that are categorized one way may have effects in other areas. For example, cerebral palsy is a developmental disability that can result in impaired movement (Colver, Fairhurst, & Pharoah, 2014). The effect of the disability may be episodic, progressive, or constant.

Models of disability

There are two predominant models for conceptualizing disability – the medical and social models. While these models can have significant impact on the lived experiences of disabled individuals, they can also shape the treatment of non-disabled individuals. What is considered to be a "normal", productive, functioning, worthy body or ability level is impacted by the views of either mode and includes physical, mental, emotional, reproductive, and other abilities.

The medical model centers on the disability/impairment in an individualistic and pathologizing manner, viewing it as a deficit to be cured or overcome (DeJong, 1979; Kattari et al., 2017; Mackelprang & Salsgiver, 2015; Watson, 2012). Under this model, it is likely that all disabilities are viewed as in need of a cure or treatment. The onus is on the individual to obtain treatment and assimilate into mainstream society.

The social model focuses on society's role in disability (Abberley, 1987; Barnes, 2013; Shakespeare, 2014). Oliver (1990) states, "it is not individual limitations … which are the cause of the problem, but society's failure to provide appropriate services and adequately ensure the needs of disabled people are fully taken into account in its social organisation." The "problem" in the social model is not the disability itself – rather, it is the lack of spaces that are accessible to individuals using mobility aids such as wheelchairs, for example.

Policies

Many policies that are not directly about disability impact the lives of disabled individuals – as people with disabilities have other intersecting identities, the impact of policies on disability might be direct or indirect. Perhaps the most well-known piece of U.S. legislation around disability is the Americans with Disabilities Act (ADA) of 1990. This federal law protects the civil rights of disabled individuals, aiming to ensure they "have the same opportunities as everyone else to fully participate in public life" (Thompson, 2015, p. 2,296). While the ADA is "the nation's first comprehensive and broadly applicable law prohibiting discrimination in employment on the basis of disability" (Rothstein, 2015, p. 2,221), its passage had to be painstakingly fought for by disabled and allied activists (Fleischer & Zames, 2011). Despite huge positive shifts in accessibility, the implementation the ADA remains lacking in many areas needed to ensure a wide range of access. The ADA also lacks a mechanism for enforcing the protections it declares, leaving it susceptible to watering-down through state and federal judicial decisions (Dunn, 2018).

Federal marriage equality was passed in the United States in 2015, expanding the legal right to marriage to any two consenting adults. This also impacted transgender individuals with partners of genders differing from their own, if one or both of them had not legally updated their sex marker; for example, if a trans man were still legally considered a woman, he would not have been able to marry his cisgender female partner. For individuals receiving disability benefits from the state, it is still not so simple. Because eligibility for Social Security benefits depends (in addition to other factors) on one's household income, some individuals lose their benefits if they marry a partner (Social Security Administration, n.d.). For disabled adults who require the consent of a legal guardian, often a parent, for medical procedures or legal agreements, this also means that their legal guardian must "sign off" on their marriage (Brown & McCann, 2018; Harris, 2018).

For individuals with more than one partner, the situation often has more dynamics – decisions over who will become the legal guardian or legal spouse, for example. Additionally, being non-monogamous may provide a broader support network for TNB disabled individuals who are sometimes viewed by society to be undeserving or undesirable (Iantaffi, 2010). Future policies and best practices should work to address the erasure of these relationships so that all committed relationships can be recognized.

There are many competing ideas of what is and is not a disability, how disabled people should act and what steps they should take to treat/cure their disability, and even what language they should use about their own bodies and conditions. This has parallels to the TNB community – shifting language, policing of identities, medical/social models, and more. In both TNB and disabled communities, there are differing identities, experiences, and needs. Recognizing these multiple truths while striving for best practices that meet the needs of our clients is necessary.

AT THE INTERSECTION OF TRANS AND DISABLED

Just as not all individuals who might be identified as disabled by others' parameters use the language of "disability" to refer to themselves, neither do all individuals who might be considered transgender or nonbinary by others identify as part of the TNB community. Being trans and/or disabled are also two identities that are cross-cutting in terms of culture – no matter one's race, socioeconomic status, religion, and other social identities, an individual may also be TNB and/or disabled. Thanks to recent surveys, we are better understanding the experiences of TNB/disabled individuals. The 2015 U.S. Trans Survey is the largest transgender-specific study to date, with 27,715 respondents. Of these, 39% had one or more disability – as compared to 15–20% of the general population (James et al., 2016; United States Census Bureau, 2012, 2015). Further, the disabled respondents ($n=6,456$) of the 2010 National Trans Discrimination Survey reported significantly higher rates of discrimination when accessing mental health centers, rape crisis centers, domestic violence shelters, and drug treatment programs, as compared to their non-disabled TNB counterparts (Kattari, Walls, & Speer, 2017).

While individuals who are both TNB and disabled certainly face increased stigma and might be more vulnerable to discrimination, there are also many strengths that these individuals might experience as a result of this combination of identities and experiences. For example, support networks of TNB/disabled individuals might be stronger or more understanding of one another. Some disabled individuals may feel that their experiences that stem from being disabled help them understand or experience their gender (or vice versa). Others might feel that being both TNB and disabled are integral parts of what makes them unique. Still, others might *not* have this connection to being TNB/disabled. It is important not to generalize these experiences and not to assume that transness/disability are always the most important components of someone's identity.

As the language used by both TNB and disabled individuals is constantly shifting, depending on cultural norms, pinpointing how to more accurately communicate our experiences, and other considerations, it should be of no surprise that language around the experiences of individuals who are both TNB *and* disabled also shifts. Even among TNB and disabled individuals, there are many conflicting ideas and conceptualization around language and identity – and there are many parallels. Recently, some individuals who are neurodiverse, experience mental illness, or have a neurological condition, coined a word to convey the fact that their genders are linked to these experiences. "Neurogender" is either a standalone identity or an umbrella term used by some neurodiverse individuals whose gender is linked to their neurodiversity (Neurogender, 2016).

Transitioning

Being disabled sometimes interacts with a TNB person's transition – that is, the steps they take to exist more authentically, whether that is internally, socially, legally, or physically. Because of the wide array of disabilities and the fact that transitioning is very individualized, it is important to recognize that there is not a single narrative around transitioning as a disabled person. For individuals who express themselves in ways that do not align with societal norms for the gender they were assigned at birth, there may be a variety of interactions with their disabilities (Iantaffi, 2010). Tactile sensitivities might limit the texture of fabric able to be worn or how tight/loose clothing must be. Chronic pain may limit one's ability to bind or wear certain shoes, and differences in mobility may impact what kinds of clothes or makeup a person is able to put on or take off without assistance. Chemical/scent sensitivities can limit the ability to use makeup. For individuals who require assistance when dressing, this might impact their access to packing, binding, trying out new kinds of clothing, wearing wigs, fastening jewelry, et cetera.

While some health conditions might interact with hormone therapy (HT) or gender-affirming surgeries, research on both short and long term impacts remains sparse. Often the focus on such interactions is negative. However, knowledge of potential positive interactions is also necessary. Testosterone can help increase muscle development, which might alleviate certain kinds of chronic pain. Some TNB individuals report a mood-stabilizing impact of HT. Exploring the positive side effects of HT with a client's help can reframe what often becomes a focus on negative interactions.

Medical interactions

Both TNB and disabled individuals might have negative experiences in health care settings. In the U.S. Trans Study (James et al., 2016), 30% of trans individuals reported having a negative experience when seeing a health care provider in the past year. However, 42% of disabled people in the sample had a negative experience. Additionally, trans people with disabilities (59%) were also more likely than non-disabled trans individuals (31%) to be experiencing psychological distress.

Transness has been pathologized and, at moments of time, considered a disability or mental illness in and of itself within dominant discourse. An example of this is the inclusion of Gender Identity Disorder (GID) in the 2000 DSM-4. The diagnosis of GID is discussed in the literature as a "problem" in need of "treatment" (Byne et al., 2012; Meyer, 2012). While consumers and health care providers have fought for progress, the medical model of disability still persists today and can define whose experiences of gender are validated. Because people with disabilities can be unjustly seen as lacking capacity, agency around gender expression and other gender-affirming activities can be limited by external forces.

Medical decisions related to gender are already met with great bureaucracy within the health care setting, and disabled TNB people may experience even more barriers. Some report additional barriers to service, including increased requirements or expectations around "proving" their gender in order to receive gender-affirming care (Drescher, Cohen-Kettenis, & Winter, 2012; Khan, 2011). For example, if a person is neurodiverse and seen as not being able to make decisions around their own gender, a clinician may deny access or require the patient to go through additional steps to "prove" their TNB status.

Some disabled people require the permission of a legal guardian for medical procedures or legal transactions, such as changing one's name or gender marker. For disabled individuals seeking HT or gender-affirming surgeries, this might prove to be a larger barrier than any impact of physical or other disability. Even with the approval and support of a medical provider (if they are able to access affirming medical providers), without the signature of their legal guardian, even updating one's name is impossible. Moreover, some providers' offices might not be accessible regarding exam tables, sensory needs, etc., requiring TNB/disabled individuals to have to choose between a provider who is accessible and a provider who is trans-affirming. Because research and known outcomes are sparse, and many health care professionals receive minimal training on serving these communities, finding providers able to provide gender-affirming care to disabled individuals can be a formidable barrier. When referrals to resources are provided for *either* trans services *or* disability-related services, many resources may not be accessible/affirming to trans individuals *with* disabilities.

Race

People of color who are both TNB and disabled may have an additional set of experiences that should be considered. Representation of individuals who are TNB is often limited to thin, White, non-disabled individuals – including in fashion, support spaces, pre/post-surgery photos, and more. People of color with disabilities are disproportionately targeted by law enforcement – over half of Black U.S. citizens with disabilities will be arrested before they reach age 28 (Mccauley, 2017), and they are disproportionately likely to experience police violence (Perry & Carter-Long, 2016). Being a person of color and disabled together and separately increases odds of incarceration and police violence due to the multi-level systems of oppression at play. Due to the impact of the ongoing stigma and oppression faced by POC, there are additional barriers to accessing mental and physical health care with providers often still lacking in the competencies needed to provide affirming care. This impact reaches policy and research, as well, with an ongoing lack of research on the experiences of individuals who are POC, TNB, and disabled. As with other sub-populations, it is integral to recognize the breadth of experiences encapsulated in each of these three components of identity/culture (POC, TNB, disabled) and to not approach any one of these groups as monolithic.

Parallels of experience

Table 23.1 provides an overview of some of the topics discussed in this chapter, as well as brief examples of some of the many implications.

TABLE 23.1 Main chapter topics and implications for trans/disabled individuals

Social model	Gender and transness are social constructs that are not consistent over time and across cultures. Internal, social, legal, and physical transition (in addition to medical transition) are considered options to alleviate dysphoria or move towards gender euphoria.	Society disables people with impairments through the promotion/maintenance of exclusionary beliefs, practices, structures and systems that bar full participation in mainstream daily living (Anastasiou & Kauffman, 2013)
Medical model	Gender is considered tethered to one's biological sex at birth (the assumed combination of one's chromosomes, organs, secondary sex characteristics, genitals, etc.) and is either not seen as able to be changed *or* medical transition is seen as the only viable way to transition. Intersex individuals are viewed as having a "problem" needing to be corrected.	Disability is the result of bodily dysfunction or pathology; therefore, it should be treated to assist individuals in participating/assimilating in mainstream culture with no or minimal adaptation made to the individual's environment or context.

(continued)

TABLE 23.1 (Continued)

Gatekeeping	Medical standards of care deem when it is appropriate or allowable for trans individuals to pursue a medical transition. The best known example of this is the WPATH standards of care.	The government defines what constitutes a disability for employment/benefit purposes. Fuels the idea of not being "disabled enough"/"stealing resources" in a capitalist frame-work. Physical accessibility as gatekeeping: literally kept out of social, educational, employment spaces.
Informed consent	Providers work with patients to ensure they are aware of the impact and possible side effects/outcomes of the medical components of transition that are being pursued. The patient has more control over when steps towards transition goals are taken.	Using medical and psychological evaluation tools establishes boundaries regarding how medical and legal decisions are made. Has the ability to both disempower and protect disabled people. NASW Code of Ethics states (1) informed consent ensures client agency in treatment and (2) the ability to provide informed consent is not static, and it is a social worker's responsibility to enhance the client's ability to provide informed consent when possible.
Identity vs person-first language	For example, "trans man" versus "man who is transgender", "man with a history of transition", or "man of trans experience".	It can be a vehicle for creating community, a reclamation of language that has been asserted forcefully onto someone, and/or a term that acknowledges someone's lived experiences. Having the ability to have a preference between identity and person-first language is necessary.
Access to language & community	Individuals with a lack of access to the internet or urban centers may have trouble finding language that resonates with their experience of gender. This may be especially true for POC or Indigenous individuals. Colonizers attempted to wipe out those who did not fit their idea of the "correct" way to perform gender, resulting in information on culturally-linked genders being harder to find.	Through the disability rights and justice movements, disability has become a uniting identity where a community can combat isolation, create shared resources, develop political power/representation.

IMPROVING SERVICE PROVISION TO TRANS AND DISABLED INDIVIDUALS

Social work values

The NASW Code of Ethics (2017) outlines the expectation that social workers demonstrate awareness and sensitivity to all cultures and interest groups, and "seek to understand the nature of social diversity and oppression with respect to … mental and physical ability" (p. 10). Beyond this call, many components of the Code of Ethics address issues pertinent to the treatment of TNB/disabled clients.

Self-determination

It is the role of social workers to assist clients in identifying and clarifying their own personal goals. When working with TNB and disabled individuals, social workers must reflect this professional value by respecting client choices without prioritizing their own perceptions of client safety over honoring client's decisions or engagement in medical or health management decisions.

Dignity and worth of a person

Social workers are tasked with the duality of being responsible both to our clients and to society at large. In many cases, these interests are harmonious, and our responsibilities as direct care practitioner and activist align – using practice knowledge with multiply-marginalized populations can enhance our capacity for civic participation. Our social location and privilege as educated professionals can amplify client voices in the political arena; this cycle of the impact of both micro- and macro-level work can inform each other to better enhance our ability to support our clients in addressing their goals and needs, and create change in the larger context we work in.

Competence

Very little formal practice knowledge exists for working with TNB and disabled clients. The NASW Code of Ethics states that when standards of practice for an area or population are still emergent, social workers should seek out existing educational opportunities, training and supervision, and consultation with the community when available to prevent harm to clients and increase competence in their work (National Association of Social Workers, 2017).

Accessibility

From as far back as 1st century B.C.E., there is known documentation of architecture and the broader spatial environment designed for an idealized body (Padovan, 2002). While societal definitions of the normative ideal body differ and have transformed over time, our environments are designed with this body in mind. The bodies that spaces are designed for are typically representative of what is most useful to the economy or political state while having severe consequences for those who deviate from this norm. In the United States, examples of this include the "ugly laws" of the 19th and 20th centuries that prevented people with non-normative bodies from using public spaces (Hamraie, 2017).

Accessibility, or the extent to which space, service, or activity is usable for all, is desirable for more than disabled people. Accessibility efforts often have secondary benefits for other users. For example, signage that employs graphics may be intended to assist people who are low-vision but also may assist people whose primary language is not the dominant one. Increased accessibility in spaces makes use easier for all. For example, ramps and elevators designed for wheelchair users decrease burden in accessing the building for those who are able to use stairs.

When applying concepts of accessibility to social work practice, it can be helpful to utilize a universal design framework. Universal design (UD) is the way an environment is made to maximize independent use and customizability for the most amount of users (Disability Act of 2005). Universal design includes seven principles: equitable use, flexibility in use, being simple/intuitive to use, ensuring information is perceptible, tolerating error, ensuring low physical effort is possible, and ensuring the size/space provided is appropriate (Centre for Excellence in Universal Design, 2014). Universal Design is a proactive approach that ensures steps are taken that make spaces and resources accessible to a broader range of individuals.

Accessibility extends beyond physical impairments. For example, offering telehealth services may eliminate the barrier of public transportation for someone who cannot physically access a space, but also for those with mental health or financial barriers that impact the ease of public transportation use. The availability of all-gender bathrooms accommodates both TNB people, as well as the safety, comfort, and use of several other types of users. Maintaining a fragrance-free space can increase access for individuals with sensitivities to chemicals or scents. It can be very helpful to include a description of the physical space and information on how to request an ASL interpreter or food that is allergy-friendly on your organization's website. While our clients are able to advocate for themselves, the onus to do so should not always fall on them. Being proactive reflects a commitment to meeting our clients' needs, whether they are TNB, disabled, both, or neither.

CONCLUSION

As social workers we must continue to educate ourselves before our first TNB/disabled client enters our practice. Being aware of potentially impactful experiences, policies, and needs, whether these are positive or negative, is one step towards being able to provide competent care to this population. With the breadth and depth of parallels in experiences related to being TNB and/or disabled, improving our competency with this population can also improve our abilities as social workers overall. Practicing informed consent, advocating for increased accessibility of spaces/services, implementing and enforcing proper policies, using accurate and inclusive language, and honoring our clients' autonomy are all necessary.

CLASS ACTIVITY

Work in small groups to determine some real-life examples of the impact of these various topics for individuals who are both trans *and* disabled. Fill in parts of the table, then discuss. Whose experiences are still being left out? What is social work's role in this on a micro or macro scale? Were a variety of trans and disabled identities/experiences considered?

Topic	Examples of Impact	Clinician/Provider's Role
Social model		
Medical model		
Gatekeeping		
Informed consent		
Access to community		

ADDITIONAL READINGS/RESOURCES

Aber, K. (2017). When anti-discrimination law discriminates: A right to transgender dignity in disability law. *Columbia Journal of Law and Social Problems, 50*(2), 299–341.

Ballan, M., Romanelli, M., & Harper, J. (2011). The social model: A lens for counseling transgender individuals with disabilities. *Journal of Gay & Lesbian Mental Health, 15*(3), 260–280.

Berne, P., & Sins Invalid. (2016). *Skin, tooth, and bone: The basis of movement is our people (A disability justice primer)*. San Francisco, CA: Sins Invalid.

Chin, M. (2018). Making queer and trans of color counterpublics: Disability, accessibility, and the politics of inclusion. *Affilia, 33*(1), 8–23. doi:10.1177/0886109917729666

Clare, E. (2015). *Exile and pride: Disability, queerness, and liberation*. Durham, NC: Duke University Press.

Clutterbuck, A. (2015). Rethinking Baker: A critical race feminist theory of disability. *Appeal: Review of Current Law and Law Reform, 20*, 51–70.

Kattari, S., Olzman, M., & Hanna, M. (2018). "You look fine!": Ableist experiences by people with invisible disabilities. *Affilia, 33*(4), 477–492. doi:10.1177/0886109918778073

Kattari, S. K. (2015). "Getting it": Identity and sexual communication for sexual and gender minorities with physical disabilities. *Sexuality and Culture, 19*(4), 882–899. doi:10.1007/s12119-015-9298-x

Piepzna-Samarasinha, L. L. (2018). *Care work: Dreaming disability justice*. Vancouver, BC: Arsenal Pulp Press.

Snorton, C. R. (2017). *Black on both sides: A racial history of trans identity*. Minneapolis, MN: University of Minnesota Press.

Wahlert, L., & Gill, S. (2017). Pathological, disabled, transgender: The ethics, history, laws, and contradictions in models that best serve transgender rights. *Kennedy Institute of Ethics Journal, 27*(2), 249–266. doi:10.1353/ken.2017.0017

Wickenden, M. (2019) "Disabled" versus "nondisabled": Another redundant binary? In A. Twum-Danso Imoh, M. Bourdillon, & S. Meichsner (Eds.), *Global childhoods beyond the North-South divide* (pp. 123–144). Palgrave Studies on Children and Development. Cham: Palgrave Macmillan.

Wilson, N., Macdonald, J., Hayman, B., Bright, A., Frawley, P., & Gallego, G. (2018). A narrative review of the literature about people with intellectual disability who identify as lesbian, gay, bisexual, transgender, intersex or questioning. *Journal of Intellectual Disabilities*, 22(2), 171–196. doi:10.1177/1744629516682681

REFERENCES

Abberley, P. (1987). The concept of oppression and the development of a social theory of disability. *Disability & Society*, 2(1), 5–19.

Anastasiou, D., & Kauffman, J. (2013). The social model of disability: Dichotomy between impairment and disability. *Journal of Medicine and Philosophy*, 38(4), 441–459.

Andrews, E. E., Forber-Pratt, A. J., Mona, L. R., Lund, E. M., Pilarski, C. R., & Balter, R. (2019). #SaytheWord: A disability culture commentary on the erasure of "disability". *Rehabilitation Psychology*, 64(2), 111–118.

Barnes, C. (2013). Understanding the social model of disability: Past, present and future. In C. Barnes (Eds.), *Routledge handbook of disability studies* (pp. 26–43). Milton Park, Abingdon, Oxfordshire: Routledge.

Brown, M., & McCann, E. (2018). Sexuality issues and the voices of adults with intellectual disabilities: A systematic review of the literature. *Research in Developmental Disabilities*, 74, 124–138.

Byne, W., Bradley, S., Coleman, E., Eyler, A., Green, R., Menvielle, E., … Tompkins, D. (2012). Treatment of gender identity disorder. *American Journal of Psychiatry*, 169(8), 875–876.

Centre for Excellence in Universal Design. (2014). What is universal design: The 7 principles. Retrieved from http://universaldesign.ie/What-is-Universal-Design/The-7-Principles/

Collier, R. (2012). Person-first language: Noble intent but to what effect? *Canadian Medical Association Journal*, 184(18), 1977–1978. doi:10.1503/cmaj.109-4319

Colver, X., Fairhurst, X., & Pharoah, X. (2014). Cerebral palsy. *The Lancet*, 383(9924), 1240–1249. doi:10.1016/S0140-6736(13)61835-8.

Crocker, A. F., & Smith, S. N. (2019). Person-first language: Are we practicing what we preach? *Journal of Multidisciplinary Healthcare*, 12, 125–129. doi:10.2147/JMDH.S140067

DeJong, G. (1979). *The movement for independent living: Origins, ideology, and implications for disability research*. East Lansing, MI: Michigan State University, Center for International Rehabilitation.

Drescher, J., Cohen-Kettenis, P., & Winter, S. (2012). Minding the body: Situating gender identity diagnoses in the ICD-11. *International Review of Psychiatry*, 24(6), 568–577.

Dunn, D., Andrews, E., & Anderson, N. (2015). Person-first and identity-first language. *American Psychologist*, 70(3), 255–264.

Dunn, P. L. (2018). A review and history of Supreme Court rulings related to Title I of the Americans with Disabilities Act. *Rehabilitation Professional*, 26(1), 19–27.

Fleischer, D., & Zames, F. (2011). *The disability rights movement: From charity to confrontation*. Philadelphia, PA: Temple University Press.

Gernsbacher, M. (2017). Editorial perspective: The use of person-first language in scholarly writing may accentuate stigma. *Journal of Child Psychology and Psychiatry*, 58(7), 859–861. doi:10.1111/jcpp.12706

Hamraie, A. (2017). *Building access: Universal design & the politics of disability*. Minneapolis, MN: University of Minnesota Press.

Harris, J. E. (2018). Sexual consent and disability. *New York University Law Review, 93,* 480–557.

Iantaffi, A. (2010). Disability and polyamory: Exploring the edges of interdependence, gender and queer issues in nonmonogamous relationships. In M. Barker & D. Langdridge (Eds.), *Understanding non-monogamies* (pp. 160–165). Milton Park, Abingdon, Oxfordshire: Taylor & Francis.

James, S. E., Herman, J. L., Rankin, S., Keisling, M., Mottet, L., & Anafi, M. (2016). *The Report of the 2015 U.S. Transgender Survey.* Washington, DC: National Center for Transgender Equality.

Kattari, S. K., Walls, N. E., & Speer, S. R. (2017). Differences in experiences of discrimination in accessing social services among transgender/gender nonconforming individuals by (Dis)ability. *Journal of Social Work in Disability & Rehabilitation, 16*(2), 116–140. doi:10.10 80/1536710X.2017.1299661.

Kattari, S., Lavery, A., & Hasche, L. (2017) Applying a social model of disability across the life span, *Journal of Human Behavior in the Social Environment, 27*(8), 865–880. doi:10.10 80/10911359.2017.1344175

Khan, L. (2011). Transgender health at the crossroads: Legal norms, insurance markets, and the threat of healthcare reform. *Yale Journal of Health Policy, Law, & Ethics, 11*, 375–418.

Krahn, G. L., Walker, D. K., & Correa-De-Araujo, R. (2015). Persons with disabilities as an unrecognized health disparity population. *Ameircan Journal of Public Health, 105*(S2), S198–S206. doi:10.2105/AJPH.2014.302182

Luo, Y., Xu, J., Granberg, E., & Wentworth, W. M. (2012). A longitudinal study of social status, perceived discrimination, and physical and emotional health among older adults. *Research on Aging, 34*(3), 275–301. doi:10.1177/0164027511426151

Mackelprang, R. & Salsgiver, R. (2015). *Disability: A diversity model approach in human service practice,* 3rd edition. New York: Lyceum Books.

Mccauley, E. (2017). The cumulative probability of arrest by age 28 years in the United States by disability status, race/ ethnicity, and gender. *The American Journal of Public Health, 107*(12), 1977–1981. doi:10.2105/AJPH.2017.304095

Meyer, W. (2012). Gender identity disorder: An emerging problem for pediatricians. *Pediatrics, 129*(3), 571–573.

National Association of Social Workers. (2017). *Code of ethics.* Retrieved from www.social-workers.org/About/Ethics/Code-of-Ethics/

Neurogender. (2016). *Neurogender.* Retrieved from https://gender.wikia.org/wiki/Neurogender

Oliver, M. (1990, July 23). *The individual and social models of disability.* Paper presented at joint workshop of the Living Options Group and the Research Unit of the Royal College of Physicians. Retrieved from https://disability-studies.leeds.ac.uk/wp-content/uploads/sites/40/library/Oliver-in-soc-dis.pdf

Padovan, R. (2002). *Proportion: Science, philosophy, architecture.* New York, NY: Taylor and Francis.

Perry, D. M., & Carter-Long, L. (2016, March). Media coverage law enforcement use of force and disability. *Ruderman Family Foundation,* 1–42. https://rudermanfoundation.org/wp-content/uploads/2017/08/MediaStudy-PoliceDisability_final-final.pdf

Rothstein, M. (2015). Innovations of the Americans with Disabilities Act: Confronting disability discrimination in employment. *JAMA, 313*(22), 2221–2222. doi:10.1001/jama.2015.3417

Shakespeare, T. (2014). *Disability rights and wrongs revisited* (2nd ed.). London, UK: Routledge, Taylor & Francis Group.

Smart, J. (2011). *Disability across the developmental life span: For the rehabilitation counselor.* New York, NY: Springer.

Social Security Administration. (n.d.). *Benefits planner; disability.* Retrieved from www.ssa.gov/planners/disability/

Thompson, A. (2015). The Americans with Disabilities Act. *JAMA, 313*(22), 2296.

United States Census Bureau. (2012). *Americans with disabilities: 2010.* Retrieved from www.census.gov/prod/2012pubs/p70-131.pdf

United States Census Bureau. (2015). *2015 American community survey 1-year estimates: Disability characteristics.* Retrieved from http://factfinder.census.gov/faces/tableservices/jsf/pages/productview.xhtml?pid=ACS_15_1YR_S1810&prodType=table

Watson, N. (2012). Researching disablement. In N. Watson, A. Roulstone, & C. Thomas (Eds.), *Routledge handbook of disability studies* (pp. 93–150). New York, NY: Routledge.

World Health Organization. (2006). *International Classification of Functioning, Health, and Disability, 2001.* Geneva, Switzerland.

CHAPTER 24

Trans/nonbinary and the religious, secular, and spiritual

Kate M. Curley, Heather Brydie Harris, and Sage Marie Tyler Warren

INTRODUCTION

Discrimination towards trans/nonbinary (TNB) identified people is well documented and pervasive across many demographic differences (James et al., 2016). Discussions on religious, secular, and spiritual (RSS) belief systems and TNB identities are often fraught with difficult conflicts between the TNB and RSS identities (Glaser, 2008). In fact, in a recent nationwide study on TNB individuals and communities, researchers found that nearly one in five (19%) TNB individuals who had ever been part of a faith community left due to experiencing rejection, marginalization, and/or discrimination within their faith community (James et al., 2016). Notably, the contention between TNB individuals and religious organizations remains antagonistic across varying religious and spiritual experiences (e.g., Mollenkott, 2001).

In this chapter, we will be intentionally using RSS affiliations as our area of analysis and exploration. The critical study of RSS identities and experiences has only recently begun aiding in the deconstruction of normative, or dominant, RSS understandings in order to birth more expansive queer categories for TNB individuals within RSS experiences. This includes recognizing the dominance of Christianity in U.S. culture. However, RSS studies, and what fits in the proverbial RSS box, is highly debated (Martin, 2017). Currently, there is no widely used term in the English language that fully captures all identities and communities that we colloquially define as "religious" or "spiritual" (Hill, 2015; Martin, 2017). This chapter seeks to acknowledge the common discourses surrounding RSS belief systems, while simultaneously working to dismantle current RSS understandings to allow for greater fluidity, or the *trans-ing* of the box itself. RSS, therefore, is used as a placeholder term to situate this work within a longer lineage of critically rethinking the categories themselves.

When the term "RSS" is used in this chapter, it encompasses all that has been classified under the critical study of religion. This includes more secular and/or humanist understandings, such as spiritualities outside of normative Christianity (such as Paganism or Satanism); as well as alternative understandings, as exemplified through the creation of sacred spaces within drag and ball scene culture(s) (Schippert, 2011). This chapter operates on the assumption that RSS is a social identity, and that it relates to the study of culture and lived experience, rather than an attempt to explain the supernatural, or to search for an ultimate truth.

BRIEF REVIEW OF THE LITERATURE

This section provides a brief review of literature, with full recognition that including everyone's narratives is impossible to accomplish, as is the case with RSS identity. Therefore, this review has the purpose of suggesting areas to explore as a human service or health care practitioner: the trans-ing of RSS categories, RSS discrimination in TNB communities, RSS disaffiliation, and unique stories of resilience and integration among TNB people. These focus areas and considerations for practitioners will be further explored in greater detail below.

Trans-ing RSS categories

The most prominent RSS ideologies in the United States (as defined by Pew Research Center, 2014) do not recognize anything outside of biologically male or female sexes, and two completely separate genders: men and women (Bockting & Cesaretti, 2001; Evans, 2017). Not surprisingly, the RSS identities of TNB individuals have not readily aligned with most current RSS research conceptualizations (Kidd & Witten, 2008). Kidd and Witten (2008) find that TNB individuals struggle with the traditional RSS standard surveys centered on Christian theology. This disconnect TNB people feel is common with RSS studies; therefore, it may skew the findings and what we think we know about RSS identities of TNB people.

Furthermore, likely due to experiencing discrimination in the RSS community itself, TNB-identified members are found to weaken their ties to formal religious institutions (Bockting, Knudson, & Goldberg, 2006). Since many TNB individuals are not bound to a formal RSS association, comprehensive analyses on TNB experiences with RSS belief systems and institutions are limited in scope. In other words, TNB individuals challenge the false religious/secular and religious/spiritual binaries in RSS experiences and identities, as seen in Ammerman (2013). TNB individuals can break these categorical boundaries of the RSS to *trans*, or move beyond the bounds of, the categories themselves.

There are several important areas of literature that center the queering and trans-ing of RSS experiences, owing particular thanks to those using tenets of critical race theory. In his discussion on queer identities and the Black church, Johnson (1998) highlights the queering of the sacred and secular as a means of reconciling church doctrines and queer identities; some TNB and queer Black Christians have transformed sites such as the nightclub, where gospel music is merged with club music, into sacred spaces where both the sacred and the erotic converge—the spirit and the flesh. In a move away from Christianity, Tinsley (2018) uses the Vodou figure of Ezili Freda, the spirit/loa of love, passion, and luxury, to depict new expressions of Black queer genders as sacred manifestations. Both Johnson and Tinsley strive within their work to align the body of queer persons as belonging to the realm of that which is sacred, while dissociating from hegemonic religious practices.

This is a part of what Muñoz (1999) termed disidentification: the practice of queer people, and particularly for Muñoz, queer people of color, to disidentify with parts of cultural norms, while not totally discarding particular parts of that culture altogether; rather, Muñoz argues, queer people transform these cultural norms. Disidentification allows for nuance: an individual may not totally disaffiliate, nor completely identify with, a specific RSS belief system; rather, they may transform it to meet their specific cultural and RSS needs. Disidentification is a means for those on the margins of sexual, gender, and racial majority culture to push back against the ideological confines of that culture without abandoning the beliefs, practices, and ideologies of that specific cultural component altogether (Muñoz, 1999). This is particularly important for TNB individuals who are affiliated with RSS communities that are based on ethnic, racial, and/or cultural significance beyond the tenets of religion specifically.

Part of trans-ing RSS as a category entails examining the multiple identity intersections at play for TNB individuals and acknowledging the whitewashing of TNB RSS identities and experiences. Independently, RSS experiences are shaped significantly by race and ethnicity in such a way that the decolonization of RSS understandings is critical for working with TNB communities of color, including RSS communities with origins in people of color's lived experiences (Henderson-Espinoza, 2013; Johnson, 1998; Phillips & Steward, 2008; Smithers, 2014).

Discrimination

TNB individuals in their RSS communities (communities of people who identify with the same RSS and gather together in some way) report being forcibly pressured to not identify or falsely identify themselves to avoid detection by other members, experiencing discrimination and marginalization, and sometimes even rejecting their RSS identity along with its community altogether (Hill, 2015; James et al., 2016; Ryan, Russell, Huebner, Diaz, & Sanchez, 2010). For example, Moore (2008) contends that the Black church, with its propensity toward *hate the sin but love the sinner* theology, formulates queer identities as taboo and creates an oppressive silence for its queer members. This is not particular to the Black church; rather, transphobia in religious spaces is ubiquitous to many RSS groups. Moore's (2008) findings of the Black church are emblematic of a larger picture. Moore argues that within Black queer cultures, Black queer cultural manifestations create new gendered expressions where whiteness has worked to construct a particular kind of gendered binary (Moore, 2008). This is exemplified through Johnson's (2008) observations of the Black church space as a place that can be both discriminatory as well as a theatrical and performative space where some queer identities are shaped. For example, the histrionics of the sermonizer and the flamboyance of the choir are two representations where Black queer religious sensibilities can be witnessed. While some TNB individuals have been able to reconcile their religious commitments and their gender identity and have remained affiliated with their RSS space, others have left non-affirming RSS sites for alternative RSS spaces, or have left their RSS traditions completely (Johnson, 2008).

Christianity is still the dominating and privileged organized religion in the U.S. and Canada, and Christian values and ethics dictate and inform societal and institutional norms for understanding and operating within RSS systems (Blumenfeld, Joshi, & Fairchild, 2009). Christian thought is notably dualistic in gender and "because our imagery and language have been one-sidedly masculine, a masculinist-shaped spirituality has resulted" (Nelson, 1983, p. 14). Although transcendent descriptors are used in the main Christian and Jewish texts (e.g., in the beginning of the Old Testament and Torah in Hebrew, God is called "elohim" which is both male and female despite all other humans being depicted as either one or the other), the transcendent, agender or omni-gender descriptors are reserved typically only for the divine, and binary gendered dualisms are the remaining normative structures for humanity and their interactions.

Although Christianity is by no means the only religious presence in the United States, looking at the dominant anti-TNB narratives from this dominant religious context does provide a glimpse into the barriers TNB-identified people have in other religious and spiritual spaces. The most commonly cited verses from the Jewish Torah in the Tanakh or the Christian Old Testament in the Bible come from Deuteronomy. For example:

1. A woman must not wear men's clothing, nor a man wear women's clothing, for the Lord your God detests anyone who does this (Deuteronomy 22:5, New International Version).
2. No one whose testicles have been crushed or whose penis has been cut off may participate in the assembly of the Lord (Deuteronomy 23:1, International Standard Version).

Citing transphobic religious doctrines such as the ones above, a person's RSS identity is often viewed as antagonizing to their TNB identity. Notably, the above quotes vary significantly across textual translations. For example, in Christian denominations, one's trans identity can be seen as "a problem" to be fixed (Leong, 2008). Due to this and the dominant Christian belief system in the United States, it is more common than not for TNB-identified people to be raised in a religious tradition whose doctrines are used as a tool of anti-trans discrimination against them in the U.S. (Oswald, 2001). Even if someone only had a religious upbringing and has since disaffiliated, the lack of familial and community support due to growing up religious and TNB may significantly impact one's psychological wellbeing (Ryan et al., 2010; Wood & Conley, 2014). Opposing viewpoints like religious doctrines that counter trans identities can also have significant negative psychological and behavioral implications for the people who are navigating these two differing communities (Mashek, Stuewig, Furukawa, & Tangney, 2006).

Being in an RSS community and experiencing instances of transphobia in the environment can lead to extreme feelings of discord and rejection by the religion, the religious community, and the higher power one believes in (Hill, 2015; Ryan et al., 2010). Following instances of discrimination, TNB-identified people can respond with adaptive or maladaptive coping strategies, and the choice between the two can be significantly impacted by one's social network—including that of their RSS community (Hill, 2015). Across multiple RSS traditions, people speak of the critical importance of others understanding or attempting to understand the integration of their trans identity and their RSS identity (e.g., Buddhism: Dillon, 2017; Indigenous Spiritualities: Driskill, 2011; Islam: Shah, 2008; Judaism: Dzmura, 2010; and Taoism; Witten, 2002). In other words, a community and its members can cause significant (un)intentional harm when they believe a TNB identity unable to be integrated into the RSS identity, even when the individual themselves believes it to be possible. This is exemplified in a study by Westerfield (2012), which demonstrated that even though Christian TNB-identifying individuals may integrate their identities internally, the perception of them in their various communities was the most harmful. Discrimination within RSS communities for TNB individuals is significant and appears to cross all RSS experiences, regardless of one's specific RSS identity.

Disaffiliation

While often related to discrimination, RSS disaffiliation provides specific concerns for TNB people. Researchers find that one in five TNB individuals who have been part of a faith community at some point will depart from this community reporting rejection, discrimination, and marginalization (James et al., 2016). Confronting departure, TNB-identified individuals are more likely to seek more general "spiritual" or non-religious orientations to their RSS identity outside of the Western Jewish or Christian traditions (Halkitis et al., 2009; Kidd & Witten, 2008). Part of this process of departure includes rejecting formal group affiliation with an RSS community (Wilcox, 2002, 2009). Interestingly, this trend mirrors what is happening nationally, where the increase in people identifying as "not religious" has been growing steadily each year since the turn of the century (Heelas & Woodhead, 2005; Pew Research Center, 2008). For this group of people who do not identify with any formal religion, religious disaffiliation has been associated with higher levels of discrimination, poorer mental health, and deteriorating conditions of physical wellbeing which are exacerbated by isolation and marginalization (Fenelon & Danielsen, 2016; Hayward, Krause, Ironson, Hill, & Emmons, 2016).

Resilience

Despite these studies on the negative tension between TNB and RSS identities resulting in decreases in mental and physical health for TNB-identified individuals, there are some small sample studies that suggest there may be alternative models.

In Kerry's (2009) study, RSS identity was found to be a critical component to long-term happiness and peace for individuals who identify as intersex. In another small sample study, Preves (2003) described how intersex individuals were able to use RSS beliefs and communities to accept and embrace their own intersex identity. While this may not be the experience for all TNB people, this potential health-promoting intersection can be life-changing for some TNB-identified people. Whether one's RSS identity is used to overcome trauma (Preves, 2003) or find happiness (Kerry, 2009), recognizing and potentially harnessing the power of the spiritual journey could be a powerful intervention for TNB people. It should also be noted that not all intersex individuals identify themselves as TNB.

Beyond intersex-specific studies, there are more general studies on LGBTQ+ populations that appear promising. In response to discrimination, Hill's (2015) research with nine Black LGBT spiritual individuals found that individuals could maladaptively cope but also adaptively cope with these instances through religion. Whereas negative coping strategies such as addiction or high-risk sexual behavior were found to further isolate and exacerbate the negative emotions related to discrimination within the RSS community, adaptive coping strategies such as recovery and self-acceptance mediated negative emotions and societal exclusion towards improved mental health. In TNB-specific studies, religiosity can increase overall health in adults, including older adults (Porter, Ronneberg, & Witten, 2013), and reduce high-risk sexual behavior (Golub, Walker, Longmire-Avital, Bimbi, & Parsons, 2010).

In another, single case study, Nicolazzo (2015) observed a case where a student found an online trans and religious community that affirmed both their gender and religious identity. There is some indication in the research that TNB people can use peer models—particularly in virtual spaces—to build community that integrates both their TNB identity and their RSS identity to increase their physical and psychological wellbeing and resilience (Nicolazzo, Pitcher, Renn, & Woodford, 2017; Singh & McKleroy, 2011).

Unique stories of integration

In two studies, almost all of the TNB individuals marked their preferred RSS identity as "not religious", "spiritual", or otherwise outside of the three dominant religions in the U.S.: Judaism, Christianity, and Islam (Halkitis et al., 2009; Kidd & Witten, 2008). Due to the unwelcoming nature of many organized RSS communities, TNB individuals have been found to reject the communal aspect of their RSS identity as described above, while still identifying with their RSS in an individual capacity (Wilcox, 2002, 2009). The existing research suggests that TNB individuals who reject RSS group affiliation may participate in what is called religious individuation, where one defines their belief system individually and outside of traditional religious institutions. For example, Wilcox (2002) applied the term "Sheila-ism" to trans women's RSS identifications named after a pseudonym of a participant in a previous study on RSS individuation. This concept is not new, but drawn from syncretism where one picks components of many religions, beliefs, and rituals to create a new personal religion which has been seen as early as the 16th century (Sastri, 2018). Sheila, as a religion or spirituality, is invented by the individual in order to integrate multiple religious and spiritual tenants while remaining inclusive of their own TNB identity. "Sheila-ism" has been described as adaptive and fulfilling for TNB individuals' relationship to their RSS identity (Wilcox, 2002).

Although Sheila-ism refers to leaving one's RSS community, integration is also possible. There are TNB narratives where meaning is found across *all* RSS identities and communities with a slightly higher concentration in more fluid spiritual traditions, such as Native American Spiritualities and Pagan traditions (e.g., Jacobs, Thomas, & Lang, 1997; Smith & Home, 2007) and volumes of stories in Christian-centered texts (e.g., Althaus-Reid & Isherwood, 2008). However, integration can be found in narratives across all traditions and identities (e.g., Buddhism: Dillon, 2017; Indigenous Spiritualities: Driskill, 2011; Islam: Shah, 2008; Judaism: Dzmura, 2010; and Taoism; Witten, 2002). Sacred texts across several religions can be interpreted to liberate or oppress TNB people. In a push to disrupt the heterosexist, cissexist, and patriarchal tendencies embedded within hegemonic Western religions, there has been a move among feminist, womanist, and queer theologians toward centering the lived experiences of the socially marginalized during the interpretation and analysis of religious texts (Monroe, 2009). While offering new interpretations of scriptures and practices have worked well for some, others have formed their own set of religious practices and/or beliefs that merge together a new, or polydox, religious practice (Coleman, 2010). Polydoxy, in contradistinction with orthodoxy, expands religious beliefs and teaching beyond their traditional forms to allow for a multitude of theologies. As Coleman (2010) writes, "Polydoxy is a full on embrace of multiplicity—of multiplicity wherever it is found—in the divine and temporal worlds" (p. 187). Polydoxy allows for multiplicity both among ourselves, our understanding of others, and religious teachings, concepts, and practices. This multiplicity has the possibility of mirroring and validating the many forms of TNB lived experiences.

WHAT THIS MEANS MOVING FORWARD

If this is the current state of knowledge on TNB RSS experiences, then what does this mean for mental health and other social-work-related practitioners? First, this chapter should clarify that any preconceived assumptions or biases a practitioner may carry with them regarding TNB individuals' relationship to RSS practices and affiliations should be critically engaged and questioned. Second, only asking what an individual's RSS affiliation is cannot guarantee an understanding of what their relationship to that RSS belief or practice involves. Practitioners should be aware of the personal, and often vulnerable, relationship between TNB and RSS identities, and do not assume that they know how RSS identity functions in any single individual's life, or how they relate to it. Inviting them to describe their RSS beliefs and affiliations as they understand them, and their relationship to that RSS, will allow them to articulate their own experience as it is felt and perceived by the individual themselves.

Fostering an open dialogue based on the articulation of their own experience allows for a greater understanding of the TNB RSS relationship. Some considerations that can be undertaken during this client-centered platform include questions, such as: What is the relationship between the individual's RSS and discrimination? Is the RSS a major source of discrimination, and/or does it function as a source of comfort and respite? Consider and respond appropriately to other intersecting identities: Does the RSS have cultural functions that are not explicitly related to RSS practice, but serve an integral role in the overall wellbeing of the individual? As a practitioner, think about how RSS identities can be a part of overarching racial and ethnic identities tied to cultural and political understandings (e.g., Two Spirit identities) (Jacobs et al., 1997).

If a disaffiliation from an RSS identity has taken place, consider the overall impact—what has changed, why, and how has this change been negative or positive in relation to the individual's overall health and wellbeing? When someone becomes disaffiliated from their RSS community, they may also experience a loss of cultural traditions, identifiers, and historicity, as well as social and political affiliations that compound upon their experience of loss. It is also crucial to recognize and understand the existence and continual development of other, and sometimes individual, RSS experiences outside of the religious/secular or religious/spiritual binary (Ammerman, 2013) and TNB individuals' RSS identities and that these experiences have potential health benefits if integration is able to occur in a meaningful and adaptive way. Allowing and encouraging religious individualization, above referred to as Sheila-ism, as a possible option in addition to nonbinary and non-traditional RSS identities and communities—while remaining cognizant of the possibilities for cultural appropriation and whitewashing of Black, Indigenous, and other people of color's religious traditions and practices—can be incredibly affirming.

As a social worker or human services practitioner, the trans-ing of RSS practices, in a culturally appropriate and responsible way, can prove beneficial to TNB individuals who are struggling with the discord or dissonance between their gender identity and their RSS affiliations. In this regard, trans-ing, as a practice and action, can be used to look for RSS meaning in non-traditional places, to blend two or more religious practices together, or disaffiliate from the negative components of an RSS while striving to keep the positive aspects of any specific RSS intact. RSS belief systems have been found to be a source of discrimination as well as a site of comfort and community with multiple meanings that intersect with other identity categories. Taking into account the pervasiveness of discrimination within and without RSS communities, while being cognizant of internalized perceptions around any given belief system, is an important consideration for social work and health care practitioners. This is especially critical in regard to belief systems that have been racialized and those associated with particular locations and regional areas (i.e., the deep South, rural, and urban). This is essential as some RSS belief systems and organizations, especially those that are racialized and associated with particular demographics, are stereotyped as being more transphobic than others. Discrimination is possible within all RSS experiences, and yet TNB individuals, families, and communities have found ways to integrate their beliefs and RSS affiliations with their gender identity and expression.

CLASSROOM ACTIVITY

The following classroom activity has been designed to help shape the lens through which social work and health care practitioners view RSS affiliations in the TNB community. Each consideration below instructs student-participants to view each other in a different era of their lives; some of those eras have already passed while others have not yet begun. This activity intends to provide students with a pathway to a deepened sense of understanding for the RSS experiences of those around them, to explore their own perceptions of how RSS beliefs and communities apply to them personally, and their levels of comfort with understanding their own lived experiences.

Instructor guidelines

To help create a space in which bonds between students are likely to form, we suggest this activity be led early in the semester, if not the first day of class. In this activity, students are instructed to pair up, which should be done based upon the needs of the students and space within the classroom. Our suggestions for pairings are: standing with toes nearly touching and looking eye-to-eye, remaining seated in a face-to-face position, forming a connection through the use of eye contact, holding hands, or another form of agreed-upon contact. The students will remain in silence while you guide them through a series of considerations in which to view each other. Students will be given approximately 30 seconds to sit with each consideration before the facilitator moves into the next consideration. Please read the prompts below and time intervals for the students participating in this activity.

Guided focus areas

1. Envision the other as a newborn baby:
   a. Consider them slowly understanding the world.
   b. Who is around them? How are they celebrating and thinking about birth?
2. Envision them growing up, feeling rejected by their RSS leaders and communities because of one of their identities (e.g., gender identity, gender expression, race, class, etc.):
   a. How could this affect their self-worth?
3. Now, envision them growing up in a healing RSS environment where they feel a sense of self-worth and validated in their identities:
   a. What does it look like when they question what they always thought they knew in an environment like this?
   b. How are they establishing new knowledge and their own selves?
   c. How are they coming to self-awareness?

Debriefing questions

1. How did this activity feel? What are your gut reactions? And why do you think these feelings and reactions showed up based on your own identities or understanding of other's identities?
2. What were some of your biases and assumptions about RSS identities that came up in this activity?
3. How much and how does RSS affiliation influence one's life transitions?
4. How might you, as a practitioner, help TNB people work through some of the challenges you envisioned in the second prompt?
5. How might you leverage resilience and multiplicity in RSS conversations with TNB people?

CONCLUSION: WHAT IS AT STAKE?

Gaining knowledge of the anti-TNB discrimination within RSS communities and systems is a necessary part of ongoing education. Each TNB individual is a person who will have their own unique relationship to their RSS identity. Practices of intentional vulnerability, as guided above, allow space to see another person in their nuanced subjectivity, particularity, and agency. The pervasiveness of discrimination, as well as the conflicts between RSS and TNB identities, have been found to have a critical impact on TNB individuals' overall wellbeing. A trans-ing of the RSS category and its practice have been shown to increase wellbeing when it aids in the positive integration of RSS and TNB identity. Disaffiliation from an RSS group can have negative or positive outcomes depending on the compounding losses associated with separating from the RSS community. Muñoz's Disidentification and Sheila-ism are two options for integrating the positive aspects of an RSS while breaking from the negative.

There is more work to be done within the study of RSS and TNB individuals, especially concerning the methods in which data is collected. The current Christian dominance, and orthodox, or binary, means of collecting RSS information does not match the needs of a demographic whose RSS affiliations resemble a multiplicity of simultaneous and fluctuating RSS identities. The same is true for categories of gender, gender identity, and gender expression. These methodological issues make data collection tenuous. For example, race and ethnicity must be considered, as racialization informs understandings of religiosity, secularism, and spirituality. Gaining insight into the function of RSS social groups for TNB individuals is a critical component to fostering positive health outcomes; including, positive internal perceptions, adaptive coping strategies, and protection against further external discrimination, isolation, and marginalization.

TNB RSS RESOURCES

Affirmation LDS
website: https://affirmation.org/
Believe Out loud
website: www.believeoutloud.com/
Center for LGBTQ and Gender Studies in Religion
website: https://clgs.org/
Dignity USA
website: www.dignityusa.org/
Equally Blessed
website: www.equallyblessed.org/
The Evangelical Network (TEN)
website: www.ten.lgbt/
Gender Identity and Our Faith Communities (HRC report)
website: www.hrc.org/resources/topic/religion-faith
Jewish Queer Youth
website: www.jqyouth.org
Keshet
website: www.keshetonline.org/
LGBTQ Humanist Alliance
website: www.lgbtqhumanists.org/
Masjid Al-Rabia, LDSN Muslim's LGBTQ Resources
website: https://masjidalrabia.org/longest-days-sacred-nights-cover
Metropolitan Community Churches
website: www.mccchurch.org/
*Michigan State University's Lesbian, Bisexual, Gay, and Transgender Resource Center Resource
    Guide on Religion and Spirituality*
website:http://lbgtrc.msu.edu/educational-resources/exploring-identities/religion-and-
    spirituality/
Muslims for Progressive Values
website: www.mpvusa.org/
Queer Dharma
website: www.queerdharma.org
Queer Disbelief: Why LGBTQ Equality is an Atheist Issue (Book)
by Camille Beredjick
Reconciling Ministries Network
website: https://rmnetwork.org/
Sunday Assembly
website: www.sundayassembly.com/
Transfaith
website: www.transfaithonline.org/
UCC Open and Affirming Coalition
website: https://openandaffirming.org/
Unitarian Universalist Welcome and Equality
website: www.uua.org/lgbtq

REFERENCES

Althaus-Reid, M. M., & Isherwood, L. (Eds.). (2008). *Controversies in body theology*. London, UK: SCM Press.

Ammerman, N. T. (2013). Spiritual but not religious? Beyond binary choices in the study of religion: Spiritual but not religious? *Journal for the Scientific Study of Religion, 52*(2), 258–278. doi:10.1111/jssr.12024

Blumenfeld, W. J., Joshi, K. Y., & Fairchild, E. E. (Eds.). (2009). *Investigating Christian privilege and religious oppression in the United States*. Rotterdam, Netherlands: Sense Publishers.

Bockting, W. O., & Cesaretti, C. (2001). Spirituality, transgender identity, and coming out. *Journal of Sex Education and Therapy, 26*(4), 291–300. doi:10.1080/01614576.2001.11074435

Bockting, W. O., Knudson, G., & Goldberg, J. M. (2006). Counseling and mental health care for transgender adults and loved ones. *International Journal of Transgenderism, 9*(3–4), 35–82.

Coleman, M. A. (2010). Invoking Oya: Practicing a polydox soteriology through a postmodern womanist reading of Tananarive Due's Living Blood. In C. Keller & L. C. Schneider (Eds.), *Polydoxy: Theology of multiplicity and relation* (pp. 186–202). New York, NY: Routledge.

Dillon, M. (2017). *Out of the ordinary: A life of gender and spiritual transitions*. New York, NY: Fordham University Press.

Driskill, Q.-L. (Ed.). (2011). *Queer indigenous studies: Critical interventions in theory, politics, and literature*. Tucson, AZ: University of Arizona Press.

Dzmura, N. (Ed.). (2010). *Balancing on the mechitza: Transgender in Jewish community*. Berkeley, CA: North Atlantic Books.

Evans, C. B. (2017). *What does God think?: Transgender people and the Bible*. Ontario, Canada: Cheryl B. Evans.

Fenelon, A., & Danielsen, S. (2016). Leaving my religion: Understanding the relationship between religious disaffiliation, health, and well-being. *Social Science Research, 57*, 49–62. doi:10.1016/j.ssresearch.2016.01.007

Glaser, C. (Ed.). (2008). *Gender identity and our faith communities: A congregational guide to transgender advocacy*. Human Rights Campaign. Retrieved from www.hrc.org/resources/gender-identity-and-our-faith-communities-a-congregational-guide-for-transg

Golub, S. A., Walker, J. J., Longmire-Avital, B., Bimbi, D. S., & Parsons, J. T. (2010). The role of religiosity, social support, and stress-related growth in protecting against HIV risk among transgender women. *Journal of Health Psychology, 15*(8), 1135–1144. doi:10.1177/1359105310364169

Halkitis, P. N., Mattis, J. S., Sahadath, J. K., Massie, D., Ladyzhenskaya, L., Pitrelli, K., … & Cowie, S. A. E. (2009). The Meanings and Manifestations of Religion and Spirituality among Lesbian, Gay, Bisexual, and Transgender Adults. *J Adult Dev 16*, 250–262. https://doi.org/10.1007/s10804-009-9071-1

Hayward, R. D., Krause, N., Ironson, G., Hill, P. C., & Emmons, R. (2016). Health and well-being among the non-religious: Atheists, agnostics, and no preference compared with religious group members. *Journal of Religion and Health, 55*(3), 1024–1037. doi:10.1007/s10943-015-0179-2

Heelas, P., & Woodhead, L. (Eds.). (2005). *The spiritual revolution: Why religion is giving way to spirituality*. Malden, MA: Blackwell Pub.

Henderson-Espinoza, R. (2013). Gloria Anzaldúa's el mundo zurdo: Exploring a relational feminist theology of interconnectedness. *Journal for the Study of Religion, 26*(2), 107–118.

Hill, P. A. (2015). *Spiritual well-being of Black LGBT individuals when faced with religious homonegativity* (Unpublished doctoral dissertation). Walden University, Minneapolis, MN.

Jacobs, S.-E., Thomas, W., & Lang, S. (Eds.). (1997). *Two-spirit people: Native American gender identity, sexuality, and spirituality*. Urbana, IL: University of Illinois Press.

James, S. E., Herman, J. L., Rankin, S., Keisling, M., Mottet, L., & Anafi, M. (2016). *The report of the 2015 U.S. Transgender Survey*. Washington, DC: National Center for Transgender Equality.

Johnson, E. P. (1998). Feeling the spirit in the dark: Expanding notions of the sacred in the African-American gay community. *Callaloo, 21*(2), 399–416.

Johnson, E. P. (2008). Church sissies-gayness and the Black church. In E. Patrick Johnson (Ed.), *Sweet tea: Black gay men of the south: An oral history* (pp. 182–225). Chapel Hill, NC: The University of North Carolina Press.

Kerry, S. (2009). Intersex individuals' religiosity and their journey to wellbeing. *Journal of Gender Studies, 18*(3), 277–285. doi:10.1080/09589230903057092

Kidd, J. D., & Witten, T. M. (2008). Understanding spirituality and religiosity in the transgender community: Implications for aging. *Journal of Religion, Spirituality & Aging, 20*(1–2), 29–62. doi:10.1080/15528030801922004

Leong, P. (2008). *Therapeutic religion: A portrait of an experimental religious environment for the marginalized, the disenfranchised, and the scarred* (Unpublished doctoral dissertation). University of Southern California, Los Angeles, CA.

Martin, C. (2017). *A critical introduction to the study of religion* (2nd ed.). New York, NY: Routledge.

Mashek, D., Stuewig, J., Furukawa, E., & Tangney, J. (2006). Psychological and behavioral implications of connectedness to communities with opposing values and beliefs. *Journal of Social and Clinical Psychology, 25*(4), 404–428.

Mollenkott, V. R. (2001). *Omnigender: A trans-religious approach*. Cleveland, OH: Pilgrim Press.

Monroe, I. (2009). Taking theology to the community. *Journal of Feminist Studies in Religion, 25*(1), 184–190.

Moore, D. (2008). Guilty of sin: African-American denominational churches and their exclusion of SGL sisters and brothers. *Black Theology, 6*(1), 83–97. doi:10.1558/blth2008v6i1.83

Muñoz, J. (1999). *Disidentifications: Queers of color and the performance of politics*. Minneapolis, MN: University of Minnesota Press.

Nelson, J. B. (1983). *Between two gardens: Reflections on sexuality and religious experience*. New York, NY: Pilgrim Press.

Nicolazzo, Z. (2015). *"Just go in looking good": The resilience, resistance, and kinship-building of trans* college students*. (Unpublished doctoral dissertation). Miami University, Oxford, OH.

Nicolazzo, Z., Pitcher, E. N., Renn, K. A., & Woodford, M. (2017). An exploration of trans* kinship as a strategy for student success. *International Journal of Qualitative Studies in Education, 30*(3), 305–319. doi:10.1080/09518398.2016.1254300

Oswald, R. F. (2001). Religion, family, and ritual: The production of gay, lesbian, bisexual, and transgender outsiders-within. *Review of Religious Research, 43*(1), 39–50. https://doi.org/10.2307/3512242

Pew Research Center. (2008). *United States religious landscape survey* (Pew Forum on Religion & Public Life). Retrieved from http://religions.pewforum.org/

Pew Research Center. (2014). *Religious landscape study* (Pew Forum on Religion & Public Life). Retrieved from www.pewforum.org/2015/05/12/americas-changing-religious-landscape/ porter

Phillips, L., & Steward, M. R. (2008). "I am just so glad you are alive": New perspectives on non-traditional, non-conforming, and transgressive expressions of gender, sexuality, and race among African Americans. *Journal of African American Studies, 12*(4), 378–400.

Porter, K. E., Ronneberg, C. R., & Witten, T. M. (2013). Religious affiliation and successful aging among transgender older adults: Findings from the Trans Metlife Survey. *Journal of Religion, Spirituality & Aging, 25*(2), 112–138. doi:10.1080/15528030.2012.739988

Preves, S. E. (2003). *Intersex and identity: The contested self*. New Brunswick, NJ: Rutgers University Press.

Ryan, C., Russell, S. T., Huebner, D., Diaz, R., & Sanchez, J. (2010). Family acceptance in adolescence and the health of LGBT young adults. *Journal of Child and Adolescent Psychiatric Nursing, 23*(4), 205–213. doi:10.1111/j.1744-6171.2010.00246.x

Sastri, M. R. (2018). *The Din I Ilahi or the religion of Akbar*. Philadelphia, PA: Franklin Classics.

Schippert, C. (2011). Implications of queer theory for the study of religion and gender: Entering the third decade. *Religion and Gender, 1*(1), 66–84.

Shah, R. (2008). Reconnecting with Allah. *Gender Identity & Our Faith Communities: A Practical Guide for Transgender Advocacy*. Retrieved from www.transfaithonline.org/fileadmin/TFexplore/HRC_Gender-Identity-and-our-Faith-Communities_2008-12_.pdf

Singh, A. A., & McKleroy, V. S. (2011). "Just getting out of bed is a revolutionary act": The resilience of transgender people of color who have survived traumatic life events. *Traumatology, 17*(2), 34–44. doi:10.1177/1534765610369261

Smith, B., & Home, S. (2007). Gay, lesbian, bisexual and transgendered (GLBT) experiences with earth-spirited faith. *Journal of Homosexuality, 52*(3–4), 235–248. doi:10.1300/J082v52n03_11

Smithers, G. (2014). Cherokee "Two Spirits": Gender, ritual, and spirituality in the native south. *Early American Studies, 12*(3), 626–651. Retrieved from www.jstor.org/stable/24474873

Tinsley, O. N. (2018). *Ezilis mirrors: Imagining Black queer genders*. Durham, NC: Duke University Press.

Westerfield, E. M. (2012). *Transgender peoples' experiences of religion and spirituality* (Unpublished master's thesis). North Dakota State University, Ann Arbor, MI. Retrieved from http://ezproxy.emich.edu/login?url=http://search.proquest.com/docview/1032563053?accountid=10650

Wilcox, M. M. (2002). When Sheila's a Lesbian: Religious Individualism among Lesbian, Gay, Bisexual, and Transgender Christians, *Sociology of Religion, 63*(4), Winter 2002, 497–513, https://doi.org/10.2307/3712304

Wilcox, M. M. (2009). *Queer women and religious individualism*. Bloomington, IN: Indiana University Press.

Witten, T. M. (2002). *The Tao of gender: Lao Tzu's Tao Te Ching adapted for a new age*. Palm Beach, FL: Green Dragon Books.

Wood, A. W., & Conley, A. H. (2014). Loss of religious or spiritual identities among the LGBTQ population. *Counseling and Values, 59*(1), 95–111. doi:10.1002/j.2161-007X.2014.00044.x

Index

Page numbers in **bold** indicate tables, n an endnote

Made in the USA
Las Vegas, NV
10 November 2020